ESSAYS IN ANCIENT GREEK PHILOSOPHY I

Essays in Ancient Greek Philosophy I

Edited by John P. Anton
with George L. Kustas

STATE UNIVERSITY OF NEW YORK PRESS

Published by
State University of New York Press, Albany

Printed in the United States of America

For information, contact State University of New York Press, Albany, NY
www.sunypress.edu

ISBN 0-87395-050-X (hc : alk. paper)
ISBN 978-0-7914-6326-0 (pbk : alk. paper)

69-14648

10 9 8 7 6 5 4 3 2 1

Contents

Preface

THE editors of this volume wish to express their appreciation for the trust which the officers and membership of the Society for Ancient Greek Philosophy placed in them when approval of the proposal to collect, select, and edit papers presented before the Society was voted unanimously at the 1967 meeting.

In accepting the responsibility to make these papers generally available (only a portion of them have previously appeared in print), we have acted in the hope of assisting in the furtherance of scholarship in this area of philosophical and humanistic studies. If the papers printed here prove a challenge to the reader and help to stimulate critical discussion and more research of the type these essays exhibit, then the purpose of this volume will have been well satisfied. Were such results to come about, the spirit and aspirations which the Society for Ancient Greek Philosophy sought to embody from the day it came into existence will accordingly be well served.

The beginnings of the Society for Ancient Greek Philosophy go back to the early 1950s, when a group of scholars feeling the need for a society devoted to the study of Greek thought undertook to form it. Special credit for conceiving the idea of this society goes to Professor Rosamond Kent Sprague, who at that time was working on her doctoral dissertation at Bryn Mawr, and is now in the Department of Philosophy of the University of South Carolina. Professors Constantine Cavarnos, C. Hillis Kaiser, John M. Robinson, and Gregory Vlastos gave generously of their time and cooperated closely with Dr. Sprague to make possible the Society's first meeting under the auspices of the Eastern Division of the American Philosophical Association held December 28, 1953, in Rochester, New York. Through the support of Professor Edwin L. Minar, Jr., of De Pauw University, the Society was able to secure agreement with the American Philological Association to hold a subsection for classical philosophy at its annual meetings. Since that time the Society has been holding two simultaneous meetings under the auspices of the Eastern Division of the American Philosophical Association and the American Philological Association, within the framework of their respective programs. Papers for these meetings have been by invitation.

The August 1964 conference in Amherst, Massachusetts, held prior to the meeting of the Fourth International Congress of Classical Studies, deserves special mention. It provided the opportunity for the Society to take on an international character. The participating scholars had come not only from the United States and Canada, but from Belgium, England, Japan, Mexico, New Zealand, and Sweden.

The presidents of the Society have been elected to the office not simply because of their life-long interest in classical philosophy and philology, but as men recognized for their contributions to the field. To date, the following have served as presidents: G. Vlastos, 1954; G. R. Morrow, 1955; L. Edelstein, 1956; R. Demos, 1957; P. Merlan, 1958; F. Solmsen, 1959; J. B. McDiarmid, 1960; P. Merlan, 1961; J. H. Randall, Jr., 1962; P. DeLacy, 1963 and 1964; L. Woodbury, 1965 and 1966; E. L. Minar, Jr., 1967 and 1968; and G. E. L. Owen, 1969–. The office of secretary-treasurer was held by Rosamond K. Sprague, 1953–56; J. M. Robinson, 1956–57; R. K. Sprague, 1957–63; and R. W. Hall, since 1963.

The papers selected for publication are arranged here in the alphabetical order of their authors' names. The papers fall into four thematic groups centering around the major periods of ancient Greek philosophy: (1) Pre-Socratics, (2) Plato, (3) Aristotle, (4) Post-Aristotelian Philosophers.

Our editorial work could not have been completed without the generous cooperation of Professors Rosamond Kent Sprague and Robert W. Hall. We are also indebted to Professors Edwin L. Minar, Jr., and Leonard Woodbury for encouragement and support. Dr. Ronald Epp, friend and former student, has given generously of his valuable time and has assisted in many special ways; his sharing in the burden of an overwhelming amount of correspondence and the industrious care with which he attended to the requisite tasks deserve special recognition. We acknowledge our indebtedness to Michael L. and Kathleen Harrington for assisting in the preparation of the indexes.

We wish to thank the Committee on Research and Creative Activity of the Graduate School, State University of New York at Buffalo, for a grant that enabled us to proceed expeditiously with our editorial task and prepare the manuscript for the printer. Professor John Sirjamaki, the Chairman of the Editorial Board of the State University of New York Press, and Mr. Norman Mangouni, the Director of the Press, have earned our deepest thanks for their generosity of mind and concern for classical and humanistic studies.

We are grateful for permission to reprint the papers that have been published in the following periodicals: *American Journal of Philology*, *Apeiron*, *Archiv für Geschichte der Philosophie*, *The Bucknell Review*, *Classical Philology*, *Harvard Studies in Classical Philology*, *The Journal of Hellenic Studies*, *The Journal of the History of Philosophy*, *The Philosophical Review*, *Phronesis*, *The Review of Metaphysics*, and *Yale Classical Studies*. Permission has also been secured from the following publishers: Les Presses de l'université Laval, Martinus Nijhoff, and Yale University Press. Full acknowledgments are given on the title page of each article reprinted in this collection.

The Editors

Introduction

I

THIS collection of essays is offered to the reader with the special aim of stimulating further interest in the exploration of the major achievements of Greek philosophy through a collection of important studies by contemporary specialists in the field. The volume is not designed to serve as a substitute for well-known historical surveys of philosophical ideas or systematic treatments of the major periods of classical Greek thought. Although the essays have been grouped in rough chronological sequence from the period of the Pre-Socratics to post-Aristotelian developments in certain important philosophical topics, the arrangement is primarily a matter of convenience.

At the heart of the present endeavor is a concern for introducing the reader to the work of scholars addressing themselves to basic topics and problems in Greek philosophy. The essays bear witness to the sobriety and carefulness with which evidence and differences of opinion have been weighed. Soundness of scholarship is combined with generous open-mindedness, we believe, in all cases—virtues which appear especially in judicious phrasing of conclusions. The reader will not fail to see that the scholars represented here are far more modest in claiming finality for their exegesis than some of the luminaries of previous generations. In these essays new evidence has often been applied profitably to correct errors of fact or emphasis made by leading scholars of the past, notwithstanding their lasting contributions and original work. It is very much to the credit of contemporary research that progress has been made toward a more reliable interpretation of Zeno's thought, for example, as compared to what Zeller wrote on the subject in 1881. The findings of Gregory Vlastos (and of Fränkel to whose work, published in 1942 and 1955, Vlastos refers), G. E. L. Owen's article in 1957–58 and D. J. Furley in 1967, provide good examples of gains in understanding the quality and scope of Greek thought.[1] Again, we refer the reader to Guido Calogero's essay in which he ably points out how a fresh exploration of the connection between logical issues and ethics can reveal why Socrates must be regarded closer to Gorgias than to Prodicus, as claimed by Wecker in the nineteenth century.[2] David Norman Levin's essay is another example of what recent scholarship can offer not only by way of settling old disputes on issues surrounding the authenticity and date of composition of a Platonic dialogue—the *Lysis* is his case in point—but also how to give more satisfactory answers to substantive questions of content and doctrine. He introduces interpretive procedures that go beyond grappling with "what Plato said," a technique widely used a generation or two ago. Michael J. O'Brien shows with cautious confidence how "their apparent inconclusiveness" need not hamper, as has often happened, the interpretation of Plato's early dialogues. Reluctant to accept the thesis and its implication, held by men of the stature of Burnet, Taylor, and Wilamowitz, that the early dialogues may correctly be read only as literary biography rather than as dialogues with developed positions in philosophy issues, O'Brien is able to give the reader a fresh and worthwhile reading of the *Laches* dispelling that indictment, at least in this case.[3] David J. Furley, working on the extant texts of Epicurus, takes a new look at the well-known paradox of ancient atomism and finds ample ground for disagreement with older authorities such as C. Bailey. Many such examples of critical discussion confirm the contributions of modern scholarship in extending and refining the attainments of the past.

The broader consideration, however, is to underline why it is that essays of the sort that make up the contents of the present volume assist the reader in understanding in certain special ways not only the general character of Greek thought that sets it apart from other periods in the philosophy and science of Western man, but also how the treatment of selected topics, when done in depth and detail, can generate on its own power appreciable comprehension of larger issues. Much clarification can be attained in the conceptual delineation of genuine problems in ancient Greek thought along with a probing into the tenability of various solutions. But the gains go even further. The reader has the comfort of perusing studies on manageable topics that can be treated without the taxing of one's attention that full-length monographs often require. But even if this be regarded only a minor advantage, there is still much merit in the opportunity here afforded for informing the reader on current conceptions of scholarship and how its findings fare in the history of the subject. This is not to say that such advantages cannot be had through acquaintance via the steady flow of pertinent literature in the printed pages of our learned journals. The special feature which these essays display in this respect is one that results from the association of the scholars involved and from the exchange of views that was made available through a public hearing from which their authors benefited.

With the introduction of new techniques for textual analysis, sharper tools for the detection and removal of errors in interpretation, and the liberal utilization of the latest findings and techniques in related fields such as the history of science and anthropology, scholars have been able to give us deeper insights into and more reliable accounts of the ideas of classical Greek thought and its development. We know more about the Pre-Socratics than was known during the nineteenth century, and the recent approaches to Platonism and Neoplatonism exhibit an impressive absence of intellectual prejudice. We do not mean to imply that contemporary scholarship is in some miraculous way immune to error or that it is thoroughly capable of exercising self-criticism without external assistance; however, the current work of philosophical scholars shows a deeper awareness of hidden interpretive assumptions that have so often colored the contributions of previous generations. One may cite the case of the influential waves of Hegelianism whether of the left or right wing variety, that underlay so many treatments, say of Plato or Aristotle and, in similarly obvious ways, dominated the understanding of the entire development of Greek thought in its diverse phases.

It is a distinctive merit of contemporary philosophy to have assisted in freeing our understanding of the past from misconceptions rooted in cultural or historical prejudice. The advances in logical theory and analytical thinking have contributed much to the elucidation of many issues and have helped bring about an appreciation of philosophical concepts previously neglected. It is to Alexander P. D. Mourelatos's credit, for instance, that he found it possible to bring together in his essay on Parmenides pertinent, fertile ideas from the writings of the Logical Positivists, and Bertrand Russell in particular, and to build an instructive parallel between contemporary conceptions of stages of thought and what he detected to be the case in Parmenides. This type of fruitful exploration of modern intellectual trends for their relevance in interpreting ancient thought has brought in many instances remarkable results; witness, for example, the new paths that Benson Mates opened towards a reconsideration of the foundation and originality of Stoic logic.[4] Although Mates's work was not done in response to the circumstance that elicited the writing of the essays printed in this volume, it nevertheless illustrates the basic point we have in mind. Of comparable orientation but with a different emphasis are the closely reasoned account of the meaning of the "Gold-Example" in Plato which Edward N.

Lee gives in his paper, and the sustained analysis which Thomas G. Rosenmeyer, Leonardo Tarán, and Kurt von Fritz undertake in their respective studies.

Much has been done in recent years to focus more carefully on the subtle connections between religious and philosophical thought in classical Greece. The topic has received so much attention that mastery of the extant literature alone requires the skills and devotion of a specialist. It is gratifying to find in some of the essays printed here investigations that contribute to recasting the issue in new molds. The traditional way of looking at the relationship of religion to philosophy had resulted in a stereotype which conceived of a one-way process from the one to the other, accompanied by the ebb and flow of tension and conflict. Charles H. Kahn directs his efforts to an examination of the extant fragments of Empedocles to show how it makes good sense to view the physical poem as being in a serious way a religious work as well. His argument helps to show that it is no longer unacceptable to approach Greek thought from the perspective of organic cultural models. Part of Kahn's essay considers how non-Greek conceptions of the soul and the immortal element in man prevent us from seeing what he regards as the correct relationship between Empedocles' two poems. The governing assumption in Kahn's essay is that of consistency in the thought and religion of Empedocles, and deserves further reflection. The issue is intimately related to the pervasiveness of rational standards in the early Greeks, and, as he aptly remarks, "the fifth century B.C. had only one standard of truth, and hence no notion of irrational faith" (p. 4).

Interpreting the place of religious elements in the cosmologies of the early Greek thinkers has been a standing concern of philosphers and theologians since antiquity. The perspective from which it was done has shifted with the winds of doctrine prevailing in each period and school. That this topic can still engage the attention of contemporary scholars comes as no surprise to the reader. What is of primary interest, however, is the special mode of analyzing the surviving fragments of the early philosophers and the different questions now being raised. In this connection, H. A. T. Reiche's paper has a double function, to exhibit in detail the complex relationship of empirical evidence to the theology of Xenophanes and, while carrying out this task, to criticize "purist" approaches, like Reinhardt's, that have relied heavily on aprioristic notions for interpreting Parmenides as well as Xenophanes. Reiche's target is the dependence of approaches appealing to aprioristic notions on Kantian principles that compartmentalize the logic of the necessary and the contingent:

> Thus in Jaeger's work appreciation of the visual roots of *prepein* is found side by side with, yet wholly unconnected to, his . . . attempt to deduce the perfection of Xenophanes' highest god from *prepon* conceived as aprioristic criterion, operative in aesthetics, ethics, and politics. A dichotomy informs Jaeger's handling of Xenophanes. The theology remains unconnected to the cosmology, and the normative criterion operative in the first is for all practical purposes stripped of its visual root-meaning and reduced to a mere postulate. . . . Proximately, at least some of this insistence that Xenophanes' deduction of the divine attributes is purely rationalistic seems to reflect the profound impact of Reinhardt's revolutionary *Parmenides* book, which coupled the attempted reversal of the accepted sequence, Xenophanes–Parmenides, with the logico-verbal view of Parmenides' *eon*. [p. 93].

These samples of criticism of underlying interpretive assumptions illustrate what may be regarded one of the central features of this collection of essays. With one or two exceptions, their authors have sought to combine analysis of concepts and close reading of textual sources with responsible assessment of related interpretations and their attendant methodological problems. Such critical evaluation of past and present contributions to the topics discussed in this volume has paid handsome dividends, and if one were to enumerate the special procedures applied, it would be proper to mention the following four: (a) In a variety of cases, scholars find it necessary to take issue with ancient authors, whether philosophers in their own right or commentators and doxographers, in order to verify through proposed tests the reliability of what is being reported on the ancient thinker under consideration. In this connection, it should hardly surprise if the accuracy of reports coming from Neoplatonic sources or the correctness of viewpoints as stated by Plato or the more literal-minded Aristotle, is often brought to question. Ancient authorities receive in these essays a fresh and reassuring scrutiny. (b) Much of the reexamination is directed against the difficulties generated in the past by scholars who confounded detached analysis of testimonies and speculative theories of intellectual history. Thus, the heritage of the nineteenth century has proved to be a mixed blessing since both its faults and original insights have sometimes been adopted without the necessary sifting required to separate the useful from the superfluous. (c) Critical discussion has been extended to include the contemporary literature relevant to each particular theme treated here. Because our authors do not accept without independent assessment the results of other authorities, it is gratifying to see how much lively debate has been carried on in the pages of this volume and how fresh insights emerge from exegetical discussions and exchange of findings. (d) Finally, these essays reveal a significant degree of disagreement even among themselves. To see how these differences can work to advance argument one step further as they use one another's analysis and point of view is one of the most constructive lessons a student can learn from exposure to the processes of creative scholarship.

II

The essays on the Pre-Socratic thinkers will disappoint the reader who is looking for facile surveys and sweeping accounts of the highlights of early Greek cosmology and the nature of reality. What these essays basically offer is an analysis in depth of fundamental problems. The exposition is done through close argument, careful delineation of topic and meticulous inspection of testimonies and evidence. The fact that the philosophies of Anaximander, Xenophanes, Parmenides and his followers, Empedocles, and Anaxagoras receive special attention must not be turned into a basis for judgment against the significance of other early philosophers of Greece. Perusal will show that these analyses and discussions encompass far more than the individual titles seem to indicate. The subthemes that come up for examination comprise a wide spectrum of philosophical problems with far-reaching implications for the entire period of Pre-Socratic thought and what follows after that.

Charles H. Kahn takes a fresh look at the alleged "two strains" of Empedocles, his mystery religion and his natural philosophy. He asks the question: "If the contradiction between his philosophic and religious views is as flagrant as most modern authors supposed, is it conceivable that Empedocles himself was unaware of that fact?" (p. 4). He takes a close look at the "contradiction" and examines the arguments offered by two types of theories that have attempted to explain it: (a) theories that talk of a "mere juxtaposition of irreconcilable elements" (Zeller, Jaeger, and Vlastos), and (b) theories that propound the hypothesis of Empedocles' spiritual development, the *Purifications* being regarded of a later date and thus reflecting a genuine change. Kahn accepts the second type of theory with modifications but rejects the insistence on the radical difference between the two poems and proceeds to show why he believes the physical poem must also be regarded a religious work.

In *On Nature*, Empedocles, the cosmologist, understands all natural processes as the combination and separation of the four elements under the influence of the contending forces of Love and Strife. Since thought and physical body seem to be identified, thought or mind is dissolved at the same time as the physical combination of the body. In the *Purifications*, Empedocles, the self-proclaimed god and seer, teaches the transmigration of the soul. This disparity cannot be explained by resorting to a theory of radical changes in Empedocles' views. Kahn argues that an interpretation can be given to show the two to be consistent. He points out that the physical poem presents a theory of the conservation of matter. The elements are not destroyed but separated. Furthermore, in Greek thought the soul which is a totality of an individual personality must be distinguished from the soul representing the God-like and immortal element in man. With these two reminders, Kahn then suggests that any one of the elements could play the role of the transmigrating daimon or the immortal soul of the religious poem. The corporeal elements are eliminated by contextual evidence in the *Purifications*, and Strife is discounted since it is depicted as the enemy of the daimon. This leaves Love as the element which corresponds to the daimon. Thus, by reconstructing Empedocles' conception of the soul, Kahn is able to reconcile the two poems.

Edward L. Minar's essay advances a reinterpretation of the characteristics of the cosmic phase in the philosophy of Empedocles. According to the conventional view, at the apogee of Love's influence the cosmos consists of a spherical, homogeneous mass which is usually characterized as static, solitary, and happy in its solitude. After a reexamination of the texts, Minar concludes: "Perhaps the question is best left undecided whether the whole was spherical either all the time or at the two extreme states. The main point to be made here is the likelihood that there was anything unique about the sphericity of Love's world, and the inappropriateness of the supposition that 'the Sphere' was a contribution to theology" (p. 46). The unity which Love brings about is not a homogeneous and static cosmos, but rather "a unity in which diverse elements cooperate to form a 'cosmos'." He sees this interpretation as having the advantage of agreement with Empedocles' eschatological notions and Empedocles' analysis of organic evolution. The reverse order of the stages of organic evolution then provides the complementary phase and characteristics for the gradual triumph of Strife. In developing his thesis, Minar argues against Vlastos, who emphasized the equality in prerogatives of the two cosmic periods (equalitarian justice). Minar insists that "any interpretation of Empedocles' cosmic periods must take account, it would seem, of the fact that for Empedocles the effects of Love are desirable, those of Strife noxious" (p. 46). It is noteworthy that in scrutinizing the relevant testimonies for the reconstruction of Empedocles' thought, Professor Minar shows how the Neoplatonists Philoponus and Simplicius have been influential in advancing ways of understanding Empedocles' theory of what the world is like at the triumph of Love: they tend to think of it as a thoroughly uniform mixture spherical in shape.

Alexander P. D. Mourelatos agrees that Parmenides B. 8. 34–41 contains a conception of the relation of mind to reality which is philosophically and historically important. The what-is is not only thinkable; it is also the end of all thinking. Mind stands committed to reality. This relation is normative, an ideal for thought. Mind tries to reach the real. Ordinary discourse or thought conceals and yet vaguely adumbrates reality. It is the goal of philosophy to "translate" ordinary thought to the primary level where what was vaguely shadowed becomes precise, clear and definite. Hence, Parmenides, like Plato, Bertrand Russell, and the early Wittgenstein, has a conception of the nature of thought as analytical and regressive. In his concluding paragraph, Mourelatos states what he finds to be Parmenides' main philosophic message: "The absurdity of mortal thinking is that it misdescribes totally what it *was intended* to describe. It is not that human names are meaningless; they are, rather, widely off the mark—*their* mark. Mortals could not have found themselves farther from the goal—*their* goal. . . . Parmenides reminds us of the relation of *pistis* between mind and reality. With the list of mortal judgments he documents the failure of the human mind to live up to this commitment" (p. 74).

Margaret E. Reesor's essay discusses what she believes to be the problem confronting Anaxagoras and how he tried to solve it. Her thesis is that he was concerned with the question "Could objects of sense perception be equated with being?" To answer this, Anaxagoras had to solve two problems: first, how could he accomplish his aim and still observe Parmenides' criterion for being, that is, that being was not divisible but continuous and all the same? Second, he had to answer Protagoras and explain to what extent sense perception is unreliable without saying that sensibles were relative to the percipient hence not existent. He met Parmenides' criterion of being with the principle that there is no smallest and used this in turn to base his theory of the continuum of the objects of sense perception. From this it followed that each entity was composed of all other entities and qualities, including all the opposites. In answer to Protagoras, who believed that the opposites and the qualities were relations, Anaxagoras asserted they were existents. He also used his theory of opposites to argue for the validity of sense perception, again *contra* Protagoras who regarded entities and qualities relative to the percipient.

A careful look at the empirical evidence related to Xenophanes' theology together with the debate about it during the last fifty years, has led H. A. T. Reiche to decide that the best way to approach the problem is through an exploration of Xenophanes' distinction of human from divine knowledge. He takes DK 21 B34; 35; 18[2] to imply: (a) unmediated *autopsy* is the surest form of human knowledge; (b) yet *autopsy* must be regarded relative to the spatio-temporally and biologically conditioned perspective of the viewer; (c) even the self-critical *sophos* can at best attain not absolute truth but only greater or lesser probability; (d) the only method by which man can improve his knowledge of the unknown so that it be more inclusive and precise is by what Alcmaeon called *tekmairesthai kai ta hexēs*, i.e., by collecting and collating empirical *tekmēria*. Reiche proceeds to show how these statements can be consistently extended to Xenophanes' theology, and by denying that this philosopher is a dualist he also denies that Xenophanes espoused "the mutual exclusiveness of the highest god and the other *theoi* and the *panta*," or that he ever taught that god-knowledge, or any knowledge for that matter, is wholly distinct from ordinary sense perception. The conclusions he reaches, namely, that it was temporal rather than spatial symmetries that furnished Xenocrates with the empirical referents of his theological thesis, that his empirical approach to available data was cultivated with full awareness of its superiority over the anthropomorphizing autopsy, and finally that the equivalence of *dokos*, *dedoxasthō* . . . *eoikota tois etymoisi* and *prepei* are equivalent expressions signifying empirical insights of maximal probability and least of minimal necessity, taken together permit an empirical account of the properties of the *megistos theos*.

The belief in the earth's immobility as a special problem, examined in passing by some of our authors, receives close consideration in John Robinson's essay. He shows that Aristotle's way of attributing immobility of earth to Anaximander is derivative, going back in fact to what Aristotle mistakenly thought Plato said in the *Phaedo* and the *Timaeus*. Robinson argues that Aristotle erroneously attributed to Anaximander the view that the earth's immobility is due to the earth's "indifference," stationed as it was at the center and equidistant from all things. He gives textual evidence to indicate that Anaximander remained within the tradition of the earliest thinkers who believed the earth to have absolute weight. In this way Anaximander brought to the foreground of scientific reflection issues such as why the earth does not fall down. The problem is solved by imagining the earth to be flat or disc shaped and supported underneath by either water (Thales) or, in most views, air. Robinson maintains that Aristotle failed to see that for Anaximander and the earliest thinkers there were two problems: (a) why the earth does not *fall down*, and (b) why it remains fixed *laterally*. The latter problem accounts for the kind of view attributed to Anaximander in the *De Caelo*, but it does not pertain to the former problem created by the earth's absolute weight.

Gregory Vlastos gives an exposition and criticism of one of Zeno's dialectical arguments against plurality. Zeno argues that if there are many existents, then the size of any one is null and is infinite. Vlastos maintains that the deduction of nullity of size is inferred from the conclusion of a previous argument. Vlastos proceeds to point out that in deducing the infinity of size the clever Zeno involves himself in a fallacy by intercalating the false premise that "the sum of every infinite set whose every member has finite size must be infinitely large" (p. 130). This fallacy Vlastos finds to be Zeno's own, since there is no trace of a similar error in any of his predecessors. Vlastos is inclined to accept the possibility that Zeno's arguments exercised a certain influence on his contemporary, Leucippus. He also observes that we have sufficient evidence to say that Zeno's other contemporary, Anaxagoras, was acquainted with Zeno's argument but must have certainly rejected the fallacious inference from it (p. 133). Nevertheless, Vlastos finds Zeno to be a skillful dialectician, considerably more advanced than Parmenides in logical technique. He defends Zeno against charges of sophistry and concludes instead that he is a showman with a penchant for melodramatic finales. Zeno had already presented an adequate argument against plurality: if the many exist, then they cannot have size and they must have size. But, determined to get the more dramatic conclusion "so small as to have no size and so large as to be infinite," Zeno involves himself in an error he could have avoided, given the mathematical sophistication of his day. Nevertheless, Vlastos concludes, Zeno is significant in the history of Western thought for far more than his dialectical skill. In assessing Zeno's substantive contribution, he states in his conclusion: "But Zeno reveals more than technical talent in this argument. In its opening part he throws out an idea new to Western philosophy: the incorporeality of Being. It is easy to miss its significance, since he exploits it only for dialectical purposes. How great is its value will be apparent if one notes that in this area the vision of the great Parmenides remained blurred and indistinct; and that without this needed clarification the whole of that great metaphysical construction hovers uncertainly on the edge of confusion" (p. 136).

Leonard Woodbury's essay, to which Mourelatos refers as important and deserving a more careful reading (p. 70), offers an interpretation of Parmenides B8, 34–41 to the effect that Parmenides believed the real world to be "expressed" both in a certain thought and name. Basic to Woodbury's argument is the observation that the antithesis of *onoma* and *ousia* can be found in later literature but is on the whole absent from the vocabulary of philosophers prior to the sophistic age. On a more technical level, Woodbury proposes *onomastai* in B 8, line 38, a reading that has drawn considerable attention in recent scholarship and is also referred to by Mourelatos, who supports the proposal but is reluctant to accept the accompanying interpretation. If the real world is "in" that-which-is, then the real world is also expressed in the form of thought "it–is" (rather than "it–is–not") and in the name "being." This is the name that does not founder on contradictions as do the names instituted by mortal men. It is the name by which the real world is truly known, in which its reality is truly expressed. Knowledge then is found in the use of a name, and Parmenides' philosophy of names leads to his ontology.

III

The works of Plato have been a wellspring of influential ideas as well as a source of philosophical problems to the inquiring mind. In the present collection the dialogues come up once again for a fresh look and a careful study and reexamination of their composition, background, thematic richness, and principles of interpretation. The relation of the Sophistic movement to Plato's thought is investigated on several occasions with the intent to fix with more precision the boundaries of certain doctrinal affinities. The titles of the essays are indicative of the range of interest and direction Platonic studies have taken in recent years. Individual works such as the *Lysis*, *Laches*, *Republic*, *Timaeus*, and the *Seventh Letter* receive close attention as do such basic themes as the relation of Forms to particulars, problems of method and structure of arguments, issues in language, logic, the philosophy of mind and theory of knowledge, ethical and political concerns, love, friendship, the place of reason in society, the concern for immortality and the persistent quest for reality.

R. E. Allen examines the relation of Forms to particulars, especially in the *Republic* and the middle dialogues. Plato faced a Parmenidean problem. Given Parmenides' criteria of reality, to wit, to be real is to be intelligible, not qualified by opposites, self-identical, and unchanging, the question arises what can be said of the sensible world which fails to satisfy these criteria? Plato rejected the alternative of maintaining the complete unreality of the sensible world and adopted the theory of degrees of being instead: sensibles were held to be intermediate between full reality and unreality (p. 165). To support this thesis Plato "proved" the existence of Forms by the argument from opposites (*Rep.* 479 A–C). The argument, however, does not establish that things qualified by opposites are less real than Forms. Plato explains the relation of Forms to particulars in terms of originals and copies. The original can exist apart from the copy, but not vice versa. The copy depends on the original for its existence. Allen argues that when the copy-theory of participation is properly understood, then one cannot accuse Plato of the difficulties engendered by the self-predication of the Forms. The relation of Forms to particulars is not that of predicates to instances of predicates but of originals to shadows or reflections. Thus, when "beautiful" is predicated of Forms and copies it is not used univocally but is systematically equivocal.

Guido Calogero's richly documented discussion supports the thesis that among the sophists Gorgias was probably more influential on Socrates than Prodicus. Welcker, the nineteenth-century German scholar, tried to show that Socrates adopted and modified the philosophical methodology of Prodicus. Calogero finds that in the *Helena* and *Palamedes* of Gorgias the Socratic ethical principle, *nemo sua sponte peccat* (*oudeis hekōn examartanei*), is clearly presupposed. Calogero's detailed analysis of the *Palamedes* reveals remarkable similarities to Plato's *Apology*. Textual comparisons indicate quite strongly that Socrates modeled his defense after the defense of Gorgias's *Palamedes* rather than the reverse. The philosophical point this article makes goes beyond the quest for antecedents of the formulation of an ethical dictum. As Calogero states, "Gorgias, envisaging the *nemo sua sponte peccat* in its most elementary form, might fall into a sort of moral indifference" (p. 183). The principle had to be grounded on firm philosophical foundations, which is precisely what Plato did.

David Gallop reviews Plato's conception of dreams, the contrast he sees between waking and dreaming, and the analogies drawn from this distinction. He finds that the results help to clarify Plato's theory of knowledge, particularly in explicating the famous Divided Line of the *Republic*. Particularly interesting is Gallop's conclusion that the dreaming-waking contrast is relevant in ascertaining the status of the *Republic* itself. The connection between dreaming-waking and image-original is taken to be of crucial significance in understanding certain aspects of Plato's thought (p. 192). It can be maintained that the *Republic* has the status of a dream and if seen as a verbal image of the Forms, is analogous to the triangles that the mathematician draws to aid him. In both cases the philosopher resorts to images to *achieve* clarity. Thus, the *Republic* is a *prophetic* dream, offering insight into the Intelligible World. But the *Republic* has dream status also because it envisages an ideal city unrealized in fact, and so may be regarded as Plato's dream of wish-fulfillment of that which he despairs of building in waking life (p. 198).

The traditional view holds that the morality developed in the *Republic* with emphasis on the Good as the end of man, on the tendance of the soul, and the moral responsibility of the indivual is foreshadowed in the *Gorgias*. Robert W. Hall argues, however, that the *Gorgias* displays a view of morality more akin to the *technē-phronēsis* ethic of the early dialogues. He stresses what he finds to be a rarely recognized moral paradox of *Gorgias*, that moral individuals are self-determined and yet they are "created" by the art of politics just as any object is created by its appropriate *technē*. In the *Gorgias*, statesmanship is not yet distinguished from ordinary *technē* as it is in the *Republic*. Given this peculiarity, the *Gorgias* would seem to lead to a disagreeable state of affairs: "There are no evil citizens, only incompetent 'statesmen'." Nevertheless, Hall does see in the *Gorgias* other elements which signify a transition to the view of morality in the *Republic*. The *Gorgias* suggests a concept of inherent value apart from utilitarian ethics by introducing a cosmic ordering principle which is the source and sustaining cause of value in all things, an obvious adumbration of the Form of the Good. Furthermore, Socrates is made in this dialogue to espouse a philosophical way of life apart from politics. In the *Republic* this culminates in the idea of the philosopher-ruler.

The subject of Edward N. Lee's article is the enigmatic gold-example in Plato's *Timaeus*. A person is making all kinds of figures in a lump of gold, continually transmuting one shape into another. Somebody points to one of them even as he is reshaping it into another form and asks, What is it? Plato then discusses three possible replies. Lee's principle of interpretation adopted with reservations from Cherniss, is the specific dialectical situation of question-and-answer in which the answerer formulates his answer keeping in mind the capabilities and character of the questioner. Lee argues that of the various answers that can be given to the particular question before us, only one is strictly correct; but if the questioner is of a certain sort, willing to accept another kind of answer, then the question should be replied to on his level. Lee then defends this scheme of dialectical encounter, which involves accommodation to the capabilities and character of the participants in the encounter, as genuine Platonic doctrine.

Donald Norman Levin's essay concentrates on the *Lysis*. He proposes a new method for identifying the main scheme of the dialogue: "By placing the last first and the first later and by ranging freely through the whole I hope not only to shed more light on the conduct of the argument of the *Lysis*, but also to demonstrate that the structure is closely interwoven and that the cleavage . . . between a protreptic introduction and a philosophical main body . . . is much less pronounced than would appear at first glance" (pp. 237–38). To identify the basic theme he asks whether this is a dialogue of the formula "What is *X*?" (viz. *Laches*, "What is courage?" or *Charmides*, "What is temperance?"). There is also another formula, found in other dialogues: "Is *X*/*Y*?" (e.g. *Meno* and *Protogoras*, "Is virtue teachable?") Neither of these formulae, however, will do in the case of the *Lysis*, especially if we take the *X* to be "friendship." Levin claims the *X* which awaits definition is not "friendship" (*philia*) but "friend" (*philos*). In the course of his discussion, he analyzes *eros* and *philia*, their relationship and place in the various dialogues and the ways in which the study of these terms throw light on the progression of meaning from a less inclusive to a broader usage. The conclusion drawn is that the *Lysis* is significant in the development of Plato's theory of *kala*, from lesser to more lofty, and finally to *auto to kalon*. The dialogue suggests that Plato had by this time conjured up the world of eternal immutable Forms.

Ronald B. Levinson's comprehensive article contributes to the debate on Plato's logical competence by a systematic survey of Plato's scattered judgments upon language. He concludes that during his long career Plato consistently held the view that, on the one hand, language or words are not to be confused with the idea or reality under investigation, and on the other, that words have great worth as instruments for instruction and discrimination. Levinson observes that Plato rejected using etymology for the inquiry into reality, but maintained the superiority of the spoken over the written word. On the positive side,

Plato implicitly formulated the law of contradiction, and characteristically guarded against the ambiguous use of words. He also regarded words as agents of human thought rather than as autonomous bearers of meaning, and in this respect Levinson attributes to him the use of stipulative definition. This point is brought out in a consideration of the *Euthyphro*, *Gorgias*, *Republic* and *Phaedrus*, first by noting the obvious Platonic habit of defining words or rather inquiring into the things which they denote. Definition of the definiendum, indicating the discriminatory and diacritical use of words, falls into two parts: (a) marking the definiendum off from other confusable entities, a task involving analysis and classification, and (b) assigning to the entity defined its proper place in the moral life and in the whole complex of being, a task which reveals the contextual aspect of the Platonic definition. Levinson agrees that the *Phaedrus* does not mark a radical change in Platonic philosophy, i.e. a turning away from the theory of Forms, but indeed adds no more than a formal elaboration of the method employed in the *Gorgias* and the *Republic.* Also among Plato's achievements are the advances made in the *Sophist* in the analysis of the structure and components of a sentence, the recognition that a sentence must be either true or false (Plato had established earlier, against Antisthenes, that there can be negative statements and false sentences), and the discrimination between assertion and denial.

Although Levinson is aware of "the importance of the ideal name as the model for the law-maker in the *Cratylus*" and he is prepared to agree that the Forms must be sought and somehow found, Rosamond Kent Sprague notes that Levinson is mostly concerned with other themes and "has, perhaps necessarily, underplayed the relationship of linguistic problems to the problems of metaphysics" (p. 368). Sprague's position is that Plato, in writing the *Cratylus*, tries to show how his concern for a theory of language is actually subordinate to the theory of Forms and that by means of the rejection of current linguistic theories one can "demonstrate the necessity for the theory of Forms" (p. 367).

J. M. E. Moravcsik studies in detail the celebrated passage 209E–212A in the *Symposium*, where Plato describes the steps on the ladder of love leading to the apprehension of the Form of Beauty. Proper understanding of this passage requires taking into consideration not only Plato's dramatization of the relationship between reason and eros but also how this interplay was carried out with the aid of a compressed outline of a theory of mind and certain basic ontological theses. Moravcsik's analysis shows that the passage involves a complex scheme of three kinds of steps: of reason, of emotion, and of creation. Their arrangement, in turn, discloses a number of significant connections between reason and eros, once their nature is fully seen, connections that shed further light on how best to approach the problem of the one and the many as it pertains to creation and the final vision of the Form of Beauty. Moravcsik's cogent argument makes clear why Beauty, as Plato conceives it in the *Symposium*, is both a common denominator and a distinct entity, and also why there is no real conflict between the two once the relation between Form and its subordinate species is cast in the right light. A substantial part of the essay is given to a discussion of the kinds of properties ascribed to Beauty. Thus, Moravcsik elucidates how the context of the passage requires certain basic distinctions on three vital issues: (a) the property of being everlasting and not subject to perishing must be seen as a necessary but not sufficient condition for being a Form; (b) to meet the criterion of sufficient condition in this case, one would have to show that the Form of Beauty is the only entity which is unqualifiedly beautiful; (c) the problems attending the issue of individuating properties can be met with the aid of the theory of definite descriptions. The distinction between Form-making and Form-individuating properties obtains in the case at hand even if Plato did not conceive the problem and its solution the way techniques of modern analysis have made possible.

The structure of the *Laches*, Michael J. O'Brien observes, is no doubt based on the opposition of *logos* and *ergon*. He argues that the dialogue rather than being inconclusive, can be seen as containing an implicit resolution in the realm of *ergon* or of personalities. The dialogue is an interaction between thought, characters, and their actions. The characters illuminate thought, and thought in turn judges the characters. Laches, the robust soldier of action, offers as a definition of courage "steadfastness of soul." Socrates' criticisms induce him to qualify the definition by including intelligence, but even this proves unsatisfactory. Nicias, the theoretical strategist, suggests that courage is "knowledge of the fearful and the safe." At the end of Socrates' criticisms of the definitions of courage propounded by Laches and Nicias, we are still left with proposals that are too general. O'Brien points out that the fault in each of these definitions corresponds to the merit in the other. Laches, who had said that courage was steadfastness, retreats quickly in the unfamiliar field of philosophical discussion. Nicias, who dwells on the theoretical aspect, falls short of his own definition in the actual battle of Syracuse in which he revealed his ignorance of what was to be feared most. Socrates alone represents the agreement of *logos* and *ergon*. At the time of his death he is both steadfast and knowledgeable of what is most to be feared: injustice rather than death. The unity of the *Laches* consists, then, not only in the harmony between the incomplete definitions of Laches and Nicias but equally in the juncture of these theoretical strands to form a practical solution in the person of Socrates himself. In the *Laches* "the purposes of the dramatist and the philosopher are in perfect agreement" (p. 132).

Martin Ostwald advances the thesis that there are two states in the *Republic*, that of the Guardians and that of the Philosophers, whereas the usual interpretation is that the Philosophers of Books V–VII are, though refined, the Guardians of Books II–IV. Ostwald undertakes to challenge the compression of the two by arguing that the state of the Guardians is a paradigmatic model developed in order to discover the principles of justice and injustice. If this is what Plato meant to propose as the ideal state, then it must not be taken as intending to serve a practical political aim. This fact, Ostwald argues, ought to be apparent from the many practical questions Socrates ignores when discussing how such a state is to function. Once the question of an actual state attaining this ideal is brought to the foreground, Socrates advocates looking for practical ways of approximating the state of the Guardians that will require the least change in actual states. What comes to prevail in the *Republic* is the view that the state of the Guardians can be approximated but not realized. This is as it should be since we must not blur the distinction between the ideal state and this world in which we are still subject to the conditions of change and decay. The point is addressed to those who are philosophers become kings or those who are now kings aspiring to become true philosophers. These philosopher-kings can bring about the required changes in three ways: by willingness to serve as guardians of the laws; by not failing to effect a model in their soul, "the constitution within" (which indeed is the ideal state of the Guardians, on which they will model the actual state); and by performing acts which will reflect both their experience and their knowledge. Plato has become convinced that the Philosopher is the only hope through which the state of the Guardians can be realized. Once again, the relationship of *logos* and *ergon* proves to be of the essence in the effort to determine the limits of the art of the possible and the contours of the vision of the ideal.

Since Beauty, Friendship, and Eros are closely related Platonic themes, it would be advantageous to read the essays by Levin and Moravcsik in conjunction with George Kimball Plochmann's discussion of the supporting themes in the *Symposium*. Plochmann is fully aware of Moravcsik's interpretation of the "ascent" passage and like both Levin and Moravcsik proposes to treat his particular subject by paying special tribute to the underlying unity of dramatic and philosophical elements that gives this and other dialogues their unique quality of style and thematic richness. Plochmann observes that in most dialogues the dialectic is controlled by the critical checking of words and definitions by a central figure, whereas in the *Symposium* the dialectic is disclosed by the sequence of characters, patterns of applause, and other incidents. Each speaker in the dialogue supports the themes of the central figure's consummate *logos*, Socrates' encomium on love. Plochmann also identifies a principle of selection which establishes the dialectical order within the speeches. To grasp the usefulness of this principle for purposes of interpretation and appreciation, one must first realize how it is that the *Symposium* must not be read simply as a statement of philosophy with a delightful background or as an instance of philosophical literature exhibiting a drama of persons, but rather as a new genre that integrates both. As Plochmann understands it, "For Plato real philosophy . . . and real poetry . . . are precisely the same" (p. 132). To argue in favor of the logical character of the subsidiary components and supporting themes, from Alcibiades' antics and Aristophanes' hiccups to the placing of the guests and their order of speaking, in this novel form of expression, is Plochmann's special task.

Thomas M. Robinson finds the passage 245C–246A in the *Phaedrus* genuinely challenging in that it contains one of the most condensed and difficult arguments, as he calls it, for the immortality of the soul. A correct analysis of this argument can hardly be given unless one is prepared to embark on a search for the logical and metaphysical issues to which it is related. (Professor Leonardo Tarán, who refers to Robinson's essay, offers a number of illuminating comments on the relevance of this passage in relation to his own efforts to decide the issue of character of the *Timaeus* and whether it makes more sense to read this latter dialogue literally or metaphorically (see Tarán's essay, pp. 394–95, note 33). Robinson defends the original reading that the soul is *aeikinētos* against Robin's *autokinētos*. As Robinson states the case for Plato, *aeikinētos* is *auto kinoun* and is the source of motion; hence it is immortal and indestructible. *Archē* and *auto kinoun* are one and the same so that there may be no cessation from being and no coming into being. These conclusions Robinson applies to the notion of soul itself. Robinson compares the *Phaedrus* passage to the final argument for immortality in the *Phaedo*, with which it has much in common. There the soul is likened to the static Ideas and yet is also said to be the principle of Life, two notions which are incompatible. Robinson suggests that the more empirical cast of the discussion in the *Phaedrus* "has its roots in the pre-Socratic tradition" (p. 347). The essay ends with a critical note on the relationship of the soul regarded as reverse of motion to the motion of the pre-cosmic chaos in the *Timaeus* 49A ff. The question is there raised whether motion in the Receptacle indicates the presence of soul. Robinson perceives that Plato is dealing with two entirely different kinds of motion; hence there seems no reason to reproach him with a lack of logic, as some of his critics have done.

Thomas G. Rosenmeyer argues contrary to most recent scholarship, especially the thesis in Richard Robinson's *Plato's Earlier Dialectic*, that for Plato hypothetical reasoning does not take an upward path and that the more general hypothesis is not, structurally, the higher. He suggests that it is misleading to think that Aristotle's logical terminology, which is ontologically conditioned, is either derived from Plato's logic or can be legitimately used as a guide to understand Plato's model of hypothetical reasoning. As a structural concept, "hypothesis" more often carries the sense of foundation, that from which to build up a superstructure. As a directional concept for logical progression, it indicates the begininning of a discussion or argument which proceeds horizontally from start to finish as a sentence progresses across the page. Drawing his evidence from the later as well as the middle and some earlier dialogues, Rosenmeyer is able to substantiate the thesis that the movement in Plato's conception of hypothetical reasoning is not a downward one but one from general assumption to specific conclusion. The significance of this interpretation is that Plato, unlike his student, Aristotle, and Plato's interpreters, *does* separate his metaphysical topography from his logic.

Leonardo Tarán's essay is a detailed consideration of the question whether the creation myth in Plato's *Timaeus* should or can be taken literally. The reader may well be aware how the literature on this controversy has affected interpretations of the Platonic corpus as a whole. Tarán's main target is Vlastos, who has given the most recent and most complete statement in defense of the thesis that Plato meant the creation of the world literally. One of the fundamental points Tarán makes is that the correct interpretation of the creation myth is tied to the problem of the origin of evil. The context of the myth shows that its purpose is "to give an account of the nature of man and of the universe to serve as the background for another mythical account, the purpose of which will be to show that the ideal state is superior and ultimately more powerful than an adversary which has greater material resources and skill but is morally inferior" (p. 373). Tarán observes that the features of the creation myth place it in a different category and ultimately concludes "that Plato purposely chose the form of a creation myth to give a systematic account of the nature of man and of the universe" (*ibid.*). Tarán bases his argument on the contradictions which he maintains Plato deliberately introduces in order to guide the reader to a systematic and metaphorical reading—contradictions that conspicuously follow once the chronological order in the account of the creation of the body and soul of the universe is given primacy.

Plato's *Seventh Letter* confronts the student with a set of problems of the highest order. Kurt von Fritz's objective is to scrutinize the meaning of the philosophic passage which boldly asserts the inherent weakness of every written statement of things that require understanding, a thesis intimately connected to what some of its interpreters have suspected to be the problem of Plato's esoteric teachings. Kurt von Fritz remarks that although most authorities in the field have decided in favor of the authenticity of the *Seventh Letter*, a new controversy has arisen which has prompted renewed attacks on the authenticity of the letter, this time from another direction. It has been proposed that the philosophic passage in the letter, assuming that the letter is authentic, can be regarded as testimony for the existence of an "esoteric" doctrine. This issue has created a serious problem of interpretation because the doctrine associated with it is not to be found anywhere in the dialogues but is claimed to have been communicated orally to a select few. Assuming the veracity of the claim, the supporters of this view have considered it a task of the first order to try to reconstruct this "esoteric" doctrine from available and presumably acceptable testimonies. In this essay von Fritz bypasses the larger issue of the authenticity of the letter to concentrate on the problems that arise in connection with the philosophic passage. He considers his primary task here "to come to the help of the *logos* of the *Seventh Letter*" and remove the misunderstandings associated with it.

IV

One of the more fascinating developments in recent approaches to ancient Greek philosophy is the steady deemphasis of the differences between Plato and Aristotle, and in turn, between Aristotle and later philosophers, in order to identify in more judicious ways their similarities and the continuity of reflective tradition in substantive issues. What now is being sought is a more methodical and reliable identification of the ingredients and pattern of philosophic activity that gave the Greek outlook its organic character. The grounds for drawing significant contrasts are undeniably there but there seems no special support forthcoming for the sort of theorizing that imported dichotomies, distinctions, and concerns which upon analysis proved to be alien to the body of Hellenic wisdom. These essays on Aristotle reflect not only sobriety in thematic treatment but an equal awareness of the danger of misinterpretations stemming from inadequate reading of evidence.

Thomas Gould investigates both Aristotle's theory of causal explanations and the possibility that Aristotle's metaphysical doctrines may have served as a basis for his ethical views. In order to discern each kind of cause, he urges us to consider not only Aristotle's doctrine of causation but also to understand how and why form, as a good being striven for, is the ultimate cause. Plato, on the other hand, for whom form is good and causes order in the world, at times admits that there are motions in the universe which are not directed to any particular good, whereas Aristotle's metaphysical views will not allow random motion or motion not caused by a good striven for. Against this background Gould proceeds to examine certain difficulties which arise in trying to fit Aristotle's treatment of ethics into his general metaphysical program. First a distinction must be drawn between human striving for well-being and necessary motions in inanimate objects because only in the case of man is error always possible. Given the possibilities of choice and error in ethical affairs, the question is: "If every motion in the universe is caused by a good striven for, and there is no such thing as random motion, what account can be given for an intelligent agent striving with less than perfect efficiency to his goal of true well-being?" (p. 453). The answer calls for a discussion of desire, appetite, and reason, which Gould places within the context of Aristotle's metaphysics, regarding intelligence as the key to man's natural fulfillment in the life of *theoria*. Given this foundation, other basic questions call for special attention: for instance, why did Aristotle actually maintain that every human urge was called forth by a form, and if he did, why does he not talk in these terms more clearly?

Joseph Owens, drawing upon various passages in Aristotle's works concerning sensible objects in human intellection, entertains the possibility that these passages might be compatible with the interpretation that the mind can find in sensible data notions that are wider than the sensible, and can see in sensible things an object, such as substance or being, that is more general than either the corporeal or the incorporeal. If this is sound Aristotelian doctrine, the mind can behold in sensible things a notion that is more universal than sensible. He brings up for special consideration the opening passage of Aristotle's *Physics* to determine whether this situation is possible in the Aristotelian noetic. The passage is shown to contain a surprising statement to the effect that one must advance from the universal to the particular. Since this seems contrary both to what might be expected and to the interpretations of most ancient and modern commentators, an analysis of the meanings of "universal" and "particular" here and in other passages is called for. Owens believes that the term *to katholou* bears one meaning (that of Book Δ of *Metaphysics*) in all passages in which it appears, including the opening one of the *Physics*. The discussion takes Owens into a detailed account of the "parts" which function as the *kath' hekasta* towards which the process of knowledge advances. He finds that in the *Posterior Analytics*, the term expresses that which is universal as a species and not just a singular thing; this permits the deduction that in the *Physics* "particular" need not mean the singular individual. Owens remarks that his interpretation of "universal" not only supports the regular and univocal meaning found elsewhere in Aristotle, but shows why the mind cannot attain in simple apprehension any concept that is common to corporeal and incorporeal things.

Arthur L. Peck begins with the question: "Can we define the field in which Aristotle believed *kinēsis* to operate?" (p. 478). Given Aristotle's four classes of *kinēsis*, Peck notes that it is inexact to say that every *kinēsis* is concerned with the realization of a form, although any one as an *archē* and a cause of motion will be informed, determined, and characterized in a definite way so as to produce as a result a thing which has a certain *ousia*, or a certain quality or quantity. The agent or efficient cause sets up in the matter a movement of a definite and specific kind, so that what is potentially *X* becomes *X* in actuality, thus acquiring the form to which is proper to the specific movement. This result is brought about by an intermediary, an *organon* to which the efficient cause imparts the movement of transmission. With this explained, Peck gives numerous illustrations from living things and artifacts. He also considers the question how far we can carry the association of movement with form. More specifically, he asks: "Can the combination of form and matter be satisfactorily applied in cases (if any) where the matter is not physical?" (p. 487). And further, "Is there a point short of the

Unmoved Mover at which form can be independent of *kinēsis*, or can be dispensed from the function of transmitting its own appropriate *kinēsis*?" (p. 488). His inquiries lead him to formulate an approach different from Aristotle's for distinguishing the various classes of movement. The cases of the Unmoved Mover and rational soul, insofar as they appear to be wholly independent of matter and thus have no movement proper to them to set up in matter, are unlike other forms.

D. A. Rees undertakes a careful analysis of what he calls the most original and remarkable aspect of Aristotle's psychology. He begins by noting the differences between Plato's and Aristotle's treatment of the subject by citing and briefly analyzing the various occurrences of *phantasia, phenomena,* and related terms and concepts in Plato, and then shows how the distinction between *phenomena* (appearance) and *onta* (reality), common to both Plato and Aristotle, is nevertheless treated differently by the two philosophers. Rees remarks that it is understandable that Aristotle's account should differ from Plato's since he abandons the Theory of Ideas, denies the Platonic *chorismos*, and assigns substantiality to the physical world. Rees also discusses the concept of imagination (*phantasia*) in modern philosophers such as Descartes, Hume, and Kant in order to contrast their view with that of Plato and Aristotle. His analysis of *De Anima* III, Ch. 3 is particularly helpful and illuminating, done in the light of modern translations of the Greek term for 'imagination'. Two major types of cases interest Rees: first, those in which the occurrence of a mental image is signified without any propositional implications; and second, those cases which, with or without reference to mental image or images, are propositional in character. According to Rees, both the propositional aspect and mental imagery are present in Aristotle's account. Certain aspects of the modern conception of 'imagination', such as scientific or poetical imagination, lie outside the scope of Aristotle's theory of *phantasia*, since Aristotle confined this power to a close dependence on that which has been perceived.

John M. Rist undertakes a reinterpretation of the Aristotelian doctrine of intellect. He proposes the reading "inside the individual soul" for the key expression *en tē psychē* which occurs at the beginning of *De Anima* III, Ch. 5. Contrary to Alexander of Aphrodisias and Averroes, and in accordance with Theophrastus, he infers that every soul contains its own Active and Passive Intellect, one moving and the other being moved. Since the Active Intellect functions "by making all things," one may reasonably say that it transforms *nous pathētikos* into a *nous noōn*. Stated in another way, ". . . it is the power which enables the

Passive Intellect to become a *nous noōn* by being made identical with the Intelligible Forms of the objects of thought" (p. 511). Rist takes the position that the perplexing features of *choristos*, *apathēs*, and *amigēs* describe only the Active Intellect, and offers arguments in favor of his interpretation that *choristos* is meant to characterize the superiority of Active to Passive. His fundamental theses are clearly stated in this challenging essay: in the individual soul there is an Active and a Passive Intellect, but it is the former that can effect the change in the latter from potency to act, admittedly a special kind of act; immortality does in fact figure in this view but solely in connection with the Active Intellect, which attains survival, but without memory or knowledge of the external world; the peculiar feature of the Active Intellect is basically its power to induce thought. If this much is admitted, Rist believes, the task of understanding the nature and functions of the Passive Intellect becomes a much easier one.

Richard Taylor opens his essay with a succinct statement on a problem of paramount importance in Aristotelian logic: "Aristotle believed that any statement which asserts or denies concerning a contingent event, that is going to occur, is neither true nor false, the world being as yet indeterminate with regard to the existence or nonexistence of such beings" (p. 522). He then remarks how this doctrine engendered enormous controversy throughout the Middle Ages, since all the scholastics declared these arguments inconsistent with the Christian outlook. In recent years, the controversy has gone in a different direction. While J. Lucasiewics, for instance, found it most useful to revive Aristotle's arguments to provide an interpretation for his three-valued logic, other recent logicians, such as C. A. Baylis, W. V. Quine, G. Ryle, and D. Williams, dismiss them as paralogisms. Taylor offers his own view of Aristotle's position, attempts a more careful formulation of the doctrine of real contingencies, indicates the sense in which the modal terms involved, viz., necessity, possible, impossible, and contingent, should be taken, and finally undertakes to meet the objections that have been raised against the doctrine. He argues that Aristotle is neither muddled in this part of his theory nor are his conclusions false; instead, he finds that "he was exceptionally profound and that at least one important part of his doctrine is true" (p. 522). Taylor also indicates how Aristotle's position has some far-reaching consequences for basic philosophic areas. In metaphysics it involves the view that time has an intrinsic order which analysis can show to be different from the characteristic order of space; in logical theory it points to an area of applicability of a three-valued logic; and in theology it makes powerful suggestions for a revision of the traditional notion of divine omniscience.

With his treatment of qualitative change G. Verbeke sheds light on a difficult but philosophically important subject. Aristotle's major concern was the possibility of translating into terms of qualitative change the most important activities of man, such as moral conduct, scientific knowledge, and technical activities. Verbeke notes the uses of quality and qualitative change in Aristotle's *Categories*, and compares them to *Physics*, VII, 3, where the arguments concern technical activity, bodily habits, habits of soul, and intellectual habits. He finds that with respect to technical activity, change in figure and shape is not really a case of alteration. Similarly, in the case of bodily habits, neither virtues (good habits) nor vices (bad habits) are alterations since for Aristotle what is entirely relative cannot be subject to alteration, generation, or change. In discussing the arguments concerning habits of soul, Verbeke concludes that the generation of moral virtues and vices is necessarily accompanied by alteration, without being itself an alteration. Again, in the case of intellectual habits, the exercise or use of knowledge is found to be neither a becoming nor an alteration. In the concluding section Verbeke advances his analyses of the nature of knowing and psychical activity and alteration a step further. He shows how the similarities between Plato and Aristotle regarding the concept of knowledge, that it is a state of rest and not motion, are found to rest basically on three factors: the etymology of *epistēmē*, the physiological conceptions of Alcmaeon of Croton, and the Theory of Ideas. Verbeke intends his findings to give support to two major theses: first, that man realizes himself fully in exerting the activity that is proper to him; and second, that the exercise of knowing or moral activity has its aims of action situated in the actions themselves and not outside or beyond them.

V

A number of substantial works in post-Aristotelian thought and Hellenistic philosophy in general that appeared in the last decade have proved influential in providing new stimulus for further studies and rekindled the quest for new interpretive ideas that would promote independent judgment based on direct acquaintance with the original sources. Thus, we have seen the publication of studies that do greater justice to the achievements of Stoic thinkers, the contributions of the Peripatetic School following the death of Theophrastus, the teachings of the School of Epicurus, the work that took place during the diverse phases of the Academy and the development of Skepsis, and, last but not least, the complex movement known as Neoplatonism. The essays on post-Aristotelian philosophy included in this volume afford samples of the quality of current work in this period in the history of Western philosophy.

John P. Anton opens his essay with an account of Aristotle's doctrine of *homonyma* as found in the first chapter of the *Categories* and discusses its place in the logic of the *Organon* in the light of difficulties that surround the textual tradition for this key passage. Settling the meaning of this doctrine requires a comparative study of the rival views on the subject held by Speusippus and post-Aristotelian commentators. It is shown that the miscellaneous materials which the Hellenistic and later commentators bring into their discussions are quite frequently alien to the issues that Aristotle had in mind. Porphyry, Dexippus, Ammonius, Philoponus, Olympiodorus, Simplicius, and Elias, all Neoplatonists, included in their comments views far more relevant to their own ontologies and logical theories than to Aristotle's. One of Anton's aims is the identification of the intellectual affiliations of the commentators and the underlying assumptions which these thinkers attributed, no doubt, in good faith to Aristotle himself. Specifically, the commentators fall short of understanding the full technical import of the *logos tēs ousias* phrase which controls the meaning of the complete formulation of *homonyma* in Aristotle's text. When the commentators took *logos* to mean both definition and description, they hardly realized they were interpolating an aspect absent from Aristotle's conception of the doctrine. As a result the commentators widened the denotation of the definiendum "homonyma" considerably beyond the controlled scope Aristotle assigned to this technical concept. This departure from Aristotle's approach to categorical and logical theory went unnoticed throughout antiquity and even beyond.

In his perceptive essay, Phillip DeLacy brings his erudition to bear on a comparative study of diverse uses of the expression *ou mallon* or *ouden mallon* as a philosophical term, noting how it underwent a number of changes during the long period of ancient philosophy and how in its more prominent uses the term came to be associated with certain persistent problems in Greek thought. The term means "no more this than that." Democritus uses it but not as a technical term. With Plato it begins to find its place in arguments and becomes a formula of refutation in that it identifies a view to be discredited as self-contradictory. Aristotle also adopts this formula of refutation in charging that certain systems in which it applies are self-contradictory. Views in which *ou mallon* figures largely as a basic feature make knowledge impossible because by obliterating differences they remove the grounds of action and moral choice. Aristotle shows how the expression obtains in his refutation of Heraclitus and Anaxagoras. When used as a universal principle, it is at once self-contradictory and untenable. Aristotle's contribution to understanding the implications of the universalization of this principle is one of high order. During the post-Aristotelian period, *ou mallon* continues to find a basic application in philosophic discussion. As DeLacy points out with ample documentation, each Hellenistic school handled the predicament of the *ou mallon* sort in its own terms, but all harken back to Aristotle's formulation. Pyrrho gave it a universal application but only to recommend through it complete suspension of judgment, *aphasia*. The Epicureans made a bold attempt to avoid the predicament but fell short of their goal especially in their theory of ethics, and similarly the Stoics escaped some of the difficulties only to encounter new ones. The scepticism of the Academy made a special effort to use *ou mallon* in restricted ways as part of their concern to elude the fatal error of self-refutation, the antecedents of which go back in large part to the insights of Aristotle and his predecessors.

David J. Furley's main theme concerns one of the most important methodological and epistemic issues in ancient atomism, early and post-Aristotelian. His essay is a painstaking examination of the problems and issues surrounding what is known as a paradox in the theories of the Atomists. In his own words: "If knowledge comes to us by means of sensation (and all senses are really varieties of the sense of touch) how are we to explain the atomist's knowledge of the basic propositions of his special theory: that the world consists of void, which is called 'the intangible', and atoms which are said to be imperceptibly small?" (p. 607). The authoritative answer modern scholarship has given to this paradox was formulated by Professor Cyril Bailey in his writings on Epicurus, and it is precisely the grounds and validity of this answer that Furley subjects to examination before proceeding with the formulation of his alternative proposal. Furley's critical look at Bailey's solution involves a fresh reading and analysis of the texts to which Bailey appealed for support. Bailey took the position that next to sense perception the Epicureans accepted a form of knowledge of the external world by which we gain access to the *adēla* or nonevident classes of subject, such as stars and the like. It is also known that whereas Epicureans were prepared to accept multiple explanations in the case of *adēla* of the meteorological sort, they made no such concessions in the case of the fundamental principles of their atomism despite the fact that these principles were admittedly not gained via sense perception. Bailey explained this discrepancy in the approach to the *adēla* by interpreting the Epicurean expression *epibolē tēs dianoias* (direct mental apprehension) to be the key notion in their theory of knowledge of principles. Furley documents his counterposition to show that *epibolē tēs dianoias* does not play the supreme part in the foundations of the atomic theory that Bailey assigned it, and, positively put, a different explanation can be formulated to show that Epicurus must be spared the charge of inconsistency although not that of simplemindedness of argument.

Audrey N. M. Rich observes that serious inquiry into the soul-body relationship started with Aristotle, though Plato was deeply concerned with the moral aspects of the problem. When Plotinus turned his attention to this topic he was substantially familiar with Aristotle's teachings, as is evidenced by the terminology and the general thrust of his inquiry. The influence of Aristotle is undeniably there but the overarching considerations that run through the *Enneads* are Plotinus's loyalty to Platonism, the profound dualism he found in it, and also a sustained suspicion and hostility toward the body, aspects conspicuously lacking in the *De Anima*. Rich's account of Plotinus's doctrines brings out significant aspects essential to a fuller understanding of his philosophy. Rich considers it important to review in detail the parts of the soul, what unites it with the body to form the *zōon*, how this complex of body and soul needs in addition the faculty of discursive thought to constitute the special case of "the man himself." It is this *koinonia* of soul and body which provides the answer to the problem of the initial embodiment of the soul and the causes originally responsible for it. In working out answers to his own set of basic issues, Plotinus found it necessary to refute the Stoic and the Epicurean views on the soul-body problem, the "attunement theory" as stated in the *Phaedo* and the Aristotelian definition of soul as the *entelecheia* of the living body. Rich offers ample documentation to show that Plotinus asserted a view that makes the soul an essence separate from any particular entity, existing prior to becoming such and such an individual and enjoying similar status after its dissociation from the body.

VI

The introductory remarks made in the preceding sections have been made by way of preface and not in the least as summaries for the original arguments and expositions presented in the essays themselves. Our purpose has been to provide a general guide to the treatment of the diverse themes which the authors found of interest and a challenge. The convergence and divergence of the viewpoints discussed in these essays and the implications they may have for an independent position on the part of the reader can only issue from a study of the essays themselves. As editors we have thought it sufficient to have made clear the nature of our enterprise as a whole and to have pointed out the themes and problems touched by the authors in their efforts to provide reliable paths to a critical appreciation of the ingenuity and originality of the Hellenic philosophic genius.

NOTES

[1] See Vlastos's essay in this volume, p. 119. For his references to the publications of Fränkel, Owen and Furley, p. 136, notes 1 and 2. For Vlastos's more recent conclusions and interpretation of Zeno's fragments, and his place in the history of Greek thought, the reader is urged to consult Vlastos's article in the *Encylopedia of Philosophy*, ed. Paul Edwards (New York, 1967).

[2] This volume, pp. 176–77, and p. 183, notes 1 and 2.

[3] This volume, esp., pp. 303–4, and p. 313 notes 1–5.

[4] Benson Mates, *Stoic Logic*. Berkeley: University of California Press, 1953.

Journal Abbreviations

AA	*Antike und Abendland*
AB	*Archiv für Begriffsgeschichte*
AFC	*Anales de Filologia Clasica*
AGP	*Archiv für Geschichte der Philosophie*
AJP	*American Journal of Philology*
AP	*Archiv für Philosophie*
APF	*Acta Philosophica Fennica*
AWL	*Abhandlungen der Mainzer Akademie der Wissenschaft und Literatur*
BFA	*Bulletin of the Faculty of Arts*
CP	*Classical Philology*
CQ	*Classical Quarterly*
Da	*Daedalus*
DR	*Downside Review*
EAC	*Entretiens sur l'Antiquité Classique*
GCFI	*Giornale Critico della Filosofia Italiena*
GGA	*Göttingsche Gelehrte Anzeigen*
GM	*Giornale di Metafisica*
HSCP	*Harvard Studies in Classical Philology*
IPQ	*International Philosophical Quarterly*
JHP	*Journal of the History of Philosophy*
JHS	*Journal of Hellenic Studies*
JP	*Journal of Philosophy*
JPh	*Journal of Philology*
JR	*Journal of Religion*
JRSS	*Journal of the Royal Statistical Society*
JTS	*Journal of Theological Studies*
Mn	*Mnemosyne*
MH	*Museum Helveticum*
NGG	*Nachrichten von der Gesellschaft der Wissenschaften zu Göttingen*
PAA	*Proceedings of the American Academy of Arts and Sciences*
PAPS	*Proceedings of the American Philosophical Society*
PAS	*Proceedings of the Aristotelian Society*
PBA	*Proceedings of the British Academy*
Phn	*Phronesis*
Phil	*Philologus*
Phx	*Phoenix*
PP	*La Parole del Passato, Rivista di Studi Antichi*
PQ	*Philosophical Quarterly*
PR	*Philosophical Review*
PS	*Philosophy of Science*
PSt	*Philosophical Studies*
RCFI	*Rivista Critica di Storia della Filosofia*
RE	*Pauly-Wissowa: Real Encyclopädie der Classischen Altertumswissenschaft*

REG	*Revue des Etudes Grecques*
RFC	*Rivista de Filosofia e d'Instruzione Classica*
RhM	*Rheinisches Museum für Philologie*
RML	*Reniconti Morali Lincei*
RP	*Revue de Philologie*
RPL	*Revue Philosophique de Louvain*
RR	*Review of Religion*
SAWW	*Sitzungsberichte der Kaiserlichen Akademie der Wissenschaften in Wien*
SBAW	*Sitzungsberichte der Bayerischen Akademie der Wissenschaften*
SHAW	*Sitzungsberichte der Heidelberger Akademie der Wissenschaften*
SP	*Studia Philosophica*
TAPA	*Transactions and Proceedings of the American Philological Association*
WKP	*Wochenschrift für Klassische Philologie*
WS	*Wiener Studien*
ZÖG	*Zeitschrift für die Öesterreichischen Gymnasien*
ZPF	*Zeitschrift für Philosophische Forschung*

PRE-SOCRATICS

CHARLES H. KAHN
University of Pennsylvania

Religion and Natural Philosophy in Empedocles' Doctrine of the Soul*

SINCE Zeller's classic work, all students of Greek philosophy have recognized that the thought of Empedocles presents two quite distinct aspects. On the one hand, Empedocles is the author of a rational cosmology which explains all processes of the natural world in terms of the combination and separation of four elements under the opposing influence of the forces of Love and Hate. Yet in his poem of *Purifications* the same author appears like a figure from another world, an inspired seer who proclaims himself a god and exhorts all mankind to purify themselves by abstaining from meat, beans, and laurel leaves. This religious teaching is just as clearly dependent upon "Orphic" or Pythagorean mystery cults as is his physical theory upon the thought of Parmenides and the Ionian naturalists. Empedocles the philosopher of nature and Empedocles the prophet of transmigration are both intelligible when taken separately. Together, they seem to compose a split personality whose two sections are not united by any essential link.

In an historical context, of course, it is possible to interpret such a duality by reference to the ambiguous spiritual tendencies of the fifth century B.C., when rationalism and mysticism had not fully asserted their rival claims nor taken up the positions of clear-cut hostility which they often occupy in the modern world. And there are in fact significant precedents in early Greek thought for such a mixture of mystery religion with natural philosophy. Pythagoras himself seems to have borrowed the outlines of his cosmology from the Milesian physicists. We find elemental physics crossed with mystic immortality in the doctrine of Heraclitus that "we live the death of the gods and they live our death."[1] The metaphysics and the cosmology of Parmenides are cast in the form

* Originally presented under the title "Panpsychism and Immortality in Empedocles" before the 1958 meeting of the SAGP in Cincinatti, Ohio. From the *Archiv für Geschichte der Philosophie*, Band 42, Heft 1 (1960): 3–35. Reprinted by permission of Walter de Gruyter & Co.

of a supernatural vision vouchsafed him on a journey to the realm of Light.

Yet even if the list of such intermarriages between philosophy and religion were considerably lengthened, it could not explain the relationship between the mystic and the rational elements in the thought of Empedocles. The problem, as Zeller put it, is that Empedocles' religious teachings "stand in no visible connection with the scientific principles" of his physics; the doctrine of transmigration and purification appear as "mere articles of faith, imperfectly appended to his philosophical scheme."[2] In fact to many scholars it has seemed that "the cosmological system of Empedocles leaves no room for an immortal soul, which is presupposed by the *Purifications*."[3] Such a radical disparity between the two aspects of Empedocles' thought led Jaeger to describe him as "a philosophical centaur, so to speak—a prodigious union of Ionian elemental physics and Orphic theology."[4]

Now this is a difficult prodigy for us to understand. If the contradiction between his philosophic and religious views is as flagrant as most modern authors have supposed, is it conceivable that Empedocles himself was unaware of that fact? Or that he found the situation a tolerable one? He cannot have consoled himself, like Averroes, by distinguishing between the conclusions of reason and the tenets of faith. The fifth century B.C. had only one standard of truth, and hence no notion of irrational faith: Empedocles makes use of the same term πίστις for belief in his physical theories and in his religious doctrines.[5] If the religion of the *Purifications* is incompatible with the cosmology of the poem *On Nature*, we are left with an unmitigated contradiction between two views expressed by the same philosopher.

Diels and Wilamowitz thought they could avoid this antinomy by transferring all of the more obviously theological fragments to the religious poem, and interpreting the latter as the fruit of a spiritual conversion in Empedocles' old age. They made the most of the fact that Empedocles' political career seems to have ended in banishment and, since the *Purifications* speak of him traveling from city to city, these two scholars attributed that poem to the last period of his life, when he had perhaps become, as Matthew Arnold imagined him,

> . . . half mad,
> With exile and with brooding on his wrongs.

In their view, the two halves of the centaur belong to different periods in Empedocles' life: the rational materialism of the physical poem is later replaced by the religiosity of the *Purifications*.[6]

As far as psychological plausibility is concerned, this hypothesis of a spiritual development for Empedocles is considerably more attractive than the usual view of his work as a mere juxtaposition of irreconcilable elements. Diels and Wilamowitz must be correct in recognizing the *Purifications* as the later of the two poems, and they may well be right in thinking that it reflects a change in Empedocles' vision of himself and his work.[7] But a difference in date and outlook between the two poems cannot possibly resolve the conflict between his philosophy and his religion, for the physical poem is also a religious work. Even if we were to follow Diels in assigning the theological fragments to the *Purifications* (although all the evidence is against this),[8] the poem *On Nature* would still not read like a tract of scientific rationalism. The proem of the work, and in particular fragment 3, brings us face to face with a religious poet whose verses breathe the spirit of mysterious, half-suppressed revelation:

> ἀλλὰ θεοὶ τῶν μὲν μανίην ἀποτρέψατε γλώσσης,
> ἐκ δ' ὁσίων στομάτων καθαρὴν ὀχετεύσατε πηγήν·
> καὶ σέ, πολυμνήστη λευκώλενε παρθένε Μοῦσα,
> ἄντομαι, ὧν θέμις ἐστὶν ἐφημερίοισιν ἀκούειν,
> πέμπε παρ' Εὐσεβίης ἐλάουσ' εὐήνιον ἅρμα
> μηδέ σέ γ' εὐδόξοιο βιήσεται ἄνθεα τιμῆς
> πρὸς θνητῶν ἀνελέσθαι, ἐφ' ᾧ θ' ὁσίης πλέον εἰπεῖν
> θάρσεϊ — καὶ τότε δὴ σοφίης ἐπ' ἄκροισι θοάζειν.

> But, ye gods, turn away from my tongue the madness of those men,
> and from your holy lips pour forth a pure stream;
> and you, the much-wooed, fair-armed virgin Muse
> do I entreat, of what is lawful for creatures of a day to hear
> drive here your well-reined chariot from Piety's hall,
> nor will you be seduced by the blossoms of honor and fame
> to pluck them in men's sight, by daring to say more than is holy
> and then forsooth to throne on the heights of wisdom.

The invocation of Calliope, the muse of lovely verse,[9] may perhaps be interpreted as a literary convention devoid of religious significance—although the fact that her chariot is to come from the realm of Piety suggests rather more than that. But what are we to make of Empedocles' appeal to the gods to "turn away from my tongue the madness of those men,[10] and pour from your holy lips a pure stream"? Why does he ask the Muse for inspiration only on those matters "which it is lawful for creatures of a day to hear"? The pious chariot of the Muse is "well-reined" (εὐήνιον) because there will be limits to her revelation: she can be relied upon not to seek glory by "declaring more than is holy."

Like the poem of Parmenides, the physical work of Empedocles is thus presented in the form of a religious revelation. Unlike Parmenides,

Empedocles insists upon the limited character of the revelation and also upon its esoteric quality: his teachings are entrusted to Pausanias alone, who is urged to keep them "mute within his breast."[11] The partial nature of the revelation makes one think of a preliminary initiation, which reserves the final disclosure for a later ἐποπτεία. In fact Empedocles adheres much more closely to the form and style of a religious revelation than does Parmenides. The poem begins and ends with an appeal for purity, and with an earnest denunciation of things impure.[12] The secret doctrine is credited with magic potency: the disciple will be able to cure old age, check or call back the winds, make rain or dry weather, and raise the dead to life.[13] Diels wished to read these promises as a scientific hope of mastering nature by the knowledge of its laws, but Empedocles' fifth-century rival in the practice of medicine, the Hippocratic author of *The Sacred Disease*, recognized the claim for what it was: a standard formula of sorcerers and medicine men, who proposed to treat epilepsy by charms (ἐπαοιδαί) and purifications (καθαρμοί).[14] And it is precisely a "healing spell" of this kind which the crowds of sufferers expect to hear from Empedocles, as he tells us in his own poem of *Purifications*.[15]

It is not only the form and spirit of the physical poem which suggests a supernatural revelation, but the doctrinal content as well. The work probably concluded with a general discussion of the nature of the gods, and with the announcement of a divinity who can only be described as a "sacred and surpassing spirit (φρήν), darting through the whole world with his rapid thoughts."[16] Its cardinal doctrine is the power of a deity "whom no mortal man has discerned":

> Fire and Water and Earth and the lofty zone of Air,
> and baneful Strife apart from these, their match in every way,
> and Love among them, equal in length and breadth;
> her must you perceive with the mind, nor sit with dazed eyes,
> she who is worshipped by mortals as instinct in their limbs,
> by whom they think loving thoughts and perform deeds of union,
> calling her by the name of Joy as well as Aphrodite;
> her has no mortal man discerned whirling among the others;
> but you shall hear the undeceptive march of my tale.[17]

The four elements had all been recognized in one form or another by the Ionians. The war between them is a central doctrine of Heraclitus. What Empedocles claims for himself is the discovery of Love and Attraction as a universal power in the physical world, on an equal footing with elemental Strife. His conception goes far beyond the poetic use of Aphrodite and Eros as symbols of the creative union of Heaven and

Earth, and even beyond Parmenides' notion of the intercourse between elemental opposites, Fire and Night.[18] Since there are four unlike elements in Empedocles' scheme, the idea of a union or harmony between them inevitably implies more than the sexual principle of an affinity between opposites. The best example of Love's work in forming natural compounds is the geometric proportion which unites the various ingredients of a mixture.[19] In this respect, every natural blend is an embodiment of Φιλότης or 'Αρμονίη.

Thus Empedocles' new divinity dominates the world of nature just as she dominates the poem in which this world is explained. When he comes to describe the fullest manifestation of this principle, Empedocles passes beyond the realm of generation and corruption to portray the perfect form of a universal Sphere within which, for a certain time, all the elements are periodically immobilized and transfigured under the absolute sway of Love.[20] Here, at the culminating moment of his cosmic poem, Empedocles presents us with a supramundane θεός, the direct counterpart to Parmenides' revelation of the perfect Sphere of τὸ ὄν, and the equivalent in early Greek thought of an apocalyptic vision.

There is, then, sufficient evidence of a religious orientation within Empedocles' poem *On Nature*. His cosmology is religious in the same sense that this term applies to the thought of Parmenides or Plato. The traditional view of it as atheistic or materialistic rests upon a confusion between the science of Empedocles and the science of the nineteenth century, or between the spirit of his poem and that of his great imitator Lucretius. There is no room for a "conversion" between the physical poem and the *Purifications*, for the author of *On Nature* is already a religious mystic who hints at his belief in immortality:

> A man wise in such matters will not surmise in his mind
> that when they are alive, in what men call life,
> then only do they exist and encounter good things and evil,
> but before mortals are composed and after they are dissolved,
> they are nothing at all.[21]

We know from Pindar that a mysterious doctrine of punishment, purification, and rebirth, comparable to that which Empedocles presents in the *Purifications*, had been taught in Acragas since the time of Theron. Empedocles must have been familiar with this teaching when he composed the physical poem.[22] He is probably referring to it in the verses just quoted, and it is not unreasonable to suppose that he has the same mystic doctrine in mind when he insists upon secrecy concerning things not "lawful for creatures of a day to hear."

If Empedocles believed in transmigration or in any form of immortality when he wrote the poem *On Nature*, all attempts to resolve the conflict between his cosmology and his religion along developmental lines are bound to fail. There is an obvious contrast between the religious attitude of the two poems, since one suppresses any direct reference to the doctrine which the other openly proclaims. And since the more revealing of the two is also the more public, it is difficult to explain this difference in terms of the audience to which they are addressed. Empedocles' own attitude seems to have undergone a change, and we must ask ourselves why. First, however, we must recognize the fact that this change does not involve the rejection of his own cosmology. The religious poem is as discreet on this subject as the physical work is mum concerning the doctrine of the *Purifications*. But in neither case does silence imply negation. Just as there are hints of the religious teaching in the poem *On Nature*, a close reading of the *Purifications* will show that they likewise presuppose Empedocles' cosmology.

The decisive moment of the physical poem is the disruption of the divine Sphere by Strife, since from this event proceeds the formation of the world as we know it. Turning to the *Purifications*, we see that this rupture of primordial harmony is paralleled by the fall of a daimon—that is, of a deified human soul—from its proper state of bliss into this "joyless place" of birth, suffering, and death. The parallel is easily remarked, for it is plainly indicated by Empedocles himself. He repeats the striking reference to "broad oaths," which seal the law of individual rebirth exactly as they ordained the physical period of the cosmos, and he tells us that the daimon fell because it "trusted in raving Strife." These formulas imply that the destiny of the human soul is grounded in the law of the universe, as revealed in the poem *On Nature*.[23]

It is therefore no trifling matter if, as many scholars have claimed, this physical cosmology is incompatible with the religious doctrine which Empedocles builds upon it. Is there or is there not a place in his physics for an immortal soul? This is the question to which some answer must be found. The chances of hitting upon the right answer will perhaps be greater if we first attempt to specify just what we mean by a "soul."

In modern usage, the term "soul" (and its various equivalents, such as *âme* and *Seele*) often refers to the conscious self in its broadest aspects—to the non-bodily reality of the whole person as seen from the inside. It may be "the essence or substance . . . of individual life, manifested in thinking, willing, and knowing," as *Webster's Dictionary* puts it.

Now if the soul is understood in such a comprehensive sense, the doctrine of its immortality naturally implies the survival of the whole person in his full individuality. And in fact the identity between the immortal soul and the concrete human being is often emphasized by the belief that the soul will eventually be reunited with its original body in some spiritualized form.

Now if this is what we mean by an immortal soul, the modern critics are certainly correct in maintaining that such a view is excluded by the cosmology of Empedocles. But it may be fairly doubted whether Empedocles or any other Greek philosopher before Christian times ever maintained the doctrine of immortality in this form. The survival they contemplate is never that of the whole human being, but of one single element of our empirical self, one whose isolated existence after death involves a complete break with the conditions of human life. The most striking example of such a break is Aristotle's doctrine of the separable νοῦς, which is eternally aware of intelligible realities but entirely unaffected by—and hence without memory of—any specifically human experience. If we disregard the metaphysical complexity of Aristotle's doctrine, it may serve to typify the Greek view of what is implied in immortality. 'Αθανασία means ὁμοίωσις θεῷ, not the preservation of human nature but an assimilation to the divine. In the case of Plato too it may be doubted whether there is any significant personal individuality for the purified ψυχή, as defined by the last argument of the *Phaedo*. In the context of transmigration, above all, there can be nothing permanent or valuable in the human condition as such. It is only the last stage on a journey which begins with the vegetable and ends with the escape into unalloyed divinity. In this view, any reunion of the soul with an individual body can only signify a blot on its condition. What lives on is not the individual human personality,[24] in fact not the man at all, but the godlike element which was lodged within his breast.

In Greek philosophy, then, there is always an implicit distinction between the soul which survives—the immortal and therefore divine principle in man—and the soul in the broader sense, as the living totality of feeling, thought, and desire. Confusion between the two is naturally facilitated by the fact that ψυχή may designate either one. In the popular conception of an afterlife, this confusion was enhanced by the old tendency to imagine the spirits in Hades as phantoms of the men who had lived on earth. So Odysseus in the underworld can recognize the ψυχαί of Ajax, Achilles, and Agamemnon.[25] But when we are dealing with a philosopher, we must be prepared to distinguish more rigorously between the divine psychic entity which lives on and the mortal complex in which it is embedded. This means, among other things, that we must separate the question of immortality from that of empirical thought or "consciousness."

In the case of Empedocles, there has been an unfortunate tendency to identify the two. Because he explains all phenomena of consciousness—all thought, feeling, and perception—by reference to the constitution of a mortal compound, most scholars have inferred that his physical theory excludes an immortal soul. How could there be good and evil for a man after death, if his "thought" (νόημα) is dissolved at the same time as the physical compound of his body? To many it has seemed that one need only raise this question to show the incompatibility between Empedocles' natural philosophy and his religious beliefs.

Yet the question is not fairly posed unless we are prepared to distinguish between the deathless soul which transmigrates and the conscious mind or thought which is the function of a particular compound. And to do so, we must first look a bit more closely at the physical psychology of Empedocles.

In the matter of consciousness, the position of Empedocles may be defined as a rigorous panpsychism. In his view, which seems to be shared to some degree by most early Greek thinkers, the faculty of feeling, perception, and thought—αἰσθάνεσθαι, νοεῖν or φρονεῖν—does not constitute a prerogative of men, or even of men and animals, but is assumed to be distributed generally throughout the natural world. From this point of view, there is really no such thing as inanimate nature. The character of any object is conceived of as a vital urge that may be described in terms of thought and volition. This conception is analogous to the "animism" which is said to characterize the attitude of many primitive peoples in their dealings with nature. But the animism of Empedocles is scarcely primitive: it is explicitly formulated as a philosophic principle. He ends the poem *On Nature* with a warning to his friend Pausanias that the truths communicated must be carefully borne in mind, or else

> they will leave you all at once, when their time comes round,
> yearning after their fellows, to return to their own dear kind;
> for know that all things have intelligence and a share in thought.[26]

This statement implies a systematic parallelism between physical objects and mental conceptions. Not only does everything have a share in thought, but every thought is treated like a thing. Apparently Empedocles recognizes no radical distinction between the two, for the constituents of the physical world and of our perception of this world are described in the same terms:

> By earth we behold earth, by water water,
> by air bright air, by fire, ravaging fire,
> love by love and strife by gloomy strife.[27]
> For out of these are all things compounded and fitted together
> and with these do they think and feel pleasure and pain.[28]

The least we can say is that Empedocles posits a one-to-one correspondence between our conscious thought or mind and the physical composition of our bodies. It seems more likely that he simply identified the two. Love and Strife are described not only as dynamic principles of cohesion and dissolution, but also as physical masses on a par with Fire, Water, Earth, and Air.[29] So mind and body are homogeneous, and external sense objects act upon us by mingling their substance with the ingredients of our nature, that is, with our body and mind at once. Sensation and philosophic instruction are described in the same concrete manner. It is hard for the truth to reach us, for the passages of entry are narrow and clogged by "wretched impacts which dull men's thoughts."[30] It is these "wretched myriads" of oncoming sensations which distract us from the truth of Empedocles' words.[31] "For men's mind is increased according to what is present," i.e., what is physically present in their bodies; when our physical condition changes, the character of our thought and perception is altered.[32] Since learning, like sensation, is introduced from without, in order to be held fast it must be thoroughly integrated into the mixture of our own nature and character, our φύσις and ἦθος.[33] If not, says Empedocles, it will hurry home to its own kind. The psychological fact of forgetting is understood as the escape of ingredients from a particular mixture.

Hence it is our physical composition or φύσις which accounts for—if it is not identical with—our psychic character (ἦθος) and thought (νόημα).[34] This is clearly seen in Empedocles' reference to the central sensorium, which for him as for Aristotle is the heart:

> nurtured in the seas of the resurgent blood,
> there what men call thought is mainly to be found;
> for the thought of men is the blood about their heart.[35]

The heart-blood plays this privileged role because it is the substance in which the elements are most perfectly blended. But the same principle applies to the body taken as a whole, as well as to each one of its parts, as Theophrastus tells us in his summary of a lost section of the poem:

Those in whom the elements are equally blended or nearly so, . . . are the most intelligent and most acute in sensation, and those closest to them are proportionately (acute and intelligent), while those with the opposite composition are the most foolish . . . And those who have an equable blend in some one part are skillful with that part. Therefore some men are good orators, others craftsmen, because the (proper) blend in one case is in their hands, in the other case in their tongue; and the same is true of other capacities.[36]

As Aristotle saw, this view of Empedocles implies not so much a single "soul" as a multitude of mental units, one for each element (since each one perceives its corresponding object) and one for each part of the body (since each has its own blend or φύσις).[37] Our psychic nature taken as a whole is a compound of these elemental and organic "souls," just as our bodily nature is a compound of elements and of their mixture in the various parts. The psychic and somatic complexes are in fact one and the same. And since there is a fragment of mind or thought corresponding to every fragment of body, the panpsychism of Empedocles implies a kind of infinite divisibility of the "soul".

It is this fragmentation of the empirical soul for Empedocles which must be borne in mind if his doctrine of immortality is to be made intelligible. On the one hand, our psychic nature at any given moment is obviously just as transitory as the physical mixture on which it is based. Not only does our mind in this sense not survive death, it does not survive any physical change whatsoever. The ratio of ingredients is altered by every bite of food, as well as every act of learning or forgetting. And the cohesion of the mixture is clearly terminated when the organism draws its last breath.

On the other hand, there can be no question of extinction, no utter destruction of psychic any more than of bodily reality. The necessary survival of the component parts of the soul is an inevitable consequence of the principle of Parmenides, which Empedocles has placed at the foundation of his cosmology. Nothing comes to be or perishes; there is only "mixture and the separation of what has been mixed."[38] Therefore death is as much an illusion in the psychic realm as in the physical. There is a continual formation and dissolution of individual compounds. But the elements of which a mind is composed are just as eternal as those of the body, for they are exactly the same.

> A man wise in such matters will not surmise in his mind
> that when they are alive, in what men call life,
> then only do they exist and encounter good things and evil,
> but before mortals are composed and after they are dissolved,
> they are nothing at all.[39]

> Fools: for they have no wits to reach long thoughts,
> who imagine that something is generated which did not exist before,
> or that anything dies away and is utterly destroyed.[40]

Whether we regard this as a religious belief or a philosophic doctrine, it clearly serves as the basis for Empedocles' whole physical system. In his view, the Parmenidean attack on generation and corruption had established the fundamental principle of permanence in nature—a principle that we may call either the conservation of matter or the conservation of mind, for the two are conceived as one.

Within the physical poem, therefore, immortality appears as the lot of every elemental ingredient in human nature. Since all of our members are deathless, all are gods. Each one of them lives on as a psychic as well as a corporeal entity, liberated from the particular mixture "which men call life." Each one of them, then, might conceivably play the role of the transmigrating daimon. But whether all of them do, or, if not, which one does, and how it may be said to "encounter good things and evil"—to none of these questions do we find an answer in the physical poem.

Now when we turn to the *Purifications*, the combination and separation of the four elements drop out of sight. We can scarcely say that there is no trace of the elements in this poem, for they are certainly reflected in the four stages of the wandering daimon, who is cast from air (αἰθήρ) to sea, from sea to earth, from earth to the blazing sun, and from the sun back to the air.[41] But nowhere in the poem is there any suggestion that these elements might constitute the nature of the fallen daimon. On the contrary, they only provide the scene within which the drama of his punishment and purification must be played out. The daimon himself is described simply as "a wandering exile from the gods," doomed

> for thrice ten thousand seasons to wander apart from the blest,
> growing into every form of mortal thing in the course of time,
> changing one for another the grievous paths of life.[42]

These various "forms of mortal things" and "grievous paths of life" correspond very well to the world of elemental transformation as it is described in the poem *On Nature*. It is a world in which the daimon is not at home. In another fragment the mortal form in which he is wrapped is described by Empedocles as an "alien garment of flesh."[43]

To say that the form of flesh is alien to the daimon is equivalent to denying that he is composed of earth, air, water, and fire, for these are precisely the constituents of flesh and blood.[44] Are we to conclude that this exiled spirit has come from a different, incorporeal world, of which the physical poem shows no trace? Do the blessed gods constitute a separate order of being, unrelated to, and incommensurable with, the natural cosmos that Empedocles has so elaborately described?[45] But why then should he emphasize the parallel between the cycle of the daimon and the period of the world by his repeated reference to "broad oaths" and to the destructive role of Strife? And how are we to conceive the relationship between this divine stranger and the conscious "thought" (νόημα) of the man whose supreme responsibility is precisely to purify the god within him? The hypothesis of an irreducible dualism between "nature" and "spirit" in Empedocles' thought may save it from the charge of contradiction, but it deprives it at the same time of any real claim to intelligibility.

Before resigning ourselves to such a desperate remedy, we must first consider the possibility of establishing a positive link between the psychology of the physical poem and the incarnate daimon of the *Purifications*. We have already noted the fact that, since all of the physical elements have a mental aspect and all are deathless, any of them might theoretically provide a seat for the wandering daimon. From the *Purifications*, however, it is clear that the banished god cannot be identified with the four corporeal elements. Empedocles is not referring to the vicissitudes of his bodily components in their previous combinations when he proclaims:

> I was once a lad and a lass,
> a bush, a bird, and a dumb fish of the sea.[46]

The punishment and purification of the daimon would be meaningless if he were doomed *by his own nature* to the eternal shuffling and reshuffling of natural compounds. The heterogeneous character of the daimon is confirmed not only by the description of his body as an "alien garment," but also by the attitude of Air, Sea, Earth, and Sun, who receive the exile only to cast him out again, since "they hate him one and all."[47] Still less is there any possibility of a positive link between the exiled god and the principle of Strife. The entire religious poem makes clear that Strife is the daimon's mortal enemy. It is Strife which has stained his godhead, as it is the elemental world in which he must be punished and purified. Hence, if the daimon corresponds to any principle in the physical poem, it can only be to the principle of Love. And most attempts to reconcile the doctrines of the two poems have in fact insisted upon a close connection, if not an outright identification, of the incarnate daimon and the physical principal of Love.[48]

The religious poem makes clear that there is some link between Love or "Aphrodite" and the godlike element in man. If it is a crime for the daimon to trust in Strife, then his true allegiance was to a different power: it must be Love who rules over the company of the blessed gods. This fact is not stated in any extant fragment of the *Purifications* but it seems to be implied, and one of the many lost verses may well have mentioned Φιλότης or Ἁρμονίη as sovereign of the pure daimons.[49] It is precisely because the daimon's homeland is a kingdom of Love that he can only appear as an exile in this world of elemental Strife, where the spirits of death and dissension have the upper hand:

> I wailed and I moaned when I saw the unfamiliar place
> where Bloodshed, Hate, and hordes of other Dooms,
> consuming Sickness, Rot, and running sores (?)
> swarm darkly over the meadow of Disaster.[50]

The divided dominion of this world between the forces of Good and Evil, Love and Hate, is systematically illustrated in the poem by a catalogue of opposing divinities, each pair of which represents the contrast between a positive and a negative force: Waxing and Waning, Sleep and Waking, "charming Certitude and dark-eyed Confusion," "bloody Quarrel and seemly Concord."[51]

Now if it is bloodshed and quarrel which have polluted the daimon and driven him from the company of the blest, it is only amity and concord which may eventually restore him to grace. What he seeks is in fact to regain a life of harmony and fellowship, where he will be permitted to share the hearth and table of the other gods.[52] And the code of purification by which he may return to this community is itself based upon a universal law of kinship. Since all nature is animate, all nature is akin; and the abstinence from bloodshed and violence against all living things is, as it were, a matter of family affection.[53]

Thus the struggle between Love and Strife dominates Empedocles' message of salvation as well as his cosmological scheme. The dramatic theme of both poems is essentially a Manichean contest between the Spirit of Good and the Spirit of Evil—between the forces of unity, harmony, and life and those of multiplicity, discord, and death. In each case the pendulum of power swings back and forth between the two according to a periodic law confirmed by "broad oaths." And in each case the present history of the world represents a transition from the rule of Love to that of Strife. In the *Purifications*, Empedocles tells us of an earlier age when ardent affection (φιλοφροσύνη) prevailed among all living creatures, while bloodshed and violence were unknown:

> They did not have a god Ares nor Uproar
> nor Zeus the king nor Kronos nor Poseidon,
> but Cypris was their queen.[54]

This Golden Age in which Aphrodite reigned supreme forms an obvious parallel to the supernatural harmony of the cosmic Sphere, within which all elements were united in the sway of Love and there was "no dissension nor unseemly quarrel in its limbs."[55]

It is precisely this parallel between the roles of Love and Strife in the two poems that constitutes the real link between them, and the fundamental principle of unity in Empedocles' thought. He seems to be insisting that the same powers prevail in the destiny of the universe and in that of man. And just as the physical Sphere suggests a supernatural harmony, so the element of Love in mortal compounds seems to stand as a physical representative for the exiled daimon.

We may recall that Φιλότης is the principle which gives unity and coherence to all natural compounds, and hence to Nature as a whole. Like her linear descendant the Venus of Lucretius, Empedocles' Aphrodite represents a force of universal vitality and creativity. But she is more than that. As Ἁρμονίη, the principle of geometric proportion, Love is responsible for the rational fitting-together of the elements and for the mental qualities which result from their symmetrical combination. We have seen that blood is the seat of intelligence because it forms a particularly smooth blend; that hands and tongue are skillful when their elements are of moderate size and proportionately mixed; that men are gifted with intelligence and keenness of perception to the extent that their components are properly blended. Hence, although the raw materials of our thought and perception are to a large extent provided by Earth, Air, Water, and Fire, the decisive form or quality of these mental acts depends upon the excellence of the mixture, in other words, upon the presence of Love. For the element of Love is not merely one ingredient among the others. As the principle of unity and symmetry it implies the positive aspect of consciousness, the pattern of intelligence and sensitivity, as Strife signifies that of dullness and stupidity. Can there be any doubt as to which principle Empedocles would have chosen to represent himself—I mean, of course, his transmigrating, divine self?

Thus we are led to agree with Cornford and his followers in maintaining that the daimon or immortal "I" of the religious poem has a place in Empedocles' physical psychology only if it is embodied in the element of Love. Such a connection between Love and the daimon suggested by the role played by "Cypris" in the *Purifications*, is confirmed by the position of Aphrodite in the poem *On Nature*. The central proclamation of Love as a great cosmic power (in fragment 17) may be compared to Anaxagoras' insistence upon the unique character of νοῦς. This is Empedocles' own version of the great discovery of his age: the recognition of the Rational or Spiritual as a distinct and dominant element in Nature. Love cannot be seen by the eyes, but only by the mind (νοῦς) or, more precisely, by the Love which is in us. For "by love we see love."[56] The element by which we communicate with this divine, creative force in the universe will fittingly stand for the divine principle embedded in man.

There is another sense in which a link between the daimon and Love is confirmed by the doctrine of the physical poem. Although all six elements are required to make up the concrete mind of the human being, it is only Love which may aspire to purification and release from the world of Strife. From the point of view of Empedocles' cosmogony, the principle of Love in man is a vestige of pre-mundane harmony, left behind in a world increasingly dominated by the hostile powers of diversity and strife. The loss of purity for this principle is represented by its admixture with other elements, in so far as they are distinguished by unlike, opposing qualities. Its release from pollution depends upon the abstinence from bloodshed, that is, from more Strife. Further obedience to this principle will, in Plato's phrase, fasten it to the flesh with new rivets. A life of purity and rationality, on the other hand, will allow the Harmony within us to increase to the point where it will be ready for release. The closing verses of the physical poem seem to afford a glimpse into the mechanism of salvation. If the divinely inspired "pure stream" of truth succeeds in penetrating within the heart,[57] a man's share of wisdom will increase, for the intelligence grows by what it meets with.[58] Hence instruction augments the mind (φρήν), while deception destroys it.[59] If a man attends to Empedocles' doctrine with pure thoughts, the truth will actually increase within him, adding to his ἦθος and φύσις. But if he is distracted by impure, erroneous concerns "which blunt men's thoughts," these truths will leave him after a certain time, "yearning for their fellows, to return to their own dear race."[60] They will return, of course, to where they have come from: the realm of Piety, the dwelling-place of the gods.[61] So, we may say, does the spirit of man, when its time of release is come. It hastens home to its fellows, back to its own dear kind.

If this hint has been properly interpreted, we see what the physical poem means by suggesting that men will experience good and evil after the dissolution of their mortal compounds.[62] Future happiness depends upon the extent to which a man's spirit—that is, his share of Love—returns to its own kind rather than to a condition dominated by Strife. Thus good fortune admits of degrees within the cycle of reincarnation. The purity and concentration of Love is presumably greater in a lion than in a laurel tree, as it is certainly greater in a man than in a beast, and in a wise man than in a fool. When a spirit like Empedocles has attained the ranks of the "seers and bards and physicians and princes among men on the earth," its complete liberation from the hostile elements is at hand.[63] When the final separation occurs, the pure spirit, no longer marked by any taint of its opposite, will experience the Good that answers to its own nature. The epistemology of Empedocles suggests what blessedness must mean for the purified daimon. By love we know love.[64]

On this view, then, the two poems of Empedocles are fundamentally compatible with one another. His conjunction of natural philosophy and mystic religion is effected by his own notion of Love or Ἁρμονίη as a complex reality, at once physical and spiritual, inherent in the symmetrical mixture of unlike components but capable of existing apart from them as an independent, imperishable entity. This is Empedocles' solution to the recurrent problems of the relationship between matter and life, body and spirit, between the animal and the god in man. Such problems do not lend themselves to final solution, and we had best not look for perfect consistency in Empedocles' view. Furthermore, there is no good reason to suppose that his two poems were conceived together as a single unit. The few clear links between them do not suggest an attempt to make their doctrines coincide point for point. On the contrary a number of years must have passed between the composition of the two works, and some of the discrepancies between them may be due to changes in Empedocles' way of looking at the subject. Above all, the poems are addressed to different audiences and speak on the whole different languages: in one case, the traditional imagery of Greek religion; in the other, the concepts and theories of fifth-century physics.

The two poems thus belong together in a loose unity, and any attempt to impose a systematic pattern upon them is bound to resort to artifice. Such is the case with Cornford's detailed interpretation, which assumes that the two works are simply alternative statements of one and the same theory. In that case the fall of the daimon must correspond exactly to the rupture of the Sphere, and his purification must culminate in a loss of separate existence, when (as Cornford claims) he is finally "merged with the other portions of Love in the unity of the Sphere. This is the physical transcription of the reunion of the soul with God."[65] But such a neat parallel between the two doctrines is not really to be found in the poems. Besides many minor difficulties,[66] the fusion of the elements in the physical Sphere does not correspond even in principle with the account of the daimons in the *Purifications*. Unlike his fellow believers in transmigration, the mystics of India, Empedocles does not imply that the purified spirit will lose itself in Deity as a drop of water loses itself in the sea. On this point the modern Orphic scholars tend to be slightly more "Orphic" than their ancient originals. If immortality in Empedocles' view cannot be defined as the personal survival of a particular human being, still less can it be identified with the escape from individuality as such. Empedocles is no more a Buddhist than he is a Christian. The terms he uses suggest the continued, harmonious coexistence of discrete individuals, very much like the celestial cavalcade of gods and spirits in the *Phaedrus*.[67] Neither the common hearths and feasting of the daimons nor the possibility that they may be guilty of perjury and bloodshed is compatible with the view that they are to be fused into a single Deity, as the elements seem to be fused within the cosmic Sphere. The fellowship of the daimons, like the breach of this fellowship, is Empedocles' symbol of a vision which cannot be translated into any other terms. It is his way of expressing the inner conviction of all mystics, that there dwells within us a fallen spirit or a portion of deity whose rightful place is elsewhere, in a realm of pure harmony and peace. Empedocles' physical doctrine of Love is an attempt to integrate this conviction within a systematic explanation of the natural world. In this context, the cosmic unity of the Sphere certainly has a religious significance, but it does not necessarily tell us anything about Empedocles' conception of the beatific life. What real connection there was between this unity and the company of the blessed daimons, we simply do not know.[68]

There is, then, no prospect of tieing up all of Empedocles' ideas into a neat system, even if we are correct in interpreting Love as the embodiment of the daimon in Empedocles' physical psychology. But such an interpretation has at least the merit of explaining how the religion of purification can appear in the background of the physical poem, and how the natural cosmology can be presupposed at more than one point in the *Purifications*. In brief, it is only this connection between Love and the daimon which can save Empedocles from the unintelligible schizophrenia that characterizes him in most modern presentations.

It seems inconceivable that this reconciliation of his religion and his natural philosophy was not designed by Empedocles himself—that it is somehow an accident, or an invention of our modern ingenuity. Yet there is one serious objection to this solution, which seems to have prevented most scholars from accepting it: namely, the lack of explicit documentary evidence. There is no clear statement of this link between Love and the daimon in any extant fragment, and no ancient author ascribes such a view of the soul to Empedocles.[69] This poses a problem of methodology, a sort of scholarly *cas de conscience*. In order to make sense of our author, do we have the right to adopt an interpretation for which there is so little direct evidence in the texts?

I think that we do. One must not lose sight of the fact that the poems of Empedocles are not literary documents of the normal type. They are well-nigh unique examples of mystic poetry from the classic period, and accordingly they pose problems which a textual analysis alone is helpless to resolve. We cannot interpret the writings of Empedocles without taking into consideration factors that are neither literary nor philosophical. If it is true (as I think it is) that the whole work of Empedocles points to a link between the religious destiny of man and the cosmic principle of Love, we must ask whether he may have had some motive for not stating this connection fully and clearly in either poem. Perhaps an explanation can be found in the special character and intention of the two works.

The poem *On Nature* observes a discreet silence on all aspects of human destiny after death. It has therefore no motive to carry its psychological analysis beyond the point of mortal dissolution, and no occasion to mention the transmigrating ego, much less to identify it with any single element in the mixture. The *Purifications*, on the other hand, are addressed to a popular audience. Despite an occasional reminiscence of the physical work, the doctrine of transmigration and release is presented here as a self-contained whole, depending for its credibility not upon Empedocles' philosophical speculation but upon his personal authority as a god among men. The doctrine of physical mixture is never mentioned; Love and Strife appear only as general principles of Harmony and Violation, Purity and Taint. The ascent to blessedness is not described in abstract philosophical terms, but in the concrete formulae and imagery of religious poetry. Most of the citizens of Acragas to whom this message was directed would scarcely be concerned to reconcile it with a complex physical theory of which they may never have heard. The poem *On Nature* was after all an esoteric work. The few who were familiar with it would discover more than one unanswered question in the *Purifications*, and would naturally turn to the master himself for an explanation.

We must remember that the links between the philosophical system and the doctrine of salvation are not indispensable for the popular diffusion of the latter. They are only required if one seeks a full understanding of all aspects of Empedocles' thought. Why should Empedocles put this understanding at the disposal of every chance comer? Why should he fully satisfy our curiosity? Is it the part of a prophet and a mystagogue to divulge all his secrets at once? On the contrary, we should rather expect him to keep a few things to himself, for private communication to his closest disciples.[70]

But if the physical poem was really an esoteric work while the *Purifications* were addressed to the general public, why does the doctrine of transmigration appear only in the latter? Why should all the citizens of Acragas hear of a matter which is not mentioned to the chosen disciple Pausanias? Here again we are asking a question which the texts do not answer. But they do suggest that the religious poem was composed at a later date, after some considerable change had taken place in Empedocles' conception of himself.[71] Now the gospel of purification must originally have been communicated to him in some private cult, presumably Pythagorean, where it was guarded by a rule of silence. When he worked out his physical system, Empedocles seems to have been motivated in large measure by the desire to lay a rational foundation for these religious teachings, and we may guess that his friend Pausanias was also an initiate. The poem *On Nature* is in fact a kind of fifth-century *Timaeus*—a synthesis of the physical knowledge of the day, conceived within a religious framework. We have seen that the religious element appears in both proem and conclusion, in the insistence on immortality and the beneficent role of Love, in the vision of the Sphere and the culminating announcement of the φρὴν ἱερή But at the moment when he composed this poem, Empedocles still felt it was not "lawful" to publish the secrets of salvation—not even in an esoteric work. He describes the temptation to do so as an impious urge "to sit upon the heights of wisdom" and "cull the blossoms of fame and honor in the sight of men."

Now at the time of Empedocles' poem, the doctrine of transmigration as such was not much of a secret. It had been parodied by Xenophanes more than a generation before, and is mentioned by Herodotus with no noticeable air of secrecy.[72] But the religious meaning of the cycle and of the abstinence from flesh does not seem to have been made public before Empedocles, and by him only in the second poem. From the Pythagorean point of view, this must have been an act of heresy and sacrilege. A trace of the scandal it created seems to be preserved in the tradition, recorded by Timaeus and Neanthes, that Empedocles was expelled from the Pythagorean society for stealing and publishing sacred doctrines.[73] It is natural to connect this surprising change in Empedocles' attitude in the second poem with his proclamation there of his own divinity. No longer mortal, Empedocles is no longer bound by mortal rules. The doctrine of the god in human form, which had reached him as a traditional teaching, has now become a fact of his own experience. The author of the *Purifications* can recall his previous incarnations and is assured of imminent release. He has thus gained such confidence in his immortal powers as "prophet, poet, doctor, and prince" that he can brave the Pythagorean injunction to silence, and can offer all men a chance to follow the way of salvation by which he himself has regained the status of divinity.

NOTES

[1] Heraclitus B 77 and B 62. All fragments are cited according to Diels-Kranz, *Die Fragmente der Vorsokratiker* (Berlin, 1954). The following works are cited below in the notes by the author's name alone: E. Bignone, *Empedocle* (Turin, 1916). H. Diels, „Über die Gedichte des Empedokles," *Berlin Sitzungsberichte* (1898), p. 396. W. Nestle, „Der Dualismus des Empedokles," *Phil.*, 65 (1906): 545. U. v. Wilamowitz-Moellendorff, „Die Καθαρμοί des Empedokles," *Berlin Sitzungsb.* (1929), p. 626.

[2] „[Die physicalischen Annahmen des Empedokles] erscheinen daher als Teile eines naturphilosophischen Systems, das . . . nach Einem Plan ausgeführt ist. Anders verhält es sich mit gewissen religiösen Lehren und Vorschriften, welche . . . mit den wissenschaftlichen Grundsätzen unseres Physikers in keiner sichtbaren Verbindung stehen. In diesen Sätzen können wir nur Glaubensartikel sehen, die zu seinem philosophischen System von anderer Seite her hinzukamen und demselben nur unvollkommen angegliedert wurden"; E. Zeller, *Die Philosophie der Griechen*, I (Leipzig 1892) p. 806; cf. ibid. 809–17 [=pp. 1001, 1004–16 in the 6th ed. by W. Nestle (Leipzig, 1920), who cites the earlier literature].

[3] J. Burnet, *Early Greek Philosophy*, 4th ed. (London 1945), p. 250.

[4] *Paideia*, Engl. tr., 2nd ed. (New York, 1945), I, p. 295, quoted with approval by G. Vlastos, who comments: " 'Prodigious' is the right word for the union of physics and theology, as it is for the junction of immortal god and mortal flesh. The one is as much of a miracle as the other, and Empedocles doubtless devoutly believed it to be such. He left us no explanation of either, and it would be futile to try to supply it by rationalizing the

theology of the mystic or mystifying the logic of the cosmologist"; *PQ*, 2 (1952): 121.

[5] For πίστις see B 3.10 and 13; B 71.1: B 114.3; and the other passages listed by Nestle (p. 548, n. 11), who also compares πίστις ἀληθής in Parmenides B 1.30; B 8.12 and 28; ἀπιστίη in Heraclitus B 86.

[6] Diels, p. 406; Wilamowitz, pp. 655–56. For the exile see πεφευγώς in Diogenes Laertius VIII 52 and κάθοδος, *ibid.*, VIII 67. In B 112, Empedocles describes himself as traveling from city to city, but his greeting χαίρετε to the citizens of Acragas does not prove that he is actually writing from abroad. The contrary seems to be indicated by the phrase ἐγὼ δ' ὑμῖν . . . πωλεῦμαι, "I go about among you an immortal god" (Burnet); „Ich aber wandle jetzt als unsterblicher Gott . . . vor Euch" (Diels, in the early editions of the *Fragmente*).

[7] The chronological priority of the Περὶ Φύσεως was contested by J. Bidez, *La Biographie d'Empédocle* (Gand, 1894), pp. 160 ff., and more recently by W. Kranz, in *Hermes* 70 (1935): 111–19, and in his *Empedokles* (Zurich, 1949). Kranz was answered by K. Reinhardt, „Empedokles, Orphiker und Physiker," *CP*, (1950): 172–77. I agree on this point with Diels, Wilamowitz, and Reinhardt, but unfortunately I cannot accept what seems to be their most decisive argument: the second invocation of the Muse in B 131 (εὐχομένῳ νῦν αὖτε παρίστασο, Καλλιόπεια). If this fragment came from the Καθαρμοί (as Diels' arrangement assumes), it would obviously constitute a backward reference to the physical poem, which begins with just such an invocation (B 3–4). But for the true place of B 131, see the next note.

[8] The λόγος ἀμφὶ θεῶν is introduced in B 131 by the invocation of a Muse, of whom there is otherwise no trace in the Καθαρμοί but who appears of course in the proem of the Περὶ Φύσεως. Bignone observed that it would be natural for Empedocles to invoke the Muse once more (νῦν αὖτε) when entering upon the last portion of his work, and pointed out the similar invocation of Calliope by Lucretius at the beginning of his last book (VI 92). From B 131 alone, then, we might conclude that there was a discussion of the gods to be found in the last section or "book" of the physical poem. Now Tzetzes actually quotes Empedocles' famous description of deity as a φρὴν ἱερή (B 134) from "the third book of the Φυσικά":

> Ἐμπεδοκλῆς τῷ τρίτῳ τε τῶν Φυσικῶν δεικνύων
> Τίς ἡ οὐσία τοῦ θεοῦ κατ' ἔπος οὕτω λέγει.

For reasons of his own, Diels wished to dismiss this statement as a "Schwindelcitate" (despite the fact that Tzetzes also assigns fr. 6 to the first book—correctly), but Stein, Zeller, and Bignone drew the more natural conclusion that B 131–34 must come from the end of the physical poem. Bignone remarked that the repetition of verses from B 29 in B 134 can find numerous parallels *within* the poem *On Nature*, none between it and the *Purifications*; and that the attack on anthropomorphism which is contained in these verses is entirely at home in the physical work, while it would be less appropriate in the religious poem, which uses traditional imagery in addressing a popular audience (Bignone, pp. 477, 631–49). Furthermore, the use of the term κόσμος for "world" (B 134.5) is much more likely to occur in a technical poem than in a popular work like the Καθαρμοί, which seems to avoid all philosophical complexities.

[9] For the Muse's name, see B 131. Empedocles may have Bacchylides 5.176 in mind, where Calliope is similarly petitioned by the poet for a chariot of song. Other poetic chariots of the fifth century (without mention of a particular Muse) are cited by C. M. Bowra, *Problems in Greek Poetry* (Oxford, 1953), p. 42.

[10] Most scholars have assumed that the μανίη which fills Empedocles with such horror must be that of dogmatic philosophers like Parmenides, who deny both the evidence of the senses and the limitations of human knowledge. This interpretation can be traced back to Sextus Empiricus, who quotes these verses to illustrate Empedocles' theory of knowledge (ἐπιπλήξας τοῖς πλέον ἐπαγγελλομένοις γιγνώσκειν παρίστησιν ὅτι τὸ δι' ἑκάστης αἰσθήσεως λαμβανόμενον πιστόν ἐστι; VII 124, cited by Diels-Kranz in the introduction to B 3). But to see how wrong Sextus can be, one need only look at his exegesis of Parmenides' proem, where the "whirling wheels" of the chariot are interpreted as a cryptic reference to the ears (VII 112).

In view of the context provided by Empedocles' own verses, it is much more natural to understand the madness in question as that of impious men who disclose more than is "lawful for creatures of a day to hear" (B 3.4–8; cf. B 2.9). As far as bold dogmatism is concerned, Empedocles' account of the precosmic Sphere can match anything in Parmenides.

Sextus and those who follow him have been led to their interpretation by the last five verses in B 3 (not quoted above), which do indeed emphasize the prudent use of sense data. But they ignore the fact that this constitutes a separate topic, introduced by the formula ἀλλ' ἄγ' ἄθρει (cf. B 17.14 and B 20.8) and marked by the shift of interlocutors from the Muse back to Pausanias.

[11] B 111.2, with B 5.

[12] Compare καθαρὴ πηγή in B 3 with καθαραὶ μελέται in B 110.2, and πολλὰ δὲ δείλ' ἔμπαια in B 2 with μυρία δειλά in B 110.7. In the Καθαρμοί, δειλός is regularly used for the misery of those who violate the precepts of purification; see δειλὸν θνητῶν γένος (B 124), δειλοί, πάνδειλοι (B 141), etc.

[13] B 111. The use of the future tense in this fragment (as in Parmenides B 10) suggests that it appeared early in the poem, not at the end where Diels has placed it. The echoes of the proem in B 110 probably indicate that these verses closed the entire work, which thus ends as it began with the opposition between purity and misery, true knowledge and dull perception.

[14] *De morbo sacro* 4, where χειμῶνά τε καὶ εὐδίην ποιεῖν καὶ ὄμβρους καὶ αὐχμούς is listed among the typical boasts of the μάγοι τε καὶ καθάρται (cf. ch. 2).

[15] B 112.11: κλυεῖν εὐηκέα βάξιν.

[16] B 134; for its place in the physical poem, see n. 8, above.

[17] B 17.18–26:

πῦρ καὶ ὕδωρ καὶ γαῖα καὶ ἠέρος ἄπλετον ὕψος,
Νεῖκός τ' οὐλόμενον δίχα τῶν, ἀτάλαντον ἁπάντῃ,

καὶ Φιλότης ἐν τοῖσιν, ἴση μῆκός τε πλάτος τε·
τὴν σὺ νόῳ δέρκευ, μηδ' ὄμμασιν ἧσο τεθηπώς.
ἥτις καὶ θνητοῖσι νομίζεται ἔμφυτος ἄρθροις,
τῇ τε φίλα φρονέουσι καὶ ἄρθμια ἔργα τελοῦσι,
Γηθοσύνην καλέοντες ἐπώνυμον ἠδ' Ἀφροδίτην.
τὴν οὔ τις μετὰ τοῖσιν ἑλισσομένην δεδάηκε
θνητὸς ἀνήρ· σὺ δ'ἄκουε λόγου στόλον οὐκ ἀπατηλόν.

[18] Cf. Hesiod *Theog.* 120; Aeschylus *Danaids* fr. 44; Parmenides B 12–13. On the other hand, the role of Aphrodite in Euripides *Hippolytus* 447–50 shows the influence of Empedocles, as does that of Eros in the speech of Eryximachus in the *Symposium.*

[19] See B 96 and B 98.

[20] B 27–29; the sphere is called θεός in B 31.

[21] B 15:

οὐκ ἂν ἀνὴρ τοιαῦτα σοφὸς φρεσὶ μαντεύσαιτο,
ὡς ὄφρα μέν τε βιῶσι, τὸ δὴ βίοτον καλέουσι,
τόφρα μὲν οὖν εἰσίν, καί σφιν πάρα δειλὰ καὶ ἐσθλά,
πρὶν δὲ πάγεν τε βροτοὶ καὶ ⟨ἐπεὶ⟩ λύθεν, οὐδὲν ἄρ' εἰσιν.

Rohde, Bignone, and others have remarked the parallel between τὸ δὴ βίοτον καλέουσι and τίς δ' οἶδεν, εἰ τὸ ζῆν μέν ἐστι κατθανεῖν, τὸ κατθανεῖν δὲ ζῆν κάτω νομίζεται; Euripides fr. 638; cf. fr. 833; Plato *Gorgias* 492E. The phrase σφιν πάρα δειλὰ καὶ ἐσθλά seems to echo the antithetic mystic formula for bliss and suffering in the afterlife; cf. *Hymn to Demeter* 480–83, Pindar fr. 121 (Bowra), Soph. fr. 119. Plato *Phaedo* 63C5: εἶναί τι τοῖς τετελευτηκόσι καί, ὥσπερ γε καὶ πάλαι λέγεται, πολὺ ἄμεινον τοῖς ἀγαθοῖς ἢ τοῖς κακοῖς.

[22] Pindar *Olymp.* II, esp. vv. 56ff.; the esoteric nature of the doctrine is hinted at in βέλη . . . φωνάεντα συνετοῖσιν. See also Pindar frs. 114–16, 127 (Bowra). Both the connection of the Second Olympian with Acragas and the close parallel between the favorable stages of reincarnation in Pindar fr. 127 and Empedocles B 146 suggest that Empedocles was familiar with this secret doctrine ,,von Haus her" (Wilamowitz, p. 660).

[23] Compare B 115.2 and 14 with B 30. For the concrete sense of πλατὺς ὅρκος, "a thick bond or enclosure," see J. Bollack, "Styx et serments," *REG*, 71 (1958): 1–35. The manner in which the Καθαρμοί thus alludes briefly to notions which have a fuller development in the Περὶ Φύσεως provides a good indication that the physical poem was composed first.

[24] Strictly speaking, a doctrine of personal immortality could scarcely be developed without a word for "person." The classical philosophers speak only of the survival of the ψυχή or νοῦς, which is not the same thing. A full study of the philosophical uses of πρόσωπον and *persona* would probably cast important light on the Hellenistic, Roman, and above all Judaeo-Christian origins of the concept of "personality." See the lexicographical survey of R. Hirzel, "Die Person," *München Sitzungsb.* (1914), Abh. 10.

[25] Only at this popular level can we speak of a Greek belief in personal immortality. Before a popular audience, Socrates alludes to the Homeric underworld and hopes to chat there with Orpheus and Agamemnon (*Apol.* 41A–C). But in the intimate seriousness of the *Phaedo* he expresses doubt as to whether he will really meet human beings in the other world, or only gods (63C).

[26] B 110.6–10:

> εἰ δὲ σύ γ' ἀλλοίων ἐπορέξεαι, οἷα κατ' ἄνδρας
> μυρία δειλὰ πέλονται ἅ τ' ἀμβλύνουσι μερίμνας,
> ἦ σ' ἄφαρ ἐκλείψουσι περιπλομένοιο χρόνοιο
> σφῶν αὐτῶν ποθέοντα φίλην ἐπὶ γένναν ἱκέσθαι·
> πάντα γὰρ ἴσθι φρόνησιν ἔχειν καὶ νώματος αἶσαν.

[27] B 109:

> γαίῃ μὲν γὰρ γαῖαν ὀπώπαμεν, ὕδατι δ' ὕδωρ,
> αἰθέρι δ' αἰθέρα δῖον, ἀτὰρ πυρὶ πῦρ ἀίδηλον,
> στοργὴν δὲ στοργῇ, νεῖκος δέ τε νείκεϊ λυγρῷ.

[28] B 107:

> ἐκ τούτων ⟨γὰρ⟩ πάντα πεπήγασιν ἁρμοσθέντα
> καὶ τούτοις φρονέουσι καὶ ἥδονται ἠδ' ἀνιῶνται.

[29] See B 17.19–20.

[30] B 2.2: πολλὰ δὲ δείλ' ἔμπαια, τά τ' ἀμβλύνουσι μέριμνας. Compare B 114 and B 133 for the difficulty truth has in reaching the mind (φρήν).

[31] B 110.6–7 (cited above, n. 26).

[32] B 106 and B 108.

[33] B 110.5.

[34] Empedocles' doctrine is directly based on that of Parmenides (B 16). Both philosophers represent, in a more rigorous way, the general fifth-century tendency to treat ψυχή as "the mental correlate of σῶμα" [E. R. Dodds, *The Greeks and the Irrational* (Berkeley, 1956), p. 138]. But both philosophers avoid the ambiguous term ψυχή and speak more concretely of νόος, νοεῖν or φρήν, φρονεῖν. (Empedocles uses the word ψυχή only once in the extant fragments, in the poetic sense of "life": B 138).

[35] B 105:

> αἵματος ἐν πελάγεσσι τεθραμμένη ἀντιθορόντος,
> τῇ τε νόημα μάλιστα κικλήσκεται ἀνθρώποισιν·
> αἷμα γὰρ ἀνθρώποις περικάρδιόν ἐστι νόημα.

[36] Theophr. *De Sensu* 10–11 = Emped. A 86.10–11. For the composition of the blood, see B 98.

[37] See Arist. *De Anima* 404b 11, 408a16.

[38] Emped. B 8.

[39] B 15 (quoted above, n. 21).

[40] B 11:

> νήπιοι· οὐ γάρ σφιν δολιχόφρονές εἰσι μέριμναι,
> οἳ δὴ γίγνεσθαι πάρος οὐκ ἐὸν ἐλπίζουσιν
> ἤ τι καταθνῄσκειν τε καὶ ἐξόλλυσθαι ἁπάντῃ.

[41] B 115.9–11.

[42] B 115.6–8:

> τρίς μιν μυρίας ὧρας ἀπὸ μακάρων ἀλάλησθαι,
> φυομένους παντοῖα διὰ χρόνου εἴδεα θνητῶν
> ἀργαλέας βιότοιο μεταλλάσσοντα κελεύθους.

[43] B 126: σαρκῶν ἀλλογνῶτι περιστέλλουσα χιτῶνι.

[44] See B 98.

[45] This is, in effect, the solution proposed by Nestle, following Rohde, *Psyche*, II, p. 183. Bignone rightly protests that such an absolute dualism

runs counter to the whole spirit of Early Greek thought and, in particular, to the parallelism of mind and body for Empedocles; but I do not see that his own interpretation of the daimon is really different from Nestle's. (See Bignone, p. 11, n. 259–68.) Their conception of the daimon as an entity distinct from the physical elements and principles seems to me excluded by Empedocles' own words: καὶ πρὸς τοῖς οὔτ' ἄρ' τι ἐπιγίνεται οὐδ' ἀπολήγει. B 17.30. And compare B 23.8–10, where the "long-lived gods" are said to be composed, like men and women, from the physical principles alone. Bignone's interpretation of ὅσσα γε δῆλα "all beings, at least, which are manifest (but not the daimons)" does not fit the context. The point is not that there are some entities which are not manifest but that of the infinite variety of apparent forms (θνητῶν ὅσσα γε δῆλα γεγάκασιν ἄσπετα) there are none which cannot be derived from these elements. The γε is therefore not restrictive but emphatic.

46 B 117.

47 B 115.12.

48 See F. M. Cornford, *From Religion to Philosophy* (London, 1912), pp. 234–42; and the same author in *The Cambridge Ancient History*, IV (Cambridge, 1926), pp. 563–69; H. S. Long, "The Unity of Empedocles' Thought," *AJP*, 70 (1949): 142–58; J. E. Raven in Kirk and Raven, *The Presocratic Philosophers* (Cambridge, 1957), pp. 348–61.

49 There is a trace of this in B 116, where Χάρις is said "to hate unbearable Ἀνάγκη." Ἀνάγκη is the principle which condemns the daimons (B 115.1), and Χάρις must be another name for Love. Ἀνάγκη is hateful to her because it deprives her of her rightful subjects or "friends." So Hippolytus (in his commentary on B 115) describes Φιλία as the good power which takes pity on the fallen souls and draws them together again.

50 B 118 and 121:

> κλαῦσά τε καὶ κώκυσα ἰδὼν ἀσυνήθεα χῶρον,
> ἔνθα Φόνος τε Κότος τε καὶ ἄλλων ἔθνεα Κηρῶν
> αὐχμηραί τε Νόσοι καὶ Σήψιες ἔργα τε ῥευστά
> Ἄτης ἀν λειμῶνα κατὰ σκότος ἠλάσκουσιν.

I follow Wilamowitz and Stein in assuming that ἀτερπέα χῶρον in Hierocles (B 121.1) is merely a Homeric paraphrase of ἀσυνήθεα χῶρον in B 118, so that the two fragments are really one. But Wilamowitz is certainly wrong in referring the meadow of Ἄτη to the underworld (p. 638). There is no place for the House of Hades in the cosmology of Empedocles: the true realm of death is this existence on earth "which men call life." It is described as a dark cave (B 120) by contrast with the region of celestial light from which the daimon has come.

Note that Κότος here stands for Νεῖκος, exactly as in the physical poem (B 21.7). Similarly Δῆρις in B 122 and in B 27a, contrasted with Ἁρμονίη in both cases.

51 B 122–23. Parmenides seems to have given a similar list of antithetic allegorical figures; see Ἔρως in Parm. B 13, *Bellum*, *Discordia*, and *Cupiditas*, in A 37.

52 B 147.

[53] B 135–41. Compare the Pythagorean principle of universal kinship as stated in the *Meno* 81d1 (in connection with the doctrine of transmigration): τῆς φύσεως ἁπάσης συγγενοῦς οὔσης. In his citation of B 128, Porphyry remarks that the recognition of this kinship prevented bloodshed in the Golden Age: τῆς γὰρ οἶμαι φιλίας καὶ τῆς περὶ τὸ συγγενὲς αἰσθήσεως πάντα κατεχούσης, οὐθεὶς οὐθὲν ἐφόνευεν οἰκεῖα εἶναι νομίζων τὰ λοιπὰ τῶν ζῴων.

[54] B 128, together with B 130. If we wish to place the Golden Age within the cosmic scheme of the Περὶ Φύσεως, it may fall very early in the present phase of the world cycle, when the Sphere has given way to individual creatures but Strife has not gained full mastery over Love.

[55] B 27a.

[56] B 17.21: τὴν σὺ νόῳ δέρκευ, μηδ' ὄμμασιν ἧσο τεθηπώς (cf. B 133 for the incapacity of the senses to apprehend divinity). For the perception of Love by Love, see B 109, cited above n. 27.

[57] B 4.3: γνῶθι διατμισθέντος ἐνὶ σπλάγχνοισι λόγοιο (with Wilamowitz's correction for διατμηθέντος: διασσηθέντος Diels). The difficulty of ingress for truth is emphasized in B 114 and B 133.

[58] B 106: πρὸς παρεὸν γὰρ μῆτις ἀέξεται ἀνθρώποισιν.

[59] B 17.7; B 23.9.

[60] B 110 (above, n. 26).

[61] B 3.1–5.

[62] B 15 (above, n. 21).

[63] See B 127 and B 146, to be compared with Empedocles' own career in B 117 and B 112.

[64] B 109.3: στοργὴν δὲ στοργῇ. Cf. B 17.23: τῇ τε φίλα φρονέουσι καὶ ἄρθμια ἔργα τελοῦσι. This would, I think, be Empedocles' answer to the question raised by Vlastos: how does the disembodied daimon get along without flesh and blood, the basis of thought? "How does he think the thoughts of love when he has nothing to think with?" [*PQ*, 2 (1952): 121].

[65] *Cambridge Ancient History*, IV, p. 569.

[66] For example, in the present world period Love must be passing out of the world as more Strife flows in: where does it go? If we identify the outgoing stream of Love with the purified daimons, their number will be complete when Strife has gained full mastery over the elemental universe. The reunion of the blessed will then coincide not with the complete unification of things by Love (i.e., not with the Sphere), but with their complete separation by Strife.

[67] This is of course no accident. The feasts and banquets of the gods at *Phaedrus* 247, in which the noblest human ψυχαί may also share, were probably inspired by the common hearths and tables of Empedocles B 147. The *Phaedrus* passage is full of Empedoclean reminiscences (cf. τὰ μὲν θεῶν ὀχήματα ἰσορρόπως εὐήνια ὄντα at 247B with εὐήνιον ἅρμα in Emped. B 3.5) and it is probably Empedocles (with Pindar) whom Plato has in mind when he begins his description of the blessed life: τὸν δὲ ὑπερουράνιον τόπον οὔτε τις ὕμνησέ πω τῶν τῇδε ποιητὴς οὔτε ποτὲ ὑμνήσει κατ' ἀξίαν (247C3).

It is more difficult to say whether the parallels between Empedocles and the mystic verses inscribed on South Italian burial plates are due to his influence on the cult poets or theirs on him. (The latter alternative is the more likely, but the tablets are not old enough to prove this.) In both cases salvation consists not in the loss of one's identity but in becoming "a god instead of a mortal" and in dwelling with the other immortals or "heroes" after paying the penalty for unjust deeds. (See Diels-Kranz, under "Orpheus" 1 B 17–20.)

There is an obvious parody of the mystic promise of bliss in Aristophanes' speech in the *Symposium:* having lost their original condition because of ἀδικία, human beings must rely upon Eros to restore it: ὅς . . . εἰς τὸ ἔπειτα ἐλπίδας μεγίστας παρέχεται, ἡμῶν παρεχομένων πρὸς θεοὺς εὐσέβειαν, καταστήσας ἡμᾶς εἰς τὴν ἀρχαίαν φύσιν καὶ ἰασάμενος μακαρίους καὶ εὐδαίμονας ποιῆσαι (193D).

68 A similar problem is posed by the incorporeal φρὴν ἱερή which flits with rapid thoughts through the whole κόσμος (B 134). The verses which introduce this divinity are almost identical with those used to describe the Sphere (B 29). What are we to make of the parallel? It tempts us to identify this φρήν with Aphrodite, the power who dominates the Sphere (so Cornford and Bignone). But the quotation of Ammonius suggests that these verses apply either to Apollo (i.e., to the great Pythagorean god of knowledge and light) or to τὸ θεῖον in general. It may be that Empedocles' polytheism permitted him to envisage divinity—even supreme divinity—under a number of intimately related, but not interchangeable aspects: Love, φρήν, and the Sphere.

69 The only possible exception is a passage in Aristotle's *De Anima* (408a 10–28), where Empedocles' doctrine of Love (φιλία) is treated as rigorously parallel to the definition of the soul as a ἁρμονία or blend of opposing elements. Aristotle's point is of course not that the ἁρμονία doctrine belongs to Empedocles, but that it is philosophically of the same type. But see the next note.

70 If Empedocles' view of the immortal soul as "Love" was in fact communicated in this way, we would have a solution to the strange mystery of the ψυχή — ἁρμονία doctrine, which first shows up in the *Phaedo* expounded by Simmias, a pupil of Philolaus, and is immediately accepted by the Pythagoreans of Phlius (*Phaedo* 86B–C, 88D; the origins of the doctrine are inconclusively discussed by Burnet, in his note on 86B6, and by R. Hackforth, *Plato's Phaedo*, Cambridge 1955, pp. 101–03). There could be no more natural place for the influence of Empedocles than among the Pythagoreans of Southern Italy and their disciples in Greece. And Ἁρμονίη is of course one of Empedocles' names for Love.

As presented by Plato and Aristotle, the ἁρμονία doctrine is no longer Empedoclean. Plato's argument turns precisely upon the fact that the "attunement" is a mere compound, incapable of existing apart from the elements of which it is composed. The theory has become practically identified with the medical conception of health as a harmony or equilibrium of diverse factors in the body. There was from the first a close link between this medical view (which can be traced as far back as Alcmaeon of Croton) and Empedocles' own theory. But if the ψυχή — ἁρμονία doctrine was really current among Pythagoreans, it must once have implied a more substantial kind of ἁρμονία: a principle of harmony that was also capable of transmigrating. That is to say, it must originally have coincided with Empedocles' conception of Φιλότης.

[71] I do not believe that Empedocles refers to himself as a god in the physical poem. Such a reference is sometimes sought in B 23.11: ἀλλὰ τορῶς ταῦτ' ἴσθι, θεοῦ παρὰ μῦθον ἀκούσας. But the exact parallel to this formula is to be found in B 4: ὡς δὲ παρ' ἡμετέρης κέλεται πιστώματα Μούσης, γνῶθι. Unlike his religious message, Empedocles presents his physical doctrine not on his own authority but on that of the Muse. And the proclamation of his divinity in B 112 strikes the reader as a piece of news.

[72] Xenophanes B 7; Hdt. II 123. Such revelations may have prompted Empedocles' prayer to the gods to avert from his tongue "the madness of those men."

[73] Neanthes and Timaeus in Diogenes Laertius VIII 54–55 (=*F Gr Hist.* II, 84 F 26; III, 566 F 14).

APPENDIX

EMPEDOCLES AMONG THE SHAMANS

In this study I have attempted primarily to reconstruct Empedocles' conception of the soul from his own point of view, and have not tried to place this doctrine within the larger context of the history of Greek religion. I have assumed, of course, that the basic tenets of the Καθαρμοί—belief in primeval sin, in punishment by reincarnation, and in eventual reinstatement by apotheosis—were not the personal invention of Empedocles, but that they reached him from the esoteric mystic tradition that is generally described as Orphic or Pythagorean. An appendix is scarcely the place to discuss this tradition and Empedocles' relationship to it. It may suffice to say that the Καθαρμοί constitute our primary source for the mystic doctrine of the soul before Plato, and that in one respect Empedocles is a more authoritative spokesman than Plato himself. For however seriously Plato's myths may be intended, it is clear that he was not a practicing Orphic or Pythagorean. Only on the funeral tablets from Petelia and Thurii do we find the doctrine of crime, punishment, and apotheosis affirmed with a direct earnestness comparable to that of Empedocles. These gold plates may provide a better clue to popular cult and belief, but the personal character of Empedocles' utterance gives us an absolutely unique insight into the intimate religious convictions of a fifth century "Orphic."

Now there is one recent interpretation of the mystic doctrine of the soul which is so provocative, and which concerns Empedocles so directly, that it can scarcely be ignored. In his brilliant book on *The Greeks and the Irrational*, Professor Dodds has sought to establish a link between the diffusion of this new view of the soul and the impact upon the Greeks of shamanistic practices and beliefs imported from the northeast, above all from the religion of the Scyths. In Dodds' chapter on "The Greek Shamans and the Origins of Puritanism," Empedocles' fragments are described as "the one first-hand source from which we can still form some notion of what a Greek shaman was really like; he is the last belated example of a species which with his death became extinct in the Greek world, though it still flourishes elsewhere." (Dodds, p. 145) It seems relevant to our topic to inquire whether Empedocles really is an example of a Greek shaman, and whether the study of shamanism offers any insight into his doctrine of the soul.

Now if by a shaman we mean no more than a sorcerer or a medicine man, the term will naturally apply to someone who claimed to be able to check the winds and raise the dead to life. But this is clearly not what Dodds has in mind, for the race of Greek sorcerers did not become extinct with Empedocles' death. On the contrary, Dodds is using the term shaman in its strict sense, for the practitioner of an archaic technique of ecstasy by which the "soul is thought to leave its body and travel to distant parts, most often to the spirit world. A shaman may in fact be seen simultaneously in different places; he has the power of bilocation. From these experiences, narrated by him in extempore song, he derives the skill in divination, religious poetry, and magical medicine which makes him socially important."[1]

True shamanism is above all represented in the religion of the Ural-Altaic peoples of north-central Asia; the word "shaman" itself comes from the language of the Siberian Tunguses.[2] However, since Meuli's classic study it has been recognized that the religious practices of the ancient world show clear traces of shamanistic influence.[3] Furthermore, an incursion of Scythian religion into Greece in the sixth or late seventh century seems to be attested by the legend of Abaris the Hyperborean who travelled over the whole earth with (or on) a magic arrow, fasting and performing feats of healing and prophecy.[4] Similar contacts between Greece and the region to the northeast are implied by the story of Aristeas of Proconnesus, who could send his soul out of his body at will, who appeared in different places at the same time, who accompanied Apollo to Italy in the form of a raven, and who told in the *Arimaspea* of his voyages into central Asia when "seized by Apollo."[5] Several examples of shamanistic trance and spirit-travelling occur in the legends of other Greek priests and prophets of the archaic age. The most striking cases are those of Epimenides of Crete and Hermotimus of Clazomenae, both of whom were credited with the power to leave the body for long periods of time.[6] The combination of this trance power with the roll of healer, prophet, and purification priest makes Epimenides the very model of a Greek shaman, as Diels remarked long ago (*Parmenides' Lehrgedicht*, p. 15). And this well-defined group of Greek ecstatics seems to provide the background for an understanding of the Orpheus myth. The magical music of Orpheus, his prophetic powers, his affinity for animals, and, above all, his descent into the underworld to bring back a soul from the dead, all suggest the idealized figure of a Great Shaman.[7] In his case, however, the specifically shamanistic motif has been tamed and transformed by the Greek imagination. Orpheus' spirit does not leave his body to travel to the infernal regions: he descends like Heracles or Odysseus, in flesh and blood.

Pythagoras too was credited with a descent into the underworld. As with Orpheus, however, this feat seems to have been understood in the traditional Greek manner as a physical journey, rather than as a trance vision like those of Epimenides or that of Plato's hero Er in the tenth book of the *Republic*.[8] But there are other links between the legend of Pythagoras and that of the early Greek ecstatics: his feats of bilocation, his identification with the Hyperborean Apollo, his connections with Abaris and with Hermotimus (whom he is supposed to have claimed as a previous incarnation), and his capacity to hear the celestial harmony "when outside of his body."[9] In the face of all this, it is possible that the historical Pythagoras—and not just the figure of legend—did in fact base his supernatural prestige upon exploits of the shamanistic type. Even so, the most decisive point for our purposes is a negative one: it is not from the shamans that Pythagoras can have learned his characteristic doctrine of rebirth. Nothing in the theory or practice of shamanism implies that human and animal souls transmigrate systematically from one body to another after death. This fact is recognized by Dodds, who suggests that the doctrine of transmigration in its general form may have been a personal contribution of Pythagoras (p. 144). It is true that the potent spirit of a dead shaman is often believed to reappear in a member of the same family or clan, but that is more a matter of legacy by possession than of a rigorous cycle of rebirth.[10] The latter has never been seriously documented for any religion beyond the reach of Greek influence—with the isolated exception of India.

Now what Empedocles shares with Pythagoras is precisely the doctrine of reincarnation. One of the fragments of the Καθαρμοί expresses his admiration for the superman who could recall his previous incarnations "in ten and twenty lifetimes of men;"[11] and this is in fact a capacity which Empedocles claims for himself (B 117). But the recollection of one's previous existences is not a shaman's trick; it presupposes the doctrine of transmigration. Nor does shamanism account for Empedocles' conception of the soul as a fallen god. The soul of a shaman is said to travel to heaven in a trance; it does not claim to have fallen from there at birth.

But if shamanism can shed no light on Empedocles' doctrine of the soul, neither does it fit the personal image of the man that is conveyed by his poetry and his legend. Empedocles' soul does not leave his body like that of Hermotimus and Epimenides. He does not ride on an arrow like Abaris or appear in the form of a raven like Aristeas. He is never seen in two places at the same time, and does not even descend to the Underworld like Orpheus and Pythagoras. Empedocles does, of course, pretend to some supernatural powers. But weather magic is not a monopoly of shamans, nor is it typical of their art. And his claims of prophecy, healing, and restoring the dead to life would be shamanistic if—and only if—these feats had been performed by means of an ecstatic trance. But to such a trance neither the fragments nor the legend make the slightest allusion.

In the absence of any such evidence for Empedocles, our conclusions can only be negative. Whatever light the comparison with Scythian and Siberian shamanism may throw upon other dark corners of archaic Greek religion, it is of no help for an interpretation of the religious ideas and personality of Empedocles. Far from providing material for the study of Greek shamanism, the case of Empedocles seems to show that the practice of ecstatic trance was no longer held in esteem. If the possession of ecstatic powers had been regarded as a source of religious prestige in the fifth century, it is scarcely conceivable that neither Empedocles nor his followers nor his later biographers should have claimed such powers for him. (It is interesting to see how little is made of the trances of Socrates, which must surely have been historical.) In this respect the contrast between Pythagoras and Empedocles is very striking. Every shamanistic trait in the legendary portrait of Pythagoras is absent from that of Empedocles. Whatever Pythagoras' historical role may have been, a later age could see him as the reincarnation of Hermotimus and the rival of Orpheus and Epimenides. But the most romantic biographers of Empedocles always knew too much of the man and his times to picture him as a shaman.[12]

Since the time of Tylor and Frazer, the use of material from cultural anthropology in historical studies has generally tended to confound the primitive and the civilized by stressing only the analogies between the two. In fact, the very same comparison may often serve equally well to distinguish the two from one another, by defining the line that separates barbarism from civilization. It is perhaps in this respect that the confrontation of Empedocles and the shamans may be most illuminating. For it enables us to distinguish the age of the Greek shamans from that of the Greek mystics. The complex figure of Pythagoras represents the point of intersection between the two. It is not surprising that shamanism should play some part in the earliest beginnings of Greek mysticism, for the shaman is as it were the mystic of a primitive society. It may well be that, as Rohde suggested, the ecstatic exploits of men like Epimenides prepared the way for Greek acceptance of the doctrine of a divine soul wandering from body to body until it can return to the gods. But by its rigor and its generality, such a doctrine is no longer primitive. It is neither an inevitable nor a common conclusion from shamanistic experience, and its appearance in Greece marks the beginning of a new era, that of philosophical mysticism. It is natural that one of the earliest representatives of the new age should be Pythagoras of Samos, a contemporary and neighbor of the Milesian natural philosophers. But Pythagoras himself is an impure example of the new type. The primitive background shows through in his own legend as well as in the curious taboos preserved by later Pythagoreans. Coming two or three generations after Pythagoras, Empedocles marks a considerable advance in the rationalizing of the mystic tradition, though he too still wears the mantle of the magician. But the doctrine as such is not bound to such circumstances. Its next appearance, stripped of all magical accessories, is in the dialogues of Plato. Pythagoras, Empedocles, and Plato represent the three major landmarks in the development of Greek mysticism. With Plato the process is complete. His conception of the soul, embodying the Pythagorean cycle of rebirth, remained definitive for the mystics as long as pagan antiquity endured.

Now there is no clear trace of this doctrine of transmigration in Greece before the time of Pythagoras, and perhaps comparative religion may after all help to define its source, or at any rate to establish its closest parallel. But in this case the best point of comparison will be provided not by a relatively backward people like the Scyths or the Mongols, but by the only civilization (outside of China) which had reached a level of intellectual development comparable to that of early Greece. The truest spiritual peers of Pythagoras and Empedocles may well be their Indian contemporaries in the age of Buddha, who also believed in the wheel of rebirth, strived to recall their previous transmigrations, and sought purification and escape through the practice of religious vegetarianism. The time has perhaps come to reconsider, in the light of modern research and with more rigorous techniques of comparison, the hypothesis developed by von Schroeder in 1884, in the first two chapters of his *Pythagoras und die Inder: eine Untersuchung über Herkunft und Abstammung der pythagoreischen Lehren*. Even if no historical link can be established, the parallel between the two religious patterns would certainly be instructive.

But that is another story.

NOTES TO APPENDIX

[1] Dodds, p. 140. M. Eliade is slightly more specific: "on ne peut donc pas considérer n'importe quel extatique comme un chaman; celui-ci est le spécialiste d'une trance, pendant laquelle son âme est censée quitter le corps pour entreprendre *des ascensions célestes ou des descentes infernales*" [*Le chamanisme et les techniques archaïques de l'extase* (Paris, 1951), p. 19, italics added].

[2] Eliade, pp. 17–18.

[3] K. Meuli, "Scythica," *Hermes*, 70 (1935): 121.

[4] Meuli, pp. 159–63; cf. Rohde, *Psyche*, II^4: pp. 90–91.

[5] Hdt. IV. 13–15; Meuli, pp. 153–59; Rohde, pp. 91–93.

[6] Rohde, II^4, pp. 94–99. Whether Zalmoxis the Thracian belongs with these men is a doubtful point; for the affirmative see Meuli, p. 163; for the negative, Eliade, pp. 350 f.

[7] Dodds, p. 147; Eliade, p. 352.

[8] A descent in the body is presupposed by the mocking story of Hermippus (in Diog. Laert. VIII, 41) that Pythagoras—like Zalmoxis—had arranged a subterranean hiding-place into which he retired. Eliade finds that such "descentes légendaires . . . n'ont pas la moindre structure chamanique" (p. 353).

[9] ἔξω γενόμενος τοῦ σώματος ἀκήκοα ἐμμελοῦς ἁρμονίας (schol. Ambros. Od. α 371, cited by Rohde, II^4, p. 420). It does not follow that this ecstasy formed part of a κατάβασις εἰς ᾅδου, as Rohde infers.

[10] See the material collected by Eliade, pp. 26–35, 88–92. The spirits of the dead generally do not take possession at birth, but when the young man is ready to undergo initiation as a shaman. A closer parallel to transmigration is suggested by the Medicine Rite of the Winnebagos, which promises immortality to its initiates by revealing the secrets that will permit them to return to earth as often as they wish (Eliade, p. 289, citing the work

of Paul Radin). But this is of course the very opposite of what reincarnation means for Empedocles, who, like an Indian mystic, wishes *not* to be reborn.

[11] Emped. B 129, according to the most likely interpretation.

[12] It is characteristic that Heraclides Ponticus, who is responsible for much that is fabulous in the legend of Pythagoras, and who dealt at length with Empedocles' revival of the woman that had lain lifeless for thirty days, seems to have treated this cure in an almost scientific spirit, as an experiment in suspended animation. Here if anywhere was the occasion for Empedocles to appear as a shaman; instead he apparently delivered a lecture on the psychosomatic causes of sleep and death. (See J. Bidez, *La biographie d'Empédocle*, pp. 24–35, who conjectures that the cure was effected by means of a magic wand like that mentioned by Clearchus. Wehrli, on Heraclides fr. 78, supposes that the inanimate woman had an apocalyptic vision, but there is no need for that; the comparison to Christ and Er is based simply on her apparent death and resurrection.)

Similar restraint in dealing with Empedocles is reflected by Heraclides' version of the myth of Er, where the eschatology of Empedocles is combined with the trance experience of Hermotimus to produce the fictitious revelation of Empedotimus. (See Rohde, II[4], pp. 94 f., n. 1; Wehrli, on Heraclides frs. 90–96, seems to have been the first to notice that Empedotimus is a composite name.) There would have been no need to invent Empedotimus if Empedocles himself had been an ecstatic.

RETRACTIONES

Looking back on this essay after some ten years, I still agree with the main features of the interpretation. However, recent studies in Empedocles have led me to revise my views on two questions which are at issue here, one tangentially and the second more essentially.

(1) I no longer believe in the four-phase reconstruction of Empedocles' cosmic cycle by Zeller and Burnet, which led me to describe the present world phase as a period of increasing strife. Jean Bollack's *Empédocle* I (Paris, 1965) has convinced me that there is only one (recurrent) world history for Empedocles, beginning with the total dissolution of the Sphere by Neikos and characterized by the continuous recreation of partial unities under the increasing dominance of Love, until (in some future moment, which Empedocles hints at but does not describe) the universal harmony of the Sphere is reconstituted and the cycle begins anew.[1] Hence all references in my article to a present state of the world in which Strife has the upper hand, or is increasingly dominant, or in which Love is yielding to Strife, should be stricken from the record. This has the effect of nullifying my note 66. And it tends rather to strengthen the analogy between the cosmic history of the physical poem and the

life history of the daimon in the *Purifications:* in both cases the pattern is one of perfect harmony yielding *at first* to a state of separation and alienation but gradually recovering its initial perfection. Insofar as the analogy holds, the Golden Age must correspond to the Sphere and not to any later moment (contra n. 54). But our knowledge of the *Purifications* is too incomplete to permit any confidence on this point.

(2) Bollack's interpretation emphasizes that Love is not a separate element over and above the basic four but is *immanent* in them as their principle of unity, homogeneity, and mutual adjustment. (Cf. Φιλότης ἐν τοῖσιν . . . μετὰ τοῖσιν ἑλισσομένην in frag. 17. 20–25, whereas Νεῖκος is δίχα τῶν, v. 19.) From this it follows that, for the physical poem at least, the purest condition of Love is not one of separation from the elements (for separation is the work of Strife) but of complete fusion with them in a perfectly homogeneous blend, where the elements cease to be distinct from one another—the condition realized in the Sphere. I am not sure how far this can apply to the daimon, but perhaps we may understand its "alien garment of flesh" as constituted not by the elements as such but by their *diversity and opposition to one another*. In its state of purity the daimon will have, or will be, an elemental body after all (cf. φίλα γυῖα in 115.3), only not one composed of *distinct* elements. The hatred which the daimon encounters in the elemental zones will reflect the fact that he, like themselves, is estranged from perfect harmony. On this view, release from strife cannot mean physical separation from the elements but rather the attainment of a new (and original) state of freedom from elemental plurality and opposition. A judgment on details had best be suspended until we have Bollack's volume on the Καθαρμοί. In any case I would no longer speak of Love as "capable of existing apart" from the elements "as an independent entity". The essential methodological point, established for the first time in recent work on Empedocles, is that his popular poem Καθαρμοί must not be used as a key for the interpretation of the esoteric work Περὶ Φύσεως, but conversely.

In response to a recent article by A. A. Long which treats many of the problems discussed here but ends by denying the compatibility of the physical and religious doctrines,[2] I would like to make clear in what sense I claim to have reconciled the two poems and the two sides of Empedocles' thought. I agree with Long (p. 275) that there is no *clear* connection between the psychophysics of the poem *On Nature* and the doctrine of the transmigrating daimon. If the connection were clear, there would be less disagreement among interpreters. What I claim is, first, that the parallels and echoes between the two poems strongly suggest that Empedocles thought of their doctrines as compatible. Hence it is the task of a sympathetic interpretation to discover what compatibility there might be. Secondly, I claim that *if* the two doctrines are compatible, then the daimon can only correspond to the principle of Love in living creatures: all other elemental constituents—insofar as they are *distinct* from Love and from one another—are excluded for the reasons given in my essay. That Empedocles *intended* the two doctrines to be compatible in this way is a legitimate inference from the fact that he has taken pains to link the two poems together by verbal echoes and by the common pattern of a conflict between Love and Strife. Whether they are *in fact* compatible is a different question altogether.

Perfect consistency in a mystic doctrine of the soul, or in any theory of mind, is a hard goal to reach. I would claim only that Empedocles has gone a long way in this direction. His theory is certainly not exempt from difficulties. One of the most acute concerns the doctrine of transmigration itself, regardless of its relation to the physical theory. This is the problem of individuation and identity: what makes a daimon one and the same as it passes from creature to creature? How can it preserve the memory of its previous incarnations? The fragments of the *Purifications* do not suggest that Empedocles ever faced up to this problem. But then, neither did Plato.

NOTES

1 See my review of Bollack in *Gnomon*, 1969, pp. 439–447. For reconstructions of Empedocles' cosmogony which parallel that of Bollack on essential points, see the articles of F. Solmsen in *Ph.*, 10 (1965): 109–48, and U. Hölscher in *Hermes*, 93 (1965): 7–33.

2 "Thinking and Sense-Perception in Empedocles: Mysticism or Materialism?" *CQ*, 16 (1966): 256–76.

EDWIN L. MINAR, JR.
DePauw University

Cosmic Periods in the Philosophy of Empedocles*

I

EMPEDOCLES[1] thought of the world-process as the product of the combination and separation of the four elements earth, air, fire, and water, under the influence of Love and Strife. The elements, as well as Love and Strife themselves, are both material, in the usual sense, and divine. The process is cyclical, and consists of a succession of phases, in each of which either Love or Strife is predominant, or gaining predominance, over the other:

> I will set forth a double doctrine: sometimes one grows out of more to exist alone, and sometimes it is separated, for more to exist, out of (the) one. Twofold is the birth of mortal things, twofold their demise; for the coming together of all begets and kills the one, and the other in turn, as things are separated, is nourished and flies apart. And these never cease their interchange, as sometimes all come together, by Love, into one, and sometimes, in turn, everything is borne apart by the hate that is in Strife. So insofar as one has learned to be born from several and several, again, have emerged as one is divided up, to this extent they are subject to birth and their life is not lasting. But insofar as they never cease constantly interchanging, to this extent they exist forever, unmoved throughout the cycle. (Fr. 17. 1–13).

What is the product of the "coming together"? It could be any sort of creature or object. Its singularity and independent existence is contrasted with the plurality of πλεόνων and πλέον' (line 2). It is, in other words, one of the mortals or mortal things of line 3. The interchange process, referred to in both its aspects of congregation and separation, causes and cancels birth, and it fosters as well as negates the process of decay. The "all" of lines 4 and 7, and the "everything" would be, on this reading, the four elements. It is clear that, in the ordinary course of

* This is a revised version of a paper presented at the 1961 meeting of the SAGP in Ann Arbor, Michigan. Reprinted with only slight variation from *Phronesis* 8 (1963): 127–45. By permission of Royal Van Gorcum Ltd.

things, both Love and Strife are at work, though at any moment one may be gaining over the other; but what is the nature of the transition from the period of one's growth to that of the other? There must be a moment at least, or an era, when each of the two reaches, or enjoys, the apogee of its influence, before beginning to decline. If these are moments, one will speak of two cosmic phases, if eras, of four. This problem has been answered in both ways, for unfortunately the evidence from the fragments of Empedocles' poems is not unambiguous.[2] It is not proposed to discuss this question here; it is enough to note that whether the periods in question are eras or moments, they should have some definable characteristics.

Empedocles makes it clear that the effect of Love is increasingly close association among the elements, so that they voluntarily seek combination with each other, while the opposite tendency of Strife is to make them hate and withdraw from one another. This means that each congregates with its own kind, so that any of them is impelled both toward its like (by Strife) and toward what is unlike it (by Love), and Empedocles uses both these impulsions in his system. There is no evidence as to what phase Empedocles used as the starting-point of his exposition, and no likelihood that any of them was thought of as primary. The period of Strife's growing influence brings the progressive disintegration of things, culminating in a state in which the four elements are completely separated from each other, and Love is presumably excluded. Her re-entry, however, and growth in power, bring about a more and more thorough mixture of the elements, a steadily increasing integration of the world.

What would be the culmination of this process? Parmenides had said, of that which exists,

> Motionless within the limits of mighty bonds, it is without beginning or end, since coming into being and perishing have been driven far away, cast out by true belief. Abiding the same in the same place it rests by itself, and so abides firm where it is; for strong Necessity holds it firm within the bonds of the limit that keeps it back on every side . . . But since there is a furthest limit, it is bounded on every side, like the bulk of a well-rounded sphere . . . (Fr. 8. 26–31, 42–43, tr. Kirk and Raven.)

This picture must have been in Empedocles' mind, and many have supposed that it provided him with a pattern of perfection. And he does say (fr. 17. 7, quoted above), "Sometimes all come together, by Love, *into one.*" This can be interpreted to mean that at the triumph of Love the world becomes a thoroughly uniform mixture, and it is tempting to think that Empedocles, influenced by Parmenides, thought of the universe as spherical in shape. Though really early evidence for such an interpretation is scanty, it is advanced by some of the commentators on Aristotle, in the Neoplatonic period. Philoponus, for example, writes,

> Again (Empedocles) says that during the dominance of Love, all things become one and produce the sphere, which is without quality, so that neither the peculiar character of fire nor of any of the others is any longer preserved in it, each of the elements shedding its particular form.[3]

Simplicius also speaks of "the sphere" (*De caelo* 528. 11, not in DK), but without explicitly denying it all quality: "Empedocles says that this cosmos comes to be under the influence of Strife separating out the elements, just as the sphere does under the influence of Love combining and uniting them."

Here it appears that Empedocles regarded the present era as one in which Strife is gaining in strength, at the expense of Love; and corroborating evidence on this point will be mentioned later. What does this mean about the cosmic, and cultural, process? Surely, for one thing, that the present is a period of decline and that the past was better—both the reign of Love, if it was an extended period, and the early part of the period of Strife's gain, when of course Love would still be very powerful. It is not surprising, then, to find Empedocles speaking elsewhere, nostalgically, of a past Golden Age (fr. 128–30). To those recent scholars who see his thought as a unity, this is one of the indications of the general parallelism between his two poems. But where precisely does the Golden Age belong? The best suggestion, along these lines, seems to be that of Kahn, who puts it "very early in the present phase of the world cycle, when the Sphere has given way to individual creatures but Strife has not gained full mastery over Love."[4] Presumably, then, there would be another similar or identical condition just before Love's complete triumph. We should have the picture, then, of "countless tribes of mortal things," and blessed daemons, living an increasingly rich and complex life, till one day they fuse into a single mass—"divine" in some sense—spherical, but otherwise, without form or quality, without motion or any other sign of life. Then, after an indeterminate period, the nearly-ideal condition—the Golden Age—suddenly reappears, or restores itself, as a result of the renewed activity of Strife, and the long process of decadence begins. This is certainly a strange conception; and though it is dangerous to expect a great and original mind to conform to canons of "common sense" or consistency, it may be suggestive to consider the possibility that we have misinterpreted the poet's meaning.

A difficult fragment is 27, whose text is given as follows in Diels-Kranz:

> ἔνθ' οὔτ' ἠελίοιο διείδεται ὠκέα γυῖα
> οὐδὲ μὲν οὐδ' αἴης λάσιον μένος οὐδὲ θάλασσα·
> οὕτως Ἁρμονίης πυκινῷ κρύφῳ ἐστήρικται
> Σφαῖρος κυκλοτερὴς μονίῃ περιηγέι γαίων.

Lines 1 and 3–4 are quoted by Simplicius, in the context of a discussion of motion and rest, as referring to the rule of Love:

> This would seem to be what Empedocles means when he says that it belongs to the necessity of things that Love and Strife hold power and cause motion alternately, and if so he also implies that a state of rest intervenes. For rest is intermediate between opposite motions. But Eudemus understands the state of rest to exist during the dominance of Love, in the sphere, when everything is combined: "The sun's swift limbs are not there descried," but as he says, "So he lay steady in the close-built hiding place of Harmony, a well-rounded sphere, rejoicing in surrounding solitude."[5]

This seems to carry the Peripatetic discussion, and also the difference of opinion as to Empedocles' meaning, back to the fourth century B.C. This disagreement is easy to understand, for of course Empedocles was not writing on the theory of motion, in Aristotelian terms. The usual description of the nature of the reign of Love and that of Strife may have developed, in part at least, from the doctrine here expressed that "rest is intermediate between opposite motions."

It is striking that Plutarch cites lines 1 and 2 as referring to the world of Strife, in a paragraph which, though syncretistic, seems clear enough about Empedocles:

> So look out and reflect, good sir, lest in rearranging and removing each thing to its "natural" location you contrive a dissolution of the cosmos and bring upon things the "Strife" of Empedocles—or rather lest you arouse against nature the ancient Titans and Giants and long to look upon that legendary and dreadful disorder and discord when you have separated all that is heavy and all that is light. "The sun's bright aspect is not there descried, / No, nor the shaggy might of earth, nor sea" as Empedocles says. Earth had no part in heat, water no part in air; there was not anything heavy above or anything light below; but the principles of all things were untempered and unamiable and solitary . . . So they were until desire came over nature providentially, for Affection arose or Aphrodite or Eros, as Empedocles says and Parmenides and Hesiod . . .[6]

Diels combined the two citations into a single fragment, choosing Simplicius' ὠκέα γυῖα over Plutarch's ἀγλαὸν εἶδος in line 1. Bignone gave the lines cited by Plutarch as fr. 26a, and thought that while they referred to the reign of Strife, fr. 27 (Simplicius' version) came from the section on Love. Kirk and Raven would insert between lines 2 and 3 the line

ἀλλ' ὅ γε πάντοθεν ἶσος ἑοῖ καὶ πάμπαν ἀπείρων,

which is quoted by Stobaeus along with line 4, making a couplet given as fr. 28 by Diels-Kranz. Given the uncertainty of the tradition, it is difficult to know which testimony we should prefer.[7] It is quite possible that, as Bignone thought, this is one of the cases of repeated lines in Empedocles, and a similar description was given, in two parts of his book, of the state of the world at the two extremes.[8] In many respects the two periods would indeed be very similar—as is understandable since Love and Strife are equal in "rights"—only that in one the elements are perfectly mixed, in the other perfectly separated, so that the evidence of this fragment would describe the world of perfect Strife at least as well as that of perfect Love. One might suppose that sun, earth, and sea are here three of the four elements, "descried"—because completely separated—during the period of Strife but in that of Love thoroughly mixed; but the expressions "sun's swift limbs" (or "shining face") and "earth's shaggy might" would in that case seem odd. He must be referring to the earth, sun, and sea as physical aggregates, components of the world as we know it, so that there is no warrant here for thinking of the "disappearance of the elements."[9] It is precisely the elements that are permanent, as the poet says many times. They "run through each other" but remain themselves. Their orderly arrangement, εἰς ἕνα κόσμον, is the work of Love, their separation into ἀκοσμία (Plutarch's word) that of Strife. It is much harder to imagine for Empedocles than for a neo-Platonist that the increasingly orderly cooperation of the elements, in the proper proportion, should be thought of as leading to the disappearance of earth, sea, and sun—or of the four elements—or to their amalgamation into an undifferentiated One.

What do lines 3–4 mean? It is commonly assumed that Harmony means Love, which provides the πυκινὸς κρύφος in which the god Sphere, who equals the rounded totality of things, is ensconced. Though 122.2, with 18, and 96.4 seem to show that Empedocles sometimes uses Harmony as a synonym of Love, it is of course not certain that we should capitalize ἁρμονίης. Could these lines too refer to Strife's reign? Even that has its own appropriate kind of "fitting-together"; at least we learn (in fr. 26. 7) that a process of "growing into one" (ἓν συμφύντα) accompanies the utter destruction (τὸ πᾶν ὑπένερθε γένηται) which Strife brings.

In any case the interpretation of line 3 is difficult. What is it to be "firmly fixed in the close-packed hiding place of fitting-togetherness" and at the same time to be the whole of things, spherical, solitary (or motionless) and happy? This does not fit Love, as we know her from other fragments, but is quite appropriate to Strife, the Empedoclean force which works for separation and hence would naturally exult in solitude. Could the poet here be reflecting satirically the views of Parmenides, and showing that the static world he had prized is really only appropriate to Strife? The latter is in fact not only bad but, in spite of his status, stupid. Intelligence, we learn from other fragments, belongs to all living things (fr. 110. 10), but increases as the mixture which Love causes becomes more perfect.[10] Strife is now victorious; segregation is complete, but what seems to him a cozy nook is in fact a prison. He does not know better than to rejoice, forsooth, in a solitude which gregarious Love would abhor.[11]

In fr. 29. 1–2, the world (under Love's rule, according to Hippolytus) is described as without wings, feet, nimble knees or sex organs, and as being "a sphere, and equal to itself in all directions." In fr. 134, speaking of Apollo in particular and of "the divine" in general, according to Ammonius, the poet gives a somewhat fuller description repeating two lines of fr. 29. He does not have a human head, no wings, feet, nimble knees, or sex-organs, "but was solely a sacred and ineffable mind, darting through the whole cosmos with swift thoughts." To Empedocles all the elements, as well as Love and Strife, are divine, and this would well apply to Love. It is quite appropriate, indeed inevitable, to think of Love as permeating the whole of the cosmic order (κόσμον ἅπαντα) of which she is the creator; but she is not the same as the spherical divinity of fr. 29, who seems to be the same as the aloof personage of 27 and 28, "rejoicing in circular solitude."[12] The parallelism of 29 and 134 suggests, too, that the idea of sphericity, as applied to gods, was for Empedocles related rather to an anti-anthropomorphic ideal, to the self-equality, consistency, and actual or potential omnipresence of divinity than to any homogeneous or motionless quality.

There are no other passages in which the word σφαῖρος or any of its derivatives is used in the actual fragments of Empedocles. It is not found in Aristotle, who in his references to the stage of Love's dominance uses the colorless expressions τὸ μῖγμα or τὸ ἕν.[13]

"Sphere" is normally feminine in Greek and it might be thought that Empedocles' use of the masculine suggests a personification. We learn from Simplicius, however (*Phys.* 1124; DK I^6 324. 16) that somewhere in the poem the neuter form was used.

Thus there is little or nothing to suggest the divine Sphere, as equivalent with the totality of things, at the apogee of Love, in the fragments themselves, in Aristotle or Theophrastus, and also not in the Peripatetic doxographical tradition through which most of our information about his physical philosophy is transmitted.[14] Neither is it attested in the partly independent tradition about Empedocles' religious views, as expressed in the *Purifications*.

In fr. 26. 3–5, Empedocles summarizes the cosmic processes:

> These things themselves exist, and running through one another they become men and the tribes of other beasts, at one time coming together by Love into a single cosmos, at other times, in turn, each being borne apart through the hatred in Strife, till growing together into one they are completely subdued.

The latter part of this seems to be paraphrased by Aristotle: "When the whole is dissolved into the elements by Strife, then fire is aggregated into one, as is each of the other elements" (*Met.* A 985 a 25; DK 31 A 37). Thus the elements at this time are collected into homogeneous masses. It has been suggested that the world was now spherical, and indeed that it may have consisted of a set of concentric spheres, presumably with Love as the outermost of them, and with Strife permeating the whole.[15]

What was the shape of the cosmos produced by Love? Empedocles would have had precedent for thinking of it as spherical. If the drum-shaped earth of Anaximander hangs free in its place because it is equidistant from the circumference, a spherical world is implied.[16] But in fr. 35, which describes the growing influence of Love, the shape is by no means unambiguous. Strife apparently has arrived "at the lowest depth of the whirl," and Love is "at the center" of it (if δίνη and στροφάλιγξ are synonyms). "All these things" (the elements) come together voluntarily to make a unity. Strife passes "out," "to the furthest bounds of the *circle*" (ἐπ' ἔσχατα τέρματα κύκλου). In addition, a passage of Aëtius suggests an elliptical or egg-shaped world:

> Empedocles said that the horizontal extent is greater than the upward measurement from the earth to the sky, that is the distance from us, the world being, according to this, more spread out because the cosmos is like an egg (DK 31 A 50).

Perhaps the world is elliptical under the more dynamic rule of Love and spherical under the static influence of Strife, and there is truth in

Simplicius' isolated comment (inconsistent with his general interpretation) that Empedocles distinguished the σφαῖρος from the κόσμος.[17]

The world is to be sure a living and divine being,[18] which at this stage attains a state of peace—of cosmos. What is more, in a protest against anthropomorphism that is reminiscent of Xenophanes, Empedocles specifies that it not only does not have members *like ours* but is equal to itself in every direction and "endless," which may mean spherical in shape; but that is not to say that it is completely homogenized, nor that it does not have "members" at all. (Indeed this would be quite inconsistent with fr. 31: πάντα γὰρ ἑξείης πελεμίζετο γυῖα θεοῖο.) The divinity of the world as a whole was a quite general assumption in Empedocles' day.

Perhaps the question is best left undecided whether the whole was spherical, either all the time or at the two extreme states. The main point to be made here is the unlikelihood that there was anything unique about the sphericity of Love's world, and the inappropriateness of the supposition that "the Sphere" was a new contribution to theology. Simplicius speaks of "Love, by unification making the sphere, which he also calls a god, though he somewhere uses the neuter: 'It was a sphere' " (*Phys.* 1124. 1; DK I[6] 324. 16). This expression seems to mean that in Simplicius' mind, though Empedocles speaks of the world as spherical, he would not have used the neuter if its name were Sphere. Elsewhere Simplicius speaks of "the sphere" in a way that scarcely seems to justify modern editors in capitalizing it, and there is nothing about the god Sphere in the doxographical reports about Empedocles' theology. Even if there were a god Sphere, he would be a veritable *Augenblicksgott*, existing only for a while at a time, at one, or two, stages in the cyclic cosmic process. It seems misleading, therefore, to speak of him as in some way different from other gods, or occupying a special transcendent position.[19]

Any interpretation of his cosmic periods must take account, it would seem, of the fact that for Empedocles the effects of Love are desirable, those of Strife noxious. Professor Vlastos emphasizes the equality in prerogatives of the two, and concludes that by the "equalitarian justice" which Empedocles conceives as prevailing in the cosmos, "were not Harmony matched to its perfect equal in Strife, there would be no created world, only the nondescript mixture of the *Sphairos*."[20] This would require us to see the complete prevalence of either one as an unfortunate though luckily temporary episode in cosmic history. The reign of Love would be as much an ἀκοσμία as that of Strife. It is of course true that they are "equal" in force and in rights, sealed by broad oaths. And Empedocles accepts the world as such a world; but this is acceptance of the ineluctable necessities of life. It is this affirmation of a heroic and tragic and characteristically Greek view which gives the tone of tender melancholy which so many readers detect in the poet, rather than any rejection of life or yearning to be free of it. The period of the growth of Love is characterized by an increasing tendency for "things" to "come together," and Empedocles makes quite clear that the things he means here are the elements.[21] Fire, water, earth, and air, that is, work together more and more congenially under Love's tutelage, in the formation of a more and more nearly perfect universe. It never achieves complete perfection, perhaps, in the usual sense, because that might seem to imply permanence, or lasting immunity to Strife. On the other hand, Empedocles may have been less enamoured of this sort of static perfection than some others. Perhaps the gay and rather complicated world to which fr. 128 (quoted below) seems to refer was more to his liking. For the kind of unity to which Love leads is precisely the complex unity in which diverse elements cooperate to form a "cosmos." On the other hand, though the primary effect of Strife is "separation," it is the elements which are separated from one another, and in this process they "grow together" into separate and, this time, really homogeneous masses, and this is tantamount to the destruction of everything save the elements themselves (fr. 26. 7, quoted above).

One of the supports of the conventional interpretation of the rule of Love is the famous couplet, fr. 17. 7–8:

> ἄλλοτε μὲν Φιλότητι συνερχόμεν' εἰς ἓν ἅπαντα,
> ἄλλοτε δ' αὖ διχ' ἕκαστα φορεύμενα Νείκεος ἔχθει.

Here it is clear, as remarked above, that the "unity" described is the opposite of the separation of the elements. In fr. 20. 2, line 17. 7 recurs. The context is different, however: ἅπαντα modifies γυῖα in the following line (εἰς ἓν ἅπαντα/γυῖα, τὰ σῶμα λέλογχε, βίου θαλέθοντος ἐν ἀκμῇ), and the unity referred to is that of a single human body. The fragment is explicitly a comparison of the work of Love and Strife in the world at large with their work in individuals (people, bushes, fish, . . .); and the εἰς ἕν is not into a quality-less mass but (line 3) βίου θαλέθοντος ἐν ἀκμῇ. In 17. 7 the text is uncertain. Some manuscripts give εἰς ἕνα πάντα, where the masculine is hard to interpret, but suggests what might have been the original reading here, found in fr. 26. 5, where these two lines are both quoted again: εἰς ἕνα κόσμον.

That the progressive development of a cosmos is one of growing complication can be seen from the lines of fr. 17 (9–13) quoted above:

> So insofar as one has learned to be born from several, and several again have emerged as one is divided up, to this extent they are subject to birth, and their life is not lasting. But insofar as they never cease their constant interchange, to this extent they exist forever, unmoved throughout the cycle.

In the context the word "unmoved" (ἀκίνητοι) seems peculiar until we realize that this is a piece of anti-Parmenidean polemic. The motionlessness or changelessness of the elements means not that they are immobile, but that they are not altered qualitatively.

Because of the influence of Love,

> who is worshiped by mortals, too, as inborn in their members,
> and by whom they think thoughts of amity and perform the works
> of concord, calling her Joy by name, or Aphrodite (fr. 17. 22–24),

are produced

> all trees, and men and women, beasts and birds,
> and fishes, nourished in deep waters, aye,
> the long-lived gods, in honors excellent

(fr. 21. 10–12, tr. Leonard), "men and the tribes of other beasts" (fr. 26. 4), those "myriad tribes of mortal things" (fr. 35. 16) of which the poet speaks so often and with such affection. In fr. 128 we seem to have an actual description of the reign of Love:

> nor unto them
> was any Ares god, nor Kydoimos,
> nor Zeus, the king of gods, nor Kronos, nor
> Poseidon then, but only Kypris queen . . .
> whom they with holy gifts were wont to appease.[22]

What impresses in the "unifying" effect of Love is not a tendency to growing *uniformity;* things are not melting together or "fusing," but becoming increasingly individual, unique, and multifarious:

> παντοίαις ἰδέῃσιν ἀρήροτα, θαῦμα ἰδέσθαι

We can tell something of Empedocles' ideal world from his eschatological notions. He adopts from the Orphics and Pythagoreans the idea of transmigration, and with it a part of the idea of the unhappiness of man's lot. It is also clear that the soul is disadvantaged by being relegated from a realm where Love rules to this world in which Strife is unhappily so prominent (fr. 118). But Kahn is right in emphasizing that "Empedocles is no more a Buddhist than he is a Christian. The terms he uses suggest the continued, harmonious coexistence of discrete individuals."[23]

In the *Purifications*, Empedocles represents himself in striking terms as having attained an exalted state:

> Friends who dwell throughout the great town of golden Acragas, up by the citadel, men mindful of good deeds, unversed in wickedness, havens of respect for strangers, all hail. I go about among you all an immortal god, mortal no more, honoured as is my due and crowned with garlands and verdant wreaths. Whenever I enter the prosperous townships with these my followers, men and women both, I am revered; they follow me in countless numbers, asking where lies the path to gain, some seeking prophecies, while others, for many a day stabbed by grievous pains, beg to hear the word that heals all manner of illness. (Fr. 112, tr. Kirk and Raven.)

The god that is each one of us (fr. 115. 5), then, if he has achieved the degree of purification which the poet thought he had reached, will in times like these, when Strife is on the increase, do the sort of thing Empedocles is doing, associating with his beloved fellows, alleviating their misery and improving their lot as best he can. Though he may feel himself an exile (φυγὰς θεόθεν καὶ ἀλήτης, fr. 115. 13), repine at his temporary lot (κλαῦσά τε καὶ κώκυσα ἰδὼν ἀσυνήθεα χῶρον, fr. 118), and long to return to the society of Love's reign (fr. 146–47), there is no reason to suppose that this would be a permanent state of bliss or salvation—or that he will wish to dissolve, or devote himself to rotating, or to contemplating complacently the circumambient solitude.

Excellent testimony as to the sort of result Empedocles attributed to the increasingly good (not necessarily more thorough) mixture of elements is provided in Theophrastus' summary of his doctrine of perception:

> Those in whom the elements are mixed equally or nearly so and not at great intervals *nor in particles too small* or too large, are the most intelligent and most keen in sense-perception, and proportionately those closest to them in this respect, and those in the opposite condition are least intelligent. Those in whom the elements are combined in loose and light texture are torpid and easily-tired. Those in whom the elemental particles are *close-fitting and broken down into small bits*, such persons are considered keen, and though projecting many things they accomplish few because of the speed of the blood's movement. But those in each of whose parts the mixture is even will be wise by virtue of this; this is why some are good speakers, some good artisans, because some have such a mixture in their hands, others in their tongues. And it is the same with the other faculties. (*De sensu* 11; DK 31 A 86. 11.)

The result of a "good" mixture, in other words, under the influence of Love, is the farthest thing from a homogeneous mass. The second italicized phrase shows that the elemental particles become very small; the first, that they do not become "too small"; rather than fusing together, they retain their specific and permanent qualities and powers. This is what produces the finest distinctions and the most highly articulated relationship of the parts of the universe. The organs become more and more keen and competent, and human beings develop more and more skills and specialties. (Incidentally, such a situation is not inconsistent with a spherical shape for the universe as a whole.)

Empedocles seems to prize harmony, cosmos, the meaningful articulation of parts into a whole. But he does not emphasize the aspect of harmony or cosmos which most pleased the Pythagoreans: the orderliness of each thing assuming and keeping its proper place. There is very little about the majesty of law, or the pleasures of hierarchy, in our poet. It is Strife that sorts things according to their kind, and endeavors to keep them in isolation. Strife is thus in a sense more orderly, in its procedures and effects, than Love is. Of course there are different kinds of harmony: Anaximander, no Pythagorean, liked κόσμος; Protagoras saw value in νόμος.

In general, one wonders whether Empedocles is as close to the Pythagoreans as is sometimes supposed. He takes a polemical posture toward their (partly heretical) follower Parmenides, and is certainly very un-Pythagorean in the open way in which he publishes his doctrines. He also seems to have shown much more interest in empirical knowledge, the details of physical and zoological science—to say nothing of his democratic politics. He is not keen on Pythagorean numerology; to be sure he speaks in terms of quantitative comparison and even of proportion, but the distinctive thing about his analysis of organic compounds is the emphasis on the qualitative.[24] The Pythagorean cosmology, on the other hand, scarcely concerns itself with qualitative distinctions but is very explicit about quantitative relationships. The *Purifications* show an influence of Orphic and Pythagorean ideas, though here too there are differences.[25]

II

Some of the difficulty in the usual interpretation of Empedocles' cosmic periods becomes more sharply apparent if we consider what correlation they may have had with his analysis of organic evolution. For while the four cosmic periods (if there are four) will not of course correspond exactly to the four stages of biological evolution of which we have some reflection in the fragments (57–62) and a fairly clear account in a paragraph of Aëtius, it seems very likely that in a system worked out in such detail the two sorts of periods were in some way correlated. Aëtius' account, which doubtless stems from Theophrastus, may be translated as follows:

> Empedocles believed that the first births of animals and plants were by no means complete, but were disjunct, consisting of parts that were not grown together. The second group, though with limbs that were grown together, were like creatures in dreams. The third group of births were of the whole-natured; the fourth group came no longer from the same kind of source, as for example from earth and water, but from one another, in some cases because of the condensation of their nourishment, in others because the beauty of the females caused an excitation of the movement of sperm. (DK 31 A 72.)

Recapitulating, the four stages are characterized by the appearance of (1) separate members or parts of animal and plant bodies (the "neckless heads" and "browless eyes" of fr. 57), (2) creatures having more than one "part" each, but sometimes in monstrous combination (the "creatures with countless hands and trailing feet" of fr. 60 and the "man-faced ox-breed" of fr. 61), (3) "whole-natured" forms, and (4) plants and animals that reproduce as now. This seems most naturally interpreted as a continuous series of stages showing the increasing complication of modes of generation during the increasing influence of Love.[26]

The cryptic description of the creatures of the third stage as "whole-natured" can best be explained by reference to fr. 62, where the same word is used:

> Now come, hear how fire, separating out, brought forth the night-clad shoots of men and tearful women; for the tale is not wide of the mark nor without knowledge. First there rose whole-natured forms from earth, having their proportion of both water and warmth. For fire sent them up, wishing to reach its like, not yet showing the lovely form of limbs nor voice nor sex-organs such as are usual for men.

Here Empedocles is describing especially the origin of human beings (as is shown by the first, and confirmed by the last line), but it is natural to assume that the same sort of description would apply to other creatures, and plants as well.[27] They spring from earth, and this is only one of many reflections of that age-old mythical idea in Greek scientific thought.[28] They will have earth in their makeup, then, and they also "have their proportion of both water and warmth" (lines 4–5). Empedocles' attention does not stray far from the mixture of elements; air is not mentioned, but it is obvious that when these creatures emerged into the air they began to partake of it, i.e. to breathe. And though the propelling force behind their origin may be Strife (for this is what causes things to seek their like, as fire does here), will they not now also begin to partake of the influence of Love? This is foreshadowed in the πω of line 7: they do not *yet* show the perfection of form or voice, or the power of sexual reproduction which we think of as characteristic of men and women, but the tendency of development is in that direction. Though still very "primitive", these people are surely not the shapeless lumps or masses of which some scholars speak.[29] In other words, the "whole-natured forms" represent a further stage in cosmic evolution beyond what might well be called the "part-natured forms" of stages 1 and 2.

It is not clear whether stages 1 and 2 are interdependent, as they would have to be if the system were to be described as truly evolutionary, in the Darwinian sense, though a comment of Aristotle shows that in the second stage those creatures tended to survive whose accidental combination of parts was such that they were fit to do so.[30] They could not, however, propagate their kind, as would be necessary for a truly evolutionary system. Not even the "whole-natured forms" of stage 3 could do that. In addition, stage 3 clearly does not depend on stage 2.

Zeller saw this process of the development of organic life as a continuous one, but most of the recent commentators have believed that the four stages must be divided between two cosmic eras: the first two in that of the growth of Love, the third and fourth in that of the growth of Strife.[31] Most, however, have avoided mentioning the absurd consequences for the detail of the system. It is reasonable enough to think of the development from scattered members to combined members as brought about by the influence of Love, and perhaps a case could be made for assigning the "whole-natured forms" to the period of Strife. But can we attribute to Empedocles the cynicism required to place the entire phenomenon of generation by sexual reproduction, under the impulsion of Aphrodite, in the epoch of Strife—and indeed the latter part of that epoch, when the whole world is approaching disintegration? There is reason to believe he thought the present a period of Strife's growth, in the statement of Aristotle that "the world is the same now in the era of Strife as it formerly was in the era of Love" (*De gen. et corr.* 334 a 5; DK 31 A 42, B 53, B 54). But surely "the same" (ὁμοίως) is as significant a word here as "now" (νῦν). He means that we have the same kind of world as then existed; and this is natural since both forces are at work in both periods.

Zeller finds it a "surprising gap" in the system that Empedocles did not have more to say about the distinguishing character of each period; but, apart from the fragmentary nature of our tradition, there was not really much to say about the process of degeneration under Strife.[32] I would suggest that in Empedocles' conception, the period of Strife's growing dominance saw the same four stages or types of organic "birth," but in reverse order. We have ample evidence that in this part of the cycle the elements cooperate less and less with each other. The constant tendency is to disintegration—from the perfect and intricate organisms we know, to forms that are "whole-natured" but much less complex, then to the "dream-like" monster forms, and last, just before the complete separation of the elements by Strife, when the combinatory influence of Love is very weak, to the pathetic "browless eyes" and "neckless heads." If this is correct, the cyclical process might be graphically represented as in the diagram (Fig. 1).

In a somewhat pessimistic spirit Empedocles diagnosed his own world as one of decay. Perhaps he thought he saw evidence of this in the increase of war or divorce or sterility, or even in an apparent increase in the incidence of monstrous births. A cyclical view of history is not necessarily pessimistic; according to temperament one may emphasize the sense of entrapment or the eventual improvement always ahead. Empedocles' doctrine of transmigration is surely inconsistent at one point with his cyclical physical theory, if fr. 147 is correctly interpreted as promising escape from the round of rebirth: "sharing with the other immortals their hearth and their table, without part in human sorrows or weariness" (tr. Kirk and Raven). This may, however, only refer to a temporary state. To be sure, ἀθανάτοις seems unambiguous, but other passages suggest that Empedocles' attitude to mortality was rather unusual. We read of "long-lived gods" in fr. 21. 12 and 23. 8, of the "springing up" of gods in fr. 146. 3; and in fr. 35 he clearly takes a favorable view of the growing power of Love, which brings forth the ἔθνεα μυρία θνητῶν as well as causing things to grow, as mortal, that "previously had learned to be immortal" (line 14). The aspect of the transmigration theory that appealed most to Empedocles was the kinship of all things, and this forms the rationale for his dietary restrictions, whatever religious or superstitious background they may have had (frs. 130, 136–41). There is not much about "sin," as a theological concept, in his thought, and the ἀμπλακίαι, by which the δαίμων may involve himself in the cycle of transmigration are moral or social rather than ritual: the shedding of kindred blood or the violation of an oath, and reliance on "raving Strife" (fr. 115. 3, 14).[33]

The highest human types or "lives," which one may go through before attaining the divinity and immortality of fr. 147, are those of benefactors of their fellow man: "and finally they come as seers and bards and physicians and leaders among men on earth."[34] The humanistic motive that led Empedocles to see as the ruling forces in nature Love and Strife, which are most familiar to us as forces in the life of man, is also the leading spirit of his physical philosophy.

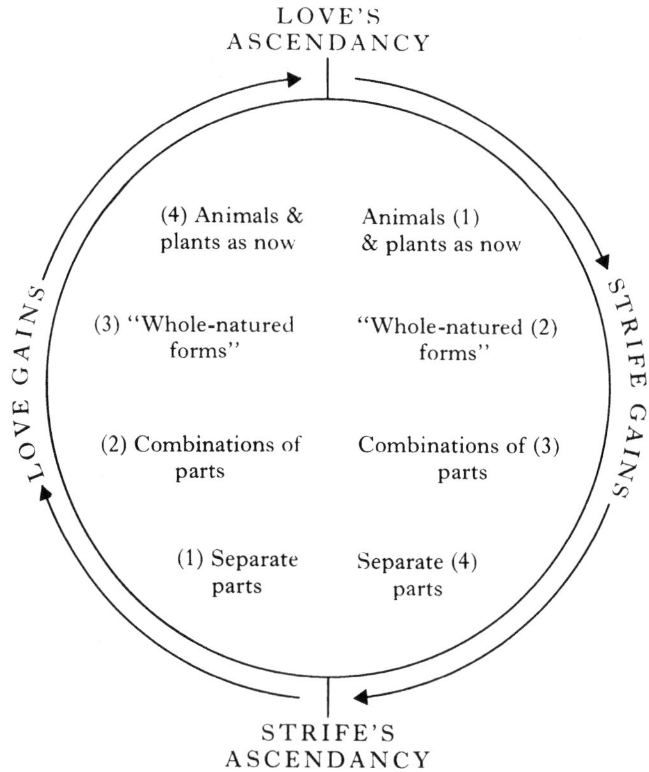

Fig. 1. Cyclical Process

NOTES

[1] I have not, unfortunately, had leisure for the kind of revision that would have been necessary to take adequate account of the ingenious and disparate interpretations that have recently appeared, especially those of Guthrie, Solmsen, Hölscher, and O'Brien.

[2] Aristotle thought there were four periods, two of activity, when Love or Strife is gaining, set apart by two intermediate periods of rest; but the lines he quotes in support do not seem to bear this meaning. (*Phys.* 8. 1. 250 b 26; cf. Zeller-Nestle, I^6, p. 971, n. 1.)

[3] *De gen. et corr.* 19. 3; DK 31 A 41. This is not an independent testimony, but merely a paraphrase of Aristotle *De gen. et corr.* 315a 3, and "very inaccurate in its inferences," as Clara Millerd points out (*On the Interpretation of Empedocles*, p. 61, n. 5). His word ἄποιον is not found elsewhere in the tradition. Cf. H. A. T. Reiche, *Empedocles' Mixture, Eudoxan Astronomy, and Aristotle's Connate Pneuma* (Amsterdam, 1960), p. 40.

[4] C. H. Kahn, "Religion and Natural Philosophy in Empedocles' Doctrine of the Soul," *AGP*, 42 (1960): 3–35, at p. 21, n. 54. This does not fully satisfy Kahn, who finally pronounces a verdict of *non liquet* on the connexion between the unity of the sphere and that of "the company of the blessed daimons" (p. 26).

[5] Simpl. *Phys.* 1183. 28; Eudemus fr. 110 Wehrli; DK 31 B 27.

[6] *De facie* 926 D–927A, tr. H. Cherniss (*Moralia*, Loeb ed., XII, p. 83).

[7] It is very clear from various Neoplatonizing explanations that Simplicius was influenced in his general interpretation of Empedocles by his own philosophical predilections. The whole system was allegorical to him, the chronological account given by Empedocles was διδασκαλίας χάριν and represented coexisting aspects of the world. In particular "the Sphere" was the symbol of the κόσμος νοητός or intelligible world. (DK 31 A 52, esp. Simpl. *De caelo* 304. 4, and ibid 141. 10, 305. 10, *Phys.* 1121. 17, 25 ff., 1186. 30 ff. Cf. Bignone, pp. 589 ff.) "The Sphere" was also, by various of the later commentators, interpreted as meaning formless matter, efficient cause, or the Stoic original fire (Zeller-Nestle, I^6, p. 975).

[8] See E. Bignone, *Empedocle* (Turin, 1916), pp. 220 ff., and the other references cited by Cherniss, *Plut. Moralia.* (Loeb) XII, p. 82, n. c. Note also that Plutarch often quotes from memory.

[9] E.g., F. Solmsen, *Aristotle's System of the Physical World* (Ithaca, 1960), p. 372, n. 16, p. 375, n. 31.

[10] "Only the delight of the *Sphairos* in his solitude is out of keeping with Empedocles' conception of the god," says Jaeger, *Theology of the Early Greek Philosophers* (Oxford, 1947), p. 141. His proposal to take μονίη as "rest" rather than "solitude" does not affect the present argument. The concept of the sphere as Love's product leads Jaeger to say, "In this way Empedocles retains the Eleatic Being as one stage in the cycle: it is the stage when the divine Love which keeps the world going has realized its dominion and become fully achieved" (ibid). The supreme achievement of the power which "keeps the world going" is to bring it to a full stop!

[11] κρύφῳ (line 3) is variously interpreted. Is it equivalent to κρυφιότης,

as LSJ think, thus meaning something like "secrecy" (Freeman), "obscurity," and hence "lurking-place," "cave" (*antre*, Zafiropulo), whether entered voluntarily, as γαίων in line 4 might suggest, or involuntarily, as ἐστήρικται suggests (so *Verliess*, "dungeon," DK)? Or is it parallel to κρυφὸν θέμεν (a conjectural reading for κρύφιον) in Pind. *Ol.* 2. 97, in which case it might mean something like "covering" (Burnet, Kirk and Raven)? If the interpretation suggested here is correct, the ambiguity may be intentional.

[12] There is no reason to attribute 134 to the *Purifications*, except Diels' assumption that anything to do with religion is from that poem. In fact Tzetzes refers to the poem *On Nature* in citing lines 4–5. Cf. C. H. Kahn, "Religion . . ." (n. 3), p. 6, n. 8.

[13] Bonitz lists the references, *Index aristotelicus* 242 a 23. That Aristotle refers to "the Sphere" with the words τοῦ θεοῦ, *De gen. et corr.* 333 b 21 (DK 31 A 40) is an assumption that begs the question at issue here. In the context of Aristotle's argument it need not mean more than "the Deity," as the Oxford translation has it. Aristotle understands Empedocles' εἷς κόσμος in the light of later metaphysical concepts of τὸ ἕν, and is thus able to castigate him for not defining adequately the relation between "the one" and the plural elements (as at *De gen. et corr.* 315 a 3 ff.). Similarly, he supposes that in bringing things together into a unity Love "destroys" everything else συνάγουσα γὰρ εἰς τὸ ἓν φθείρει τὰ ἄλλα, *Met.* B 1000 b 11). But there is nothing in his comments to indicate that the world's shape is spherical. Perhaps this is odd, if that was so, or was clearly expressed by Empedocles; Aristotle has a good deal to say, especially in the *De caelo*, about the properties of spheres.

[14] Hippolytus *Ref.* 7. 29 (DK I[6] 324. 12–16, introducing fr. 29) implies a relation between Love and the sphere, but the implication may well be that of Hippolytus himself, following the conventional interpretation. Aëtius 1.7.26 (*Dox.* 303) described the divinity according to Parmenides as σφαιροειδές, but no such word appears in the section (28) on Empedocles. Diels however proposed two conjectural restorations which are printed in DK 31 A 32, introducing both the words σφαιροειδές and Σφαῖρος. It is obvious from the text as it stands that the doxographers were concerned with the peculiar relationship of the one and many in Empedocles' cosmology and theology, and the absorption of the many into (or separation out of) the one (ἀναλυθήσεται). Usener's conjecture (DK I[6] 289. 11 n.) does justice to this. But there is no positive justification for inclusion of the idea of sphericity [indeed the first restoration is given "beispielsweise" in *RhM*, 36 (1881): 345.] The phrase τὸ μὲν ἓν τὴν ἀνάγκην (DK I[6] 289.9) is obviously wrong. For Empedocles' deity Necessity see frs. 115–16. She is an eternal oracular power, doubtless the guarantor of the oath that assures the equal rights of Love and Strife (fr. 30. 3) and so far from being identical with the "one cosmos" of Love's reign that Charis "hates unbearable Necessity" (fr. 116).

[15] E.g., Kirk and Raven, *The Presocratic Philosophers* (Cambridge, 1957), pp. 345 ff.

[16] DK 12 A 11, etc.; cf. C. H. Kahn, *Anaximander and the Origins of Greek Cosmology* (New York, 1960), pp. 53, 77.

[17] *De caelo* 139 b 16 (Schol. in Ar. 489 b 22; Zeller-Nestle I[6], p. 975, n. 7; not in DK).

[18] "But when Strife had grown great within its limbs, and sprang to its privileges as the time was fulfilled, which is fixed for them as alternate by a broad oath" (fr. 30; cf. 31, 35. 11). Fr. 27a (οὐ στάσις ουδέ τε δῆρις ἀναίσιμος ἐν μελέεσσιν) does not apply to the world as a whole, or to the god Sphere, but as Plutarch's introductory words show, to an individual human being, presumably at the time of the predominance of Love. (If it is an Empedoclean fragment at all, as Wilamowitz conjectured, and as the language seems to indicate.)

[19] E.g., Jaeger, *Theology of the Early Greek Philosophers*, pp. 142, 153; cf. Kahn, "Religion . . .," p. 21.

[20] G. Vlastos, "Equality and Justice in Early Greek Cosmologies" *CP*, 42 (1947): 156–78, at p. 160.

[21] Fr. 17, line 7 ἕν, line 9 ἕν, line 10 ἑνὸς πλέον', line 16 ἕν line 17 πλέον' ἐξ ἑνός are all explicitly explained by lines 18–20: the "more" are the four elements plus Hate and Love. And the "one" is the "one cosmos."

[22] Lines 1–4, tr. Leonard. If this fragment is from the *Purifications*, as is usually assumed, Kirk and Raven are right in seeing it as an indication of the parallelism between the two poems. However, it comports poorly with their picture of the rule of Love as an undifferentiated mass (p. 345).

[23] "Religion . . ." p. 25.

[24] Here I should disagree with Prof. Friedrich Solmsen [*Aristotle's System of the Physical World* (Ithaca, N.Y., 1960), pp. 372 f. and "Tissues and the soul," *PR*, 59 (1950): 446 f.], and with Kirk and Raven, who speak of "the *exact* proportion in which these substances are compounded" (p. 335; my italics). This is to ignore the line εἴτ' ὀλίγον μείζων εἴτε πλεόνεσσιν ἐλάσσων "either a little more of it or less of it with more of the others" (fr. 98. 4), as well as the word μάλιστα "about" (line 1). Empedocles seems to give an exact ratio in 96 and in the paraphrase of Aëtius (DK 31 A 78), but 98 shows that, though he thought there *was* a certain ratio in each case, he did not place great importance on stating it with mathematical precision.

[25] He *may* be referring to Pythagoras in fr. 129, though the κείνοισιν of line 1 is more likely the people of the golden age of Love; cf. ἦν δέ τις ἐν κείνοισιν with fr. 128. 1: οὐδέ τις ἦν κείνοισιν. (Jaeger doubts the identification, *Theology*, p. 151.)

[26] "Die Entstehung der Tiere und Menschen dachte sich Empedokles durch mehrere aufeinanderfolgende Vorgänge vermittelt, die ebensoviele Versuche einer immer vollkommeneren Vereinigung ihrer Teile darstellen" (Zeller-Nestle I[6], p. 986.)

[27] This seems to follow from the parallel with the Aëtius passage, where "animals and plants" are mentioned. Cf. Zeller-Nestle I[6], p. 987, n. 2.

[28] W. K. C. Guthrie, *In the Beginning* (London, 1957), ch. 2.

[29] E.g. Bignone, *Empedocle*, p. 450 et passim: *masse integre*. Diels-Kranz have *rohgeballte Formen*, Zeller-Nestle *unförmliche Klumpen* (I[6], p. 987), Tannery *formes indistinctes* (*Pour l'histoire de la science hellène*, p. 344). Similarly Holwerda (*Commentatio de vocis quae est* φύσις *usu* . . .,

p. 69): "μελέων φύσις (fr. 63) significat 'membrorum globus horribilis' idemque designat atque οὐλοφυὴς τύπος, qui homo, ut e fragmenti versu ultimo apparet, incerti erat sexus." I do not find the examples persuasive by which Holwerda seeks to show (pp. 68–70) that φύσις may mean not only *statura*, but also *monstrum, massa, moles*. These are τύποι; it is clear from LSJ that τύπος is primarily a blow, then the impression made by the blow—a seal-impression, an engraving, or the like. It is used by extension of many kinds of "types," but always of a *shape*. Sometimes the shape may be vague or undetermined, but never shapeless. The word οὐλοφυής is given the suitably ambiguous translation "whole-natured" by John Burnet, *Early Greek Philosophy*[4] (London, 1930), pp. 214, 243), and he is followed in this by Kirk and Raven (p. 338). Whether the root φυ-here has the sense of "existence," "being," "nature," or of "growth," the compound should mean something like "existing as a whole" or "single-growing." Simplicius' definition of it (*Phys.* 382. 17 ff.) is clearly influenced by his general interpretation. The only authority cited by LSJ for the word from the classical period, other than Empedocles, is Aristotle *PA* 693 a 25, where Peck's translation is "one uninterrupted whole."

[30] Ar. *Phys.* B 198 b 29; DK 31 B 61. Cf. Simpl. *Phys.* 371. 33.

[31] Zeller-Nestle I[6], p. 988, n. 2.

[32] Ibid, 978 f. We need not worry about the "Ausscheidung der Elemente aus dem Sphairos" (p. 979); Zeller himself, when he discussed the details of *Weltbildung*, noted that the separation ἐκ πρώτης . . . τῆς τῶν στοιχείων κράσεως (Ps.-Plut. *Strom.* ap. Eus. *PE* 1. 8. 10; DK 31 A 30) must refer to the beginning of Love's mixing activity. (κρᾶσις would seem an odd word to denote the totally-separated world of Strife; but the whole phrase, including the late word στοιχείων reads like a generally-phrased introduction to the main part of the sentence, reflecting the summarizer's views). Aristotle is simply wrong in stating that Empedocles omits to discuss world-formation under Love (*De caelo* 301 a 14; DK 31 A 42), as Cherniss points out (*Presocratics*, p. 194).

[33] This is of course not to deny that these concepts are frequently important in religious thought; but it seems misleading for Kirk and Raven (p. 350 f.) to generalize this into a doctrine of "the primal sin and fall of man."

[34] Fr. 146. 1–2. There seems slight warrant for rendering πρόμοι as "princes," giving a monarchist ring to this democrat's sentence. (Freeman, *Companion* p. 174, cites this line as showing "aristocratic bias.") It is a poetic word in which the etymological connexion with πρό seems to have remained strong. According to LSJ it always is equivalent to πρόμαχος in Homer.

ALEXANDER P. D. MOURELATOS
The University of Texas at Austin

Mind's Commitment to the Real: Parmenides B 8.34-41*

ταὐτὸν δ' ἐστὶ νοεῖν τε καὶ οὕνεκέν ἐστι νόημα·
οὐ γὰρ ἄνευ τοῦ ἐόντος, ἐν ᾧ πεφατισμένον ἐστίν
εὑρήσεις τὸ νοεῖν· οὐδὲν γὰρ ἢ ἔστιν ἢ ἔσται
ἄλλο πάρεξ τοῦ ἐόντος, ἐπεὶ τό γε Μοῖρ' ἐπέδησεν
οὖλον ἀκίνητόν τ' ἔμεναι· τῷ πάντ' ὄνομ' ἔσται [*or* ὀνόμασται]
ὅσσα βροτοὶ κατέθεντο πεποιθότες εἶναι ἀληθῆ,
γίγνεσθαί τε καὶ ὄλλυσθαι, εἶναί τε καὶ οὐχί,
καὶ τόπον ἀλλάσσειν διά τε χρόα φανὸν ἀμείβειν.

One need not know very much about the history of ancient philosophy—one might just barely make out and translate the words "same," "thought," "being," "Fate," "name," to sense that this is an important and fascinating text. Indeed, it is one of those *topoi* which regularly exercise the ingenuity of students of Greek philosophy. An interpretation of it often colors, or reflects, one's understanding of the metaphysics and epistemology of early Greek philosophy as a whole. In proposing to undertake here yet another argument on the analysis of the passage, I do not aim for anything like certainty or finality of exegesis. This would be too much to hope for, when we are working at such small scale, and all the more so in the case of pre-Socratic studies, where the evidence itself is limited and fragmentary and our controls over language and background only too imperfect. Rather it is through an analysis of this passage that I can explain most clearly and directly a certain conception of the relation of mind to reality for which I also find evidence in other texts, in some of the characteristic aspects and themes of Parmenides' poem, and which I consider philosophically

* Presented at the 1967 meeting of the SAGP in Boston, Massachusetts. An expanded version of this paper appears as chapter 7 of my book, *The Route of Parmenides: A Study of Word, Image, and Argument in the Fragments* (New Haven, Yale University Press, 1970). The present version is published in this collection with the kind permission of Yale University Press. I am indebted to Professor Gregory Vlastos for criticism of earlier drafts and for his kindness in allowing me to read a paper of his, which remains unpublished, entitled " 'Names' of Being in Parmenides."

and historically important. So let me proceed directly to the analysis, not pausing to review or to formulate the *status quaestionis*,[1] but taking up points of controversy as they arise.

I

Our text is not a fragment out of context; it occurs momentously in the climactic section of the poem's central argument, which we, more or less, understand. If we approach B 8.34 ff. as continuous with what has preceded,[2] then we find ourselves in possession of two important clues for understanding the controversial first line. (a) The presumption is that ταὐτόν refers back to the subject under discussion in B 8 as a whole, viz. ἐόν, "what-is."[3] It must therefore function as subject in B 8.34, not as predicate. (b) Since B 8.34–41 is preceded by a deduction of the "completeness" of ἐόν,[4] it is only logical to check for a possible connection between the key words, νοεῖν and νόημα, of B 8.34 and the argument that what-is is οὐκ ἀτελεύτητον, "not incomplete" (cf. also B 8.42 τετελεσμένον).

If we pursue this second clue, what comes to mind immediately is the many passages from the epic in which a τέλος-word expresses the fulfilment of a thought, wish, or prophecy. The closest parallel is *Il.* 18. 328: "But Zeus does not fulfill (τελευτᾷ) all thoughts (νοήματα) for men." Also of interest in this connection is the expression τελέωμεν μῦθον, "let us fulfill the thought" (*Od.* 4.776–77), and the formula-line αὔδα ὅ τι φρονέεις· τελέσαι δέ με θυμὸς ἄνωγεν, "speak what you intend, and my heart prompts me to fulfill it." In a recent study of the τέλος-words in Homer, Z. P. Ambrose observes: "τελεῖν does not only mean 'to do.' It means 'to do, or make, or act in full accord with some plan, command, prayer, promise or prophecy.' "[5] Again: "The essence of the action of the Homeric verb τελεῖν . . . is to transform concept into fact, whether this concept be a promise or a plan or a prophecy."[6] All of this suggests strongly that the connection between B 8.34–41 and the completeness proof from which it grows ought to be sought in the familiar idea of τελεῖν νόημα. Simplicius evidently saw this connection, as we may gather from his paraphrase: "for the sake of (ἕνεκα τοῦ) the thinkable, and it would be the same to say 'of being,' is thinking, since being is its τέλος" (*Phys.* 87.17–18). Most critics would disregard this comment as a misleading Neoplatonist gloss.[7] This is unfair to Simplicius, considering that the association of νόημα with τελεῖν is as old as Homer.

If we respect the presumption that ταὐτόν refers back to ἐόν, and if we do not ignore Simplicius' gloss, then the most plausible translation of B 8.34 would read:

And the same thing is to be thought [*or* "to be known"] and (is) wherefore is the thinking [*or* "knowing"].

I have construed the Greek as: ταὐτὸν δ' (subject) ἐστὶ νοεῖν τε (first predicate) καὶ ⟨ἐστὶ⟩ οὕνεκέν ἐστι νόημα (second predicate).[8] It is only fitting that a man who conceives of νοεῖν as a "quest" should avail himself of the syntactic form ἐστὶ νοεῖν = "is to think of" = "is to be thought of." Statements of the form "it's there to know, to apprehend, to think of" are exactly what we should expect from Parmenides.

In his recent edition of the Parmenides fragments, L. Tarán avoids a similar construction ("The same thing can be thought and is the cause of the existence of thought") on the grounds that it is "tautological and makes no sense in the context of Parmenides' argument."[9] I frankly do not see the tautology in the translation cited by Tarán: the idea that the intentional complement and the cause of thought are one and the same is not a truism, but a metaphysical thesis which requires argument (cf. Descartes on the distinction between "objective" and "formal" reality). At any rate, I would like to show that the translation which I gave above, far from being tautological, is charged with a sense which is both striking philosophically and appropriate at this juncture of the argument.

There is an important difference between ἐστὶ νοεῖν and οὕνεκέν ἐστι νόημα. The first tells us that ἐόν "is there to think, to know," i.e., that it is accessible and available—perfect, complete and fully actual as it is—that nothing prevents our knowing it. In other words, the first half of B 8.34 is a permission clause (though we need not translate "can be thought").[10] As a permission clause, it does not by itself exclude other objects of thought, nor does it oblige mind to be directed to ἐόν. It has, in effect, the form of a hypothetical: if you should choose to seek ἐόν, you will find it. But the second clause is stronger. It suspends the "if" and it cancels alternatives: thought is ἕνεκεν the what-is, i.e., the latter constitutes its goal, or constitutes the compelling authority to which thought must submit.[11] The two clauses are complementary. The first guarantees the presence or the availability of a certain object; but it posits no obligation for mind to seek it. The second posits the obligation, but gives no guarantee of the object's availability. The first clause says "you may," the second clause says "you must." Already this gives a pregnant, far from tautological sense to B 8.34. But we have only begun to draw out the significance of this very rich line.

It will be recalled that οὕνεκα or οὕνεκεν has three uses: (a) "wherefore," (b) "because," (c) "that" (= ὅτι, ὡς). Use (c) is generally regarded as a specialized case of (b).[12] Most recent critics would interpret the οὕνεκεν of B 8.34 under (c),[13] whereas I have argued in favor of (a). Yet, I suspect that the other two senses are also involved in the thought of B 8.34. What made possible the transition from (b) to (c) was precisely the conception of the subject-matter of an utterance or thought as the cause which prompts the thought or utterance.[14] Note that we can say indifferently "final" or "efficient" cause: facts *compel* us to think of them as they are; and the object of our desire *invites* or *elicits* appropriate thoughts from us. An important feature of the translation which I favor is that it expresses a doctrine which a Greek speaker could formulate after reflection on the etymology of conjunctions such as ὅ, ὅτι, and οὕνεκεν. That reflection on etymologies (real or supposed) is one of the characteristic devices of pre-Socratic thought is familiar enough, and requires no argument. I am not suggesting, of course, that Parmenides simply recorded his understanding of the etymology of οὕνεκεν="that" in the line under discussion. What I am saying, rather, is that the line gains in poetical force by using a certain word to explain a conception which (conception) already controls another and familiar use of that same word.

Let us also not forget that this is a line about mind *and* reality. We learn something about each from it. Of reality it says that it is identically the same in expectation, or in anticipation, and in actuality. The very same thing which prompts thought (οὕνεκεν) is there for us to know (ἐστὶ νοεῖν). This obviously continues the argument for οὐκ ἀτελεύτητον, "not incomplete," in the section immediately preceding. Parmenides' ἐόν has the integrity of Zeus' own word to Thetis:

> οὐ γὰρ ἐμὸν παλινάγρετον οὐδ' ἀπατηλὸν
> οὐδ' ἀτελεύτητον, ὅ τί κεν κεφαλῇ κατανεύσω.
>
> No (word) of mine is revocable, nor deceptive, nor unfulfilled
> when I bow my head in assent to it. (*Il.* 1.526 f)

It is quite otherwise with the things of δόξα. As Parmenides might have put it, ἄλλα ἐστὶ νοεῖν καὶ ἄλλα οὕνεκέν ἐστι νόημα, they are other in the knowing than they were in anticipation. This is an aspect of their "faithlessness" (cf. B 1.30). Conversely, ἐόν shows its good faith (cf. B 1.29 ἀληθείης εὐπειθέος) in being identically the same as object given (ἐστὶ νοεῖν) and as object yearned for (δίζησις, οὕνεκέν ἐστι νόημα). So the guiding idea of πίστις (cf. πείθειν B 1.16, 8.39; Πειθώ B 2.4; πίστις B 1.30, 8.12; πιστός B 8.50) is implicit in B 8.34, as well as the idea of the completeness of what-is.

From the viewpoint of mind, B 8.34 contains the striking doctrine that νόημα is about, or for the sake of, or is compelled by, ἐόν. This is a new element in the argument. So far the ἐόν has been presented as something unfamiliar and remote: something lying "far from the beaten track of men." The idea that it is the οὕνεκεν of thought (without qualification) appears here for the first time. We should now examine B 8.34 together with its sequel.

> And the same is to think of and wherefore is the thinking. For not without what-is, ἐν ᾧ πεφατισμένον ἐστίν, will you find thinking. For no other thing, but what-is, either is or will be, since it was just this thing that Fate shackled to be whole and immobile (B 8.34–38).[15]

We must, for the moment, leave the difficult expression, ἐν ᾧ πεφατισμένον ἐστίν untranslated. The rest of the text can be construed independently. What should not be missed is the emphatic concatenation of references to ἐόν: ταὐτόν, "the same thing"; οὐ γὰρ ἄνευ τοῦ . . ., "not without the . . ."; ἐν ᾧ, "in [on, upon] which"; οὐδὲν . . . ἄλλο πάρεξ τοῦ . . ., "not any other thing except the . . ."; τό γε, "specifically this." The phrase "you shall not find thinking without what-is" should be understood on the basis of a Platonic parallel, *Sophist* 237D, probably a deliberate imitation of Parmenides' language, put in the mouth of the Eleatic Stranger:

> We speak the word "it" at each instance with reference to something-that-is (ὄντι); for it is impossible to speak it all by itself, naked and deserted (γυμνὸν καὶ ἀπηρημωμένον), as it were, by all the things-that-are.

To paraphrase Plato: you shall not find the word "it" naked, or deserted by the things-that-are. To paraphrase Parmenides: you shall not find thinking naked or deserted by what-is.

Against this background it would appear, *a priori*, that the sense of ἐν ᾧ πεφατισμένον ἐστίν is, roughly, "to which (scil. the ἐόν) it (scil. τὸ νοεῖν) refers" or "to which it is addressed." But the usual translation, "in which it is expressed [*or* "revealed"]," is rather far from this sense. Most readers would concede that this is at best an unsatisfactory rendering. For it is not at all clear how we should interpret the doctrine that thought is expressed *in* what-is.[16] Besides, the Greek πεφατισμένον ἐστίν carries the sense of the present perfect (cf. πεφάτισται) much more prominently than does the English "is expressed." But the translation "in which it has been expressed" becomes even more strange.[17]

The key to the phrase is, I believe, not in the participle πεφατισμένον (from a rare verb, the semantics of which are unavoidably obscure), but in the phrase ἐν ᾧ . . . ἐστίν. The usual translation assumes that ἐν has vaguely locative or instrumental force. It has been overlooked that the ἐν together with εἶναι can have an idiomatic sense "to depend on, to rely upon, to be under the authority of" (cf. English "it's up to").[18] What is perhaps even more significant: this use appears to have its paradigm in the ancient image of God "holding" the fate, or the fulfilment, or the outcome of all things:

> ἀλλ' ἤτοι μὲν ταῦτα θεῶν ἐν γούνασι κεῖται
>
> But these things lie on the knees of the gods. (*Il.* 17.514)

Of special interest for Parmenides is the affinity of this conception with words such as πεῖραρ and τέλος:

> νίκης πείρατ' ἔχονται ἐν ἀθανάτοισι θεοῖσι.
>
> The *peirata* of victory are held by the immortal gods. (*Il.* 7.102)
>
> ἐν τοῖς γὰρ τέλος ἐστὶν ὁμῶς ἀγαθῶν τε κακῶν τε.
>
> On them (scil. on Zeus and Poseidon) rests the *telos* for good and evil. (Hes. *Op.* 669)
>
> Ζεῦ πάτερ . . . πᾶν δὲ τέλος ἐν τὶν ἔργων.
>
> Father Zeus . . . and the *telos* of all labors rests with you. (Pindar *Nem.* 10.29)

If this is indeed the force of ἐν ᾧ . . . ἐστίν here, then the relevant parallel out of the few occurrences of φατίζω is obviously the one in which the verb has some of the force of "to promise": τῷ τῆς θεᾶς σὴν παῖδ' ἄλοχον φατίσας, "having promised your unwed daughter to the son of the goddess" (Eur. *Iphig. Aul.* 135). In Parmenides φατίζω occurs once again at B 8.60. The goddess uses the word to announce her description of the physical world "so that no mortal opinion may outstrip you." As used here the verb becomes still one more token of the relationship of πίστις between her and the Kouros. The goddess φατίζει and the Kouros is asked: κόμισαι, "guard, cherish, preserve" (B 2.1).[19] This clearly belongs with the πιστὸς λόγος (B 8.50) and the solemn hand-shake (B 1.23). So in B 8.60 φατίζω means not only "I explain, I show, I make plain" but also "I give, I bestow, I commit, I entrust." Correspondingly, a πεφατισμένον νόημα would be a thought not only "spoken" or "declared," but also "bestowed" or "committed."

Now if the main connection of the phrase is ἐν ᾧ . . . ἐστίν, then πεφατισμένον is a circumstantial participle.[20] This makes any and all of the following translations possible:

> on which it depends, once solemnly declared;
> on which it depends, having been solemnly declared;
> on which it depends, inasmuch as it has been solemnly declared.

Or combining all three into a single paraphrase:

to which it stands committed.[21]

We should now look at the sequel of B 8.34 from the double standpoint, once more, of ἐόν and νοεῖν. With respect to the first, the themes of πίστις and of the οὐκ ἀτελεύτητον are still recognizable, although subdued. At least part of the force of B 8.35 is that ἐόν will not desert or abandon its trustee, τὸ νοεῖν. Again, when we read that this is because "Fate shackled it," we think naturally of the bonds of trust (πίστις), which, in this case, bind reality to its station, as well as to the other party, mind or discourse. Similarly, part of the force of "there is and will be [note the pairing of present and future] no other but what-is," is that in an imagined interval (*per impossibile!*) between thought and its realization in ἐόν, there will be no tricks, no substitutions, no adulteration.[22] The reason given (ἐπεί) for the continued firm attachment of what-is to mind is immobility, just as the οὕνεκεν of B 8.32[23] assigned the complete or accomplished nature of what-is to the immobility deduced for it in B 8.26–31.

But the more important points are made with reference to mind. It will be convenient to assign numbers to the clauses of the sequence so that we may study the logical structure:

1. And (δέ) the same is to think
2. and is wherefore the thinking.
3. For (γάρ) you shall not find thinking without what-is,
4. to which it stands committed.
5. For (γάρ) no other either is or will be except the what-is,
6. since (ἐπεί) it was just this (τό γε) that Fate shackled, so as to be whole and immobile.

Clause 1 needs no explanation. The whole argument up to this point has the force of "it's there to think!" It is, as I argued earlier, the second clause which contains the radical suggestion: ἐόν is not just available; it is that which always compels and attracts mind. It would seem to me that the entire sequel of B 8.34, including (as I will try to show) B 8.38–41, is elucidation and support for this radical claim. The most direct way to bring this out is to cast B 8.34 ff. into the form of a dialogue:

1. *Goddess:* And that very same thing is there to think, and is also the wherefore of thought.
2. *Kouros:* Yes, I see what you mean about it's being *there*. We have been talking in terms of a journey to it all along. But what's this about its being the "wherefore" of all thought?

3. *G*. You shall not find thinking without what-is.
   K. Why?
4. *G*. Because (γάρ) it stands committed to it.
   K. I don't see that. Why should mind be committed specifically to what-is and not, say, to *X* or *Y* or *Z*?
5. *G*. Because (γάρ) there simply neither *is* nor *will* there be any other thing (for it to be committed to).
   K. Why not?
6. *G*. Because it is only what-is (τό γε) that was properly bound by Fate to be whole and immobile. (*Implication*: All other *X*'s, *Y*'s and *Z*'s are loose and faithless.)

What makes me think that this, or something very like it, is the correct interpretation of this passage is that emphatic concatenation, which I pointed out earlier, of references to ἐόν. It is natural to assume that this continued focus on the ἐόν is intended to serve as an exclusion. It must obviously exclude candidates to the status of being the οὕνεκέν ἐστι νόημα. The conclusion reached is that ἐόν is the actual and implicit object of all thought because nothing else could possibly be its object. The whole argument amounts to this:

1. ἐόν is a possible object of mind.
2. No other entities could possibly fill that role.
3. So ἐόν is not only a possible but a necessary object of mind.

It is important to appreciate the radical character of the doctrine of B 8.34–38, as I have translated and explicated the text here. Parmenides is telling us that νοεῖν and νόημα as such (the text is unqualified) are necessarily implicated with, or bound to, ἐόν. It is not simply the μῦθος or the λόγος of the goddess, but human thought as well, the νοεῖν of ordinary mortals no less than that of the privileged revelation to the Kouros, which is tied to what-is.[24] So the revelation of the Parmenidean poem has the characteristically philosophical mood of making explicit that which is implicitly possessed or yearned for by all men.

Against this interpretation one could cite B 6.5: "helplessness in their breasts steers their distracted mind (πλακτόν νόον)." Moreover, in B 16 we find a νόος which changes according to the state of "limbs that have wandered much (πολυπλάγκτων)," and in B 7.2 and B 8.17 νόος-words appear in contexts which imply that mind could actually take the route not of ". . . is . . ." but of ". . . is not . . .". How can we reconcile this with the doctrine of B 8.34 ff. on the interpretation given here?[25]

Actually, the conflict is much less serious than it appears at first sight. Although νόος and its derivatives is primarily an "achievement" or "success" word (in Ryle's sense), it is quite natural that, on occasion, it should appear in contexts which bear the sense of task or failure.[26] So the oxymoron of the expression πλακτὸς νόος does not involve a logical inconsistency. A similar oxymoron may be found in B 2, where Parmenides announces plural routes which εἰσὶ νοῆσαι, "are for thinking," but then allows only one of them.[27]

Moreover, to say that mind is always "with," or "on account of," or "committed to" the real does not mean that these two entities exist all along and for all men in the same relation which was established for the Kouros as a result of the revelation. That would have made the revelation unnecessary. The relation belongs not to the realm of fact or to psychology, but to an ideal, or normative realm—at the level of one's logical subconscious.

In other words, when we speak of a "necessary relationship between mind and reality" we ought to keep distinct the two aspects of (a) "universality" and (b) "norm" or "propriety" in this modal term.[28] So to say, "You shall not find thinking without what-is, to which it stands committed," need not mean that thinking is already there, attached to what-is. It's not everyone who is aware of the involvement—just *you* (the Kouros) and only *from now on* (the future tense, ἔσται, may very well have this significance), as a result of a challenging argument. One might compare the familiar experience of hindsight: "That *must* be what I had in mind!"[29]

Now like the subconscious of psychoanalysis, the logical subconscious has its ways of making itself felt even at the surface. Elements in the factual or conscious level reflect and reproduce the ideal order which obtains in depth. Something of this sort can be seen in the structure of the argument in B 2 to B 8. The openly negative route is unquestionably wrong. No one wants to take it. But mortals think and speak in terms which obscure or disguise from them the fact that they have actually veered off course, that they are now travelling the negative route. The purity of their intentions, as it were, conceals their πλάνη, "error, wandering." The challenge of B 6 and B 7 was precisely that it confronted mortals with this fact. And it takes most of the argument of B 8 to make good this "contentious challenge." Mortals are "two-headed" in just this sense: they *really* want τὸ ἐόν, but due to their ineptness (ἀμηχανίη) they land with τὸ μὴ ἐόν.

The concept of νοεῖν, νόος appears at three levels here. At the deepest level we come to see in a clear and rigorous sense that νοεῖν is of, about, because of, or for the sake of, what-is (as the latter is understood after B 8). At the surface level, this "ontological commitment" is felt as a preference for expressions couched in positive terms. But in between the two, a certain gap develops between intention and performance. The fault is not on the side of what-is, for it has πίστις. It is we who, somehow, violate our implicit pledge (cf. πεφατισμένον) to the real.

The interpretation I am developing here will be clarified if we consider some instructive parallels. The philosophy of Logical Atomism, formulated and defended by Russell and Wittgenstein in the early decades of this century, postulated three stages in the relation of thought to reality similar to the three stages distinguished above. At the most primary level, simple, primitive names stand in a direct relation of reference to the simple constituents of the world. The latter are minimal sense data according to Russell; for Wittgenstein they are "atomic objects," entities which are defined only as the limit of analysis (Wittgenstein refused to commit himself on their nature). At any rate, these "atoms" are quite unlike the objects or things we acknowledge in everyday experience. At this familiar level, we operate with names such as "Tom" or "Fido" or "Homer." Names of this sort do not refer directly to real constituents; they are abbreviations for more or less elaborate descriptions. By successively analyzing these descriptions toward greater explicitness and precision, we finally reach the real atoms, which constitute their ultimate, although implicit, reference. It is in this transition that confusion sets in. We fail to understand our own tacit rules of translation from the familiar to the primary level.[30]

In an ideal or normative sense,[31] all thought is "of" or "for the sake of" these elementary constituents. But it is only through philosophic argument and elucidation that we come to realize this. So the task of philosophy is to make explicit something to which we are already committed. This notion of implicit ontological commitment is formally analogous with the Parmenidean conception, expressed by means of the phrases: οὕνεκέν ἐστι νόημα and ἐν ᾧ πεφατισμένον ἐστίν.

There are, of course, ancient parallels for this conception of the relation of discourse to reality. We immediately recognize the analytical or reflective outlook of the tradition of logical atomism as one of ancient lineage: it goes back to Plato. What is especially interesting for an interpretation of Parmenides is that Plato employs the preposition ἕνεκα or ἕνεκεν at climactic points of philosophic argument to introduce the ultimate or supreme object of all inquiry.[32] Moreover, in a number of these passages ἕνεκα appears framed by metaphors which one associates with Parmenides. This use of the preposition both illustrates and serves to mediate the characteristically Platonic conception of knowing as a process of retrieval or recollection. The preposition points like an arrow to the object of our philosophic quest. We "know" it before we *know* it. We permanently belong to it and it belongs to us, but we have somehow become estranged. Whether at the small scale of a philosophic conversation, or at the larger scale of a life-long quest, it is the hold of this relationship which makes inquiry possible. The analogy between Plato's "recollection" and psychoanalysis (Freud), or philosophical analysis (Russell, Wittgenstein, Moore), is one that has been explored often enough. So I must not dwell on it here. What I wish to suggest is that something of this analytical or regressive conception of the nature of thought is already present in Parmenides.

I would further like to suggest that Parmenides was not the only one of the pre-Socratics to conceive of inquiry in these terms. Recall how Heraclitus speaks of the *Logos*: it is the common and permanent possession of all men; and yet, this, which is most intimately and securely theirs, is precisely what men fail to acknowledge (Diels-Kranz 22 B 72). Men are asleep: they are not alert to the realities of this one, common world (22 B 1, cf. 22 B 30). They are not aware of that which is most obvious (22 B 56), and this is absurdly paradoxical, for "how could one fail to notice that which never sets?" (22 B 16). They are like deaf people; they are present and yet absent (22 B 34). They are like travellers who have forgotten where the route leads (22 B 71). So the goal of philosophy must, of necessity, be one of self-knowledge (22 B 101).

I find it illuminating to place Heraclitus B 2 next to Parmenides B 8.34–36:

> 22 B 2 διὸ δεῖ ἕπεσθαι τῷ ξυνῷ· τοῦ λόγου δ' ἐόντος ξυνοῦ ζώουσιν οἱ πολλοὶ ὡς ἰδίαν ἔχοντες φρόνησιν.
>
> For this reason it is necessary to follow the common; and while the *Logos* is common, the many live as if they had a mind of their own.
>
> 28 B 8.34–36 ταὐτὸν δ' ἐστὶ νοεῖν τε καὶ οὕνεκέν ἐστι νόημα· / οὐ γὰρ ἄνευ τοῦ ἐόντος, ἐν ᾧ πεφατισμένον ἐστίν, / εὑρήσεις τὸ νοεῖν·
>
> And the same is there to think and is wherefore the thinking; for not without what-is, to which it stands committed, will you find thinking.

To the expression "common" (ξυνόν) in one text corresponds ταὐτόν, "the same," in the other. What Heraclitus says by way of polemic Parmenides says more as a diagnosis. The points registered are, of course, different: as different as the Heraclitean λόγος is from Parmenides' ἐόν. But there is common ground between the two passages to this extent: the λόγος or the ἐόν is not just *there*, it is not just a proposal or a challenge; it is, rather, the correct, and obligatory, and implicit object of all φρόνησις or νόημα.

II

Against this background, I now would like to argue in support of the reading ὀνόμασται for the end of line 38. Leonard Woodbury, in an important article[33] which, curiously, has not received the hearing it deserves from recent editors, pointed out that this reading (orthographically odd, but cf. B 9.1) is superior to the preferred ὄνομ(α) ἔσται by criteria both of palaeography and interpretation.[34] I will not undertake to repeat Woodbury's arguments here, but I will cite what he considers a telling weakness in the text ὄνομ(α) ἔσται, viz., that this is intelligible only in the translation "will be *mere* name," where the crucial word is the gloss supplied by the translator. The interpretation which Woodbury develops from the text ὀνόμασται is not altogether convincing. He interprets τῷ as referring to an unnamed subject "the world," rather than to ἐόν, which is the more obvious candidate.[35] But Woodbury's text is attractive independently of his interpretation. The translation would read:

> B 8.38 . . . With respect to this thing have all names been spoken . . .[36]

I would add three more considerations in support of Woodbury's text with the translation just given. (a) With ἐόν as the subject of the proofs of B 8 there is the same presumption that τῷ refers to ἐόν as there was at B 8.34 that ταὐτόν has that reference. (b) After the emphatic τό γε, just one line above, the hearer or reader would most naturally take τῷ as the demonstrative pronoun. Indeed, the whole weight of that chain of references to what-is which begins at B 8.29 (8 pronoun references, and ἐόν featured 4 times) makes it most unlikely that τῷ should not be taken with that reference. The parallelism of ἐν ᾧ at B 8.35 and τῷ at B 8.38, both after the main caesura, is especially strong.[37] (c) The present perfect ὀνόμασται is very appropriately placed between the πεφατισμένον ἐστίν of B 8.35 and the πεποιθότες of B 8.39 and τετελεσμένον ἐστί of B 8.42.[38]

If we are to do justice to the translation given above, we should pause to clarify the logic of the Greek concept of "naming" or "calling." Expressed variously by verbs such as ὀνομάζειν, καλεῖν, λέγειν, it involves basically the same three part relation which we find in a familiar use of English "to call":

> And God (*A*) called the light (*B*) Day (*C*).

Between *A* and *B* we have a subject-object relation which is roughly one of referring, pointing, singling out. The element *C* functions as an internal object of the verb: it spells out the "content" of the verb's action (it gives what the older grammars used to call the "effected" as distinct from the "affected" object of the verb). This places *C* in a relation of apposition to *B*. Indeed, this apposition amounts to identity. For it is precisely in the logic of the sentence given to authorize the statement:

The light is Day.

In Greek this relation of *A–B–C* could be expressed in either of two ways. One would be the exact counterpart of the syntax with "to call" in the example given: Subject—Direct Object (accusative)—Internal Object (accusative).[39] Another is the construction we find in B 8.38: *A* ὀνομάζει *C* (=the internal accusative) ἐπί (on, with reference to) *B*.[40]

The most important thing to appreciate about either of these constructions is that the element *C* carries meaning prior to entering in this three-term relation. The same holds for "to call" in the sentence cited above. If we say "God called the light Day," we are allowed to ask "Why?" And we are entitled to an explanation of the form "because light is of such-and-such character." (The Bible, it will be recalled, proceeds to give just such an explanation in a vast number of similar passages: "She shall be called Woman, because she was taken out of man"; "And Adam called his wife's name Eve; because she was the mother of all living.") In other words, *C* is treated as an abbreviated description. This is borne out by such permissible paraphrases as:

It will be spoken of *as* Day.
It will be known *by* the name of Day

The name is understood here as a verbal recipe which will help us select or recognize the phenomenon. In Greek the tendency to give explanations after statements of the form "*A* called *B–C*" is very strong indeed.[41]

To return to the text of B 8.38–41: since ὀνόμασται is passive, the element *A* will be an understood βροτοῖς, "by men." The element *C* is in ὅσσα βροτοί, etc., "the things which mortals, etc." This relative clause attaches itself to an understood internal subject ὀνόματα. Finally, the element *B* appears in the dative τῷ. As we saw just now, "to speak names" does not in this context mean "to utter sounds," but rather "to (meaningfully) describe." The immediate paraphrase is: It is this which mortals are describing when they say . . .; mortals have called it *Y*, but it actually is *X*.

On the translation defended here, B 8.40–41 appears as a list of types of utterance made by mortals. They say: (a) "came to be" and "ceased to be"; (b) "is" and "is not"; (c) "alters its place" and "transmutes color and/or shape."[42] What makes these types of judgment "mortal," in the pejorative sense, is not so much that they conjoin contradictory ideas; rather each of the conjuncts is objectionable by itself. This holds for the "is" of mortals as well as for the "is not." The "is" of mortal thinking is one which can easily turn back into "is not." Similarly, they expect that "is not" could have a determinate sense. So the list is, in effect, a disjunction of six types of mortal judgment. Parmenides is telling us: no matter what it is that mortals say, they must say it with reference to what-is.

We are now in position to appreciate a parallel, often noticed, between B 8.38–41 and certain passages from Empedocles:

> Not for one of all mortal things is there a growing-to-be (φύσις), nor is there attainment of baneful death; there is, rather, only mixing and alternation of the ingredients mixed: it is with reference to these that the name of growing-to-be is spoken among men (φύσις δ' ἐπὶ τοῖς ὀνομάζεται ἀνθρώποισιν). (Diels-Kranz 31 B 8)
>
> And when they [scil. the constituents] emerge in the air having been mixed on (the pattern of) man, or on that of the kind of wild beasts, or on that of plants, or on that of birds, *that* they then call getting-to-be (τότε μὲν τὸ λέγουσι γενέσθαι) and when they fall apart, *that*, correspondingly, they call unhappy death. They do not speak by the Right of Justice (ᾗ θέμις οὐ καλέουσι),[43] but by Convention I speak so myself (νόμῳ δ' ἐπίφημι καὶ αὐτός). (31 B 9)[44]

The Empedoclean doctrine involves the following logical steps: (1) Men speak in terms of coming-to-be and death. (2) This language is untrue or unfaithful to the facts—there is no θέμις in it—because there are no such processes in reality; there is only mixing and unmixing. (3) These are the processes which the language of generation and perishing refers to, but which it misdescribes. But one may comply with accepted usage, provided he understands the true or real counterparts of expressions such as "birth" and "death."[45]

Here, once again, we see the three moments in the relation of discourse to reality which we found earlier in the tradition of logical atomism, in Plato, and in Heraclitus. Empedocles is not simply attacking the language of mortals: he is also interpreting it. He shows how it is in touch, ultimately, with the real processes of the world, though *prima facie* it conceals and obscures these processes.

So in Parmenides B 8.38–41 we have the culmination of the thought of B 8.34, and of the proof of "completeness" from which this section on thought and reality grows. We might represent the course of the argument in a scheme like the following: (1) The ἐόν is complete, accomplished. (2) The ἐόν itself is available to mind but is also that which compels and attracts mind. (3) Mind is implicitly committed to the ἐόν. (4) There could be no other object for mind to seek. (5) All human discourse has the ἐόν as its only true and ultimate reference.

We see, then, that the three clauses at the end of lines 34, 35, and 38 are strictly parallel, indeed equivalent: οὕνεκέν ἐστι νόημα, "wherefore is the thinking," = ἐν ᾧ πεφατισμένον ἐστίν, "to which it stands committed" = τῷ πάντ' ὀνόμασται, "with reference to it have all names been spoken." The effectiveness of the whole passage lies precisely in this logical *crescendo*: the same thought is given successively stronger and more explicit statements.

To convey my understanding of B 8.38–41, I gave, earlier, the paraphrase: mortals call it *Y*, but it actually is *X*. This is normally how we should understand the passage from what we know of the construction ὀνομάζειν ἐπί τινι. For as we saw, "to name *X* (as) *Y*" in Greek does not mean to attach the sound "*Y*" to *X*, but rather to describe *X* in terms of *Y*, which is thus assumed to already have meaning independently of its naming relationship to *X*. So the relevant categories for interpreting this passage are not meaningfulness versus meaninglessness but truth versus falsehood.[46] The parallel from Empedocles bears this out. Human discourse describes the world in terms which are false to the world's reality.

This parallel between Parmenides and Empedocles has a wider context. The standard conceptual frame for pre-Socratic speculation on the φύσις or ἀλήθεια of things was, what I would like to call, speculative predication: "*Y* really is *X*." Of this conceptual frame the following are simple variants:

(a) What they believe to be *Y* is really *X*.
(b) What they call *Y* is really *X*.
(c) The so-called *Y* is really *X*.

To (b) and (c) the formula (d) is like a corollary:

(d) It is really with reference to *X* that the expression "*Y*" is employed.

This verbal frame, in any of the four versions, must have appeared again and again in explanations of natural phenomena by the early "physicists." Recall Xenophanes B 32:

ἥν τ' Ἶριν καλέουσι, νέφος καὶ τοῦτο πέφυκε
πορφύρεον καὶ φοινίκεον καὶ χλωρὸν ἰδέσθαι.
What they call Iris [a goddess of such-and-such attributes] that too
is in its nature a cloud which looks gleaming and purple and green.

What is absent from such "physiological" applications of the verbal frame is the element of extreme surprise, paradox, and irony which we find in Parmenides' text. It is this element which makes B 8.38–41 such a fitting climax to the argument of B 8 as a whole. The deductions have taught us that what-is is ungenerable, indivisible, immobile, fully completed. And now we hear that it is that very thing which mortals describe as "coming to be," and "perishing," etc. The disparity could not be more dramatic. The gulf between implicit promise and actual performance could not be greater. This is precisely why τῷ appears without a connecting particle, in asyndeton. Like Heraclitus' B 2, these lines reveal the total estrangement of men from that which is most properly and intimately theirs. This point gets lost, of course, in the translation "mere name." For the whole rhetoric of this passage depends on a confrontation of task with performance. The absurdity of mortal thinking is that it misdescribes totally what it *was intended* to describe. It is not that human names are meaningless; they are, rather, widely off the mark—*their* mark. Mortals could not have found themselves farther from the goal—*their* goal. This is exactly what was meant by the "backward-turning route." With the words τῷ . . . ὀνόμασται, "with respect to it have been spoken," and πεποιθότες εἶναι ἀληθῆ, "having trusted [scil. mortals] that they be true," Parmenides reminds us of the relation of πίστις between mind and reality. With the list of mortal judgments he documents the failure of the human mind to live up to this commitment.

NOTES

[1] See Leonardo Tarán, *Parmenides: A Text with Translation, Commentary, and Critical Essays* (Princeton, 1965), pp. 120–44; Jaap Mansfeld, *Die Offenbarung des Parmenides und die menschliche Welt* (Assen, 1964), pp. 65–66, 84–85, 101–02, 141–42.

[2] Most critics would regard B 8.34–41 a "digression" or "recapitulation" on Thought and Being: so recently Raven, in G. S. Kirk and J. E. Raven, *The Presocratic Philosophers* (Cambridge, 1957), p. 277; Mansfeld, p. 101; W. K. C. Guthrie, *A History of Greek Philosophy*, II (Cambridge, 1965), pp. 39 ff.; for Tarán's view, see below, n. 22.

[3] We find ταὐτόν τ' with reference to ἐόν only five lines above. To the

continuative τ' of B 8.29 corresponds the continuative τ' of B 8.34. The two lines are linked by what appears like a continuous chain of references to what-is: ταὐτόν τ' ἐν ταὐτῷ ... καθ' ἑαυτό ... μιν ... τὸ ἐὸν ... ἐὸν ... ταὐτὸν δ'. Cf. U. Hölscher, *Anfängliches Fragen* (Göttingen, 1968), p. 101.

4 Cf. Tarán, pp. 119 and 191.

5 "The Homeric *Telos*," *Glotta*, 43 (1965): 44.

6 Ibid, 47. Cf. E. Heitsch, "Das Wissen des Xenophanes," *RhM*, N.F. 109 (1966): 227 ff.

7 Tarán, p.120; Guthrie, II, p. 39.

8 For οὕνεκεν introducing a relative clause with the value of a substantive, cf. *Od*. 3.60 f. πρήξαντα νέεσθαι οὕνεκα ("that on account of which") δεῦρ' ἱκόμεσθα. See P. Chantraine, *Grammaire homérique*, II (Paris, 1953), p. 286, and P. Monteil, *La Phrase relative en grec ancien*, Études et commentaires, 47 (Paris, 1963), p. 267. A good parallel is Plato *Euthyphro* 6A τοῦτ' ἔστιν οὕνεκα τὴν γραφὴν φεύγω. In ἐστὶ νοεῖν we have a case of the active infinitive in passive sense: cf. Chantraine, p. 300; E. Schwyzer–A. Debrunner, *Griechische Grammatik* (Munich, 1934), p. 357. Examples from Homer are: βόες ἦεν ἐλαυνέμεν (*Od*. 18.371); ῥηΐτεροι πολεμίζειν ἦσαν 'Αχαιοί (*Il*. 18.258). Exact parallels are θάλασσα δ' οὐκέτ' ἦν ἰδεῖν (Aesch. *Pers*. 419), βουλεύματ' ἔπη τ' ἐστὶν ἀκοῦσαι (*Prom*. 1055), and ἀθάνατον ἔσχον ἀρετήν, ὡς πάρεσθ' ὁρᾶν (Soph. *Phil*. 1420). Cf. Plato *Theaetetus* 201E αὐτὸ γὰρ καθ' αὑτὸ ἕκαστον ὀνομάσαι μόνον εἴη. For an excellent discussion of this type of construction, see H. Boeder, *Grund und Gegenwart als Frageziel der frühgriechischen Philosophie* (The Hague, 1962), pp. 141–43. The most striking parallel, and one which has not been discussed so far, is in a text which obviously derives from Eleatic arguments, the Hippocratic *Art*, ch. ii: εἰ γὰρ δή ἐστι γ' ἰδεῖν τὰ μὴ ἐόντα, ὥσπερ τὰ ἐόντα, οὐκ οἶδ' ὅπως ἄν τις αὐτὰ νομίσειε μὴ ἐόντα, ἅ γε εἴη καὶ ὀφθαλμοῖσιν ἰδεῖν καὶ γνώμῃ νοῆσαι ὡς ἔστιν. The sense is clearly: "If non-beings are there to see, as beings [are], I know not how one could regard them as non-beings, those very things which would be there [for him] to see with his eyes and to know with his understanding that they are." No text could put more forcefully the idea: "It's there to see! Look at it!" The temptation to render (bookishly and unimaginatively) the first ἐστι and the εἴη of this text by "is possible" and "would be possible" should be resisted. The examples from Aeschylus and Sophocles ought to be sufficient as a deterrent. The construction which I adopt here is essentially that of Hölscher: cf. his "Grammatisches zu Parmenides," *Hermes*, 84 (1956): 390 ff., and now his *Anfängliches Fragen*, pp. 91 ff., 95 n. 16, 99. But Hölscher shoulders an unnecessary burden of proof by arguing that τε καί cannot be used to connect two subjects in an identifying proposition. His construction of the obvious Parmenidean counterexample, B 6.8 (ibid, 96 n. 20, 102), is unconvincing.

9 Tarán, p. 121. He considers it "possible," nevertheless, and his construction of the similarly worded B 3 reads: "For the same thing exists for thinking and for being" (p. 44).

10 Indeed, we must not give this translation. For it obscures the syntax, and erases the sense of presence in ἐστὶ νοεῖν. Cf. Boeder, pp. 142 f.

[11] K. von Fritz, in "Νοῦς, Νοεῖν and their Derivatives in Pre-Socratic Philosophy, Part I," *CP*, 40 (1945): 237–38, argued that the οὕνεκεν here, which he interpreted as οὗ ἕνεκεν, has the force of the "*causa efficiens* as well as the logical reason." I suggest that we interpret the word as suggesting ambiguously both a final and an efficient cause.

[12] Cf. Chantraine, p. 291; Monteil, pp. 268 f.

[13] Now also Tarán, pp. 122 f.; and Guthrie, II, pp. 39 f.

[14] See Monteil, pp. 268–69, and note esp. p. 268: "la distinction conceptuelle entre cause et objet d'un sentiment est peu nette, et aisément neutralisée." Cf. Chantraine: "les propositions déclaratives sont issues de propositions completives de cause" (p. 288); see also pp. 290–91. Specifically with reference to Parmenides, see Hölscher, *Anfängliches*, pp. 93–94.

[15] The particle γε in B 8.37 makes necessary the paraphrastic translation: "since it was just this thing that . . ." The γε here surely has the force of "specifically" or "only."

[16] Cf. Tarán, pp. 123, 126.

[17] For a review of interpretations, see Tarán, pp. 123–28. The translation, "for you will not find thinking without (finding) Being in what has been expressed," which he adopts from Albertelli, is not very plausible. It corresponds to a Greek text: οὐ γὰρ εὑρήσεις τὸ νοεῖν ἄνευ ἐόντος ἐν νοήματι τῷ, ὃ πεφάτισται. It would be very awkward if ἐν ᾧ, coming immediately after ἐόντος and emphatically after the main caesura, had to be construed as referring not to the latter but to a vaguely understood νόημα or λόγος.

[18] Cf. ἐν σοὶ γάρ ἐσμεν (Soph. *O.T.* 314); ἐν ταῖς ναυσὶ τῶν Ἑλλήνων τὰ πράγματα ἐγένετο (Thucyd. I. 74); . . . ἐν δ' ἐμοὶ τέλος/ αὐτοῖν γένοιτο τῆσδε τῆς μάχης πέρι, "let the τέλος of their fight be determined by me" (Soph. *O.C.* 422). For a discussion of this use, see Schwyzer-Debrunner, p. 458.

[19] The word may additionally have the connotation of "spread the word": cf. J. Mansfeld, "Fr. B2,1," *RhM*, N.F. 109 (1966): 95–96. But the parallels he cites in support of this are mostly fourth-century and later.

[20] The participle is similarly interpreted in Diels-Kranz and in Mansfeld, p. 84. Closely related is Hölscher's interpretation (*Anfängliches*, p. 99): he treats πεφατισμένον as subject.

[21] I take it, it is considerations such as the ones given above that motivate Guthrie's translation and gloss "in which [i.e., in dependence on, or in respect of which] it is expressed [or revealed]" (II, p. 39). I would also agree with Mansfeld's comment (p. 85) that B 8.35–36 amounts to the implication νοεῖν→ἐόν. For the sentence says, in effect, ∼(νοεῖν·∼ἐόν), which is the classical definition of truth-functional implication. Now I say "amounts" rather than "*ist klare implikative Bezeichnung*" (p. 85, his italics) since Parmenides' mode of expression is more concrete and more pictorial. But I find the rest of Mansfeld's account of B 8.34–36 confused. His explication is: "Denken impliziert dasjenige, weswegen der Gedanke ist, weil es immer schon im 'weswegen', d.h. im Seienden, impliziert ist. Parmenides behauptet hier die Umkehrbarkeit der implikativen Beziehung zwischen Denken und Seiendem: p (Denken) imp q (Seiendes), weil q imp p" (p. 85). That $p \rightarrow q$ because $q \rightarrow p$(!) is a fallacy unworthy of Parmenides. Besides, the counter-

part in the text of this double implication posited by Mansfeld is not clear. B 8.35–36 is surely of the form p→q. The "Umkehrbarkeit" must be in B 8.34. (Mansfeld often represents this, as well as B 3, by the formula p→q. But on *his* implicational interpretation of these lines, the ταὐτόν must refer to a reciprocal relation.) If B 8.34 is the coimplication p↔q, then the p→q of B 8.35–36 is not enough to support it, much less could it be "gleich-beteutend," as Mansfeld remarks a few lines above the comment cited.

22 Tarán (pp. 136, 139–44, and 193) finds a deduction of the attribute μουνογενές, "unique," in these lines. But the clause "since it was just this thing that Fate shackled" reads more like a consequence or a corollary of uniqueness, rather than a proof of it. The deduction of μουνογενές is more plausibly found in the proof of "indivisibility" (B 8.22–25). The weakness of Tarán's interpretation here is betrayed in his comment: "The characteristic of uniqueness follows by itself without a special demonstration" (p. 141).

23 I translate "therefore." It is generally recognized that lines 32–33 constitute a proof of the "complete" or "accomplished" character of what-is. So οὕνεκεν must introduce an independent clause. Contrast: Tarán, p. 118; Guthrie, II, p. 34.

24 Cf. von Fritz, 237.

25 Ibid, 236.

26 "We very often borrow achievement verbs to signify the performance of the corresponding task activities . . . 'Hear' is sometimes used as a synonym of 'listen' and 'mend' as a synonym of 'try to mend' " [G. Ryle, *The Concept of Mind* (London, 1949), pp. 149 f.].

27 Cf. also the oxymoron in Pindar, *P.* 2.61: κενεᾶν ἐλπίδων χαῦνον τέλος, "the gaping fulfilment of empty expectations."

28 By failing to draw this distinction, von Fritz, *op. cit.* n. 11, 236, exaggerates the inconsistency between passages in which νόος, etc. are connected with truth and others in which they are connected with error. Tarán's critique of von Fritz in "El significado de NOEIN en Parménides," *AFC*, 7 (1959): 123, 134 ff., is also vitiated by the absence of this distinction, and results in the unconvincing thesis that Parmenides' νοεῖν and νόος refer indifferently to a mind that knows the ἐόν and to mind in error.

29 von Fritz's final solution is, therefore, correct: "even the πλαγκτὸς νόος of mortals cannot fail to be linked up inextricably with the ἐόν (239). But I would add the qualification that in the case of mortal opinion the link is felt as normative or jussive—as an unrealized obligation. Cf. Boeder, p. 175.

30 Cf. *Tractatus Logico-Philosophicus*, 4.002, 4.112.

31 For purposes of brevity I have slurred over an important difference between Russell and Wittgenstein. The first is much more of a Platonist. For him the task of philosophy is correction no less than elucidation. In addition with the difficulty of understanding the rules of projection, we must cope with the fact that a good deal of everyday language is out of touch with reality, or represents reality in a distorted or attenuated form: "The process of sound philosophizing, to my mind, consists mainly in passing from those obvious, vague, ambiguous things, that we feel quite sure of, to something

precise, clear and definite, which by reflection and analysis we find is involved in the vague thing that we start from, and is, so to speak, the real truth of which that vague thing is a sort of shadow" (Russell, "Logical Atomism," Lecture I). Contrast Wittgenstein's view: "In fact, all the propositions of our everyday language [*Umgangsprache*: the emphasis is on its 'everyday' character], just as they stand, are in perfect logical order.—That utterly simple thing, which we have to formulate here, is not an image of truth, but the truth itself in its entirety" (*Tractatus*, 5.563). It is, of course, this doctrine which is developed in Wittgenstein's later philosophy of ordinary language. Russell's, more so than Wittgenstein's, view is the one which bears comparison with the interpretation of Parmenides I am developing here.

32 In *Phaedo* 67B the οὗ ἕνεκα points toward the ultimate fulfilment of a life-long quest which is metaphorically conceived as a journey. Similarly in *Symposium* 210A, 210E, 211C, where οὗ ἕνεκα introduces repeatedly "the beautiful itself" (cf. *Gorgias* 499E–500A). In *Republic* 510D the preposition points toward the real or ultimate subject of mathematical thinking. The word also functions to remind interlocutors of the specific or main topic of a philosophic dialogue: *Theaetetus* 184A; *Laws* 701C–D, 894B; *Charmides* 158E, 165A.

33 "Parmenides on Names," *HSCP*, 63 (1958): 145–60.

34 Ibid, 145–53. Woodbury's reading has been adopted by M. Ostwald, review of Jaeger *Festschrift* [*HSCP*, 63 (1958)], *Phx*, 14 (1960): 169, A. A. Long, "The Principles of Parmenides' Cosmogony," *Ph*, 8 (1963): 97, and Joseph Owens, *A History of Ancient Western Philosophy* (New York, 1959), p. 65. It is also defended by Vlastos in the unpublished paper mentioned above, p. 59n. Hermann Fränkel considers the passage corrupt. He proposes the emendation τῶ μάψ ὀνόμασται [*Dichtung und Philosophie des frühen Griechentums* (München, 1962), p. 408 n. 20]. I note that Ostwald would prefer to construe the τῷ as a dative of the agent. But the translation, "By it (scil. τὸ ἐόν) are all the names given . . ." (169 n. 1), which he obtains from this construction, has the meaning "The ἐόν gives all the names"—surely a bizarre and unlikely doctrine.

35 Cf. Tarán, pp. 129–31.

36 For the construction, see Woodbury, 149. It is proper to concede that the parallels are not perfect: the examples which have been adduced are all of the form ὀνομάζειν "*X*" ἐπί τινι. But there are cases of καλεῖν with a bare dative (καλεῖν ὄνομα "*X*" τινί: see *LSJ*, *s.v.* ὄνομα I. 3). An appeal to analogy in this case seems legitimate: the Diels text and translation cannot claim more precise parallels: see below, n. 38.

37 This, however, also argues against Woodbury's view (149) that the reference of τῷ is not to the ἐόν but to the "real world."

38 A series of thoughtful queries and objections voiced by Professor G. E. L. Owen at the meeting of the SAGP at Boston (Dec. 27, 1967), and stated more fully in private correspondence, has prompted me to formulate four more arguments in support of Woodbury's text. (d) In the short quotation of the line in Simplicius *Phys.* 86.31 only one out of three MSS. reads

ὀνόμασται. On the other hand, there are indications that Simplicius himself had written ὀνόμασται. The full context reads:

> εἰ οὖν ὅπερ ἄν τις ἢ εἴπῃ ἢ νοήσῃ τὸ ὄν ἐστι, πάντων εἷς ἔσται λόγος ὁ τοῦ ὄντος,
> οὐδὲν γὰρ . . . -σται [=B 8.35–38]
> καὶ τὰ ἐπαγόμενα δὲ ὑπὸ τοῦ Ἀριστοτέλους κτλ.

If Simplicius knew the end of line 38 in the form τῷ πάντ' ὄνομ' ἔσται, he would have had no reason to reproduce this clause, which is incomplete without the relative clause which defines its subject and is, at any rate, irrelevant to the exegetical point he is making. By contrast, τῷ πάντ' ὀνόμασται is a complete statement, and it supports the gloss πάντων εἷς ἔσται λόγος. (e) ὄνομα and ὀνομάζειν have a good sense for Parmenides: it is the "what-is-not" which is ἀνώνυμον; mortals go astray when they name what ought to remain nameless (cf. B 8.54); at the end of the poem, τοῖς δ' ὄνομ' ἄνθρωποι κατέθεντο does not say "they have attached a *mere* name to these (better than mere?) things"; on the contrary, it complains and charges that mortals gave them status, and conferred recognition upon them by bestowing names. So we are both unprepared to take ὄνομα in a pejorative sense at B 8.38, and, in retrospect, after we have read on into the "Doxa," such a use of ὄνομα at B 8.38 would have appeared singularly puzzling, even perverse. (f) Heraclitus B 28, in which δοκοῦντα has the force of "*no more than* opinion" does not help as a parallel for ὄνομα="*mere* name." In the Heraclitus text the sarcasm (the deflated sense for δοκοῦντα) comes through even if we do *not* supply the "nur" of Diels-Kranz. In Parmenides B 8.38, by contrast, a deflationary adjective or adverb is indispensable once we read ὄνομ' ἔσται: without it the sense is that "all things that mortals posited are a name," which presumably says that mortals express their resolutions in language, or that their beliefs are formulated in terms of names. (g) The distance from πάντ' ὄνομ' ἔσται in B 8.38 (together with its sequel) and the parallels which involve contrasts between ὄνομα and ἔργον, or the like, remains considerable. It is noteworthy that the parallels cited by H. Diels [*Parmenides Lehrgedicht* (Berlin, 1897), p. 87], as well as those found in F. Heinimann [*Nomos und Physis* (Basel, 1945), pp. 43–56] and *LSJ*, feature one or more (and typically a combination) of the following: (i) an explicit contrast with a contrary term; (ii) an adversative or disjunctive construction; (iii) ὄνομα inflected as a dative or accusative of respect; (iv) the deflationary adjective μόνον.

39 See *LSJ: s.v.* καλέω II. 1; *s.v.* λέγω III. 4; *s.v.* ὀνομάζω II. 1.

40 For examples see Woodbury, 149. The two constructions appear side by side in Parmenides B 9, in lines 1 and 2 respectively.

41 One thinks immediately of Hesiod: cf. *Th.* 144–45, 207–10, 234–35, 281–83, etc. Recall also that Hesiod's long lists (e.g., of the Nereids, *Th.* 240 ff.) consist mostly of names which can be understood easily as descriptions.

42 There is a point to the periphrasis, "bright surface," if we construe it as an indication that the διαμείβειν could involve either the surface, or its brightness, or both.

43 It is surely better to read ᾗ rather than ἥ (Diels-Kranz) to match the dative νόμῳ in the second half of the line.

44 Woodbury cites the Empedocles fragment ("Parmenides on Names," 149, 160 n. 38) only as one of the examples for the construction ὀνομάζειν ἐπί τινι.

45 Tarán, p. 143, takes note of the parallel with Empedocles B 8 and observes that the latter "adopted Parmenides' thesis that the words of mortals when used to assert things which do not exist are empty names." But that the names are empty (without any reference) is precisely what Empedocles does *not* say.

46 Here I am conscious of echoing an argument developed by Vlastos in the paper mentioned above, p. 59n.

MARGARET E. REESOR
Queen's University

The Problem of Anaxagoras*

When Anaxagoras developed his philosophy in the middle of the fifth century B.C., the objects of sense perception were under attack. Heraclitus had denounced the weakness of sense perception and called upon men to observe his logos which was both an account or explanation of the universe and the principle according to which it was organized. Parmenides separated being from the sensibles and argued that the latter were objects of opinion rather than of knowledge. Protagoras went even further. If we are to use Plato's *Theaetetus* as evidence, he argued that the sensibles were relations. They were relative to each percipient and even to the condition of the percipient at a particular moment. Since individuals had different sensations of the same object, the object itself did not have the qualities attributed to it. If one person said that something was hot, and another that it was cold, it was neither hot nor cold. Could objects of sense perception be equated with being, without breaking any part of Parmenides' canon? To what extent were sense perceptions unreliable? These were two of the questions which Anaxagoras had to answer.

In an earlier article in *Classical Philology*, I argued that the heart of Anaxagoras' philosophy lies in his thesis that there is no smallest, and that his philosophy can be reconstructed from this premise.[1] If there is no smallest, it follows that we cannot separate an entity or a quality from another entity or quality, for the very act of separation presupposes a smallest which can be separated. This is suggested in Anaxagoras' statement, "Since it is not possible that there should be a smallest, (it) could not be separated, nor could it be by itself" (59B6).[2] Since entities could not be separated from entities or qualities, all things were in all.[3] Each entity, therefore, was composed of all entities and qualities. The component entities which determined the individuality of the entity predominated over all other component entities but not in a mathematical

* Presented at the 1960 meeting of the SAGP in Hartford, Connecticut. Reprinted from *Classical Philology*, LVIII (1963): 29–33, by permission of the University of Chicago Press.

ratio. Since the seed partook of the nature of the entity, it too must have been a composite of all qualities and entities, but with predominant component entities.

The word μέρος (part or portion) occurs six times in the fragments of Anaxagoras. It is used in such sentences as "all things have a portion of everything" (59B6 and 12), "in everything there is a portion of everything" (59B11 and 12), and "there are many portions of many things" (59B12). In these passages the term "portion" must mean a quantity which is a division of a larger whole. There is no contradiction between such statements as "all things have a portion of everything" and the premise that there is no smallest. For instance, there is a portion of water in the human body, and this portion is roughly measurable, but it cannot be separated from the body, because there is no smallest or minimum of the portion.

More difficult is the interpretation of "portion" in Fragment 59B6, in which Anaxagoras writes "since the portions of the large and of the small are equal in number." In my earlier article, I compared this sentence with 59B3, "But it [I believe the subject is large] is equal to the small in number," and argued that the portions were possible numerical divisions and that Anaxagoras meant that for every plus there is a minus to infinity. Large and small are infinite in increase and diminution. This interpretation receives support from what follows in 59B6, "Since the portions of the large and small are equal in number, even in this way all things would be in all." If large and small are both infinite, there is no smallest, and consequently all things are in all.

The interpretation of the words ὅμοιος and ὁμοιομερής in Anaxagoras has also raised many problems. The word ὅμοιος means "like" or "similar." In Fragment 59B12 Anaxagoras wrote, "Mind is all alike (ὅμοιος) both great and small. But nothing else is like anything else, but of what there is most, this most clearly each thing is and was." Anaxagoras is stating that one mind is like another mind, both human and cosmic, but that one entity is not like another entity. One mind is like another, as Anaxagoras says in this passage, because it never mixes with anything else. One entity is not like another because, although each entity contains all entities and qualities, each entity has within it certain entities and qualities which predominate and give it its individuality.[4] Elsewhere Anaxagoras writes that the seeds were infinite in number and not like one another (59B4). Presumably the seeds had the same predominant component entities and qualities as the plants and animals which were to develop from them.

The term homoeomery was used by Aristotle to denote natural bodies in which each part had the same nature as the whole.[5] Lucretius also interpreted the word as signifying the homogeneity of a substance (1. 835–41). There is, however, no fragment of Anaxagoras which indicates that the entity was considered to be homogeneous, and no evidence that Anaxagoras used the term homoeomery at all. But my interpretation of Anaxagoras' philosophy would not preclude the possibility that the entity was homogeneous.

The continuum of the objects of sense perception which Anaxagoras postulated was consistent with Parmenides' requirements for being. Parmenides had argued that being was not divisible since it was all the same (28B8. 22), and that it was continuous (28B8. 6 and 25). From the principle that there is no smallest, it followed in Anaxagoras' philosophy that every quality or entity contained all other entities and qualities, and no quality or entity could be separated from any other.

Parmenides' principle that being cannot come into being or pass away and that it cannot become more or less was also accepted by Anaxagoras. This is shown in two fragments: "The Greeks do not rightly regard coming into being and passing away; for nothing comes into being or passes away, but from the things that are it is mixed and seaparated. And in this way they would rightly call coming into being, being mixed together, and passing away being separated" (59B17; cf. Parmenides 28B8. 3 and 13–15), and, "When these have been separated in this way, one must realize that all things are neither fewer nor more (for it is not possible that there should be more than all) but all things are always equal" (59B5; cf. Parmenides 28B8. 47–48).

Anaxagoras speaks of a separation within the primordial cosmic mixture brought about by speed or force and controlled by mind. He assigned to the mixture the cosmic opposites, the moist, dry, the warm, cold, the bright, dark,[6] the earth and the seeds [59B4].[7] If the hypothesis I have stated is correct, then each of the three groups must have contained the other two both before and after the separation. When the *nous* caused the mixture to revolve, the parts became separated (59B9 and 12). What did this separation mean? The separation brought into existence the conditions of our world as we know them. It produced the earth, the aether, clouds and rain (59B15–16). Earth was formed when earth and the qualities which predominated in earth, such as the thick, wet, cold and dark, came together. The separation also created conditions necessary for nourishment, growth, dissolution, and change of quality.

Birth took place when the mixture of the components in the seed was such that the entity about to be realized predominated in it. In the sperm, hair, nails, veins, arteries, sinews and bones, which were at first unseen because of their smallness, increased in size and gradually became separated from one another (59B10). Death was the dissolution of the mixture and the return of the components to the mass. Growth was due to the addition of parts, similar to those which predominated in the entity, from the nourishment which the entity received. For example, as Aristotle wrote, bread contained flesh, bones, veins, sinews, hair, nails and wings; and water possessed wood, bark and fruit (59A45, 15–18). The problem for Anaxagoras was to explain why wood was not edible, or why flesh was not in the wood. Flesh was, as a matter of fact, in the wood, but in so small a portion that it could not contribute to the growth of flesh. Change of quality was likewise explained in terms of the mixture and separation which takes place within the entity (59A52).

A proportionately large number of fragments deal with the opposites and deserve special attention. From the thesis that there was no smallest followed the unity of opposites. In my earlier article, I argued that large and small were inseparable because they were infinite in degree.[8] The same conclusion appears to hold true for the cosmic opposites. Anaxagoras wrote, "Things in the cosmos have not been separated from one another nor has the warm been cut off from the cold with an axe nor the cold from the warm" (59B8). We can infer that the opposites which were cosmic were found in entities also. A piece of iron, for instance, could be hot or cold. Presumably the hot and the cold were thought to mix with the iron.

More light on the opposites is found in another fragment of Anaxagoras in which he wrote, "To itself each is both large and small" (59B3). As I pointed out in my earlier article, the antithesis of πρὸς ἑαυτό is, of course, πρὸς ἄλλο. Anaxagoras was arguing that, while every entity is small or large compared with another entity, when no comparison is made, the entity is both large and small. Similarly, an entity would be both sweet and bitter. From this passage we can infer Anaxagoras' answer to Protagoras. The opposites and the qualities were existents, and not as Protagoras had believed relations.[9] They were not relative to the percipient.

In two passages Anaxagoras uses black and white as examples. In one, he argued that snow was black. Snow was frozen water, and water was black; therefore, snow also was black (59A97). Elsewhere, he stated that we are not able to judge the truth because of the weakness of our sense perceptions. He illustrated this by taking two colors, black and white, and pouring one into the other drop by drop. The sight, he said, could not distinguish the gradual change of color.[10] These statements illustrate the inseparability of the opposites, black and white, and the weakness of sense perception. Sense perception was unreliable because, although an entity had both opposites, the senses could distinguish only one.

It is possible also that Anaxagoras found unity in the parts of the spectrum. He referred to the seeds as having all kinds of shapes, colors and flavors (59B4). Although it is possible from the wording of the Greek to infer that each seed had one shape, color and flavor, I do not think that this is what is meant. The experiment which was made by pouring black and white into each other drop by drop could be made with adjacent colors in the spectrum, such as blue and green or orange and red, and the result would have been similar. It could have been inferred—and I believe it was inferred by Anaxagoras, although there is no evidence for this—that each color was in every other color and that an entity which had one had all. The same point may be made in regard to shapes and flavors. The shape of one rectangle fused into that of another, and an oval into a circle. One flavor similarly blended with another.

In the *De sensibus* (27) Theophrastus states that for Anaxagoras sense perception came about through the opposites, for the like is not acted upon by the like.[11] Professor Cherniss has argued that this passage is based on Aristotle's misinterpretation of Anaxagoras and the confusion of interaction with the principle of psychological contrast.[12] If this is the case, Anaxagoras' sense perception was probably based on the same principle of like to like which was used by the other Presocratics. One sentence in this part of the *De sensibus*, however, sounds like a quotation from Anaxagoras himself. Theophrastus in describing Anaxagoras' account of touch and taste, gives a list of opposites, warm, cold, sweet, sour, drinkable and non-drinkable, and at the end (28) writes, "For he (Anaxagoras) says that all are in us."[13]

If Theophrastus were correct in his interpretation how could the opposites have been used in Anaxagoras' theory of sense perception? Theophrastus appears to believe that every individual had both the contraries of a pair of opposites, and all the pairs, and that one contrary of a pair of opposites was known by the other. For example, we know the cold by the hot (28). We seem to have a scale of degrees of hot and cold, infinite in increase and diminution, similar to the scale of large and small.[14] The temperature of the body is part of this scale, and when it comes into contact with another part of the scale (in this case, external to the entity) sensation results. In sight the eye has all the colors, and both contraries of every pair of colors, but the pupil of the eye has a predominant color. A stronger color outside the pupil may be reflected in it, and, if this happens, sight occurs (27 and 37). As Theophrastus explains, colors are reflected in each other (37).

Why were the opposites so prominent in Anaxagoras' philosophy? Anaxagoras was arguing that entities and qualities, that is, the objects of sense perception, were reality, and that they formed a continuum which observed the criterion of Parmenides' canon. But the validity of sense perception had been questioned by Protagoras, who appears to have held that entities and qualities were relative to the percipient. Anaxagoras, therefore, was concerned to prove that the sensibles were existents and not relative, since otherwise they could not be considered constituents of being. For this reason he had to discuss the problem of the opposites and the nature of sense perception. Further, if as I have argued, Anaxagoras' philosophy rested upon the premise that there is no smallest, some discussion of large and small was required here also.

There is no reason to believe that the opposites were elements or that the opposites determined the nature of the seed. We know nothing about the seeds except that, as we may assume from the name, their components and predominant parts were the same as those in the entities which were to be derived from them.

NOTES

[1] "The Meaning of Anaxagoras," *CP*, LV (1960): 1–8.

[2] The subject of this sentence is ambiguous. In my earlier article (*op. cit.*, 3), I stated that there were three possibilities: the great and the small, the opposites, and the entities. All references to the fragments of Anaxagoras are to be found in Diels-Kranz, *Frag. d. Vorsokr.*[6] (Berlin, 1952).

[3] The phrase "all things" has caused considerable difficulty. Did "all things in all" mean every natural substance in every other natural substance or every artifact in every natural substance? For instance, did it mean that wood was in gold or that a table was in gold? Artifacts are mentioned only once in Anaxagoras (59B4), and in a context in which they have no bearing on the problem. But the examples which Anaxagoras uses include natural substances such as hair and flesh (59B10), and when Aristotle and later writers speak of the homoeomeries as the elements of Anaxagoras, they draw their examples from natural substances only (*De gen. et corr.* 314a 17 and 19, 314a 27, *De caelo* 302a 32). The term entity, therefore, should probably be limited in its meaning to exclude artifacts.

4 Since it followed from the premise that there is no smallest that anything which shared in the mixture permeated the whole, if mind had shared in the mixture, all entities and qualities would have had mind, and would have been able to think. Further, mind is never an object of sense perception and the mixture was composed only of such objects. A. Wasserstein, "A Note on Fragment 12 of Anaxagoras," *CR*, LXXIV (1960): 4–5, emended this passage from ἕτερον δὲ οὐδέν ἐστιν ὅμοιον οὐδενί to ἕτερον δὲ οὐδέν ἐστιν ὅμοιον. The reasons for the emendation are, I believe, inadequate.

5 *Phys.* 203a 23–25 and *De gen. et corr.* 314a 17–20.

6 To these may be added the thick and the rare, 59B12 and 15.

7 There were seeds of those things which were to become entities after the separation: that is, there were seeds of plants and animals. There is no evidence for seeds of artifacts.

8 *Op. cit.*, 2.

9 Plato *Theaetetus* 152 ff. and Aristotle *Met.* 1007b 18–25 seem to indicate that Protagoras was a relativist. For a different point of view see F. M. Cornford, *Plato's Theory of Knowledge* (London, 1935), pp. 34–36.

10 59B10 and 21. See W. Kranz, "Die ältesten Farbenlehren der Griechen," *Hermes*, XLVII (1912): 129.

11 I have used for Theophrastus' *De sensibus* the edition of H. Diels, *Doxographi Graeci* (Berlin, 1879), pp. 507–10.

12 H. Cherniss, *Aristotle's Criticism of Presocratic Philosophy* (Baltimore, 1935), p. 301, n. 40.

13 Unfortunately, the MSS reading of this sentence is corrupt. Diels (*Dox. Graec.*, p. 507. 18) reads πάντα γὰρ ἐνυπάρχειν ἐστιν ἐν ἡμῖν, printing ἐστὶν with an obelus. In editing the same sentence in *Frag. d. Vors.*[6], Diels substitutes φησὶν for ἐστιν. The latter reading is accepted by G. M. Stratton, *Theophrastus and the Greek Physiological Psychology before Aristotle* (London, 1917).

14 See my previous article, *op. cit.*, 2.

H. A. T. REICHE
Massachusetts Institute of Technology

Empirical Aspects of Xenophanes' Theology*

The evidence concerning Xenophanes' theology[1] and the intensive debate over the past half-century concerning the meaning of that evidence combine to suggest that one of the less controversial ways of approaching it is by way of Xenophanes' distinction of human from divine knowledge. Thus DK 21 B 34; 35; 36; 18[2] are now generally taken to imply

(1) that unmediated autopsy is the surest form of human knowledge (B 36+35);[3]

(2) that even so the temporal (B 34, 4; 18) and spatial (A 41a) limitations of the individual observer restrict and distort what he actually does see; that when directed toward data rubricated as "divine," in particular, biological and cultural expectancy-patterns further distort autopsy (B 14; 15; 16) in ways peculiar to species (therio-, anthropomorphic) and sub-species (hippo-, Aithiopomorphic); that, in sum, even autopsy is relative to the spatio-temporally and biologically conditioned perspective of the viewer;[4]

(3) that, given this built-in relativity of autoptic knowledge, even the self-critical *sophos* can at best attain not absolute truth but only greater or lesser probability (*dokos*, B 34, 4);[5] and

(4) that the only method, by which man can improve his knowledge of the unknown, so as to obtain results ever "better" (B 18, 2) in terms of inclusiveness and precision, is by what Alcmaeon (DK 24 B 1) calls *tekmairesthai kai ta hexēs*, i.e., by collecting and collating empirical *tekmēria*.

Xenophanes' omission to allow for any exceptions to this procedure means that he wants it applied to all aspects of reality, i.e., to *anthrōpoi*, to the subjects (remaining to be specified) of the predicates *theoi* and

* A revised version of a paper originally presented under the title "Xenophanes and the Axiomatization of the God-Concept" at the 1961 meeting of the SAGP in Atlantic City, New Jersey.

panta, and to the subject (also remaining to be specified) of the predicates *heis*, *megistos*, and *theos*; that, in short, being real, being the object of knowledge, and being open, directly or indirectly, to empirical inspection and induction are meant to be synonymous.

Yet if such is the logical consequence of Xenophanes' statements, it has not so far been consistently extended to Xenophanes' theology, even by those who have themselves stressed the visual-empirical basis of what the Presocratics mean by knowledge. The reasons for not drawing this consequence sort themselves into two partially overlapping groups, some deriving from the content of what Xenophanes says about the gods, god, and the physical universe, others deriving from the form in which he says it.

Under the first heading there are essentially two arguments.

(1) The first centers on Xenophanes' clear distinction, in spatial terms some claim, of the greatest god from the *panta* (B 25). This is taken to mean that, like Aristotle's Unmoved Mover, Xenophanes' god must be spatially outside the *panta*, the more so as he is immobile and the *panta* moving (by his agency).[6] Yet Aristotle's famous testimony (*Met.* A 5, 986 b 18=A 30) that the Colophonian εἰς τὸν ὅλον οὐρανὸν ἀποβλέψας τὸ ἓν εἶναί φησι τὸν θεόν proves that Aristotle did not think the distinctness of the *theos* from the cosmos (B 25) to imply physical separateness, as it does in the case of his own Unmoved Mover. Besides, had he thought this implication to exist in the case of Xenophanes' god, he would certainly have claimed it as precedent, however *agroikon* and *psellizon*.[7] It does not follow, however, that Aristotle and Theophrastus therefore thought Xenophanes a pantheist (as against a panentheist), let alone that there is an unresolved contradiction between Aristotle's claim that the moving *holos ouranos* served Xenophanes as the model of his theology and the clear fact that Xenophanes conceived of that god as immobile.[8] These difficulties are really predicated on a false disjunction. For insofar as motions are in fact periodic, they are traditionally thought of as *akinētoi kata kyklon*, whether or not these motions are spatially circular.[9] At the level of the circumpolars, of course, temporal and spatial periodicity had always been seen to coincide, witness Homer's statement that Ursa Major "turns about in the same place . . . and alone is never plunged in the waves of the Ocean" (*Il.* XIV 488). The problem arose at the next lower level. Were the remaining fixed and planetary stars to be conceived in terms of that coincidence, too, or was their evident temporal periodicity to be conceived in terms of spatial patterns not necessarily, if at all, circular? The Milesians and, later on, Parmenides opted

for the former, Xenophanes and Heraclitus for the latter alternative. Thus, the Xenophanic *sophos* finds temporal periodicity availing itself of such spatial analogues as rectilinear, non-reciprocating, parallel motion (for the sun: A 41a); reciprocating, "meandering" motion (for the daily and secular[10] tidal motions: A 33, p. 123, 1 ff.), wholly irregular motion (as that connected with the origin of organisms from, and their return to, earth: B 26), and no doubt others. What matters is that all these various non-circular motions are yet temporally periodic, symmetric. For that is the necessary and sufficient reason of their being classified as "cyclical" and hence "immobile." There is then no contradiction between Aristotle's claim that the (sc. moving) *holos ouranos*[11] is the model on which Xenophanes patterned his greatest god and Xenophanes' own characterization of that god as immobile. The empirical character of this god, by the same token, appears to be grounded in his ability to "encompass and control all" (in the solemn wording of Ionian natural theology) by way of their temporal periodicities.

(2) There is Xenophanes' ascription to his *megistos theos* of omniscience, i.e., of knowledge unrestricted by any spatio-temporal and biological relativity of perception (B 23; 24; 25; 34, 1; 36). Obviously this means that this god is "all mind." The controversy turns on the meaning of mind in this context. Does Xenophanes mean that, instead of possessing individual sense-organs, god has, or even is, a "common sensorium," i.e., is endowed with a wholly non-anthropomorphic combination of mind and body;[12] or that he lacks any kind of a body at all, i.e., is immaterial (in the sense not notoriously documentable till after Anaxagoras) and therefore invisible?[13] The evidence overwhelmingly favors the first of these alternatives.

Turning to arguments deriving from the form rather than the content of Xenophanes' theological statements, we find essentially three.

(1) There is the assurance with which the same Xenophanes, who argues the tentative, empirical character of human knowledge, describes his highest god. This assurance, some hold, is nothing short of absolute certainty, hence inherently underivable from empirical knowledge, hence a rationalistic contamination of what on Xenophanes' own grounds ought to be but tentative, empirical knowledge.[14] Yet the indicative mood of all the theological predications concerned, positive as well as negative, and the reference to *aiei* in B 25, 1 do not necessarily imply a certainty greater than that consistent with empirical extrapolation from the *panta* (B 25; 34, 2, 4). To claim that they do is to import an antithesis between absolute, rational certainty and tentative, empirical knowledge,

which ignores the fact that extrapolation from experience does provide a degree of certainty intermediate between the two extremes cited. Xenophanes' theological statements, in particular, should not be assimilated to the rationalistic extreme until and unless the prior question, "Is there an empirical object—other than the spherical cosmos of the Milesians—inspection of, and extrapolation from, which would yield Xenophanes' predicates *heis*, *theos*, and *megistos*?" has been posed and definitely answered in the negative, neither of which has happened to date.

(2) There is the fact that Xenophanes' negations of physical and moral anthropomorphisms precede his affirmations (the moral ones being either lost or deliberately omitted).[15] This has been taken to mean (a) that for Xenophanes there is a necessary connection between all instances of empiricism and perspectivist relativism, (b) that the effort to avoid this relativistic empiricism is the necessary and sufficient explanation of Xenophanes' *via negativa*, (c) that the resulting negations, in turn, are the necessary and sufficient explanation of his affirmations concerning god.[16] In short, it is not the non-empirical status of Xenophanes' theology which is here deduced from his alleged certainty, but his alleged certainty which is deduced from his determination to avoid relativistic empiricism by avoiding, if not affirmation *per se*, yet all empirical affirmation.

The trouble with this argument is that it imputes to Xenophanes the confusion of contrary and contradictory. Xenophanes, the theologian, is tacitly taken to deny any except the most radical alternative to autopsy with its notorious, anthropomorphic biasses (see above, p. 88). He is made the advocate of an empiricism which produces necessary (apodeictic) insights into the nature of godhead precisely because it confines itself to negations. True, the difference between the construction of *eidenai* with *amphi*+genitive (as in B 34, 2 εἰδὼς ἀμφὶ θεῶν τε καὶ ἅσσα λέγω περὶ πάντων) and the (hypothetical) construction of *eidenai* with direct object (i.e., εἰδὼς τοὺς θεούς) is the measure of the difference between intellectual knowing and sensuous inspection.[17] Yet it does not necessarily follow that Xenophanes thinks of god-knowledge, or any knowledge for that matter, as wholly distinct from ordinary sense-perception. Parallels like Pindar, *Ol.* I 35 ἔστι δ' ἀνδρὶ φάμεν ἐοικὸς ἀμφὶ δαιμόνων καλά argue otherwise.[17A] To claim that it does follow, is to prove too much and, by that token, to shoulder the burden of proof. The evidence does not in fact require us to assume that Xenophanes is here asserting anything more sanguine than the following: lacking god's capacity for synaesthetic autopsy of *to saphes*, man must content himself to collect, collate, and critically (i.e., of course, intellectually) extrapolate from such autoptic experiences as he does find available to him ἀμφὶ θεῶν τε καὶ περὶ πάντων. Whatever visual information men find thus available (B 36), let that (sc. be properly collated and interpreted and then) be accepted as the best provisional account available (ταῦτα δεδοξάσθω μὲν ἐοικότα τοῖς ἐτύμοισι, B 35). For, after all, δόκος δ' ἐπὶ πᾶσι τέτυκται (B 34, 4). Wilamowitz's emendation of Plutarch's *dedoxasthai* into *dedoxasthō* rightly articulates the desirability of such acceptance. Obviously, what men are here enjoined to accept is something qualitatively different from the uncritical ethnomorphism of Ethiopians and Thracians and such common anthropomorphic notions as that gods are born, wear clothes, etc. (B 14). A critical stage of intersubjective and indeed inter-ethnic collation à la Hecataeus must be meant to intervene before one can truly say that something has been verified by all mortals and not merely individuals and tribes. Yet B 14 proves that even this is not enough. Even if secured, a *consensus gentium*[18] would still be flawed by anthropomorphisms. Note that the inadequacy of that *consensus gentium* is still a function not of the object but of the subject of the consensus. It is wholly independent, that is, of Xenophanes' replacing the spherical by a non-spherical universe[19] as the basis of his religious universalism,[20] i.e., as the alternative to the inevitable distortions, anthropomorphic and other, of all autopsy individual, tribal, and collective. Xenophanes' point is that only the physical explanation, which the *sophos* alone can supply, will remove such religious anthropomorphism as is bound to disfigure even a *consensus gentium* (B 14). He alone can demonstrate that the *panta*, including such ancient *theoi* as Gaia, Pontos, Helios, and Iris[21], are physical processes. By physicalizing them, however, Xenophanes definitely does not mean that they therefore cease to be *theoi*. Quite the contrary. Only now that they have been de-anthropomorphized and physicalized, do they become *theoi* properly speaking. In this respect Xenophanes remains perfectly consistent with the natural theology of his predecessors. The rational transparency of physical processes is not an argument against, but for, their divinity.[22] The clear implication of Xenophanes is that all the anthropomorphic gods of all mythologies can thus be retranslated into the physical, meteorological, and astronomical processes from which they stem.[23] They will thus provide empirical indications (*tekmēria*) toward the *megistos theos*. That even after the helping hand of the *sophos*, the *consensus gentium* will still fall short of absolute certainty, i.e., of identity with the *sensorium commune* of the *heis theos*, Xenophanes seems to accept as a fact of life. When he complains that "Homer and Hesiod have attributed to the gods all manner of *athemistia erga*" (B 11; 12), his very wording implies, therefore, (a) that there are in fact *theoi* (B 36; 34, 2), (b) that these are empirical, (c) and specifically, that they involve, not anthropomorphic persons, but physical processes, which (d) exhibit, not random behavior, but precise temporal symmetries, and (e) that mythology errs by ignoring points (c) and (d). Here, too, is the key to Heraclitus' statement that certain details of the Dionysiac cult would be shameful, were it not for the identity of Dionysus with the (sc. non-anthropomorphic) Hades (DK 22 B 15).

(3) There is, finally, Xenophanes' use of the normative *prepon*-category to motivate the theologically central assertion that the highest god is immobile. By exposing the visual roots of this category, Pohlenz[24] did for *to prepon* what Fränkel had earlier done for *eidenai*. Yet even as Fränkel did not extend his own insight to Xenophanes' god-knowledge, so Pohlenz and his successors did not, and for similar reasons, extend their insight to Xenophanes' theological use of the *prepon*-category. They continued to treat it as a purely aprioristic norm specifying the logically necessary connection of god's essence with certain predicates,[25] i.e., with the contradictories of certain, indeed all, empirical predicates. Thus, in Jaeger's work[26] appreciation of the visual roots of *prepein* is found side by side with, yet wholly unconnected to, his (necessarily circular) attempt to deduce the perfection of Xenophanes' highest god from *prepon* conceived as aprioristic criterion, operative in aesthetics, ethics, and politics. A dichotomy informs Jaeger's handling of Xenophanes. The theology remains unconnected to the cosmology, and the normative criterion operative in the first is for all practical purposes stripped of its visual root-meaning and reduced to the level of a mere postulate.

Xenophanes' own words, Aristotle's testimony and Pohlenz's findings to the contrary notwithstanding, Xenophanes' cosmology is correspondingly reduced to the role of illicit point of departure for equally illicit inferences concerning a theology that is wholly discontinuous with it. The theological meaning of the *prepon*-category is made to appear, if not as the illegitimate child, yet as involving the complete functional re-adaptation, of its primary, empirical meaning. Proximately, at least some of this insistence that Xenophanes' deduction of the divine attributes is purely rationalistic seems to reflect the profound impact of Reinhardt's revolutionary *Parmenides* book, which coupled the attempted reversal of the accepted sequence, Xenophanes—Parmenides, with the logico-verbal view of Parmenides' *eon*.[27] Ultimately, no doubt, it reflects the

Kantian conviction that the necessary and normative is inherently underivable from the contingent and empirical.

In expanded translation, ἐοικότα τοῖς ἐτύμοισι (B 35) would have to be rendered as "verifiably like, resembling, the true state of affairs." The critical activity of the witness is as indispensable to the process of establishing the objective *etyma* as it is to the process of determining the true winner(s) in a contest such as the one described at *Iliad* XXIII 361.[28] The procedure is no more aprioristic than that of Homer's judges. Now *prepei* and *eoiken* are in fact synonyms. Once again, therefore, the burden of proof devolves upon those who insist, for reasons not clearly supported by the evidence at hand, that *oude min epiprepei* does not and cannot mean "it is not like him (in terms of intersubjective, critical *dokos*)" just as *eoikota tois etymoisi* means "verifiably like, resembling, the truth." Both terms imply (a) cautious extrapolation from empirical data and (b) results, which though less than absolutely certain are yet far more solidly grounded than any known alternative. A brief survey of the meanings of *prepein* will now make this clear and prepare, at the same time, for a look at the actual empirical data underlying οὐδὲ μετέρχεσθαί μιν ἐπιπρέπει ἄλλοτε ἄλλῃ in B 26.

In *prepein* one must distinguish three meanings:

(1) As an intransitive verb it denotes someone performing in an outstanding manner before witnesses. The particular area of his feat may be added in the grammatical form of an accusative of specification (e.g., *boēn.*) Men and gods alike can be conspicuous or outstanding in this way. Even Zeus can be πρέπων δι' αἰθέρος (Euripides, *Hel.* 216). The presence of witnesses is implied as *conditio sine qua non* of establishing who is thus shining forth and in what respect, and of having the facts, thus established, formally certified (if need be) by verbal praise and gifts.

(2) As a transitive verb it has now come to denote the witness' judgement on someone who has set a pattern of *prepein* in the first sense. This judgement conflates empirical (historical) survey with extrapolation from that empirical survey so as to project the future trend and, by that token, the expectations plausibly invested in that agent's future performance. The information which, if it was given at all, accompanied the agent's own acts of excellence in the form of an adverbial qualifier, now finds itself catapulted to the status of grammatical subject. It is now adjudged at once "characteristic" of (*eoiken*), and "probable" (*eikos*) for him. To the extent that the agent fails to live up to that expectation, he is taken to fall short of his own standard.

(3) The implication that, by deceiving our expectations, the agent falls short of his own standard, now hardens into a criterion at once ontological and moral. Performance-patterns are socially valued as the necessary and sufficient revelation of a man's true identity. As his past behavior thus acquires for each person the definitional cogency of a class-concept, it becomes binding upon him with the quasi-logical force of an either/or disjunction. The point is that what is established by extrapolation from empirical data as maximally *probable* is, at the same time, the *necessary* minimum of identity. No need, once again, to think Xenophanes' clear recourse to normative categories as implying the absolute transcendence of empirical *dokos*. For example, if failure to act shamefully has in fact been found to characterize the behavior of agencies classified as "divine," violation of that rule proves that those responsible are not, in fact, gods. That, of course, is Euripides echoing Xenophanes (*Belleroph.* fg. 292, 7; cf. *HF* 1345=C 1), but Xenophanes himself apparently was fond of such disjunctions, especially in combatting mythological anthropomorphisms (A 13).[29]

The socially sanctioned obligation to view one's performance-record as the definition of one's essence is matched, on the side of the witness, by his obligation to formalize his testimony, if need be, by laudatory word and gesture. Both obligations then transparently originate in immemorial social pressures associated with so-called "shame-cultures," not in logical cogency pure and simple. No need, therefore, to associate the theological meaning of *prepein* with a "later," post-Parmenidean phase of Greek thought. The link between the witness' testimony (by word or gift) and the particular performance honored remains symbolic equivalence. The honor must be "like," and therefore true to, the thing honored. Suffice it to refer to the criterion governing the selection of sacrificial victims and to the *communicatio idiomatum* between what is thought befitting to godhead, on the one hand, and to the liturgical transactions of the witness, on the other—right down to the *dignum et iustum* of the Eucharistic prayer. There exists an important, but neglected, piece of confirmatory evidence: Pindar, *Nem.* X 3 *Hēras dōma theoprepes.* Even if this passage were not demonstrably unrelated to myth-critique, it would still be above suspicion of Xenophanic influence, since Pindar, though a younger contemporary of Xenophanes, is notoriously averse to philosophy. The meaning of *theoprepes* here can be explained in terms of van der Leeuw's definition of sacred space as "that locality that becomes a position by the effects of power *repeating themselves* there or *being repeated* by man. It is the place of worship . . ."

(italics mine).[30] Thus it is the periodic and perfectly empirical epiphanies of Hera (however conceived) which define Argos as evidently "like, befitting Hera." What this passage proves, of course, is that the empirical inspection of deity's (sc. periodic) epiphanies is part of immemorial religious tradition, and that the later (Stoic) use of the term *theoprepes* in technical, philosophical contexts, like Xenophanes' own theological use of *prepein* (B 26), marks but the adaptation of an older, liturgical *terminus technicus* that comes endowed (like, e.g., *douloprepes*) with a meaning at once empirical and generic.

To sum up our conclusions so far:

(1) (a) Aristotle's choice of the expression *holos ouranos* and (b) Xenophanes' refusal to accept the Milesians' spherical universe combined to argue that it is temporal, not spatial symmetries, which furnish Xenophanes with the empirical referents of his theological predications.

(2) The progressive collection, collation, and extrapolation of empirical data, not apriorism, was found to be at once the true alternative to anthropomorphizing autopsy and fully consistent with the Milesian tradition of natural theology. We found further support for this conclusion in

(3) the equivalence of *dokos*, *dedoxasthō . . . eoikota tois etymoisi*, and *prepei* as embodied in the famous negation of B 26, all three expressions signifying empirical insights of maximal probability and, by that token, of at least minimal necessity.

There is no reason, then, for not interpreting the theological fragments, B 23–26, in a manner consistent with these conclusions. It will be well to start with the attribute *megistos* in the light of the first two conclusions cited. If it was the observation primarily of temporal symmetries, not (except in the case of the circumpolars) circular orbits which inspired Xenophanes' theology, then the superlative, *megistos*, refers to some one (*heis*), largest period, which (in the hieratic terminology of natural theology) "encompasses and governs all" other, lesser periods—in the form, presumably, of their lowest common multiple.[31] For many of the periods involved would, of course, be incommensurable like, typically, solar day, lunar month, and solar year. Xenophanes' extrapolation to such a Greatest Period would be the measure of the role which empirical *dokos* plays even within his characterization of the supreme, non-anthropomorphic deity. If, as here suggested, Xenophanes conceives his supreme (*megistos*) deity in terms primarily temporal, not spatial, then to be "the greatest among gods and men" is, in effect, to be the period of periods. Inevitably, this deity's rule takes the form of what

Anaximander[32] calls the "assessment" by which Time controls the "time-limits" of, i.e., the submultiples of itself applicable to, each process in a purely immanent fashion. Since it is self-enforcing, this control is self-witnessing, too. It does not need man's recognition. Man, however, does well not to disregard it. To do so, whether willfully or not, is as self-liquidating as proper recognition is self-rewarding.

Now individual periods, biological and calendaric, are known to have been observed from time immemorial, as witness the cycles of royal tenure and sundry festivals.[33] In length these empirical cycles vary all the way from, say, the solar day to the 8-year luni-solar, 12-year Jupiter, and 1460-year Sothis (Sirius) period. Even truly cosmic periods like Heraclitus' Great Year and perhaps already Pherecydes' Chronos-Kronos (DK 7 B 1) remain, at least in their submultiples, perfectly empirical. Thus, Heraclitus' $10{,}800^{a}$ is the product of the 360^{d} that is the approximate mean between lunar and solar years and the $2 \times 15 = 30^{a}$ of one human generation.[34] Likewise in Xenophanes the divine "period of all periods" transcends but does not by that token negate experience.

Nor is Xenophanes' resulting combination of "chronomorphic" henotheism and a critique of traditional mythology altogether unparalleled. Whatever Pindar's personal reservations about Orphism, there is the striking parallelism of

<table>
<tr>
<td>νόμος ὁ πάντων βασιλεὺς
θνατῶν τε καὶ ἀθανάτων (fg. 152 Bowra)
χρόνος ὁ πάντων πατὴρ (Ol. II. 17)
ἄνακτα τὸν πάντων ὑπερβάλλοντα
χρόνον μακάρων (fg. 14)</td>
<td>~</td>
<td>'Αθανάτων καλέω καὶ
θνητῶν ἁγνὸν ἄνακτα
οὐράνιον Νόμον . . . φύσεως
τὸ βέβαιον . . . ἀεὶ τηροῦντα
νόμοισιν κτλ.
—Orphei Hymni 64,
Quandt</td>
</tr>
</table>

With all due allowance for its dependence on the Pindaric fg. 152, the Orphic hymn's first line does seem to share with Pindar dependence on a common Orphic source.[35] Comparable Orphic influence has, of course, long been claimed for Xenophanes B 23.[36] Moreover, even in his myth-critique Pindar justifies his silences and emendations precisely by Time's role as guarantor of a perfect, if morally neutral, equilibrium of deity's cooperative presences in human *areta*.[37] Zeus, Nomos, and Chronos are, in function at least, synonymous. Xenophanes, too, as we shall presently see, thinks of the supreme temporal period as morally neutral. How account for these phenomena? Pindar's notorious distaste for Milesian cosmology, unqualified by comparison to that of Xenophanes, precludes direct Milesian influence. We are left with an Orphic source common to both, compounded certainly in Xenophanes' case by indirect exposure (by way of Solon's immanent Dike) to the Milesian model of Nature as self-regulating. Therefore, the case for taking Xenophanes' supreme god as the monarch Time, controlling all things by "assessing" their immanent time-limits, does not rest alone on the assumption, however probable, of Xenophanes' selective affiliation to Anaximander. Nor does it require us to assume more than a contingent periodicity of all events ("if A, then B, but not necessarily A"), of indeterminate moral connotation at that. If grasped by the *sophos*, it will enable him to avoid choices that necessarily entail the compensatory, opposite extreme and so enable him to help others secure the social stability (*eunomiē*) they all seek. If it is ignored, as it is by those preoccupied with traditional myths, luxuries, and athletic success, those ignoring it will find themselves victims of cycles as empirical and relentless as Solon's *koros—hybris—atē* cycle.[38] Ignorance condemns one to repeating, instead of escaping (wherever possible) these cycles. The reasoning is strikingly similar to that later advanced by advocates of the mixed constitution. Good and bad, then, are not attributes of the periodicities governing natural and political reality alike. They are contingent consequences of man's learning, or failing to learn, the empirical conditions that will minimize his involvement in these periodicities. Alas, there is no reason to suppose that Xenophanes' fellow-Colophonians or Eleans were any readier to grant the empirical status of these periods, let alone the exceptional social utility of those proclaiming them, than were Heraclitus' fellow-Ephesians, when they expelled Hermodorus although, or rather precisely because, he was *onēistos* (DK 22 B 121).

This is why mythology's imputation of anthropomorphic immoralities (*aischra*) to the gods is rejected not on the grounds that they are immoral but "practically useless" (*ouden chrēston*, B 1, 23), and why Xenophanes' own *sophiē*, by contrast, is said, ultimately, to generate *eunomiē* and wealth. Mythology, then, is not useless because it says immoral things about the gods, but it says such things because, like infatuation with athletic prowess and Lydian luxury, it puts men literally and dangerously out of touch with the (cyclical) realities.[39] Differently put, the issue between Xenophanes and Homer turns not primarily on moral content at all, but on verifiability. The traditional alternatives, viz., the sociological and the rationalistic ones, but trivialize the real issue. According to the one, it is Xenophanes, the virtuous burgher, who righteously protests the loose, uncivic morality of the Olympians (so, roughly, W. F. Otto); according to the other, he attacks in the name of enlightened rationalism and individualism the dogmatic obscurantism of political reactionaries (so, roughly, Snell). What he does say, is that mythology, athletics, and luxury—unless enlightened and relativized by natural theology with its grasp of the cyclical nature of all processes—are at once symptom and cause of man's self-incurred ignorance and vulnerability. For those ignorant of the amoral law of temporal symmetries are evidently condemned to be victimized by it. In one respect, however, Xenophanes tempers the wholly amoral quality of his supreme deity (morality, obviously, being not the only possible alternative to immorality).[40] He conspicuously fails to suggest that the highest god, any more than his subsidiaries, jealously obstructs man's efforts to improve his grasp of periodicities by observation and induction and so improve his chances of survival. Deity consents to being rendered predictable by, and thus innocuous to, man and actively helps him to bring this about. Hence Xenophanes' plea that men pray τὰ δίκαια δύνασθαι πρήσσειν (B 1, 15–16).

What follows for Xenophanes' supreme deity? His argument seems to rest on two empirical facts, one positive, the other negative—

(1) The countless, incommensurable periods of reality are in fact coordinated, i.e., there is a chronological world-order.

(2) There is no empirical evidence for an external agency responsible for this coordination. (It is tempting to take this as an empirical alternative to Anaximander's famous argument from negative sufficient reason within a purely geometric model: DK 12 A 26.)

By extrapolation from these two facts Xenophanes infers—

(3)—a controlling agency immanent to (i.e., distinct, though not separate from) the several empirical periods taken jointly, i.e., presumably, in the form of their least common multiple. Any numerical value, (whatever the actual time-unit employed) thus assigned to the supreme deity would satisfy the two characteristics of *dokos* (see above, p. 96). It would be at once probable and a necessary minimum.[41] Probability would attach to any particular measurement, the more so since many periods are presumably as yet undiscovered. It would be a necessary minimum of truth, at the same time. Xenophanes' lines about the cumulative character of human insight (B 18) should probably be interpreted in this light. "Yet the *gods* have not revealed *all things* to men from the beginning; but by seeking men find out better *in time*." Taking up the italicized phrases in reverse order, one ought perhaps to render *chronō zētountes* as not merely "in the course of time" but also quite literally as "through, i.e., by means of (sc. the noting and measuring of), time"; *panta* not just as "all things" but more specifically as "all periods (sc. and multiples thereof) below the level of the supreme one"; *theoi* not just as "gods" but (with Apollodorus, *p. theôn*, *FGrHist* 244 F 352) as πάντα . . . ἃ δύναμιν ἔχειν ἑώρων (cf. B 36). In any case, the highest god clearly "controls" the countless, incommensurable periods in question by some procedure implicit in his "encompassing" them. His control over them is, in effect, conceived in terms of a largest period monitoring its components by a continuous and concurrent activity of quasi-intellectual self-differentiation and self-integration.[42] For this god is "all" (*oulos*) synaesthetic awareness and, like Solon's Dike, omniscient.

It is tempting to construe this as Xenophanes' resolutely empirical alternative to the early Pythagorean notion that "unit" spontaneously "inhales", and so limits, the unlimited (Aristotle, *Met.* N 1091a 17–18 = KR 312), thereby "generating" not only the number-series (i.e., the Decad) but also the three-dimensional universe. Xenophanes agrees that the supreme god is one or unit (*heis*, B 23 + Aristotle's εἰς τὸν ὅλον οὐρανὸν ἀποβλέψας τὸ ἓν εἶναί φησι τὸν θεόν, A 30). But on empirical grounds he refuses the consequences, viz., that this unit "inhales" sc. the unlimited (A 1) and thus "generates" its components, *theoi*, *panta*, and the rest. The "mortals" whom in B 14 Xenophanes attacks for holding (*dokeousi*) that the gods are born (*gennasthai theous*) must then include the sophisticated followers of Pythagoras alongside the plainer ones of Homer and Hesiod. The first abet a subtler, the second a cruder version of anthropomorphism. The collocation here of poetic and conceptual mythology foreshadows the Epicurean habit of treating the Academics as pseudo-scientific perpetuators of the very mythology they pretend to combat.[43] In any case, the *aiei* of B 26, 1 precludes not the periodicity, but *genesis* (and *phthora*) of the cosmos. Aristotle's rejection of the Pythagorean model for deducing a γένεσις ἀιδίων ὄντων (*Met.* N 1091a 12), taken together with his testimony on Xenophanes in *Met.* A (A 30), confirms the earlier impression that he saw in Xenophanes a forerunner, however *agroikos*, of his own doctrine of cosmic eternity (*De Philosophia* vs. *Timaeus*).

(4) Xenophanes speaks of this highest god as "shaking" (*kradainei*)[44] all things, of doing so effortlessly (*apaneuthe ponoio*), and as not, in the process, having to move about, for this is not "like him" (*oude min epiprepei*). The *kradainei* must be related to the timing-function of this supreme "assessor." It is uniquely appropriate to the suddenness and discontinuity of temporal *tropai*.[45] From the point of view of the highest god, then, "shaking" must be the physical analogue of his continuous,

"introspective," monitoring of the various periods. Yet this activity does not involve either motion or locomotion. Xenophanes presents both points as no less empirical than the immanent world-order itself: "*it is not like* god to move about." The expression cited can be read as Xenophanes' empirical alternative to the logic, ostensibly so similar, by which Anaximander establishes the geocentricity of his cosmos: "for it behoves (*prosēkei*)[46] that which is established at the center and is equally related to the extremes, not to be borne (*pheresthai*) one whit more either up or down or to the sides . . . so that it stays fixed by necessity (*hōst'ex anankēs menein*)" (DK 12 A 26). Anaximander derives his assurance, so e.g., KR p. 135 hold, "from a brilliant leap into the realms of the *a priori*." Xenophanes, in any case proceedsempirically. Indeed, in the name of empiricism he fights on two fronts at once: against Homer's anthropomorphism and also against the aprioristic version of non-anthropomorphism, associated with Anaximander's sphericity and circular orbits. For it is on empirical grounds that he denies the reality of circular orbits (except, apparently, in the case of the circumpolars). Refusing the temptation to interpolate complete geometric, let alone circular, models from the vast variety of spatially isolated yet temporally periodic phenomena (last and first visibility, tides, coming to be and passing away,[47] etc.), he never succumbs to the temptation to postulate celestial archetypes of circular motion—movement in the plane of the ecliptic and in that of the fixed stars—as Plato was to do, in the *Timaeus*.

The point of his denying even circular motion to the highest god, then, is not that such would be incompatible with immobility—it is not[48]—nor that it is "not seemly" in some purely *abstract* sense for god to rotate like e.g., Ursa Major[49] or to move about like the stars, deities subsidiary to him, in pursuit of fuel.[50] It is that in point of empirical fact (critically collated) all cosmic processes seem to be coordinated instantaneously and in some way internal to their temporal periods. This body of observation is then translated into three complementary attributes of the supreme god, viz., (a) the immanence of the controller in the processes controlled, (b) the synaesthetic (B 24) and presumably omniscient awareness of the controller, and (c) the controller's ability to exercise his control without the need for physically displacing himself (B 26) relative to what he controls. No doubt, all three of these attributes are clearly at variance with Homeric anthropomorphism. Yet the anti-Homeric polemic is clearly not primary but a mere corollary, however important, of Xenophanes' attempt to account for the empirical datum of a chronological world-order. By analogy, the same must be true of Xenophanes' specification of the physical circumstances attending the supreme god's exercise of his control. "He causes all things to tremble" (*panta kradainei*), we are told, "by the power of thought alone" (B 25). Now *kradainei*, so far from seeming anti-Homeric, actually evokes Zeus moving his brows and so causing Olympus to tremble in *Il.* I 530. Scholars have therefore treated it as a deliberate reminiscence of Homer's famous description of Zeus' majesty,[51] or, at least, as an allusion to the animistic notion of a lance trembling as it yearns to strike home, or of the trembling leaves of the mythic world-tree.[52] Two considerations, however, are fatal to this reading, viz., the character at once empirical and chronological of Xenophanes' earlier description of the supreme, controlling deity, and the monumental awkwardness of supposing Xenophanes to evoke (without irony) Homer and/or mythology at the very climax of his anti-anthropomorphic polemic. The first consideration is decisive. Within the context of the supreme god's assessing individual limits of time, *kradainei* would, as said, seem to be a metaphor for an empirical aspect of periodization. Physical tremor, though lacking any literal relevance to the temporal world-order, is a perfect metaphor for the temporal reversals (*tropai*) that processes characteristically undergo every time they reach their temporal limits (*metra*).

Can we go farther still? Xenophanes' use of a physical metaphor to convey one of the key-features associated with temporal periodicity and the peculiar combination of mental activities and physical immobility, by which he has the supreme god assess and supervise this periodicity, evokes one traditional image in particular. The physical tremor, in conjunction with Xenophanes' denial that the supreme god "walks to and fro," suggests that this metaphor, however modified, is in fact the ancient (Pherecydean) notion of Time's Loom. Time is here presumably pictured as walking to and fro in front of his loom—*histon epoichomenē* is, of course, standard for Homer's weaving women (*Od.* V 62; X 222; *Il.* I 31)—as he casts the shuttle with the woof of fate back and forth across the vertical warp-threads, whose length represents the overall length of time available for subdivision (periodization) in each individual case. It is the casting of the shuttle which, every time it strikes the frame, causes the loom to tremble. Notice that Xenophanes retains the tremor set up by the moving shuttle, but denies the need for Time to walk back and forth in the process.[53] Clearly, the immanent conception of Time's working has here replaced the simpler, anthropomorphic one. In effect, Xenophanes is retaining the traditional picture of Time's Loom, but at the price of eliminating (a) the difference between weaver and loom and (b) the motion of the shuttle itself, by accelerating it to the speed of thought itself. This amounts to a de-anthropomorphizing "correction" (*diorthōsis*) of what Goethe (*Faust* I, 513–14) has the Geist say of himself in good Pherecydean fashion:

> "So schaff' ich am sausenden Webstuhl der Zeit und wirke der Gottheit lebendiges Kleid."

NOTES

[1] This revised and rewritten version of the original paper of 1961 is based on material from a book-length study, about to be concluded, on the criterion "like, befitting deity" from its Greek beginnings through Cappadocian theology and beyond till the eighteenth century.

[2] Unless DK and the number of the author are added, all A and B references are to Xenophanes (DK 21). Greek lettering is avoided except in the case of longer phrases and entire lines.

[3] So Fränkel, "Xenophanesstudien," *Hermes* 60 (1925): 184 ff.. Heitsch, "Das Wissen des Xenophanes," *RhM*, 109 (1966): 193–235 makes, in effect, three important qualifications: (a) even in the *Iliad* (Z 150, etc.) *isasin* and *idmen* are only mediately autoptic (211); (b) Hesiod's Muses do not themselves have autoptic knowledge of what preceded their own birth (*Theog.* 53–62, 915–17 [197]); (c) even when they do have such knowledge, they can still choose between truth and falsehood (*Theog.* 27 [198]).

[4] Note, of course, that Xenophanes' downward extension of this perspective relativism to the animal world (B 15) is purely hypothetical. For, in Alcmaeon's terminology, animals have in fact only *aisthēsis*, not *xynesis* (men, *aisthēsis* and fragmentary *xynesis*; gods alone, perfect *xynesis* and *saphēneia*). Still, Xenophanes does not deny that oxen, horses, and lions have *aisthēsis* of theological data—only that they lack the *xynesis* to realize that what they see is in fact *theos* and the hands to paint or sculpt it.

[5] This is as true of the *sophos* when he *etyche tetelesmenon eipōn* as it is of ordinary men. Untersteiner, *Senofane* (Firenze, 1955) p. ccxxv, n. 36, takes *epi pasi* not as neuter but as masculine and to contrast with the *sophos*; though even the *sophos* would not know it if he did hit upon the *saphes* as against merely the optimal *dokos* available.

[6] Thus Fränkel (above, n. 3) makes all human knowledge consistently empirical, including theological knowledge, but avoids the consequence of a this-worldly god by taking Xenophanes' negative, empirical statements about god to mean that on empirical grounds alone god must be transcendent, i.e., beyond the physical world and space itself. Similarly, Lumpe, *Die Philosophie des Xenophanes von Kolophon* (Munich, 1952) p. 35, holds that "seine Methode ist somit weder rein empiristisch noch rein rationalistisch; er gelangt vielmehr durch spekulative Durchdringung der empirischen Gegebenheiten zur Erkenntnis erfahrungstranszendenter Realitäten." *Pace*

Reinhardt, *Parmenides*[2] (Frankfurt, 1959), pp. 116 ff., (who suppresses B 23 in favor of the monotheism of *De X.*, equates all forms of divine immanence with pantheism, and therefore makes Xenophanes into a dualist) the present paper denies the mutual exclusiveness of the highest god and the other *theoi* and the *panta* (see below, p. 92). Fränkel, *Dichtung und Philosophie des Frühen Griechentums* (New York, 1951), pp. 428, 431–32, 434, and Luther, "Wahrheit, Licht und Erkenntnis in der griechischen Philosophie bis Demokrit," *AB* 10 (1966): 51–52 both locate X.'s god outside the world, the latter inconsistently adding that X. "seine empirische Theologie inkonsequenterweise mit spekulativen Gedanken versetzt."

[7] So rightly Kirk and Raven, *The Presocratic Philosophers* (Cambridge, 1960) (=KR), p. 172.

[8] *Pace* KR, ibid.

[9] As they are not in the case of Empedocles, for example, who coins the phrase ταύτῃ δ' αἰὲν ἔασιν ἀκίνητοι κατὰ κύκλον (DK 31 B 17, 12=B 26, 13).

[10] "The clear exposition of a cyclical theory supported by concrete evidence is indisputable, *and once again shows that Xenophanes must be seriously reckoned with*"—comment KR p. 179 (italics mine). This just assessment of his "physical ideas," however, does not prevent KR from doubting that X. was "fully conscious" of the relation of the lesser deities to their superlative (170) or that he could have "precisely located" that god with respect to the world (172).

[11] As I have argued elsewhere (*Empedocles' Mixture, Eudoxan Astronomy, and Aristotle's Connate Pneuma* [Amsterdam, 1960], pp. 111, 116–17), *holos ouranos* here is equivalent to *to . . . holon kai pan* of *De Coel.* I 278b 9–22, echoes Plato's analogical use of *ouranos* at *Timaeus* 32B 8–34B 5, and reproduces Aristotle's (lost) praise of X. in *De Phil.* I for heralding his own, albeit exclusively astronomy- and orbit-oriented, version of cosmic piety. Jaeger (orally) concurred, thus in effect modifying his exclusively astronomical reading of *holos ouranos* in *Diokles von Karystos* (Berlin, 1938), p. 147 and *JR*, 18 (1938): 133=*Scripta Minora* (Roma, 1960), II, p. 174. Cf. also the approval by Untersteiner, "Il περὶ φιλοσοφίας di Aristotele," *RFC*, 88 (1960): pp. 347–48, and *Aristotele, Delle Filosofia* (Roma, 1963), pp. xii, 133–35. KR rightly translate "whole world."

[12] So Kurt von Fritz, "*Nous, noein* etc." *CP*, 40 (1945): 228 ff.

[13] Fränkel, *Dichtung* (above, n. 6), p. 429, n. 10, and *Wege und Formen Frühgriechischen Denkens* (Munich, 1955), p. 285, n. 2 stresses X.'s role as pioneering the theology of Anaxagoras and, ultimately, Aristotle.

[14] So e.g., Lumpe (above, n. 6) pp. 33–35.

[15] Deichgräber, "Xenophanes περὶ φύσεως," *RhM*, 87 (1938): 27 ff. explains this in terms of the metaphysical rather than ethical meaning of X.'s theology. Gigon, *Der Ursprung der griechischen Philosophie* (Basel, 1945), p.191 disagrees, holding the loss of ethical affirmations to be accidental and the reference to the *prepon* in B 26 to be ethical in any case, not to mention B 11 and 12. Against both views see this paper, below, p. 98.

[16] Such, in schematic form, is the reasoning of Heitsch (above, n. 3), 217–19. He effectively Kantianizes Lumpe's "erfahrungstranszendente

Realitäten" into "tatsächlich unvorstellbar, da jenseits möglicher Erfahrung"!

[17] So rightly Heitsch (above, n. 3), 222.

[17A] Cf. below, n. 37.

[18] Cf. Oehler, "Der Consensus omnium als Kriterium der Wahrheit in der antiken Philosophie und der Patristik," *AA*, 10 (1961): 103–29. Xenophanes is briefly mentioned with reference to his myth-critique only (104).

[19] For a good statement of the case against Xenophanes' assuming a spherical universe, see Untersteiner (above, n. 5), pp. lxx–lxxvi.

[20] Aristotle, *De Phil.* consciously revives Xenophanes' notion that consensus, properly refined by physical science, concerning the universe provides the basis of religious universalism. As a Platonist, however, he redefines that cosmos as spherical and pretends to maximal certainty where Xenophanes allows only maximal probability. On Aristotle, see Jaeger, *Aristotle*[2] (Oxford, 1948), p. 166.

[21] Gigon (above, n. 15), p. 178 notes that the *panta* of B 34, 2 but explicate what had remained implicit in Hesiod, adding "Das Alles, von dem er redet, sind eben auch die Götter, sofern es Gaia, Pontos, Helios oder Iris sind." Kahn, *Anaximander* (New York, 1960), p. 156, n. 3, too, correctly surmises that the *theoi* are the elements, fixed and errant stars.

[22] For the basic principle, see Stenzel, *Metaphysik des Altertums* (Munich, 1931), pp. 28–9, and Jaeger, *The Theology of the Early Greek Philosophers* (Oxford, 1947), *passim.* Thus neither the sun's physicality nor its periodic rekindling at the start of its diurnal linear (not orbital) motion prove that Xenophanes thought it unqualified for divinity, let alone that his reported admiration for Thales' ability to predict solar eclipses must be understood ironically (*pace* Steinmetz, "Xenophanesstudien," *RhM*, 109 [1966]: 15, and scholars there cited).

[23] In at least one passage, *Met.* 1074a 38, all too lightly dismissed by Ross, *ad loc.*, Aristotle makes the same point, except that he has typically narrowed the cosmological to an astronomical matrix of myth.

[24] Pohlenz, "τὸ πρέπον, etc.," *NGG*, (1933), 53 ff.

[25] Deichgräber (above, n. 15), 29.

[26] Jaeger, *Paideia* II (New York, 1943), pp. 213, 402, n. 71, and (above, n. 22) 49–50.

[27] Jaeger himself would not infrequently tell about the deep excitement which that book stirred upon its appearance in 1916.

[28] So rightly Luther (above, n. 6), 36, in criticism of Heidegger's and Bultmann's view of *alētheia* as exclusively object-bound.

[29] In the pseudo-Aristotelian *De MXG* these simple disjunctions appear expanded into a scholastic system of dilemmas, where truth is approached indirectly through successive negations in the form of *reductio ad absurdum.* Reinhardt (above, n. 6), pp. 91 ff., notoriously defended the source-value of this treatise on several grounds. Methodologically, the proven reliability of the two sections on Melissus and Gorgias, he held (cf. pp. 36 ff.), favors the reliability, however unproven otherwise, of the section on Xenophanes'

theology. Gigon (above, n. 15), pp. 192–93, and "Die Theologie der Vorsokratiker," *EAC*, I (1952): 142–43, and Steinmetz (above, n. 22), 49–71 concur. It is claimed, moreover, that not only Simplicius' equivocations on finitude vs. infinity and motion vs. immobility, but also Hippolytus' list of 5 divine predicates agree with *De MXG*, and that, since Hippolytus follows Theophrastus, so does *De MXG*, either directly (so Reinhardt, p. 93 n.) or indirectly, by way of Theophrastus' *Physics* (so Steinmetz, 51). In conjunction, both arguments are taken to prove the source-value of *De MXG*, notwithstanding what Untersteiner (above, n. 5), pp. xxii ff. has shown to be the Megarian character of *De MXG*'s negative theology. Consistently, this Megarian dialecticism is treated as but the distillation and systematization of Xenophanes' own intentions. Steinmetz (53–71) goes as far as denying not only the fact but the very intention of consistency to Xenophanes' positive statements and tries to support this by citing what Xenophanes says about the sun and deity. Thus, Reinhardt's argument becomes a closed system, immune to contrary evidence derived from Xenophanes' own words. Xenophanes' negations confirm, his affirmations do not touch, the value of *De MXG*.

Now Hippolytus' list is, in fact, incomplete. It lacks the crucial equivocations, which in *De MXG* occupy the sixth and seventh places. As for Simplicius, he need not have mistaken *De MXG* for Theophrastean to have thought it as reliable a source as Theophrastus and Aristotle (so rightly Zeller-Nestle I^7, pp. 630, 639). The methodological argument, which argues from analogy with the trustworthiness of the sections on Melissus and Gorgias, overlooks that the post-Parmenidean dialecticians named are inherently more congenial to the Megarian approach than the earlier Eleatics. By simply ignoring a number of notorious inaccuracies concerning the latter, found in *De MXG* (cf. Zeller-Nestle I^7, p. 636, n. o), Reinhardt's argument begs the question. In the case of Xenophanes, in particular, it not only lacks support by, but actually conflicts with, the primary evidence. The conflict of X.'s alleged equivocation on the mobility vs. the immobility of god with B 26 is a case in point and suffices to destroy the credibility of *De MXG* except where vouchsafed by Xenophanes' own words. This remains true even if (as Steinmetz tries to show) *De MXG* did reproduce Theophrastus. No appeal to the authority of the Eresian could exempt us from the obligation to disallow any statement at variance with the primary evidence. As late as Aristotle, the consistency and empirical (cosmological) reference of Xenophanes' theological statements stand uncontested. The break occurs after Aristotle, when ontology is reduced to dialectic—a process completed by the time of *De MXG* and perhaps begun (on Steinmetz's view) as early as Theophrastus. Yet whatever the exact date of that reduction, the fact remains that the correct, cosmological understanding of Xenophanes' theology is one of its obvious casualties.

[30] *Religion in Essence and Manifestation* (London, 1938), p. 393; cf. also 398: "Thus, man does not make or select but only discovers shrines, by the act of orientation."

[31] Contrast the Pythagorean view of time. The temporal continuum,

like the spatial one (the 3-dimensional universe) and the number-series (the *dekas*), is generated by unit differentiating itself as it "inhales," and so limits, the surrounding unlimited (Aristotle, *Met.* N 1091a 13=DK 58 B 26=KR # 312). The *sphaira tou periechontos* (Aristotle, *Phys.* Δ 218a 33+Aet. I 21, 1=DK 58 B 33), with which Pythagoras reportedly equates *chronos*, can thus only be the actual, astronomical *ouranos*, conceived as at once a spatial and a temporal continuum. By the same token, the *hen*, which Pythagoras is said to have predicated of this *ouranos* (Aristotle, *De Pyth.*, fg. 11 Ross=DK 58 B 30) must be the *hen* not before but after its self-differentiation into the spatio-temporal continuum of the rotating skies. If the resulting Pythagorean equation, *chronos*=sky, does reflect Pherecydes' name, *chronos* or Kronos, for the sky (so Zeller-Nestle I[7], p. 546, n. 1), it invests it with new, precise, and definitional force. Xenophanes may or may not have understood Pherecydes' oscillating nomenclature, Kronos or *chronos*, on analogy with his own explanation of Iris as the rainbow (B 32) and therefore as a legitimate anticipation of his own *megistos theos*. (Our discussion of *kradainei*, below p. 102, rather suggests that he did.) Yet whatever his view of Pherecydes, Xenophanes definitely rejected the characteristic Milesian and Pythagorean leap from periodicity to whole circular orbits, on the grounds that such geometrizing exceeds controlled extrapolation from experience. All he claimed to see when looking (not at the *ouranos* alone but) at the *holos ouranos* (see above, n. 11) was a vast number of temporal periodicities manifestly culminating in one (*heis*) largest (*megistos*) period. To Xenophanes, then, the intuition of the continuum comes at the end, not the beginning, and in temporal, not spatial terms. Reinhardt's claim (above, n. 6), pp. 116–17, that the very contrast of spherical god and nonspherical universe proves the "transcendence" of the former is thus clearly untenable.

32 So plausibly KR p. 120.

33 Cf. e.g., Frazer, *The Golden Bough* (New York, 1922), pp. 321, 324–25.

34 DK 22 A 13, with Gigon, *Untersuchungen zu Heraklit* (Leipzig, 1935), pp. 70 ff.

35 So rightly Heinimann, *Nomos und Physis* (Basel, 1945), pp. 67–70.

36 See Rathmann, *Quaestiones Pythagoreae Orphicae Empedocleae* (Halle, 1933), pp. 62–64.

37 Like Xenophanes, Pindar is a sharp critic of mythology's immoral tales about the gods. Unlike him, however, he is too conservative to accept the relevance of Ionian cosmology (fg. 197), to dismiss mythology as inherently false because anthropomorphic, or to admit any doubt concerning athletic prowess as evidence of divine epiphany. This suffices to preclude the influence of Xenophanes (*pace* Ziegler, "Die Persönlichkeit des X.," *Satura Viadrina* [Breslau, 1921], p. 113), let alone of Parmenides (*pace* Dornseiff, *Pindars Stil* [Berlin, 1921], p. 127). At the same time, Pindar's myth-critique is too radical to be a mere continuation of the moralizing tendency of the *Odyssey* as compared to the *Iliad*. His maxim, *de deis nil nisi bene*, is habitually cited out of context and thus misunderstood. Three

passages are basic to a proper understanding of his policy. First, *Ol.* I. In order, ostensibly to absolve the gods of unbecoming gluttony (52), Pindar absolves Tantalus of serving up his son, Pelops, to them. He motivates this adjustment of the tradition by saying that, unless one confines those tales to the ἀμφὶ δαιμόνων καλά, one incurs the guilt of blasphemy. Now as proof that Tantalus' alleged attempt to trick the gods into cannibalism (28b–29) is objectively false, Pindar appeals to the evidence of subsequent history (32–34): the gods' continuing support of the charioteer's prowess at Olympia (106 ff.). Next, *Ol.* IX. Heracles' power to battle the very gods is itself evidence of divine assistance. In effect, *nemo contra deos nisi deus ipse.* Note that Pindar first tells the story of Heracles' *theomachia* and only then censures it, on the grounds that to associate the gods with battle is blasphemous (35 ff.). Note once again the reference to time (*para kairon*, 38). His point is, or should be, perfectly clear. Blasphemy derives from objective error; what is erroneous is not the story of the gods battling Heracles, but the omission of that story to add that without divine assistance even Heracles could not have undertaken to battle them in the first instance. The point that without divine assistance there is no excellence, not even for Heracles, is made twice (28, 103), framing the actual story of the combat. What makes the traditional version "untimely" (*para kairon*) is not its ostensible impiety, but its omission to add that divinity is present on both sides, and the *aprepes* thus part of a more inclusive view of *theoprepeia*. In retrospect, we now understand why in *Ol.* I Pindar cites the gods' subsequent hallowing of Tantalus' offspring as proof that Tantalus could not in fact have tried to trick the gods into cannibalism. His argument is at once immanent and indirect. So evil an act could never entail the forgiveness implicit in Pelops' subsequent, god-given triumph. Hence not it, but at most the theft of nectar and ambrosia can have occurred. Finally, there is Pindar's decision (fgg. 70+152) to praise Geryon for courageously defending his right against Heracles' superior might, favored though that is here by Zeus. Pindar does not say that the Nomos ruling gods and men is identical with, only that it includes, the triumph of might over right, just as it includes failure besides success. The Nomos in question, then, expresses (1) the necessary connection of *areta* and divinity, (2) the superiority of that connection to considerations of justice/injustice and/or success/failure, witness the combat of Hector and Achilles, Heracles and the gods, Geryon and Heracles, (3) the crucial role of temporal succession, in addition to simultaneity, in guaranteeing the perfect balance between the gods' support of just and unjust, successful and unsuccessful *aristeiai*. Over a sufficiently long time-span, then, the ἀμφὶ δαιμόνων καλά will turn out to be perfectly neutral with respect to just or unjust, success or failure. Once it is seen that the *Nomos basileus* is not identical with, but merely includes, the triumph of might over right, the rest falls into place. Pindar's preference not to say (*sigōmi*) what is μὴ Δὶ φίλτερον (fg. 70, 3) turns out to mean the opposite of what it is habitually taken to mean. It means that Pindar will suppress moralistic criticism not although criticism is justified, but because it is unjustified. Given the traditional association of deity with *areta* and of Zeus' will with self-revelation in order of time, there is nothing surprising about Zeus favoring such unjust *areta* as that of Heracles here at some points of that time. M. Treu, "Νόμος Βασιλεύς: alte und neue Probleme", *RhM*, 106 (1963), 193–214, recognizes that to Pindar immoral is no less "god-given" than moral *areta* (213), but overlooks Pindar's concurrent use of time as the order in which both offset each other in the long run. Thus he can speak of a theological dilemma, supposedly original with Pindar, and actually praise him for the "intellectual honesty" of not attempting a resolution (214). Pindar's silences, then, have no primary connection with Puritan scruples. Insofar as they do not suppress, but complement theological half-truths, they are relative, not absolute silences. What is emended in the light of subsequent experience (*Ol.* I 32–34) is only the association of deity with anything less than *areta.* Provided it is associated with *areta*, moral labels, success or failure, cease to matter. Convinced that human excellence is a locus of divine epiphany and on the basis of a record stretching from the mythical past to the agonal present, Pindar in effect concludes that deity is not good and weak but omnipotent, if morally neutral. It is the *total record of deity throughout historical time*, which enables him to assess the truth-value of a given myth. The equation of excellence and deity is clearly of Homeric origin. Yet where does Pindar get his notion of time as the dimension in which the moral neutrality of that equation becomes manifest? Not certainly from philosophers like Anaximander and Heraclitus, however close to his point of view a sentiment like Heraclitus' τῷ μὲν θεῷ καλὰ πάντα καὶ δίκαια (DK 22 B 102, which Porphyry appropriately cites, on *Iliad* IV 4, to refute the alleged *aprepeia* of the gods enjoying or even participating in battle). That his source is Orphic, instead, is suggested by the tabulation on p. 97.

38 Solon 5, 9 Diehl-Beutler, with Jaeger, *Paideia* I² (New York, 1945), pp. 139–45.

39 Phylarchus' report on B 3 has been taken to mean that Xenophanes thinks the Colophonians' adoption of Lydian luxuries responsible for their succumbing to the Lydian conquest of B.C. 560 ff. and thus, indirectly, for his own exile (after B.C. 555) by the pro-Lydian tyrant: so Steinmetz (above, no. 29), 31 ff. It should be clear, however, that history is here cited in support of the broader thesis, already adumbrated in B 2, 19–22, that the wrong values, viz. concern with sports and luxury instead of with expert-knowledge of sequences and cycles, cause men to be victimized by precisely such sequences as that of luxury and the loss of the ability to resist attacks, domestic *and* foreign, upon their liberty. Prosperity falls along with it. What athletic victories do not increase, luxury actively destroys.

40 So rightly Cornford, *Principium Sapientiae* (Cambridge, 1952), p. 147.

41 Similarly, the definition of the gods as the *kreittones* is minimal in the sense that it delimits them from everything below.

42 Approaching the matter from a wholly different direction, Untersteiner (above, n. 5), p. clxii, says that the *theoi* express the *scindibilità elementare dell' Uno.*

43 On this, cf. the third section of my paper, forthcoming in *RhM*, 112

(1970), "Cosmological Polemics and Mythological Models: Plato, Aristotle, Lucretius."

[44] Calogero's proposal ("Senofane, Eschilo, e la Prima Definizione dell' Onnipotenza di Dio," *Studi di Filosofia Greca* [Bari, 1950]: 33–55) to read *kraainei* instead of *kradainei* neglects the limitations, natural and rational, of the power of Xenophanes' supreme god, however superlative with respect to his subsidiaries. Cf. also the good remarks of Untersteiner (above, n. 5), p. clxxiv, n. 26.

[45] On *tropai* as "keine Entwicklung, ein Umschlag" and its Heraclitean equivalents, *amoibē* and *metapiptein* (DK 22 B 90; 88), see Gigon (above, n. 34), pp. 65–66. Cf. ibid p. 86 on the sun's *metra* of B 94 as necessarily temporal, not spatial.

[46] This term, too, not the latently visual *prepei*, is the one used by the dialectical *De MXG*, e.g., 977a 17, 24; 978a 4.

[47] For a specific instance of the sort of thing Xenophanes is refusing, cf. Alcmaeon DK 24 B 2.

[48] See above, p. 90.

[49] Cf. PMag. Par. 4.700=I 96 ff., Preisendanz, where Ursa Major is described as ἡ κινοῦσα καὶ ἀντιστρεφοῦσα τὸν οὐρανόν, κατ' ὥραν ἀναπολεύουσα καὶ καταπολεύουσα.

[50] This doctrine, of course, Xenophanes A 38; 40 shares with Anaximenes DK 13 A 7 and Heraclitus DK 22 B 6; 30.

[51] So Jaeger (above, n. 22), p. 212, n. 3.

[52] So Untersteiner (above, n. 5), p. clxxiii.

[53] For Time or Fate as the weaver, cf. Onians, *The Origins of European Thought* (Cambridge, 1954), pp. 349–50; for time as qualitative, not homogeneous, ibid., pp. 411–15. The fact that the earliest Greeks conceived the process of time (and fate) as the movement of a circle around the earth (cf. Onians, pp. 442 ff.) may explain the doxographers' tendency to misrepresent circular time as a spatial *periechon*; see e.g., Aet. 1.21.1 on Pythagoras and the comment of Untersteiner (above, n. 5), p. lxxv.

JOHN ROBINSON
Windham College

Anaximander and the Problem of the Earth's Immobility*

In the course of his review of the reasons given by his predecessors for the earth's immobility, Aristotle states that "some" attribute it neither to the action of the whirl nor to the air beneath's hindering its falling:

> These are the causes with which most thinkers busy themselves. But there are some who say, like Anaximander among the ancients, that it stays where it is because of its "indifference" (ὁμοιότητα). For what is stationed at the center, and is equably related to the extremes, has no reason to go one way rather than another—either up or down or sideways. And since it is impossible for it to move simultaneously in opposite directions, it necessarily stays where it is.[1]

The ascription of this curious view to Anaximander appears to have occasioned little uneasiness among modern commentators. On the contrary, it has been accepted—quite justly, if it is to be accepted at all—as evidence for the early abandonment in Greek thought of the notion of an absolute up and down.[2] The only commentator, so far as I know, to reject outright Aristotle's ascription of this view to Anaximander is W. A. Heidel, who never developed at any length his reasons for doing so.[3] Nevertheless Heidel seems to be entirely in the right, and I propose to provide in this paper what I hope will be more solid grounds for rejecting the explicit testimony of Aristotle.

Let us begin by seeing what the passage asserts. It formulates the general principle that a body will stay put if two conditions are fulfilled: first, that it is "stationed at the center" of whatever contains it, and second, that it is "equably related to the extremes" of that container. A body in this state is ὅμοιος. It is further implied that the earth is a body that fulfills these conditions, and that this is the reason why it does not move out of its place.

* Presented at the 1953 meeting of the SAGP in Rochester, New York.

The meaning of the first condition seems clear enough. If the earth is the body in question, and what contains it is the οὐρανός, then "to be stationed at the center" will mean "to be equidistant from every point on the circumference of the οὐρανός." The second condition is fulfilled when the earth is "equably related to the extremes" of the οὐρανός, but we are not told in what respect it must be equably related to them. For further light on this point we must turn to the account of the matter given by Hippolytus, who is drawing on what may be supposed to be Theophrastus' version of our passage. According to this account, Anaximander held that the earth is suspended in mid-air "by reason of its equidistance from all things (διὰ τὴν ὁμοίαν πάντων ἀπόστασιν)."[4] It is difficult to see what "all things" can refer to unless to all points on the circumference of the οὐρανός; otherwise the explanation would entirely lack plausibility. On the other hand, if this is all that the passage asserts, it is evident that the second condition adds nothing to the first. All that is necessary is that the earth be located at the center.

Now, what was the immediate source upon which Aristotle was drawing for the formulation of this view? It is, I think, evident that he was drawing upon certain passages in the *Phaedo* and in the *Timaeus* in which we find Plato putting forward a very similar view. The evidence for this is clear enough from an examination of the language of the passage in the *De Caelo*, the similarity of which to the language of the dialogues has not failed to catch the attention of commentators.[5] But the similarity is not merely verbal. In the *Phaedo* once more we have the earth's immobility offered as a particular case of a general principle, namely that "a thing which is in equilibrium and placed in the center of something homogeneous (ὁμοίου) will not incline in one direction rather than another, but being equable (ὁμοίως δ' ἔχον) will remain steady (ἀκλινές)."[6] The earth, being spherical, *is* in equilibrium; and, being placed at the center of the οὐρανός, which is uniform, it does not move in any direction.

But it is not quite clear what is meant by the "uniformity of the heavens" (ὁμοιότητα τοῦ οὐρανοῦ). As Burnet has pointed out, ὁμοιότης cannot refer to homogeneity of substance or density, for the world is not homogeneous in substance.[7] But if this is so, the word must refer to the space itself which is taken up by the οὐρανός, and by the "uniformity of the heavens" will be meant, then, merely its equidistance in every direction from the earth taken as a center. To say this, however, is simply to repeat in another form what has already been stated, namely that the earth is situated in the center. As we have seen, Aristotle preserves this redundancy by saying that the earth must not only be located at the center but must also be equably related to the extremes. It is unnecessary, I think, to labor this point further, for a number of modern commentators have already expressed either openly or by implication their belief that Plato is the immediate source of Aristotle's formulation of the view he attributes to Anaximander.

That Aristotle drew his formulation of the view from Plato does not, of course, prove that the view itself was not held by Anaximander. But neither is there any indication, either in the *Phaedo* or the *Timaeus*, that Plato drew his account from Anaximander. Aristotle is our *sole* evidence for the existence of the view prior to Plato. Hippolytus, of course, ascribes the view in question to Anaximander; and Aëtius, in a passage we shall deal with presently, ascribes a similar view to Parmenides and Democritus. But it is almost certain that they do not speak from first-hand knowledge, and that their information comes from Theophrastus, and so ultimately from Aristotle. The passage in the *De Caelo*, then, which is before us, constitutes the only direct evidence we have for the belief that Anaximander dealt with the problem of the earth's immobility in this way.

We may now turn to the evidence against Anaximander's having held the view imputed to him by Aristotle—evidence supplied in large measure by Aristotle himself in other passages in the *De Caelo*.

A little consideration will show that this theory of the earth's immobility is founded upon the supposition that the earth has no absolute weight, that is, that it has no natural tendency to fall. According to Aristotle, the earth, because of its equidistance from the extremes, will move neither sideways *nor up or down*. The possibility of the earth's moving upward we may ignore; this does not appear to have presented itself as a problem to any of the Presocratics. But the possibility of its falling down presented them with a very acute one; for these thinkers, unlike Plato, thought of the earth as having weight, and therefore as requiring some sort of support. Aristotle himself is evidence for the preoccupation of earlier thinkers with this problem, and it is clear from his account that most of them supposed the earth to be supported by air:

> Anaximenes, Anaxagoras and Democritus say that the flatness of the earth is the cause of its staying where it is; for it does not cut the air beneath it but covers it like a lid. This seems to be the way of flat-shaped bodies; it is difficult even for the wind to move them because of their power of resistance. The same immobility, they say, is produced by the flatness of the surface which the earth presents to the air which lies beneath it.[8]

Similar statements in the doxographers and even in the medical writers attest to the presence of a single tradition in early cosmology: the belief that the earth is absolutely heavy and requires support.

The only apparent exception to this view (aside, of course, from the passage in the *De Caelo* whose accuracy is in dispute) appears in a statement by Aëtius: "Parmenides and Democritus say that the earth, being equidistant in every direction, remains in equilibrium, having no reason to fall one way rather than another; hence though it quakes it does not move."[9] The idea is the same as that expressed in the report of Aristotle: the earth, being equidistant in every direction from the οὐρανός, remains balanced. Being no more inclined to move one way than another, it does not move at all.

Now we know to start with that this report is quite false so far as it concerns Democritus, for we know that Democritus regarded the earth as flat, and we know from Aristotle's own account that those thinkers who held the earth to be flat did so because the immobility of the earth—specifically its failure to fall—necessarily involved its being flat.[10] That is, it is only on the basis of its being flat that we can account for the earth's staying up by riding upon the air. But why need the problem of the earth's support arise at all unless it is because the earth is thought of as absolutely heavy? And if the earth *is* heavy, then clearly there *is* a reason for Democritus why the earth should fall one way (*i.e.*, down) rather than another, and Aëtius' report must be erroneous.

Whether Aëtius correctly attributes this view to Parmenides is more difficult to decide because of the slightness of our knowledge of the details of Parmenides' cosmology. Nevertheless, we have enough information to allow us to draw conclusions that are highly probable, and these make it unlikely that Aëtius' report can be trusted.

What is important for our purposes, as the above consideration of Democritus has shown, is the shape of the earth in Parmenides' cosmology. We have two pieces of evidence bearing on this, both of which come from Diogenes Laertius. In his life of Parmenides, Diogenes states that "he was the first to represent the earth as spherical (σφαιροειδῆ) and as situated in the middle."[11] But elsewhere he gives a rather different account. We are told, he says, that Pythagoras was "the first to call the heavens a cosmos and to describe the earth as στρογγύλη; but Theophrastus says that Parmenides was the first to do this."[12] The first of these statements is of little value. Diogenes uses the same word, σφαιροειδῆ, to describe the earth of Anaximander, which we know to have been flat.[13] Moreover, the assertion that Parmenides was the first to place the earth in the center is contrary to all the evidence. Of more importance is the second account, which comes from Theophrastus and implies that Parmenides himself used the word στρογγύλη to describe the shape of the earth. The majority of the commentators take στρογγύλη to mean, here, "spherical" as opposed to "flat" (πλατεῖα)—apparently on the ground that the words στρογγύλη and πλατεῖα are used as antonyms in the *Phaedo*.[14] But passages from other authors might be cited to the contrary. The author of the "Hippocratic" treatise *Head Wounds*, for example, writing toward the end of the fifth century, distinguishes between weapons that are στρογγύλα and weapons which are περιφερέα, though περιφερής is the word which Plato himself uses in the *Phaedo* to describe the spherical earth.[15] "It is certain," as Heidel has pointed out, "that in the fifth century the term in question was not used exclusively or even generally with reference to a sphere."[16] On the other hand, it *is* frequently used in connection with a cylindrical shape.[17] Hippolytus, for example, describes the earth of Anaximander as στρογγύλον, κίονι λίθῳ παραπλήσιον: "round, like a stone column."[18] The word is used again to describe the earth of Diogenes of Apollonia, which was almost certainly disk-shaped.[19] Thus in both cases where the term is used to describe the shape of the earth in connection with earlier thinkers it has the same meaning. There is no reason to suppose that it had a different meaning as applied to the earth of Parmenides. On the contrary, the fact that Parmenides uses σφαῖρα to describe the sphere of being and στρογγύλη to describe the earth suggests *prima facie* that he distinguished between the use of the two words. The likelihood that Parmenides did treat the earth as a flat disk is increased by Aëtius' description of the earth as the midmost of a series of concentric rings, unique only in being solid—a way of speaking that strongly suggests that it is shaped like a disk.[20] If this is true, then there is good reason to believe, arguing upon the lines pursued above in connection with Democritus, that Parmenides regarded the earth as heavy; and this is confirmed by the statement of Pseudo-Plutarch that "the earth arises from the sinking down of the dense"—the "dense" being the heavier part of the original mixture.[21] But if Parmenides thought of the earth as heavy, it is clear that he could not have supposed, any more than Democritus, that there is no reason for the earth to move one way (*i.e.*, downwards) rather than another.

I have been at pains to establish the fact that all our evidence points to the existence of a single tradition among the earliest thinkers, one presupposing that the earth has absolute weight, and accounting for its support by imagining it to be flat. That Anaximander belonged to this tradition is not difficult to establish; indeed had he departed from it in the manner imputed to him by Aristotle, the failure of succeeding thinkers to comment upon the fact would be completely inexplicable. We know that before Anaximander Thales thought of the earth as heavy, for he felt obliged to explain its staying up by supposing that it floated upon water.[22] That Anaximander followed him in thinking of it as heavy is evident from the fact that in accounting for the disposition of the parts of the cosmos he makes use of the same process of separation (ἔκκρισις, ἀπόκρισις) which subsequent thinkers make use of in accounting for the coming together of the heavier elements at the center and the lighter at the periphery.[23] It was for this reason that, like Thales before him, he was faced with the problem of the earth's support—a problem which he was obliged to solve (following the line of thought so succinctly indicated by Aristotle himself) by conceiving it as a flat disk, a cylinder having a depth one-third its breadth.

On the basis of this evidence I hold that the view imputed to Anaximander by Aristotle not only *was* not but *could* not have been held by him. Simplicius, aware of the impossibility of fastening such a view upon Anaximander, departs so far from Aristotle as to say that Anaximander attributed the immobility of the earth "*both* to the air's holding it up *and* its equilibrium and 'indifference.' "[24] Consider for a moment the significance of this statement. We have in it the first suggestion that the problem of the earth's immobility is not a simple but a complex problem. On the one hand there is the problem of the earth's *support*—of explaining why it does not fall; on the other there is the problem of the earth's lateral fixity—of explaining why it is that the earth does not move to one side or another. Much of the confusion in Aristotle's discussion in the *De Caelo* springs from the fact that he fails to realize that these are two entirely different problems. For example, in the midst of a discussion of why the earth does not fall, he ascribes to Empedocles the view that "it is the swiftness of the motion of the heaven as it swings around in a circle that prevents the earth from moving."[25] He is speaking here of those thinkers who attribute the earth's position at the center to the vortex (δίνη); "for all of them say that this is the cause, arguing from what happens in liquids and in air, where the larger and heavier things always travel to the center of a vortex. Hence all who hold that the heaven came into being say that the earth travelled to the center for this reason."[26] Now it is evident from this context that Empedocles can only have meant to explain in this way why it is that the earth does not move *sideways*, *i.e.*, in the plane of the whirl. Being heavy, it is carried to the center and held there by centripetal force. But the whirl does not prevent the earth from falling, and Empedocles recognizing this, supplied an additional cause for its being held aloft by supposing, with his predecessors, that it is flat.[27] Aristotle mistakenly thinks of Empedocles as representing a tradition other than that represented by Anaximenes, Anaxagoras and Democritus, regarding the cause of the earth's immobility, because he fails entirely to see that for earlier thinkers there were *two* problems involved: one of explaining why it does not move sideways, and quite another of explaining why it does not fall.

We have seen that earlier thinkers met the latter problem by imagining the earth to be supported from below, either by water (in Thales' case) or by air; and we have seen that according to Aristotle himself *all* of them accounted for the earth's lateral fixity by making use of the whirl as a principle of explanation sufficient not only for the original separating-out of the light from the heavy but also of the continuing maintenance of this separation. In the fragmentary accounts which we have of Anaximander's thought there is ample evidence of his having made the same sort of use of the whirl as a principle of explanation as we find in later thinkers.[28] We have, therefore, to regard with equal suspicion Aristotle's account of Anaximander's views even with regard to the problem of the earth's lateral fixity.

At the same time it is perhaps a little easier to see how Aristotle could have come to the mistaken conclusion that Anaximander held the view ascribed to him in the *De Caelo*. An earth held in the grip of the vortex would *in fact* be in a condition of ἰσορροπία or ὁμοιότης in as much as it would be driven in upon the center with equal force from all sides; and it would be equidistant from all points on the periphery of the vortex for the same reason. A poetically worded reference to this state of affairs could very easily have been misconstrued by Aristotle as a *causal* account of the earth's immobility.[29] Whether this is what happened we have, of course, no way of knowing; but it seems to me clearly impossible in the face of the available evidence to take seriously Aristotle's ascription of the view of the *Phaedo* and the *Timaeus* to Anaximander.

NOTES

[1] Aristotle *De Caelo* II. 13, 295b 10 ff. I have followed Stocks and Burnet in rendering ὁμοιότης as "indifference." The word suggests better than "likeness" or "similarity" the dynamic aspect of the situation.

[2] See most recently Charles H. Kahn, *Anaximander and the Origins of Greek Cosmology* (New York, 1960), pp. 76 ff. I have discussed Kahn's

acceptance of Aristotle's testimony in a review article, "The Framework of Greek Cosmology," *RM*, XIV (1961): 676–84.

[3] W. A. Heidel, "The δίνη in Anaximenes and Anaximander," *CP*, I (1906): 279–82; see also *The Frame of the Ancient Greek Maps* (New York, 1937), pp. 68–69.

[4] Hippolytus, *Ref.* i.6 .3 (DK 12 A 11).

[5] See, for example, Stocks' note on *De Caelo* II. 13, 295b 12 in the Oxford translation. Stocks rightly points out that although Aristotle borrows the language of the *Phaedo* his understanding of it was faulty.

[6] Plato *Phaedo* 108E–109A. Cp. *Timaeus* 62D–63A.

[7] John Burnet, *Plato's Phaedo* (Oxford, 1911), note on *Phaedo* 109A6.

[8] Aristotle *De Caelo* II. 13, 294b 13 ff.

[9] Aëtius iii. 15. 7 (DK 28 A 44).

[10] Aëtius iii. 10. 5 (DK 68 A 94) and Aristotle *De Caelo* II. 13, 294a 9 ff.

[11] Diogenes Laertius ix. 21 (DK 28 A 1).

[12] Diogenes Laertius viii. 48 (DK 28 A 44).

[13] Diogenes Laertius ii. 1 (DK 12 A 1). Cp. [Plut.] *Strom.* 2 (DK 12 A 10) and Hippolytus *Ref.* i. 6. 3 (DK 12 A 11).

[14] Plato, *Phaedo* 97D.

[15] *On Head Wounds* iii. 24 Withington. Plato, *Phaedo* 108E. For the date of *Head Wounds*, see Withington in the Loeb *Hippocrates* iii, xxv.

[16] W. A. Heidel, *The Frame of the Ancient Greek Maps* (New York, 1937), p. 74.

[17] Theophrastus, for example, in his *History of Plants* (v. 6. 5) describes unsquared logs as ξύλα στρογγύλα. In another place (*History of Plants* vii. 4. 5) he speaks of a certain plant as στρογγυλόκαυλον: "having a round stalk." In both cases the reference is to something cylindrical.

[18] Hippolytus *Ref.* i. 6. 3 (DK 12 A 11).

[19] Diogenes Laertius ix. 57 (DK 64 A 1). Cp. John Burnet, *Early Greek Philosophy* (London, 1930), p. 357.

[20] Aëtius ii. 7. 1 (DK 28 A 37).

[21] [Plut.] *Strom.* 5 (DK 28 A 22).

[22] Aristotle *De Caelo* II. 13, 294a 28.

[23] As W. A. Heidel observes ["The δίνη in Anaximenes and Anaximander," *CP*, I (1906), 281] "the whole range of Greek philosophy connects ἀπόκρισις and ἔκκρισις with the δίνη."

[24] Simplicius *De Caelo*, 531–32.

[25] Aristotle *De Caelo* II. 13, 295a 17.

[26] Aristotle *De Caelo* II. 13, 295b 10 ff.

[27] So much is clear from Aëtius ii. 8. 2 (DK 31 A 58). The "tilting" referred to here and in connection with other thinkers (*e.g.*, Aëtius iii. 12. 2 [DK 68 A 96] for Democritus) implies a flat earth.

[28] For the rôle of the δίνη in the thought of Anaximander and his successors I would refer the reader to my *Introduction to Early Greek Philosophy* (Boston, 1968), Index, *s.v.* "Vortex."

[29] That Anaximander expressed himself in "somewhat poetical language" we know from Simplicius *Phys.* 24. 18 (DK 12 B 1).

GREGORY VLASTOS
Princeton University

A Zenonian Argument Against Plurality*

THE two surviving fragments of this argument make up between them some 65% of all that has come down to us of Zeno's original treatise.[1] On this one ground, if on no other, they have a high claim on the attention of anyone interested in becoming acquainted with the authentic Zeno. The problems they present are great but, one may hope, not insuperable. How much progress has already been made one may judge by comparing the best of the recent studies, Fraenkel's,[2] with the best of the older ones, Zeller's.[3] The present study picks up where Fraenkel's leaves off, and this may help explain why it devotes so much more space to the discussion of his views than to those of other scholars.

(I) *Reconstruction of S1*

Simplicius,[4] to whom we owe the preservation of our two fragments ("B1" and "B2," I shall call them hereafter, by their numbering in Diels-Kranz),[5] makes it clear that they formed parts of a longer train of argument.[6] Of this our B1 was the concluding section, being preceded (contrary to Diels' mistaken numbering) by our B2. This in turn was preceded by another argument, which I shall call, arbitrarily, "S1." Here Simplicius (139. 18–19) tells us—and this is all he says about it—Zeno had "previously (*i.e.*, prior to B2) demonstrated that nothing has size due to each of the many (existents) being self-identical and one." Though only a paraphrase, and an incomplete one, this is entitled to respect, for it is written by a man who has an original text[7] not far from his eyes, having just cited from it verbatim our B2, and about to cite shortly after our B1. So taking our stand on Simplicius' paraphrase—the deduction of absence of size from self-identity and unity—we can proceed to look for the other premises which would have authorized this surprising inference. Now it so happens that we have a fragment of Melissus (B9), where absence of size is inferred from unity. I translate literally, and number the sentences for convenient reference:

* Presented at the 1957 meeting of the SAGP in Cambridge, Massachusetts.

[M1] If it exists,[8] it must be one;

[M2] but if it is one, it must have no body.

[M3] But if it had thickness, it would have parts,

[M4] and then it would not be one.

Now by pasting the data of Simplicius' paraphrase on this fragment of Melissus we can produce the following reconstruction of S1:

[Z1] If anything exists, it must be one and self-identical.

[Z2] But if it is one and self-identical, it can have no size.

[Z3] For if it had size, it would have parts,

[Z4] and then it would not be one and self-identical.

[Z5] Thus, if the many exist, none of them can have size.

This is a sufficient solution to the problem of supplementing the data in Simplicius with premises that would be quite acceptable to an Eleatic yet still so plausible in themselves that assent to them could be elicited from non-Eleatics by easy supporting moves: *e.g.*, for [Z3], "If it has any size at all, it must be also two halves of that, four quarters of it, and so forth"; and for [Z4], "If it has two parts, then it is two things, hence no longer one,[9] and then how could it be the same as itself, since *it* is one?"

The main hazard of the reconstruction is obviously at [Z3], [Z4], which fill in a middle term for the inference certified by Simplicius: from unity and self-identity to absence of size. Can we get some independent confirmation of this suggestion? It seems that we can, for a part of it, *i.e.*, for Zeno's arguing, as did Melissus, from the (supposed) incompatibility of "x is one" with "x has parts" and the entailment of "x has no size" by "x has no parts": "Alexander says that the second argument, the one from dichotomy, [Arist., *Phys.*, 187a 1–2], is Zeno's, who argues that if being had size and were divisible, it would be no longer one but many . . ."[10] Since "divisible" here = "has parts,"[11] this is good support for this part of the reconstruction. Its confirmatory value would not be appreciably reduced if, as seems probable, Alexander was echoing here not S1 as such but a part of another of Zeno's arguments against plurality.[12] There would be nothing to keep Zeno from using some of the same materials in different arguments.[13]

(II) *The Argument of B2*

As cited by Simplicius (139. 10–11), the demonstrand was: "That which has neither size nor thickness nor mass, would not even exist";[14] the proof ran:

[1] "For if it were attached[15] to another existent, it would make [the latter] no larger.

[2] For, having no size, it can contribute nothing in respect of size when attached.

[3] And thus [it follows] already that what is attached would be nothing.

[4] If, indeed, something will not decrease another by detachment from it, nor increase it by attachment to it, it is clear that what was attached or detached was nothing."

As is clear at [3], and also at [4], Zeno, in good Eleatic fashion, takes "would be nothing" as equivalent to "would not exist" in the demonstration. Let us give him this equivalence: we have more pressing things to worry about. What is to be proved is, "If *x* has no size, *x* is nothing." The supposed proof: "If *x* has no size, it can add none to *y* by attachment to *y* (=[2]), hence cannot increase *y* (=[1]), hence is nothing (=[3])." But this last step is astonishing. How could one possibly infer "is nothing" from "cannot increase *y*"? All one could infer from the latter is "is nothing *in respect of size*," *i.e.*, "has no size." But this we already know as the hypothesis at [2] and [1]. Could it then be that Zeno has *confused* "*x* has no size" with "*x* is nothing"? Impossible. These two propositions are, respectively equivalent to the antecedent and consequent[16] in the demonstrand. Unless they were perfectly distinct in Zeno's mind there would have been no argument. What could be happening then? Could it be trickery? Fraenkel (pp. 20 ff.) has so argued: the phrase at [3] which I have translated "what is attached would be nothing," τὸ προσγινόμενον οὐδέν [ἐστιν], he argues, "can be taken to mean 'no increase takes place' . . . or [alternatively] 'that which is added is nothing'," and Zeno is counting on getting the phrase with the vital, second, sense past the reader's defences by having it slip by in the innocent, first, sense. Is Zeno then a slippery character, a sophist? Let us not get drawn into this argument, but only ask how effective the suggested trick would really be. προσγενομένου had been used just before, at [2], to mean quite unambiguously (in the usual translation) "that (existent) which is added." Why should the reader (unless he were half asleep when he read that sentence) be expected now, one sentence later, to take the very same word in the different sense of "the increase"? But suppose he did; then he would know (unless he is still nodding) that the argument has not advanced an inch ("*x* would not increase *y*" at [1]; "no increase takes place" at [3]), and Zeno's thumping claim at [3] of having "already" proved the essential point would be inane. A reader who could be fooled by such a manoeuvre would scarcely be worth fooling.

I wish to suggest another way of construing the argument. Suppose we were to take "If [1], then [3]" as an enthymeme. What would be the missing premise? Obviously

> [0] That which would not increase another by attachment to it, or decrease it by detachment from it, would be nothing.

Given this as the major, and [1] as the minor, [3] would follow smoothly. And if we now look at [4] above, it will be evident, I trust, that it is only verbally different from [0]. Zeno's argument then becomes formally correct if we take it as follows: "If [2], then [1]; and [1], given [4], implies [3]." What may occasion surprise is that [4] should then be left to bring up the rear, instead of heading the procession or, in any case, preceding [3].[17] But this reversal of the formal order is done often enough in a conversational argument. Cf. "A and B must be equal, for they are both right angles. It is clear, I take it, that all right angles are equal." A similar reversal in Zeno's argument would incur no fault of inference, nor would it break any rules of exposition, for there were none to break at this time and for a long time after. The more serious question would be whether Zeno is entitled to [0] as a premise. Since this is clearly a dialectical argument, this question boils down to: is [0] the sort of premise that Zeno's readers would have passed as unquestioningly true? Were it not for the conclusion of the immediately preceding S1, the answer would surely be: "Yes, no one would think of disputing [0], except one who had already formed the notion of incorporeal existence, and this could not be claimed for anyone prior to the Eleatics." But now that Zeno has just finished proving to the reader that no existent has size, it does seem awkward to expect him to admit a proposition which so obviously contradicts that conclusion. An alert reader might have balked at this point, retorting: "You are asking me to assume [0], having already implied it is false." But Zeno could have replied: "You have been assuming it long before this argument began. Are you so fully persuaded now of the conclusion of S1 that you are prepared to surrender all of your previous beliefs that will not square with it? If so, I welcome you as a brother in the Eleatic faith, and there is no need of further argument with you. It is only the unconverted I am addressing now, who have not yet taken stock of the effect of the preceding argument on their familiar dogmas, [0] among them. Their innocence serves my purpose. By letting them keep [0] for the time being, I can set off another explosion whose blast effect should be still greater on their stolid minds."

Certainly Zeno would have produced a more elegant argument had he denied himself after S1 the use of any premise which clashes directly with the conclusion of S1. The beauty of his other extant fragment against plurality, B3, is that it achieves just this effect. His performance here is definitely clumsier by contrast.[18] But it is still a tolerable form of dialectical argument and this, I submit, is a sufficient reason for accepting this interpretation of his text in preference to either of the above alternatives which involve, respectively, confusion and deception.

(III) *B1: Translation and Explanation*

Translation

1. But if [the many][19] exist, each must have some size and thickness, and one [part] of each[20] must extend beyond the other [part of the same existent].

2. And the same reasoning applies to the projecting [part]. For this too will have size and some [part] of it will project.

3. Now to say this once is as good as saying it for ever: for no such [projecting part] of it will be the last or without one [part similarly] related to the other [part].

4. Thus if there are many, they must be both small and large: so small as not to have size; so large as to be infinite.

Analytic Paraphrase

1. If [P], then [Q], and then [R]:[21]

 [P] There are many existents.

 [Q] Every existent has size.

 [R] Given any existent, *a*, there will be two existents, *b* and *c*, which are non-overlapping parts of *a*.

2. If [Q], then also [S]:

 [S] Given *c*, there will be two existents, *d* and *e*, non-overlapping parts of *c*.

3. If [R] and [S], then [T]:

 [T] The series *a*, *c*, *e*, *g*, . . . whose every term is related to its predecessor as *c* to *a*, has no last term.

4. If [P] (and ???),[22] then [U] and [not-U]:

 [U] The size of *a* is null.

 [not-U] The size of *a* is infinite.

Commentary

There have been two broadly different constructions[23] of the reasoning in *1* to *3*, pursuing alternative interpretations of ἀπέχειν at *1*, προύχοντος and προέξει at *2*. One of them goes back to Zeller,[24] and has enjoyed the

—DIAGRAM HERE—

support of excellent scholars, notably Fraenkel's,[25] who translates ἀπέχειν "to be at a distance from," and takes the sense to be: two parts, front and back, are separated by an intervening core. In that case my [R] would have to be re-written as

[R′] Given any existent, *a*, there will be three existents, *b*, *m*, and *c*, which are non-overlapping parts of *a*, and such that *b* is separated from *c* by *m*.

Similarly my [S] would have to be re-written as

[S′] Given *c*, there will be three existents, *d*, *n*, and *e*, non-overlapping parts of *c*, such that *d* is separated from *e* by *n*.

My [T], on the other hand, would be unaffected: this, no more and no less, would be inferred from [R′] and [S′], as from [R] and [S]. This is my main objection to Fraenkel's interpretation: Why should Zeno use more elaborate machinery to get his [T] when a simpler one would suffice? As for the wording, it is (at the least) compatible with the more economical construction, in that it refers to two parts at the first division, with no allusion to an intervening third[26] at *1* or thereafter: *2* (and, by implication, *3*) refers only to the "projecting" part; and προέχειν, in its standard sense, "project, jut out from," is normally said of *contiguous* parts, one of which is thought of as sticking out from or extending beyond the other;[27] the same sense is possible, though not standard, for ἀπέχειν, whose meaning in *1* must in any case be the same as that of προύχοντος at *2*.[28]

Now we can see how the argument goes. That [P] implies [Q] is a carry-over from B2. That [Q] implies [R] takes us back to [M3] and [Z3] in Section (I) above. One may conjecture that the reasoning would be: if something has bulk, it must be spread out in space, so you can distinguish in it a "here" from a "there"; having such contiguous, non-coincident and non-overlapping, parts or regions, Zeno, might have explained, is part of what we *mean* by having size. The discrimination of any two such parts in any existent I shall refer to as a "division", though no such word appears in Zeno's text,[29] or even in my analytic paraphrase. It will be simply a convenient name for the process by which we get the two parts, *b* and *c*, at *1*, *d* and *e* at *2*, or any subsequent two thereafter.[30] That no physical cut or fission is intended here is quite obvious, and none would have been warranted anyhow, without further assumptions, since no property of existents except their size is specified at [Q]. Thus the problem, insoluble for the engineer, of pursuing the division past the smallest particle he can split with his present tools, does not arise. That no part reached by such division will be the last follows by reiteration of the reasoning which warrants [R] and [S] or even analytically from [R] alone: a supposed last term in the *a*, *c*, *e*, *g*, . . . series would have to be an existent (since only existents are members of the series), yet not have the two parts prescribed by [R] for *any* existent.

(IV) *The Deduction of Nullity of Size*

How get past [T] to the dilemma in the conclusion? The answer must have seemed obvious to Zeno, since he gives not a word to justify, or even outline, the transit.[31] But what would he have said, if pressed for an explanation? Let us start with the first part of the contradiction which, he thinks, he has proved to follow from the refutand: "Thus if [P] there are many, then [U] they must be . . . so small as not to have size." Is [U] supposed to follow from the preceding argument in B1? Or is it meant as the consequence of something or other *before* B1? Here are two possible justifications of [U]: "*jI*" and "*jII*", let us call them. Offhand, the first might seem the better bet, for one would ordinarily expect [U] to be the direct upshot of the close-packed argument which immediately precedes it. It has been so taken by some authorities.[32] How then would the derivation go? Let T. L. Heath speak for this view:[33] To prove that, if there are many, each will be so small as to have no size, Heath explains,

> Zeno relied on the infinite divisibility of bodies as evident; assuming this, he easily proved that division will continually give smaller and smaller parts, there will be no limit to their diminution, and [i] if there is a final element, it must be absolutely *nothing*. Consequently, [ii] to add any number of these *nil*-elements . . . to one another, even in infinite number, will give *nothing* as the total.

Had Zeno followed this line of reasoning, he would have blundered, as can be easily shown: Heath's [i] will do only as a hypothetical whose antecedent must be false for Zeno, since it is contrary to [T] above, and also because the consequent of [i] is false, being contrary to [Q] above. As for Heath's [ii], it would be similarly unobjectionable if taken only as a hypothetical, sc. "*if* there were final members of zero magnitude, the aggregate magnitude of an infinity of them would indeed be zero." But what would this do to establish the demonstrand (our [U]), that the magnitude of each of the many existents is zero? Nothing. To derive this from Heath's [i] and [ii] Zeno would have to *assert* the antecedent of [i]; and this he could only do by contradicting, as has just been shown, two things he has previously asserted in B1.[34]

But what would this prove? Unless we are prepared to settle matters of historical fact by issuing unlimited credit to our philosophical heroes, we cannot regard the blunder in *jI* as a sufficient reason for thinking it could not have been Zeno's. We can, however, concede that if he did make such a mistake, it would not have been so arbitrary as it appears in Heath's reconstruction; he would not, we may assume, pursue a line of argument providing two good grounds precluding the existence of final elements of null magnitude, and then turn right around and for no reason at all assert their existence. Could there have been any such reason? To see that there could have been we may turn to an argument in Simplicius of uncertain authorship, not included in Diels-Kranz, but listed as a Zeno fragment by Lee and defended by him as genuine.[35] Since Simplicius gets it from Porphyry, I shall call it "the Porphyry text." Here is a fairly literal translation,[36] with reference marks interspersed:

> Parmenides had another argument which was thought to prove by means of dichotomy that being is only one, and that it is without parts and indivisible.
>
> [A] For, he says, if it is divisible, let it have been cut in two, then each part in two. This is being done continually, then clearly, he says,[37]
>
> [1] either there will be left certain final, smallest, atomic magnitudes, infinite in number, and the whole will then consist of smallest magnitudes, infinite in number;
>
> [2] or else it will vanish and be dissolved into nothing, and will then consist of nothing.
>
> These conclusions are absurd. Hence it cannot be divided, but will remain one.
>
> [B] Further, since it is all alike throughout, if it is divisible, it will be divisible throughout (πάντῃ)[38] alike, not just here but not there (τῇ μέν, τῇ δὲ οὔ).[39] It will be clear that, once again, nothing will

> remain, but it will vanish, and, if it is to have components, it will consist of nothing. For if any part of it is left over, it has not yet been divided throughout. From all this, he says, it is evident that being will be indivisible, without parts, and one.

Conspicuously absent from this argument is any mention of *infinite* divisibility. But that the assumption is made at [A2] and [B] is certain.[40] For since [A] is the case in which the division is finally stopped by "atomic magnitudes," [A2] must be the remaining alternative: no "atomic magnitudes", hence infinite divisibility. The same, *a fortiori*, at [B], for this takes up where [A2] leaves off, adding nothing except the stipulation that being is "divisible *throughout*," thereby closing off the [A1] possibility left open before. How then does the writer get to the conclusions of [A2] and [B?]—His key moves are the opening ones: "let it have been dichotomized" at [A]; "let it have been divided throughout" at [B]. In other words: suppose that the operations which are said to be possible in the hypotheses ("divis*ible*"; "divis*ible* throughout") have been carried through to a finish, or completed. The conclusion which interests us then appears as a necessary condition of this completion: so long as any part of being is left undivided, the division of being has not been completed; it can have been completed only when being has wholly "vanished." But what makes the writer so sure that his key moves are authorized? To put in the most blatant form the assumption he is making, let us have him reply:

> Suppose the hypothesis had been instead, '*x* is mechanically divisible.' I would then be obviously authorized to assume that it is logically possible to carry out completely the mechanical division of *x*. By the same token, from '*x* is infinitely divisible' I am entitled to infer that, on this hypothesis, the completion of the infinite division of *x* is logically possible.

What is being assumed here is that the *logical* (no less than the grammatical) relation of "infinitely" to "divisible" is parallel to that which ordinary adverbs like "mechanically," "smoothly," "cheaply," etc., might bear to "divisible." The assumption is, of course, mistaken, for it leads to a contradiction: Since "infinitely"="endlessly,"[41] and "completion"="ending,"[42] it follows that "the completion of the infinite division of *x* is logically possible"="the ending of the endless division of *x* is logically possible." But this brings into the open the contradiction that remains concealed even when the assumption is put in the ultra-explicit form of the imaginary argument above, for even there it is far from obvious that the relation of "completion" to "infinitely" is the same as that of "ending" to "endlessly." How much more plausible the whole argument would be when this assumption itself is masked by excluding "infinitely" from a place in the explicit premises, as the whole argument of the Porphyry text succeeds in doing. The extent of its plausibility we may judge from the fact that the core of [B] is reproduced point for point in an argument which Aristotle cites[43] as the very one which was "believed to necessitate atomic magnitudes";[44] and Aristotle talks[45] as though it was so believed by Democritus. Zeno too then *could* have subscribed to the same reasoning; and having reached by this route the conclusion that infinite divisibility entails dissolution into final elements of null magnitude, he could have carried the results over into B1, and could then easily have taken *jI*, contradiction and all, in his stride. All this, *if* the argument in the Porphyry text is really his. But is it?

Citing it from Porphyry, where, as we saw, it is ascribed to Parmenides, Simplicius remarks: "It is worth considering whether this argument is really Parmenides', and not, as Alexander thinks, Zeno's" (140.23). For opposing the Parmenidean authorship, Simplicius gives an excellent reason: "No such argument figures among the Parmenidean [texts]."[46] But when suggesting its derivation from Zeno, all he can offer in support is "that most of our information refers the puzzles from dichotomy to Zeno."[47] This is meager evidence indeed: the cited statement is consistent with the existence of several original "arguments from dichotomy" by early writers other than Zeno, and for any number of later pastiches. Did Alexander then have a better reason? Not likely, else Simplicius would have mentioned it to strengthen his case. And there is internal evidence against its ascription to Zeno: (*1*) it argues constructively for the Eleatic thesis that Being is one and indivisible, after the manner of Parmenides and Melissus, not destructively against the non-Eleatic thesis that "there are many," which is the only thing Zeno did when arguing on plurality according to both our primary[48] and secondary[49] evidence; (*2*) the form of the arguments is quite different from that of Zeno's extant arguments against plurality, both of which fall very self-consciously into the "If *P*, then *C* and not-*C*" pattern, the predicates in *C* and not-*C*, being carefully phrased to heighten the felt contrast: so small as to be null *and* so large as to be infinite at B1; finite (in number) and infinite (in number) at B3. In the Porphyry text this pattern is altogether absent at [B], while [A] offers *alternatives* at [1] and [2] ("either . . . or . . ."), not a *conjunction* ("both . . . and . . ."), and makes no effort to exploit the contrast by finding at [2] pat antitheses to the predicates at [1]. With the materials of [A] Zeno would surely have produced a razor-sharp "*C* and not-*C*" conclusion from the hypothesis, or even a couple of them: finite in size *and* null in size; infinite in number *and* null in number. Nor would it have been like him to bluster at [1], saying its conclusion is "absurd," instead of parading its absurdity. What is it, anyhow? None is now visible to the naked eye.

So the case against the ascription of the Porphyry text to Zeno is strong, while that for it could hardly be weaker.[50] But this text has at least shown us the only plausible route by which Zeno too would have inferred final elements of null magnitude from infinite divisibility, *if* he had ever done so: by way of the assumption that "is infinitely divisible" entails "its complete division is logically possible." Let us then scan his other fragments to see if he shows any tendency to take this path in any of them. He certainly does not in the Race-course and Achilles, both of which proceed on precisely the opposite assumption: that their respective series, being infinite, can *not* be traversed. Nor does he in B3: the number of existents, Zeno argues here, must be infinite "because there are always other (existents) between any (given) existents, and again others between these." Here too the argument would have been ruined if Zeno thought that this infinite process *could* be completed. So far, then, as we can judge from his other work, Zeno did not make the assumption that would have led to [U] via *jI*.

We could, therefore, rule against *jI* by merely availing ourselves of a principle of exegesis analogous to the "innocent if not proved guilty" rule of the common law: given two constructions of a text, both of them equally consistent with the evidence, prefer the one more favorable to the author's intelligence. Such *jII* would certainly be: it would suppose Zeno to be inferring that *a* is "so small as to have no magnitude" from the conclusion of S1 that *a* has no magnitude. The inference is harmless to the point of triviality, and Fraenkel's suspicion of "precarious" logic here—"Smallness, i.e., little magnitude, can hardly be ascribed to a thing which actually possesses none" (p. 200)—seems unfounded: one could indeed object to an inference like "*a* has no size, therefore it has a very small size," since "very small size" does suggest some finite size, all the more so in the context of B1, where "some size" at *1* and "size" at *2* are used to *mean* a finite size. But I can see no good reason to object to "*a* has no size, therefore *a* is so small as to have no size," for "no size" in the consequent quite clearly precludes the reservation of a finite size. So logically *jII* is as impeccable[51] as *jI* was disreputable, and has a sterling claim to the benefit of the doubt. What is more, it has some slight positive evidence in its favor: Simplicius writes as though *he* believed *jII*. With both [U] and [not-U] clearly before him—he starts off by citing it at 139.8–9—he refers to B1 (by citation, 141.1 ff.) *only* as providing proof of [not-U], infinity of size;[52] and since he does not tell us how [U] is proved, but does refer (by paraphrase, 139.18–19) to the proof of nullity of size at S1, it seems reasonable to assume that he thinks this *was* the proof of the first horn. To be sure, it remains possible that he misunderstood Zeno's argument. But had he done so, it is more likely that he would have misunderstood it in the direction of *jI* (since, as we have seen, he is willing to credit Zeno with the text from Porphyry, and hence to believe that Zeno did deduce null size from infinite divisibility). And since his knowledge of the text was better than ours, his apparent interpretation of it in the direction of *jII* may be allowed to decide in its favor.

(V) *The Deduction of Infinity of Size*

Having exonerated Zeno from a fallacy in the deduction of [U], it would be pleasant if we could render him the same service in the deduction of [not-U]. This unfortunately is out of the question. That *a* is "so large as to be infinite" could have been derived, so far as I can see, from nothing but the immediately preceding argument, and only by intercalating the certainly false premise that the sum of every infinite set whose every member has finite size must be infinitely large.[53] Only one proposal to save Zeno from this error is even worth discussing: Fraenkel's, to the effect that *apeira* could mean here "indeterminate," no less than "infinite," and Zeno was exploiting the *double entendre* to make "the conclusion sound far stronger than it really is" (p. 197). But I find this third allegation of slippery logic no stronger than the ones I rejected above. This one can be disposed of on purely linguistic grounds: we do not know of a single case in which *apeiron* means "indeterminate in respect of size (or, of number.)" When it does mean "indeterminate," as in a fragment of Philolaus (B11) or in Plato's *Philebus* (23c 9 ff.), it expresses simply lack of form or definiteness in general. Neither in these cases, nor in any other classical text known to me,[54] is *apeiron* used as modifier of size or number to mean "large or small or medium, we don't (or, can't) know which." What we do find is, in poetic or popular usage, *apeiron* for "indeterminately *large*," *i.e.*, "vast, enormous."[55] And this, of course, would not save Fraenkel's thesis, for even if we supposed it (as Fraenkel does not) to be the meaning of *apeira* here, it would convey an inference as fallacious as if it did mean "infinite": to infer that the sum of the $b+d+f+\ldots$ series is enormously large would be as bad a mistake (indeed, a worse, more whimsical, one) as to infer that it is infinitely large.

There is then no escaping the sense of "infinite" for *apeira*, and we must, therefore, reconcile ourselves to the thought that our clever Zeno here walked into a booby-trap. How are we to explain the mishap? The simplest explanation would be that it was due simply to his ignorance of the arithmetical theorem (whose first preserved statement is in Aristotle),[56] that the sum of a series will not exhaust a finite quantity, no matter how far the series may be extended, if its terms decrease in constant ratio.[57] I do not find this a convincing explanation. Zeno's arithmetic, properly used, would surely have taught him all he needed to know in order to explode his fallacy by this method. Thus, if he made 3/4 the ratio of division, he could have seen that when the series had just two terms, *b* and *d*, the sum would be $3a/4+3a/16=15a/16$; when it had three terms, *b*, *d*, and *f*, the sum would be $63a/64$; and that the same thing would happen no matter how many terms he put into his series, the sum being always less than *a*, since the last term added would never be the whole of the difference between *a* and the sum of the preceding terms but always 1/2 of that difference. Naturally, there is no means of proving, and no particular reason for assuming, that Zeno did any such figuring. Let us suppose him averse to such calculations or even incapable of them. He could still have satisfied himself on the essential point by simply reasoning as follows: "Since all the magnitudes included in the series are non-overlapping parts of *a*, their sum will always fall short of the magnitude of *a* by just that part of *a* which remains as yet *un*included in the series—as some part always must, since the series is infinite." There is nothing especially recondite about this reasoning, and the gist of it would be intuitively apparent in the simplest of diagrams, such as the one at Section III, above: if Zeno used a two-dimensional figure to represent *a*, and moved in division from left to right, it would be perfectly clear that his procedure would never allow him to get past the right-hand extremity of *a*, or, indeed, to ever get *to a*.

Conversely, we would do well to remind ourselves that knowledge of the Aristotelian theorem did not offer sufficient protection against Zeno's fallacy. Thus Simplicius, who expounds Aristotle's formula quite intelligently in commenting on *Physics* 206 b 3, solemnly asserts in other contexts that "that [whole] which consists of infinitely many magnitudes would have infinite magnitude."[58] Or, to keep closer to the classical era, we have the same idea in Epicurus:

> . . . neither must we allow that [bodies] of finite size may decrease *ad infinitum*. For once one says that there are an infinite number of bodies, of no matter what size, in a given thing, it becomes impossible to understand how the size of the latter could still be finite. For [each of] the infinitely many bodies has some size; no matter what may be this size, their [aggregate] size would then be infinite.[59]

There must have been some tacit assumption which would have made it seem obviously true that any collection of an infinite number of sizeable parts would have to be infinitely large: so very obviously, that even someone who knew all about Aristotle's theorem (as Simplicius certainly did, and some of Epicurus' associates almost as certainly)[60] would not think of applying it to the present case, but infer forthwith infinity of size for the container from infinity of number of the parts contained. I cannot imagine what this could be except that *the collection had a smallest member*. This would be quite sufficient to make the conclusion seem a matter of course: given an infinity of non-overlapping parts the least of which has some finite magnitude, it would be obvious that the aggregate magnitude would be infinite. "But would not this contradict [T] above?"—Certainly, since "smallest" entails "last." But the contradiction need not have been apparent even if carried to the closest proximity with [T]. It could even be imported into the explication of [T], and still not strike the eye, as *e.g.*, in "all the members of this series, *down to the very smallest*, must have some finite size." And if the italicized phrase aroused misgivings, they could be suppressed with, "the members of the series are arranged in order of decreasing size, so there must be a part smaller than any part,[61] and this could only be the smallest." The plausibility of this assumption seems to me very great. It expresses the tendency to extrapolate from what remains true of the series so long as it has a finite number of terms to what would be the case if *all* its terms were present in it. Zeno's best hope of checking this tendency lay in making the assumption as explicit as possible. Had he actually said, "The series $b+d+e+$ . . . must have a last member," his chances of noticing the contradiction with [T] would have immeasurably improved. He threw this chance away when he treated the inference as something much too obvious to deserve a place in his text.

Lacking support in textual evidence,[62] the suggestion I have made is merely a hypothesis as to *why* Zeno made the fallacy in the deduction of [not-U]. But that he did make the fallacy is no hypothesis. It is as much of a certainty as any we can hope to reach in such matters. Since there is no trace of a similar error before Zeno's time, he must be reckoned the inventor of this fallacy. And since his arguments had a considerable currency, he must also be reckoned its most important propagator. It may thus have been his influence that reached down to the end of the fourth century to provide Epicurus with a bad reason for atomism.[63] It was certainly at work in the middle of that century, for Zeno is mentioned as the source of arguments which led Xenocrates to that metaphysical and mathematical oddity, the doctrine of indivisible lines.[64] It is a reasonable presumption, though of this we have no direct evidence, that he also exercised some influence on the founder of the atomic hypothesis, his contemporary, Leucippus.[65]

But on another of his great contemporaries, Anaxagoras, Zeno's arguments fell flat. Anaxagoras' knowledge of Zeno's book may now be more than a general presumption, for some close echoes of Zenonian diction have been recently noticed in two of his fragments.[66] Acquainted with Zeno's arguments, yet making infinite divisibility a cardinal principle of his physics, Anaxagoras must have certainly rejected Zeno's fallacious inference from it in B1. This is perfectly plain from the very form in which he states his adherence to the principle of infinite divisibility:[67]

> B3 For of the small *there is no smallest*, but always a smaller, for it is impossible that what is should not be . . .
>
> B6 . . . Since *the smallest cannot exist* . . .

In the italicized words Anaxagoras explicitly repudiates that assumption which, if I am right, was just the source of Zeno's fallacy.[68]

(VI) *Some Conclusions*

1. *Of "Pythagorean" point-atoms, no sign*

It has been held by scholars of the highest eminence, and is still widely believed today, that Zeno's polemic was specially directed against a theory, supposedly held by the Pythagoreans of his time, that the ultimate components of the universe had the indivisibility of geometrical points and the extensive magnitude of physical bodies.[69] Elsewhere I have questioned the existence of trustworthy evidence that the Pythagoreans entertained any such theory at this time.[70] Here we may consider Zeno's side of this supposed polemic. From the foregoing analysis of one of his arguments against plurality, what may we learn of its target?—The refutand of the whole argument is "many exist," and what it professes to show, if true, would be true of any existents: none have size, and all have infinite size. The premises used in the deduction are, in the first case, the self-identity and unity of any existent, which no one would have denied; in the second, the capacity to increase other things when attached to them, to decrease them when detached from them, which all non-Eleatics would impute to all existents. The scope of the argument then is perfectly general: all being, real or supposed, is its theme. Where then are the famous point-atoms? There is no mention of them or allusion to them in the fragments we have studied, and not once have we found it necessary to bring them into the elucidation of the sense of Zeno's words.

But Aristotle, in a reference to B2, writes as follows:[71]

> Further, (i) if unity itself were indivisible, then, according to Zeno's postulate, it would be nothing. (ii) For, he says, that which makes [something else] no larger, when added, and no smaller, when subtracted, is not an existent, (iii) evidently assuming that being is magnitude. (iv) And, if a magnitude, it must be corporeal, for this [has magnitude] in all dimensions,[72] while other [magnitudes], do make [other things] larger when added in one way but not in another: *e.g.*, a plane [may increase a plane] and a line [may increase a line], but (v) a point and a unit [can increase anything] in no way whatever. (vi) But though his theory is of a low order, and the possibility of an indivisible thing can be justified even to him[73] —for such a thing [*sc.* a point] when added *would* increase the number, though not the size—still, how can a magnitude arise from one, or any number, of such [indivisible] things? This would be like saying a line could arise from points.

Now if we did not have the original fragment, we would find it difficult to sort out reportage from inference in this whole passage, and could then have good excuse for invoking Aristotle's witness for talk of the indivisible point-unit in Zeno's argument. Yet even then an attentive reading might have made out the difference between (ii), which is clearly credited to Zeno ("he says"),[74] and everything after it, since already at [iii] Aristotle is telling us what is *implied*[75] by the Zenonian doctrine at (ii), without saying that this implication was mentioned by Zeno himself; while at (iv) and (v) we are at a still further remove from the paraphrase at (ii), for these are only implications of (iii).[76] Yet it is just this "instructive passage" which Burnet thinks *proves* that Zeno's first argument against plurality "refers to points."[77] Ross too cites (v) in this passage as one item of evidence for the view that "what Zeno is attacking is the building up of the world out of points and units";[78] his other item is Simplicius, 99.10, "(vii) But here, as Eudemus says, he [Zeno] refuted the One—for he speaks of the point as the One." But this is unintelligible apart from the context, where the "here" refers to the long extract from Eudemus that Simplicius (97.11–99.6) has just finished quoting. The relevant lines are, "(viii) but the point he [Zeno] assumed was nothing.[79] [ix] For he held that what does not increase [another thing] when added, nor decrease (it) when subtracted, is not an existent" (97.15–16). Here it is quite clear that not even Eudemus claims to be reporting any *statement* of Zeno's about the point: this Zeno "assumed" (τιθέναι), he says, *i.e.*, must have thought so, since he held (ix). Thus the point unit, which made its first appearance in our texts in Aristotle's argument at (iv) above, continues to accompany the paraphrase of B2, though still without any claim that Zeno said this or anything else about the point. It is only at (vii) that this distinction rubs off at last, and the explanation, "for he speaks of the point as the One," reads as though *Eudemus* said that Zeno said that the point is "the One." But since we have the original of Eudemus's statement, we can see that not even he said that Zeno said any such thing.[80]

2. *Dialectical Histrionics*

If I had to judge Zeno's character on no other evidence than that supplied by his performance in this argument against plurality, my verdict would be: (1) He is not an impostor, even in play: three distinct imputations of sophistry have been examined, and not one of them, I have argued, is sustained by the evidence.[81] (2) But he is very much of a showman.[82] His theatrical taste is written all over its design. When he reached the end of B2, he had already proved to his satisfaction that, if the many exist, they cannot have size, and that they must have size. This of itself, if valid, would be an ample refutation of the pluralist thesis; hence everything thereafter would be logically supernumerary. But for Zeno this sequel is the climax of the whole argument, contriving the far more spectacular contradiction, "so small as to have no size, so large as to be infinite." Had he been less intent on getting this melodramatic finale, he would have been spared the logical gaffe by which he got it. The mistake was avoidable, since Anaxagoras avoided it without benefit of any intervening improvement in logical or mathematical apparatus.

3. *Advance in Logical Technique*

But Zeno's argument, for all its faults, marks a great advance in philosophical argumentation, as one can see by comparing it with the only important previous venture in this medium: Parmenides. One part of Zeno's argument, the first six lines of B1, is a brilliant piece of logical exposition, incomparably more precise, rigorous, and economical than any surviving fragment of earlier philosophical prose. The architectonics of the whole argument are also impressive. Three distinct inferential sequences are joined to form a unified argument, exhibiting, probably for the first time in a philosophical context, the *reductio* in its most powerful form, "If *P*, then *C* and not-*C*. [Therefore, not-*P*]."[83]

6. *A Substantive Contribution*

But Zeno reveals more than technical talent in this argument. In its opening part he throws out an idea new to Western philosophy: the incorporeality of Being.[84] It is easy to miss its significance,[85] since he exploits it only for dialectical purposes. How great is its value will be apparent if one notes that in this area the vision of the great Parmenides remained blurred and indistinct; and that without this needed clarification the whole of that great metaphysical construction hovers uncertainly on the edge of confusion.[86]

NOTES

1 This paper was presented as "research in progress" to a meeting of the SAGP. In subsequent years—and most particularly during 1963 and 1964—I worked intensively on Zeno's fragments and reached on some points conclusions differing from views expounded in this paper. I have pointed this out to the editor of the present volume, explaining to him that I would not have the opportunity at this time to go through this paper and bring it into line with my later conclusions. He requested its publication on these terms. Readers who may wish to compare what I say here with subsequent findings may consult my article on Zeno in the *Encyclopedia of Philosophy*, ed. Paul Edwards (New York, 1967), where my conclusions on the interpretation of Zeno's fragments and on his place in the history of Greek thought are stated summarily. For more detailed discussions of special problems the following may be of interest: review of H. Fränkel, *Wege und Formen Fruehgriechischen denkens*, in *Gnomon* 31 (1959): 193 ff.; "A Note on Zeno's Arrow," 11 (1966): 3–18; "Zeno's Race Course," with an Appendix on the Achilles, *JHP* 4 (1966): 95–108. For subsequent publications on Zeno's first two arguments against plurality, consult especially, G. E. L. Owen, "Zeno and the Mathematicians," *PAS*, 58 (1957–58): 199–222; D. J. Furley, *Two Studies in the Greek Atomists* (Princeton, 1967), Chapter 5, on Zeno.

2 H. Fraenkel, "Zeno of Elea's Attacks on Plurality," *AJP* 63 (1942): 1 ff. and 193 ff. I shall refer to this hereafter solely by the author's name. [The same paper, with few changes, has been translated in Fraenkel's *Wege und Formen Fruehgriechischen Denkens* (Munich, 1955).] For references to other studies, see Fraenkel and the commentaries in H. D. P. Lee, *Zeno of Elea* (Cambridge, 1936) and P. Albertelli, *Gli Eleati* (Bari, 1939).

3 *History of Greek Philosophy*, trans. S. F. Alleyne (London, 1881), I, pp. 614 ff.

[4] *Commentary on Aristotle's Physics* 138.3 ff. To this book I shall refer solely by its author's name.

[5] *Fragmente der Vorsokratiker*, 6th ed. (Berlin, 1951).

[6] For the correct reconstruction of the order of its various sections see Fraenkel, pp. 17 ff. The same order in Albertelli, *op. cit.*, p. 204.

[7] Most probably Simplicius' book did not purport to be a complete text of Zeno's original treatise (else why only οἶμαι at 99.17, and why appeal to nothing better than the πλείστη ἱστορία at 140.24?). Yet Simplicius was confident that he knew at least parts of Zeno's own book. He refers to Zeno's "treatise" at 140.28 (also at 139.5), the same term he used for that of *e.g.*, Parmenides (144.28), Anaxagoras (163.7), and Diogenes (151.25–28).

[8] A variant text would yield, "If being exists . . ."

[9] Cf. Plato *Meno* 77A7.

[10] Simpl. 138.3–5 (included under Lee 7).

[11] Cf. Alexander *ap.* Simpl. 127.20–25. Cf. the transition from "having parts (μέρη)" to μεμερισμένον in Plato, *Sophist* 244–E245A. Both of these passages make it clear that the "parts" and "divisions" envisaged in such arguments are *not* necessarily physical cuts and do *not* assume the necessity of intervening wedges to keep one thing apart from another in order to justify the propriety of referring to them as distinct parts of the whole or of the whole being divisible or divided in this way. As will be noticed below (Section III) there is no reference to splits or fissions in the derivation of parts, and parts of parts, at B 1; and there is obviously none in the dichotomies of the Race-Course (Arist., *Phys.* IV. 2, 233a 21 ff., 239 b 14 ff.).

[12] A reconstruction of it (the probable sense, not the wording) may be of interest: "If (a) there are many, then (b) each of them would have to be one, for (c) the many are a multitude of ones; but (not-b) none of them could be one, for (d) each would be divisible *ad infinitum*, hence (e) each would be infinitely many." Evidence for (a) as the refutand of several of Zeno's arguments: Plato *Parmenides* 128D 5–6; Simpl. 139.5. For the form of the *reductio*: B1 *sub fin.*; B3; Plato *Parmenides* 127E 1–2. For "if (a), then (b), for (c)": Eudemus *ap.* Simpl. 99.7 (=Lee 6; echoed by Philoponus in Lee 2 and 8; cf. also Plato *Parmenides* 165E 5–7, and Arist. *GC* I 7, 325a 9). ἑνάδων in Eudemus (and in Philoponus) can hardly be Zeno's; its first known use (and only one, even by Plato) is at *Philebus* 15A; Eudemus is clearly *not* quoting; and that part of his phrasing which suggests that Zeno argued for the non-existence of *any* "one" may be dismissed as careless paraphrasing or misunderstanding, similar to that of Alexander *ap.* Simpl. 127.20.25. For "(not-b), for (d)": Themistius f. 12.1 (=Lee 1). For "(d), hence (e)": Alexander *ap.* Simpl. 183.4 but without "*ad infinitum*" at (d), and "infinitely" at (e), which Alexander may have omitted because they are logically pleonastic, though very much in Zeno's style—see below, section (VI) at 2(2). The original of these last two items was clearly not in Simplicius' text, else he would not quote Themistius' paraphrase (139.19) of the first, nor would he remark of the second, "I think there was no such argument in Zeno's text (99.17)."

13 Zeno must have had a fair number of arguments against plurality in his book ("40" in Proclus *in Parm.* p. 694.23 is doubtless a padded figure, but even so a testimony to the large total with which he was credited), and, in spite of his great inventiveness, could hardly have avoided some duplication of vital premises.

14 Not printed as a direct quotation in Diels, though both the diction and the stylistic turn of the first clause mark it off as Zeno's.

15 The usual translation of προσγίγνεσθαι/ἀπογίγνεσθαι in this fragment is "to be added/subtracted." This loses the more concrete flavor of the original: cf. Melissus B7 (4). There is good reason to think these words were never the ordinary terms for "adding/subtracting": they could not take the active voice, nor supply derivatives for "addition/subtraction" to compete with πρόσθεσις, ἀφαίρεσις.

16 "That which has no size" would be the minor term, "nothing," the major, and "that which would not increase another by attachment to it," the middle term.

17 Other objections to this construction are: (i) we would expect in lieu of εἰ γὰρ at the start of [4]; but δὲ *can* introduce a statement giving the reason for the preceding—Liddell & Scott, *s.v.*, I.3; (ii) since τὸ προσγιγνόμενον has been used at [3] to refer to the existent which has no size (the logical subject of [1], [2], and [3]), one would normally expect ἀπογινομένου, προσγινομένου at [4] to have the same reference; but in that case the second part of [4] would be a mere reiteration, contrary to Zeno's habitual economy.

18 Even this could have been overcome by changing the order: instead of S 1–B 2–B 3, he could have made it B 2–B 1 (lines 1–7)–S 1—B 1 (lines 7–9); note that S1 does not invoke any *premises* which directly contradict anything in B 2 and B 1.

19 Equally possible grammatically is "(it [*sc.* each of the many] exists)," as in Fraenkel, 195 and n. 72. But this makes the "each" in the next clause stylistically repetitious.

20 For this construction of αὐτοῦ, partitive, and referring to ἕκαστον see Fraenkel, n. 67. This had already been seen by W. A. Heidel in *PAA*, 48 (1913): 724, but has been ignored in both Diels (-Kranz) and the English translations. Correctly understood in R. Mondolfo, *L'Infinito nel pensiero dei Greci* (Florence, 1934), p. 246, n. i: he sees that the expression can only mean that of each existent one part *deve distare dell' altra.*

21 Strictly construed, the grammar of *1* would yield "If [P], then [Q and R]." But since Zeno would justify [R] by [Q], the logical sequence has to be as above.

22 The reason for the question-marks, if not already obvious, will soon become so.

23 See Albertelli, p. 207, for the main pre-1939 references.

24 *Op. cit.*, pp. 616–17.

25 Pp. 193 ff. Fraenkel's construction is different from Zeller's in so many ways (beginning with the translation), that it may be misleading to think of it as a version of Zeller's theory. It is that *only* in respect of assuming

that Zeno operates with two terms separated by a third at each step of the argument, rather than with just two contiguous terms.

26 Or to "front" and "back" parts, assumed in Fraenkel's interpretation. A projection need not be towards the front.

27 Zeno's use of the term in this fragment is most probably due to his thinking of the first term in each division as being much larger than its twin. If *b* is much larger than *c*, it would be natural to think of *b* as the base and of *c* as a "projection" from it. I have ignored this point in the accompanying diagram, using the more convenient 1/1 ratio as the *principium divisionis*.

28 That which is said to ἀπέχει at *1* is termed the προύχοντος at *2*. (And cf. ἀπέχουσιν in Arist., *De Part. Anim.*, 655a 31–32.)

29 Though scarcely foreign to Eleatic thought or vocabulary. Cf. διαιρετόν at Parmenides B8.22, διῄρηται at Melissus B 10.

30 It is thus evident that the series of divisions, D_1, D_2, D_3, . . ., matches term for term the series of "projecting" parts, *c*, *e*, *g*, . . . Each is denumerably infinite, and, having a first term, can have no last.

31 A gap in our text is, of course, possible at this point, but there is no good reason to suppose it. That there was none in Simplicius' source is as good as certain, for, to my knowledge, he never presents a broken citation as though it were unbroken in any of his dozens of quotations from the pre-Socratics. And it is hard to see how the break could have been made by an earlier copyist or editor: why should anyone want to give the argument through [T], and then skip the links to the conclusion?

32 *E.g.*, P. Tannery, *Pour l'histoire de la Science Hellène* (Paris, 1887), pp. 254–55; T. L. Heath, *History of Greek Mathematics* I (Oxford, 1921), p. 275; Lee, *op. cit.*, p. 30. I discuss Heath's construction as the most plausible one. For Tannery's cf. n. 34, below. Lee's is ingenious, but would, in effect, make [not-*U*] a necessary premise for the deduction of [*U*].

33 *Loc. cit.* This is not Heath at his best. He seems to be unaware of the contradiction in the reasoning he imputes to Zeno. I suspect he was misled by Tannery (*loc. cit.*) to whom he does not refer, but whose very wording he echoes.

34 Tannery's construction (*loc. cit.*) leaves Zeno free from this fallacy, but only by shifting on Zeno's "adversary" the burden of asserting that there are final elements. But if that is the way the "adversary" is going to behave, how did he get past our [T], or even to it: was he so careless as to agree to [R]?

35 The second in his Zeno fragments. For the defence, see his commentary. Albertelli (*op. cit.*, p. 185) cites it along with Philoponus 80.23 ff. (=Lee 3) as examples of "fanciful and partly arbitrary reconstructions of Zenonian reasoning" by later writers.

36 Partly indebted to Lee's.

37 In Lee the wordi κἄπειτα τῶν μερῶν ἑκὰτερον δὶχα, καί τούτου ἀεὶ γενομένου, δῆλον φησιν are omitted without explanation.

38 πάντῃ also in Aristotle, *GC* I. 2, 316a 16 ff. and 325a 8, and only in these two passages in Aristotle with this meaning, to my knowledge.

39 τῇ μέν, τῇ δέ in Arist., *De Gen. et Corr.* (hereafter abbreviated to "GC"), I. 8, 325a 10 as the contradictory to πάντῃ.

40 At [A1] also, for nothing less than an infinite number of divisions is required to produce an *infinite* number of these atoms from a single original thing; but that "final" terms do result would also entail that the series of divisions is *not* infinite. This is a muddle, the worst I have encountered in this inquiry.

41 In a sense which has nothing to do with *temporal* endlessness, but is simply the logical endlessness of a series of divisions (n. 37, above) which can have no last term, since it is infinite, denumerable and has a first.

42 In the same sense, i.e., reaching the final terms of the series of terms produced by the series of divisions. [A1] speaks openly of "final" terms; [A2] and [B] imply the same thing, since their "nothings" are not regarded as existing *outside* the series (in which case their existence would be logically harmless) but as members *of* the series, hence necessarily its last members.

43 *GC*, I. 2, 316a 15 ff.; cf. n. 38, above. The main difference is "body" here in place of "being" in the Porphyry text, and a far more verbose and explicit argument, whose goal is to establish pluralistic atomism, not (as in Porphyry) Eleatic monism. But the structure of the two arguments is the same. This one runs: if a body is "divisible throughout," its complete division is logically possible, but cannot be complete so long as any part remains undivided; hence, when the division has been completed, the body will have been dissolved into extensionless points or bare "nothings" (316a 28). For a better comprehension of this argument, the sense of the difficult line, 316a 20, should be taken to be just that indicated at n. 37, above: bisect (divide κατὰ τὸ μέσον) similarly (ὡσαύτως: *a* to get *b* and *c*; then *b* and *c* to get *d* and *e*, and *f* and *g*, respectively; and so forth) and completely (καὶ ὅλως δέ, *i.e.*, until no part is left undivided; Joachim's rendering [the Oxford translation, followed also in the Loeb] "by any other method," is very strained and in any case unnecessary, since a simple translation makes good sense).

44 *GC*, I. 2, 316b 35.

45 Without actually saying so. Cf. *GC*, I. 2, 316a 14; cf. H. Cherniss, *Aristotle's Criticism of Presocratic Philosophy* (Baltimore, 1935) p. 113, but note also the striking similarities with *GC* 325a 8–10, noticed at nn. 38 and 39, above, and further that the inference from infinite divisibility to the dissolution of existents into non-existents is endorsed by Epicurus, *Ep. ad Hdt.* 56, and seems to be echoed also by Lucretius, I. 746–56.

46 For "texts," not "traditions" (so Lee, p. 22), to be supplied after τοῖς παρμενιδείοις, cf. Simplicius 116.6 and 19, also 144.28.

47 Lee (p. 31) thinks "Simplicius clinches his argument [for the Zenonian authorship of the Porphyry text] by quoting this argument [B3] from Zeno's own book as being sufficiently similar to the argument in question [that of the Porphyry text] to justify him attributing it to Zeno." But the subject of φέρεται at 140.27 is the same as that of ἀπομνημονεύεται just before, which can only be the ἐκ τῆς διχοτομίας ἀπορία, *not* the Porphyry text as such.

48 B1, B3.

49 Plato, *Parmenides*, 127 E ff.; Simplicius 139.5 ff., 141.10.

50 Its authorship must remain unknown, though we may surely list Melissus as an important source for [B]. He too argued formally for the same demonstrandum (cf. his B 9 and B 10), and made explicit use (at his B 7) of the Parmenidean premise that being is "all alike," from which the key proposition is derived at the start of [B] that being must be "divisible throughout" and not "just here, but not there": both of these expressions occur, as we have seen (nn. 38 and 39, above) at *GC*, I. 8, 325a 3–13, which seems to be principally a report of Melissean doctrine (the initial argument, "no motion, if no vacuum," is properly his [B7 (7–10)], and the next one, "no plurality if no vacuum" is most likely to be his, since he is the only Eleatic known to have used the non-existence of a vacuum as an explicit dialectical premise).

51 There might still be the objection that "so small as to have no size" is linguistically idiosyncratic. But Zeno does want a special effect here: to make the contrast with "so large as to be infinite" at [not-U] as loud as possible. Is it too loud? Not for his purpose; he wants to startle.

52 The strength of this link in the argument would be doubled by Fraenkel's (p. 17) brilliant emendation of ἄπειρον for ἀπείρων of the MSS. at Simplicius 139.15. For then Simplicius' epitome of B 1 at 139.17–18 would be attached directly to [not-U], instead of merely, as on the present reading to [Q]. But I am not sure the emendation is correct: the style of ἄπειρον, etc. seems a little too spry for Simplicius.

53 Also, of course, the unobjectionable premise that the magnitude of *a* equals the sum of the series $b+d+f+h+\ldots$ (cf. the diagram at III, above).

54 Fraenkel (*loc. cit.*) also refers to Aristotle's use of *apeiron* at *Phys.* III. 6, to refer to a convergent series. But here *apeiron* is predicated of the series (not of its sum, as it would have to be in our fragment) and does mean "infinite."

55 Good example in Liddell and Scott, *s.v.* B.1.

56 *Phys.*, III. 6, 206b 7–9. For the best translation and explanation see T. L. Heath, *Mathematics in Aristotle* (Oxford, 1949), p. 106.

57 There is, of course, nothing in the premises of Zeno's argument to *require* (a) that the $b+d+f+\ldots$ series decrease in constant ratio, or (b) that the assumed magnitude of *a* be finite. But both (a) and (b) are *consistent* with the premises, so that if their addition sufficed to defeat the conclusion (as it does) the dialectical force of the whole argument would be ruined.

58 *Physics* 142.14; cf. also 168.34–169.1, 459.23–24, 460.2–4, 462.3–5; *De Caelo* 608.15. From ibid, 459.25–26 it would appear that Eudemus held the same view. Eudemus, needless to say, is a competent historian of mathematics, and so perhaps is Simplicius himself (cf. pp. 60 to 69 of his *Physics*).

59 *Ep. ad Hdt.*, 56–57. For some comment, see my "Minimal Parts in Epicurus," *ISIS*, 56 (1965): 121–47, at p. 141 and notes.

60 Cf. the paper cited in the preceding note, p. 127 and notes.

[61] Which would even be true if taken to mean, "given any part, there is always a smaller." In spite of verbal appearances, the two statements would be *contraries*. Cf. Bertrand Russell, *Our Knowledge of the External World*, revised edition (London, 1926), pp. 141–42.

[62] But cf. n. 68, below.

[63] I suspect that the equally fallacious argument at Lucr. I. 615–22 also comes from Zeno: its affinity to his B 3 is obvious, and it can be recast into the same, "If *P*, then *C* and not-*C*" form—If any part, *a*, of the universe, *u*, is infinitely divisible, then the number of parts in *a* and *u* is equal (since infinite in both) and unequal (since *u* has all the parts of *a* and also all the parts of parts other than *a*).

[64] Ps.-Arist., *De Lineis Insec.* 968a 18 ff., 969a 26 ff., 969b 16 ff. All these references are to the Race-Course. But 968a 3–7 looks like a reference to our B 1, though without ascription to Zeno. Cf. also Philoponus, *Phys.* 84.15 ff. The testimony of Alexander *ap.* Simplicius 138.10 ff., and of Simplicius himself, 140.13 ff. and 142.16 ff., is not so clear.

[65] Cf. Aristotle, *Phys.* I. 3, 187a 2–3.

[66] J. E. Raven, "The Basis of Anaxagoras' Cosmology," 48 (1954): at 126–28.

[67] We are fortunate in having these original fragments, for from Simplicius (461.7–9) and from *De Caelo* 608.15 one might have gathered that Anaxagoras did make the same fallacy. But note that Simplicius does not profess to be paraphrasing at this point, but only to be drawing an inference (συννοεῖν) from the foregoing. He assumes that the inference he would draw (sc. that everything is infinitely large: n. 58, above) from the premise that everything has an infinite number of parts would also be drawn by Anaxagoras. The only thing in Anaxagoras' fragments that might lend color to this imputation is the last sentence of B 3, and it is significant that Simplicius did *not* cite it in support of his interpretation. I would translate, "in relation to itself each thing is both great and small," and would interpret: when we take a thing just by itself, the determinations "large" or "small" become matters of indifference; a grain of sand is small only by comparison, say, to a stone; taken by itself there is no more reason for calling it "small" than "large."

[68] That Anaxagoras should be so emphatic on this point (note that "no smallest" at B 3 is strictly unnecessary: the sentence might as well have read simply "of the small there is always a smaller" as the next one does read "and of the large there is always a larger") could mean that he thought this was the source of Zeno's fallacy.

[69] The best statement of the theory is still that of its originator, Paul Tannery (*op. cit.*, chapter on Zeno). For influential adherents: Burnet, *Early Greek Philosophy*, 3rd ed., (London, 1920), pp. 310 ff.; Cornford, *op. cit.*, pp. 58 ff.; H. Cherniss, *op. cit.*, p. 43 and pp. 155–61. Raven (*op. cit.*, 126) speaks of this view, with some reason, as now "generally accepted." But *contra*, e.g., G. Calogero, *Studi sull'Eleatismo* (Rome, 1932), pp. 115 ff.; N. B. Booth, "Were Zeno's arguments directed against the Pythagoreans?", *Ph*, 2 (1957): 95 ff.

70 *Gnomon*, 25 (1953): 31–32.

71 *Meteo.* 100b 7–19. I have made liberal use of the Oxford translation.

72 I am adopting Fraenkel's (p. 18) deletion of ὄν at line 11. Without the deletion the sense would still be pretty much the same.

73 *I.e.*, even if we were to assume that what Zeno says at (ii) is true.

74 A perfectly adequate paraphrase of the closing part—[4] at (II), above—of our B2. The substitution of "added/subtracted" for "attached/detached" in the original (cf. n. 15, above) is scarcely culpable in this context.

75 ὡς δηλονότι. For other uses of this expression to mark a constructive inference see *Phys.* I. 4, 189b 10, *De Caelo* I. 10, 279b 28.

76 Similarly at (i) Zeno is not represented as having *said* that unity, if indivisible, would be nothing, or even that what is indivisible would be nothing. "Zeno's *axioma*" is clearly what Zeno *assumed*, *i.e.*, (ii): cf. Cherniss' excellent paraphrase, *op. cit.*, p. 43, n. 165.—As for "theory" at (vi), it refers to (ii)+(iii)+(iv)+(v), *i.e.*, to what Zeno "says" *and* what follows from it.

77 *Op. cit.*, p. 317.

78 *Commentary on the Metaphysics*, I, p. 246. But Ross does not explain why he thinks this is the case. Shortly before (p. 245) he appears to be recognizing that (ii) is all that Aristotle ascribes directly to Zeno.

79 Even if μηδὲ ἕν were the correct text here (so Diels; but μηδέν or μηθέν in the same quotation, Simplicius 139.1), the sense would still be "nothing" ("not even one").

80 But even if Eudemus were professing to be giving us at (viii) information of what Zeno said, the gift would be of dubious value, since Eudemus seems to be following not Zeno's text but Aristotle's paraphrase: his reference to "point" at (viii) and his shift to προστιθέμενον, ἀφαιρούμενον and use of [οὐ] τῶν ὄντων εἶναι at (ix) reveal his direct dependence on the Aristotelian passage.

81 *I.e.*, that of the fragments. As for the secondary evidence, the best of it, Plato's, is ambiguous: at *Parmenides* 128AB Plato puts the gravity of Zeno's argument on a level with that of Parmenides himself; at *Phaedrus* 261D ff. he associates Zeno with the orator who makes the same things take on contrary appearances, and thus seems to think of him as an artificer of deception, whence Cornford (*op. cit.*, pp. 67–68) infers that "Plato seems to have thought of him as a mere sophist." But note that Plato does not impute to Zeno *intentional* deception or deliberately sophistical arguments, and that in calling him the "Eleatic Palemedes" associates him with inventors (cf. *Republic* 522D, *Laws* 677D), not charlatans. The reference to Zeno as a professional sophist (taking fees) is only in *I Alc.* (119A).

82 Here I meet Fraenkel (pp. 193, 206) half-way.

83 The *reductio* is, of course, also Parmenides' stand-by; but he does not cast his arguments in the form which would exhibit the fatal consequences of the refutand as a pair of contradictory propositions.

84 On the above reconstruction of S1, "no existent has size" would be true for Zeno, since it follows from [Z1], [Z3], and [Z4], not one of which

he would have reason to doubt. This conclusion gets some added support from the fact that it would preserve consistency with the pattern of argumentation suggested at *Phaedrus* 261D 7–8, which may be expanded and rephrased in the light of *Parmenides* 127E 1–2 as, "If there are many, then each would be both homogeneous and heterogeneous, both one and many, both at rest and in motion." It will be noticed that the first term in each of the contradictory pairs—"homogeneous" (ὅμοια; cf. Parm. B 8.22 and Mel. B 7.1), "one," "at rest"—would be a true predicate of Eleatic Being. So would the first term of the corresponding pair—"no size and infinite size"—in the present argument.

[85] I too have missed this prior to the present study: I ascribed the innovation to Melissus [*Gnomon*, 25 (1953): 34–35]. Since Zeno's book was written in his youth (*Parmenides* 128D), it is reasonable to assume that it preceded any writings by Melissus.

[86] I cannot attempt to defend here my view that the incorporeality of Being is entailed by Parmenidean doctrine, but is not *asserted* by Parmenides probably because he himself did not clearly see the entailment.

LEONARD WOODBURY
University of Toronto

Parmenides on Names*

> ταὐτὸν δ' ἐστὶ νοεῖν τε καὶ οὕνεκεν ἔστι νόημα.
> οὐ γὰρ ἄνευ τοῦ ἐόντος, ἐν ᾧ πεφατισμένον ἐστιν,
> εὑρήσεις τὸ νοεῖν· οὐδὲν γὰρ ἢ ἔστιν ἢ ἔσται
> ἄλλο πάρεξ τοῦ ἐόντος, ἐπεὶ τό γε Μοῖρ' ἐπέδησεν
> οὖλον ἀκίνητόν τ' ἔμεναι· τῷ πάντ' ὄνομ(α) ἔσται,
> ὅσσα βροτοὶ κατέθεντο πεποιθότες εἶναι ἀληθῆ,
> γίγνεσθαί τε καὶ ὄλλυσθαι, εἶναί τε καὶ οὐχί,
> καὶ τόπον ἀλλάσσειν διά τε χρόα φανὸν ἀμείβειν.
>
> (B 8.34–41)

THIS is the text that is printed by W. Kranz in the sixth edition of H. Diels's *Die Fragmente der Vorsokratiker* (Berlin 1951).[1]

No one is astonished to find a queer verse in Parmenides, but line 38 appears to be unusually eccentric. The editors attempt to translate it: "Darum wird alles *blosser* Name sein," but the italics seem to betray their embarrassment. And no wonder; for the line is full of oddities. The singular is singular indeed, and when it is forced to mean "mere Name," by which is meant "meaningless as mere Name," it begins to look stranger still. The antithesis of ὄνομα and οὐσία does indeed occur in later literature, but it is unlikely, on general grounds, to be used before the sophistic age. ὄνομα and ἔργον, on the other hand, although found in the contemporary text of Heraclitus, cannot be fitted into this passage.[2] The use of the future tense is to say the least surprising, although at a pinch it may be taken as the *futurum consequentiae*, of which philosophers, being given to drawing inferences, are said to be fond. It may be that even goddesses, in the act of making revelations to privileged men, may experience moments of recognition of a necessity in things, when they pass from the ignorance of the past into the knowledge of the future, and that they do not possess an unchanging knowledge of a timeless reality; it may be, although we should not expect Parmenides to

* A slightly revised version of a paper presented at the 1957 meeting of the SAGP in Washington, D.C. Reprinted from the *Harvard Studies in Classical Philology*, LXIII (1958): 145–60 (published in honor of Werner Jaeger), by permission of Harvard University Press. Square brackets are used in the notes to indicate revised and new notes.

speak as if this were the case. Still, even these peculiarities might be acknowledged and dismissed as harmless, were it not for the incongruity of the verse with its context.

Let us look first at what follows. The editors translate the next line thus: "was die Sterblichen *in ihrer Sprache* festgesetzt haben, überzeugt, es sei wahr," and this is, I think, clearly right. The ellipsis is easy after what has preceded, but if confirmation of this interpretation is needed, it is found in B 19.3: τοῖς δ' ὄνομ' ἄνθρωποι κατέθεντ' ἐπίσημον ἑκάστῳ. The meaning of the two lines is this: all the institutions (of speech) that mortal men have established in the belief that they are true will (turn out to) be Name. This is either disappointingly barren or alarmingly pregnant. If "Name" means no more than "word," then the lines make a true, but empty and tautologous, statement. If, on the other hand, it means what it says, we are left to conjecture of what the institutions of speech can be a name.

In the lines that precede Parmenides makes the point that nothing, not even thought, can exist apart from that-which-is, for *Moira* holds the that (which is) in bonds, so that it is whole and immovable. Or, to put it differently, the that must be and must be whole and immutable; all else is, as it were, excluded and cast into not-being. Then our sentence follows, preceded by "therefore." The difficulty is: what is the connection of thought which is thus explicitly indicated? How does it follow from the exclusion of not-being that the institutions of speech are (or will be) Name? Parmenides goes on to give examples of the institutions of speech that he has in mind: becoming and perishing, being and not-being, change of place and play of color. These terms, as we are told elsewhere, are used in combination by mortal men in their contradictory accounts of things.[3] They mark the road of δόξα, not the road of truth. Parmenides is therefore, on the accepted interpretation, making the inference that all institutions of speech made by mortal men are false. But how is this point made clear by stating that they are Name? Only, so far as I can see, if the reader is to supply for himself the assumption that none of these names refers to anything real and all of them are given to figments of the imagination.[4] Parmenides will then be understood to argue that, since that-which-is exists whole and unchangeable, all the terms used by mortal men which describe a different kind of world must be false, because they name something that is imaginary but not real. This would be intelligible, but Parmenides does not, here or elsewhere, give us any ground for making the assumption. Indeed, if he held this view, it would be crucial for his conception of δόξα. It is incredible that he should have omitted all mention of it in his treatment of the road of δόξα but have required that it be supplied silently by the reader in a quite different context. Finally, if Parmenides held for this reason that all names instituted by men are false, we must enquire how he would have justified his own assertion of the necessity of saying, as well as thinking, "it-is."

Whatever fault may be found with Parmenides' verses, everyone must recognize that in rigor of argument his poem is unrivaled among contemporary thinkers. Before charging him with a fault in argument, we are obliged to consider whether the defect may not lie in the text. This must in any case be inspected.

These lines are quoted, as part of a long fragment of Parmenides' poem, by Simplicius in his commentary on Aristotle's *Physics* (146.7–14). He apparently had the complete text before him; at any rate, he quotes at length, because, as he says, copies of Parmenides were scarce in his day. Diels, in the apparatus of his edition of Simplicius, reports the readings of the MSS thus: "πάντ' ὠνόμασται DEF (later πάντ' ὄνομ' ἔσται cf. p.87.1): πᾶν ὄνομ' ἐστὶν a" (a is the Aldine edition of 1526). The correction that Diels here proposes is based on a reading in an earlier passage of Simplicius' commentary (87.1), in which only two and a half lines are quoted. There his apparatus gives the following note: "τῷ πάντ' ὄνομ' ἔσται a: τῶ πάντ' ὄνομα ἔσται F: τῶ πάντ' ὀνόμασται E . . . τῶ πάντ' οὔνομα ἔσται D." This time F, which Diels judged to be of lesser authority,[4a] and the Aldine edition give the reading that he commends, whereas E has a variant of the reading given by the MSS in the long fragment; D supports F in its division of words but may betray the influence of ὠνόμασται in its unmetrical οὔνομα.

Both here and in his edition of the *Vorsokratiker* Diels has preferred the reading πάντ' ὄνομ' ἔσται, in spite of the powerful considerations that point in the other direction. These arise from the following facts: he attributes inferior authority to the MSS in which this reading occurs; in the passage in which Simplicius is quoting at length and so most likely to be following closely his text of Parmenides, the MSS are unanimous in giving ὠνόμασται; in his brief quotation Simplicius has chosen to end with line 38, thereby implying that πάντ' is comprehensible without the following lines, as it may be if πάντ' ὀνόμασται is read but can hardly be with the alternative reading. Diels's principal reason for rejecting such considerations was, I suppose, that ὠνόμασται is unmetrical and ὀνόμασται ungrammatical.

The latter is indeed rare but, I believe, authentic.[5] It occurs as a variant again in another passage of the same commentary of Simplicius (180.9–12), in which he quotes another fragment of Parmenides (B 9). The following is Diels's text of the first two lines[6]:

αὐτὰρ ἐπειδὴ πάντα φάος καὶ νὺξ ὀνόμασται
καὶ τὰ κατὰ σφετέρας δυνάμεις ἐπὶ τοῖσί τε καὶ τοῖς . . .

In his apparatus Diels reports: "ὀνόμασται aF[1]: ὠνόμασται DEF[2]." The former has the weaker authority, but is of course preferable on metrical grounds.[7] Moreover, in yet another passage of Simplicius' commentary (31.3–7) there is a paraphrase in prose of a portion of Parmenides' argument (B 8.56–59). This portion deals with the two opposite principles which are the basis of the opinions of mortal men and was followed at a short interval, as Simplicius says (180.8), by these lines. The paraphrase states that the one principle comprises the rare, the hot, light, and so on; ἐπὶ δὲ τῷ πυκνῷ ὠνόμασται τὸ ψυχρὸν καὶ ὁ ζόφος κτλ. The verb, which does not occur in the text of which the paraphrase is made, has been borrowed, it is conjectured, from these lines, which were found a little further on; or it may have been taken from the lost lines that intervened. In either case the form ὀνόμασται must have occurred in one of Parmenides' hexameters.[8] There seems to be no reasonable doubt that the form was used by Parmenides; it may have been pressed into service in verse by others as well.[9]

If we return now to the lines of Parmenides with which we began, we see that ὀνόμασται has better manuscript authority and does not deserve the suspicion with which it is regarded. However, one further difficulty remains. Plato, in a passage of the *Theaetetus* (180D), refers to those who, like Melissus and Parmenides, opposed the doctrine of flux and affirmed that all things were one. He quotes the following verse:

οἷον ἀκίνητον τελέθει τῷ παντὶ ὄνομ' εἶναι.

The same line is also quoted by the invaluable Simplicius, who says (29.16–18): ἀκίνητον αὐτὸ ἀνυμνεῖ καὶ μόνον ὡς πάντων ἐξῃρημένον. In another place (143.10) he gives it with a minor variant in some MSS (πάντῃ in aDF). Some scholars, relying on Simplicius' μόνον, correct οἷον to οἶον, rightly I think.[10]

Diels and others have taken this to be the same verse, a little distorted by Plato, who was notoriously lax about looking up his quotations, and copied faithfully from him by Simplicius. If this is correct, it must be granted that this quotation of the text supports ὄνομ' ἔσται rather than ὀνόμασται.

Fortunately, there is little reason to suppose that it is correct, as Cornford has shown in an illuminating argument.[11] Why should Simplicius, who apparently had the text of Parmenides before him and quotes from it often, have on this occasion copied Plato's misquotation? If he did, it is clear that he cannot have supposed it to be the verse with which we are concerned, for he was able to quote this twice, exactly or with substantial exactness, in its context. Plato, for his part, had studied Parmenides closely. It is incredible, Cornford argues, "that he produced a verse meaning '*It is sole, immovable. The All has the name "Being"*' out of the end and the beginning of two sentences meaning 'Since Destiny has fettered it *so as to be whole and immovable; therefore all those things will be a (mere) name* that mortals have agreed upon', etc. This is not a case of 'arbitrarily completing a single ill-remembered verse.' It is hard to conceive the mental process that could generate such a hybrid in the most slovenly brain. Plato was not slovenly, and he had a deep respect for Parmenides." We must conclude that this is a different verse and irrelevant to our present purpose. The tradition of the text favors ὀνόμασται.

Furthermore, if ὀνόμασται is accepted, τῷ cannot mean "therefore," as it is commonly translated; for the institution of names is not a consequence of the exclusion of not-being. In order to understand, it is necessary to recognize the construction, ὀνομάζειν (or καλεῖν) ἐπί τινι.[12] It occurs often enough, being found, for example, in Parmenides, Empedocles, Thucydides, Euripides, and Plato. It is used of the relationship between names and reality, as in Plato (*Parmenides* 147D): ἕκαστον τῶν ὀνομάτων οὐκ ἐπί τινι καλεῖς; (*Theaetetus* 185C): ᾧ τὸ ἔστιν ἐπονομάζεις καὶ τὸ οὐκ ἔστιν. The dative with τίθεσθαι occurs without ἐπὶ in Parmenides (B 19.3): τοῖς δ' ὄνομ' ἄνθρωποι κατέθεντ' ἐπίσημον ἑκάστῳ and in Herodotus (1.148.1): ὀρτήν, τῇ ἔθεντο οὔνομα Πανιώνια.[13] It is regular with καλεῖν, as in Plato (*Politicus* 279E): τούτοισι . . . τὸ μὲν ὄνομα "ἱμάτια" ἐκαλέσαμεν; (*Cratylus* 385D): καλεῖν ἑκάστῳ ὄνομα.[14] I have noticed no other certain example of the simple dative with ὀνομάζειν,[14a] though there is a probable parallel in Hesiod (fr. 116.2 Rzach: 235.2 Merkelbach-West): καὶ οἱ τοῦτ' ὀνόμηνʼ ὄνομ' ἔμμεναι.[15] In the construction with which we are concerned it is evidently conceived that the name is put on, or given to, that which is named. It is usually the case that either the name is identified by the use of ὄνομα or the nominee by that of ἐπί, but such constructions may dispense with both, as in ὀνομάζειν or καλεῖν τινί τι, or in Plato's τίθεσθαι τινί τι (*Theaetetus* 157B; *Cratylus* 392D and 402B).[16] In the passive ὀνομάζεσθαι ἐπί is used with specific names as subjects, as in Empedocles (B 8.4): φύσις δ' ἐπὶ τοῖς ὀνομάζεται ἀνθρώποισιν: "The name of φύσις is given to these by mankind." καλεῖσθαι is used similarly, but with the simple dative, as in Euripides (*Hec.* 1271–73): τύμβῳ δ' ὄνομα σῷ κεκλήσεται . . . κυνὸς ταλαίνης σῆμα.

The meaning of the lines now appears: "With reference to it (the real world)[17] are all the names given that mortal men have instituted, in the belief that they were true, becoming and perishing, being and not-being, change of place and play of color."[18] On this interpretation, lines 38–41 follow smoothly upon the verses that precede. The names that mortal men give *must* be given to that-which-is, because there *is* nothing else to which they can refer.[18a]

The names that mortal men institute, although false and deceptive, are not mere fancies or illusions of the mind. They are accounts of the one real world, to the existence of which men's beliefs are at times committed. But men's convictions are not steadfast, because they have accepted the authority of appearance (δόξα) and are held fast in the contradictions of the dualism to which this testifies. The road that they have chosen can never lead them to truth, because it must forever turn back upon itself in contradiction, affirming and denying in turn the being of the world. The names which they set up as signposts along the way share necessarily in this fatal error. They say, as Parmenides points out, that it comes to be but also perishes, that it is but also is not, that it suffers change of place and play of color. All the names that mortal man make contain the light of truth, but this is inevitably snuffed out by contradictions.[19] The question remains: is there any name, not made by men, of which the light cannot be put out?

In order to seek an answer, it is necessary to consider the difficult lines at the beginning of our passage. First, thinking is said to be the same as οὕνεκεν ἔστι νόημα. Then Parmenides continues: "For you will not find that thinking without that-which-is, in which it is expressed. Nothing is or shall be apart from that-which-is, since *Moira* bound that so as to be whole and unmoved."

Probably the commonest way of taking οὕνεκεν is to give it the meaning of τὸ οὗ ἕνεκα.[20] The verse then means: "thinking is the same as the purpose (or the foundation, or cause, or necessary condition) of thought." The latter term is then identified with the "that-which-is" of the next line and "thinking" is supplied as the subject of "is expressed." The meaning attributed to οὕνεκεν seems dubious, but what condemns the interpretation is the sense that it ascribes to Parmenides. He is made to distinguish that-which-is from thinking in two ways: it is the purpose or cause of thinking and it is that in which thinking is expressed. But on the other hand thinking is the same as that-which-is, since both are identified with the purpose of thought. It is not easy to conceive how these statements can be reconciled so as to form a consistent whole; for, if that-which-is is the purpose or cause of thought as well as the bearer of its expression, then it must be something more than thought: but if it is the same as thought, then it may indeed be thought's expression, but it can never be the cause of thought or the bearer of thought's expression. The usual means of escaping the dilemma is a recourse to either idealism or realism. Either that-which-is is reduced to a product of mind, or else thinking is limited by an objective reality. Theoretically speaking, these lines of escape are open, but who will say that Parmenides' own words, or those of his contemporaries, point clearly in either direction?

It is better to take οὕνεκεν in the sense of "that,"[21] which is common in Homer. This meaning provides the translation: "thinking is the same as the thought that it-is." It is evident that we have here a statement of the form that thinking must take. We are reminded of that way of which Parmenides says (B 2.4) that it belongs to Conviction and follows after Truth: it asserts that "it-is." Thinking can take no other way than this, and it must follow that it then takes the form of the thought that "it-is."

This is the correct road to the truth about the real world. Anyone who thinks at all must think this, for the only alternative is the thought, "it-is-not." Parmenides, as is well known, did not distinguish clearly between the meanings of "is." Most statements about the world that contain this word were existential, and consequently negative statements of this form connoted nonexistence. But Parmenides is in search of the right road to the truth about reality. For him a negative existential statement about the world cannot provide such a road, for it can only mean that the real world does not exist. A road that denies the existence of its destination cannot lead anywhere. This is the sense that we must attribute to Parmenides' doctrine that the way of not-being is neither thinkable nor speakable.[22] It is evident that he cannot have meant that no statement of this form can be made, since he himself formulates such a statement before duly rejecting it. He does not mean that the vocables cannot be uttered, nor that the statement has no meaning. What he denies is that it can refer to anything real. It is impossible that the object of this thinking, which is the real world, should be nonexistent. If we are to think about the real world at all, we must think that "it-is" and cannot think that "it-is-not."

It is now possible to grasp the movement of the argument in these lines. Thinking can take only one form ("it-is"), because thinking of this kind and that-which-is are inseparable (and so thinking can never be found "with" anything else, nor in any other form than "it-is"). This is because (there cannot be anything else, "with" which thinking might be found, since) that-which-is is unique, being necessarily whole and unmoved. The argument moves from thinking to that-which-is. It asks why thinking can take only one form and answers that the necessity of being, which makes that-which-is unique, does not permit an alternative. It is evident that Parmenides finds in being a limitation upon thought and cannot therefore have held any view that reduced being to thought.

On the other hand, it is no more likely that he regarded thought as determined by being. We may grant that it is possible that the mind is somehow limited by an objective being, but Parmenides goes further than that: he says that thinking must take the form "it-is," and that that-which-is-not can be neither thought nor spoken. How could the mind be compelled, by a necessity not its own, not merely to take a certain form, but to use a certain word? How could an objective being compel the mind to use the expression, "it-is" and to refrain from saying "it-is-not"?

Parmenides' words simply do not give a clear statement of either of these theories. It seems prudent, therefore, to seek another account of his thought, preferably one that is less sophisticated than either of these, and so more appropriate to the early fifth century B.C. It is plain that Parmenides conceives of a necessary relation between the thought "it-is" and the real world. The question is: what is that relation?

The answer is to be found, I believe, in the second line of our passage. There, in the course of saying that thinking and that-which-is are inseparable, Parmenides adds a most significant, though subordinate, clause. He speaks of "that-which-is in which it is expressed." The "it" is generally held to be "thinking," although doubts have been felt about this.[23] Now if Parmenides said that thinking is expressed in that-which-is, we face the same metaphysical dilemma as before. He could not, in that case, say either that that-which-is is an expression of thinking or that thinking is determined by that-which-is. There would be an "expression" of thinking, but it would carry beyond the mind to find itself "in" that-which-is. Burnet indeed notices the difficulty and translates, "*as to which* it is uttered,"[24] but I cannot reconcile this version with Parmenides' Greek. It seems better to ask whether it would not be preferable to supply a different subject.

I believe that we must supply as subject here, just as in so many other passages, the real world,[25] which appears often in the fragments explicitly as "this" (τὸ or αὐτὸ) and implicitly in the formula "it-is." In our passage it is emphatically present in the recurrence of the article in the immediately preceding lines, first in the repeated τοῦ ἐοντος, then in the pointed τό γε, and climactically in the τῷ of line 38. Parmenides would then say that the real world is expressed in that-which-is and would thus state definitely how he conceived the relation between "it-is" and the real world. Thinking must take the form "it-is," because the real world is "expressed in" that-which-is, and consequently in the thought, "it-is." Conversely, "it-is-not" is unthinkable and unspeakable, because the world is not "expressed in" it.

Parmenides' imagery points in the same direction. He does not say that he is searching his mind or his experience in order to find truth. He is in search of the right road. This implies that a right road exists, among the thoughts or words that are in use, and leads only to truth. It is not something that man can make, nor a means that he devises to any of his ends. It is something to be discovered: it is the track—and contains the expression—of the real world itself. It must lead to truth, because the real world is "in" it. When we think of the real world by means of the thought that "it-is" and conceive of it as "that-which-is," and severely eschew the opposite thoughts, we have found that track and cannot fail of its goal. This thought teaches us how to conceive of the real world, and so constitutes the only way by which the mind can achieve its purpose in the apprehension of truth. We must conceive of the real world, not as "it," but as "that-which-is," if the world is to become intelligible. We can grasp it only in its aspect as being; that is to say, as expressed in that-which-is.

However, Parmenides, I take it, conceives of a necessary expression of the real world as the manifestation of the world, not to the mind alone, but in language as well. "That-which-is" and "it-is," even considered as words, evidently contain expressions of the world, since the one contains, and the other implies, the "that." The expression of the world is necessarily to be found in "being" as well as in being. Parmenides says repeatedly that we are compelled to speak, as well as to think, in a certain way.[26] There are correct forms of words, with which thought cannot dispense, which it must use if it is to follow the right course. "That-which-is" and "it-is" are such forms. Both are, of course, uses of the word "being," which, when used of the real world, is necessarily true, because the real world is seen to be "in" its uses. "Being" is more than a word: it is the world's name.

It now becomes profitable to consider the fragment that Cornford discovered in the quotations made by Plato and Simplicius. It runs thus, in its emended form:

οἷον ἀκίνητον τελέθει τῷ παντὶ ὄνομ' εἶναι.

It does not, it must be admitted, seem at first sight a likely verse to be chosen as the epitome of Parmenides' philosophy. Yet Plato certainly quoted it to serve that purpose, and Simplicius, who quotes it twice, appears to give independent testimony for the text. What can be made of it?

Cornford commented as follows: "the only suspicious word is τελέθει, which (according to Diels, *Vors.* Index) the Presocratics never use to mean 'is.' Empedocles uses τελέθειν (once) and ἐκτελέθειν in their proper sense 'to arise,' 'to grow'—an association that Parmenides would avoid in speaking of his changeless Being." On this ground Cornford felt justified in conjecturing τε θέλει and compared a famous fragment of Heraclitus: ἓν τὸ σοφὸν μοῦνον λέγεσθαι οὐκ ἐθέλει καὶ ἐθέλει Ζηνὸς ὄνομα (B 32). He then proposed placing this new verse after B 19 at the end of the poem in this way:

⟨τούτων οὐδενὶ πίστις ἔνι· μοῦνον γὰρ ’Ανάγκη⟩
οἷον ἀκίνητον τε θέλει τῷ παντὶ ὄνομ’ εἶναι.

and translated: "but all these names are false; for Necessity is willing that the All should *only* be called one and immovable." An attractive consequence of this conjecture is that it would provide a definite echo of the language of Heraclitus as well as a rejection of his doctrine.

Now it is true that τελέθει does not occur in the surviving fragments of Parmenides' poem, but Parmenides cannot have avoided it for the reason that Cornford gives.[27] Although εἶναι is his most characteristic word, he does not hesitate to use πέλειν in its place, presumably for metrical reasons. Yet this word has similar connotations of becoming and change,[28] and Parmenides does not refrain from using a verb of motion even of the immovable that-which-is, as in his ἐὸν γὰρ ἐόντι πελάζει (B 8.25; cf. 8.46–47). The use of τελέθει is possible in Parmenides and is evidently attested independently by Plato and Simplicius. If it were nevertheless to be rejected, a simpler emendation could be found in τε πέλει.

In either case we have a verse of not more than Parmenidean uncouthness. Its meaning, I take it, would be: "One and unmoved is the name of the all—'being'." The main construction of the sentence is similar to that in another fragment of Heraclitus[29]: τῷ οὖν τόξῳ ὄνομα βίος, ἔργον δὲ θάνατος (B 48). Although τὸ πᾶν does not occur elsewhere in what is left of Parmenides' poem, it is used by other early philosophers, occurring several times in Empedocles (B 13,14,39.3), for example. Moreover, the MSS of both Plato and Simplicius, with substantial agreement, attribute the expression to Parmenides. Still, it is worth noticing that Parmenides, who uses πᾶν often enough in apposition to the subject of the verb "is," does not elsewhere use τὸ πᾶν. It is possible that παντὶ had for him, in this case also, an appositional function. If this is correct, the effect of the word is to give strong assurance that the name applies to all of reality whatsoever, just as in another passage (B 8.33) it serves to make plain that, as reality is lacking in nothing, so that-which-is-not would be completely defective. It is well to observe that ἐόν also occurs sometimes with, and sometimes without, the article; πᾶν may have been used similarly. On this interpretation the meaning of the verse is: " 'Being' is the one and unchanged name of all of it."[29a]

Cornford's fragment gives direct confirmation in this way of the interpretation suggested for B 8.34–36. "Being," in its various verbal forms, is the correct name and "it-is" the correct thought, by means of which we attain to truth. The verse that states this is most important for the understanding of Parmenides. Plato was therefore, so far as we can see, perfectly justified in quoting it as the type of the Parmenidean philosophy of rest. Indeed, I cannot find in our fragments any other verse that would have served his purpose equally well. The verse says, it is true, rather more than he needs, since he is not here concerned with names at all. Nevertheless, if no better text was available, Plato was quite ready to turn whatever he could find to his purpose.[30] This is quite evident from his choice of Homer's mention of "Ocean, the well-spring of all things, and mother Tethys" (*Il.* 14.201 and 302) as the first statement of the philosophy of movement. The verse of Parmenides required a good deal less interpretation in order to serve as an example on the one side than Homer's innocent mythology needed on the other.

The view which we have now attributed to Parmenides, that reality is expressed in a certain thought and name,[31] is of course common among unsophisticated people.[32] The name speaks the truth about things: ὄνομα ὄρνις; the *nomen* is an *omen.* In a famous passage of the *Agamemnon* (681–698) the chorus reflect on the name of Helen and wonder who it was who named her so truly—perhaps some one unseen who spoke the name happily with fore-knowledge of what was to be. For she was "Hell-on-ships, hell-on-men, hell-on-cities." Sophocles' Ajax, brooding over the disaster that has befallen him, groans αἰαῖ and then asks who would have thought that his name would so truly fit his tragic fate (430–433). The Aeschylean chorus conceives that Helen's name may fit the disaster that she was to become: that is "expressed in" Helen. Sophocles is, as usual, more subtle. The form of the old belief is preserved, for the name proves true and the truth is conceived as a fitting of name to fate. But it is not made clear, as in Aeschylus, that this is the work of divinity, or even of nature; and the correspondence between name and fate, whether real or fancied, is a matter of surprise as much as of wonder. The lines do not seem to bear the full weight of the old meaning, and yet to reduce the idea to a conceit is to make it trivial and insipid. Sophocles, on this as on other occasions, knew how to balance the old form against the new rationalism. It will be remembered that even Aristophanes, who could weigh with precision the verses of Aeschylus and Euripides, did not venture to set a line of Sophocles in the balance.

Once the real thing is recognized as "in" that-which-is, the true name is not only the "fitting" or the like, but the "being," name. Herodotus provides a good example. He tells us (6.50.3) that Cleomenes asked Crius what his name was; and the other told him τὸ ἐόν.[33] We are likely to translate: "he told him what it was." But it would be better to turn τὸ ἐόν as "his true name," and better still as "his real name": that is, not simply the name which men give to him, but the name by which the real man is truly known—that in which his reality is expressed.[34] Even Plato, who did not believe that reality was to be found in any names or statements, nevertheless preserved the old connection between the λόγος and being, although in an altered form: for "being" (εἶναι) is for him the λόγος that we give of reality (οὐσία).[35]

It is now possible to see the meaning of what has seemed at once the plainest and the most inscrutable of Parmenides' statements:

τὸ γὰρ αὐτὸ νοεῖν ἐστίν τε καὶ εἶναι (B 3).

These words appear to say that thinking and being are identical, but what they mean is harder to determine. Some commentators take the statement at its face value, and some of these are willing to accept the consequence that being thinks.[36] Others, who rightly reject the attribution of such a view to Parmenides, attempt to force the words to mean that the same thing can be thought and can be. This in turn is said to mean that only that which can be thought can be, and being is thus reduced to the thinkable. But the interpretation is hard won—if won it is—from the text and there is much in Parmenides that prevents us from attributing such a view to him. The best suggestion was made by Heidel,[37] who related this fragment to B 8.34 and so took the meaning to be that thinking is the same as thinking that it (the object of thought) is. There is, in other words, one and only one right form of thought. This interpretation accords very well with the view that there is one correct name and thought, which we have found reason to ascribe to Parmenides. The difficulty about Heidel's interpretation is that it requires the reader to supply νοεῖν again with εἶναι, and it is not very clear that such an ellipsis is regular or even possible.

It seems better to accept the simplest version, that thinking and being are the same, and to consider, in the light of what we have learned, what that can mean. "Being," as we saw, is more than a word: it is the name of the real world. Not even thought can dispense with it, but must take the form of the thought that "it-is." If we now go a step further and ask what is the meaning of that name and that thought, we are reminded that, in fifth-century Greek, νοεῖν serves for "mean" as well as for "think." τί ποτ' οὖν νοεῖ τὸ ὄνομα; What can be the meaning of that name? The answer can only be that it means the being of the real world, or, in Parmenides' terms, τὸ ἐόν. It is now customary to translate this as "that-which-is," but it would probably be more exact to turn it as "that-as-being" or "that-in-being," for Parmenides says that it is "in" this that the real world (the "that") is "expressed." There is a reciprocal relation between the world and "being." On the one hand, "being" (εἶναι), considered qua name, is only a name; but, as the name of the world, it is being itself (equally εἶναι). On the other hand, the world (τὸ) is expressed in that-in-being (τὸ ἐόν), which is the world named. Name and world are reciprocally dependent, since a name implies that world of which it is a name and the world, which must find expression, can find it only if the name is used of itself.[38] The name refers to the world but means the world in being.

νοεῖν has been until now translated, for convenience' sake, as "mean" or "think," but these renderings will no longer suffice, since it now appears what is implied when νοεῖν is used, as by Parmenides, not of a word or a thought, but of the name of the world. The object of νοεῖν is that-in-being, and in consequence νοεῖν can here stand only for that knowledge which perceives the world as it is. Knowledge of being can be found only in the meaning of the name, "being." Parmenides' philosophy of names leads directly into his ontology. But we have no text that asserts the identity of knowledge with its object, of νοεῖν with τὸ ἐόν. The text that has so often been thought to make this assertion says in fact something quite different. It says that νοεῖν is the same as εἶναι, and this must mean that knowledge, like the right thought and meaning, can be found only in the use of the name. The only way is a μῦθος ὁδοῖο, ὡς ἔστιν.

Werner Jaeger has taught us to take seriously the theological significance of Parmenides' proem and to see at the heart of his philosophy a "Mystery of Being."[39] What I should venture to propose to him is that the meaning of the goddess's revelation is that the world is expressed in "being," and that Parmenides' holy mystery is the reality of a name.

NOTES

[1] My best thanks are due to the John Simon Guggenheim Memorial Foundation of New York for the grant of a Fellowship in 1956–57, which provided me with the leisure necessary for the writing of this paper.

[2] For examples of these antitheses, cf. H. Diels, *Parmenides: Lehrgedicht* (Berlin, 1897), pp. 86–87; F. Heinimann, *Nomos und Physis* (Basel, 1945), pp. 52–56.

[3] Cf. B 6.8–9; 8.55–59; 9 etc.

[4] Cf., for example, Plat. *Republic* 493BC for a clear statement that δόξα is named.

[4a] [A. H. Coxon, in *CQ*, 18 (1968): 70–75, now argues, against Diels, that F is "the main representative of the better tradition of the text" of Simplicius' commentary on Arist. *Phys.* 1–4.]

[5] For the loss of the temporal augment in the reduplication of the perfect tense, cf. Herodotus' use of forms such as ἀρτέαται (1.125.3; cf. 6.109.6); οἰκέαται (1.142.4); ἅρμοσται (3.137.5); οἴκισται (4.12.2, where Hude, however, prefers οἴκηται). Cf. R. Kühner, *Ausführliche Grammatik der griechischen Sprache* besorgt von F. Blass 1.2[3] (Hanover, 1892), pp. 19–21; E. Schwyzer, *Griechische Grammatik* 1 (Munich, 1939), p. 655.

[6] P. Von der Mühll has conjectured νενόμισται at B 9.1, with references to Plato's *Republic* 515B and T. Nissen in *Phil*, 91 (1936): 271, n. 2: cf. Heinimann, *Nomos und Physis* (see n. 2 above) p. 49, n. 17. On the similarity between ὀνομάζω and νομίζω, cf. Heinimann, *loc. cit.* and E. Laroche, *Histoire de la racine* NEM – *en grec ancien* (Paris, 1949), pp. 222; 238, n. 9a. But the conjecture has no support either in the MSS of Simplicius or in the scholion; no parallel for νομίζω ἐπί with dative is adduced and no explanation given of the meaning to be attributed to the expression in a text that is earlier than the radical sophistic antithesis of νόμος and φύσις. It is evident that B 6.8 does not confirm the proposed construction of B 9.1–2.

[7] Cf. Pind. *Ol.* 9.50 (Turyn), where the correct reading is ὀνύμασθεν but one MS gives ὠνύμασθεν.

[8] For examples from Homer of forms of the perfect or pluperfect tenses in which the initial vowel is not lengthened in a place in which the metre would forbid lengthening, cf. ἀλιτήμενος (*Od.* 4.807) and ἱέρευτο (*Il.* 24.125). Cf. also P. Chantraine, *Grammaire homérique*[2] 1 (Paris, 1948), pp. 421–22.

[9] The form may have been used by Theognis: cf. *Studies in Honour of Gilbert Norwood*, *Phoenix* Suppl. vol. 1 (1952), p. 33.

[10] Cf. Plato's own interpretation and Parmenides B 8.36–37. It is unlikely that οἷον is Plato's word for introducing a quotation, since he seems not to use it for this purpose: for Plato's formulas in quotation, cf. J. Labarbe, *L'Homère de Platon*, Bibl. de La Fac. de Philos. et Lettres de L'Univ. de Liège fasc. 117 (Liège, 1949), pp. 39–40. For a parallel to the asyndeton of οἷον ἀκίνητον cf. B 8.27. For the confusion of οἷος and οἶος, cf. Schol. on Pind. *Nem.* 4.151.

[11] Cf. F. M. Cornford in *CR* 49 (1935): 122–23; *Plato's Theory of Knowledge* (London, 1935), p. 94, n. 1.

[12] For the construction, cf. R. Kühner, *Ausführliche Grammatik* besorgt von B. Gerth 2.1[3] (Hanover and Leipzig, 1898), p. 319, n. 1. Cf. ἐπίφημι, ἐπιλέγω, ἐπονομάζω, ὄνομα ἐπιφέρω, κτλ.

[13] On ὄνομα τίθεσθαί τινι, cf. *LSJ s.v.* ὄνομα I.2 and Kühner-Gerth, *Ausf. Gramm.* 2.1[3], p. 45.

[14] On ὄνομα καλεῖν τινι, cf. *LSJ s.v.* ὄνομα I.3.

[14a] [In all earlier editions of Pollux, beginning with the Aldine edition of 1502, that I have been able to consult, the text of 10.137 includes the sentence: ὠνόμασται δὲ τῷ κιβωτίῳ παραπλήσιόν τι σκεῦος κανδύταλις. E. Bethe in the second volume of his edition, published as vol. 9 of the *Lexicographi Graeci* in 1931, gives ὡμοίωται δὲ τῷ κιβωτίῳ [παραπλήσιόν τι σκεῦος] κανδύτανες. His apparatus reports no more than: ὡμάταιε τῷ II (II is the common source of F and S). But on p. xviii of his first volume of 1900 he had written: "Ceterum saepius quam adnotavi codices vel codicum archetypi pusilla quaedam variant, ex gr. verba λέγεται, ὠνόμασται, καλεῖται, καλοῦσι." It remains therefore unclear what is the reading of the MSS, while the evidence provided by Bethe, though corrupt, is slightly closer to ὠνόμασται than to ὡμοίωται, which he prefers. In sense ὠνόμασται seems to be superior, as Pollux is primarily concerned with distinctions of names rather than of objects and the reading ὡμοίωται is tautologous with παραπλήσιον. If παραπλήσιόν τι σκεῦος is an interpolated gloss on the rare name, the latter argument disappears, but the text containing ὠνόμασται then runs more easily.]

[15] [The construction is not quite certain enough to make it by itself a decisive parallel. It is possible to suppose that τοῦτ' ὀνόμηνʼ is the equivalent of a verb of saying and οἱ is a possessive dative with the dependent ὄνομ' ἔμμεναι. There are several objections to such a construction. First, in early Greek, names are names *of* something and when given are given *to* something. Parallels are therefore urgently required to support the view that τοῦτ' ὀνόμηνʼ could give an independent sense, "he pronounced this name." Then, Greek usage develops what grammarians call a "pleonastic" or "epexegetic" infinitive in dependence upon a verb of naming. Cf. *LSJ s.vv.* ὀνομάζω II.2 and καλέω II.3.b; also n. 34 below and especially *Pind. Ol.* 9.63–64: μάτρως δ' ἐκάλεσσέ νιν/ἰσώνυμον ἔμμεν, which shows how to take the Hesiodic verse. Finally, if it is granted that we have here a naming construction and that the nominee is indispensable, the position of οἱ is evidence that the dative was either governed by τοῦτ' ὀνόμηνʼ or jointly by this expression and by its relation with the dependent clause. It seems therefore probable, if one judges by the passages cited by *LSJ*, that the verb governs the noun or pronoun and does not develop into a verb of saying, although it may be influenced by such verbs: cf. H. W. Smyth, *Greek Grammar* (Cambridge, Mass. 1956), sections 1615, 1981; cf. also section 2011; Kühner-Gerth, *Ausf. Gramm.* 2.2[3], pp. 9–11, 2.1[3], p. 44. For a parallel case, the development of the meaning and syntax of νομίζω, cf. Laroche, *Hist. de la rac.* NEM- (see n. 6 above) p. 225. The Hesiodic construction appears to have something in common with the syntax of ὀνομαίνω in the sense, "promise," "designate" (cf. n. 31 below), as in Hom. *Od.* 24. 341–42: ὄρχους δέ μοι ὧδ' ὀνόμηνας/δώσειν πεντήκοντα. In

fact, Hesiod's usage may be brought under the general rule that in naming constructions the dative may be used of the nominee in place of the accusative, ὄνομα καλεῖν τινι in place of ὄνομα καλεῖν τινα.]

[16] [The use of κεῖσθαι with the simple dative, even when not a naming construction, offers an illuminating parallel. Cf., e.g., Archil. fr. 70.2, D[3]: Λεωφίλῳ δὲ πάντα κεῖται and *LSJ s.v.* κεῖμαι IV.5.]

[17] For examples of similar asyndeton, cf. B 1.4, 15, 20; 8.50, 54.

[18] The parallel in Heracl. B 67 will be evident: it is the one Fire that is named, but many names are given to it.

[18a] [The varied arguments that have now been brought forward by L. Tarán, *Parmenides* (Princeton, N.J., 1965), pp. 120 ff., especially pp. 129–36 against this reading and interpretation are fatally weakened by his failure to mention the evidence of the MSS, to supply any instance of the use of ὄνομα in an earlier text in the sense required ("mere name"), or to consider how older views might be revised in the light of a new interpretation.

W. J. Verdenius has now published an illuminating study, "Der Logosbegriff bei Heraklit und Parmenides" [*Ph*, 11 (1966): 81–98; 12 (1967): 99–117], in which he argues for a general view of Parmenides that has important similarities to my own. However, he rejects (114, n. 51) the reading of B 8.38 which is defended here. Apart from grammatical doubts, his objection seems to be that it would be incompatible with Parmenides' distinction between the world of being and the world of change to connect that-which-is with the names used by men. Nevertheless, he himself conceives of the basic Parmenidean distinction as one between "absolute and relative reality," in which the latter reflects, represents, or approximates (117) the former. He therefore agrees that ὄνομα cannot be "mere (or meaningless) name" and concedes to it at least a relative value, like that of all things in the world of appearance. He does not, so far as I can see, face the question why ἔστι (which is an ὄνομα according to Cornford's fragment and is certainly used by the speech of mortal men) has an absolute value for Parmenides. He denies that the infinitive γίγνεσθαι could be an ὄνομα of a substantive such as τὸ ἐόν. No reason is given for this judgment, but if he means that it must be a ῥῆμα rather than an ὄνομα, it is sufficient to reply that the distinction is unknown before Plato (*Cratylus* 399 AB, 425A, 431B; *Sophist* 262A) and that the infinitive is an ὄνομα in Cornford's fragment (as is the finite ἔστι in Plato, *Theaetetus* 185C and verbs generally when not used predicatively in Arist. *De Interpr.* 3). In general, it seems that Verdenius' theory can easily accommodate the view that the divine name and human names have parallel functions. His theory may in fact be improved by such an adjustment, for it might explain why the two worlds are related in the way shown.]

[19] This statement obviously has implications for the interpretation of the much-discussed fragment B 16. Here it must be sufficient to point to the presence of νόος in the context of the way of opinion.

[20] This interpretation, which goes back to Simplicius (*Phys.* 87.14; 144.23), was adopted by Diels, and by many others after him. For a collection of translations reflecting this interpretation, cf. E. D. Phillips in *PR*, 64 (1955): 550 ff.

[21] This interpretation has been preferred by many, including Heidel, Fränkel, Von Fritz, and Cornford: cf. W. J. Verdenius, *Parmenides: Some Comments on his Poem* (Groningen, 1942), p. 39, n. 2.

[22] Cf. B 2.7–8; 8.16–17.

[23] It is not necessary for my present purpose, nor indeed possible in a short paper, to criticize the variety of scholarly opinions that have been put forward in interpretation of this passage. Cf., however, Phillips and Verdenius in nn. 20 and 21 above.

[24] Cf. J. Burnet, *Early Greek Philosophy*[4] (London, 1930), p. 176.

[25] This is the view of Verdenius, *Parmenides* (see n. 21 above), p. 32. [But cf. now *Mn*, ser. 4, 15 (1962): 237, where he finds the subject to be ἀλήθεια in the sense of "the true nature of things."]

[26] Cf. B 2.7–8; 6.1; 8.8, 17, 50–52, 53; 19.

[27] I am indebted to Professor F. Solmsen for pointing out to me that Plato, who quotes Hes. *Op.* 122 twice, gives in one passage (*Cratylus* 398A) καλέονται, but in the other (*Republic* 469A) τελέθουσιν.

[28] Cf. *LSJ s.v.* πέλω with Parm. B 6.8; 8.11, 18, 45.

[29] For examples of the construction, cf. Kühner-Gerth, *Ausf. Gramm.* 2.1[3] p. 45.

[29a] [The comments of L. Tarán, *Parmenides*, pp. 133–36, are hard to follow. On. p. 134 he finds in the line the meaning "all things are one," but on the following page he states that "the last part of the line contains the assertion that Being is the name of all." Tarán does not show how it is possible to construe the line in such a way that it yields both translations, and he is further embarrassed because he holds that Parmenides cannot have held either doctrine. He is therefore inclined to think that the text is corrupt or that Plato "either misquoted the fragment or purposely parodied line 38 in order to make it fit his context." But he neither assesses the corruption nor explains what Plato may have intended by his misquotation or parody, or what Simplicius, who had the text of Parmenides at his elbow, may have taken it to mean.]

[30] It is perhaps worth mentioning that Plato elsewhere (*Parmenides* 142A), when dealing with an undifferentiated One such as that of Parmenides, thinks it worthwhile to make, in addition to other criticisms, the point that such a One cannot have a *name*.

[31] Cf. the use of ὀνομάζω, ὀνομαίνω, φατίζω, (ἐπι)φημίζω in the sense of "promise," "betroth," "devote," etc. The act of specifying by name has a power of its own.

[32] Cf. E. Cassirer, *The Philosophy of Symbolic Forms* (New Haven, Conn., 1953–55), 1.117–19; 2.40–41. In describing the function of language in mythical thinking, Cassirer writes (2.40): "in all this the basic presupposition is that word and name do not merely have a function of describing or portraying but contain within them the object and its real powers."

[33] For many examples of the use of τὸ ἐόν, cf. J. E. Powell, *A Lexicon to Herodotus* (Cambridge, 1938), *s.v.*

[34] Cf., e.g., Herodotus' use (1.95.1; 116.5) of ὁ ἐὼν λόγος and (7.143.1) of τὸ ἔπος εἰρημένον ἐόντως. The account and the word are not merely true,

but real. Cf. E. Boisacq, *Dictionnaire étymologique de la langue grecque* (Heidelberg and Paris, 1938), p. 291 for the connection of ἐτά, ἐτάζω, ἐτεός, ἔτυμος, ἐτός and ἐτήτυμος with ἔσ-τι. The notion that reality is a result of naming seems to underlie the construction of a "pleonastic" εἶναι in dependence upon a verb of naming. Cf. Plat. *Protagoras* 311E: σοφιστὴν... ὀνομάζουσι... τὸν ἄνδρα εἶναι; Pind. *Ol.* 9.63–66 and *Pyth.* 9.63–65; and *LSJ s.vv.* ὀνομάζω II.a and καλέω II.3.b. Cf. n. 15 above.

[35] Cf. *Phaedo* 78D. At *Cratylus* 425D, E Plato warns explicitly against taking words in this way. R. B. Levinson in *RM*, 11 (1957): 39 writes that "for Plato language is, as Friedländer has well put it, something *with* which, not *from* which, knowledge accrues."

[36] Cf. Phillips (see n. 20), 547–52.

[37] Cf. W. A. Heidel in *PAA*, 48 (1913): 720.

[38] It follows from this reciprocal dependence that not only the world, but also the right "way" to it, *is*: cf. B 8.18. The right way, like Crius's name in Herodotus, should be called "being" as well as "true." This notion appears to underlie the construction noted in Emped. B 8.4 and Parm. B 8.38–41 and such expressions as καλεῖν ὄνομά τινι, (see p. 149 and n. 14 above): the name is also a thing, and so it may be named or called, as well as given to something. If naming is a kind of fitting together of two *things*, it does not matter whether we say that the fitting A is applied to B or that A is fitted to B. ἐπώνυμος may be used either of the name that is given to someone or of the thing that is "named on" (as we should say, "gives its name to") the person: cf. Hom. *Od.* 19.409 and Soph. *Aj.* 574; in both cases name-thing fits on (ἐπί) the person. But when naming becomes a purely mental act names may be given to things in the sense of being taken to refer to them. They cannot any longer be fitted to, or "named on," them.

[39] Cf. W. Jaeger, *The Theology of the Early Greek Philosophers* (Oxford, 1947), p. 107.

PLATO

R. E. ALLEN
University of Toronto

The Argument from Opposites in *Republic* V*

REPUBLIC V (475A–480A) contains one of the first statements in European philosophy of the doctrine of degrees of being and reality. Plato there distinguishes two types of object, νοητά and δοξαστά, two Worlds, the Worlds of Knowledge and Opinion. And he holds that, of these Worlds, that of Knowledge is the more real.

This distinction has sometimes been read as purely epistemic, resting not on things, but on our (often defective) knowledge of them: there is one world, not two, though it may be apprehended in two ways. But this view is patently at odds with the text. Knowledge and opinion are δυνάμεις, "faculties," to be distinguished and defined by their objects, no less than by the state of mind they produce (477D), and Plato clearly states that the fallibility and unclearness of opinion is rooted in the relative unreality of opinables (479C).

The unreality of opinables is a paradox, but a paradox which is also a solution. Plato faced a Parmenidean problem, that of reconciling the sensible world with criteria of reality it cannot satisfy. To be real is to be intelligible, not qualified by opposites, self-identical, and unchanging. The sensible world is none on these things, and it therefore cannot be real. But an unreal world is a philosophical embarrassment, especially when it happens to be a world in which we live. To say that it is in *no* sense real is impossible; for it must in some sense exist even to be illusion. The alternative is to suppose that there are degrees of being and reality, and this alternative Plato chose: There are objects of opinion; they are qualified by opposites; and they are *not* fully real. Plato held true what Parmenides had held impossible, that "things that are not are" (DK 7). The objects of opinion are intermediate between full reality and complete unreality.

* Read before the Society for Ancient Greek Philosophy (hereinafter abbreviated as SAGP), December 27, 1961 at New Haven, Connecticut. Reprinted by permission from *The Review of Metaphysics*, XV (1961): 325–35.

This thesis he supported by a proof of the existence of Forms based on an argument from opposites (*Rep.* V 479A–C). Everything beautiful is ugly: everything just, unjust; everything holy, unholy. What is double is no less half, and the same is true of large and small, light and heavy. Such things as these have an ambiguous character: they are "neither real, nor not real, nor both real and not real, nor neither real nor not real."[1] They whirl about between being and not-being, objects of opinion, not of knowledge. The objects of knowledge are αὐτὰ ἕκαστα, the Forms, which are fully real and not qualified by opposites.

This argument is admirably brief and succinct, and singularly unconvincing. It does not, by itself, demonstrate that Forms exist, nor that things qualified by opposites are less than fully real. For that, certain missing premisses must be supplied.

2. The opposites Plato mentions are all contraries: both of each pair cannot apply at the same time and in the same respect to the same thing. It has therefore sometimes been thought that Plato condemned the reality of sensible objects on the ground that they are internally self-discrepant or self-contradictory—a time-honored defense for theories of degrees of reality.

Within an Idealistic system, such a view is not absurd. If one regards space, time, and physical objects as mental constructions produced by inadequate understanding, it is not unreasonable to regard contradiction as the invariant symptom of that inadequacy. So Bradley, for example. But the Idealist does not suppose that what exists may be self-contradictory; on the contrary. He supposes that what exists may *appear* to be self-contradictory—as indeed it sometimes does. Strictly, Idealism does not suppose that there are degrees of reality, but only that there are degrees of understanding.

Whatever may be the merits of this view, it is not Plato's. There is nothing in the middle dialogues to suggest that there would not be degrees of reality even if there were no minds: the mind discovers its objects, and does not produce them. Therefore, if Plato's ground of complaint against δοξαστά is that they are self-contradictory, he must have held that contradictions not only appear to exist, but exist.

This is a view only a skeptic or a fool could hold, and Plato was presumably neither. To attribute it to him is to assume that he used a fallacious argument to reach an absurd conclusion, and contradicted himself to boot. For earlier in the *Republic* (IV 436B, E), with physical examples in mind, he had rejected as impossible the view that anything can be incompatibly qualified. The premisses of the argument from opposites do not imply the inconsistency of δοξαστά; and in light of his expressed opinions, there is no reason to suppose that Plato thought they did.

The argument assumes that anything qualified by one opposite will be qualified by the other,[2] and further, that this joint qualification is consistent. What type of predicate will satisfy those conditions? The prime candidates, are plainly relational predicates, especially comparatives, since joint qualification follows from the internal logic of such terms. To say, for example, that a thing is tall is implicitly to say that it is taller than something else; compared to some third thing, properly chosen, it will also be short. Plato's examples of large/small, double/half, light/heavy, are relational in just this sense, a fact of which he was aware (cf. *Rep.* IV 438B ff.). It is because they are relational that such opposites imply their opposites,[3] and introduce no genuine contrariety into the things they jointly qualify.

The argument also treats evaluative opposites as relational. There is nothing beautiful which is not ugly, no good which is not evil—a concise statement of the vanity of mortal longings, perhaps, but not, one assumes, of mortal logic. It is not enough to suppose that the same things may be good and bad in different respects; for there would then be no internal reason why something should not be good, or bad, in every respect, and so not qualified by opposites. If evaluative opposites are to imply their opposite, and not to imply contradiction, they must be relational; to say of anything that it is good must be to say that it is better than some things and worse than others, and therefore also bad. If this account of Plato's use of evaluative predicates is sound, it will follow from his argument that there are Forms such as Ugliness, Injustice, and Evil. Those Forms are mentioned by name at *Republic* V 475E–476A.

3. The argument from opposites is offered to prove that Forms exist. Its sense becomes clearer in Book VII (523A ff.), where it is held that reflection is provoked when the same object produces two opposite impressions, and not provoked when such opposition does not occur. Consider, for example, the fingers of a hand. One is larger, the other smaller, a third between them in length. They are all equally fingers, and the mind is therefore not compelled to reflect on what it means to be a finger. But with the *size* of these fingers it is different, for sight presents two opposite qualities with equal clearness, declaring that the third finger is both large and small. When this happens, the mind is driven to

question what the senses mean, and so comes to regard largeness and smallness as distinct things, confusingly mingled in the thing seen. In asking what is meant by large and small, the mind is led to distinguish objects of intelligence from objects of sight.[4]

This is an important argument. Its sense may, I think, be put, however little in Plato's terms, as follows. If it is granted that opposites imply opposites, then the sense or meaning of the terms which connote them cannot be identified with the things to which those terms apply. If F and G are opposites, then "F" and "G" differ in sense. But *ex hypothesi*, whatever is an F is also a G, and *vice versa*. Therefore, if the meaning of "F" and "G" were identical with the things which are F and the things which are G, the meaning of "F" and "G" would be identical. Which is absurd. In short, if opposites imply opposites, the sense of the terms which connote them cannot be "just the things we see." (Cf. *Parmenides* 130D.) Nominalism is impossible: there is a logical distinction between the intension and the extension of comparative or relational terms. Combined with the theory that the meaning of a term is what it refers to, which Plato in the middle dialogues characteristically assumes, the distinction becomes ontological; the argument from opposites establishes what it was introduced to prove: that Forms exist.

It also throws light on the question of what sorts of Forms there are. Substantive terms such as "finger" have no contraries (cf. *Phaedo* 104A–B, 105A, *et passim*), and are not relational. The argument from opposites does not establish Forms for such terms, and the discussion of 523A ff. strongly suggests that there are no such Forms (cf. esp. 524D, 9–525A 2). This is presumably why Socrates in the *Parmenides* is in doubt whether substantival terms do not refer to "just the things we see," and why the only clear Forms in the middle dialogues are opposites. The Shuttle of the *Cratylus* (389B) and the Bedstead of the *Republic* (X 596B) are plainly chosen for their value as examples; the substantives used in the final proof of immortality in the *Phaedo* (e.g., "fire," "three," "soul") are not said to refer to Forms, though the opposites connected with them (e.g., "hot," "odd," "life") seem so to refer; and the often-cited remark at *Republic* X 596A, that we may posit (τίθεσθαι) a Form answering to every common term of discourse, is perhaps no more than a prescription for philosophical method, not an ontological claim at all. It seems likely that, in the middle dialogues, there are no Forms of substances.

But if the argument from opposites establishes the existence of Forms, and helps to determine what sorts of Forms there are, it does not directly establish that things qualified by opposites are less real than the Forms which qualify them. That conclusion follows, if it follows at all, from the inner character of the relation between Forms and particulars.

4. What is that relation? The context in which the argument occurs helps provide an answer.

The distinction between the Two Worlds is drawn in order to define the nature and objects of the philosophical life, and to distinguish it from that of the "lovers of sights and sounds" who superficially resemble philosophers. The latter delight in beautiful tones and colors and shapes, and the works of art into which these enter, but they lack the power to apprehend Beauty itself, and are unwilling to follow a guide who would lead them to it (476B–C). The mental state of such men is that of a dream, and their dream is the dream of opinion. Dreaming is defined as believing that a likeness is not a likeness, but an original, believing "a resemblance not to be a resemblance, but the very thing it resembles" (476C). Philosophers, on the other hand, know the original of these likenesses, know that there is such a thing as Beauty itself, and recognize both it and the things that partake of it (τὰ ἐκείνου μετέχοντα) without confusion. Such men are awake, not dreaming; have knowledge, not opinion. The objects of knowledge are Forms; it is clearly implied that the objects of opinion are the likenesses of Forms in the sensible world. τὰ μετέχοντα are εἰκόνες or εἴδωλα. Forms, their originals, are παραδείγματα (cf. *Republic* V 472C 4–5, 472B, 479A; VI 484C–D). μέθεξις is copying.[5]

This conclusion is confirmed, if confirmation is needed, by a parallel argument in the *Phaedo*. In the second proof for Anamnesis (73B ff.), the Equal itself is distinguished from particular equal things on the ground that particular equals—sticks and stones, for example—sometimes seem equal to one thing but not to another,[6] whereas Equality never seems to be inequality. It follows that equal things and the Equal itself are ἕτερα ὄντα.

What is the relation between them? Particular equals "fall short" of Equality, and are "deficient" with respect to it (74D 5–7, E104, 75A 2–3, B4–8). Their deficiency is teleological: they "wish" to be like the equal (74D 10); they "desire" to be of its nature (75A 2), and desire it urgently (75B 7). This discussion applies to every Form (75C–D); it implies that the relation of particulars to Forms is one of frustrated finality.

Since goals have no reality apart from the things that pursue them,

Forms are not goals. Purposive activity, for Plato, is exemplified by the craftsman, looking to a model and producing copies. Those copies are different in kind from their original: as the painter looks to a bed and produces a picture of a bed, so the carpenter looks to the Form of a shuttle and produces a shuttle that can be made and broken[7] (cf. *Republic* X 596B–E, *Cratylus* 398B). Particulars are "deficient" because they are a different sort of thing from the Forms they resemble. Their relation to Forms is analogous to the relation of a reflection of a bed to the bed reflected. They "fall short" of their Forms as the reflection of a bed falls short of a tired man's hope. In the *Phaedo*, as in the *Republic*, participation is copying.[8]

5. The copy theory of participation sheds important light on what Plato meant by saying that Forms are not qualified by opposites. In the *Hippias Major*, Hippias remarks to Socrates, "You seem to me to be seeking the reply that Beauty is something of such a sort that it will never appear ugly to anyone anywhere." Socrates replies, "Now you understand me beautifully." (291D, cf. 289C, 292E, 294A–B; *Lysis* 217E). In *Symposium*, Diotima puts the claim still more strongly (211A; cf. *Phaedo* 74B–C, 102D–103A, 103B:

> (Beauty itself) is not beautiful in one respect and ugly in another, nor beautiful at one time and at another not, nor beautiful in one relation and ugly in another, nor beautiful here and ugly there so that it is beautiful to one man but not to another.

The point of this strenuous affirmation is not merely that Beauty itself is not identical with ugliness or qualified by it: it is that the Form of Beauty is the exemplar of beauty. It is supremely beautiful, and other things cannot approach it in beauty[9] (*Symposium* 211D). In the *Phaedo*, Socrates remarks that "If there is anything else beautiful besides the Beautiful itself, it is so because it partakes of that Beautiful."[10] The denial that Beauty itself is in any sense ugly is merely the obverse of the thesis that Beauty itself is *just* beautiful, *pure* beauty, αὐτὸ τὸ καλὸν εἰλικρινές[11] (*Symposium* 211E 1; cf., e.g., *Republic* V 478E 1–3, *Phaedo* 66A 2–3). Forms are not qualified by opposites because they are purely what they are; particulars, because they fall short of their Forms and are mere resemblances of them, are mixtures of opposites.[12]

6. If the foregoing analysis is correct, the argument from opposites in *Republic* V is intimately connected with what has sometimes been called self-predication. No Form is qualified by its opposite: Beauty

itself, for example, is not ugly. The obverse of this proposition is that Beauty itself is beautiful, and as we have seen, Plato in some sense believed that obverse true.

This line of reasoning grates harshly on the logical ear: it seems to confuse two distinct senses of "not." Cows are not purple because they are some other color. Middle C is not purple because it is not any color at all. That Beauty itself is not ugly is plainly a truth of the latter kind: it is not the sort of thing that *could* be ugly, and to suppose otherwise is to suppose nonsense. But just as Beauty itself cannot be ugly, neither can it be beautiful; to make such a claim is to commit a type confusion, to assimilate the Form to its particulars. The inference from "Beauty itself is not ugly" to "Beauty itself is beautiful" would appear to be vicious, not valid.

Further, it *is* vicious, *if* Plato was committed to self-predication, and confused Forms with their particulars. But he did not. Forms stand to particulars, not as predicates stand to instances of predicates, but as originals stand to shadows or reflections. Participation is copying. The bearing of this analogy on the question of self-predication is direct.

Let us suppose (the figure is not original) a group of people chained fast in a cave, and so situated that all their lives they have seen nothing but shadows and reflections on the wall before them. Because they are not acquainted with the originals of their reflections, they will believe that the reflections are themselves originals. They will talk about what they see, and their language will suit their situation. For example, they may call bed-images beds, and shuttle-images shuttles.

Next let us suppose that one of the group (we might call him Socrates) is released, made to turn around, and so for the first time to see the originals of his shadows. He will find himself subject to a peculiar linguistic strain: he will have no words appropriate to these new objects. Ordinary beds, the ones to which he is accustomed, are in fact images of an original which he is now privileged to inspect. Yet that original is not in the ordinary sense a bed at all. But since ordinary beds are images of it, he will find it natural to call it too a bed; only in order to prevent confusion, he may specify the peculiar sort of bed he means: he may call it, not merely a bed, but the Bed itself. By so doing, he would mark the fact that the original Bed is not, in the *ordinary* sense, a bed; for a bed in the ordinary sense is merely an image.

If Socrates returned to his companions in the cave, and had to answer questions about what he had seen outside, he might reply as follows. "You call this a bed, and that a bed, but in truth those are not *real* beds at all. They are merely reflections (you know what a reflection is, since you have seen reflections of reflections) of the one real bed, the Bed itself." If he were asked whether the Bed itself is a bed, his reply would no doubt be, "How not? Of course it is a bed, and preeminently a bed. Ordinary beds are mere images of it. But please understand, I mean something very different, in calling it a bed, from what I mean when I call these things that we are used to seeing beds. For they are only reflections of the Bed. To say that the Bed itself is a bed is in some sense trivial—who could think otherwise?—and I mention it only in order that you may understand that the Bed itself is the original of those other beds.

This figure is easy for the imagination to grasp; but as an illustration, it is not wholly apt. "Beauty itself is beautiful" is equivalent to "Beauty itself is not ugly." But no parallel equivalence holds for substantival terms like "bed," since substantival terms have no opposites; and we have found reason to believe that Forms are posited only for terms which have opposites. To present the copy theory of participation, then, in terms of substantives, is to sacrifice exactness of thought for ease of understanding; but this is no great flaw. It may be difficult, perhaps impossible, to *imagine* that beautiful things are resemblances of Beauty itself in a manner analogous to the way in which reflections of a bed are resemblances of that bed. But there are many things which we cannot imagine which we can yet understand. The illustration chosen here is of course Plato's; and though perhaps inaccurate, it serves its purpose well.

The bearing of the figure on the issue of self-predication is obvious. It is natural to call copies and originals by the same name. To do so is merely to emphasize their community of character, the fact that copies are resemblances of originals. But the same term has a different significance when applied to these different sorts of things. What appears to be self-predicative language in Plato is in fact only the natural result of construing participation in terms of resemblances and originals; and it reflects a very different view of the relation between universals and particulars than any we are now accustomed to accept. Self-predication, the type confusion many critics have claimed to find in Plato's Theory of Forms, is a mare's nest.

7. To sum up: Particulars are resemblances of Forms, and depend upon them both for their character and their existence. Because they are resemblances, particulars fall short of their originals, and because they

fall short, they fail to satisfy the criteria of reality. For example, they are qualified by opposites, not εἰλικρινές. They therefore cannot be said to be real. But neither are they wholly unreal, for they are resemblances, however deficient, of real things. And so, in a perfectly legitimate and intelligible sense, they are both real and not real: real in that they *are* resemblances, not real in that they are *resemblances*. The copy theory of participation and the theory of degrees of reality are not two theories, but one. That theory reconciles the existence of the sensible world with criteria of reality it cannot satisfy.

NOTES

[1] 479C 3–5, following Adam and Cornford.

[2] That joint qualification holds in every case, and not merely in some, follows from the sense of 479B–C, and also from the fact that if any F thing were *purely* F, it would *be* F (cf. 478E 1–3).

[3] Opposites such as these admit of no logical extreme. For example, there is no largest, or smallest, possible thing, a fact which anyone familiar with the Zenonian problems of infinity, and their treatment by Anaxagoras, must surely have known (cf. *Philebus*, 24A–25A).

[4] This discussion should be carefully distinguished, as Plato suggests at 523B from that of 602C ff., where sense error and the illusions of perspective lead to qualification by opposites. The fact of sense error does not imply that Forms exist, but only that we sometimes misapprehend particulars, a type of misapprehension to be dispelled by counting, weighing, and measuring. What is at issue in 602C ff. may be the difference betweein εἰκασία and πίστις; it is clearly not the difference between δόξα and ἐπιστήμη. The argument from opposites turns on the fact that particulars *are* (and do not merely seem) qualified by opposites. Measurement will only confirm the appearance that my third finger is both large and small (cf. VII 523B 5–7).

[5] Similarly, the image analogy is central to the interpretation of the figures of the Sun, Line, and Cave, which carry forward the discussion of the Two Worlds (cf. VI 507A–C).

[6] This analysis of the argument requires reading τῷ . . . τῷ in 74B 8–9, and translating, "Do not the very same things—equal sticks and stones—sometimes appear equal to one thing but not to another?" This reading and translation are supported by 74A 9–10: φαμέν πού τι εἶναι ἴσον, οὐ ξύλον λέγω ξύλῳ οὐδὲ λίθον λίθῳ . . . The argument, so read, is that of *Republic* V. See also *Epistle VII*, 344A–B.

[7] The final expression of this view of finality is the *Timaeus*, where the universe is the artifact of a divine Craftsman, looking to Forms as his model. It is not certain that this figure should be taken literally: the teleology of the *Phaedo* (97B ff.) in many ways similar to that of the *Timaeus*, perhaps significantly makes no explicit reference to a craftsman-god. There is good reason to hold, with Cornford, that the Demiurge is not a distinct entity, but a symbol of the rationality of the world-process. If this is true, μέθεξις is not

literally μίμησις; but this does not touch the question of whether particulars are resemblances of Forms, but only that of how they come to be resemblances. It seems clear that Plato regarded particulars quite literally as εἴδωλα, even though perhaps not literally as μιμήματα.

[8] At 74D 8–E 4, Socrates remarks: "When anyone sees something and thinks, 'This thing I now see wishes to be like something of a different sort but falls short and cannot be of such sort as that—it is inferior'—the man who happens to think this must have known in advance, I suppose, the thing which he says the other resembles, but falls short of." ἄλλο τι τῶν ὄντων is ambiguous: it may mean "a different thing" or "a different *sort* of thing": the latter meaning is prescribed by 74C 7–9. Particulars resemble, and differ in type from, Forms. Cf. *Phaedo*, 100A 1–3: "I certainly do not agree that the man who examines τὰ ὄντα in λόγοι is examining them ἐν εἰκόσι to a greater degree than the man who examines them in ἔργα." Both λόγοι and ἔργα are images of τὰ ὄντα—though the former are doubtless the more revealing. For ἔργα in this sense, see *Cratylus*, 389C 1. Note that "ὄντα" differs in sense in 74D 10 and 100A 2: in the former passage, it is generic, including both originals and likenesses, whereas in the latter, it includes only originals.

[9] The following brief remarks are perforce dogmatic. They are meant to supplement the argument of "Participation and Predication in Plato's Middle Dialogues," *PR*, LXIX (1960), 147–64. Reprinted in *Studies in Plato's Metaphysics*, ed. R. E. Allen (London, 1965).

[10] 100C cf. 74A, which seems clearly to assume that the Equal itself is pre-eminently equal.

[11] The "is" here is most conveniently taken as the "is" of identity, though this does not bring out the full evaluative sense of the statement, the fact that to say that Beauty itself is beautiful is to say that it is pure beauty, unalloyed with ugliness in any way. In fact, the "is" used here is a sense of "is" peculiar to exemplarist systems. To say that Beauty is beautiful is to say that it is the exemplar of beauty in things, and to emphasize the community of character between exemplar and exemplifications. So in certain medieval systems, to say that God is good is to use a unique sense of "is." Goodness cannot be predicated of God, since His nature is not composite: He is His goodness, and does not merely have it; and other things are called good only through their relation to Him. But the statement is not, strictly, an identity statement: it is clearly not the same as saying that God is God, or that He is wise.

[12] There is a problem here which should be mentioned, one kindly pointed out to me in discussion by Prof. Raphael Demos. It is this: Forms are themselves qualified by opposites: opposites such as sameness and difference, unity and plurality—syncategorematic characters. Thus, if qualification by opposites is the basis of the distinction between particulars and Forms, that distinction cannot be maintained: Forms would themselves become particulars. The answer to this problem is, I think, this: it is not mere qualification, but the *manner* of qualification by opposites, that is at the heart of the distinction. There is no indication that Plato ever regarded

syncategorematic characters as exemplars or paradigms; on the contrary, the second part of the *Parmenides* is perhaps a *reductio ad absurdum* of this view. Thus forms are not resemblances of such characters. Therefore the deficiency which characterizes the relation of particulars to Forms does not characterize the relation of Forms to syncategorematic characters. This is another way of saying that if Forms are exemplars, syncategorematic characters are not Forms. There is thus no ground for treating Forms as another kind of particular.

GUIDO CALOGERO
University of Rome

Gorgias and the Socratic Principle *Nemo Sua Sponte Peccat*[*]

MORE than a century ago the great German scholar Welcker tried to confirm the tradition that amongst the sophists the real master of Socrates had been Prodicus. Welcker called him his "forerunner."[1] In our century this valuation was once exaggerated to the extent of maintaining that the "principle of Prodicus"—that is, the care for the exact distinction and usage of the meanings of synonyms—had been the starting-point for every sound development in logic, whereas the methodological pattern presupposed by Socrates in his discussions was, on the contrary, a *Prinzip der absoluten Vieldeutigkeit*, a principle of absolute equivocation and ambiguity, and therefore the starting-point for every kind of trouble in that field.[2]

Of course, the connection of Socrates with Prodicus was justified by the fact that both, in their conversations, appeared frequently to be dissatisfied with certain answers or expressions of their interlocutors, and therefore discussed the meanings of certain terms used by them. But the difference between the two approaches was very sharp, as appears from every passage of the Socratic dialogues of Plato, in which Prodicus is introduced to explain the demands of his synonymics in the midst of the debate.[3] He wants everybody to use, for example, the verb εὐφραίνεσθαι in some cases and the verb ἥδεσθαι in some others, following what he thinks to be the right usage, the ὀρθότης ὀνομάτων; whereas Socrates does not care what kind of words one may use, but is only interested in what one really expresses by these words, that is, the meaning which he gives to them. Both search for meanings of words: but Prodicus' question is: What *does it* mean?—and Socrates' question is: What *do you* mean?—Prodicus says: ἀνδρεία means this, θρασύτης means that: so you shall use ἀνδρεία in the first case and θρασύτης in the second; Socrates asks: What do you mean by ἀνδρεία? (τί λέγεις τὴν ἀνδρείαν;). He does not care for

* Presented at the 1956 meeting of the SAGP in Claremont, California. Reprinted by permission from the *Journal of Hellenic Studies*, LXXXVII (1957): 12–17.

correct speaking: he himself likes to speak εἰκῇ τοῖς ἐπιτυχοῦσιν ὀνόμασιν (as he says in Plato's *Apology*, 17C). He is interested in the real thing, in what is meant, in the human behavior which has to be chosen and in the human valuation which has to be given. So Prodicus is the forerunner of all those people who try to determine the proper meanings of the words of a language and to put together its vocabulary for the right usage of those words so long as the passage of time does not change their meanings; and also of those people who write treatises on logic or semantics in the belief that the right knowledge of the meanings of a language is the best method for reasoning well. Socrates, on the contrary, is the perennial master of the real way of reasoning well, stressing not so much logic but dialogic, that is, never pretending to know the true meaning of what has been said by others before ἐξετάζειν them and never pretending to be immediately understood by others without διδόναι λόγον to them, in that incessant dialogue which is the moral life of men.

Now this Socratic ideal of the dialogue is strictly connected with the basic principle of his ethics, *nemo sua sponte peccat* (οὐδεὶς ἑκὼν ἐξαμαρτάνει). As a matter of fact, only a person who understands that nobody acts in a certain way without preferring it to any other possible way of action of which he is aware, can be interested in finding out the reasons for such a preference, without being certain in advance that they are wrong.[4] Now, this principle is clearly presupposed in the *Helena* and in the *Palamedes* of Gorgias. This sophist, therefore, might well be considered as the forerunner of Socrates with more reason than Prodicus, although none of his interpreters, as far as I know, seems to have suspected such a connection.[5]

Let us view the main argument of the *Encomium on Helen*. After having briefly recalled her origin and beauty, Gorgias begins the treatment of the real subject of his speech, which is not so much a eulogy as an apology, as was remarked by Isocrates.[6] Gorgias wants, as he says, "to subject her story to critical examination, and so rescue her from ignorant calumny."[7] His point is that she acted as she did because she was irresistibly compelled to do so. As long as such a compulsion is supposed to have been determined by Τύχη or by 'Ανάγκη or by the Gods or the violence of a man, there is no question: her innocence is obvious. But now Gorgias maintains that she was irresistibly compelled, and therefore deprived of any αἰτία, even if the compulsion was only enacted through πειθώ, persuasion: and this despite the fact that βία and πειθώ were for his contemporaries the precise technical terms used to express the opposition between coercive and non-coercive behavior, as the distinguishing characters of tyranny and democracy, of slavery and freedom.

This is evidently the main contention which Gorgias has to prove, and so he devotes to it the seven central paragraphs of his speech (8–14: seven precede and seven follow), beginning with the expression of his conviction that although his task may appear difficult, it will be easy for him to fulfil it: εἰ δὲ λόγος ὁ πείσας καὶ τὴν ψυχὴν ἀπατήσας, οὐδὲ πρὸς τοῦτο χαλεπὸν ἀπολογήσασθαι καὶ τὴν αἰτίαν ἀπολύσασθαι ὧδε.[8] And here immediately follows the famous passage on the power of the *logos*, which has always been considered as the most typical expression of Gorgias' philosophy: λόγος δυνάστης μέγας ἐστίν. . . . This power is not only the emotional force of poetry, λόγος ἔχων μέτρον, or the magic wizardry of incantations: it is also the power which we would call the persuasive force of reason:

> (13) "That Persuasion, when added to speech, can also make any impression it wishes upon the soul, can be shown, firstly, from the arguments of the meteorologists, who by removing one opinion and implanting another cause what is incredible and invisible to appear before the eyes of the mind; secondly, from legal contests, in which a speech can sway and persuade a crowd, by the skill of its composition, not by the truth of its statements; thirdly, from the philosophical debates, in which quickness of thought is shown easily altering opinion."[9]

Gorgias expatiates on this subject of the various forms of the influence exerted by λόγος and its πειθώ upon the soul; but the conclusion is always the same, and it is clearly expressed in §12: λόγος γὰρ τὴν ψυχὴν ὁ πείσας, ἣν ἔπεισεν, ἠνάγκασε καὶ πιθέσθαι τοῖς λεγομένοις καὶ συναινέσαι τοῖς ποιουμένοις. ὁ μὲν οὖν πείσας ὡς ἀναγκάσας ἀδικεῖ, ἡ δὲ πεισθεῖσα ὡς ἀναγκασθεῖσα τῷ λόγῳ μάτην ἀκούει κακῶς. Persuasion by λόγος is equivalent to abduction by force, as nobody can fail to "consent to what is done" if he "agrees to what is said"; in other words, nobody can help acting in accordance with the considerations to which he has been brought. In Socratic terms, οὐδεὶς ἑκὼν ἐξαμαρτάνει, nobody does anything, which may appear wrong from a better point of view, without considering it ἀγαθόν from his point of view. And even if this point of view is the visual perception of those objects which induce us to fall in love with them, the situation does not change, as Gorgias says in the last section of his speech: εἰ γὰρ ἔρως ἦν ὁ ταῦτα πράξας, οὐ χαλεπῶς διαφεύξεται τὴν τῆς λεγομένης γεγονέναι ἁμαρτίας αἰτίαν. ἃ γὰρ ὁρῶμεν, ἔχει φύσιν οὐχ ἣν ἡμεῖς θέλομεν, ἀλλ' ἣν ἕκαστον ἔτυχε· διὰ δὲ τῆς ὄψεως ψυχὴ κἀν τοῖς τρόποις τυποῦται (§15). We see the things as they happen to be, not as we want them to be! And what follows seems to anticipate some well-known Socratic analyses of the nature of fear and courage, as dispositions of the soul depending upon its way of seeing things as δεινά or θαρραλέα, which we find in Plato's *Protagoras* and *Laches*.[10] The general conclusion is repeated in §19: if Eros is a god, gods are irresistible, εἰ δ'ἐστὶν ἀνθρώπινον νόσημα καὶ ψυχῆς ἀγνόημα, οὐχ ὡς ἁμάρτημα μεμπτέον ἀλλ'ὡς ἀτύχημα νομιστέον. There is no need to change here, with Weidner and Immisch, νομιστεόν into οἰκτιστέον, or to add ⟨ἄξιον ἐλέου⟩ with Reiske: Gorgias has already said, at the end of §7, δίκαιον οὖν τὴν μὲν οἰκτῖραι, expressing the same idea of the ἔλεος, "compassion," deserved by the κακοί inasmuch as they are ἀμαθεῖς, which is so common in the Platonic passages concerned with the Socratic principle κακὸς ἑκὼν οὐδείς.[11]

Let us now look at the *Palamedes*. The hero defends himself by proving, first, that he could not have carried into effect his supposed treason even if he had wanted to, and, secondly, that he could not have wanted to perform the actions of which he is accused, even if he had had the opportunity of performing them. The first part of the defence, which is by far the shorter of the two, does not concern our problem (as the first part of the *Helena* did not). But the second part is a continuous reassertion of the principle which we know as the basis of Socrates' ethics. Right from the beginning, in §13, Palamedes asks: What motive could I have had? And the reason given for this question is a statement of that principle: οὐδεὶς γὰρ βούλεται προῖκα τοὺς μεγίστους κινδύνους κινδυνεύειν οὐδὲ τὴν μεγίστην κακότητα εἶναι κάκιστος. The formula οὐδεὶς βούλεται προῖκα εἶναι κάκιστος corresponds almost literally to the formula οὐδεὶς ἑκὼν κακός. Only a few lines farther on, the same presupposition is expressed in the following passage: ἀλλ'ἴσως ἑκόντες ἑκόντι παραδώσουσιν, μισθὸν τῆς προδοσίας ἀντιδιδόντες; ἀλλά γε ταῦτα πολλῆς μωρίας καὶ πιστεῦσαι καὶ δέξασθαι· τίς γὰρ ἂν ἕλοιτο δουλείαν ἀντὶ βασιλείας, ἀντὶ τοῦ κρατίστου τὸ κάκιστον; (§14). As a matter of fact, the impossibility of "choosing the worst instead of the best" is a typical point frequently underlined by Socrates in the demonstration of his principle. At the beginning of §16 we read the sentence καὶ μὴν οὐδ' ἂν τιμῆς ἕνεκα τοιούτοις ἔργοις ἀνὴρ ἐπιχειρήσειε καὶ μέσως φρόνιμος, which presupposes the idea that a reasonable man cannot do things which he judges harmful to himself. And §18 insists: κακῶς δὲ παθεῖν οὐδὲ εἷς ἐπιθυμῶν πανουργεῖ. And §19: δισσῶν γὰρ τούτων ἕνεκα πάντες πάντα πράττουσι, ἢ κέρδος τι μετιόντες ἢ ζημίαν φεύγοντες. This theme of the κέρδος seems to anticipate the subject of the *Hipparchus*, whose connection with the principle *nemo sua sponte peccat* I think to have proved sufficiently.[12] Finally, in §25 Palamedes says that he cannot be accused at the same time of two opposites, wisdom and madness: the accuser, who does so, τὸν αὐτὸν λόγον λέγων πρὸς τοὺς αὐτοὺς ἄνδρας περὶ τῶν αὐτῶν τὰ ἐναντιώτατα λέγει (a sentence in which has been found an echo of contemporary discussions about the logical rule which was later to be called the Law of Contradiction). And here follows §26, to which we shall compare a corresponding passage from Plato's *Apology of Socrates:*

> *Palam.* 26 Βουλοίμην δ'ἂν παρὰ σοῦ πυθέσθαι, πότερον τοὺς σοφοὺς ἄνδρας νομίζεις ἀνοήτους ἢ φρονίμους. εἰ μὲν γὰρ ἀνοήτους, καινὸς ὁ λόγος, ἀλλ' οὐκ ἀληθής· εἰ δὲ φρονίμους, οὐ δήπου προσήκει τούς γε φρονοῦντας ἐξαμαρτάνειν τὰς μεγίστας ἁμαρτίας καὶ μᾶλλον αἱρεῖσθαι κακὰ πρὸ παρόντων ἀγαθῶν. εἰ μὲν οὖν εἰμι σοφός, οὐκ ἥμαρτον· εἰ δ'ἥμαρτον, οὐ σοφός εἰμι. οὐκοῦν δι' ἀμφότερα ἂν εἴης ψευδής.

> Pl. *Apol.* 25D Τί δῆτα, ὦ Μέλητε; τοσοῦτον σὺ ἐμοῦ σοφώτερος εἶ τηλικούτου ὄντος τηλικόσδε ὤν, ὥστε σὺ μὲν ἔγνωκας ὅτι οἱ μὲν κακοὶ κακόν τι ἐργάζονται ἀεὶ τοὺς μάλιστα πλησίον ἑαυτῶν, οἱ δὲ ἀγαθοὶ ἀγαθόν, ἐγὼ δὲ δὴ εἰς τοσοῦτον ἀμαθίας ἥκω, ὥστε καὶ τοῦτ' ἀγνοῶ, ὅτι, ἐάν τινα μοχθηρὸν ποιήσω τῶν συνόντων, κινδυνεύσω κακόν τι λαβεῖν ἀπ' αὐτοῦ; . . . Ταῦτα ἐγώ σοι οὐ πείθομαι, ὦ Μέλητε, οἶμαι δὲ οὐδὲ ἄλλον ἀνθρώπων οὐδένα· ἀλλ'ἢ οὐ διαφθείρω ἤ, εἰ διαφθείρω, ἄκων· ὥστε σύ γε κατ' ἀμφότερα ψεύδῃ.

Gorgias' passage, even taken by itself, is completely Socratic in its content: every word might have been said by Socrates in a Platonic dialogue. But even more astonishing than this coincidence between the main principle of the defences of Helen and Palamedes and that of Socrates' ethics, is the similarity of this passage to that from the *Apology* which we have placed side by side with it. They end practically with the same sentence, after two formulations of a dilemma which is also substantially the same, because it refers always to the principle *nemo sua sponte peccat*, according to which nobody can, at the same time, ἁμαρτάνειν and be σοφός or διαφθείρειν and do so ἑκών.[13] Now, the coincidence between Gorgias' *Apology of Palamedes* and Plato's *Apology of Socrates* is not limited to this passage, but permeates the entire structure of both works. In order not to take too much space with quotations, we only mention, for each subject, the corresponding passages (indicating both works with the initials of their authors, and with an X. Xenophon's *Apology*, when the correspondence extends to it too).

> Death is not the real issue: everybody is condemned to die: G. 1; P. 38C–D; X.27.
> Real issue: if ἀποθανεῖν happens δικαίως or not: G. 1; P. 34E–35C: X. 28.
> Death is preferable to αἰσχρόν behavior or repute: G. 35; P. 38E–39B.

Judges who may condemn people to death should not decide in one day: G. 34–35; P. 37A–B.
If you kill me, my fame will cause you to be blamed: G. 36; P. 38C.
I could not go elsewhere as an exile: my hosts would become suspicious, and it would be a βίος οὐ βιωτός,[14] in Greece as well as ἐν τοῖς βαρβάροις: G. 20; P. 37C–E; cp. *Crito* 53B–54A.
Not only am I not guilty, but I am your εὐεργέτης: G. 30; P. 36C (the best proof of my innocence is my entire life: G. 28–29; X. 3).
I will not use lamentations and prayers, in order to move you to pity: I will only διδάσκειν τὸ ἀληθές: G. 33; P. 34C–35C, cp. 38D–E; X. 4; 9.
Interruption of the ἀπολογεῖσθαι by a διαλέγεσθαι with the accuser: G. 22; P. 24B ff.; X. 19 ff.

Now we can understand why in the enumeration of the most important sophists made by Socrates in Plato's *Apology* (19E) Gorgias comes first, before Prodicus, and why the first hero put to death by an unjust sentence, whom Socrates thinks he may meet in Hades, is Palamedes (41B). Not only must he have heard Gorgias presuppose in his discussions the same principle upon which he was to base his ethics;[15] he must also have clearly remembered Gorgias' *Apology of Palamedes* when he pronounced before his judges his own apology, of which we certainly have the best document in Plato's work. After all, this information is definitely given to us by Xenophon, who presents Socrates himself as recalling Gorgias' *Apology* in his *Apology* (26): παραμυθεῖται δ'ἔτι με καὶ Παλαμήδης ὁ παραπλησίως ἐμοὶ τελευτήσας. ἔτι γὰρ καὶ νῦν πολὺ καλλίους ὕμνους παρέχεται 'Οδυσσέως τοῦ ἀδίκως ἀποκτείναντος αὐτόν. Josef Morr[16] has well argued that this passage cannot be an allusion to Euripides' *Palamedes* (fr. 588 Nauck), and that ὕμνοι and ὑμνεῖν may refer also to prose works: as a matter of fact, Gorgias himself (fr. 5b Diels-Kranz) seems to call his encomia ὕμνους. Moreover, Morr (who had strongly underlined the coincidence between Gorgias' *Palamedes* and Xenophon's *Apology of Socrates* as to the point that everybody is already condemned by nature to die, without noting, however, the far more numerous coincidences, in this and in other points, with the Platonic *Apology*), quotes Xen. *Mem.* IV, 2, 33: Τὰ δὲ Παλαμήδους οὐκ ἀκήκοας πάθη; τοῦτον γὰρ δὴ πάντες ὑμνοῦσιν ὡς διὰ σοφίαν φθονηθεὶς ὑπὸ τοῦ 'Οδυσσέως ἀπόλλυται. In connection with this interpretation, according to which Odysseus had accused Palamedes because he was envious of his σοφία, Morr refers to Gorgias' *Palamedes* (25: σοφίαν μου κατηγορεῖς) in order to show that the situation here is the same, and that therefore this is the work quoted by Socrates in Xenophon.

This may be true or false, but in any case Xenophon was particularly influenced by Gorgias, and certain aspects of this influence may confirm what we have seen concerning the relation between the sophist and Socrates. Nestle, who has carefully studied the sophistic heritage in Xenophon,[17] recognizes for instance Gorgias in the διδάσκαλος τῶν παίδων about whom Cyrus is told by his father in *Inst. Cyri*, I, 6, 31. He ἐδίδασκεν τοὺς παῖδας τὴν δικαιοσύνην . . . , μὴ ψεύδεσθαι καὶ ψεύδεσθαι, καὶ μὴ ἐξαπατᾶν καὶ ἐξαπατᾶν, καὶ μὴ διαβάλλειν καὶ διαβάλλειν, καὶ μὴ πλεονεκτεῖν καὶ πλεονεκτεῖν. Διώριζε δὲ τούτων ἅ τε πρὸς τοὺς φίλους ποιητέον καὶ ἃ πρὸς ἐχθρούς. Καὶ ἔτι δὲ ταῦτα ἐδίδασκεν ὡς καὶ τοὺς φίλους δίκαιον εἴη ἐξαπατᾶν ἐπί γε ἀγαθῷ καὶ κλέπτειν τὰ τῶν φίλων ἐπί γε ἀγαθῷ. Now, if this διδάσκαλος is really Gorgias,[18] it is also easy to see that his doctrines are very similar to certain *loci communes* of the ethics of Socrates, who liked to show, in his criticism of the traditional ἀρεταί, how what is good from the point of view of a single ἀρετή in certain cases is not good in other cases; for example, that which is good with reference to friends may not be so as regards enemies, and so on.[19] On the other side, Nestle agrees with Hertlein and Ritter, who see a symbolic representation of both the destiny and the fundamental moral principle of Socrates in the portrait of the man of whom Tigranes tells Cyrus that his father sentenced him to death because he thought that he was corrupting him, whereas the man was, in fact, so καλός κἀγαθός, that he advised the son not to be angry with the father for this: οὐ γὰρ κακονοίᾳ τινὶ τοῦτο ποιεῖ, ἀλλ'ἀγνοίᾳ· ὁπόσα δὲ ἀγνοίᾳ ἄνθρωποι ἐξαμαρτάνουσι, πάντα ἀκούσια ταῦτα ἐγὼ νομίζω (*Inst. Cyri*, III, 1, 38). And so we see that in the main educational work of Xenophon, it is Socrates and Gorgias who seem to be present, as masters of the youth, worthy to be idealised together; Gorgias maintaining points familiar also to Socrates, and Socrates reasserting his *nemo sua sponte peccat*.

Anyway, be it as it may with Xenophon, the presence of the aforementioned principle in Gorgias' *Helena* and *Palamedes* is evident, we believe, after our analyses of their contents. G. Bux[20] was right in remarking that the "logical" structure of both those discourses has nothing to do with the εἰκός of Teisias and Corax. Neither defence presupposes any likely reconstruction of facts individually connected with the personal situation of Helen or of Palamedes—as, for instance, all other defences of Helen in Greek literature do, including the very inept one of Isocrates.[21] They are based only on general arguments, which could be employed by any other person accused of adultery or treason. But it is no use to say that this type of argumentation is an *apagogischer Schlussbeweis*, whose presence in both defences as well as in the Περὶ τοῦ μὴ ὄντος reveals all of them to be only exercises in Eleatic dialectic.[22] What is important is the real content of this *Beweis*: and this, we have seen, is nothing else than the sum of the considerations, upon which the *nemo sua sponte peccat* of Socrates is based.

The date of Gorgias' discourses is not certain, but no one has thought that they might have been written after 410 B.C.[23] As it is also quite unlikely that they were composed by the very old Gorgias after the death of Socrates, there is no reason to change the ancient view that the *Defence of Palamedes* influenced Socrates' own defence as well as its descriptions by Plato and Xenophon, and not *vice versa*. At the same time, the idea of the irresistible power of λόγος and πειθώ, so brilliantly outlined in the *Helena*, coincided with the οὐδεὶς ἑκὼν κακός of Socrates, but also confronted him with the most important problem of moral conduct. In fact, Gorgias, envisaging the *nemo sua sponte peccat* in its most elementary form, might fall into a sort of moral indifference. Everybody could act only according to his persuasions: so everybody could dominate the others if he was able to persuade them![24] Against this new tyranny of the *logos*, which was both threatening the independence and directing the behavior of the ψυχή in her most intimate realm (by the way, even this idea of the soul as the seat of consciousness and moral conduct, in which Burnet and Taylor saw the most important element of Socrates' philosophy, has been found present in Gorgias' discourses), Socrates had to find a remedy. And this was not a repudiation of the *nemo sua sponte peccat*, but the discipline of the πειθώ by the διάλογος. Everybody acted according to his private reasons, but everybody had to διδόναι λόγον of these reasons and to αἰτεῖν λόγον of the reasons of the others, in order that the better ones could exercise their better πειθώ. So the μέγιστον ἀγαθόν was for Socrates the ἐξετάζειν through the διάλογος, both in this life and in any other possible life[25]: and the κατὰ βραχὺ διαλέγεσθαι was the only civic discipline necessary in order to check the μακρολογία of the rhetors and their possibly bad πειθώ.[26] But this was not enough for Plato, who was not only a teacher but a politician as well, and did not possess the quiet Socratic patience to wait for the slow results of the διάλογος. The reason why we find the manifesto of his new position in a dialogue entitled *Gorgias* is probably that he could not discuss the faith in πειθώ and οὐδεὶς ἑκὼν κακός and διάλογος of his master Socrates without beginning by a discussion of the faith in πειθώ and οὐδεὶς ἑκὼν κακός of the master of Socrates himself.

NOTES

[1] "Prodikos von Keos, Vorgänger des Sokrates," in *RhM*, 1832 and 1836, reprinted with additions in *Kleine Schriften*, II (Bonn, 1845), pp. 393–541. Socrates himself says, in Plato's *Meno* 96D, that Prodicus had been his teacher. But even if this is not a joke, to study under somebody and to be a disciple of him are not the same thing.

[2] S. Ranulf, *Der eleatische Satz vom Widerspruch* (Copenhagen, 1924); and cf. my criticism, "Una nuova concezione della logica prearistotelica," in *GCFI*, VIII (1927): 409–22.

[3] See e.g. the passages quoted in Diels-Kranz, 5th ed. 84A, 13–18.

[4] May I refer for this to my article "Socrate" in *Nuova Antologia* (November, 1955): 291–308, and cf. *The Message of Socrates* ("Civilization, the Past and the Future: the Athens Meeting 1966," Amsterdam, Elsevier, 1967, pp. 9–23) and *Filosofia del dialogo*, 2nd ed., Milan, 1969.

[5] *Helena* and *Palamedes* are still considered only as "exercises" by K. Freeman (*The Pre-Socratic Philosophers*, 2nd ed., Oxford, 1949, p. 359) and as "jeux d'esprit" by E. Dupréel (*Les Sophistes*, Neuchâtel, 1949, p. 61), although he has carefully analysed many aspects of Gorgias' ethics. As to the interpretation of Gorgias by M. Untersteiner (*I Sofisti*, Turin, 1949, pp. 114–248), I find it very difficult to understand it, even in the English translation by K. Freeman (*The Sophists*, Oxford, 1954, pp. 92–205).

[6] *Laudatio Helenae*, 14–15. That Isocrates' quotation of the γράψαντα περὶ τῆς Ἑλένης really refers to Gorgias and not to another apologist of Helen, is now generally accepted.

[7] §2. The quotation is from the summary given by K. Freeman in her *Ancilla to the Pre-Socratic Philosophers*, 2nd ed. (Oxford, 1952), p. 131.

[8] The feeling of the difficulty of his task is again expressed by Gorgias some lines farther on, if the beginning of §9 has, as I think, to be read with Immisch δεῖ δὲ κᾶδοξα δεῖξαι τοῖς ἀκούουσι (all other readings give a poor sense).

[9] From the summary of K. Freeman (see above, note 7), which is here almost a complete translation.

[10] Compare, for example, what §§16–17 say about the φόβος as engendered in the soul by the notion of a "future danger" with the definition of δεινά as μέλλοντα κακά and θαρραλέα as μέλλοντα ἀγαθά and of the ἀνδρεία as ἐπιστήμη τῶν δεινῶν καὶ τῶν θαρραλέων, in *Laches* 198B ff.

[11] This principle, which is clearly ascribed to Socrates also by Xenophon and Aristotle, was evidently considered so important by Plato that he never disowned it through all his life, although he did not follow it in many developments of his philosophy. Cp. e.g. *Apol.* 25D–26A; *Protag.* 345E; *Hipp. Minor* 376B; *Hipp. Maior* 296C; *Gorgias* 488A, 509E; *Republic* 336E, 589C; *Tim.* 86D–E; *Leg.* 734B, 860D. By the way, as in *De iusto* 374A Socrates quotes this principle as expressed by "a poet" who said οὐδεὶς ἑκὼν πονηρὸς οὐδ' ἄκων μάκαρ (which seems to be Epicharmus fr. 7 Diels-Kranz with the last two words so changed from ἄταν ἔχων), and as in *Protag.* 345E he ironically finds it expressed in Simonides' poem, I wonder whether this sort of play with ancient poets (which is referred to also in Plato's *Apol.*

22B) may not have been extended by Socrates also to Homer. In this case, οὐδεὶς ἑκὼν ἐξαμαρτάνει may have been the witty inversion of K372 ἑκὼν δ' ἡμάρτανε φωτός. As a matter of fact, some MSS. (quoted by Allen, *ad. loc.*) say at this point that some people changed the first hemistich to that of Λ350, reading therefore καὶ βάλεν, οὐδ' ἀφάμαρτεν, ἑκὼν δ' ἡμάρτανε φωτός. They probably wanted to restore the harmony between Socrates and Homer, showing that the ἑκὸν ἁμάρτημα of Diomedes was not a real ἁμάρτημα, otherwise it could not have been ἑκόν!

[12] See my commentary on the *Hipparchus* (Florence, 1938), where I have also tried to show that there are many reasons to believe in its authenticity.

[13] It is also to be remarked that a few lines before Socrates had asked Meletos: ἔστιν οὖν ὅστις βούλεται ὑπὸ τῶν συνόντων βλάπτεσθαι μᾶλλον ἢ ὠφελεῖσθαι; (25D), which corresponds to the μᾶλλον αἱρεῖσθαι κακὰ πρὸ παρόντων (or προχείρων ὄντων, if one prefers Radermacher's to Diels' conjecture) ἀγαθῶν of Gorgias' passage; whereas the term ἁμαρτήματα, corresponding to ἐξαμαρτάνειν and ἁμαρτίας of Gorgias, appears in what immediately follows in Plato's *Apology* (26A).

[14] Gorgias' ἀβίωτος βίος (20) and βίος οὐ βιωτός (21) literally correspond to Plato's βίος οὐ βιωτός, which appears just a little farther in his *Apology* (38A). It is to be remarked that such expressions, according to the "Wort-index" of Kranz in Diels' *Vorsokratiker*, are used only here in all the pre-Socratic period (ἄβιος in Antiphon has just the opposite meaning). I cannot, therefore, understand why Untersteiner, in his commentary on this passage (*I Sofisti: testimonianze e frammenti*, II, Florence, 1949, 123–4), says that Gorgias' ἀβίωτος βίος is an "espressione empedoclea," quoting Empedocles fr. 2, 3 as reading ζωῆς ἀβίου. This is only a conjecture of Scaliger, the text given by Sextus is ζωῆσι βίου.

[15] And possibly also discuss topics which became at the same time well-known points of departure for Socratic discussions: for example, the relation between ἀδικεῖσθαι and ἀδικεῖν (*Palamedes*, 31, and cf. *Crito*, 49B ff.) or the idea that one has to help friends and injure enemies (*Pal.*, 18).

[16] "Des Gorgias Palamedes und Xenophons Apologie," in *Hermes*, LXI (1926): 467–70.

[17] W. Nestle, "Xenophon und die Sophistik," in *Phil*, XCIV (1939–40): 31–50. On the influence of Gorgias upon Xenophon see also H. Schacht, *De Xenophontis studiis rhetoricis*, Berl. Diss. 1890, and K. Münscher, in *Phil*, Suppl. Band 13, 1920, 3.

[18] Nestle sees in Gorgias' philosophy the common source of what is said in this passage, in Δισσοὶ λόγοι, 3, and in Plato, *Republic*, 331E ff.

[19] Every criticism by Socrates of the single traditional ἀρεταί in the early Platonic dialogues might be quoted as an example for this (e.g. the discussion of the σωφροσύνη in *Charmides*: σωφροσύνη is not equivalent to walking in a slow and dignified manner, because in certain cases it is more σῶφρον to hurry, and so on).

[20] "Gorgias und Parmenides," in *Hermes* (1941): 393–407. Certain coincidences between *Palamedes* and Plato's *Apology* had also been noticed

by H. Gomperz (*Sophistik und Rhetorik*, Leipzig, 1912, pp. 9–11) in his defence of the authenticity of Gorgias' discourses.

21 The history of the defences of Helen has been studied by M. S. Khafaga, "Absolutio Helenae," in *BFA* (Cairo, 1950): 85–98, which unfortunately I was unable to trace. The fact that Gorgias' discourses do not consider any individual circumstance of Helen's and Palamedes' actions, but generally prove every adultery or treason to be either impossible or unintentional, had been stressed also by H. Gomperz (*Soph. und Rhet.*, p. 11 ff.) But, considering such demonstrations simply as absurdities, he saw in them only the proof that Gorgias' discourses were mere jokes.

22 Through a similar reduction of the real arguments to their external structural pattern H. Gomperz (*Soph. u. Rhet.*, pp. 1–35) had already arrived at the conclusion that the Περὶ τοῦ μὴ ὄντος was a pure display of rhetorical ability, no less than *Helena* and *Palamedes*. I believe that I have proved, on the contrary, that also the Περὶ τοῦ μὴ ὄντος is neither a joke nor an exercise, but a highly ironical *reductio ad absurdum* of the Eleatic philosophy (especially of Zeno): see the chapter on Gorgias in my *Studi sull' Eleatismo* (Rome, 1932: a translation in German is being published by the Wissenschaftliche Buchgesellschaft in Darmstadt).

23 *Helena* is placed by Preuss (*De Eurip. Helena*, Leipzig, 1911) between the *Troades* and the *Helena* of Euripides, in 414 B.C., and by Pohlenz [*NGG* (1920): 166] before the *Troades* (see also K. Freeman, *Pre-Socr. Philos.*, p. 363). The *Palamedes* is dated before 411 by E. Maas [in *Hermes*, XXII (1887): p. 579.]

24 In Plato's *Gorgias* 452D–E Socrates asks Gorgias what he thinks to be the μέγιστον ἀγαθόν, and how he can give it to men: he answers that it is the πείθειν τοῖς λόγοις, because it ensures the ἄρχειν ἑκάστῳ, making everybody else a δοῦλος. The same idea ὡς ἡ τοῦ πείθειν πολὺ διαφέροι πασῶν τεχνῶν—πάντα γὰρ ὑφ'αὑτῇ δοῦλα δι' ἑκόντων ἀλλ' οὐ διὰ βίας ποιοῖτο—is attributed to Gorgias in *Philebus* 58A–B. So πειθώ, which was the essential instrument of any democratic opposition to a tyrannical βία, becomes the instrument of a new sort of tyranny (βία δι' ἑκόντων), until it is checked by διάλογος.

25 Plato, *Apology* 38A, 41B; and cf., for the interpretation of these passages, my article "Socrate" quoted above, note 4.

26 This explains also the fundamental value of the opposition between the sophistic μακρολογία and the Socratic κατὰ βραχὺ διαλέγεσθαι in Plato's *Protagoras*. According to Dupréel ("Sophistes," 80–81), *Gorgias* 449B–C might be considered as a proof that the κατὰ βραχὺ διαλέγεσθαι was at least less alien to Gorgias than to Protagoras. This could be another sign of his particular proximity to Socrates. In any case, the only one who had not understood anything at all was poor Prodicus. Confronted with the choice between μακρολογία and βραχυλογία, he just recommended a moderate length! (μόνος αὐτὸς ηὑρηκέναι ἔφη ὧν δεῖ λόγων τέχνην· δεῖν δὲ οὔτε μακρῶν οὔτε βραχέων ἀλλὰ μετρίων: *Phaidros*, 267B).

DAVID GALLOP
Trent University

Dreaming and Waking in Plato*

ALLUSIONS to dreams, or to the contrast between dreaming and waking, are frequent in Plato's writings. They occur in most of the major dialogues, sometimes repeatedly in a single work. This paper will review the evidence for Plato's conception of dreams,[1] and will explore his use of analogies from dreaming to express some central ideas in his theory of knowledge and philosophical method. Some miscellaneous passages from various dialogues will be briefly discussed in Part I. Part II will aim to throw some light upon the distinctions between different levels of cognition in *Republic* V–VII.[2] Part III will consider the application of the dreaming-waking contrast to the *Republic* itself.

I

Dreams are sometimes mentioned only in passing and have no discernible bearing upon the philosophical argument. But even from such casual allusions, we can gather something of their import in more significant contexts.

They are, as we might expect, commonly associated with mistakes, delusions, or false expectations. In the *Statesman* (290B) the Eleatic Stranger says that he was not dreaming when he asserted a certain view, meaning that he was not mistaken. At *Lysis* 218C Socrates begins his refutation of a promising theory with the words: "It looks as if we have had a golden dream." He uses the same phrase in the *Theaetetus* (208B), after exploding an interpretation of a theory that he has heard in a dream himself (201E ff.). Earlier he has said: "You have never, *even in sleep*, gone as far as to say to yourself that odd numbers must be even, or anything of that sort" (190B). At *Philebus* 65E he says: "No one ever saw wisdom or intelligence being or becoming disgraceful, whether waking or dreaming." Such mistakes are, apparently, too gross even for a

* A revised paper which was originally presented under the title "The Platonic Dream" at the 1965 meeting of the SAGP in Providence, Rhode Island.

dreamer. But this in itself implies that dreams are, typically, the domain of error.

On the other hand, they are sometimes veridical.[3] At *Charmides* 173A Socrates echoes the Homeric distinction between dreams that come through gates of ivory and those that come through gates of horn. Dreams in Plato are frequently of the latter kind. The dreamer's vision is significant, even if opaque. Here we encounter the common notion of a prophetic dream, a supernatural vision or abnormal experience, in which divine commands are given, or truths revealed, that are not accessible to waking consciousness. Thus in the *Apology* (33C) dreams are one source of Socrates' conviction that he must continue his mission to the people of Athens. In the *Crito* (44B) he can base his prediction that the sacred vessel will arrive next day upon a dream, whose meaning, for once, is said to be "all too clear." In the *Phaedo* (60E) he explains that he has been writing verses to test the meaning of a recurrent dream bidding him cultivate the arts.[4]

These allusions do not imply that Plato subscribed to popular belief in the significance of dreams,[5] or that the dreamer can always recognise their true significance himself. The *Timaeus* (45E–46A) offers a scientific account of them in terms of residual internal "motions":

> When some stronger motions are left, they give rise to images answering in character and number to the motions and regions in which they persist—images which are copies made inside and remembered when we are awake in the world outside. (trans. F. M. Cornford)

Later in the same work (71A–E) a special explanation is given of prophetic dreams. They are supposed to be images perceived by the irrational part of the soul upon the smooth surface of the liver. However,

> No man in his normal senses deals in true and inspired divination, but only when the power of understanding is fettered in sleep or he is distraught by some disorder, or, it may be, by divine possession. *It is for the man in his ordinary senses to recall and construe the utterances*, in dream or in waking life, of divination or possession. (71E)

The dream requires interpretation, but the dreamer himself cannot provide it. Socrates, we may recall, found the poets less competent than their audience at interpreting their own works (*Apology* 22B). In the *Symposium* (175E) he remarks, ironically, that his own wisdom is a poor thing, "disputable like a dream," in contrast with the clear vision of Agathon the poet. The poet's vision, he implies, is obscure in comparison with the philosopher's, and his expression of it is ambiguous. The dream figure here suggests the obscurity of poets that is derided more openly elsewhere.[6]

This charge of obscurity is extended in the *Phaedrus* to written works of any kind, philosophic ones included. Any writer's belief that his work possesses much stability or clarity is said to be a reproach to him.

> For ignorance of what is a waking vision and what is a mere dream-image of justice and injustice, good and evil, cannot truly be acquitted of involving reproach (277D).

The contrast between waking and dreaming here perhaps represents the difference between a clear or thorough grasp of concepts obtained through oral dialectic, and a vague or partial understanding derived from the written word.[7] In this respect, Platonic dialogues have the status of dreams themselves. They too are enigmatic and subject to misinterpretation (275E). Yet they offer some degree of enlightenment, if interpreted aright.

In the *Meno* (85C), after the slave's geometry lesson, true opinions are said to have been stirred up in him "as if in a dream." Just as elements from previous waking experience are recollected in dreams, so the slave's prenatal acquaintance with mathematical truths is recollected in his lesson. But the lesson leaves him still unequipped with a deductive proof of his theorem. True opinions have been aroused, but not yet "tethered" by an understanding of their grounds, and thus converted into knowledge. The waking experience has not been recovered with clarity or completeness. Here again, dreaming is used to express a correct, but as yet inadequate, apprehension of truth.[8]

Two other passages are worth noticing. In the *Theaetetus* (157E–158E), dreams create an initial objection to Protagorean subjectivism: it cannot be the case that all experience is true, for dreams and hallucinations are delusive.[9] Socrates argues, however, that this objection is ill-founded. For there are no adequate criteria for distinguishing waking from dreaming,[10] or for regarding one order of experience as false and the other as true. In both states "our mind strenuously contends that the convictions of the moment are certainly true" (158D). The dreamer therefore has as good a claim to truth as the waking man. The experience of each is "true for him."

Socrates has asked Theaetetus how we should prove at any given moment that we are not dreaming. Yet in certain passages we encounter the idea that, in some profound sense, we generally are. In a difficult section of the *Timaeus* (52B–C), we are told that space is:

> apprehended without the senses by a sort of bastard reasoning, and hardly an object of belief. This indeed is that which we look upon *as in a dream* and say that anything that is must needs be in some place and occupy some room, and that what is not somewhere in earth or heaven is nothing. Because of this *dreaming* state, we prove unable to rouse ourselves and draw all these distinctions and others akin to them, even in the case of the *waking* and truly existing nature, and so to state the truth. (trans. F. M. Cornford)

Two points seem to be made here. First, we do not perceive space directly, but divine its existence from what we do thus perceive.[11] Secondly, we are disposed, incorrectly, to regard space as a necessary condition of any existence whatever. Our normal awareness is, as it were, spatially conditioned. We can transcend it only in mathematics and philosophy, and even then only intermittently and with conscious effort. While we are engrossed in the sensible world, we pass our time in a waking dream. We remain in what Aldous Huxley called "the quasi-hypnotic trance in which most human beings live and from which it is the aim and purpose of all true philosophy, all genuinely spiritual religion, to deliver them."[12] This brings us to the central thesis of the *Republic*.

II

In *Republic* V, after Socrates has affirmed the need for philosophers to be rulers, he contrasts them with "lovers of spectacle" (φιλοθεάμονες), and says that the latter "live in a dream" (476C8).[13] For he argues, a man is dreaming, whether he be awake or asleep, if he mistakes a likeness for that which it is like. This is the mistake that the φιλοθεάμων makes. He fails to distinguish between the many beautiful things of sense experience and the Form of Beauty itself. By contrast, the philosopher who does make this distinction, lives "very much awake" (D4). Similarly, in Book VII, a man who cannot define the notion of good is said to be "dreaming and dozing through his present life," and "before he awakens here he will arrive at the house of Hades and fall asleep for ever" (534C–D).

To interpret the dream figure in these contexts, we may consider the kind of experience of which our dreams consist. Typically, they are (1) *unclear*, (2) *incoherent*, and (3) *ephemeral*: (1) their images are less clear than those of waking consciousness; (2) they juxtapose elements unrelated in waking life; and (3) they are short-lived in comparison with waking experience. These features, although not common to all dreams, are characteristic of them. They are the basis on which we occasionally ascribe a "dream-like quality" to our experience, or wonder seriously (i.e. outside philosophy) whether we are dreaming or not. They are also precisely the respects in which Plato treats the sensible as "inferior" to the intelligible world, belief as "inferior" to knowledge.

(1) Belief is said not to exceed knowledge in *clarity* (σαφήνεια), or ignorance in unclarity (ἀσάφεια). It is "darker" (σκοτωδέστερον) than the former, but "brighter" (φανότερον) than the latter (478C). The cognitive states of the Divided Line are proportioned in respect of degrees of clarity (σαφήνεια; 511E). Objects in the visible world are placed between "being" and "not-being" on the ground that they will appear neither "darker" than the latter nor "brighter" than the former (479C). (2) Their lack of clarity is connected with their *incoherence*, *viz.* their propensity to manifest contrary qualities. The many beautiful, just and holy things will also appear ugly, unjust and unholy (479A). The same applies to things large and small, heavy and light, double and half (479B). The senses report the same thing as both hard and soft, thick and thin (523–4). A state that is really neither pleasant nor painful can appear to be both (583E–584A). Things seen may appear to be both straight and bent, concave and convex (602C). (3) Since phenomena are thus incoherent, our judgments about them are *unstable*. The soul, when beholding the world of change, "shifts its opinions hither and thither" (508D).[14]

By contrast, the objects of the Intelligible world, and the judgments made by mathematicians and philosophers about them, possess the clarity, coherence, and stability of normal waking vision. Mathematicians define their terms clearly. Their propositions are logically ordered, mutually consistent, and eternally true. The mind is unshakably convinced of their truth once they have been demonstrated.[15]

The same advantages would be available for judgments of value, if philosophy were all that Plato hoped that it might become. Dialectic would provide a "science of values," by means of which practical questions could be infallibly solved. The solutions would be unaffected by the personal view-points or interests of those who reached them, like answers to questions of size and number obtained by measurement and calculation. "Value" knowledge would enable waking vision to replace dreaming in human affairs. The dreamer's private world[16] of subjective judgment would be abandoned for the public world of waking men, sharing a common intellectual experience, and solving their problems objectively by means of agreed procedures.

The philosopher ruler's training in these procedures would provide him with a rationale for those judgments of value that he had learned to make uncritically when young (401E–402A). This perhaps gives point to the suggestion (414D–E) that the guardians' early education happened to them "as if in a dream." In context, this strange story is supposed to bolster up the myth of their autochthonous origin. In a sense, however, their early education *was* dream-like, for it exposed them to sensible images of Beauty and other Forms, which they would see directly only later in life when trained in dialectic.

So far, philosophy and mathematics alike have been treated as "waking" states in contrast with other levels of cognition. Yet there is one place in Book VII where even mathematicians are said to be dreamers:

> Geometry and the studies that accompany it are, as we see, dreaming about being, but the clear waking vision of it is impossible for them as long as they leave the assumptions which they employ undisturbed and cannot give any account of them. (533B)

In what sense does a mathematician's failure to question his assumptions make him a dreamer? Despite the discussion in the *Theaetetus*, it is natural to take dreams as lacking any foundation in external reality. In particular, internal coherence within a dream is no guarantee of its truth. Hence to call the mathematician a dreamer is to imply that despite coherence within his system, he may be saying nothing known to be true.[17] His terms may be clearly defined and his propositions logically ordered, but his whole system may be no more than the consequence of verbal definitions and unquestioned assumptions. So long as these remain unchallenged, his conclusions must remain purely hypothetical. To establish their categorical truth is the task of dialectic.

Like the φιλοθεάμονες of Book V, however, mathematicians remain unaware of their limitations. They too confuse images with originals, for they too are content with mere "images," i.e. with terms and definitions (λόγοι),[18] whose real designata they feel no need to question.

The connection between the dreaming-waking and image-original contrasts now becomes of crucial significance. The dreamer is one who sees an image of an object and not the object itself. According to Dodds,[19] the Greeks did not speak as we do of *having* a dream, but always of *seeing* a dream—ὄναρ ἰδεῖν, ἐνύπνιον ἰδεῖν. That Plato thought of dreaming as seeing an image is especially clear from the *Sophist* (266D), where a real house is contrasted with a painted one, and the latter is described as "a man-made dream for waking eyes." To paint a picture is to produce a kind of dream, and to see a dream is to see a kind of picture. Moreover, as already noticed, the dreamer fails to recognise that the object before him is a mere picture, and will not acknowledge the existence of any reality beyond it.

We can now grasp the relevance of the dreaming-waking contrast to the Divided Line. Just as the "objects" of the Line (ἐφ, οἷς) are related, in respect of reality (ἀλήθεια), as image to original (510A8–10, 511E2–4), so the cognitive states (παθήματα) are related in respect of clarity (σαφήνεια 509D9, 511E2–4), as dreaming to waking. We have already seen how this applies to the contrast between belief and knowledge in Book V. We have also seen how an analogous contrast is drawn in Book VII between mathematics and dialectic. It remains to apply the dreaming-waking contrast to the lower segments of the Line. In what way could it be held to symbolise the relation between εἰκασία and πίστις?

This is more difficult. The state of εἰκασία is nowhere referred to as "dreaming," and it is hard to see how a man in εἰκασία could make a mistake analogous to that of the φιλοθεάμων or the mathematician. For the "objects" assigned to his segment of the Line are shadows and reflections; and even the most unenlightened of men do not normally mistake these for the objects that cast them, or refuse to distinguish between such images and their originals.

But the passage about εἰκασία is densely compressed. Socrates says that he is leaving a great deal out (509C7). If this entitles us to read between the lines, the objects of εἰκασία need not be confined to those expressly mentioned. They may be supposed to include the "appearances" presented by physical objects, more especially those that misrepresent their real nature, and thus afford the philosopher a basis for distinguishing "real objects" from "sense-data."[20] If this is accepted, the dreaming-waking contrast will be applicable here too. In εἰκασία there will be a failure to distinguish "image" from original. For this is the condition of the "plain man," who draws no distinction between sensible appearances and the physical objects that produce them. He does not recognise the dependent and ephemeral character of "appearances," that would be aptly symbolised by shadows and reflections. The qualities of dream images noted earlier, their lack of clarity, coherence and stability, are shared by shadows and reflections, and characterise the appearances of a physical object in its interaction with perceiving subjects. For these appearances are numerous, changing and transitory, whereas the object is unitary, unchanging and permanent. The differences between a physical object and its appearances are thus precisely analogous to these between a Form and the objects that fall under it. Εἰκασία is the state of one who does not recognise these differences, whereas πίστις is the condition of one who does.

On this view, πίστις involves the drawing of a distinction between Appearance and Reality *within* the physical world. It is the state of those who understand the physical structure of objects, both natural and artificial, which causes their appearances.[21] Such observers are not limited, like the prisoners forecasting shadows (516C–D), to empirically based predictions of phenomena, for they have a grasp of their physical causes. At this level we also find craftsmen, concerned with the production and tendence of "things grown and things constructed" (533B). They are contrasted with those who cater for the "opinions and desires of men," i.e. presumably, those who exploit the ignorance, emotions and appetites of ordinary people, with poetry, sophistry and rhetoric.[22]

III

The foregoing interpretation can be summarised in the following diagram:[23]

Book V

"Objects"	"Cognitive States"
Forms A	Philosopher "Waking"
Sensibles B	φιλοθεάμων "Dreaming"

Books VI–VII

"Objects"		"Cognitive States"
Forms	Aa	Dialectician νόησις "Waking"
Verbal Images	Ab	Mathematician διάνοια "Dreaming"
Material Things	Ba	Natural Scientist πίστις "Waking"
Images	Bb	Plain Man εἰκασία "Dreaming"

What, in this complex scheme, is the status of the *Republic* itself? We might expect it to exemplify the thesis of Book V that the philosopher lives "very much awake." Yet it does nothing of the kind. It has, rather, the status of a dream. It is a mere image of what it portrays, an expression of philosophic vision that shares the defects inherent in all written works. It is, in the words of the *Phaedrus*, "a mere dream-image of justice and injustice, good and evil."[24] It provides an image appropriate to the Ab level of cognition, a verbal picture of the Forms.

First, it is a prophetic dream. Through its use of images, it offers a prophetic insight into the Intelligible world. In Book IV, when about to define justice in the individual, Socrates says:

> Finished, then, is our dream and perfected—the surmise we spoke of, that, through some god (κατὰ θεόν τινα), at the very beginning of our foundation of the state, we chanced to hit upon the original principle and a sort of type of justice. (443B–C)

The principle in question is that each man should perform one function, that the shoe-maker should stick to his last. This has proved to be an image (εἴδωλον) of justice (443C4–5), for it was adopted throughout the construction of the city, and thus foreshadowed the definition of justice as the performance by the parts of city and individual of their respective functions. When the principle is understood in its profoundest, i.e. its psychological, sense, it is seen to enshrine the true account of justice that has been sought. In this sense the dream has proved veridical, and can thus be ascribed to "some god."[25]

In Book IX Socrates speaks of the perverted sexual desires and murderous impulses that emerge in the dreams of outwardly decent men, and that are gratified by the tyrannical man in waking life. He contrasts such dreams with those of one who retires to sleep after gratifying his appetites in moderation and soothing his spirited element. The "best part of him" is then left free "in isolated purity to examine and reach out towards and apprehend some of the things unknown to it, past, present or future," and it is then that "he is most likely to apprehend truth" (572A–B). Here there are striking affinities between the dreamer and the philosopher. Both are released from the limitations of their ordinary awareness. Dreaming, as Dodds has said,[26] is "the sole experience in which [normal men] escape the offensive and incomprehensible bondage of time and space." It is just such an escape that the philosopher achieves in his contemplation of timeless and non-spatial Forms. Moreover, like the dreamer of this passage, he can discover truth only when the clamour of appetites and emotions is stilled, and reason has undisturbed access to her own objectives.

Thus there is a sense in which the philosopher, although wide awake compared with other men, is himself a dreamer. Moreover, and paradoxically, in order to impart his vision to others, he must, as it were, re-enter the dreaming state. To convey a clear view of Justice and Man, Ruler and City, he must resort to images, specifically to the construction of a dream city.

The paradox is well illustrated on two successive pages of the *Statesman*. When discussing the nature of examples, the Eleatic Stranger describes our experience as "knowing all things in a dream, yet knowing nothing when we are once again awake" (277D2–4). Here the dream in which we may "know all things" seems to be the philosophical understanding of an abstract concept by means of an illustration. But later, after using an example to explain the rôle of examples in general, the Stranger proposes that they use another one to understand the nature of the statesman's art, "in order that it may become waking instead of dreaming experience for us" (278E10). By this he means, presumably, that when they have defined the statesman, they will have a clear grasp of his nature instead of their present vague idea. In this latter passage, dreaming represents an unphilosophical *lack* of clarity, whereas in the former it represents a use of images to *achieve* clarity, such as we find in the *Republic* itself.

One further aspect of dreaming in the *Republic* remains to be noticed: the notion of wish-fulfilment. This appears most strikingly in the passage already mentioned from Book IX, where bad impulses are said to be gratified in the dreams of decent men. But it recurs elsewhere. In the *Theaetetus* (173D), philosophers are said to be immune from worldly interests. Indeed they are so unworldly that "to take any interest in the rivalries of political cliques, in meetings, dinners and merry-makings with flute girls never occurs to them *even in dreams*." Their fantasies are, perhaps, of a more elevated kind. At any rate there is some evidence that the ideal city of the *Republic* should be counted among them. In constructing it, the dreaming-waking contrast is linked with the difference between fantasy and fact, theory and practice, words and deeds. The image of the ideal city is a dream, just because it is a city in words, unlikely to be realised in action.

When introducing his plan for women and children in Book V, Socrates expresses the fear that his audience will think him merely indulging in visionary talk (450D),[27] and he compares himself with idle thinkers who pretend to themselves that their wishes are already granted (458A). He goes on to argue that his plan is *not* impracticable or visionary (οὐκ ἀδύνατά γε οὐδὲ εὐχαῖς ὅμοια), that the city is "not altogether a vision (μὴ παντάπασιν ἡμᾶς εὐχὰς εἰρηκέναι), but that though difficult, it is in a way possible" (540D). But the tone of these passages is pessimistic and the argument carries little conviction. The city, he says, could be realised "most easily" by separating children under the age of ten from their parents, and training them *de novo* (541A–B). Since he has hinted earlier (501A3–4) that such extreme measures would not be at all easy, to admit that they afford the "easiest" means of realising the city is only to recognise its extreme improbability.

The dream status of the city is strongly suggested in a well known passage from Book VII. When telling his trained philosophers that they must go back into the Cave, Socrates says to them:

> In this way both for us and for you (ἡμῖν καὶ ὑμῖν) the city will become a waking reality, and not a dream, like most existing cities, which are peopled by men who fight one another for shadows and wrangle for office as if that were a great good. (520C–D)[28]

One may suspect a *double-entendre* in this cunningly worded sentence. The city will become "a waking reality and not a dream" in two senses. "For you," because it will be ruled by "you" philosophers, and not by the dreamers who now contend for power. In this sense it is existing cities that are the dream ones, and only the ideal city that is "real." But in another sense it is the ideal city that is the dream. Only when philosophers become kings will it become feasible, "see the light of the sun" (473E). Only when they re-enter the Cave will the city become more than the dream that it now is "for us"; that is, for Socrates and his friends who have been founding it in words. If, as Cornford once suggested,[29] Plato "enjoyed framing the studied ambiguities forced on him by his dramatic method," this is a case in point.

The *Eighth Epistle* makes similar use of the waking-dreaming contrast. It ends by exhorting the relatives and friends of Dion to strive "until like a heaven-sent dream presented to waking eyes, the plan which has been pictured by us in words be wrought by you into plain deeds and brought to a happy consummation" (357D).[30] Similarly, the end of the *Laws* (969B) looks forward to seeing "as an accomplished fact and waking reality that result which we treated but a short while ago in our discourse as a mere dream." Much earlier (746A), the Athenian Stranger had criticized his own programme as impossible of complete fulfilment. For this would require that the citizens should accept all that is dictated to them by the law-giver, "almost as if he were telling nothing but dreams, or moulding so to say, a city and citizens out of wax." This would apply equally well to the city of the *Republic*, combining the two figures, dreaming and sculpture, repeatedly used to describe it.

We have interpreted the *Republic* as a prophetic dream. It provides a verbal image of Justice, Ruler and City, and thus expresses an insight into the Intelligible world. But we may perhaps say that Plato hardly expected its fulfilment in the world of action. Dreaming, like painting, was the solace of his political inertia. If our argument has been correct, the dream of a just society was the refuge of one who despaired of building it in waking life.

NOTES

1 This subject has also been discussed by H. D. Rankin, "Dream/Vision as Philosophical Modifier in Plato's *Republic*," *Eranos*, LXII (1964): 75–83. A richly detailed and wide-ranging account of the Greek attitude to dream-experience is given by E. R. Dodds in *The Greeks and the Irrational*, Ch. IV.

2 This part of the paper is closely related to my article "Image and Reality in Plato's *Republic*," *AGPh*, 47 (1965) and, like it, owes much to an interpretation of the Divided Line that I learnt from the late John Austin. I am also grateful to Professor Gregory Vlastos for written comments on an earlier version of the present paper, which have helped me in making extensive revisions.

3 "Veridical" in the sense that they are, somehow or other, fulfilled in *subsequent* waking life (or "come true"). Dreams are seldom veridical in the sense that they correctly represent a *contemporary* state of affairs in the external world. This latter sense, familiar in modern epistemology, has little application to dreams. (See N. Malcolm, *Dreaming*, pp. 66–69.)

4 For prophetic dreaming, cf. also *Laws* 800A.

5 See *Laws* 909E–910A, *Epinomis* 985C, and Dodds, *op. cit.*, pp. 108, 125.

6 *Republic* 332B, *Lysis* 214D, *Protagoras* 339 ff.

7 This cannot be certain, since the construction to be placed upon ὕπαρ τε καὶ ὄναρ in 277D10 is doubtful. The above translation and interpretation are Hackforth's (*Plato's Phaedrus*, p. 161, n. 3). To take ὕπαρ and ὄναρ adverbially, qualifying ἀγνοεῖν, deprives the contrast of any obvious point. Why should ignorance of justice and injustice, good and evil, be censured both in waking and dreaming subjects?

8 Interpretations of the dream in this context vary. According to E. S. Thompson (ed. *Meno*, p. 140) the slave's opinions are still "fluid and insecure." J. Gould (*The Development of Plato's Ethics*, p. 136) says that the reference is to their "instability" and "apparent strangeness." R. S. Bluck

(ed. *Meno*, p. 33. n. 2) thinks that the slave has had "only a dreamlike memory of the truths concerned aroused in him, and there is little or no ἀκρίβεια." This seems more likely than Bluck's later suggestion (p. 311), that the arousing of the slave's opinions is comparable with the *recalling* of a dream. Rather, it has been comparable with his *having* a dream, which is itself an imperfect recall of waking vision.

[9] Similarly at *Philebus* 36E dreams and deranged states offer some support to the thesis that not all pleasures (or pains) are true. Socrates suggests, and Protarchus agrees, that any one denying that pleasures (or pains) can be false would have to deny that one could, whether dreaming or waking, mistakenly believe that he experienced pleasure (or pain). Unfortunately the ensuing discussion does not return to this point. But dreaming might well be supposed *prima facie* to provide instances of false pleasure.

[10] This passage contains an odd puzzle. In agreeing with Socrates that waking and dreaming are hard to distinguish, Theaetetus remarks: "The conversation we have just had might equally be one that we merely think we are carrying on in our sleep; and when it comes to thinking in a dream that we are telling other dreams, the two states are extraordinarily alike" (158C). Dreams in which we think we are telling other dreams are uncommon. Even if conceivable, e.g. dreaming about a psychoanalytic interview, they seem a bizarre and inept illustration of the point. With Heindorf's reading of ἄττα for ὀνείρατα in C6 the text would mean: "When in a dream we think we are relating something, the two states are extraordinarily alike." This does little to remove the difficulty. For why should dreams in which something is related (no matter what) be singled out as *specially* similar to waking experience? Other proposed emendations (e.g. reading ὕπαρ for ὄναρ in C 5) face similar objections. If we keep the O.C.T. reading, it is possibly no coincidence that later on Socrates recounts a philosophical theory which he calls "a dream in exchange for a dream" (201E). Is the dialogue in some sense "a dream in which other dreams are told"? If such dreams were specially hard to tell apart from waking life, Theaetetus' doubts about the status of their conversation would have more point than he realises. This would not make his statement any more plausible, but it would give it some dramatic significance.

[11] A. E. Taylor (Commentary on *Timaeus*, note on 52B3) denies that the passage means that we lack a clear vision of space itself. He takes it to mean only that "with regard to it [space] we dream with our eyes open." However, the dream figure does also seem to be connected with the idea that we apprehend space "by bastard reasoning," i.e. that its existence is not perceived, but has to be inferred.

[12] *The Devils of Loudun*, pp. 20 ff., quoted by E. R. Dodds, ed. *Gorgias*, p. 10.

[13] From now on all references are to the *Republic* unless otherwise noted. P. Shorey's translation in the Loeb Classical Library is used throughout, with minor modifications.

[14] Cf. *Protagoras* 356D, where the "power of appearances" is said to lead us astray and confuse our judgments. See also *Phaedo* 79C, where the

soul is said to "wander and be disturbed and dizzy as if drunk," when it uses the senses.

[15] Cf. *Meno* 98A.

[16] The use of dreaming as a symbol of subjectivity is strongly suggested by Heracleitus' observation that the waking share one common world, but the sleeping turn aside each into a world of his own (fr. 89). See W. K. C. Guthrie's discussion of this fragment in his *History of Greek Philosophy*, I, pp. 427–31. The privacy of dream contents is also suggested by the expression τὸ ἐμόν ἐμοὶ λέγεις ὄναρ used by Adeimantus (563D) to mean "You are telling me what I already know." "My own dream" is, presumably, what I know better than any one else.

[17] See 533C. A similar point is made in a different connection at *Cratylus* 436D. *Cratylus* 439C is also worth noting. Socrates there raises a question about which he says he "often dreams," namely whether there is any Form of Beauty, Good and so forth. A science of values, if there were such a thing, would be exposed to the same doubt that the *Republic* explicitly entertains regarding mathematics: *are* there such things as Beauty and Goodness, or is our "science" no more than a system of coherent propositions based upon verbal definitions? If so, does it deserve the name "science"?

[18] The case for regarding the mathematician's objects as λόγοι, "verbal images," has been argued in the article referred to in note 2 above.

[19] *Op. cit.*, p. 105.

[20] For this view of the objects of εἰκασία cf. H. J. Paton, "Plato's Theory of *Eikasia*," *PAS*, XXII (1921–22). See also D. W. Hamlyn, "*Eikasia* in Plato's *Republic*," *PQ*, VIII (1958). This interpretation can be supported from the treatment of painting in Book X. The painter of an ordinary bed is there said to make "an apparent bed" (κλίνη φαινομένη, 596E), or to represent "the appearance as it appears" (τὸ φαινόμενον ὡς φαίνεται, 598B). His work is φαντάσματος μίμησις, i.e. he reproduces the appearance of the bed. Here Plato treats the "appearance," the single partial aspect captured by the painter, as an *image* of the bed—σμικρόν τι ἑκάστου ἐφάπτεται, καὶ τοῦτο εἴδωλον, B 7–8. The sensible appearance is related to the physical object as image to original, and is thus an appropriate "object" for εἰκασία. I am grateful to Professor J. L. Ackrill for drawing this line to my attention, but am fully responsible for the use here made of it.

[21] I feel less certain now (1968) of the above interpretation of εἰκασία and πίστις than when I wrote the original version of this paper. (1) The interpretation does not make it clear whether shadows and reflections in the literal sense should be included as objects of εἰκασία or whether they merely symbolise "appearances." To understand them only symbolically is perhaps to place too great a strain on the text. On the other hand, if they are understood both symbolically and literally, εἰκασία will have at least two quite disparate sets of objects. (2) The contrast between plain men and philosophical sophisticates is not the same as the contrast between those who know and those who are ignorant of the structure of physical objects. These distinctions cut across each other, whereas the above interpretation runs them

together. It is natural, perhaps, to associate them closely, since a causal theory of perception is often used to support the dichotomy between real objects and their appearances. But this hardly justifies blurring the two distinctions.

22 This contrast recalls the distinction in the *Gorgias* 464B ff. between genuine and pseudo-arts. The genuine craftsman aims to benefit rather than to please, and his methods are scientific, not merely empirical.

23 The lettering is Austin's. It brings out clearly the proportions holding between different segments of the Line. The ratio A:B (as between "objects") symbolises the relationship between image and original, and (as between "cognitive states") the relationship between dreaming and waking.

24 But see note 7 above.

25 "God," we have been told earlier, "neither changes himself nor deceives others by visions or words or the sending of signs in waking *or in dreams*" (382E–383A). Hence the passage in the *Iliad* where Zeus sends a deceitful dream to Agamemnon has been duly marked for expurgation.

26 *Op. cit.*, p. 102.

27 μὴ εὐχὴ δοκῇ εἶναι ὁ λόγος. Liddell and Scott give "prayer" as the primary sense of εὐχή. They translate εὐχαῖς ὅμοια λέγοντες (499C4–5) "building castles in the air." Aristotle uses πολιτείαν τὴν κατ' εὐχὴν γινομένην to mean a utopian constitution (*Politics* 1295a 29–30). This use of εὐχή is an interesting derivative. It embodies the idea that prayers are seldom granted (just as dreams seldom come true) in real life. Hence to call something a "prayer" is *eo ipso* to suggest that it will *not* come about. Our own use of "dream" often has the same implication.

28 καὶ οὕτω ὕπαρ ἡμῖν καὶ ὑμῖν ἡ πόλις οἰκήσεται, ἀλλ' οὐκ ὄναρ, ὡς νῦν αἱ πολλαὶ ὑπὸ σκιαμαχούντων τε πρὸς ἀλλήλους καὶ στασιαζόντων περὶ τοῦ ἄρχειν οἰκοῦνται, ὡς μεγάλου τινὸς ἀγαθοῦ ὄντος.

29 *Mind* (1932): 174.

30 For ὕπαρ ἀντ' ὀνείρατος in the sense of "reality as opposed to mere fantasy," cf. also *Ep.* III, 319B.

ROBERT W. HALL
University of Vermont

Techne and Morality in the *Gorgias**

THE *Gorgias* has usually been taken to herald a new beginning in Platonic morality because it presents at least in outline the morality of the *Republic* with its emphasis on the inward ordering of the soul, and implies the moral responsibility of the individual. The Socratic–Platonic emphasis on the tendance of the soul emerges in the analogy which Socrates draws between the art of politics which cares for the soul and the art which looks after the well-being of the body.[1] The "new" morality is apparently embodied in Socrates' stress on the fact that all that a man does, he does for the "good." "Good" is supposed to be quite close to if not identical with man's true good as conceived by Plato. "Good" has even been taken to be an anticipation of the idea of the good.

Although there is something new in the *Gorgias*, I think that on the whole the dialogue displays a view of morality which is quite similar to the utilitarian ethic grounded on the knowledge and values of *techne* so characteristic of the early dialogues. As a result of its espousal of a utilitarian ethic patterned after the procedures of *techne*, the *Gorgias* displays a little-noticed moral paradox as striking as that of the *Lesser Hippias*' affirmation that if morality is akin to the knowledge of an art, then he who consciously and deliberately does evil is morally better than one who unwittingly does wrong. The moral paradox in the *Gorgias* stems from the assumption that moral individuals are self-determined; they act spontaneously or autonomously; (this is Plato's meaning although he does not use such terminology). Yet these moral beings are "created" by the art of politics and the practisers of that art much as any object is created by its appropriate *techne*.

By this I mean that the raw material or subject matter upon which an art is applied is in a real sense passive in the process of creation in that

* This is a revised version of "The Moral Philosophy of the *Gorgias*," a paper presented at the 1962 meeting of the SAGP in New York, New York. Reprinted with only slight variation from Professor Hall's *Plato and the Individual*, (The Hague, 1963). By permission of Martinus Nijhoff.

the shaping or molding which results in the final object of the art is the work of the craftsman. The wood which is being turned into a shuttle by the craftsman contributes nothing but "subject matter" to the artistic process and the finally completed object. The craftsman, however, does not act arbitrarily or capriciously. As a craftsman he is guided by the essential nature or form (εἶδος) of the product which he is creating. Through his activity and technical knowledge he seeks to impose order and an approximation of the relevant form upon the materials appropriate to his craft.[2]

Although this passivity of the object of an art in the creative process is most clearly seen in those arts that produce tangible products such as agriculture, carpentry, ship-building, it also extends to such arts as geometry and calculation. To my knowledge Plato nowhere states explicitly this passive character of the object during the process of its realization. But I think that is implied in Plato's theory of *techne*. The significant factors determining the development of the raw material into the finished product are the craftsman and his knowledge of the form of the object.

One passage in the *Gorgias*, however, does strongly suggest the passivity of the object during the creative process. Socrates compares the activity of the good statesman in producing morality in his citizens to the activity of the craftsman. The true statesman is

> just like any other craftsman, who having his own particular work in view, selects the things he applies to that work of his, not at random, but with the purpose of giving a certain form to whatever he is working upon. (503D–E)

Here Socrates emphasizes the craftsman's role in applying the appropriate form to the material upon which he is working. Applying this generalization to specific *technai* Socrates goes on apparently to stress the function of the craftsman in bringing to completion his activity with the production of the object of his art:

> You have only to look, for example, at the painters, the builders, the shipwrights, or any of the other craftsmen, whichever you like, to see how each of them arranges everything according to a certain order, and forces one part to suit and fit with another, until he has combined the whole into a regular and well-ordered production (τεταγμένον τε καὶ κεκοσμημένον πρᾶγμα); and so of course with all other craftsmen, and the people we mentioned just now, who have to do with the body-trainers and doctors; they too, I suppose, bring order and system into the body. (503E–504A)

The combination and ordering of the various parts of the proposed object into one whole can apparently only come about through the activity of the craftsman. There is no indication that the various parts containing the raw material spontaneously come together or suggest to the craftsman how he might join them into a "regular and well-ordered production."

Of course some products of artistic activity may seem to belie the predication of passivity. Is not a healthy, upright well-developed body active in attaining that condition under the direction, to be sure, of a trainer? Is not the patient in a sense active following the commands of a doctor even to the extent of engaging in certain activities to regain his health which is the object of medicine and the activity of the doctor? But to return to the elements of artistic production, it seems that the man who follows the direction of the trainer or the doctor, no matter how active he may be, is still following the directions and mode of procedure set down by the craftsman with his knowledge of the form of the object of his art. In arts of this type the activity of these objects is still fundamentally passive. It is done at the behest of another. And from Socrates' inclusion of the trainers and doctors in his mention of the craftsmen of objects more obviously passive in their production such as houses and ships, it would seem that he means to attribute to their objects the same sort of implicit passivity.

But it is paradoxical that an individual who contributes nothing to the attainment of his morality and who is completely "shaped" by an external agent is, in any significant sense, moral. Yet, this result follows from the portrayal in the *Gorgias* of the statesman as a craftsman of moral citizens without any of the conditions found in the *Republic*, which would limit the parallelism between the activity of the statesman and that of the craftsman. Chief among these conditions is the relation of the philosopher rulers' "craft" to the world of forms and the idea of the good. This condition also would distinguish statesmanship from the realm of *technai*. Although statesmanship is analogous to *techne*, in fact it is not a *techne* in a strict sense.

In the course of the development of this view of statesmanship as a *techne* in the strict sense, Socrates rejects Gorgias' attempted definition of *techne* as that art concerned with the "greatest of human affairs . . . and the best" as "ambiguous and by no means clear" (451E). Though Gorgias does finally offer a logically adequate definition of rhetoric (455A), Socrates finds it unacceptable because as defined by Gorgias, rhetoric is a matter of routine (ἐμπειρία), and has "no account to give of the real nature of things it applies, and so cannot give the cause of any of them" (465A). Rhetoric is irrational and only a sham art because along with the other sham "arts" of flattery, it does not provide for the "best advantage" (βέλτιστον) of the body and soul. Surely, however, Socrates is guilty of the same lack of clarity which he earlier levelled against Gorgias when he claims that, in contrast to flattery, "medicine and gymnastic, justice and legislation always bestow their care for the best advantage of the body and soul'. . ." Obviously gymnastic and medicine bring about and maintain the "best advantage" of the body in its health. But what is the "best advantage" of the soul which the twin arts of legislation and justice create and sustain? To say "health" of the soul is hardly to provide an explanation.

It may be suggested that "best advantage" means the inward moral condition of the soul apart from any utilitarian consequences. But not only does the absence of any analysis of the soul as a substantial entity suggest the contrary, but it appears likely that this ambiguity is resolved in favor of a utilitarian connotation of "best advantage." Further, the application of these arts to the securing of the "best advantage" of the soul results in the little-noticed moral paradox that morality is attained not by the individual and his own efforts, but by the statesman.

These consequences are the result of the application in ethics of *techne-phronesis* and its values. Such results provide another stage in what seems to me to be Plato's effort to discredit the utilitarian ethic grounded on the values of *techne* and after the model of *techne-phronesis*. *Techne-phronesis* may in some respects be superior to the opinion of the masses or of the Sophists and rhetoricians, but in the *Gorgias* it provides an unsatisfactory standard of good and an inappropriate explanation both of the winning of morality by the individual and of his moral regeneration.

Socrates' attempt to show that the rhetoricians or orators have the least power in cities "since they do nothing that they wish to do practically speaking, though they do whatever they think is best," culminates in an avowal of the utilitarian values of benefit (ὠφέλιμον), profit (λυσιτελοῦν), or advantage (χρήσιμον). Distinguishing between means and ends, Socrates affirms that the means, those intermediate things which are neither good nor bad, are done "for the sake of good things" (ἕνεκεν τῶν ἀγαθῶν) (467E ff.), such as "wisdom, and health and wealth and everything of that kind." It would be premature to interpret the usage of "the good" in the singular as in ". . . it is for the sake of the good that the doers of all these things do them" (468B) to mean the form of the good or even some abstract human good. The use of "good" is merely another way of referring to the good things which are the objects of our desire.[3] These "good things" are clearly utilitarian. They reveal the values of the existing society. Intermediate things are done for the sake of things good in a conventional utilitarian sense. An ill man takes drugs for health; merchants sail the seas for commercial advantage. To generalize:

> If a man does something for an object, he does not wish the thing that he does, but the thing for which he does it. (467D)

The relevance of this passage to Socrates' claim that the rhetoricians "do nothing that they wish" although they do whatever "they think best," refers to a wrongness in the choice of means to a desired end rather than in the selection of ends. Socrates condemns the unintelligent and, hence, wrong choice of means to attain an end. The ends which the rhetorician may desire are conventional goods. Yet, his profession of rhetoric makes him powerless to choose intelligently the appropriate means to attain these goods: "Do you," asks Socrates of Polus, "regard it as a good, that a man does what he thinks to be best, without having intelligence" (νοῦν) (466E)? Intelligence does not connote in this context, it seems to me, knowledge in any special Platonic sense like knowledge of the idea of the good. It is unlikely that Plato at this stage of his thought, at least, used terms in a consistent, technical, rigorous sense. Intelligence here connotes knowing how best to attain whatever ends one may have in view. Without the ability to make effective use of his supposed power to choose appropriate means for a desired end, an apparently all powerful rhetorician is actually without power.

Socrates points out that "we wish to slaughter people or expel them from our cities or deprive them of their property" (468C), not for itself but for the good it brings; such actions are beneficial (ὠφέλιμον) because they lead to the desired for good thing. Such means if profitable or beneficial may bring about wealth, prosperity, and the other qualities conventionally assumed to be the objects of one's interest and actions. But to achieve that conventional object, we must know whether our chosen means will bring about the end. Exiling the wrong person, or taking away a powerful individual's property, may not bring about the desired for end of social stability or of maintaining power, or of personal advantage. Insofar as a rhetorician desires a good thing, he does nothing that he wishes, to paraphrase Socrates, although he does what he thinks best to attain his desired good. He does nothing that he wishes because the object of his wish, a conventionally good thing, is not attained because of his ignorance of the appropriate means to it.

Polus' attempts to win the day by glorifying the sheer exercise of power meet a sharp rejoinder from Socrates. Exercise of power is valued only if it is just (468E ff.). Socrates here expands his earlier notion that great power as a good thing exists only in doing what one thinks fit when one receives advantage or profit (conventionally understood) from doing it. Such advantage seemed to depend on selecting the proper means to achieve a good thing. Now the emphasis appears to be placed on the just character of the action, "just" apparently in the sense of conforming to the existing conventional legal and moral standards. Emphasis on the moral quality of action supplements rather than replaces the advantage in securing the appropriate means for achieving a good thing. The appropriate means for securing a good thing can only be means in accordance with justice and morality. Acting justly, in short, is to one's advantage or profit conventionally understood.

In his demonstration that to suffer injustice is better than to commit injustice (474A ff.), Socrates seems to arrive at a concern for the inward nature of the soul. The worst evil that could befall the soul is injustice. Yet the means Socrates employs to effect this conclusion reveal predominantly utilitarian values. Bodies, colors, figures, sounds, observances, laws, studies are beautiful (καλόν) in a moral-aesthetic sense if they have some benefit (ὠφελία), or "use for some particular purpose," or provide pleasure (474D).[4]

Polus's interpretation of Socrates' definition of the beautiful as the pleasant (ἡδονή) or the good (ἀγαθόν) (475A) is revealing. Polus identifies what Socrates terms the beneficial with the good, and Socrates does not object to this interpretation. It would follow then, that the ugly is that which is painful or evil. Hence if, as Polus agrees, the commission of injustice is uglier, or not as beautiful as the suffering of injustice, it must exceed the latter in evil or lack of advantage, for obviously it is not more painful. But injustice is not that which is intrinsically evil (any more than justice is intrinsically valuable), but that which is disadvantageous or not beneficial in the sense of not having a "use for some particular purpose." Even in an apparent emphasis on the condition of the soul, then, utilitarian values prevail. Injustice is evil in that it is disadvantageous, and provides no use or benefit in a purely utilitarian sense.

The utilitarian connotation of "good" or good things is apparent in Socrates' refutation of the Calliclean thesis that pleasure and the good are the same. We must distinguish between good and bad pleasures, for the good is the object of all our actions:

> The good (τὸ ἀγαθόν) is the end of all our actions, and it is for its sake that all other things should be done, and not it for theirs . . . Then it is for the sake of good things (τῶν ἀγαθῶν) that we should do everything, including what is pleasant, not good things (τἀγαθά) for the sake of the pleasant. (499E–500A)[5]

But nothing approaching the form of the good of the *Republic* is here implied, not even a universally applicable human good outside of what may be beneficial and useful in a conventional utilitarian sense. Socrates clearly brings out this conventional interpretation of "good" in his conversation with Callicles, which leads to the above affirmation that the good is the object of all our actions.

> Well, then, what you now state, it seems, is that some particular pleasures are good, and some bad; is not that so?
>
> Yes.
>
> Then are the beneficial ones good (ἀγαθαί), and the harmful ones bad?
>
> Certainly.
>
> And are those beneficial (ὠφέλιμοι) which do some good (ἀγαθόν) and those evil which do some evil?
>
> I agree.
>
> Now are these the sort you mean—for instance, in the body, the pleasures of eating and drinking that we mentioned a moment ago?
>
> Then the pleasures of this sort which produce health in the body, or strength, or any bodily excellence—are these good (ἀγαθαί), and those which have the opposite effect bad (κακαί)?
>
> Certainly.
>
> And similarly in the case of pains, are some useful (χρησταί) and some base (πονηραί)?
>
> Of course.
>
> So it is the useful (χρηστάς) pleasures and pains that we ought to choose in all our doings? (499C–E)

Here Socrates identifies the good (ἀγαθόν) with the useful (χρηστόν) or ὠφέλιμον as Polus did earlier in restating Socrates' criteria for the beautiful. In this passage those things are good which contribute to the physical well being of the individual. Taken in conjunction with his earlier discussion (467C–468D) of the subordination of "things neither good nor bad" to the attainment of the good things such as widsom, health, wealth, and the like, Socrates seems again to be within the realm of the utilitarian values of *techne-phronesis*. The good which is the object of all our actions signifies nothing more than conventional utilitarianism, which entails a life full of "good things" in the sense already described. Thus Socrates' argument against Callicles's initial acceptance of hedonism seemingly concludes not only with a distinction between good and bad pleasures, but with a repetition by Socrates of a utilitarian criterion of this distinction, and amounts to a definition of good in terms of utility.

The inadequacy of this utilitarian standard comes out most clearly in the analysis of its attainment through securing morality within the individual's soul. Not only do the values of *techne* and *techne-phronesis* color the meaning of "good" and "beautiful", but the adoption of an art of politics (πολιτική) devoted to the care of the best advantage of the soul (464B) presents serious problems in the formation of an ethical view which should allot to the individual the major responsibility for acquiring virtue. The analogy between the arts which minister to the body and the two subbranches of the art of politics which tend the soul strengthens the interpretation of a kind of moral passivity of those individuals tended by the art of politics. The primary concern of any craftsman is the welfare of the objects of his art, not of himself or of the betterment of the art. Applied to the two arts which look after the well being of the body, gymnastic and medicine, this means that the practitioners of these arts are charged with the physical health of the citizens. The craftsman of gymnastics issues commands for exercise which result in the bodily strength and well being of his charges. When necessary, the physician practices the related art of medicine to rid a temporarily ill body of its unhealthy condition. In both activities the craftsman deals with the citizen as an object of his art. The citizen himself contributes nothing. He gains, or regains, as the case may be, bodily health through tendance of his physical condition by following orders given by experts.

To liken without qualification the branches of the art of politics to these two arts is to make both the initial winning of morality and the regaining of moral health the function of experts other than the individual concerned. An unobjectionable procedure in gaining and preserving physical health becomes unacceptable when applied to the gaining and preserving of morality. To imply, as the *Gorgias* does, that the individual himself is inactive or passive in becoming just and in moral regeneration is to indulge in a moral paradox as striking in its way as that of the

Lesser Hippias. The paradox in the *Gorgias* follow consistently from the assumption that tendance of the soul is like any other art, especially that unnamed art which in its two subdivisions of gymnastic and medicine looks after bodily well being. The practiser of the political art which cares for the soul's moral well being can give an account of "the real nature of the things it applies, and so can . . . tell the cause of any of them" (465A). But Socrates' analogy between the art of politics and all other arts does not allow a role for the acquisition of his morality to the individual himself. He puts the art of politics on all fours with the other arts in the respect that in achieving the welfare of the object of the art, the object itself contributes nothing.

The achievement of the morality of the individual is solely the responsibility of the craftsman, the statesman. Any adequate analysis of morality entails the moral responsibility or the autonomy of the individual. No matter how the morality of his action is determined, whether by the nature of his motive or merely the character of his action, his moral worth is his own responsibility and achievement. Others may provide the conditions surrounding his eventual attainment of morality, but the actual acquisition of morality as well as moral regeneration must be the individual's own doing. Plato in the *Republic* explicitly affirms the moral responsibility of each individual.

In the *Gorgias*, Socrates' discussion of the manner in which morality is attained, as well as the way in which justice or moral regeneration is brought about, indicates that despite its superiority to the empiricism of rhetoric, science as *techne-phronesis* is inadequate for the moral tendance of the soul. Socrates' refutation of Polus' contention that it is better for the wrongdoer to escape all punishment than to pay the penalty for his crime clearly brings out the incongruous passivity of the agent in his moral regeneration (476A–481B).

Arguing along lines applicable to the many arts that employ instruments or tools in making their respective products, Socrates generalizes, "If a man does (ποιεῖ) anything . . . there (must) be something which is also acted (πάσχον) upon by the doer of the thing . . ." This thing "suffers" what the agent does and "the effect such as the agent's action makes it . . ." If x affects y in manner z, then y is affected by or acted upon by x in manner z. Socrates selects his examples from the wide class of arts or crafts that entail some sort of operations on their appropriate products (476B–D). "And if the striker strikes hard or quick, the thing struck is struck in the same way"; "if one burns, something must be burnt"; and finally, "if one cuts . . . something is cut . . . if the cut is large or deep or sore, the cut made in the thing cut is such as the cutter makes it." These examples drawn from the procedures of various arts illustrate the general principle applicable to most if not all arts, "that the patient (or object) receives an effect of the same kind as the agent's action" (476D).

Turning next to the desirability of just punishment Socrates applies the general principle that the patient suffers the quality which the agent inflicts. If the person is punished justly, he thereby "becomes better in soul" (βελτίων τὴν ψυχὴν γίγνεται); "he who pays the penalty," is "relieved from badness of soul . . . the greatest evil" (μεγίστου κακοῦ) (477A). Yet, outside of his bringing himself to the courts to undergo just punishment, the unjust individual is passive while undergoing the purgative powers of punishment which result in his moral regeneration. He is like an object which receives the impress of an action inflicted upon it. It appears as though the very act of just punishment makes the unjust man just by cleansing him of his injustice. But if this is so, an external agency alone can effect the wicked man's regeneration and make him "better in soul."

Being better in soul is not further explained by Socrates. It implies the removal of evil (πονηρία) from the soul in the form of injustice, ignorance (ἀμαθία), or cowardice (477B). Ignorance is an important factor in the individual's wicked condition. Its removal would require participation by the individual, but Socrates does not develop its implications for moral responsibility here, as he does in the later dialogues. Since justice is fair or beautiful (καλόν), it is either pleasant or beneficial. Since it may be painful, justice must be beneficial (ὠφέλιμον) (478B). He who suffers just punishment is thereby benefited.

"Benefit" has a utilitarian connotation. A quality of soul which prevents the happiness of the criminal is removed by one other than the criminal. Happiest is he who never has had need of punishment, he who undergoes just punishment is happier by far than he who escapes altogether (478D–E). The vindication of punishment lies in the removal by the just punisher of the evil in the soul which prevents happiness. Ridding the soul of evil is accompanied by the appearance of happiness. The benefit which the justly punished individual receives appears in a negative sense as the removal of evil from his soul, positively as the return of happiness. Just punishment is beneficial or advantageous and therefore, fair or beautiful.

Yet, as stressed earlier, the so-called moral regeneration of the wicked man is the product of legal justice, a sub-art of the art of politics and its practitioner, the judge or whoever is responsible. The criminal has as little to do with the regaining of moral health as the patient has with his physical health. Both are tended by experts other than themselves, a tenable position in medicine but hardly so in morality.

Complete reliance on experts for the moral regeneration of the criminal is underscored in Socrates' verbal tiff with Callicles. Again the analogy with the medical art is significant, for it brings home the external quality of such regeneration. Just as the doctor does not allow his patient to satisfy his desires indiscriminately, so the true statesman in dealing with the unjust soul must "restrain its desires and not permit it to do anything except what will help it to be better" (βελτίων) (505B). Although again the meaning of "better" may be ambiguous, the external quality of the wicked man's betterment is clear. He does not control his own desires; by forbidding him certain desires the statesman seeks to improve his spiritual health just as the doctor betters his patient's condition by denying him the satisfaction of certain desires. But the control by the statesman of the wicked individual's harmful desires again denies the individual's participation in his own moral regeneration. This account in the *Gorgias*, as I have already suggested, stands in sharp contrast to Plato's later treatment of the reform of the individual through a change in his inward nature by removing the ignorance which causes the evil action. The individual himself achieves a condition of wanting to do what is right and restraining his harmful desires.

Socrates' account of the art of the true rhetorician or statesman, the practiser of legislation, which is the other sub-art of the art of politics, inhibits any contribution by the citizen, the "object" of the statesman's art, to the attainment of his "good," or moral condition of soul. The object of the statesman's art is the tendance of the citizens' souls to make them as good as possible. The true statesman constantly says and does what is best (βέλτιστον) whether or not his listeners find it pleasing. The statesman, then, has a special art or craft to perform. He is

> the good (ἀγαθός) man, who is intent on the best when he speaks, [he] will surely not speak at random in whatever he says, but with a view to some object . . . He is just like any other craftsman, who having his own particular work (ἔργον) in view selects the things he applies to that work of his, not at random, but with the purpose of giving a certain form (εἶδος) to whatever he is working upon. (503D–E)

In following out the procedures of his art, the statesman *qua* craftsman has precisely the same relation to his object, the moral tendance of the souls of his citizens, as "painters, builders, shipwrights, or any of the other craftsmen, whichever you like," have to their respective objects. The significant feature of this relation is to the complete and utter passivity of the object upon which the craftsman works. He himself imposes order on the object. Each craftsman

> arranges everything according to a certain order, and forces one part to suit and fit with another, until he has combined the whole in a regular and well-ordered production (τεταγμένον τε καὶ κεκοσμημένον πρᾶγμα). (503E–504A)

Every object or product of a *techne* which is a "regular and well-ordered production" is good or useful (χρηστή). Order (κόσμος) and regularity (τάξις) not only make a good or useful house, ship, or some such object, but also a soul which is useful and good. The ambiguous connotation of χρηστόν as good or useful is quite appropriate to its application in the crafts and arts. An object made by a craftsman is good only insofar as it is useful for carrying out some purpose. A well-ordered and regulated soul, then, is not only good, but in some sense useful. An orderly soul is temperate, and as a consequence of its temperance is just and pious, doing what is fitting to both gods and men (507A–D).

But how can a soul act virtuously if its excellence is due to another's activity, i.e. the statesman? The temperate soul is also courageous; thus, in effect, the unity of the virtues is reducible to temperance. It is quite inexplicable how a soul can so act which has achieved its excellence through the art of another rather than through its own efforts. The temperate man, the good man, "does well (εὖ πράττειν) and fairly whatever he does; and he who does well is blessed and happy" (507C). The ambiguity of εὖ πράττειν, which can mean, as noted earlier, either doing or faring well, enables Socrates to establish a relation of necessary entailment between technically proficient action—doing well, and happiness—faring well.

Excellence of soul is but one of many excellences achievable in all products of the various arts and sciences. The excellence (ἀρετή) of any thing, implement or tool, body, or living thing, is secured by "an order or rightness or art which is appropriate to each". (506D) The orderly and regular condition of soul constituting its excellence or *arete* is imposed entirely from outside the soul by the legislator. But moral excellence presupposes a responsibility and spontaneity which is belied by the unqualifiedly external manner for achieving temperance and the other virtues. Although passages in the *Republic* suggest a similar relationship between the philosopher-ruler and the citizens he tends, they are qualified or complemented by passages which point out that although the philosopher can be taken perhaps as a necessary condition for the winning of justice by the ordinary citizen, it is the individual himself who must finally attain his own justice through doing what is "within and in the true sense concerns one's self and the things of one's self . . . (*Rep.* 443D).

Socrates, at 516A foll., emphasizes in a negative manner the moral passivity of the citizens. Socrates likens the care of the statesman for his citizens to that of a shepherd for his herd. We blame the shepherd for the worsening of his flock. So Socrates contends should it be with the supposedly great statesman of Athens. If the facts showed that Pericles and others left the citizens "wilder" and hence "more unjust and worse" after their tenure in office than before, they could not be considered as true statesmen. To argue that the analogy between the shepherd and the statesman is a limited one, and that the statesman can not be held to be completely responsible for the moral condition of the citizens as the shepherd is for physical well being of his flock, is to admit that statecraft is not one among many *technai* but in some significant respects unique. But in the *Gorgias*, Socrates, as far as I can see, places no qualification on statesmanship as an ordinary *techne*. It is as much a *techne* as medicine, carpentry, or charioteering. The "products" of each of these *technai* can not be bad in their respective ways if their creator is a true craftsman. What is impossible with the art of the charioteer is also impossible with the art of the statesman:

> Good drivers . . . do not keep their seats in the chariot at the first race to be thrown out later on, when they have trained their teams and acquired more skill in driving! This never occurs either in charioteering or in any other activity (ἔργῳ).

In a real sense, then, there are no evil citizens, only incompetent "statesmen."

In the discussion thus far, then, the *Gorgias* has markedly displayed the influence of the utilitarianism of the values of *techne-phronesis*. Terms such as good (ἀγαθόν), beautiful (καλόν), order (κόσμος), regularity (τάξις), and excellence (ἀρετή) embedded in the utilitarian values of *techne* are applied without modification to ethical values. Although Socrates rejects hedonism, it is clear in the *Gorgias* that, with an exception soon to be noted, his discussion moves within the realm of a *techne*-oriented ethic, one that is beneficial in the utilitarian sense in bringing about conventional or popular happiness.

Here as in the *Protagoras*, Socrates seems to stress the significance of having an art of politics governing the welfare (in a utilitarian sense) of the soul rather than the opinion that makes up the habitude (ἐμπειρία) of the rhetoricians and sophists. But the art of politics in its two branches of legislation and justice so closely resembles the other arts that it denies the individual's role in acquiring morality or in bringing about his moral regeneration. They are, rather, the products of the arts of legislation and justice.

The fact that the philosopher-ruler of the *Republic* is described in terms reminiscent of the true rhetorician or statesman of the *Gorgias* should not obscure two points. First, nowhere is the latter's science described as anything more than a *techne-phronesis*. Secondly, the philosopher-ruler only provides the necessary conditions – the proper environment, the appropriate education, whereby the individual himself may order his soul morally. But in *Gorgias*, the true statesman, it seems clear, produces the moral condition (or moral regeneration) of the individual soul, as any *techne* through the efforts of the craftsman makes the appropriate object of art.

At the same time however, the *Gorgias* breaks with the *techne*-oriented ethics of the earlier dialogues by eliciting a source of value or goodness which transcends the standard of utilitarianism. Probably to indicate that he is not presenting Socrates's own doctrine, Plato prefaces Socrates' account with a reference to the fact that "wise men (σοφοί) tell us." (507E) Here, as in 493A and the *Meno* 81A, Plato resorts to the same or similar devices to separate the views of the Platonic Socrates from his own views or the views of others with which he agrees, in this case the Pythagoreans. What these wise men tell us is that:

> heaven and earth and gods and men are held together by communion and friendship, by orderliness, temperance, and justice; and that this is the reason why they call the whole of this world by the name of order (κόσμου), not of disorder or dissoluteness. (507E–508A)

As the basis for such order, Plato enunciates a sustaining principle of all things underlying both law and nature, and hence resolving their conflict upheld by Callicles. With this principle Plato has gone beyond the ordinary commonplace arts and crafts, medicine, shipbuilding, weaving, shoemaking, and the like, to grasp a truly cosmic ordering principle. Such a principle or standard of value is that of geometrical equality or proportion (ἰσότης γεωμετρική) (508A), a transcendent ordering principle, which as the source and sustaining cause of value in all things, for the first time in this study foreshadows the *Republic*'s form of the good.

Moreover in this brief section (507D–513C), Socrates introduces the philosophic life, a life devoted to philosophy which exists in isolation and which is distinguishable from the life and activity of the true statesman or rhetorician. Only, it seems, in the *Republic* are the two ways of life, the philosophic and the political, reconciled in the life of philosopher-ruler. The *techne-phronesis* which provided the model for the good or orderly soul is rejected as worthless, both as a model for the ethical life and as means to a utilitarian existence. Man's most important consideration is not how long he may live, but how he may "best (ἄριστα) live out his allotted span of life." (512E)

The context allows a moral connotation to "best" hitherto denied to its cognates because of the utilitarian character of their contexts. The affirmation of the cosmic principle of geometrical equality and the exaltation of the philosophic life indicate a new line of ethical development and an emphasis on the intrinsic value of *arete* and its vindication on a principle which transcends the values and knowledge of a *techne* influenced ethic. Tendance of the soul takes on a more Platonic view, stressing its inherent worth apart from the beneficial consequences noted in the earlier dialogues. At the same time there is the theme of limitation of the moral life to those few philosophically gifted, so eloquently declaimed in the *Phaedo*.

Along with its suggestion of a new cosmic ordering principle and its exaltation of the philosophic life, then the *Gorgias* performs an important therapeutic service. Not only does it reject hedonism, but it shows implicitly the impossibility of patterning a theory of the moral education of the individual along the lines of a *techne*. The moral spontaneity of autonomy so necessary for morality requires effective action by the person himself who is to be moral. The *Gorgias* sets up an analogy between the artist and the object of his craft, and the statesman and the making of moral citizens. Yet this requires considerable qualification not found in the *Gorgias*, that clearly allocates to the individual citizen the making of his own morality with some assistance from the statesman.

Although the *Gorgias* does not, as does the *Republic*, suggest the extension of morality to all individuals under the proper condition, it does in its espousal of the philosophic way of life and its introduction of the geometrical principle of equality suggest a concept of inherent value apart from the utilitarianism which dominates other early dialogues.

NOTES

[1] Cf., for example, Werner Jaeger's treatment of the *Gorgias* in *Paideia* II (New York, 1944), pp. 126–60, especially p. 132. J. Moreau makes much of an alleged autonomy of the soul in the *Gorgias*; cf. his *La Construction de L'Idéalisme Platonicien* (Paris, 1939), p. 204 ff., especially p. 207.

[2] The *Cratylus* also implies a passive aspect to the object of a craft in the process of production. When the craftsman makes a shuttle, for example, he must have his mind on the form (εἶδος) of the shuttle. The wood upon which the form of the shuttle is somehow impressed is apparently quite passive, cf. *Cratylus* 389A ff. *Republic* X, 596B, like the above passage from the *Cratylus*, emphasizes the significance of the form (unlike the *Cratylus*, "idea" here would apparently refer to the theory of forms, but the difference is not significant for our discussion) in the activity of the craftsman. This passage together with the *Charmides* 165D ff., *Euthydemus* 280C ff., allows no active function to the object of the *techne* in the process of creation but regards it simply as the product. The emphasis appears to be on the activity of the craftsman conditioned by his knowledge of the nature of or form of the object he is seeking to create. It would not be far wrong to consider the object in the creative process as a gradually emerging effect which stems from the activity of the craftsman.

[3] In the *Gorgias* 468A–C, the plural ἀγαθῶν or ἀγαθά is usually translated in the singular as the good. Jowett, Hamilton, Helmbold and Schleiermacher consistently do so. Lamb (whose translation of the *Gorgias* is used here with some modification) translates in 468A in the plural: "Then do people do these intermediate things . . . for the sake of good things (ἕνεκεν τῶν ἀγαθῶν), or the good things (τἀγαθά) for the sake of the intermediate." But immediately following he renders τὰ μεταξὺ δήπου τῶν ἀγαθῶν "the intermediate for the sake of the good." The remaining relevant instance of the plural in 468A–C, τὰ γὰρ ἀγαθὰ βουλώμεθα, Lamb translates in the singular. Croset and Bodin, the Budé editors, like Lamb translate ἀγαθῶν and ἀγαθά in 468A in the plural: "Ces choses neutres, quand on les fait, les fait-on en vue de celles qui sont bonnes, ou les bonnes en vue des neutres," but unlike Lamb, they go on, "Les neutres evidement en vue des bonnes," translating ἀγαθῶν in the plural. But in the remainder of the passage the Bude editors render ἀγαθά (468C) in the singular, translating τὰ γὰρ ἀγαθὰ βουλώμεθα as "Car nous voulons notre bien." Their translation of this last phrase suggests the reason for the general tendency of translators to render the Greek plural of "good" in the singular. For scholars usually view the *Gorgias* here and at *Gorgias* 500A as presenting the true "good for man" which is the final end of man's actions, or even as presenting the form of the good as the goal of man's endeavor. Cf., for example, Jaeger, *Paideia*, II, p. 135, and J. Hirschberger, "Die Phronesis und die Philosophie Platons vor dem Staate," *Phil*, S.B. XXV (1932): 135–36. In his edition of the *Gorgias*, Dodds (pp. 235–36) suggests, that "the good" signifies the "good for the agent." I agree with this interpretation if it is not taken as embracing a "general conception," as Dodds puts it, of the actor's good. Rather, "good" means good things; the agent seeks not "the good" but good things

for himself. Good in the plural can be better understood, as Dodds suggests, to stand for the various good objects of desire as in the *Protagoras* (358C–D) and *Meno* (77C). I think that this interpretation has additional plausibility if it is noted that the intermediate things are actions or things which are means for good things such as wisdom, health, and wealth.

[4] On the ambiguity of καλόν cf. E. R. Dodds' commentary on the *Gorgias* (Oxford, 1959), pp. 249–51.

[5] All those translators mentioned in n. 3 above translate the Greek plural of good in this passage in the singular, obscuring, I think, still further the essentially utilitarian character of the *Gorgias*, which is implied in "good things" but not as clearly in "the good."

EDWARD N. LEE
University of California at San Diego

On the "Gold-Example" in Plato's *Timaeus* (50A5-B5)*

At *Timaeus* 50A5–B5, Plato presents a concise, enigmatic illustration of the "Receptacle" or "All-receiving Nature." He imagines someone moulding figures of all kinds in a lump of gold, and continually remoulding each and all into all the others. Someone else then *points* to one of these shaped pieces of gold and asks, "What is it?" (τί ποτ' ἐστί). Plato comments on three possible replies to this question:

(i) μακρῷ πρὸς ἀλήθειαν ἀσφαλέστατον εἰπεῖν ὅτι χρυσός,

(ii) τὸ δὲ τρίγωνον ὅσα τε ἄλλα σχήματα ἐνεγίγνετο, μηδέποτε λέγειν ταῦτα ὡς ὄντα, ἅ γε μεταξὺ τιθεμένου μεταπίπτει,

(iii) ἀλλ' ἐὰν ἄρα καὶ τὸ τοιοῦτον μετ' ἀσφαλείας ἐθέλῃ δέχεσθαί τινος, ἀγαπᾶν.

In the present paper, I shall discuss the interpretation of these three replies. By far the fullest account of them to date is by Prof. Cherniss.[1] He has effectively refuted many earlier views, but I am not fully persuaded by his own interpretation, and in Part I of this paper I attempt to show some difficulties in his reading. Then (II–III) I shall advance and defend an alternative interpretation of my own: first (II) defending in detail my way of construing Plato's language here, then (III) explaining the philosophical doctrine expressed by the passage, so construed, and defending the claim that it is genuinely platonic doctrine. To conclude (IV), I shall comment briefly on the place of the example in its wider context in the *Timaeus*.

I

I find four major difficulties with Cherniss' reading. First, it involves an equivocal view as to the relation between the three main components. On the one hand, Cherniss holds that (i) and (ii) go closely together as contrasted answers to the one question posed in the context: "[(ii)] being

* This is a slightly revised version of a paper presented at the 1965 meeting of the SAGP in Providence, Rhode Island.

the forbidden reply to the question τί ποτ' ἐστί, to which [(i)] is the correct answer."[2] But, on the other hand, he also holds that (ii) and (iii) go closely together as contrasted answers to some other question to which (ii) is the forbidden answer, and (iii) the correct reply: "τὸ τοιοῦτον here [in (iii)] is the abbreviated alternative to the forbidden ταῦτα ὡς ὄντα [in (ii)]."[3] He thus finds two correct alternatives to (ii)—which is to say, his view of (ii) is basically equivocal. To support his reading of (ii), Cherniss requires a certain shift in the reader's understanding of the question to which (i), (ii) and (iii) provide answers. The initial question is specifically asked about some one thing that the asker points at (50A7–B1). On the recommended answer (i), we are to say that that is gold (for it remains gold, in the midst of all its other changes); what we are not to say, is (ii) that what the questioner points at is a "triangle," "square," or any other of the passing shapes.[4] But in order to progress beyond this point in the text, Cherniss needs to take the basic question in a somewhat different sense: that question must now specifically concern the shapes that come to be in the gold, for it is only as an answer to that question that (iii) can be called for, as a new corrective to (ii). To support such a shift in sense, Cherniss accords a rather marked, subject-switching force to 50B2 δέ, and punctuates his translation so as to convey the shift by placing a semi-colon between (i) and (ii), with only a comma between (ii) and (iii). The required shift is rather elusive, but we can perhaps fairly bring it into relief by amplifying slightly upon his translation. (The arrow-brackets are in the original; only the words in square brackets are my additions:)

> [When the questioner asks what it is that he is pointing at,] by far the surest answer so far as truth is concerned is to say "gold"; but as to the triangle and all the other figures that were coming to be in it, [if it is *those* he means to ask about,] ⟨the surest thing is⟩ never to say "these are," since they ⟨i.e. what would be denoted by "these"⟩ [i.e. those things that he is pointing at] are changing even while one is making the statement, but to be content if with some assurance he may be willing to accept ⟨the statement⟩ "What is such and such ⟨is⟩." [i.e., if he really wishes to know what the square or triangle *is*, then be content if he will agree that "what is such and such is—the triangle and the other figures."]

The following dialogue may help to make these answers, and the necessary shift, more clear:

> (Y is moulding all sorts of shapes in some gold.)
>
> X.1—(X, pointing to the thing in Y's hands, asks,) "What is that?"

(i) Y.1—"This is gold."
X.2—"Why don't you say that it's a triangle? It looks like one."

(ii) Y.2—"Just then it did, but look: I have made it into something else even while you were speaking, so I couldn't properly have said, 'what you are pointing to *is* a triangle.'"
X.3—"I see, but what *about* those figures that you are moulding in the gold?" [τὸ δὲ τρίγωνον read with subject-shifting force; cf. Cherniss' "but as to the . . . figures".]

(ii) Y.3—"What about them? What you are pointing at is clearly not the triangle, the square, or any other figure, for I make it into something different even as you speak."
X.4—"But if *that* is not (a? the?) triangle, what is? What would you refer to by the term 'triangle'?"

(iii) Y.4—(Remembering the contents of *Timaeus* 49D–E) "What is such and such. I mean (cf. 49E5) what is permanently of such and such a nature, and always recurs alike in all these cases: *that* is what I mean by 'triangle,' and I would be content if you would accept that answer too."

In this schema, Y.2 and Y.3 represent the two interpretations of (ii), one set in contrast to (i) (=Y.1), and the other to (iii) (=Y.4). To secure both senses of (ii) in the context, we require the shifts in the understanding of the question at issue that are represented here by X's questions. Since, on Cherniss' view,[5] the entire gold-example serves as a brief illustration of all the preceding lines since 49C7, these required shifts would of course receive support from the wider context. None the less, it seems to me that they strain our passage to the limit. Though that might not be decisive in itself, some other difficulties combine with it to weigh strongly against Cherniss' reading.

My second difficulty with Cherniss' reading is the plural ταῦτα in answer (ii). The vivid emphasis on pointing in 50A7–B1 clearly showed that some *one* thing is denoted, and one question asked about it (δεικνύντος δή τινος αὐτῶν ἓν καὶ ἐρομένου τί ποτ' ἐστί). The first reply prescribed is clearly singular,[6] and Cherniss sees that (ii) must also have a basically singular force: "[(ii)] must mean 'never to say that *these* are' in the sense 'never to say "*this* is triangle," "*this* is square," etc.' "[7] But despite the singular question so vividly imagined in the context, Cherniss maintains that Plato's mention of the various possible shapes (τὸ δὲ τρίγωνον ὅσα τε ἄλλα σχήματα ἐνεγίγνετο) abruptly attracts the deictic pronoun into the plural. Many interpreters have held that ταῦτα refers specifically *to* those most obvious plurals in the context (τὸ δὲ τρίγωνον ὅσα τε ἄλλα σχήματα) but Cherniss rejects that reading[8] and must accordingly hold that the ταῦτα is drawn into the plural by those terms, though referring not to them, but to some *one* subject which (in each case) we would point at and inquire about.[9]

My third, and most general difficulty with Cherniss' reading is the supposed parallel with 49D–E which he relies upon at every turn in his interpretation. (In particular, it underlies his view of the (ii)–(iii) antithesis as saying that not ταῦτα but τὸ τοιοῦτον should be called "triangle," "fire," or whatever.)[10] In point of fact, that parallel is quite defective: (a) in 49D–E, we find four different complex references to the qualitatively invariant aspect of becoming (49D5–6 τὸ τοιοῦτον ἀεί and the other τὸ τοιοῦτον phrases in D6–7, E5–6, and E6–7[11]). Cherniss takes 50B4 τὸ τοιοῦτον as an abbreviated allusion to these phrases,[12] but he gives no explanation why Plato here omits the essential temporal modifiers so carefully retained and varied in all four instances in 49D–E. Furthermore (b), to secure a (ii)–(iii) antithesis "exactly parallel"[13] to 49D–E, Cherniss has to omit 50B4 ἐὰν ἄρα, B4 καί and B4–5 μετ' ἀσφαλείας . . . τινος. He provides no explanation for the presence of these terms, nor does he explain the precise force of B5 ἀγαπᾶν in this context. For all these reasons—and because I feel that the entire (ii)–(iii) antithesis based on 49D–E requires a strained equivocation in our understanding of the context (see the first objection above)—I find it difficult to believe that the parallel with 49D–E is proper to our passage.[14]

Still another reason for this view, and my fourth and final difficulty with Cherniss' reading, concerns the lines immediately following the gold-example. In 50B5 ff., Plato says that ὁ αὐτὸς λόγος holds of the Receptacle. He then explains his meaning in a way that fits *only* the (i)–(ii) antithesis, and makes no use of (iii) at all. His remark at 50B6–8 (it must always be called the same . . .) parallels answer (i) in the gold-example: we are always to reply, "it is gold," for that much about it remains the same. In addition, 50B8–C4 parallels comment (ii): the Receptacle never truly takes on any of the characters that it receives, although it may appear to do so. Cornford brings out the parallel clearly:

> The Forms, "in some strange manner that is hard to express," impress their characteristic qualities on the Receptacle. But the Receptacle does not itself possess any of these characters or qualities, *any more than gold in itself possesses a triangular shape.* The qualities do not belong to it; they only pass in and out, like images crossing a mirror.[15]

Plato's own explanation in 50B8 ff. thus seems to undercut one of Cherniss' arguments for a parallel with 49D–E. Cherniss supports that parallel by comparing B3–4 ἅ γε . . . μεταπίπτει with 49E2–4 φεύγει . . . φάσις.[16] They are indeed similar passages, but Plato's explanation shows that the clause within the gold-example makes a special and rather different point. At 49E2–4, Plato cited the "fugitivity" of phenomenal individuals as a reason why they cannot provide a stable, definite referent for such terms as "this" or "fire" or "water" or the rest. At that point, his aim was to say that we should properly refer these terms to something else (to τὸ τοιοῦτον ἀεί). But at 50B3–4 he is explaining why we should not speak of the gold as being of-any-particular-shape: not because we *should* refer such shape-words elsewhere (though Plato does believe that) but because these transitory shapes have no real *hold* upon the nature of the gold, and cannot be said to be what it *is* (i.e. cannot rightly answer the question τί ποτ' ἐστί). In 50B2–4 Plato is concerned with talk about the Receptacle, not about triangle or fire.

II

The cumulative effect of the difficulties I have indicated is to leave me unconvinced by Cherniss' reading of the gold-example. My own interpretation will be very different from his, yet my basic orientation toward the passage follows a principle which Cherniss himself has done more than any other commentator to establish. As Cherniss emphasized,

> The whole sentence from 50A7 to the end . . . is determined by the hypothesis that someone asks a question . . . and is framed as the recommendation of a reply to that questioner . . .; and consequently the person who asks the question, not the thing about which he asks, must be thought of as the one who will accept or decline to accept this answer [i.e. as the subject of 50B5 ἐθέλῃ].[17]

In other words, the passage depicts in miniature a specific dialectical situation of question-and-answer; it presents the schema of a dialectical encounter, and it is in the context of that encounter that Plato's recommendations are made.[18] This fact is the key to the passage, as I shall try to show. I first set forth the main lines of my reading, and then offer a defense of its details.

The basic antithesis or contrast in our passage is not between (i) and (ii), nor (ii) and (iii), but between (i) and (iii); or rather—since (i) and (ii) go closely together as two sides of the same coin—between the (i)–(ii) complex and (iii). It is a contrast between the best reply (μακρῷ πρὸς ἀλήθειαν ἀσφαλέστατον) and a second-best reply (one to be offered only under the specific dialectical circumstances cited, and to be accepted only μετ' ἀσφαλείας . . . τινος). That (iii) is only a second-best reply is shown particularly by the καί (indicating that the point which follows is an addition to the "surest" answer stipulated in [i]–[ii]), as well as by ἀγαπᾶν (as often in Plato, the force of the verb is "to settle for" or "acquiesce in" something—"to be content with it," *even though* it falls short of the ideal one might desire).[19] But what is the answer that we may, in certain cases, be content with? What does the τὸ τοιοῦτον in (iii) signify? I believe the phrase is not, as it were, in quotation-marks; it is not itself the content of the answer to be made, but refers back *to* the kind of answer meant: the very one proscribed in (ii), an answer in terms of τὸ τρίγωνον ὅσα τε ἄλλα σχήματα. For this use of τὸ τοιοῦτον, see particularly *Laws* VIII.838E2–3: ὅπως δὲ αὖ τὸ τοιοῦτον ἐθέλοντας λέγειν πάντας δυνατὸν ἔσται ποτὲ παρασχεῖν; "How can he ever make everyone willing to say that sort of thing"—where τὸ τοιοῦτον refers to the views about sexual relations discussed earlier. In sum, our passage depicts a dialectical encounter, a context in which only one sort of answer is strictly correct, but where—*if* our questioner is of a certain sort, a person willing to accept another kind of answer as well—we should be content to speak to him at his level, and reply to his question in that other way. If someone points toward something appearing in a place before him and asks, "What is that (to which I am pointing)?" the strictly sure and true reply (i) would be to say that it is the Receptacle (=gold in the example). If we wish to speak "most securely with respect to truth" we must (ii) avoid replying with the name of the particular appearance that happens to present itself (for that term will not tell what that to which he is pointing [i.e. the Receptacle] *is*). *However* (iii), in the event that our questioner is someone willing to accept that sort of answer, too, in that special dialectical situation, we may be content with (settle for) that strictly improper reply (ii), instead of insisting on the proper answer (i). I shall now offer more detailed support for this interpretation, support first for my analysis of the language in 50B1–5, then for my attribution to Plato of the doctrine that I find in the passage.

Answer (i) poses no problems. In answer (ii), in accord with the majority of commentators, I take ταῦτα to refer directly to the preceding plurals, and would translate the passage thus: "but as for the triangle and all the other figures that were coming to be in it, never to speak of those—which alter even while one speaks—as being." However, the exact force of the B3 phrase μηδέποτε λέγειν ταῦτα ὡς ὄντα needs to be carefully explained. Both (i) and (ii) are given here as guides for answering the single question τί ποτ' ἐστί, asked about some single thing to which the questioner is pointing. We cannot construe the B3 phrase to mean "never to speak of those as being" in the sense "never to answer with the words 'those exist' (nor even, in each separate case, with the words 'the triangle exists' or 'the square exists' or whatever)." We cannot, for such bare assertions of existence would be an absurdly incongruous reply to the question τί ποτ' ἐστί. What else can then be meant by the phrase "to speak of something as being"? I believe the answer is provided by *Sophist* 263B9, a passage closely parallel to 50B3.[20] Plato there defines a false statement as one which says about X things other than what is (the case about X) (263B7 ἕτερα τῶν ὄντων). It is one which Τὰ μὴ ὄντ' ἄρα ὡς ὄντα λέγει (B9): "says that not-beings are beings" in the sense that it "states things which are not (the-case-about-X) as being (the-case-about-X)."[21] In this passage, "to speak of something as being" is not "to say of it, 'it exists'," but rather "to speak of something else's being *it*": i.e., it is to speak of *its* being-what-something-else-*is*; or, better, of its being-the-case-about (holding true of) some subject specified in the context. I believe *Timaeus* 50B2–4 is very similar. There "to speak of the triangle (etc.) as being" does not mean "to say that they *exist*" (which would be no answer to the question in the context); rather, it means "to say that *they* are what the-object-that-the-questioner-points-to *is*"; in short, it is to give "triangle" (etc.) as the answer to the question τί ποτ' ἐστί. The gist of the relation between (i) and (ii) is thus the following: "if someone should point and ask you such a question, the surest answer is to tell him that it is gold, and never to reply that it is a triangle or any other of those changing shapes."[22]

On Cherniss' view, the ἀλλά introducing (iii) is parallel to those in 49D5 and D6. It sets up a (ii)–(iii) antithesis "exactly parallel" (128.3) to that in 49D–E, and has what Denniston calls its "eliminative" role, "substituting the true for the false." On my view, there is no such (ii)–(iii) antithesis, no parallel to 49D–E. The ἀλλά introduces an affirmation opposed to the earlier clauses as a conditional exception to the general rule they state.[23] The whole collocation ἐάν ἄρα καί might be taken together,[24] but I believe the καί belongs with τὸ τοιοῦτον, not with the verb; it emphasizes the questioner's willingness to accept the answer cited in (iii), *over and above* the strictly "safest" answer given in (i).[25] With the ἐὰν ἄρα collocation ("emotional," not inferential, ἄρα) notice Denniston's remark: "ἄρα in a conditional protasis denotes that the hypothesis is one of which the possibility has only just been realized: 'If, after all.' "[26] We cannot make a mechanical application of such judgments, of course, but Plato's use of the particles here does seem (to me) to mark a somewhat sudden or "just realized" quality about the exception that he abruptly allows for in (iii).[27]

As noted in Part I above, 50B4 τὸ τοιοῦτον lacks the temporal qualifiers so carefully varied but consistently conjoined with that phrase in 49D–E. That fact appears to me to undermine any parallel with 49D–E, and I take it instead that τὸ τοιοῦτον refers back to the preceding answer (one in terms of "triangle" and so forth).[28] The words μετ' ἀσφαλείας . . . τινος stand (as indicated by the τὶς) in contrast to 50B1 μακρῷ πρὸς ἀλήθειαν ἀσφαλέστατον. The word ἀσφάλεια seems here to mean an inward feeling of security or confidence, the qualified (τὶς) sense of certainty with which someone might accept the less-than-safest reply. I have found no exact parallel for such a subjective meaning of the term, but it easily and naturally takes on that connotation from the context here.[29] Though the word ἐθέλειν often functions as a mere auxiliary, it has a more important role here. The nuance conveyed by the use of both ἐθέλειν and δέχεσθαι is an emphasis upon the voluntary, the spontaneous and sincere character of the questioner's acceptance: it is not for form's sake nor argument's sake that he accepts the answer, but because it represents the degree of dialectical insight this speaker can attain.[30] 'Εθέλειν in Plato often has such a dialectical role, indicating readiness to engage in an argument or to maintain (or agree to) some position.[31] Perhaps the best example is *Parmenides* 133B: the problems about "participation" can be surmounted only by a man of wide experience and natural ability, *willing* to follow through a long and difficult argument (ἐθέλοι δὲ . . . ἕπεσθαι). There is perhaps also a nuance to the use of δέχεσθαι here. It stands in contrast to the fuller dialectical security of answer (i)–(ii), and so conveys the idea of *simply* accepting or agreeing to answer (iii), without pressing on to scrutinize those weaknesses that make the statement strictly invalid. Compare *Cratylus* 421D7–9: Λέγω γὰρ οὖν εἰκότα. οὐ μέντοι μοι δοκεῖ προφάσεις ἀγὼν δέχεσθαι, ἀλλὰ προθυμητέον ταῦτα διασκέψασθαι. So too, in *Timaeus* 50B5, δέχεσθαι signifies one's passive acquiescence in a kind of reply that has not been subjected to (and could not withstand) full dialectical scrutiny.[32]

The verb ἀγαπᾶν appears to me to give the strongest support for the present reading. It *can*, of course, mean "to delight in fully," "cherish," or "be (wholly) content with."[33] Very often, however, and especially in dialectical contexts and in conjunction with a conditional clause, the verb (and its relations) have the sense "to rest content with" or "to settle for" something less than the ideal. Here are various examples, first from non-dialectical, then from dialectical contexts:

(A) 1. *Republic V.* 475A9–B2: If men desirous of honors cannot get them from the great, they are content to get them from the small: κἂν μὴ ὑπὸ μειζόνων . . . ὑπὸ σμικροτέρων . . . τιμώμενοι ἀγαπῶσιν.

2. *Protagoras* 328A8–B1: ἀλλὰ κἂν εἰ ὀλίγον ἔστιν τις . . . ἀγαπητόν.

3. *Laws* IV. 684C7–9: Men wish that their treatment should be pleasant, but should be thankful if it takes only *small* pain: τὸ δέ γ' ἐστιν ἀγαπητὸν . . . εἰ καί τις μετὰ λύπης μὴ μεγάλης δύναιτο κτλ.

4. *Laws* IV. 705A1–2: a city-site is too close to the sea, ὅμως δὲ ἀγαπητὸν καὶ τοῦτο.

5. *Laws* IV. 718D5–7: εἰ καὶ μὴ μέγα τι, σμικρὸν δέ, . . . πᾶν ἀγαπητόν.

6. *Laws* V. 735D7: a tyrant could take the best and strongest measures, but someone without such power, if he can so much as (D6 εἰ καί) effect the mildest measures, will be quite content to do even that much—ἀγαπώντως ἂν καὶ τὸ τοιοῦτον δράσειεν (cf. England *ad loc.*).

7. *Republic* V. 472B–473B: we cannot *fully* realize the Forms in actions, but should be content to come as close as we can; (ἀγαπᾶν in 472C1, C3, and 473B2).

(B) 1. *Theaetetus* 207A3–7: we cannot list *all* the parts in a wagon, but would be content, when asked to define it by enumerating its parts, if we could list a few: ἀλλ' ἀγαπῷμεν ἂν ἐρωτηθέντες ὅτι ἐστὶν ἅμαξα [cf. 206E6–7 τί ἕκαστον, and the question in *Timaeus* 50A7–B1], εἰ ἔχοιμεν εἰπεῖν κτλ.

2. *Theaetetus* 164C9: Socrates chides himself for being content with (ἀγαπᾶν) a purely verbal argument.

3. *Cratylus* 439B6: What method men *should* use to discover truth is too much to decide; ἀγαπητὸν δὲ καὶ τοῦτο ὁμολογήσασθαι—that they ought not to go about it through names, etc.[34]

4. *Sophist* 241C7–9 and *Meno* 75C1 (less clear cases).

This small selection of cases will suffice to show the sense "to settle for" or "acquiesce in" somewhat inferior circumstances.[35] That sense fits easily with the exception-making force we found for ἀλλά and the additive force of καί, as well as the other details. However, it seems to me difficult to take ἀγαπᾶν here in the sense required by Cherniss' reading of a (ii)–(iii) antithesis that parallels 49D–E, the sense of a true, full contentment with the dialectically *proper* answer—full satisfaction with the *ideal.* Even if we do read B4 ἀλλά as parallel to those in 49D5 and D6, the reasons for the ἐὰν ἄρα conditional, and especially for B4 καί, remain most unclear. Furthermore, 49D–E gave a schema for talking about fire and water (or whatever) in a manner ἀσφαλέστατα μακρῷ (49D3). If there *is* a (ii)–(iii) antithesis parallel to 49D–E, why is the ideal answer here said to be accepted only μετ' ἀσφαλείας . . . τινος? And why ought we to be *content* if it is only accepted thus?

III

To defend the present reading further, it is time now to show that the doctrine we have found expressed in the passage is genuinely platonic doctrine, consistent with other dialogues and legitimately attributable to Plato himself. Up to this point, we have seen that the gold-example presents us with the schema of a dialectical encounter. The most proper answer under the circumstances there is that prescribed in (i)–(ii), yet Plato advises in (iii) that we may be content with a strictly improper answer under certain conditions: we may agree (for agreement's sake) in cases where our questioner does not perceive the need to seek the fuller, stricter truth of the matter. Clause (iii) advises a concession, instead of a rigid insistence on the strictly true account. In short, it advises a reply which is "more dialectical," in exactly the sense of *Meno* 75D5–7: ἔστι δὲ ἴσως τὸ διαλεκτικώτερον μὴ μόνον τἀληθῆ ἀποκρίνεσθαι, ἀλλὰ καὶ δι' ἐκείνων ὧν ἂν προομολογῇ εἰδέναι ὁ ἐρωτῶν. Moreover, precisely that manner of agreement was, as many have remarked, the hallmark of Socratic dialectic, epitomized at Xenophon, *Memorabilia* 4, 6, 15: ὁπότε δὲ αὐτός (sc. Socrates) τι τῷ λόγῳ διεξίοι, διὰ τῶν μάλιστα ὁμολογουμένων ἐπορεύετο, νομίζων ταύτην τὴν ἀσφάλειαν εἶναι λόγου. Part of the point here is no doubt the every-day examples used in his talk (*Gorgias* 490E–491A), but central too is his reliance on the step-by-step agreement and response of interlocutors, and the consequent accommodation of his teaching to their capabilities. Such accommodation remains a basic principle of Plato's later dialectic, as of his theory of persuasion. We find it in the "midwife" speech of the *Theaetetus:* just as midwives are the best match-makers (149D–150A), so Socrates can judge which students deserve to stay with him, and which may be sent off to Prodicus (151A–B). At *Politicus* 277C the principle is stated clearly: for those who are able to follow it, a verbal definition of any living creature is much better than a picture or model; but for others, those will suffice:

> γραφῆς δὲ καὶ συμπάσης χειρουργίας λέξει καὶ λόγῳ
> δηλοῦν πᾶν ζῷον μᾶλλον πρέπει τοῖς δυναμένοις
> ἕπεσθαι· τοῖς δ' ἄλλοις διὰ χειρουργιῶν.

Still another version of the principle is indicated soon after in the *Politicus*. At 285D–286A, Plato distinguishes between Forms that have sensibly apparent images and those (by far the more important cases) that do not. In the case of the former, he says, if someone asks for an account of them, we *can*—if and when we *want* to reply without taking pains and without going into a discussion—simply indicate the sensible likeness:

> τοῖς μὲν τῶν ὄντων ῥᾳδίως καταμαθεῖν αἰσθηταί τινες ὁμοιότητες πεφύκασιν, ἃς οὐδὲν χαλεπὸν δηλοῦν, ὅταν αὐτῶν τις βουληθῇ τῷ λόγον αἰτοῦντι [sc. by asking τί ποτ' ἐστί ?] περί του μὴ μετὰ πραγμάτων ἀλλὰ χωρὶς λόγου ῥᾳδίως ἐνδείξασθαι·

Plato clearly does not believe that any terms can really be ostensively defined, nor that any matters can be adequately dealt with χωρὶς λόγου (n.b. *Sophist* 218C1–5). It is not the same thing at all to say that some Forms have readily discernible sensible images, and to say that one can adequately treat those matters just by pointing those images out. Plato does maintain the first, but all he says about the latter is that, when we *want* to, we can deal with certain questioners just by ostensive presentation of an image, χωρὶς λόγου. When would we want to do so? Presumably, when (as said at *Politicus* 277C) our questioner is not one of those who is able to follow out a lengthy *logos*. If one of those "able to follow" asks us, "what is fire?"[36] we may embark on a *logos* of the lengthy mathematical sort that Plato gives in *Timaeus* 53C ff. But if one of "the others" inquires, we may simply strike a match or point to some flame, and *show* him some of that stuff, saying, "this is fire."[37] By the same token, if one of those "others" points at some fire and asks us, "what is that?" we may be content to say that it is fire. (We may be content, because he is marked as one of those "others" precisely *by* his willingness to accept that sort of answer with the sort of ἀσφάλειά τις realized in dialectical agreement at an unexamined verbal level.[38]) The genuinely proper, strictly secure reply [sc. that given in (i)–(ii)] is reserved for τοῖς δυναμένοις ἕπεσθαι.

According to *Phaedrus* 275E, one of the major faults with written works is that they cannot thus accommodate their message to their readers' specific capabilities (cf. 276A6–7, E6). According to *Phaedrus* 271C10–272B2, the art of persuasion rests precisely on such an accommodation of one's *logos* to the hearer's aptitudes. It must adjust thus to his level, for it achieves its end of ψυχαγωγία (261A) not by force, but by his voluntary acquiescence.[39] If that acquiescence must to some extent be won by various irrational devices,[40] yet it must also make some plausible appeal to whatever degree of rationality the hearer has. For the great majority of men, capable of right opinion but not of νοῦς (*Timaeus* 51E), a partial or mythical account will serve (cf. *Timaeus* 29C–D). Such devices as the noble lie of the *Republic*, the *Timaeus*' myth of a creation or the theology of *Laws* X are Plato's "way of getting across to the masses veracities and sanctities whose formal essence was beyond their grasp."[41] So long as the devices of persuasion win the wills of unenlightened, "unawakened" men to voluntary compliance with the law, we must be content with that, and not insist upon accounts too elevated for their understanding.[42] Indeed, were we to force on them the strictly *true* account—if we told everyone they are but dreaming and that their image-world is not truly *real* (n.b. *Timaeus* 52B3–C5)—we might only make ourselves appear ridiculous and so relinquish any influence upon events. Therefore a skillful dialectician, a man who understands the weakness and complexity of mortal human nature, will be content with what agreement he can get, and not force on his interlocutors truths more advanced than they are ready to accept. In the dialectical encounter visualized in the gold-example, the most proper answer is that specified in (i)–(ii). When someone points at an appearance and asks its nature (τί ποτ' ἐστί), the only genuine, perduring *nature* that he really points to is the "Receptacle" (*Timaeus* 49E7–50A2). There is no form or character truly existing *there* where he is pointing; for the Form itself cannot be "there" (cf. 52A3) nor be a "this," while the phenomenon does not truly in-form the Receptacle (50C1–2), and itself has only fleeting image-being, not that of the really real (52C2–D1); hence no reply in terms of forms or characters (τὸ δὲ τρίγωνον ὅσα τε ἄλλα σχήματα ἐνεγίγνετο) can truly tell the nature of that-which-is-pointed-out. The proper answer therefore should avoid such predicates entirely. However, these considerations are more than most people can accept,[43] and in the event that our questioner is someone willing to accept that improper kind of reply (in addition to the best or surest one), we may be content to give him that as an answer: ἀλλ' ἐὰν ἄρα καὶ τὸ τοιοῦτον μετ' ἀσφαλείας ἐθέλῃ δέχεσθαί τινος, ἀγαπᾶν.

IV

Even if my argument is accepted, misgivings may no doubt remain as to *why* Plato makes this passing concession in this context. I have no real answer to that, and can only reply that any interpretation of the gold-example leaves it *somewhat* enigmatic. As we noted in Part I, Plato goes on to deal directly with the Receptacle (at 50B5 ff. ὁ αὐτὸς δὴ λόγος), and in doing so he makes use of (i) and (ii), but not of (iii). Thus he himself did not wholly integrate the passage in its context. Nor do ancient testimonies seem to help. Aristotle only once refers to the gold-example, but he is puzzled by it, too, and comments only on clause (i).[44] Simplicius quotes at length from the gold-example[45], but he stops at 50B4 μεταπίπτει, and thus omits clause (iii) entirely! The explanation he provides in the context clearly shows that he took the gold-example as an illustration of the Receptacle.[46] He quotes lines 49E6–50A4 with it, and apparently takes it that αὐτοῦ πέρι in 50A5 refers back only to lines 49E7 ff., in which the subject of the Receptacle (ἐν ᾧ) was introduced. (Cornford took much the same view,[47] but Cherniss holds[48] that it illustrates all of 49C7–50A4.)

None of this really dispels the enigma, nor is anything likely to do so. We can say that at *Timaeus* 49–50 Plato is concerned with the logic of statements involving ostension.[49] He seeks to distinguish the stable or invariant factors which enter into the constitution of the transitory occurrences at which we point. With characteristically vivid imaginative force, he does this—not by imagining the effects of slow, relentless processes of change (cf. Melissus B7), nor by contemplating the "certain uncertainties" over vast extents of time (cf. the ode in Sophocles' "Ajax" 646–683); instead he imagines an artisan ceaselessly moulding some gold (why *gold*?) into all varieties of shapes. Around this vivid image he then builds a dialectical encounter in which various possible replies are discussed, and then adapts the whole to his exposition of the obscure "all-receiving nature." Perhaps—given such a complex array of purposes—the enigmatic character of the passage was quite unavoidable.

NOTES

1 Harold Cherniss, "A Much Misread Passage of the *Timaeus* (*Timaeus* 49C7–50B5)," *AJP*, 75 (1954): 113–30, at 125–27. Henceforth all references to Cherniss' view will be to this article—usually by page and line number, thus: "128.6"=page 128, line 6.

2 126.4–6; cf. n. 18, lines 3–7.

3 127.25–26; cf. n. 19, *sub fin.*

4 This is the first of Cherniss' views of (ii) referred to earlier. Cf. his n. 17, lines 3–18, and last 3 lines; also n. 18, lines 3–7.

5 Cf. 125.1–2, 127.24 and 128.1–6. Against this part of Cherniss' view, see my third objection below.

6 As Cherniss says, "ὅτι χρυσός stands for τοῦτο χρυσός ἐστι" (126.7).

7 N. 17, end of first paragraph; my emphasis. Cf. lines 4–5 of second paragraph (quoted n. 9 below), and n. 18, lines 5–7.

8 N. 17, second paragraph.

[9] To appreciate the difficulty here, compare these passages in Cherniss: (a) n. 17, para. 2, lines 4–5 (a quote from A. E. Taylor, with Cherniss' comment in brackets): "the figure [i.e., the golden figure to which one would point and say: 'this is . . .'] would be actually changing as you spoke." (b) n. 18, lines 3–5: "the golden shapes (i.e. the phenomena) [note the plural] to which the naïf answerer is likely to point and say 'these are triangles, squares, etc.' "

[10] Cf. p. 127, last 5 lines: τὸ τοιοῦτον replaces ταῦτα as the subject of the statement.

[11] Cf. Cherniss, p. 115, n. 3 on these phrases.

[12] Cf. p. 128, bottom paragraph. Also *AJP*, 78 (1957): 246 (top).

[13] 128.3.

[14] On my own view—cf. II and III below—that parallel is dropped, and τὸ τοιοῦτον has a different role.—I am well aware that Cherniss' whole interpretation of 49D–E has been challenged by Gulley (*AJP*, 81 [1960]: 53–64). I have shown elsewhere that his challenge fails completely, but I cannot deal with that point here; see my paper, "On Plato's *Timaeus* 49D4–E7," *AJP*, LXXXVIII (1967): 1–28, at 15–20.

[15] Cornford, *Plato's Cosmology*, p. 184, my italics; cf. also p. 181.

[16] Page 125, n. 17, lines 7–11, p. 126, n. 18, lines 5–8.

[17] Cherniss, 126–27.

[18] Details will be added below, but the dialectical character of the passage is sufficiently proved by the question posed (ἐρομένου τί ποτ' ἐστί), and by the language of (iii): Plato often uses ἐθέλειν of dialectical readiness to say something, answer a question, or participate in a discussion; he usually uses ἀποδέχεσθαι for accepting an answer, but δέχεσθαι is also found (n.b., *Sophist* 247D6 ἐθέλοιεν ἂν δέχεσθαι καὶ ὁμολογεῖν [cf. 247E6]). We shall see that ἀγαπᾶν and ἀσφάλεια also fit this dialectical orientation.

[19] Cf. especially *Timaeus* 29C7–D1: ἀλλ' ἐὰν ἄρα μηδενὸς ἧττον παρεχώμεθα εἰκότας, ἀγαπᾶν χρή, μεμνημένους ὡς . . . φύσιν ἀνθρωπίνην ἔχομεν, κτλ. Remarking upon ἀγαπᾶν here, A. E. Taylor spoke of "its usual sense in classical Greek, 'to put up with,' 'not to grumble at.' We should prefer exactitude to approximation, and certainties to probabilities, but where the former are not to be had, we must 'put up with,' 'be decently contented with' the nearest approximation we can get." (*Commentary on Plato's Timaeus*, p. 75)

[20] Cherniss (at 126.10) cites *Sophist* 263B9 to support his reading, but his other examples there significantly differ from the *Sophist* passage, and are closer to his view of 50B3. At *Laws* 643D8–9 the ὄντα is clearly copulative, and accompanied both by an explicit subject and predicate term: λέγομεν ὡς τὸν μὲν πεπαιδευμένον ὄντα, τὸν δὲ ἀπαίδευτον (cf. *Laws* 886D4–8); that is not the case at *Sophist* 263B. (At *Laws* 641C8–D1, the verb is not εἶναι.)

[21] As Moravcsik points out, περὶ σοῦ is understood from 263B5 (cf. B11) in both B7 and B9 (his "Being and Meaning in the *Sophist*," *APF*, 14 [1962]: 76–77). Instead of his "relational being," however, I would speak (as above) of the being of *facts*: of its being (or not being) the *case* that so-

and-so. Cf. Cornford, *Plato's Theory of Knowledge*, p. 213, n. 1: "τὰ μὴ ὄντα, things which are not the fact," and p. 214, lines 5–6: "what is (the fact)"; also Moravcsik, *op. cit.*, p. 63 with n. 1.

22 This is of course the same (i)–(ii) antithesis that Cherniss sees in the passage (see Part I above). The reading of 50B3 given here was also that of Moreau in his 1939 book, *L'Ame du Monde* . . ., p. 16: "quant au triangle et à toutes les autres figures que cette masse revêt, jamais il ne faut donner ces attributs *comme étant ce que la chose en question est*" (my emphasis).

23 Cf. the passage from Aristotle cited in n. 27 below.

24 Cf. *Charmides* 168A10: an ἐπιστήμη of itself as well as others is absurd, "if, indeed, there really *is* such a science" (ἐὰν ἄρα καὶ ἔστιν). Also *Phaedrus* 257C3 ἐὰν ἄρα καὶ ἐθελήσῃ ("if he *should* be willing, after all" [cf. Verdenius, *ad loc.* in *Mn*, ser. 4, 8 (1955): 283, with pp. 266–67 *ad* 228E1]).

25 The καί might also be taken—though I think this less likely here—to mean "even": "If he is willing to accept even that sort of answer . . ."

26 Denniston, *The Greek Particles*², p. 37.

27 We may perhaps compare a passage in Aristotle (*Cat.* 11a, 26–29): particular branches of knowledge are not properly spoken of as relative to something else, *but if, after all*, they are to be spoken of thus, it is in virtue of their genus (knowledge) that they *too* can be called relative: ἀλλ' εἰ ἄρα κατὰ τὸ γένος καὶ αὗται πρός τι λέγεται. In *Timaeus* 50B4–5, there is a strong cumulative force from the exception-marking ἀλλά, the "sudden" or just-realized ἐὰν ἄρα, and καί denoting the addition of something over and above the earlier items. These, coupled with the contrast between μακρῷ . . . ἀσφαλέστατον and μετ' ἀσφαλείας τινος, and the particular force of ἀγαπᾶν (see below), all suggest a much looser relation between (iii) and (i)–(ii) than that which Cherniss finds.

28 For τὸ τοιοῦτον as a loose backward reference to the sort of thing said just before, cf. *Laws* 838E2–3 (quoted above), *Parmenides* 131B9, *Meno* 75E4 (cf. *Laws* 683E8). Sometimes, of course, it is a more specific reference to the preceding words (cf. *Phaedrus* 261E5, *Republic* 562E6, *Laws* 694C9 and *Sophist* 241D8), but that is not the case here.

29 The words δέχεσθαι (close to ὁμολογεῖν, cf. *Sophist* 247D6) and ἐθέλῃ permeate the clause with a subjective air that readily infuses itself with ἀσφάλεια. Compare the controversy over ἀσφάλεια in *Ev. Luc.* I. 4. J. H. Ropes persuasively argued that the ἀσφάλεια there "is that of the person who is to know, not . . . the facts or doctrines"; and that "the mind of a Greek, when he associated 'security' with 'knowing,' naturally turned to the security of the knowledge itself, rather than that of something else which was in some way related to the knowledge" (*JTS*, 24 [1923]: 69–70).

30 We shall return to the connection between this voluntariness, Platonic *Peitho*, and the ἀσφάλειά τις when examining the meaning behind Plato's inclusion of the third component.

31 Various dialectical cases: *Theaetetus* 170C6, 172B3, 177C9 (with διαμάχεσθαι, etc.); *Theaetetus* 184E8, *Sophist* 247D1, 6, *Cratylus* 431A6

(with ὁμολογεῖν, συγχωρεῖν); *Theaetetus* 196D5, *Parmenides* 131C9 (εἰπεῖν); cf. *Republic* 506C5, E4. Often, Plato uses the term ἐθέλειν in methodological discussions strongly colored by a background of ethical evaluations. The "digression" in the *Theaetetus* has two good examples: if an orator can be made to forsake his petty bickering and is then *willing* to turn his attention to abstract moral traits in themselves, he will see what a poor thing his usual chatter is: ἐθέλειν at 175C1 and 177B3. With the latter, and B2 λόγον δέῃ δοῦναί τε καὶ δέξασθαι, cf. *Cratylus* 426A2–3: an appeal to foreign-language origins to "explain" the meanings of words is a dodge (like a *deus ex machina*) used only by τῷ μὴ ἐθέλοντι λόγον διδόναι κτλ.

32 With *Cratylus* 421D, quoted just above, compare *Timaeus* 29C–D, quoted (in part) in n. 19 above; Plato there continues, saying it is fitting men accept a "likely account" in these matters (τὸν εἰκότα μῦθον ἀποδεχομένους). The myth in the *Timaeus* is one level of approach to the truth, a possible stopping-point for those willing to accept it, though there are more abstract or advanced degrees of insight to be had, for those "willing" and able to pursue them. The εἰκὸς μῦθος has (at least) the function of πειθώ, inducing certain kinds of people to accept a reverential feeling for the cosmos, much as the Prefaces of the *Laws* have the role of πειθώ, inducing acceptance of the laws. N.b., *Laws* IV. 723A4–7, with A5 δέξηται and 684C2–3, τοὺς νόμους οὓς ἑκόντες οἱ δῆμοι . . . δέξονται. Cf. H. Görgemanns, *Beiträge zur Interpretation von Platons Nomoi* (1960), pp. 30–56 and *passim*. As at *Laws* IX. 875A–D (notice ἐθέλειν there) the techniques of Peitho are a concession to the ἀσθένεια of human nature (*Laws* 875A2, B7, *Timaeus* 29D1, 68D–69A, etc.)—or at least that of the many (*Laws* 875D2–3, 718D–E; cf. *Timaeus* 51E5–6, 53D6–7).

33 A. E. Taylor's statement quoted earlier (n. 19 above) does express one common sense of the verb, but is of course too limited; cf. *LSJ s.v.*

34 Rather different is *Cratylus* 430A1: Ἀλλ' ἀγαπητὸν καὶ τοῦτο, which approaches an impersonal statement of sufficiency: if Cratylus will admit even this much, Socrates has enough to refute him. (Cf. 430A3 καὶ γὰρ ἂν καὶ τοῦτο ἐξαρκοῖ, and the similar passage at *Sophist* 247C9–D1: εἰ γάρ τι καὶ σμικρὸν ἐθέλουσι συγχωρεῖν . . . ἐξαρκεῖ [sc. for refuting them].)

35 Cf. Ingemar Düring's observation on Plato's use of ἀγαπᾶν, "expressing an attitude of philosophic resignation" (*Aristotle in the Biographical Tradition* [Goteborg, 1957], p. 351). The clearest cases of that use seem to be *Republic* V 472B–473B and *Timaeus* 29C–D (with *Critias* 106B–107D).

36 E.g., by asking τί ποτ' ἐστί, τὸ πῦρ; Cf. *Politicus* 285E2 τῷ λόγον αἰτοῦντι.

37 "τοῦτο πῦρ ἐστι" Cf. *Politicus* 277C . . . πρέπει τοῖς δυναμένοις ἕπεσθαι, τοῖς δ' ἄλλοις . . . With *Politicus* 277C and 285E, compare *Parmenides* 133B8–9 (cited above) ἐθέλοι δὲ πάνυ πολλὰ καὶ πόρρωθεν πραγματευομένου τοῦ ἐνδεικνυμένου ἕπεσθαι, and notice *Timaeus* 53C3 συνέψεσθε. See also the earlier references for "dialectical" ἐθέλειν given above (n. 31).

38 N.b. χωρὶς λόγου in *Politicus* 285E and *Sophist* 218C1–5, with which cf. *Phaedrus* 263A, and (especially) *Timaeus* 48B6–8 (with 51B7–C5).

[39] N.b. *Philebus* 58A8–B2: ἡ τοῦ πείθειν [τέχνη] . . . δοῦλα δι' ἑκόντων ἀλλ' οὐ διὰ βίας ποιοῖτο. On the entire subject, see C. P. Segal's stimulating paper, "Gorgias and the Psychology of the Logos," *HSCP*, 66 (1962): 99–155.

[40] Cf. Segal *passim* on ἀπάτη, γοητεία and τέρψις. Think too of ἐπᾴδειν in the *Laws*, and the "psychagogic" role of the liver at *Timaeus* 71A–72C!

[41] Gregory Vlastos, in *RR*, 13 (1949): 277.

[42] Cf. n. 32 above, and Görgemanns' book (cited there) on *peitho* and its role as a concession to human ἀσθένεια (pp. 155–61 and *passim*).

[43] Only few achieve clear conviction about the Forms (cf. *Parmenides* 133B–C, *Timaeus* 51E); the many remain within that "dreaming" state (*Timaeus* 52B–C) in which we fail to draw the requisite distinctions.

[44] *De Gen. et Corr.* II. 1, 329a 13–21. See Shorey, *AJP*, X (1889): 63–65.

[45] *In De Caelo*, p. 636, 22–27 (Heiberg).

[46] Ibid. 636, 27–637, 19 (n.b., 636, 28–29).

[47] *Plato's Cosmology*, pp. 181–85 [n.b., 181 (bottom), 183 (top), and 184 (bottom—quoted in Part I above)].

[48] 125.1–2.

[49] Compare Stilpo's argument in *Diog. Laert.* II. 119 (107, 18–20 [Long]); and cf. *Cratylus* 429B–431A and *Politicus* 285D–286B.

DONALD NORMAN LEVIN
Rice University

Some Observations Concerning Plato's *Lysis**

LET us concede that the *Lysis*** is not some alien intrusion into the Platonic Corpus—so Ast and Socher claimed long ago[1]—but a genuine work of Plato. Even in the nineteenth century those who thought this dialogue spurious were only an embattled few.[2]

But, though the majority were agreed that Plato himself had penned the *Lysis*, they could arrive at no consensus regarding the date of composition. The rise of the science—or pseudo-science—of "Sprachstatistik"[3] did not eliminate controversy. Recurrence or non-recurrence of τί μήν and πῶς δ' οὔ apparently meant one thing to one scholar, something else to another. Soberer spirits tried to find some way of harmonizing their stylometric researches with what could be deduced from analysis of the content of the various dialogues. Did scholarly agreement result? Hardly. The lateness of the *Parmenides*, *Sophist*, *Politicus*, and *Laws* (which had hardly been open to doubt even in the pre-statistical era) continued to be acknowledged.[4] Yet in the case of the *Lysis* there was such great divergency of opinion that Verdam, von Arnim, and Wilamowitz could call the dialogue respectively fourth, fifth, or sixth in order of composition (making it thereby more or less contemporaneous with its companions from Tetralogy V, the *Charmides* and *Laches*),[5] whereas Ritter and Raeder placed it fourteenth or fifteenth, directly ahead of the *Symposium*,[6] and Pohlenz went so far as to claim that its publication not only directly preceded that of the *Symposium*, but also postdated the appearance of the *Phaedrus* among Plato's works.[7]

Quot eruditi, tot ordines dialogorum. Rather than inflict yet another chronological scheme on the scholarly community[8] I shall take my cue from Monsieur Robin. Restricting his concern to those dialogues in which Plato's formulations regarding love and friendship are expounded, playing down stylometrics, moreover, in favor of other forms of com-

* Presented at the August, 1964 meeting of the SAGP at Amherst, Massachusetts.

parison, he arrives at the following progression—one which ought to have been obvious generations before his time:

Lysis (early)
Symposium (middle)
Phaedrus (late)[9]

So much for chronology. Having granted not only that the *Lysis* is genuine, but also that it antedates both the *Phaedrus* and the *Symposium*—whether it precedes or follows the *Charmides*, its "twin brother," according to some,[10] or the *Protagoras*, or any of the other allegedly early "aporetic" dialogues need not concern us[11]—let us turn now to questions of more than ancillary interest.

Alas! Among those who move beyond such considerations in order to grapple with "what Plato said" (*pace* Paul Shorey)[12] there is little agreement concerning the import of the *Lysis*. Pohlenz, for example, declares that the scope of this work, like that of the *Phaedrus*, is restricted to παιδικὸς ἔρως.[13] Frankly I think that this statement does disservice to both dialogues. Von Arnim thought likewise, and was so forceful in denunciation[14] as to cause Pohlenz to back away from his original position.[15]

Radically different, but not much more satisfying, is the suggestion, put forth by Grote a century ago. "To multiply defective explanations," he avers, "and to indicate why each is defective, is the whole business of the dialogue."[16]

I shall not add any further examples—at least for the moment. Actually not a few explorers of the thought conveyed in the *Lysis*, despairing, no doubt, of any satisfactory overall categorization, reduce their own contribution to running restatement of and commentary on the content of the several conversations which constitute the dialogue. This technique—if technique be the right name (and I do not mean to imply that scholars who attempt a summation invariably neglect to avail themselves of it)—has been iterated so often[17] that my choosing to resurrect it now would hardly arouse much excitement, let alone interest, had I not chosen also to combine sparing use with an innovation or two. Instead of doggedly citing or paraphrasing every significant proposition or dialectical link from *Lysis* 203A1 to 223B8 I shall start at the end of the dialogue before even considering the beginning. A pause for clarification or for mulling over some possible deeper significance will be inserted wherever necessary. By placing the last first and the first later and by ranging freely through the whole[18] I hope not only to shed more light on the conduct of the argument in the *Lysis*, but also to demonstrate that the structure is closely interwoven and that the cleavage alleged by some between a "protreptic" introduction (up through the first conversation between Socrates and Lysis) (203A1–211A8) and a "philosophical" main body of the dialogue (211A9 ff.)[19] is much less pronounced than would appear at first glance.[20]

Let us begin, then, with the aftermath to ἀπορία. Socrates, always alive to the humor of a difficult situation, observes that he, old man that he is, and Lysis and Menexenus have all three made themselves ridiculous in their inability to complete a simple definition, when it is so manifest that their mutual relationship provides in itself an illustration of that which was to be defined (223B3–8). After a whole series of complex discussions the speakers find themselves back whence they began: they can point to isolated examples, but so far[21] no general principle has been enunciated to their satisfaction.

Just before this, as a pair of slaves was arriving to guide his teen-aged interlocutors home from the gymnasium, Socrates reconsidered all the blind alleys into which their joint endeavor had strayed (222E3 ff.). The term awaiting explication, he notes, can be identified neither with "the beloved" (οἱ φιλούμενοι) nor with "the loving" (οἱ φιλοῦντες). Both equivalances were ruled out in the course of Socrates' first talk with Menexenus (211D6 ff.). Nor can it be equated either with "likes" (οἱ ὅμοιοι) or with "unlikes" (οἱ ἀνόμοιοι). The one possibility was disproved during the second conversation between Socrates and Lysis (213D6 ff.), the other in an ensuing discussion (215C3 ff.) into which Menexenus found himself drawn. Not even equation with "the good" (οἱ ἀγαθοί), which would have so gladdened the soul of Socrates, could it only have been upheld, turns out to be valid. Invalidity was an inevitable consequence of the previous determination that, contrary to the supposition of many, "like is no friend to like" (215A4 ff.).

This catalogue of failure reaches a sort of climax with Socrates' mention of "those akin by nature" (οἱ οἰκεῖοι),[22] unhappily dismissed from consideration only a short time before (once again the incompatibility of similars turned out to be the stumbling block), despite what had seemed a promising start (221E3 ff.).

Lest he try everyone's patience by extending the list further Socrates classifies other discarded possibilities as τὰ ἄλλα ὅσα διεληλύθαμεν: "all else that we have discussed" (222E5). Undoubtedly he has in mind "the evil" (οἱ κακοί), no sooner mentioned than rejected out of hand (214B8–D7),[23] as well as "the morally neutral," "those who are neither good nor evil" (οἱ μήτε ἀγαθοὶ μήτε κακοί),[24] initially brought into the discussion during Socrates' second interview with Menexenus (216C1 ff.).

Up to now I have refrained from acknowledging just what it was that Socrates and his companions were so anxious to define. I have done so deliberately in the hope that a few misconceptions might be cleared up in the interim. The *Lysis*, like a number of apparently early dialogues, poses a crucial question which may be reduced to the formula "What is X?" "What is courage?" (ἀνδρεία) Socrates asks in the *Laches*. In the *Charmides* he raises a similar query regarding temperance (σωφροσύνη).[25]

There exists, however, another type formulaically expressible as "Is X Y?" One rather noteworthy instance is shared between the *Protagoras* and the *Meno:*

> ἆρα διδακτὸν ἡ ἀρετή;
>
> Is virtue [X-term] teachable?
> [Y-term: not predicate adjective,
> really, but quasi-substantive:
> "a teachable thing"][26]

In the latter dialogue, as a matter of fact, the formula undergoes several modifications at the outset. "Is virtue teachable?" Meno's initial question to Socrates, may be codified as "Is X Y^1?" Immediately Y^1 gives way to Y^2 as Meno asks, "Or is it not teachable, but to be acquired through practice?" (ἢ οὐ διδακτόν, ἀλλ' ἀσκητόν). Still further questioning on Meno's part introduces the possibility that Y^1 and Y^2 must both be rejected in favor of Y^3 or Y^4. "Or is it neither to be acquired through practice nor to be learned?" (ἢ οὔτε ἀσκητὸν οὔτε μαθητόν), Socrates' interlocutor would like to know, "Is it inborn instead or imparted to mankind in some other fashion?" (ἀλλὰ φύσει παραγίγνεται τοῖς ἀνθρώποις ἢ ἄλλωι τινὶ τρόπωι).[27]

Obviously the same sort of inquiry occurs in the *Lysis*, with οἱ φιλούμενοι as Y^1, οἱ φιλοῦντες as Y^2 . . . We need not go through the rest of the list. It is time now to consider the other term which remains constant. If we interpret the "What is X?" and the "Is X Y?" of this dialogue simply as "What is *friendship*?" and "Is *friendship* such and such?" we shall be considerably in error. To put it succinctly, the X which awaits both some sort of definition and identification with some Y is not "friendship" (φιλία), but "friend" (φίλος). This is made clear throughout the discussion. Note Socrates' final words, which I now cite in full:

> ἐροῦσι γὰρ οἵδε ἀπιόντες ὡς οἰόμεθα ἡμεῖς
> ἀλλήλων φίλοι εἶναι—καὶ ἐμὲ γὰρ ἐν
> ὑμῖν τίθημι—οὔπω δέ, ὅ τι ἔστιν
> ὁ φίλος οἷοί τε ἐγενόμεθα ἐξευρεῖν.

> They will say in taking their departure that we think ourselves to be *friends* to one another—indeed, I count myself in your number—but that we were incapable of ascertaining *what a friend is.*[28]

Confession of inability to deal with this question of the type "What is X?" is, of course, preceded by the admission that, no matter which Y was brought under consideration in the series of "Is X Y?" questions which dominate the dialogue, a satisfactory equivalent for X could not be found. Ἀλλ' εἰ μηδὲν τούτων φίλον ἐστίν, resignedly comments Socrates, ἐγὼ μὲν οὐκέτι ἔχω τί λέγω: "But if none of these [i.e. the several Y's] is *friend*, for my part I have nothing more to say." Socrates will speak again, to be sure—with possibly even a hint that all is not lost.[29] But as things stand now, all meaningful discourse has ceased.

Having attempted to translate Socrates' words, I am conscious of an ambiguity which ought not to be passed over without comment. In the protasis of the condition should I have taken τούτων not as partitive genitive with μηδέν, but as some other type of genitive (possessive, or possibly objective) with φίλον? If so, that latter adjective—or is it really a substantive?[30]—would have to play a new role also. It is one thing to say "if none of these is friend," quite another to say either "if nothing is their friend" or "if nothing is friend to them."

This apparently minor grammatical difficulty is linked with much larger problems which beset the whole. Had Plato chosen to allow Socrates and his followers to essay a definition of φιλία rather than of φίλος,[31] perhaps the discussion would have proceeded, if not without difficulty, then at least with somewhat less tendency for the dialectics of the inquiry to prove abortive. What is φιλία, really, but a *relationship* between φίλοι?

Of course Socrates himself, though he might have extracted from an interlocutor an admission of its correctness, would hardly be likely to take much satisfaction in so simple, not to say tautologous, an explanation as this. It has been alleged, for example, that φιλία lies at the very center of the political thinking expressed in the Platonic dialogues and epistles.[32] Possibly too, had this been the term to be defined in the *Lysis*, Socrates would have taken up the questions posed for him by latter-day expositors:

> Is φιλία quite distinct from ἔρως?
> Are they really one and the same?
> Does the former subsume the latter?

The expositor's own response may depend upon which dialogue he has been lately reading—or even upon which part of a given dialogue.

Casting a glance at *Phaedrus* 255E1–2 (καλεῖ δὲ αὐτὸν καὶ οἴεται οὐκ ἔρωτα ἀλλὰ φιλίαν εἶναι), but leaving *Laws* 837A–B[33] conveniently out of account, Wilamowitz finds Plato to share in what he takes to have been a more or less universal opinion in antiquity: friendship and love are two basically different relationships ("zwei grundverschiedene Verhältnisse").[34] For this reason too he argues—wrongly, I think—that the *Lysis* is much less closely connected with the *Symposium* than most Platonic scholars are willing to admit.[35]

Grube, however, not only reaffirms the kinship of the *Symposium* and the *Lysis*, despite what Wilamowitz has said, but justifies his reaffirmation with a claim that in both works ἔρως, the species, is subsumed under the genus φιλία.[36] In his eagerness to demonstrate that the generic term must include the "passionate love" of the older Hippothales for Lysis as well as Lysis' more normal friendship with his contemporary Menexenus—"or else," he warns, "the whole introduction is singularly irrelevant"—Grube defines the special term much too narrowly. In view of the behavior of Hippothales, the would-be pederast *par excellence*, "sexual desire" might be an adequate translation for ἔρως in the *Lysis*—at least at the outset. But in a later passage equivalence with φιλία seems almost to be assumed.[37]

Nevertheless Grube himself, if I am not being overcharitable, apparently realizes that ἔρως so conceived does not suit the *Symposium*, except (here I am carrying charity even further, since he says nothing of the sort) as a preliminary error to be corrected through the remarks of the several speakers.[38] "We are therefore justified"—if I may quote Grube directly—"in tracing the *development* [emphasis mine] of Eros through the *Lysis* to the *Symposium*, as is usually done . . ."[39]

Levi is one of those who follow this "usual" procedure. His assertion that the theory of ἔρως set forth in the *Symposium* resolves many of the difficulties left unresolved in the *Lysis* with respect to φιλία[40] could hardly be labeled revolutionary. Yet note his willingness to consider ἔρως identifiable with φιλία—provided that it signify a love which is pure and not an egotistical and sensual passion.[41]

However, what Levi has just rejected describes exactly the emotion experienced by Hippothales. And in the *Lysis* it is called not φιλία, but ἔρως.[42] The former term does not even enter the picture until the conversation with Hippothales has been terminated and Socrates turns his attention to the two comrades—φίλω γάρ ἐστον, he says to them (207C8)—Lysis and Menexenus. Addressing *them*, not Hippothales, he cites the old proverb to the effect that community of property is the rule among friends (κοινὰ τά γε φίλων λέγεται) and deduces therefrom that Menexenus and Lysis will differ little from one another, "if the two of you," he remarks, "are telling the truth about friendship" (εἴπερ ἀληθῆ περὶ τῆς φιλίας λέγετον) (207C10 f.). Even in replying to Socrates' good natured banter the two boys react in unison. I cite three successive responses:

> Wherefore the two of them laughed.
> (ἐγελασάτην οὖν ἄμφω) (207C6)
> "Quite so!" the pair responded.
> (πάνυ γ', ἐφάτην) (207C9)
> The two assented.
> (συνεφάτην) (207C12)[43]

The contrasting manner of the two interviews, that with Hippothales enamored of Lysis, yet unable to establish a relationship, and that with Lysis and Menexenus, bound so closely to each other that they speak as one, not only serves to indicate that ἔρως is not identical with φιλία—that the latter is the genus, the former the species would not be ruled out[44]—but also paves the way dramatically for the ensuing discussion of whether "opposites attract" or "like cleaves to like" as well as for the puzzlement over the necessity or non-necessity of reciprocation.[45]

It ought to be clear by now that ἔρως is something more than "passionate love." In the *Symposium* and *Phaedrus* its scope will be increased to the point where ἔρως will take over most or all of the role assigned to φιλία in the *Lysis*, as well as new functions not mentioned or perhaps only hinted before. But in the *Lysis* already φιλία too seems to be considerably more inclusive than "friendship" as we conceive it. "The Greek word is ambiguous," Shorey remarks, "being used also for what we should speak of as *love*" [emphasis mine].[46]

Earlier I begged the question by defining φιλία tentatively as a relationship between φίλοι. Now I propose to beg the question further by classifying as φίλοι those whose conduct can be described via the verb φιλεῖν. But if the noun φιλία is ambiguous, meaning normally "friendship," though *in extenso* "love" of every sort, the verb φιλεῖν is ambiguous in just the opposite way. Normally, it means "to love";[47] but "be a friend to," the equivalent of φίλος εἶναι, an expression employed regularly in the argumentation of the *Lysis*, is another possibility.

Unfortunately φίλος εἶναι proves no less fraught with ambiguity than were φιλία and φιλεῖν.[48] First of all, φίλος could be a noun. "Friend" is the most obvious translation. One is hardly likely to render the Greek word as "lover": that is the meaning attached rather to the noun ἐραστής, the very term which Plato employs in the *Lysis* to denote persons such as Hippothales, just as he indicates their accustomed behavior through the use of the verb ἐρᾶν. This verb, like φιλεῖν, can mean "to love." But it often has connotations quite distinct from those with which φιλεῖν is regularly associated.

Plato, however, is no respecter of vulgar norms. Just as the ἔρως of the *Symposium* comes more and more, in the course of the several speeches, to resemble what is called φιλία in the *Lysis*, so the ἐραστής of the larger dialogue (actually the personified ἔρως himself, as Socrates demonstrates when it is his turn to speak) (199C3 ff.) shows progressively less resemblance to Hippothales, Lysis' aspirant lover, while taking on lineaments already familiar from the discussion of the role of the φίλος undertaken by Socrates, Lysis, and Menexenus. Similarly in the *Phaedrus* there is a movement toward a truer conception of the lover's role, once the false eroticism of the speech ascribed to the orator Lysias (230E6–234C5) has been effectively dispelled.[49]

But an ἐραστής, be he sensualist or sage, must direct his emotions toward some object. The beloved of a pederast like Hippothales may be called ὁ παῖς—literally "boy," but here no doubt "darling" or "favorite":[50] a meaning shared not only with the relatively unambiguous τὰ παιδικά[51] (comparable, it would seem, to Latin *deliciae*),[52] but also, apparently, with ὁ καλός. In fact it is the question τίς ὁ καλός; (204B1 f.) which inaugurates Socrates' probe into the love-life of Hippothales.

Now it happens that καλός (translated most frequently as "beautiful," but also as "handsome," "noble," "brave," "fine," "good," "excellent," and much more)[53] is one of the widest ranging terms in the Greek vocabulary. But out of this seeming chaos is evolved the philosophical hierarchy central to Plato's *Symposium* (210A4–211D1): from beautiful bodies (τὰ καλὰ σώματα) through a series of ever more exalted impersonal and intangible καλά stepwise all the way to the Idea of the Beautiful (αὐτὸ τὸ καλόν).

In the *Lysis*, however, where a comparable progress to the Good (τὸ ἀγαθόν)—which, if conceived already as the Idea of the Good,[54] would subsume even τὸ καλόν[55]—is not sketched out until long after the termination of Socrates' talk with Hippothales, whatever ambiguity of language lurked in that interview could have been minimized still further, had Socrates been content to prune his vocabulary of expressions like ὁ καλός and refer to the beloved, the passive partner in the relationship, always as ὁ ἐρώμενος, the lover, the active partner, always as ὁ ἐρῶν.[56] Early in the conversation (in fact, immediately after having proclaimed his awareness that Hippothales is in love)[57] Socrates employs this very terminology to indicate his own divinely bestowed power quickly to recognize one who loves and one who is loved (γνῶναι ἐρῶντά τε καὶ ἐρώμενον) (204C2).

Analogous distinctions are imported into Socrates' first conversation with Menexenus. But, whereas it was quite clear earlier that ὁ ἐραστής, "the lover," was identical with ὁ ἐρῶν, "one who loves,"[58] it is not at all clear that ὁ φίλος must be the same as ὁ φιλῶν, the active partner in a friendship. We noted earlier that φίλος could be a noun and that "friend" was how it ought to be translated usually.[59] However, φίλος can also be an adjective exhibiting the same amphibious nature as the Latin word *amicus*. The same distinctions occur in both tongues: the noun is construed with the genitive case, the adjective with the dative. But *amicus*, whether it means "friend of" or "friendly to," seems to be active always, comparable to *amans*, "one who loves," never—so far as I can discern—to *amatus*, "one who is loved."[60] Such is not the case where φίλος is concerned. Whatever the status of the noun, that of the adjective is ambiguous: it can mean not only "friendly to" (active), but also "dear to" (passive).[61]

The latter significance was apparent toward the close of Socrates' first discussion with Lysis. Having been advised already that it is not his youth, but his lack of training which renders him ineligible to engage in certain activities, no matter what his personal wishes may be, the boy is now questioned pointedly (210C5 f.):

> ἆρ' οὖν τωι φίλοι ἐσόμεθα καί τις ἡμᾶς
> φιλήσει ἐν τούτοις, ἐν οἷς ὦμεν ἀνωφελεῖς;
> Shall we then be *dear* to anyone and will anyone
> *love* us insofar as we are useless?[62]

"Now then," adds Socrates, once Lysis has responded in the negative, "neither does your father love you, nor, insofar as he is useless [καθ' ὅσον ἂν ἦι ἄχρηστος in the original], does anyone love anyone else" (οὐδὲ ἄλλος ἄλλον οὐδένα φιλεῖ) (210C7 f.).

If, indeed, the notion put forth here and constantly reiterated throughout the dialogue, namely that friendship must be based on utility, is one of the rocks on which the whole discussion founders[63]—for it is on this account that Socrates disallows the pairing of like with like, despite evidence to the contrary from life itself,[64] and denies that the good man (ὁ ἀγαθός), self-sufficient as he is, can be anyone's friend[65]

—ambiguous terminology constitutes not another rock merely, but a congeries of vicious shoals.

True, there are occasions where Socrates is allowed to engage in clever word-play without damaging the main line of the argument. In the course of the exchange with Lysis to which we have been giving attention he deftly brings together a series of etymologically related expressions (φρονεῖν, μέγα φρονεῖν, μεγαλόφρων εἶναι, ἄφρων εἶναι) whose ambiguity, already noticeable, when they were isolated from one another is enhanced by their interrelationship in the present context.[66]

But the ambiguity of φίλος is a much more serious matter. Perhaps it is only after the rest of the dialogue has become familiar to us that we recognize a foreshadowing of trouble already in the supposedly simple and non-technical first interrogation of Lysis by Socrates. "If, accordingly, you become wise, my boy," Socrates avers, "all will be friendly to you" [φίλοι with dative, take note: the adjective, but in an *active* sense][67] "and to you", he continues, "all will be οἰκεῖοι—for you will be useful [χρήσιμος] and good" [ἀγαθός] (210D1–3).

Once again utility seems to be the *sine qua non* of friendship.[68] Not until later will Lysis' or anyone else's being good as well as useful turn into a stumbling block on the paradoxical ground that no other person can be of any use to the good man.[69] For the moment, at least, it is asserted that, should Lysis fail to become wise and useful and good, no other person will be friendly to him (φίλος again, and once again, active) neither parents nor οἰκεῖοι (210D3 f.).

Twice over I have deliberately left this last term untranslated. Already in these first two appearances what will later mean "akin by nature"[70] is included in the same context with φίλος in the active sense. Clearly οὔτε ὁ πατήρ . . . οὔτε ἡ μήτηρ οὔτε οἱ οἰκεῖοι signifies "not father nor mother nor members of the household,"[71] whereas "and all will be *on familiar terms* with you" seems to be the meaning of καὶ πάντες σοι οἰκεῖοι ἔσονται.

Thus in this initial encounter of Socrates and Lysis the way has been prepared for concentrated inquiry, beginning with the question of whether φίλος actually designates the active or the passive party to the relationship (212C8 ff.) and terminating with the attempt to demonstrate that the basis of friendly relations is τὸ οἰκεῖον, the fact of a "natural affinity" (221E3 ff.).[72]

I promised earlier to avoid a dogged itinerary through the dialogue from 203A1 to the end. Nor shall I attempt anything of the sort for any of the individual conversations. Instead I should like to consider what of value remains after the shipwreck of every effort to explain who is friend to whom and why.

En route it might be worthwhile to scrutinize yet another rock or set of shoals. The argument, or rather, the several arguments in the *Lysis* foundered not only on ambiguities of language and on the insistence that a friend be useful, but also on Plato's refusal to acknowledge gradations. This problem is closely related to the other two, of course. Ὅμοιος means "similar," yet need not imply total equality; ἀνόμοιος means "dissimilar," yet need not be synonomous with ἐναντίος. Hence it would be possible for two individuals to resemble one another (to be ὅμοιοι, that is) and yet differ enough (that is, be ἀνόμοιοι) to allow each to complement the other's deficiencies. Such being the case, it would be possible to justify both seemingly contradictory propositions: "like goes with like" and "opposites attract."

Furthermore, by avoiding mutual exclusiveness Plato could have effected a successful rapprochement with his conception of τὸ οἰκεῖον. Affinity does not preclude mutual need. In fact, it was in explanation of how ἐπιθυμία οὗ ἂν ἐνδεὲς ᾖι ("desire for what is lacking") operates as a cause of friendship (replacing the previously discredited supposition that the presence of evil, κακοῦ παρουσία, was responsible)[73] that τὸ οἰκεῖον was brought into the discussion. For τὸ οἰκεῖον here means not only "that which is akin by nature," but also, if the implications of possible synonymity with τὸ ἐνδεές may be included, "that which is one's own but of which one has been up to now bereft."[74] The analogy with the formulations assigned to Aristophanes in Plato's *Symposium* (189C2–193D5) should be quite obvious to everyone.[75]

It is indeed fortunate that later dialogues have salvaged conceptions such as this out of the shambles occasioned in part by too rigid insistence that τὸ οἰκεῖον is simply τὸ ὅμοιον (already jettisoned, thanks to a refusal to recognize distinctions and gradations) under another name.[76] The *Symposium* is, of course, the chief beneficiary of this salvage operation. Not the speech of Aristophanes alone, but other speeches as well owe something to the *Lysis*.

Nowhere is this indebtedness more manifest than in Socrates' confutation of Agathon (199C3–201C9) and subsequent report (201D1–212C3) of an alleged conversation with Diotima.[77] That ἔρως which is personified and portrayed by Socrates, in contrast to what Agathon had asserted, as bereft of τὸ καλόν and of the several ἀρεταί, yet eager to possess them all, as being in a state midway (μεταξύ) between wisdom and ignorance, yet desirous of attaining the former—which, of course, means that he is φιλόσοφος in the truest sense—corresponds very closely to the active "friend" depicted in the latter part of the *Lysis*. He too happens to be not σοφός, but φιλόσοφος.[78] He can be classified neither as evil nor as good: he is "morally neutral" (οὔτε ἀγαθὸς οὔτε κακός).[79]

The object of his affections, on the other hand, is *not* morally neutral, and certainly not evil, but desirable (φίλος in a passive sense) and good (ἀγαθός). No, that is not quite right. We must take cognizance of a most significant shift in gender. When one person cares for another, the real love-object, according to Socrates' formulations, is not the latter individual, but that for the sake of which (οὗ ἕνεκα) he is loved. Hence there exists the hierarchy tersely put into words by Glaser:

> Primär ist das φίλον, sekundär der φίλος.[80]

Glaser is right too in stating that this order of precedence does not contradict the stepwise progress which Diotima purportedly set forth for Socrates' benefit.[81] I should have preferred a more positive declaration, however. The movement from lesser to more lofty καλά, and finally to αὐτὸ τὸ καλόν—I have already noted it in passing[82]—clearly is derived from the *Lysis* and should be seen as a development of the theory therein expounded to combat an infinite regress. If the passive φίλος is "dear" to the active (and, conversely, if the active is "friendly" to the passive) for the sake of something else which is deemed "desirable" (φίλον τι), and that latter in turn has been sought for the sake of yet another φίλον τι, the seemingly endless chain of subordinate and superior φίλα will terminate in a πρῶτον φίλον ("prime love-object" or "prime desirable") whose close correspondence with αὐτὸ τὸ καλόν of the *Symposium* is undeniable, just as it is undeniable that both may be equated with the Good (τὸ ἀγαθόν),[83] the ultimate goal of all endeavors.[84]

That in the *Lysis*, as in the *Symposium*, Plato has already conjured up the world of "eternal, immutable forms"[85] can there, then, be any doubt? Granted, the terms εἶδος and ἰδέα have not yet joined the technical vocabulary of Platonism. It would be a mistake, surely, to draw any inferences regarding the Theory of Ideas from *Lysis* 204E5 f. (πολλοῦ δεῖς τὸ εἶδος ἀγνοεῖν τοῦ παιδός) or from the sequence κατά τι τῆς ψυχῆς ἦθος ἢ τρόπους ἢ εἶδος at 222A3, where the last word seems to be merely a reinforcement of the two nouns preceding. On the other hand, the noun παρουσία and the verb παρεῖναι, whether it be "whiteness" or "evil" which makes its "presence" felt,[86] indubitably foreshadow not only the language, but also the substance of the mature "Ideenlehre" to be found in the middle dialogues.[87]

A hint of what is to come may be discerned also in the designation of the "prime desirable" as φίλον . . . τῶι ὄντι (220B1 f.; B4) and ὡς ἀληθῶς . . . φίλον (219D4 f.), whereas the great mass of φίλα, which turn out to be "desirable" only for *its* sake, turn out also to pose a danger of deceiving us (219D2 f.), inasmuch as they are little better than "images" (εἴδωλα) of that which is truly to be sought.[88]

Lest we be deceived, nevertheless, though from a different quarter, let us not take our leave of the *Lysis* without dispelling the impression that the argument yields up only negative results. The theory of reciprocity is abandoned, to be sure, as is the widely held view that similarity or the not quite so widely held view that dissimilarity forms the basis of friendly relations, not to mention the apparently original doctrine of τὸ οἰκεῖον. Of course, it is hardly surprising that evil should be eliminated not only as a final, but even as an efficient cause—if terminology usurped from Aristotle may be allowed this once—and that its place should be taken by a more acceptable and morally untainted ἐπιθυμία οὗ ἂν ἐνδεὲς ᾖι.[89]

And what is it that is lacking and is thus become the prime object of desire (πρῶτον φίλον)? It is the Good (τὸ ἀγαθόν), the ultimate goal which remains always in view to Plato and Platonists no matter how much else must be abandoned as dialectically unacceptable.[90]

NOTES

** All references to the *Lysis* or to other Platonic works are keyed to John Burnet's Oxford Classical Text (5 vols., first published 1900).

1 F. Ast, *Platons Leben und Schriften* (Leipzig, 1816), pp. 428–34; J. Socher, *Über Platons Schriften* (Munich, 1820), pp. 137–44.

2 S. Cholava's denial of Platonic authorship on the grounds of inexact or erroneous dialectic, uncharacteristic modes of thought and speech, unusual behavior of the interlocutors, and unsatisfactory composition of the whole ["Über die Unechtheit des Dialogs *Lysis*," *ZÖG*, 9 (1858): 793–802 (Cholava I)] was promptly attacked by J. Kvičala, "Über Platons *Lysis*," *ZÖG*, 10 (1859): 275–84 (Kvičala I) [H. Bonitz appended a sympathetic "Anmerkung zu dem vorstehenden Aufsatze," pp. 285–88]. Cholava's reply, "Bemerkung zu dem Aufsatze von I. Kvičala über Platons *Lysis*," *ZÖG*, 10 (1859): 589–91 (Cholava II), stimulated a "Gegenbemerkung" from Kvičala, pp. 591 f. (Kvičala II).

3 L. Campbell and W. Dittenberger are among the pioneers. Cf. in particular, the former's editions of various Platonic dialogues (published at Oxford from the 1860's onwards) and the latter's "Sprachliche Kriterien für die Chronologie der platonischen Dialoge," *Hermes* 16 (1881): 321–45.

4 Sir D. Ross, in *Plato's Theory of Ideas*2 (Oxford, 1953), p. 2, performs a most useful service in placing side by side the chronological

sequences proposed by H. von Arnim [cf. p. 234 of his "Sprachliche Forschungen zur Chronologie der platonischen Dialoge," *SAWW*, 169 (1911–12): 1–235 [von Arnim II: von Arnim I is a Programm—a procurable copy of which has thus far eluded my search—entitled *De Platonis dialogis quaestiones chronologicae* (Rostock, 1896)]], W. Lutosławski (*The Origin and Growth of Plato's Logic* (London, 1897), H. Raeder (*Platons philosophische Entwickelung*[2] (Leipzig, 1920), C. Ritter, see not the earlier works ([Ritter I, II and III respectively: *Untersuchungen über Platon* (Stuttgart, 1888); *Neue Untersuchungen über Platon* (Munich, 1910); *Platon: sein Leben, seine Schriften, seine Lehre* (2 vols., Munich, 1910–23)], but the much later *Die Kerngedanken der platonischen Philosophie* (Munich, 1931), [Ritter IV]; cf. not *Platonische Liebe* (Tübingen, 1931) [Ritter V], but the still later "Unterabteilung innerhalb der zeitlich ersten Gruppe platonischer Schriften," *Hermes*, 70 (1935): 1–30 [Ritter VI], and U. von Wilamowitz-Moellendorff [*Platon*, (2 vols., (Berlin, 1909–19); I[5] (Berlin, 1959); II[3] (Berlin, 1962))].

5 So far as I am aware, there has been very little inclination to vouch for the authenticity of the *Theages*, the "black sheep" of the tetralogy.

6 See the comparative table assembled by Ross (above, n. 4: Lutosławski could bring himself neither to confirm nor to deny that the *Lysis* was Plato's own) as well as H. D. Verdam, "De ordine quo Platonis dialogi inter se succedant," *Mn*, N.S. 44 (1916): 255–94 (which includes ad fin. a comparison of the schemes of Verdam, Ritter, and Raeder). Verdam dates the *Lysis c.*397 B.C., but A. Wirth [*AJP*, 16 (1895): 211–16] insists on 394 B.C. as *terminus post quem.*

7 M. Pohlenz, *Aus Platos Werdezeit* (Berlin, 1913) [Pohlenz I], p. 367. This chronology, along with other of Pohlenz' proposals (see the discussion below and accompanying nn.), was vigorously assailed by H. von Arnim *Platos Jugenddialoge und die Entstehungszeit des Phaidros* (Leipzig and Berlin, 1914) [von Arnim III]. Pohlenz defended himself first in a review of von Arnim's book, *GGA*, 178 (1916): 241–72 [Pohlenz II] (on the relationship of the *Lysis* to the *Symposium* and *Phaedrus*, see pp. 251–60), again (von Arnim having attacked anew, "Platos Lysis" *RhM*, N.F., 71 (1916): 364-87 [von Arnim IV], even as Pohlenz was warding off the initial onslaught,) in an article wearily entitled "Nochmals Plato's *Lysis*," *NGG*, (1917): 560–88 [Pohlenz, III].

8 Without committing myself necessarily thereto, I should like to call attention to the arrangement set forth by G. Vlastos when I studied under him at Cornell University in the early 1950's:

Group I (Socrates utilizes ἔλεγχος in his professedly agnostic role): *Ion, Laches, Lysis, Charmides, Euthyphro, Hippias Maior*

A group unto themselves: *Apology, Crito*

Group II (Theory of Ideas given mature expression): *Gorgias, Protagoras, Meno, Cratylus, Phaedo*

Group III (after 388 B.C.): *Republic, Symposium, Phaedrus*

Group IV: *Parmenides, Politicus, Theaetetus, Sophist*

Group V: *Timaeus, Philebus, Laws*

[9] L. Robin, *La théorie platonicienne de l'amour* (Paris, 1908; new ed. 1933), ch. 2 (pp. 53–120).

[10] E.g., H. Mutschmann, "Zur Datierung des platonischen *Lysis*," *WKP*, 35 (1918): 428–31 (see especially 430). Cf. von Arnim II (above, n. 4), who accords priority to the *Lysis*. His list of "Zwillingbrüder" includes *Gorgias* and *Meno*, *Symposium* and *Phaedo*, *Sophist* and *Politicus*.

[11] That the *Lysis* could have been written during Socrates' lifetime is no longer seriously entertained, since hardly anyone allows much credence to the anecdote recorded by Diogenes Laertius (3.35):

> φασὶ δὲ καὶ Σωκράτην ἀκούσαντα τὸν Λύσιν ἀναγιγνώσκοντος Πλάτωνος, " 'Ηράκλεις," εἰπεῖν, "ὡς πολλά μου καταψεύδεθ' ὁ νεανίσκος." οὐκ ὀλίγα γὰρ ὧν οὐκ εἴρηκε Σωκράτης γέγραφεν ἀνήρ.

Possibly the final statement is true, however, not only of the *Lysis*, but of the Platonic dialogues in general. Cf. Pohlenz II (above, n. 7) 252. My own surmise is that the anecdote itself grew out of the preoccupation of the rhetorical schools with what this or that celebrity "might have said" on this or that occasion (i.e., "How would Socrates have reacted, had he been present at a recitation of one of Plato's works?"). Cf. Wilamowitz' suggested explanation of how an anti-Callimachean epigram (*Anthologia Palatina* 11.275) came to be ascribed to Apollonius (*Hellenistische Dichtung* (Berlin, 1924), II, p. 97, cited with qualified approval in the course of my own discussion of the poem in question, *TAPA*, 93 (1962): 162, n. 24).

[12] Shorey's book of the same name (Chicago, 1933) [Shorey III] is useful, so far as it goes. But to find out "what Shorey said" about Plato and Platonism one must repair also to other of his works, notably "The Unity of Plato's Thought," *University of Chicago Decennial Publications*, 6 (1903): 129–214 [Shorey I], a most salutary piece of writing, in my estimation. Shorey II, for our purposes (much that is relevant to Plato intervenes), is "The Alleged Fallacy in Plato's *Lysis* 220E," *CP*, 25 (1930): 380–83.

[13] Pohlenz I (above, n. 7), p. 370. See also n. 36 below.

[14] Von Arnim III (above, n. 7), p. 60.

[15] See Pohlenz II (above, n. 7), p. 258 and n. 2, who meekly replies that he had meant only to attract notice to the extension of the concept of ἔρως which may be observed in the *Phaedrus* and *Lysis*. I remain unconvinced.

[16] G. Grote, *Plato and Other Companions of Socrates* (London, 1865 and several subsequent editions), I, p. 516.

[17] Tedium increases rapidly after the first few encounters. Robin's exposition, *op. cit.*, (above, n. 9), pp. 3–8, stands out, however, thanks to its wonderfully Gallic (hence possibly somewhat un-Platonic) lucidity.

[18] To my knowledge, no previous scholar has proceeded in exactly this way. However, F. Horn, *Platonstudien* (Vienna, 1893), after having recapitulated the argumentation of the dialogue in detail (pp. 103–8) commences his several pages "Zur Erläuterung" (pp. 109–19) with a reexamination of the last of the three large sections into which he thinks the *Lysis* to be divided.

[19] See, for example, von Arnim III (above, n. 7), p. 70.

[20] Von Arnim took issue with those who assumed that the first part had

been written for the sake of the second. I myself think that they are right. Still, there may be some merit in von Arnim's assertion that Plato has constructed the conversation with Hippothales and the initial interrogation of Lysis in such a way as to disprove the old slander that Socrates was guilty of corrupting the youth of Athens. Cf. Wilamowitz (above, n. 4), I, p. 141, who believes the rehabilitation of Socrates as educator to have been a common aim of the *Lysis* and *Charmides*. Although he claims to detect signs of friction between the author's philosophical and artistic aims, Wilamowitz urges that they not be studied in isolation from one another.

21 The fact that Socrates has prefixed οὔπω rather than οὐ to the clause which terminates in οἷοί τε ἐγενόμεθα ἐξευρεῖν (223B7 f.) may indicate that he retains some glimmer of hope for an eventual solution.

22 This expression originally denoted members of the same household (οἶκος or οἰκία), and was applied both to family and to retainers. Cf. below p. 15. Extension beyond the confines of the household to include all who share some affinity is clearly indicated in the suggestion of Socrates that Lysis and Menexenus might be φύσει πῃ οἰκεῖοι vis-à-vis one another (221E6; cf. 222A5).

23 However "evil" in another sense (τὸ κακόν as a causative agent) figures very prominently in later discussion (217A3 ff.; see also below, pp. 246-48) before being eliminated altogether from consideration.

24 T. Becker, "Zur Erklärung von Platos *Lysis*," *Phil*, 41 (1882): 284–308, who translates τὸ μήτε ἀγαθὸν μήτε κακόν as "das Indifferente" (299), expresses astonishment that A. Westermayer [I have not yet been able to lay hands on a copy of the latter's *Der Lysis des Plato zur Einführung in das Verständnis der sokratischen Dialoge* (Erlangen, 1875)]—apparently his favorite whipping-boy, as Pohlenz was von Arnim's (cf. above, n. 7, and p. 237 with nn.)—would have the temerity to regard "das relativ Gute" as an accurate interpretation of the original.

25 R. Robinson, *Plato's Earlier Dialectic*² (Oxford, 1953), p. 49, would add the *Euthyphro*, where "the Holy" (τὸ ὅσιον) and the *Hippias Maior*, where "the Beautiful" (τὸ καλόν) is to be defined. He disjoins, however, the *Gorgias*, *Meno*, and *Republic* I (he too, like so many previous scholars, prefers to classify the last as a separable "early dialogue") on the ground that all three "abandon the question 'What is X?' for the question 'Is X Y?' " (concerning which latter see the discussion immediately below).

26 Robinson recognizes the presence of the "Is X Y?" question in the *Meno* (cf. n. 25 above), yet strangely groups the *Protagoras* with the *Ion*, *Hippias Minor*, *Apology*, and *Crito*, which dialogues, he avers, "never raise the question at all." Or have I misunderstood his not entirely clear language? Does he mean to say that some works of Plato start with "What is X?" then shift to "Is X Y", while others either dispense with both or bring up the latter without ever having considered the former?

27 Cf. Aristotle, *Nicomachean Ethics*, where the problem is acknowledged (I. 9, 1099b 9–11: ὅθεν καὶ ἀπορεῖται πότερόν ἐστι μαθητὸν ἢ ἐθιστὸν ἢ καὶ ἄλλως πως ἀσκητόν, ἢ κατά τινα θείαν μοῖραν ἢ καὶ διὰ τύχην παραγίνεται) and an Aristotelian solution proposed.

28 Cf. above, p. 238. "The explicit question of the *Lysis*," Robinson contends, *loc. cit.* (above, n. 25), giving precedence to the "Is X Y"? question "is not what friendship is, but what its condition is." I should prefer that he had said "not what friendship is, but the conditions under which one becomes a friend." Just before the first interrogation of Menexenus (212A8 ff.) Socrates himself, having noted the astonishing ease and speed with which Lysis and Menexenus have taken to one another (211E8–212A4), admits that he is at a loss to explain this or anything of the sort (212A5 f.):

οὐδ' ὅντινα τρόπον γίγνεται φίλος ἕτερος ἑτέρου οἶδα

29 See n. 21 above.

30 Cf. διδακτόν in the "Is X Y?" question cited above, p. 5. Observe, however, that διδακτόν in predicate position, is clearly a Y-term, whereas φίλον, though apparently in predicate position also, was always X, so far as the preceding discussion in the *Lysis* was concerned.

31 I count some seven occurrences of the former in the *Lysis:* 207C11; 214D7; 216B1; 219A4; 220B3; 221D3; 221E4. Though its appearance is never without significance (most of the passages in which the noun occurs will be discussed below), there can be no mistaking the fact that φιλία is not the term to be defined.

32 See W. Jaeger, *Paideia* (tr. G. Highet), II (Oxford, 1943), pp. 174 f.

33 Concerning this passage see n. 36 below.

34 *Op. cit.* (above, n. 4), I, p. 143. Cf. II, p. 68, where Wilamowitz again cites a belief in basic difference, but ascribes it to "griechisches Empfinden" rather than to the ancients in general.

35 He prefers to see a tight bond between the *Lysis* and the *Charmides*. Cf. above, n. 20.

36 G. M. A. Grube, *Plato's Thought* (London, 1935; repr. Boston, 1958), p. 92, n. 1. Cf. J. J. Verbrugh, *Über platonische Freundschaft* (Diss., Zürich, 1930), p. 22, who views the *Lysis* as a preparation for the *Symposium* and who consequently thinks it quite wrong to assume a sharp boundary between the two concepts. Without claiming, as did Pohlenz before he had been rebuked by von Arnim (above, p. 237 and nn. 13–15), that in the *Lysis* it serves as sole subject, P. Friedländer, *Platon* II² (Berlin, 1957), p. 94, nevertheless claims that an atmosphere of Attic παιδικὸς ἔρως can be sensed from the beginning of the dialogue to the end. Behind the φιλία overtly presented he finds ἔρως to be constantly lurking. Cf. *Laws* VIII, 837A8 f., which Friedländer translates as "Wenn Freundschaft heftig wird, so nennen wir sie Liebe." But is not Plato simply talking of genus and species, as Grube suggested (though he did not cite this passage)?

37 I.e., at 221E3–5 (cited in part by Friedländer, *loc. cit.* [above, n. 36], p. 95, along with Socrates' statement at 211E2 f.: πρὸς δὲ τὴν τῶν φίλων κτῆσιν πάνυ ἐρωτικῶς [sc. ἔχω] to show the close connection between the two concepts throughout the dialogue):

τοῦ οἰκείου δή, ὡς ἔοικεν, ὅ τε ἔρως καὶ ἡ φιλία καὶ ἡ ἐπιθυμία τυγχάνει οὖσα, ὡς φαίνεται, ὦ Μενέξενέ τε καὶ Λύσι.

K. Glaser, "Gang und Ergebnis des platonischen *Lysis*," *WS*, 53 (1935): 47–67, thinks φιλία to be subsumed under ἐπιθυμία (p. 58). Cf. the suggestion of von Arnim III (above, n. 7), p. 40 that ἔρως in the broadest sense = ἐπιθυμία without reference to pederasty. If Glaser is right (ἐπιθυμία, at any rate, is shown in the dialogue to function as a sort of efficient cause; cf. below, pp. 246, 248), perhaps we should interpret this passage as an indication not of interchangeability of the three terms, but of progression from the less to the more inclusive.

[38] Note particularly Pausanias' distinction between a vulgar (πάνδημος) and a heavenly (οὐρανία) Aphrodite and concomitantly between a vulgar and a heavenly Eros (180D3 ff.). The *Lysis* and the *Symposium* diverge markedly also in another not unimportant respect. In the latter dialogue ἔρως is endowed with a personality from the outset; such is not the case ever for either ἔρως or φιλία in the *Lysis*.

[39] *Loc. cit.* (above, n. 36). I have broken off at the point where Grube takes issue with Wilamowitz' denial of close kinship between the two dialogues.

[40] A. Levi, "La teoria dell' ἔρως nel *Simposio* di Platone," *GM*, 4 (1949): 290–97 (Levi I). See p. 290 especially, as well as p. 295 of "La teoria della φιλία nel *Liside*," *GM*, 5 (1950): 285–96 (Levi II).

[41] Levi II (above, n. 40), p. 293.

[42] See especially 204B7 f.:

. . . οἶδα γὰρ ὅτι οὐ μόνον ἐρᾷς, ἀλλὰ καὶ πόρρω ἤδη εἶ πορευόμενος τοῦ ἔρωτος.

[43] Though it may have been already obsolescent in his lifetime, Plato rarely neglects an opportunity to employ the dual. Its use with reference to Lysis and Menexenus is both deliberate and appropriate.

[44] Hence I discern no real disharmony between *Laws* H 837A8 f. and *Lysis* 221E3–5 (see above, nn. 36 f.), if the latter be interpreted as I suggested at the end of n. 37 above.

[45] The thesis that careful characterization of the several speakers is not mere "dramatische Einkleidung" (I forget whether it is von Arnim who introduces this expression; yet the viewpoint that the *Lysis* does not hang together is certainly his: see above, p. 238 and nn. 19 f.), but an essential feature closely linked with the philosophical tenets set forth in the dialogue receives vigorous affirmation from R. G. Hoerber. See his "Character Portrayal in Plato's *Lysis*," *CJ*, 41 (1945–46): 271–73 [Hoerber I], and (with most of the same material incorporated, pp. 24 f.) the subsequent "Plato's *Lysis*," *Phn*, 4 (1959): 15–28 [Hoerber II].

[46] Shorey III (above, n. 12), p. 115. I have deliberately suppressed the remainder of the sentence:

though passionate love is usually eros

inasmuch as our previous discussion ought to have made clear that Plato, at least, goes well beyond the usual.

[47] A. E. Taylor, *Plato, the Man and his Work*[4] (New York, n.d.), p. 65, n. 2, while admitting the multiplicity of possible meanings for φιλία (see also below, p. 244 and n. 61), insists that φιλεῖν "can only be rendered 'to

love.' " In certain contexts, however (outside the *Lysis*, as it happens), the verb can carry a specialized meaning akin to that of the Latin *osculari*. Similarly the noun φιλότης, though etymologically related to φιλία, may convey connotations of passion. See, for example, Mimnermus 1.1.3 ff.:

κρυπταδίη φιλότης καὶ μείλιχα δῶρα καὶ εὐνή,
οἷ' ἥβης ἄνθεα γίγνεται ἁρπαλέα
ἀνδράσιν ἠδὲ γυναιξίν . . .

However, φιλότης has quite a different significance (=ἰσότης, especially where good men are concerned) for Aristotle, *Nicomachean Ethics* VIII, 5, 1157b36 f. Also, of course, Φιλότης is the preferred term in Empedocles' Περὶ φύσεως, appearing regularly as the counterforce to Νεῖκος, whereas Φιλίη recurs there only rarely.

48 On the prevalence of "Vieldeutigkeit" throughout the *Lysis* (practically every important term turns out to be ambiguous, as will be shown in the discussion below) see S. Ranulf, *Der eleatische Satz vom Widerspruch* (Diss., Copenhagen, 1924), pp. 26–40. A catalogue of ambiguous expressions to be found in the various dialogues is inserted at pp. 184 ff. (for the *Lysis* see p. 185).

49 Even apart, however, from preoccupation with rhetoric and style, the *Phaedrus* ventures into new territory not really explored in the other two dialogues: e.g. μανία. The notion that love was a sort of madness already seems to have become a cliché. Consider the ribbing to which Hippothales is subjected (*Lysis* 205A7 f.: οὐχ ὑγιαίνει, ἔφη ὁ Κτήσιππος, ἀλλὰ ληρεῖ τε καὶ μαίνεται). Nevertheless, there is no effort here to evolve a theory of μανία as concomitant of love on a more exalted plane.

50 Were it not for the article (*N.B.*, ἡ παῖς="girl"), not even the sex of the beloved would be clear. But even with the article restored παῖς remains an ambiguous term, since in some contexts it can mean "servant" or "slave," whether or not the individual in question is still an adolescent. Consider too the fact that pederasty smacks often of exploitation. But these ambiguities apparently are not important enough to merit attention in Ranulf's catalogue (see above, n. 48).

51 This latter is really a technical term. Accordingly it occurs far more often in the interview with Hippothales and Ctesippus (204D6; 205A2; 5; B3; E2; 4; 5; 206C3) than does ὁ παῖς (204E6; 205B8).

52 *Pueri delicati* (note the etymological connection) constitute almost a professional class of male courtesans. But pederasty was never so much in vogue among the Romans (who deemed it an alien vice) as among the Greeks. Hence the term *deliciae* is applied more often to females, as are expressions such as *mea vita* and *mea lux* (literally "my life" and "my light"), utilized so frequently by Catullus and his fellow poets. Concerning the not inconsiderable erotic vocabulary which developed at Rome see especially R. Pichon, *De sermone amatorio apud latinos elegiarum scriptores* (Diss., Paris, 1902).

53 Consider too the combination καλὸς κἀγαθός, which supposedly characterizes the true gentleman. There may be a play on this significance

also in Socrates' admonition to Hippothales (205E4–7) to avoid fruitless pursuit of a beloved who shuns him: else he will render himself ridiculous by becoming τοσούτωι μειζόνων . . . καλῶν τε καὶ ἀγαθῶν [probably neuter here, but the genitive is conveniently ambiguous] ἐστερημένος. Note that Lysis himself is called καλός τε κἀγαθός at 207A3.

[54] A. C. Pacheco, *Plato's Conception of Love* (Diss., Notre Dame, 1942), p. 7, is not alone in detecting "germs of the Theory of Ideas" already in the *Lysis*. Concerning the significance in the dialogue also of παρουσία and of the πρῶτον φίλον cf. below, pp. 246 (with n. 73) and 247 (also p. 248) respectively.

[55] This is made clear, at any rate, in the *Republic*. See also the discussion of "Le Beau" and "L'idée du Bien" contributed by Robin (above, n. 9), 226 f.

[56] Actually ἐραστής, invariably active in meaning, is just about synonymous with the latter.

[57] Cited above, n. 42.

[58] Cf. n. 56 above.

[59] See above, p. 242.

[60] Perhaps it is possible to translate *amans* and *amatus* respectively as "he who acts the part of a friend" and "he who is befriended"; but normally *amare*, like φιλεῖν, is rendered "to love," whereas *amicus*, like φίλος (let us restrict our attention to the nominal use for the moment) is usually "friend." Cf. above, p. 242 and n. 47.

[61] " 'Friendly', " explains Taylor, *loc. cit.* (above, n. 47), "means definitely 'a person feeling affection' and 'dear' a 'person toward whom affection is felt.' " W. Eckert, *Dialektiker Scherz in den früheren Gesprächen Platons* (Progr., Schwabach, 1906–07) in the course of his discussion of the *Lysis* (pp. 85–98) neatly distinguishes between φίλος with genitive (nominal and active) and φίλος with dative (adjectival and passive). He cites this as a difficulty. The real difficulty, however, so far as Plato conceives it, is not that φίλος can be either noun or adjective, but that both the adjective and the noun seem susceptible to either active or passive interpretation.

[62] In the interest of idiomatic expression I have translated the combination ἐν τούτοις, ἐν οἷς as if it were really καθ' ὅσον (which appears, as a matter of fact, directly afterwards at 210C8 (cited below)).

[63] L. Stefanini in his chapter on the *Lysis* [*Platone*[2] (Padua, 1949), I, pp. 180–86] has effectively put his finger on the problem. But there are other problems too in the *Lysis*. Hence I cannot accept fully the conclusion which Stefanini draws at p. 185:

> Svariando di motivo in motivo il *Liside* illustra l'unico argomento: in una concezione utilitaristica della vita morale non esistono ragioni dell'amicizia.

This doctrine is finally rejected by the Stoics. See Diogenes Laertius 7.124 (cited by C. Huit, *Séances et Travaux de l'Académie des Sciences Morales et Politiques*, N.S. 41 [1894]: 636, n. 2, who notes, on the other hand, that Socrates is credited with such views not only in the *Lysis*, but also in Xenophon's *Memorabilia*).

[64] Not only the poets (with only slight modification Homer, *Odyssey*,

p 218, ὡς αἰεὶ τὸν ὅμοιον ἄγει θεὸς ὡς τὸν ὅμοιον, is cited at 214A6), but also the natural philosophers, notably Empedocles and Democritus (for a listing of relevant fragments see Diels' Index [*VS*⁹, III, p309 f.] s.v. "ὅμοιος Substantiv"), stress the mutual attraction of similars. Those who assert that like is hostile to like (see Hesiod, *Works and Days*, 25 f., somewhat garbled in quotation at *Lysis* 215C8–D1) and that attraction occurs rather between opposites (which notion is overthrown in turn by Socrates and his interlocutors) appear to have been in the minority, though the eminent Heraclitus is included among them. However, I sense a paradox in Empedocles' formulations: what brings "likes" together (air with air, fire with fire, etc.) is the ascendancy of Strife; whereas the ascendancy of Love causes a redistribution of such a sort that dissimilar entities are brought into juxtaposition.

[65] Aristotle, be it noted, makes room in his *Nicomachean Ethics* both for friendships geared to convenience or mutual advantage, though he finds them to be impermanent and not very exalted, and for φιλία τῶν ἀγαθῶν, something quite distinct to which he accords high honor. That Plato does not conceive of utility in the common fashion is quite credibly argued by Horn (above, n. 18), p. 111.

[66] Ranulf (above, n. 48) takes note of this combination in his catalogue, p. 185. He translates μέγα φρονεῖν (with which μεγαλόφρων εἶναι may be equated) both as "grosse Einsicht besitzen" and as "edelmütig und hochsinnig sein." One would have supposed that the objective of this byplay was to show that pride in oneself must be conjoined with knowledge and understanding. However, in his more detailed discussion of the passage (p. 29) Ranulf indicates some dissatisfaction with Socrates' procedure. Leaving Ranulf's objections aside, I think the interplay between the two meanings of μέγα φρονεῖν to be most *à propos* in view of the earlier conversation in which Socrates advised Hippothales against continuing to sing Lysis' praises, lest he render the boy insufferably proud. The present interview with Lysis came about, after all, in order that Socrates might demonstrate to Hippothales the proper way for an ἐραστής to address an ἐρώμενος (i.e., with gentle reproof rather than with conceit-inspiring laudation).

[67] Cf. above, p. 244 and n. 61.

[68] Cf. above, p. 244 and n. 63. But see also n. 65.

[69] Cf. p. 244 above.

[70] Cf. above, p. 238.

[71] Cf. above, n. 22.

[72] *Lysis* 221E3–5 is cited above, n. 37. The opposition between οἰκεῖον and ἀλλότριον is noted several times over in the dialogues: e.g. *Charmides* 163C4–6. At *Lysis* 222C3 ff. and *Symposium* 205E6 f. the former term is paired with τὸ ἀγαθόν, the latter with τὸ κακόν. See Glaser (above, n. 37), p. 60; von Arnim III (above, n. 7), p. 59; A. Guzzo, *GCFI*, 9 (1928): 391.

[73] Here is the language, at least, of the Theory of Ideas. Cf. J. Moreau, *La construction de l'idéalisme platonicien* (Paris, 1939), pp. 153 f. But two oddities ought to be noted. In view of its negative nature, the status of τὸ κακόν as a "form" is somewhat questionable. Moreover a distinction is

drawn (217C3 ff.) between a "presence" whose influence is permanent and that which produces only a temporary or apparent change.

[74] Much unnecessary controversy has arisen over the interpretation of 221E2 f.:

ἐνδεὲς δὲ γίγνεται οὗ ἄν τι ἀφαιρῆται

The text too is disputed. Codd. give τις: Stephanus, with whom Burnet seems to be in agreement, prefers τι. Heindorf would change ἐνδεές to ἐνδεής; Eckert (above, n. 61), p. 95, n. 116, approves. No one, so far as I know, has proposed to replace ἀφαιρῆται with something else. But some are annoyed at the suggestion that τὸ οἰκεῖον, which will be mentioned before the end of 221E3, could be equated with that which has been snatched away. The best course, I think, is to take the verb not too literally: "what is lacking" can then be understood as "that which is at least potentially one's own".

[75] Considerable insight into the significance of this speech (which he deems a "capolavoro") is shown by Levi I (above, n. 40), pp. 294–97. Also worthy of notice is Levi's sympathetic evaluation (pp. 292 f.) of the doctrines set forth in the speech of the physician Eryximachus (*Symposium* 185E6–188E4).

[76] It is left for posterity, e.g., Glaser (above, n. 37), p. 64, to observe that "ähnlich" and "verwandt" are not identical.

[77] Some scholars argue that the lady from Mantinaea serves as a convenient mouthpiece for the expression of Platonic doctrines alien to the thinking of the historical Socrates.

[78] The same distinction between "wise" and "loving wisdom" (note the use of the neuters τὸ σοφόν and τὸ φιλόσοφον) will be found at *Phaedrus* 278D3–6. Whether or not this belongs among the "purely verbal quibbles" to which Shorey I (above, n. 12), 141, n. 77, makes passing reference, there can be no doubt that the theory of reciprocity between friends (either of whom could then be φίλος both actively and passively: i.e., at once φιλῶν and φιλούμενος) not only seems to be contradicted by those numerous instances in which affection is answered by hostility, but is also dealt a body blow by Socrates' insistence that consideration be give to a series of compounds (φίλιπποι, φιλόρτυγες, φιλόκυνες, φίλοινοι, φιλογυμνασταί, even φιλόσοφοι) (212D5 ff.) applicable only to the active partner in an obviously one-sided relationship. Plato has been accused, moreover, of misconstruing the Solonian couplet (=fr. 13 Diehl[3]) cited at 212E3 f.:

ὄλβιος, ᾧι παῖδές τε φίλοι καὶ μώνυχες ἵπποι
καὶ κύνες ἀγρευταὶ καὶ ξένος ἀλλοδαπός.

Actually the status of the crucial adjective is ambiguous. φίλοι could be predicate adjective in agreement with several subjects (as Plato seems to have interpreted) or simply an attributive modifying παῖδες (as Plato's critics think Solon meant to indicate), in which latter case the quotation would not really be relevant to the problem with which Socrates and Menexenus are grappling.

[79] See also above, p. 238 and n. 24.

80 Loc. cit. (above, n. 37), p. 63. "Primär ist das Eidos," Glaser adds (p. 65), explaining himself more fully (be it noted that Plato does not yet use the term εἶδος itself in this sense; see below), "und die Verwandtschaft mit ihm, sekundär die Freundschaft mit Menschen, die es gemeinsam haben."

81 Ibid., n. 20. With regard to the relationship between "soul" and "thing" Glaser recommends consultation of the *Phaedrus*.

82 See p. 243 above.

83 Cf. above, p. 243 and n. 55. On the introduction of a transcendental *summum bonum* "long before *Republic* VI" see H. Gauss, *Philosophischer Handkommentar zu den Dialogen Platos*, III, ii (Bern, 1954), p. 108.

84 Cf. Aristotle's reference at the beginning of the *Nicomachean Ethics* to τἀγαθόν, οὗ πάντ' ἐφίεται.

85 See above, n. 54. Frankly, I am surprised at the dearth of interest in the *Lysis* manifested by most authors of books or monographs on "Platonische Ideenlehre" (P. Natorp not excepted). Some mention the *Lysis* not at all, others (to one or two of whom I have made or shall make reference in these notes) allow only a passing nod.

86 Cf. *Charmides* 160D6 f. (ἐννοήσας ὁποῖόν τινά σε ποιεῖ ἡ σωφροσύνη παροῦσα) and 161A8 f. (σωφροσύνη δέ γε ἀγαθόν, εἴπερ ἀγαθοὺς ποιεῖ οἷς ἂν παρῇ, κακοὺς δὲ μή). 217D is one of the passages in the *Lysis* (the other is 218A–B, where the distinction between σοφός and φιλόσοφος (cf. above, p. 17 and n. 78) is demonstrated) to catch the attention of P. Brommer, Εἶδος et Ἰδέα (Diss., Utrecht, 1940), p. 27.

87 I should agree with those whose chronology of the Platonic corpus places the *Phaedo* in close proximity to both the *Symposium* (which it probably follows) and the *Republic* (which it probably precedes).

88 Cf. F. Susemihl, *Die genetische Entwickelung der platonischen Philosophie*, I (Leipzig, 1855), p. 20. Yet a note of caution (excessive caution, in my opinion) is sounded in the very next paragraph:

Das höchste Gut ist keineswegs der Begriff des Guten.

Had he been discussing Aristotle rather than Plato, Susemihl's comment might have been more to the point.

89 Cf. above, p. 246.

90 "Das wichstigste Ergebnis des *Lysis*," observes Horn (above, n. 18), p. 118, "ist mithin die Feststellung des absoluten Werthes des Guten . . ." He adds, and I should agree, that the *Lysis* does not deserve the subordinate role usually assigned it. In view of the status of the Good as the cornerstone of Plato's ethics and in view of the frequency with which this dialogue is echoed in later Platonic works, there may be considerable justification for Horn's claim that the *Lysis* lays the groundwork for the whole Platonic Corpus. Huit (above, n. 63), p. 641, however, scales down the positive content of the dialogue to a view of friendship as "la tendance commune de deux âmes semblables et différentes vers le bien souverain."

RONALD B. LEVINSON
University of Maine

Language, Plato, and Logic*

ANALYTICAL philosophy, with its reduction of traditional epistemological and metaphysical issues to problems in the analysis of language, may with a certain exaggeration be described as "a series of question marks on Plato." He is variously appraised: on rare occasions, he is acclaimed as himself essentially an analytical philosopher;[1] more often, he is castigated for exemplary errors in logical syntax, to the corruption of all later thought.[2] Others write of Plato's deficiencies in dialectic, his blithe unawareness of the dangers of ambiguity, and the consequent confusions in his thought,[3] while still others conduct debates over the *Parmenides* in which Plato's logical acuity is the one issue on which both sides agree.[4]

The present paper will be concerned with some logical questions but, as my title implies, language (i.e., natural language) will preponderate over logic in the stricter sense. Thus it is my hope by bringing together Plato's scattered judgments, explicit and implied, upon language as "an instrument of instruction and discrimination" (*Cratylus*), to contribute indirectly to the current debate over Plato's logical competence.

My paper falls naturally into the following divisions: after a short historical foreword (section I), I shall consider

II. The dialogue *Cratylus*, Plato's most extensive survey of the nature of language and its relation to truth and reality.

III. Plato's theory and practice of language as revealed in his other dialogues, in two aspects:

* Presented at the 1955 meeting of the SAGP in Boston, Massachusetts. A somewhat modified treatment of the same topic entitled "Language and the *Cratylus*: Four Questions," was published in, and permission obtained from, the *Review of Metaphysics*, 11 (1957): 28–41. For publication of the paper in this volume, minor editing of the manuscript, verification of references, and checking of the citations from the Platonic text have been done by Professor Levinson's wife, Elizabeth J. Levinson, Ph.D. and by Charles F. Virtue, Professor Emeritus of Philosophy, and David Tatem, Associate Professor of Classics, both at the University of Maine.

A. Rejections of theories and techniques present in his environment.

B. Positive achievements.

IV. Plato's conception of language as related to knowledge and reality.

I. *Plato's Predecessors*

1. Plato's grapple with the theme of language will seem less a phantom strife if viewed against its culture-historical background and in relation to the speculations already in the field.

Not to be overlooked is the influence of Greek religion, especially the oracles, and of the older poetry, all of which encouraged the belief that words may be vehicles of a divine truth, but that they require special skill and ingenuity for their understanding. Among philosophers, Heracleitus had at least played with the cryptic meanings suggested by paranomasias such as the name Zeus and ζῆν (*zēn*), "live," ξὺν νῷ (*xun nōi*), "with mind," and ξύνῳ (*xunōi*), "common" or "shared"; and upon this hint, perhaps reenforced by Pythagorean–Orphic fantasies, that later follower of Heracleitus, Cratylus, was to erect the doctrine of the "natural rightness of names."

2. The sophists of the fifth century gave lively attention to the theme of speech. Thus Protagoras did much to develop the foundations of Greek grammar, on which Plato was to build, distinguishing the kinds of sentences, the tenses, and the parts of speech, while Hippias advanced the classification of the letters and syllables, and Prodicus (of whom more will be said below) developed a "synonymic."

3. Destructive criticism was also rife. Parmenides, the first thinker of record to raise critically the question of the relation between words and thought, had branded "all that mortals in their speech have agreed upon"—his own verbally expressed theory apart—"a mere name,"[5] and had denied that it was possible to speak or think of "what is not." This distrust of ordinary language was in later days developed by the Megarians, the heirs of Parmenides, and exploited by their clowning counterparts, the eristics. The negative position was reenforced by Antisthenes, who according to Aristotle argued against the possibility of anything beyond tautologous definitions of the type, "Man is man," and denied the possibility of contradiction,[6] while at the same time he declared that "the study of words is the beginning of education."[7]

4. Meanwhile, Protagorean relativism had tended in the field of language to the belief that words refer by convention, and refer to

individual experience only; and Democritus, from his base in atomism, devised specific arguments in support of the view that language is a product of chance (τύχη).

5. Amidst this confusion, according to the view I support, Plato chose as his anchorage the Socratic assumption that human reason is capable of arriving at adequate verbally stated meanings through a critical pursuit of definition, and between logical nihilism, on the one hand, and an irresponsible occultism, on the other, sought a middle path.

II. *The "Cratylus"*

Omitting regretfully much that is required for a full appreciation of the dialogue, I shall consider only those features directly relevant to my special theme.

1. Whether to adhere to the traditional early date or, with Allan and others,[8] to promote the *Cratylus*, in view of its thematic affiliations, to the near neighborhood in time of the *Theaetetus* and the *Sophist*, is not to me of primary importance, since I reject the assumption of major shifts and developments in Plato's thought; the important thing is the detailed correspondence between the *Cratylus* and the whole group of later dialogues, and the fruitfulness of considering them in close mutual relation. Similarly, I shall not feel it necessary to enter here into the question, perennially debated, of the historicity and personal standpoint of Cratylus. Suffice it to say that in the dialogue he serves as point of departure for Plato's rejection of three uncongenial views: the Heraclitean doctrine of unqualified Flux; a neo-Heraclitean or mystical Pythagorean interpretation of language, having three components; and the Megarian-sophistic denial of the possibility of false statement.

2. The first result reached by the dialogue is a definition of the ideal name in terms of its function. The topic of the dialogue is the "rightness of names," which latter must be understood to include what we should call verbs, in their infinitive and participial forms; adjectives; and nouns. Are names "right" by nature, or by mere custom and convention? The question is initially met by Socrates' demonstration that names can be "right" in both ways. To do so, he develops the concept of the "Nomothete," an ideal "custom-establisher" or name-maker, who imposes names as customs, to be sure, but in accord with the nature of the ideal Name, to which he looks (ἀποβλέπω) as model (389D). Like the ideal Statesman of the *Politicus*, the ideal Nomothete can best be understood as the fusion of the everyday actuality of past lawgivers with an ideal; he is both those ancient and very human inventors of language

who will be mentioned later in the dialogue, and also what we may call a "regulative norm" of words as tools of thought. The names he makes will be fit "instruments for instruction and discrimination." The word used, διακριτικόν (388C), and the accompanying comparison of the name's function with that of the weaver's shuttle in dividing the threads, implies the familiar Platonic notion of the assignment of the entities named, to classes, an indication borne out by the requirement laid down later in the dialogue that names must be given to the subclasses which make up a typical Platonic "grid" or network of related classes (see below).

3. The second chief result of the dialogue is its rejection of the view, never elsewhere seriously considered by Plato, that names are capable in themselves of conveying knowledge about reality. Plato, it is true, believes it possible that many names were created in past times as capsule descriptions of their objects, by word-makers who sought to express in them the natures of things. Some basic words may be phonic imitations or sound-pictures, which owe their possibility to the natural fitness of certain sounds, such as *r*, *o*, *d*, to express certain basic qualities of things, such as motion, roundness, or stability. And here Plato proposes half-seriously an investigation into the structure of language, which is to start by classifying in named categories and sub-categories the sounds and, correspondingly, the qualities, and is then to examine their correlations as found in actual words (424B–425B).

Plato seriously believes, also, that many other words have been formed as compounds of these basic words, and though he warns us, by many a disavowal of certainty, against accepting too readily his specific etymologies, some of which are obviously fantastic, he permits his Socrates to present a great array of these, and among them to propose that perhaps the ancients, believing that Flux is good, called "the harmful" τὸ βλαβερόν, from τὸ βουλόμενον ἅπτειν ῥοῦν, "that which seeks to halt the flow," and that "the beautiful," τὸ καλόν, has been symbolically named in honor of mind or intelligence, which is "that which gives names," τὸ καλοῦν. Somewhat later in the dialogue, Socrates is made to present equally plausible derivations which imply that to their makers, stability and not Flux seemed good. All these names for Plato are unquestionably of human origin. Time has so altered them that much reconstruction is needed before we can even guess their meaning. They are not consistent in what they imply. And what if their makers erred? Only independent knowledge can tell us which of these would-be imitative names convey truth.

4. A third point of great importance is Plato's recognition of the necessity of convention in names. Imitative names must always be imperfect—such is the very nature of imitations; and time and human caprice introduce into them innumerable changes, so that they must be understood by custom. Many names, moreover, cannot be imitative, such as personal names, and those of the innumerable array of numbers. In all such cases, the name transfers meaning from mind to mind only by convention, and can do so only between those who have prior knowledge of the thing named (433E). Again, the necessity of attaining knowledge independently of words is presupposed.

5. Of major importance for Plato's later thought is this further conclusion: meaningful false statement is possible. Cratylus had maintained that names cannot be false, since one cannot say "what is not"; for him, the name Hermogenes, taken by Cratylus as meaning "son of Hermes," and implying good fortune in money-making or skill in speech, cannot be the name of one who has neither; it is either another man's name, or a mere noise. Now it is to be observed that throughout the dialogue, Plato treats names as capable of truth or falsity; nor is this as illogical as it seems, since the application of the name is regarded as an implicit proposition. Plato proceeds to show that just as a picture of a woman can be attributed to a man or the reverse, so a name can be wrongly attributed, and in such a case will be wrong or "false"; and he goes on to say that if this is true of "names" (ὀνόματα), it is true also of "phrases" or "predicates" (ῥήματα) and of statements (λόγοι), which are the combinations of these (431B). Here he implies, though to the irritation of interpreters he does not make explicit what the terms mean to him in this context, that he already has the conceptions of subject, predicate, and statement so familiar to readers of the *Sophist*.

6. The *Cratylus* concludes with a demonstration that since names themselves cannot provide knowledge either of their own "rightness" or of reality, and since if all is Flux neither stable knowledge nor anything truly knowable can exist, the Forms must be sought and somehow found.

7. In summary, we can say that though Plato has found language faulty and of human origin, liable to falsehood and error and containing always an unpredictable element of convention—thus far he has allowed Protagoras and Democritus their due—he has also saved it from the utter futility to which the Megarians and, in effect, Antisthenes, had condemned it. Capable in its instructive and classificatory power of being the immediate copy of the Ideal Name, of serving well the dialectician, and of conveying, between those who have prior knowledge,

authentic truth, it is high in potential dignity and worth. But Plato remains convinced that outside of language, knowledge is an attainable ideal.

III. *Theory and Practice of Logical Language in the Other Dialogues*

I propose now, in the second main section of this paper, to bring together in summary form a selection from what Plato has told us elsewhere than in the *Cratylus* relevant to this theme. The material will fall into two subdivisions, of which the first will recount Plato's rejections of a number of fifth and fourth century theories and techniques of language study or manipulation; here there will be some overlap with the rejections seen in the *Cratylus*. The second subdivision will recount Plato's own proposals and corresponding practice.

A. *Plato's Rejections*

1. That Plato rejected etymology as a reliable organ of inquiry into the nature of reality, the *Cratylus* gave us reason to believe, and this conclusion a survey of the other dialogues confirms to the hilt. At the same time we note the by no means negligible role he did assign it, though not as part of his substantive thought. Philologically considered, there is no reason to doubt that some of his derivations are seriously offered, in the sense that he believed them at least probably correct; indeed, in some instances, by the standards of modern philology, so they truly are (e.g., in *Phaedo* 90D, the name Hades, Ἅιδης from ἀειδές, "unseen"). But their primarily non-philological character is confirmed by the suggestion, in *Politicus* 295E and *Laws* 714A, of two separate derivations for the important word νόμος, "law." In addition, Plato continued to speak of the men of early times as having assigned names which they formed out of still older words, sometimes with great propriety (e.g., *Laws* 800A, 816B, 957C). The sovereign point to note, however, is that Plato's etymologies subserve what in a large sense may be called rhetorical ends, and are never advanced as independent guides to knowledge.

2. A second method of linguistic study, rejected by Plato, is that study of synonyms mentioned above, which Plato presents as having been devised and practiced by the sophist Prodicus of Ceos. Readers of the *Cratylus* will recall the reference made to him near the beginning of the dialogue (384B) where Socrates, being asked to discuss the correctness of names, disclaims knowledge he might have had "if I had attended the 50 drachma course of Prodicus, which, he says himself, gives a man a complete education on this topic." The quoted words

carry an obvious coefficient of satirical depreciation, often but not always present in Plato's many references to this sophist. Only once does Prodicus receive at Plato's hands a compliment, when at *Euthydemus* 277D Socrates makes a serious appeal to his principle of the correctness of names, in order to clarify an ambiguity; but the size of the compliment is considerably diminished in the immediate sequel, when the whole body of such knowledge is characterized as a mere prelude to serious inquiry into the reality of things.

The *Protagoras* offers the most instructive account of Plato's attitude, for there we have Prodicus depicted in action, as the expert in the art of discriminating or "dividing" words—the same term which Plato was later to apply to the process he invented for dividing and redividing classes. Here (*Protagoras* 337A–C) Prodicus is shown making a pompous and empty little speech in which pairs of generically equivalent words are unnecessarily contrasted. At a later point in the dialogue, beguiled by Socrates, Prodicus assists in robbing a passage from Simonides of its meaning by applying his verbological technique. Plato's implied criticism of Prodicus in both passages comes to this: he has violated the *Cratylus*' precept that subordinates the "rightness of names" to an inquiry into the thing signified. In the first instance Prodicus was shown pointlessly distinguishing between words which in the context were in no real danger of being confused; such words are indeed confusable, if we have at hand a Prodicus to devise an ingenious confusion as a preliminary to restoring them, histrionically, to their pristine distinctness. Similarly, in the Simonides passage, the vanity of the method is for Plato sufficiently revealed by the variety of interpretations of the poem which result from its application and the impossibility of deciding between them—not to mention the impossibility of understanding the poet's own meaning—as long as one remains within the area of word-criticism as Prodicus understands it.

If, as has often been suggested since Grote undertook to vindicate the sophistic movement, Plato has interposed his prejudice between us and the real Prodicus, I can only say that for our present purpose Plato's reason for rejecting the "Prodicean" method remains untouched by the possible fact that Plato has unjustly fastened it onto a much more able and significant man. The Prodicus whom Plato shows us has, strictly speaking, no theory of language. He is interested neither in how words might be used to express difficult new conceptions, nor in how to understand the thought of persons who had used the words in senses perhaps other than those he approved. He has only a technique for constructing a kind of dictionary, a manual of diction by which one might be assured that in employing such-and-such a word in such-and-such a sense, one was conforming to the usage of polite Athenian society. Useful in itself, this technique is neither logical nor ethical in its aim.

3. Plato's often-quoted depreciation of the written word in the *Phaedrus*, and also in the part of the *Protagoras* which we have just had under view, is relevant in this connection: the helpless word, unable to talk back in correction of its misinterpreters, needs its parent to come to its aid, and cannot answer the questions of those who desire further explanation of its meaning (*Phaedrus* 275D–E); the poets whose works we read cannot themselves explain their meanings, nor can we be sure which to choose among the different interpretations placed upon them by supposed authorities (*Protagoras* 347E). The author of the *Seventh Letter* has gone further in the same direction, so far, in fact, as to declare (341C–E, 342E–343A, 344C–D) that "on really serious subjects, no man of sense will ever dare to entrust his thoughts to language, when it is unchangeable, as in writing" (trans. Bury, Loeb Library).

But whether or not one accepts the *Letter*, with its extreme development of the principle, the *Phaedrus* passage retains a clear and defensible sense, implied by the *Cratylus*, and underlined by the fate of the Simonides poem in the *Protagoras*: it is the oft-told semantic tale that to persons who have no knowledge of the things or concepts signified by the words, or for whom the words bear other significations, written language does not convey the thought intended. Only in face-to-face discussions, often repeated, when thought is restated in different words, can obscurities be explained, and mutual understanding be reached; only living language is worthy of a man's best thoughts. As we shall see below, this principle has possible bearing on Plato's policy, so distinct from Aristotle's, of eschewing in his writings almost entirely the use of technical terms.

4. The last of Plato's denials to be reckoned with is his early and late refusal to be halted by sophistic barriers to constructive thought, either by those arguments resting on a technique of patent verbal ambiguity, illustrated in the *Euthydemus*, or by the logico-linguistic contentions of the more serious surviving representatives of the Parmenidean denial of non-being. It is the eristics against whom Plato directs his criticism, for example, in the *Theaetetus* (154D–E, 199A), where he speaks of their habit of battering one another's arguments with counter-arguments and "dragging words about as they please" from pointless love of combat; words used in this fashion Plato must set himself to

discredit. From the other side, as we learned from the *Cratylus*, Plato recognized that the issues raised by the less frivolous among these disputants touched the validity of language as the tool of thought, and this recognition roused him to vigorous efforts in its behalf.

B. *Plato's Positive Contributions*

The negative evidence as to Plato's outlook tells a clear and consistent story, in consonance with the *Cratylus*, and requires only to be enlarged and not corrected by the positive evidence now to be supplied, partly by Plato's explicit statements, but chiefly by the eloquent proof of his practice throughout the dialogues.

1. One very conspicuous use that Plato made of "words"—I should like to emphasize the quotation marks—was to seek to define them, or rather to ask what the things were which they denoted: to ask, "What is piety? Justice? A sophist?" and so forth. We shall examine first the pursuit of definition in the early and middle Platonic dialogues and in the *Phaedrus*, the date of which is disputed, in order to see what it is that Plato is aiming at in this process, and whether the clarification of concepts he attempts is logically justifiable.

a. Let the *Euthyphro* serve as our example of an early dialogue of search, ending in failure to define τὸ ὅσιον, "holiness" or "piety." The Socrates who meets us here, however much he is still the historical man, is yet for our purposes interchangeable with Plato as his fully accredited spokesman.—We are struck immediately with a contrast between the method of Socrates and that of Cratylus or of Prodicus. From the very start there is no suggestion that any significance attaches to the word ὅσιον in its character as word. The *word* is not piety, and there is nothing to be learned from the examination of its shape or sound, or from its supposed derivation; nor does Socrates assume that light on the nature of piety can be gathered by citing examples of how the word ὅσιον was used by men of old, Simonides or Homer: usage settles no questions in philosophy; and if Euthyphro had preferred to discuss the nature of piety or reverence for the gods under some other name, the Socrates of the *Charmides*, at least, as we shall see below (section III B 3a), would have been content to investigate the meaning of that term, instead. In short, Socrates and the author of the *Euthyphro* are not thinking *about* words but *with* them.

In confirmation of this claim, observe the immediate attachment of the reported conversation to the moral and religious realities of the Athenian scene, and the problems that they present to any honest mind.

Here, in the shadow of the courtroom where Socrates is destined to be condemned on an ambiguous charge of impiety, a professional pietist, himself engaged in entering a charge of impiety, is invited to reflect a little more deeply upon the nature of this familiar thing, piety, and its opposite. Socrates contrives to bring to Euthyphro's belated attention in rapid but logically ordered succession a set of "Prolegomena to Any Future Theology," revealing the inadequacies and contradictions of traditional notions about the gods, and implying the conditions to which an acceptable religious philosophy must conform. Piety must be subsumed, it is suggested (11E), under justice, and religion thus related to the foundation of the moral life, from which there is grave danger, underlined by the tales of dissension among the gods, that it may become estranged, to the injury of both. In sum, the *Euthyphro* puts its readers on their way toward an organized community of values, within which the meaning of piety must be functionally determined. This purpose the dialogue fulfills in the absence of a formulated answer to the initial question, or perhaps, one could even say, by means of its failure to arrive at the missing formula.

b. Much that I have said of Plato's purpose in pursuing definition in the *Euthyphro* is true more abundantly of ensuing dialogues of the transition period. The *Gorgias* is a case in point. There, as will be remembered, a definition of rhetoric is in request; the presence of the famous rhetorician for whom the dialogue is named attaches the discussion to issues of serious political and educational concern. Again as in the *Euthyphro*, though here the search is much more elaborately developed, we find Socrates exploring the thing or concept in question in its relations to kindred concepts and to basic concerns of human life. Socrates is saying, in effect, "Let us assume that rhetoric means what you, Gorgias, and your pupil, Polus, by your practice and by your explicit claims take it to mean: that art of speech which is the 'artisan of persuasion.' Let us then consider what this entails. If, within persuasion as a whole, we distinguish the kind that imparts knowledge from the kind that produces belief only, to which kind does rhetoric belong? Whom and on what subjects does it persuade? With knowledge on the part of the persuader, or without? With consequences which, in a thoughtful moment, the teacher of persuasion would himself approve?" And so on (*Gorgias* 453–61).

Out of the material facts thus elicited Socrates constructs (463) a "grid" or scheme of relationships between rhetoric, thus conceived, and seven other arts aimed at the benefiting or pleasing of soul or body, in order that the actually discreditable place of this supposed sovereign among the arts may stand revealed, and proceeds once more to show, this time from the point of view of the possessor of the art, that what it can accomplish is not what, in the ultimate sense, is either good or genuinely desired. Here again Plato's conception of the legitimate and fruitful handling of questions asking, "What is X?" has been made clear. The meaning of X can be discerned only in the light of a full exploration of its relations, not only to its closer kin among the arts—though these relations will help to delimit it and distinguish it from those other X's with which it may be confused—but also to the widest context in which it admits of being placed.

c. But the outstanding example, in the grand manner, of what the *Euthyphro* and the *Gorgias* were adduced to show, is expectably, the *Republic*. The miracle of method by which Plato has converted a rejected stone of the *Charmides* (the phrase τὰ ἑαυτοῦ πράττειν, "to do one's own task," there suggested as a definition of temperance) into the cornerstone, the definition of justice, in the *Republic*, is worth pondering. Book I had supplied an arsenal of defective weapons for attacking the problem of defining the capital term. The radical flaw in all these efforts, including the Thrasymachean, was their naïve trust in the adequacy of "three words," taken alone, to embrace within their scanty boundaries the immensity of the moral and political universe. How is it, then, that Plato seems to have done the trick with the same three words with which Critias, in the *Charmides*, had failed?

The obvious answer is, once more, that Plato was extremely well aware of the power and the limitations upon the power of words. In the instance before us, eschewing a direct attack, he has used the word "justice," his definiendum, as a point of departure for what might seem a long detour which enables him to discover an initial anchorage for the word, viz., the hypothetical community operating on such a plan that each class and individual is performing a task of its own and in keeping with its own natural fitness. At this point it becomes possible to revert to the original question and to produce, as a not unsuitable verbal formula, τὰ ἑαυτοῦ πράττειν. But "justice" is by no means yet defined. The meaning of the three words must first be extended to embrace a similar correspondence of functions and natural fitness within the individual soul. The remainder of the *Republic* provides a continually increasing depth of meaning to the formula, which is ultimately made to include the oneness of the harmonious city, and the vision attained by the philosopher-kings. We are shown what justice means to the city and the soul which possesses it, and what is its place in the realm of ordered being.

d. In adducing the *Phaedrus* as my last illustration of Plato's theory and practice of the defining art, I find myself in partial conflict with what seems to be the current consensus regarding its relation to Plato's thought. According to the reigning view, the *Phaedrus* expounds a method of dialectic constituting an innovation of decisive importance in Plato's philosophical development, finding expression only in the period after the *Republic*, and carried forward without a break into the later, dialectical dialogues. To me it appears, on the contrary, that the greater explicitness and complexity of the divisions found in the *Phaedrus* are the simple result of the topic—which is, precisely, the method of composition, written or spoken. The *Phaedrus* adds no more than the formal analysis and elaboration of the method employed both in the *Gorgias* and in the *Republic*.

In the *Gorgias*, the wider classes of persuasion and of the arts of tendance are broken down into their constituent classes; just so, in the *Phaedrus*, the wider classes of madness and of rhetoric are dissected. The untroubled surface of the *Republic* is apt to conceal from the casual reader the complexity of detailed articulation and classification immediately below, such as the correlated trisections of types of soul and types of social function and the corresponding tetrads of virtues; but on occasion, in the Divided Line, Plato makes his divisions so explicit that they become a logical diagram. In each such case, there is refusal to stop at the level of the linear definition; the analysis is widened to include the structure of relations of the area, large or small according to the purpose in view, within which the definiendum has its place. Its definition thus becomes, initially at least, a process of marking it off in an almost literal sense from other confusable entities. There remains ideally one further step (and it is seen in all three of the positive dialogues we have been considering), the assigning of the entity defined to its proper place in the moral life and beyond that, in the universal theatre of being.

If the parallel just drawn is accepted, I am entitled to bring the *Phaedrus* under one head with the three dialogues already discussed, as a further and more refined example of one central Platonic insight, viz., the value of contextual definition. That the method of the *Phaedrus* is continuous with that employed in the *Sophist* and *Politicus* and described in the *Philebus* (and also referred to, as we have seen, in the *Cratylus*) is not matter of dispute. We have therefore to deal with a method of multilinear definition, present at least as early as the *Gorgias*, which reveals its discriminatory power in its analysis of relations, while grounding apprehension of the essence of the thing defined on a metaphysical doctrine of immediately knowable substances, the Forms. To quote Plato in confirmation of Plato, let me cite as a singularly apt comment the maxim occurring in the *Cratylus* (438E): "How are we to learn about things except by the way that is most likely and most right—through one another if they are related, and through themselves?" Plato is not hoping to discover the essence of a transcendental entity in a few miraculously and inherently significant words.

2. We have next to observe Plato's skillful way of preventing the looser habits of common sense from passing themselves off as genuine reports of reality, and his awareness of the pitfalls into which the careless user of language may fall.

a. As the reader of the *Republic* well knows, Plato is always willing to halt the progress of his argument in order to clear up a confusion of this sort. An outstanding instance is the longish section of this dialogue (436A ff.) where the threatened contradiction between the unity of the soul and the plurality of its motions prompts him to a logical disquisition (436C) on the ambiguity of the unqualified statement that something is in motion or at rest, in the course of which he states, without naming, the essential notion of the Law of Contradiction. Once it has been grounded on this stabilizing principle, Plato is telling us, thought can proceed with confidence; it is set free to incorporate its conclusions in words that remain under its control. Has it discovered that something is at rest? The discovery may be true or false, but it cannot be contradicted by the statement that something else, or the same thing in some other respect, is in motion. Aside from the question whether any metaphysical truth is here at stake, the ground has been cleared for the critical and rational use of language.

b. Plato's intellectual superiority to the words at his disposal, his ability importantly to transcend their limitations, comes clearly before us once more in the passage immediately following (438B ff.), where we see him inventing means for conveying another idea for which no precise verbal expression was available in current Greek. Plato is undertaking to distinguish between what we would call "unqualified" and "qualified correlates" such as the pairs, "thirst, pure and simple" and "drink, pure and simple," and "much thirst" and "much drink." This is then summed up in a general statement, after which, taking pains to avoid misunderstanding, as he says explicitly (438D–E), he explains that the qualifications of the two members of a pair are not necessarily the same:

"knowledge of health" is not "healthy knowing." The passage shows that Plato recognized, in this particular relationship of action and the object of action, the principle of "relational univocity," although he may on occasion have chosen to violate it (*Gorgias* 476B ff.) and may even in some instances have done so unawares.

c. A little later in the *Republic* (454A), another threatened contradiction prompts Plato once more to warn us of the need for watchfulness against ambiguity. Socrates, by a pleasant little fiction, pretends to have let himself and his interlocutor drift into that sort of pointless contentiousness, or eristic, into which many fall, against their wills, all for the lack of making the necessary divisions and distinctions between classes or kinds (εἴδη). It has been agreed that to different natures, different pursuits must be assigned, and yet it has also been said that men and women—who are surely of different natures—must have the same pursuits; can both be true? "How potent a thing is this same eristic!" Socrates exclaims, and goes on to say, in effect, "How many good folk are taken in by it, and find themselves pursuing words while they imagine they are engaged in profound argument! Thus through failure to distinguish one sort of difference of nature, which is relevant, from others that are not, we have been sadly led astray." Plato, it is true, conceives the two things that have been confused as ontological realities and not, as modern logic considers them, mere conceptual classes. But this should not blind us to the fact that Plato is here talking logic, and distinguishing between two senses that an ambiguous word may bear. We may note in anticipation of a later topic that this passage is among those which best display Plato's vocabulary for expressing the concept of ambiguity.

3. I wish now to reenforce the above conclusion by appealing to certain passages in which Plato has, as it were, anticipated some of his modern critics by an explicit rejection of naïve dependence upon the authority of words to determine meaning and a refusal to regard them as more than the heteronomous agents of human thought.

a. The *Charmides* retains a position among the dialogues presumably preceding the *Republic*. It is therefore the more significant, as furnishing evidence of Plato's early arrival at a high level of sophistication, that this dialogue contains a curt and unqualified refusal to recognize an autonomy of words. Critias has argued that temperance is τὰ ἑαυτοῦ πράττειν or ἐργάζεσθαι, which may be roughly translated, "to do one's own task" or "deed," but that it is not τὰ ἑαυτοῦ ποιεῖν, "to do one's own work"—and gives as his reason the statement that the word ποιεῖν, "work," as he far-fetchedly appeals to Hesiod to confirm, includes in its connotation some dishonorable activities, incompatible with the honorable nature of temperance. Socrates replies: "I have heard Prodicus make just such distinctions ten thousand times," and adds a sentence (163D) which deserves quoting and underscoring as a revelation of Plato's insight into the functional relation between the word and the thought: "I give you the right to assign any meaning you like to any term you choose to employ; only make it clear to me whatever the thing is to which you are applying any term you use." Or, in other and more modern words: "Specify your referent and you may employ whatever symbol you choose." In the face of recent warnings against insinuating the future into an ancient thinker by presenting his doctrine in modern dress, one might hesitate before attributing to Plato so modern a concept as that of the "stipulative definition"; but would it not take a present-day Prodicus to discriminate between these two forms of Plato's statement?

b. A passage from the *Phaedrus* moves along parallel lines. Here (263A–E) we are shown the importance of stipulated meanings for the rhetorician who aspires to be master of a genuine art. Socrates explains that there are two classes of things, those whose "names" are indisputably clear, e.g., iron and silver, and those that, like justice and goodness, give rise to diversity of interpretation and dispute. The skilled speaker who intends to deal with one of these latter, of which "love" is surely one, must recognize it as such, and act accordingly. Hence if Lysias' speech is to pass muster, he must have compelled us "at the beginning of his discourse on Love . . . to conceive it as a certain definite entity, with a meaning he had himself decided upon." In these unambiguous terms Plato has declared the necessity, for a responsible rhetoric no less than for dialectic, of unambiguity.

4. At this point the path of our inquiry into Plato's hermeneutics of words leads us back to consider a piece of unfinished business that arose in the course of our exposition of the *Cratylus*. One might expect to find that the man who announced the ideal of words as the tools of instruction and discrimination, fit for the use of the dialectician, would himself go at least some part of the way toward closing the gap between actual speech and the ideal. In this expectation one would not be wholly disappointed. Plato never at any time attempted (so far as can be known) to carry out the systematic examination of the Greek language put forward as a possibility in the *Cratylus*, or to compose words on the phonic model, nor did he abate one whit his warning against over-valuing the word itself, as we shall see. But to some extent even in his mid-period, and

especially in his later years, when questions of logico-linguistic precision were being given central consideration, and when, in the Academy, he was directing an educational program, he put into linguistic form some of the results of his inquiries and of his pedagogic invention.

In my study of the matter I have found theoretical confirmation and much practical aid in Lewis Campbell's extensive survey and detailed tabulation of the language of the later dialogues.[9] Campbell has collected an impressive display of examples showing the moulding influence of Plato's thought upon his language in every region of his concern, and provides long lists of his verbal inventions. Here it will not be possible to give more than a few samples of what will be found in Campbell, together with one or two of my own gathering from earlier dialogues.[10] Plato's inventions are of two sorts:

a. Growing out of Plato's practice of logical division are a number of words that Plato has taken over intact, or slightly altered, from common usage, and employed in a new sense. They include terms for special mental functions (διάνοια and εἰκασία; *Republic* 511D–E); for logical division (τομή, διχάζω, διχοτομέω; *Politicus* 261A, 264D, 302E); for logical opposition (ἀντίθεσις and ἀντίκειμαι; *Sophist* 257E, 258B, both well on the way to becoming Aristotle's terms for the opposition between propositions); and for classes of different degrees of inclusiveness (γένος, *Parmenides* 129C; ἄτμητος, *Phaedrus* 277B; and ἄτομος, *Sophist* 229D). Another sort of term is the pedagogical-satirical adaptation of κολακική (*Gorgias* 502D) to mean "flatterology."

If the question is raised whether Plato is fully conscious of his own verbal innovations, we are fortunate enough to find him, in the *Theaetetus*, supplying us with an answer. In this dialogue many careful discriminations of terms are made, and on one such occasion (198A ff.), when it is necessary to distinguish between learning and knowing and between latent knowledge and full awareness, Plato proposes the temporary assignment of a specific Greek word to each conception, and carries out his argument successfully by means of them. Thus Plato has shown how with full awareness he can combat the unscrupulous wordster or avoid the errors of innocent confusion with the scrupulous use of that "diacritical tool," the word.

b. The examples just given display Plato's almost austere moderation; novelty has been procured at the cost of minimal departure from the track of usage. But new formations are also found, and among them one destined to a distinguished philosophical career: ποιότης (*Theaetetus* 182A). This is the first appearance in extant literature of the word "quality," put forward by Plato with apologies for its uncouthness. An amusing example is "misology," "hatred of reasoning" (*Phaedo* 89D). More spectacular, though in general much less serviceable and enduring, are the many terms invented for subdivisions reached in διαίρεσις, itself a word adapted by Plato from the related meaning given it by Prodicus. These include such mildly humorous constructions as εἰδωλοποιική (*Sophist* 235B), "the art of making images," and δοξομιμητική (*Sophist* 267E), "the art of notion-dissembling."

Here again Plato has explained what he is about, and has supplied an additional caveat against our thinking that he attached any exaggerated importance to his creations. Plato's "Eleatic Stranger" avers (*Sophist* 267E) that the ancient word-makers were remiss in making distinctions between kinds and failed to supply us with a sufficiency of names; hence he is obliged boldly to coin a name to suit the present need. And in the *Politicus*, where many such names have been devised, Plato's Stranger compliments his young interlocutor (261E) for his observing comment that the exact form of the name just proposed does not matter: "If you preserve such an indifference to mere names, you will be proclaimed richer in wisdom when you are old."

5. "Plato does not technicalize his terms"—thus Shorey has stated, with a connotation of approval, what is often expressed in the form of a rebuke by those who see in Aristotle's development of a fixed philosophical vocabulary an effective remedy for Plato's neglect of terminological precision, with its consequent harvest of ambiguity and error.[11] I shall not here decree a settlement of this dispute, but I think that the area of conflict can be significantly reduced by a careful inspection of certain logical or methodological devices whereby, in my opinion, Plato very largely compensates for the absence of a technical vocabulary, and in some respects achieves a happier result. Accordingly, I shall try to show the means Plato employs and the degree of clarity he does achieve and then to suggest his reasons for not having taken Aristotle's course.

a. Let us examine first one of Plato's most striking devices, a species of logical "shock treatment," which I shall call "misinterpretation followed by correction." This is the characteristic procedure in the Socratic dialogues, in which Socrates asks a question which is not understood, and the interlocutor's answer goes awry; in another typical case, Socrates himself feigns to misunderstand the interlocutor's suggestion and turns it into an absurdity (*Hipp. Maj.* 287E, *Meno* 72D ff.; *Charm.* 161C ff., *Rep.* 338C). In both cases clarification results. The whole proceeding is a technique for avoiding oracular obscurity or long harangues; interlocutor and reader alike achieve clarity and this without the use of any term not part of the general store.

b. A second closely related technique often found in the dialogues, particularly in the *Republic*, is the practice of stating first a highly complicated notion in full panoply and incomprehensibility, and then, by successive restatement, interspersed with illustrations, making the ordinary everyday words take on precise meaning *pro tempore* for the purpose at hand, while leaving them free to drop back into the pool of ordinary meaning when this purpose shall have been served. We have cited an illustration of this in section III B 2b above.

c. A third recurrent practice is that of constantly varying and replacing the words and phrases used to designate even his most characteristic and frequently employed concepts. An outstanding illustration is the language in which he expresses his doctrine of the Forms. As is well known,[12] his vocabulary displays an extraordinary variety and range. Whether he will employ εἶδος or ἰδέα or οὐσία, αὐτὰ καθ'αὑτά or τὰ ὄντως ὄντα, ὃ ἔστι καλόν or αὐτὸ καλόν, παρουσία or μέθεξις or μίμησις—is not, as is sometimes confidently asserted, simply a function of Plato's philosophical development, a key to the chronology of the dialogues (though I am not denying that frequency-counts, here as elsewhere, may tell us something of value). In some passages this variety of usage appears to function primarily as a means of bringing into sharp focus the aspect of the Ideas relevant to the particular purpose: certain descriptions are peculiarly suited to the Ideas in their transcendental character, as heavenly models, as objects of raptured contemplation; others better serve to bring out the structured order of the Forms as the paradigms for the logical classification of concepts. Sometimes when no difference of meaning is intended the motive of literary variety seems to operate and two or more such terms are employed interchangeably (e.g., *Politicus* 262D–E). A related practice is that of using two or more closely related parables or metaphors, as in the *Republic*, where the Cave and the Line illustrate the same conceptions, but emphasize now one, now another of the meanings they symbolize.

d. By this use of overlapping terms and expressions Plato contrives to indicate a kind of nuclear meaning determined by the area of significance common to all the terms employed, comparable to the unshaded area of overlap in a set of logical circles. This technique, which I shall call "clarification by overlap," could be illustrated by a swarm of texts from various dialogues, too numerous to be cited here. Many of them are short passages where Plato uses in close proximity several words conjointly expressive of a single notion, and perhaps adds a statement of his principled distaste for that method of Prodicus which would restrict him to a single term;[13] in other cases he varies his phrasing of a concept within the limits of a single dialogue,[14] or rejects an opponent's attempt to introduce a difference of words which does not answer to a relevant difference of meaning.[15]

e. Passing over these briefer instances, I shall present as my final example a concept which, like the earlier cited Theory of Forms, is not limited to a particular dialogue, and which enjoys the further advantage of prominence in recent Platonic debate. The following table draws from passages some of which have been already analyzed here, a number of Plato's multiple expressions describing verbal ambiguity, distributing them under captions for whose categoreal imperfection some favor must be asked. My translations have been made painfully literal in order to escape suspicion of having improved Plato by modernizing him.

Agents, motives, and causes of ambiguity

Phaedo 101E: ἀντιλογικοί, "disputatious persons"

Republic 454B: ἄκοντες ἀντιλογίας ἅπτεσθαι, "unintentionally to fall into contradiction"

Theaetetus 164C: ἀντιλογικῶς, "in disputatious fashion"

Phaedo 101C: κομψείας, "subtleties"

Republic 436D: κομψευόμενος, "contriving subtleties"

Sophist 259C: κομψός, "subtle"

Republic 454A–B: ἐρίζειν, ἔριδι, ἐριστικῶς, "wrangling," "disputatiously"

Theaetetus 168B–C: συνηθείας ῥημάτων τε καὶ ὀνομάτων, ἃ οἱ πολλοὶ ... ἕλκοντες, "the accepted meanings of words and phrases which most men pervert"

Theaetetus 199A: ἕλκων (ὀνόματα), "perverting [words]"

Sophist 259C: τοὺς λόγους ἕλκων, "perverting words"

Sophist 259D: τἀναντία ... προφέροντα ἐν τοῖς λόγοις, "bringing up verbal oppositions in argument"

Republic 454A: μὴ ... κατ' εἴδη διαιρούμενοι τὸ λεγόμενον ἐπισκοπεῖν, "not applying the proper distinctions in examining what is said"

Republic 454A: κατ' ... ὄνομα διώκειν τοῦ λεχθέντος τὴν ἐναντίωσιν, "pursuing oppositions on the basis of words"

Republic 454C–D: τὸ εἶδος τῆς ἀλλοιώσεως ... τεῖνον, "the kind of difference that is relevant"

Ambiguity itself

Charmides 162A: ᾐνίττετο, "he was riddling" (i.e., uttering obscure sayings, as poets do; said with irony, of an ambiguous phrase)

Republic 332B: ᾐνίξατο, "he was riddling" (as above)

Theaetetus 152C: ᾐνίξατο, "he was riddling"

180A: αἰνιγματώδη, "riddling"

Euthydemus: 300D: ἐξημφοτέρικε τὸν λόγον, "he made the argument ambiguous" (said of a double antinomy)

Republic 479B–C: ἐπαμφοτερίζειν, "equivocate" (said of a riddle)

Euthydemus 278B: τὴν τῶν ὀνομάτων διαφοράν, "the difference in [the sense of] the words"

Theaetetus 164C: τὰς τῶν ὀνομάτων ὁμολογίας, "the similarities of the words"

Sophist 256A: οὐ . . . ὁμοίως εἰρήκαμεν, "we did not mean the same thing"

Phaedrus 263A: ἀφισβητοῦμεν ἀλλήλοις τε καὶ ἡμῖν αὐτοῖς, "we are at odds with each other and with ourselves" (about the meaning of words)

Phaedrus 263C: ἀμφισβητησίμων, "disputable" (terms)

Theaetetus 198C: ἀμφισβητήσεις, "contradictions" (between words)

Sophist 259B: πολλαχῇ μὲν ἔστι, πολλαχῇ δ' οὐκ ἔστιν, "in many ways things *are*, and in many ways *are not*"

Sophist 218C: τοὔνομα . . . ἔχομεν κοινῇ . . . τὸ δ' ἔργον . . . καλοῦμεν . . . ἰδίᾳ, "we all use the same word, but each one names by it an object which is his alone"

Republic 454A: τοῦ λεχθέντος τὴν ἐναντίωσιν, "the contradiction in what is said"

Cratylus 437A: ἀμφίβολον, "ambiguous" (word)

Ambiguity characterized and investigated

Symposium 187A: ἴσως τόδε ἐβούλετο λέγειν, "but perhaps he means to say this"

Republic 331E: ὅ τί ποτε λέγει, "whatever he may mean"

Theaetetus 206C: (cf. 206E): τί ποτε βούλεται τὸν λόγον ἡμῖν σημαίνειν, "what he wishes to indicate by [the word] λόγος"

Symposium 187A: πολλὴ ἀλογία, "entire irrationality" (of a saying)

Symposium 187A: τοῖς . . . ῥήμασιν οὐ καλῶς λέγει, 'he does not express himself well in words"

Phaedrus 263A: ἄλλος ἄλλῃ φέρεται, "opinions divide in all directions"

Republic 437A: ἀμφισβητήσεις, "contradictions" or "verbal oppositions"

Sophist 259B: ἐναντιώσεσιν, "verbal oppositions"

The foregoing parade of instances should serve to illustrate the danger of assuming that Plato lacks a conception simply because he has not summed it up in a single or a very few specialized terms.

f. And here I will offer the promised conjectural explanation of why Plato refused to accept the aid that a permanent staff of expert words might have given him. Perhaps Socrates was an all but sufficient reason; certainly no lively image of that great informal converser could have been conveyed through the medium of a fixed vocabulary, and much of Plato's initial energy was directed to that goal. Nor did the Socratic influence end there. Plato's conception of dialectic, to which free Socratic inquiry had pointed him the way, required a continual shifting of the frontiers of language, a burning of verbal bridges behind him: the *relevant* distinctions must be sought and found, and this pursuit must never degenerate into a hunting of words (διώκειν κατ' ὄνομα). He would have felt that he was surrendering his philosophic freedom if he should confine his language within the straitjacket of a professional jargon. To the very end, moreover, Plato wanted to carry his respondent along with him, whether it was the young Glaucon at the moral crossroads or the gifted young Theaetetus to be initiated. He could imagine encouraging some benighted son of the law-courts to leave his sordid concerns and mount the steep road to the giddy heights (*Theaetetus* 175C–D); and the neglected education of Cleinias and Megillus, those good grey men, was waiting to be improved in the course of a long summer day's walk, in the *Laws*. For purposes such as these, a technical vocabulary would have been an outright encumbrance.

6. My inventory of Plato's handling of language for logical ends must not omit that familiar entry, his solution in the *Sophist* of the problems associated with false statement and false belief, a topic touched upon more than once in earlier pages. Taking into account also what other dialogues report, I shall direct attention to four points.

a. Comparison with the *Cratylus* shows the *Sophist* providing some novelties in the categoreal equipment required for the analysis of logical discourse, though it is difficult to say precisely how many, since the changes are sometimes only the more explicit statement of what was present in less developed form. But in the history of logic, as of mathematics, it is notorious that improvements in formal clarity and compactness of statement are entered among the assets. In the case before us, formal and material advance can be discerned in the following respects:

i. An explicit analysis of the "sentence" (λόγος) into "noun" (ὄνομα) serving as subject, and "verb" or "predicate" (ῥῆμα), which must possess temporal reference (*Sophist* 261D–262E).

ii. A recognition that a sentence must be either true or false, this property being called, in contrast to the Aristotelian usage, its "quality" (ποιόν τι) (*Sophist* 262E, 263A).

iii. Discrimination between assertion and denial (φάσις and ἀπόφασις) (*Sophist* 263E–264A).

b. In formulating his theory of the statement as requiring for its truth or falsity the presence of both subject (ὄνομα) and verb or predicate (ῥῆμα), Plato appears to deny what he had asserted in the *Cratylus*, viz., that a single name (of thing or action) can be true. But this contradiction is only apparent. In the *Cratylus* what is intended is the application of the name, which constitutes an implicit statement to the effect, "This object possesses the nature, or identity, intended by the name." In the *Sophist*, however, the single name (of thing or action) is conceived as standing alone, in mid-air, as it were, and under such circumstances it cannot be considered as true in anyone's logic. In the *Sophist*, moreover, it must be observed that the names employed are conceived as already valid, established as signifying the things intended: no doubt is raised, e.g., that the names "Theaetetus" and "flying" really signify the person and act in question. In other words, the results of the *Cratylus* may be said to be presupposed.

c. The *Sophist* picks up and introduces into its far more inclusive frame, the problem of false statements, for which the *Cratylus* had found a partial solution in the analogy between portraits and their originals. There the falsity consisted in bringing up to the actual man Hermogenes his own name, conceived as the inappropriate word-picture, "son of Hermes"; here in the *Sophist* the falsity lies in bringing up to the symbol for the young man Theaetetus the inappropriate symbol for flight. In each case it is insisted by Plato's representative that the name, or statement, is really about the person in question, and is really a name, or statement; these moves in the argument are made in order to render impossible the two usual escapes from admitting that false assertions can be made, escapes which were illustrated by Cratylus when he declared Hermogenes' name to be either that of another person or a mere noise.

The novelty actually present in the *Sophist* consists rather in the relating of the naming process, and the combination of names in statements, to the explicitly expounded dialectic of the Forms or ideal genera (the μέγιστα γένη) and their mutual interpenetration (κοινωνία), whereby each form is shown to be capable of participating both in the Form of the Same and in the Form of the Other (this is summed up at 258D–259B). The statement or sentence (λόγος) is now called the "weaving together of Forms with one another," συμπλοκὴ ἀλλήλων τῶν εἰδῶν (259E), and "the weaving together of nouns with verbs" (262D), and is therefore conceived as a pair or group of symbols such that each refers the entity it signifies to its proper class; if the sentence is false, one of the entities "is not," in the sense that it is "other" (263B); i.e., the class of one of its entities participates in the Class of the Other in relation to the class of the other entity.[16] This explanation of the way in which Plato is interpreting false statement depends on recognizing the part played by names, adopted or invented, in referring entities to their proper classes or εἴδη, as these classes are discovered by the process of classification or διαίρεσις—a means of reference which has been discussed above (section III B 4b), and which is also mentioned in the *Cratylus* (424D).

In the *Cratylus* Plato had assigned to his ideal Nomothete the task of appointing instructive and "diacritical" names but had left us with only the barest indication of how to give concrete meaning to such an enterprise. In the *Sophist* and in the other dialectical dialogues that blank space is filled with the full-blown method of διαίρεσις. And when Plato adds the theory of the μέγιστα γένη and the interpenetration or mutual exclusion of the Forms, he has provided a framework of conceptual relations for the whole group of problems common to the *Sophist* and the *Cratylus*. Plato has here in the *Sophist* elaborated and applied what we may call with some degree of modernization a logic of class-inclusion, and has made it so flexible a logical instrument that it has seemed to many recent critics to imply a palinode, a rejection of his earlier naïve Realism of the Forms. In my view, however, this conceptual logic remains for him, at the same time, an undiminished metaphysic of the Forms, an analysis of the structure of Reality. Thus Plato, though still burdened, as most contemporaries will feel, with the "syntactical error" of the substantialized predicate, has at this price escaped those graver entanglements in the grammar of the verb "to be" which were hindering thought in his day.

d. Of substantial importance to our concern is the topic with which my survey of the *Sophist* will conclude: the relation of thought to language implied by the account (263E ff.) of "inner speech," a phenomenon already noticed in the *Theaetetus* (e.g., 189E) and scheduled for further handling in the *Philebus* (38C–E). In the *Cratylus*, Plato had followed the example of his predecessors in the field and had couched his discussion of language chiefly in terms of names, a fact which continued to exert a restrictive influence upon the discussion. It is, therefore, newsworthy to find the wider horizon supplied by the virtual equivalence assumed in these other dialogues between thought and language, in their simple and no less in their more complex forms. In the *Theaetetus*, the explicit recognition of this hand-and-glove relation had not availed, in the absence of the Forms, to establish the possibility of false opinion. But here in the *Sophist*, once the theory of the interpenetration and mutual exclusion of the Forms has been set forth and employed to settle the problem of spoken falsehood, the close association of thought with language is of substantial assistance to Plato in his attack upon the problem of false opinion.

It would, however, be a mistake to infer that on any level Plato would materially identify word and thought. Thought, rather, selects its own verbal counters, by means of which it carries forward its dealings with the world (*Theaetetus* 177E). On the highest level, words can no longer appear. Unfortunately the relevant texts are few; we are nowhere (unless in *Letter VII*) offered a discussion of this issue in terms. But the *Republic* account (532A–B) of νόησις as achieving immediate contact with the intelligible real seems to me decisive.

IV. *Plato's Conception of Language as Related to Knowledge and Reality*

It may be asked whether the ontological status accorded to language in the *Cratylus* remained in force throughout the long remainder of Plato's thinking life, and concomitantly, apart from any radical shift, whether his later writing does not contain at the least some further clarification of points relevant to this issue, which the *Cratylus* left implicit or even obscure. Some of the evidence required for an answer has already entered our exposition, but many fresh texts remain unadduced. A brief synthesis is in order.

From the position so emphatically asserted at the end of the *Cratylus*, Plato never for a moment withdrew: language is no oracle, no fountain of verity in its own right. The wisdom of words is vicarious only.

Retained from first to last is the corollary refusal to allow words to replace ideas as the subject-matter of genuine inquiry and, along with this, the counter-principle that when an argument is suspected of turning upon a merely verbal hinge, or, put in Platonic terms, when it appears possible that our word does not represent a proper εἶδος, subdivided to the requisite degree, it is our dialectical first duty to inquire minutely into the logical interrelations it conceals.

In further agreement with the *Cratylus*, but going beyond it in explicitness and fulness of development, are a number of vindications of the power of language to stand off the cripplement and self-contradictions which Megarian puzzles and Heracliteanism had prepared for it. The refutation of Protagorean relativism in the *Theaetetus*, and the construction of a workable logic of negation and falsehood in the *Sophist*, are evidence of Plato's faith in the potentiality of language when rightly understood to function as the chief instrument of rational thought. This recognition of the natural amity between reason and speech is expressed in the doctrine that mental activity (with the limitations earlier noted) is a mute internal language, and audible speech a reflection of thought on the stream of breath.

Many are the tributes paid to the power of language as medium for the imitation of reality: λόγοι are by no means inferior to ἔργα as images of what is real (*Phaedo* 100A); words more than facts partake of truth and can more adequately present the perfect city, declares the *Republic* (472E–473A); pictures in words serve better for the instruction of those who can understand than pictures visible to the eye (*Politicus* 277C). But no finer encomium is elsewhere offered in the span of Plato's writing than in the *Timaeus* (47B), where speech is assigned, as its final cause, along with sight and hearing, the task of bringing the soul to harmony with the "untroubled periods" of cosmic reason, "whereto speech contributes the largest share," serving as "an ally against the discord which has grown up in . . . our soul, to bring her into order and into unison with herself."

And, finally mention must be made of the "epistemological digression" in *Epistle VII*, which at a first reading may appear to go far toward cancelling out the handsome compliments that we have been hearing Plato pay to words. To relieve this embarrassment, I shall make use of a *deus ex machina* in the person of Glenn Morrow, who in his *Studies in the Platonic Epistles* (Urbana, Illinois, 1935) pp. 61 ff., has done the almost un-do-able: in equitable argument, luminously expressed, he has interpreted the Platonic *Letter* in such wise as to bring its content into harmony with the standpoint at which the Plato of the late period had arrived. I should be disingenuous in suggesting that I am personally able to accept Professor Morrow's position without reservation. But among my agreements with him, most relevant to my theme is his recognition that the *Letter* is preaching good Platonic doctrine when it warns us, with one hand, against confusing the word itself with the reality of which we are in search, while with the other it directs us to the word, and especially to the living, spoken word, as to an indispensable aid;—in short, in total agreement with the *Cratylus*, it reaffirms faith in the word as the "didactic and diacritic tool" of thought.

NOTES

[1] A. J. Ayer, *Language, Truth, and Logic* (London, 1936).

[2] B. Russell, *History of Western Philosophy* (New York, 1945).

[3] The work of Richard Robinson, including *Plato's Earlier Dialectic*, 2nd. ed. (Oxford, 1953), *Definitions* (Oxford, 1950), and articles in *Mind* ["Ambiguity," L (1941): 140–55; "Plato's Consciousness of Fallacy," LI (1942): 97–114] and *PR*, ["Forms and Error in Plato's *Theaetetus*," LIX (1950): 3–30] has been an important stimulus to the writing of this paper.

[4] Gilbert Ryle, in *Mind* ["Plato's Parmenides," I and II, XLVIII (1939): 129–51, 302–25]; G. Vlastos, and W. Sellars in *PR*, ["Third Man Argument in the *Parmenides*," LXIII (1954): 319–49; LXIV (1955): 438–48; LXV (1956): 83–94; and "Vlastos and the Third Man," LXIV (1955): 405–37].

[5] Diels, Fr. 8, 11.38–9.

[6] Arist. *Metaph.* △ 29, 1024b 34.

[7] Epict. *Diatr.* I, 17, 12.

[8] Jowett, 4th ed., III, p. 10. Ross assigns the earlier date, chiefly for the reason (which I reject) that the Ideas as they appear here seem to him not yet transcendent.

[9] *Plato's Republic*, eds. Jowett and Campbell (Oxford, 1894), II; pp. 260–fin. See also the Introduction to Campbell's edition of *Sophist* and *Politicus*, pp. xxiv ff.

[10] Plato's priority in using these words as indicated has been confirmed by reference to the new Liddell and Scott.

[11] Richard Robinson, *Mind* (1941), "Ambiguity," and 1942, "Plato's Consciousness of Fallacy."

[12] See Ross, *Plato's Theory of Ideas*, p. 228, where a table of 17 such terms is presented, without exhausting Plato's resources.

[13] E.g., *Protagoras* 358A, ἡδύ, τερπνόν, χαρτόν, 358E, φόβος, δέος; *Meno* 75D–E, πέρας, τελευτή, ἔσχατον; *Cratylus* 384D, ξυνθήκη, ὁμολογία, νόμος, ἔθος; *Letter VII* 342B, στρογγύλον, περιφερές, κύκλος.

[14] *Cratylus* 393D, 394C, 432E, ἡ οὐσία ἐγκρατής, τῇ δυνάμει ταὐτὸν φθεγγόμενα, and ὁ τύπος ἔνεστι.

[15] *Cratylus* 433E, 434E, 435C, ξυνθήκη, ἔθος, ὁμολογία.

[16] The difficulty found by Robinson, *PR*, (1950): (11–12) in accepting Cornford's view that the present passage exemplifies the use of the theory of the μέγιστα γένη appears to me to vanish when it is recognized that the key words τὰ ὄντα, ἕτερα τῶν ὄντων, and πολλὰ . . . ὄντα περὶ ἕκαστον . . . , πολλὰ δὲ οὐκ ὄντα appearing in 263B, refer back explicitly to 258D–259B. Robinson's paraphrase of 263B obscures this similarity by unnecessary modernization of the language.

J. M. E. MORAVCSIK
Stanford University

Reason and Eros in the "Ascent"-Passage of the *Symposium**

IN *Symposium* 209E–212A—one of the best known passages of the Platonic corpus—Plato describes a series of steps leading to the apprehension of the Form of Beauty. Although much has been written on this passage, there is a need to subject both the account of the process of ascent as well as the description of the object of final vision to closer scrutiny than others have done before. Several commentators emphasize that both reason and eros play important roles in the ascent.[1] It is also well known that the object of final vision is one of the Platonic Forms. In this paper an attempt will be made to determine the exact nature of the roles and interrelations of reason and eros, and to give a detailed account of what Plato says about the Form of Beauty.

Plato's own summary of the ascent—211C 1–D 1—distinguishes only movements across four levels; from the interest in the beauty of bodies to that of institutions and practices, from there to the beauty of the sciences, and then the final movement to the apprehension of the Form of Beauty. This summary is, however, only a rough outline; although the four levels mentioned are significant within Plato's scheme of the ascent, an account of the complexity of the actual series described will have to go beneath the relative simplicity of this fourfold division. A survey of the steps described indicates that three types of steps make up the ascent. There are steps of reason, i.e., events of knowing, grasping, understanding, etc., but also steps of emotion such as loving, preferring, showing disdain, and steps of creation, in particular the creation of discourse. Accordingly, it might not be inappropriate to present a scheme that does justice to this complexity. Within the scheme R-steps, C-steps, and E-steps will mark the steps of reason, creation, and eros. The E-steps can be divided further into positive and negative ones. The possibility of

* This is an extensively revised version of a paper presented at the 1960 meetings of the SAGP in New Haven, Connecticut.

this scheme shows the distinctness of reason and eros,[2] while its detailed structure should give us a better understanding of Plato's theory of mind.

Applying the scheme to a translation of the text yields the following results.

E1. "he should love one body" (210A 7)

C1. "and engender within it beautiful discourse" (210A 7–8)

R1. "after this he should realize that the beauty of any one body is akin to the beauty of any other body" (210A 8–b1)

R2. "and if one is to pursue beauty in accordance with form[3], it is folly not to regard beauty in all bodies as one and the same" (210B 2–3)

E2. "having considered this one is to become the lover of all beautiful bodies, and restrain one's zeal toward the one, disdaining it and thinking little of it" (210B 4–6)

E3. "and after this to honor beauty in the soul more than that beauty which is in bodies so that if a proper soul had even a little bloom, this would suffice for loving and caring for it" (210B 6–c1)

C2. "and to seek and bring into being discourse that improves the youths" (210C 1–3)

R3. "in order that he may be forced to behold beauty in practices and laws[4]" (210C 3–4)

R4. "and to see that all of these belong to the same kind" (210C 4–5)

E4. "so that he may show disdain toward the beauty of bodies" (210C 5–6)

R5. "and after the practices he should be led to the sciences so that he may see the beauty of these" (210C 6–7)

R6. "and looking at beauty in the many, not with regard to the one instant like a servant caring for the beauty of one child or man or practice, being a miserable slave limited in thought; but turning toward the wide sea of beauty, contemplating it" (210C 7–d4)

C3. "he would generate much beautiful and noble discourse and thoughts contained in abundant philosophy" (210D 5–6)

R7. "until thus strengthened and nourished he shall grasp the knowledge of the following sort of beauty" (210D 6–E1)

(In 210E 1–6) there is a brief interlude, and then a statement of how one must proceed in proper sequence, and how one suddenly comes to see the Form of Beauty; all previous labors were for the sake of this final step. In 210E 6 following, a description of the Form of Beauty is given.)

The verbs in all of the R-steps ("realize," "regard," "see") belong to that standard vocabulary within which Plato expresses his views about intellectual processes. In E1, E2, and E3 the notion of eros enters explicitly to define the positive and negative attitudes that seem to be called for. The verb in E4 is "ἡγήσηται", suggesting the work of reason, but the compound expression within which the verb is placed appears also in E2 (210B 6) which is clearly a step determined by eros. To think little of something, in the context of this passage, is to stop loving it and to develop aversion for it. As we shall see later, a better way to put this is by saying that we must transcend certain objects as ultimate objects of over-all aspirations.

If we extract the C-steps from the series, the lower half of the ascent yields the following Platonic "equation":

E1 : R1 : R2 : E2 equals E3 : R3 : R4 : E4.

In view of the frequent occurrence of such mathematical analogies in other dialogues—the most famous being the "Divided Line" of the *Republic*—one need not argue that this structure was intended by Plato. Its significance, however, needs to be established. The most obvious feature of the equation is that the E–R–R–E sequences can be assigned to two distinct levels; the first takes place on the level dealing with the beauty of bodies while the second is concerned with the love of souls and the beauty of practices. Another point emerging from the consideration of this structure is that neither do we have reason or eros dominate the other, nor do we have a simple cycle of mutual dependence (that would be the E–R–E–R pattern).

It is convenient to label the move from one level to the other the "transcategorical move". Our scheme brings out the important point that the transcategorical move is the work of eros alone; it is an E–E step. The explanation for this must be found in the detailed examination of the nature of E-steps and R-steps.

E1 and E3 are both positive, they both initiate a series of steps on a given level, and their objects are particular entities. (The beginning of E3 might not seem to be love of a particular, but the main emphasis of the whole step is the love of one soul.) These steps alone among the ones making up the lower half are yielding steps of creation. In contrast with these, E2 and E4 do not yield creations, they are negative, and are directed towards objects on a general plane (E2 showing partial and E4 complete disdain).

The R-steps also fall into a pattern; R1 and R2, and again R3 with R4 represent intellectual moves consisting first of recognizing common features of a plurality of instances, and then isolating the common element and grasping its unity. R. G. Bury had probably this in mind when he described the role of "nous" in this passage as generalization and identification.[5] It is crucial to note, however, that this is not the only work of "nous," and that the relation between unities on any given plane and their instances is not the only "one and many" relation described in the passage. For in addition to seeing the unity within each level, the mind has to grasp also that all of the levels are "akin"; they are, one might say, species of beauty. The mind has to see how the species are related, and then has to apprehend the Form of Beauty both as the common denominator among the levels and as an object in its own right.

Thus we see two "one and many" relations exhibited in the passage. There is the relation between different species or kinds of beauty—bodily, spiritual, intellectual—and their instances, and then there is the relation between the different kinds and the Form of Beauty. Only the grasp of the second unity gives complete understanding, and if knowledge is restricted to knowledge of Forms, then only the grasp of the second unity yields knowledge. This shows that the second "one and many" relation is more important for Plato than the first. Indeed, this can be supported also by passages from other dialogues; e.g. in the preliminary discussion in the *Meno* (71E–73A) Socrates' objection to his opponent is not that the latter confuses particular instances with the common denominator to be found among instances, nor that the latter provides as an answer to the question: "what is excellence?" only references to particulars, but that he mentions in his answer only many kinds of excellences instead of giving an account of excellence in general. These considerations show that already in the middle period dialogues not only is the relation between concrete instances and abstract properties in the center of focus, but also the relation of species and genus (though it must be pointed out that in the middle period dialogues Plato does not show explicitly how these two relations differ and his views about participation are answers only to questions about one of the two relations.) In order to make the transitions between levels intelligible we must assume that for Plato, each level—properly understood—"points beyond itself." For example, the beauty of moral practices and institutions is that the principles governing these can be given a priori justification, thus leading one to consider the beauty of the sciences and dialectic. Each type of beauty is incomplete in itself; only the final vision brings one into contact with an entity that is beautiful "in itself."

These characterizations of E-steps and R-steps enable us to

characterize the transcategorical move. The fact that the work of eros is required indicates that for Plato the move from one kind of beauty to another is not merely a matter of grasping common elements within pluralities, as he describes the move toward understanding unity within a given plane. The mind is turned towards a new kind of beauty by the negative feelings toward instances on the old level, and the formation of new eros toward an instance on a new level. Since this initial E-step precedes the R-steps on that level we must interpret it as eros without a clear conception as to the nature of the object loved or aspired to. Yet it must carry with it some belief ("doxa") about the nature of the object, else it could not set in motion an intellectual sequence terminating in the grasp of the unity of a kind of beauty. Aesthetic appreciation turns into appreciation for moral qualities, and that, in turn, is transformed into appreciation of the beauty of abstract intellectual systems.

This account of the transcategorical move suggests that the steps are causally interrelated. This is not the only way of reading this passage. One might think of the stages of ascent merely as stages on life's way, a series of destinations offering increasingly greater awards. To be sure, some of the phrases connecting the steps (210A 9, B 1, B 6, C 4, C 7) indicate merely conjunction and temporal succession, but the participial construction at 210B 4 and the occurrences of "ἵνα" with the subjunctive (210C 3, C 5–6, C 7) can be taken as suggesting causal linkeage. Finally, two passages clearly imply causal connections. In 210C 3 R3 is linked to E3 by stating that the soul along the path will be "forced" to turn to something new. Again, in 210D 6 we find that the "strength and nourishment" provided by the previous steps helps the soul to arrive at R7.

What is the causal relationship between the steps? It cannot be the case that Plato intends each step to be a necessary condition for the one following. For this would entail the claim that nobody can appreciate the beauty of mathematics without having appreciated bodily beauty. On the other hand, we cannot suppose that the steps are sufficient conditions for their successors. Such a view would entail that once someone takes the first step on this path, he will always arrive at the terminal point, sooner or later. Not only is this a strange view, but there is evidence that Plato did not hold it. For both in R5 and in the final summary Plato refers to the fact that the soul making this journey has to be "led right." Thus the general picture emerging is that of a series of steps that are, in some important way, contributory causes of their successors. The nature of this contributory causal role needs to be spelled out for R-steps and E-steps respectively.

One of the main ways in which R-steps guide eros is their function as revealing new possible objects of aspiration. As will be argued below, the eros of this passage is not "blind passion"; i.e., the various E-steps involve aspirations toward an object or objects on account of their nature. It is nous, in the form of R-steps, that reveals the natures of various entities that might become objects of desire and aspiration. It is important to note that in this capacity the R-steps are indeed a guiding and not a blocking force. The role of reason in this passage is not to issue injunctions against certain objects as things to be aspired to, but to help the soul transcend previous aspirations by revealing objects more worthy of eros. This guiding role, however, does not seem to be sufficient for exhausting what Plato describes as the nourishment and strengthening of the soul. The other main role of reason comes closer to what philosophers call today efficient causation. That is to say, not only do the R-steps reveal new objects, but the steps considered as processes create a general condition in which aspirations toward new objects may arise. If we interpret the causal effects of R-steps in this dual way, then the *Symposium* can be read as consistent with the Platonic view, expounded elsewhere, that all shortcomings are somehow due to the failings of reason. This view is quite misleadingly put at times as the claim that all evil is due to ignorance. On the interpretation proposed here, Plato believes that all shortcomings are due either to ignorance (lack of knowledge of certain objects) or lack of reasoning (lack of sufficient amount of reasoning going on in the soul, thus not creating conditions for new and higher aspirations to arise).

Before we spell out the causal roles of the E-steps, a general characterization of eros as presented in this dialogue is called for. The translation used in this essay, "aspiration," itself calls for justification, for this is not the usual way of interpreting eros. But from 205–206 it becomes clear that Plato is using "eros" in a wide sense, including any over-all desire or wish for what is taken to be good. The qualification "over-all" is needed, for Plato is not talking about momentary impulses but about wishes, desires, aspirations that determine the ultimate goals of one's life. Thus eros is not blind passion; it is the wish or desire (the language of 205 admits of either translation) for things deemed on account of their nature to be worthy of having their attainment become a man's ultimate goal. Plato points out that he is deliberately extending the meaning of "eros"; he remarks that men call only part of all of this by the term "eros"; by redefinition Plato is pouring new life into a traditional terminology.

Once we realize that by "eros" Plato means in this passage "aspiration," it is easy to see not only that as such it must be accompanied by some belief with regard to its object, but also that there is no underlying process called "eros" over and above the various E-steps. The E-steps represent varieties of aspiration, and there is no such thing as an underlying process called "aspiration" in addition to the varieties represented. This interpretation is supported not only by our account of the E-steps and their connection with R-steps, but by the passage referred to above where Plato suggests that what people usually call "eros" is only a part of what is really eros. Here Plato implicitly divides eros into parts, and there is no suggestion that there is a psychological substratum for these.

From this characterization a number of conclusions can be drawn. First, E1 is not mere sexual desire; rather, it is the love of bodies for the sake of bodily beauty that can be abstracted and contemplated on a general level. It is also the sort of "eros" that yields the creation of discourse. Thus although E1 has a clearly erotic aspect, it cannot be identified with sexuality (unless one is to suggest that according to Plato one has to overcome one's sexual desire towards one person and direct it towards many). Further textual evidence for this interpretation is given by 209, where Plato suggests that the creative products of the poets or the statesmen are more worthy than the products of the creative efforts of average men in sexual union. Thus the move from mere sexual interest to some sort of aspiration, presumably aesthetic, is made before the ascent is begun. In short, many people never arrive even at E1.

From this point and the point about eros being the sum of "parts", i.e., various aspirations, we can draw the further conclusion that eros is not a raw motivating power, or some simple primitive force that holds sway over men. It is not the energy behind an ontological elevator, pushing souls up the ladder; or a force or fund of energy that underlies all activities.[6] As a further consequence we can see that Plato's theory of eros is not related to modern theories of sublimation as has been thought at times.[7] For if it were so related, then not only would we have to start with mere sexuality but also one would have to construe the R-steps as blocking rather than guiding eros. Nor is the ascent equivalent to the Freudian theory of sublimation in reverse.[8] Plato is not assuming that everyone desires the contemplation of the Form of Beauty and that only the inability to understand higher goals leaves men with simple sexual desires as their over-all dominant motive.

After all of these negative characterizations it is time to turn to positive statements. We saw that the ascent assumes the ability on the part of some to arrive at E1, and not to have mere sexual satisfaction as their dominant goal. How such a "pre-ascent" move is to be achieved is not discussed in the *Symposium*; we must leave open, however, the possibility that Plato—in contrast with current fashionable psychological speculation—does not regard the man of mere appetites as somehow the "natural state." He regards man as reasoning and groping for ways of life that allow the expansion of reasoning activities in the "natural" state, and would perhaps say that the man of mere sexual appetite is "brutish" and requires therapy.

About the over-all aspirations we can conclude one thing with certainty. Both *Meno* 77–78 and *Symposium* 205 show Plato believing that these over-all aspirations aim at what people take to be good for them. The ascent-passage shows that these aspirations do not turn back upon themselves; our aspirations are not simply to the effect that whatever needs we have, these should be satisfied. Eros is always "other-directed"; i.e. it is for objects of pursuit that lie outside the soul, and the pursuit becomes the pattern along which a human life is organized. Thus in general one can say about the causal influence of eros on the mind that eros is what pushes the mind to new investigations. It "keeps the mind restless" by forming negative attitudes toward objects on a plane which has been understood already, and creating the need and motive for further exploration.

How is this interplay of reason and eros linked to acts of creation? Each of the three C-steps is linked to one of the four levels on which the ascent is based, and each involves the creation of "*logos*," by the lover or the loved one.[9] The first two C-steps are the effects of E-steps, but the third is the result of an R-step. Although not much is said about the nature of what is created, one can draw inferences from the level at which the creation takes place, and the step that precedes it. The first C-step takes place on the aesthetic level, at which the soul has not yet attained knowledge, and indeed it has not yet concentrated on what is beneficial to the souls of men, since this comes only at the second level. Given this information and the reference to Homer in the preceding passage as a creator, it is safe to assume that C1 results in poetry. C2 appears on the level at which concern is for the soul, and its product is said to be improving people. Still, this creation too is the result of an E-step and it takes place prior to the appreciation of the sciences. Thus the creation represented in C2 is also based on opinion, or belief, and not knowledge. In view of these facts, one can assume that the products of C2 are discourses, with moral or merely intellectual and elenchtic emphasis, that improve young people. Only the third act of creation is linked to an R-step: the product is identified as philosophy, and it is hardly necessary to point out that the link to an R-step that involves appreciation of the sciences indicates that this "product" is based on knowledge and not mere belief. The causal role of these acts of creation can be seen in the following way. Attention to poetry may inspire love toward a person, but it also turns attention to the characteristics of the loved object, thus facilitating the grasp of aesthetic beauty in general. On the second level again, discourse that improves a person not only helps to increase devotion to that person, but also helps to focus attention on the nature of the beauty of souls, thus leading to a grasp of beauty in general on that plane. Finally, the production of philosophy obviously helps a soul to the final comprehension of the Form of Beauty.

As one surveys the lower half of the ascent, the question arises whether the progress achieved is a matter of more and more inclusive aspirations or of a complete change in general aims in life. In the light of this question we can distinguish between an "inclusive" and an exclusive interpretation of the ascent. According to the inclusive version our eros widens as we make progress from stage to stage; we do not abandon physical and aesthetic love for the love of spiritual beauty, nor do we jettison the latter in favor of love of the sciences. We enrich our appreciations according to this view by keeping the former interests and adding to these newer ones. According to the exclusive interpretation the former objects of aspiration are not kept but are totally replaced by the new objects. The presence of the negative E-steps is a formidable support for the exclusive interpretation. This conclusion can be made more palatable by pointing out that given our account of eros, such a view does not entail the ascription of an asexual, passionless ideal to Plato. Our over-all aspirations do indeed undergo drastic change according to the ascent-passage, but this leaves open the possibility that other sub-ordinate desires and passions are still vital parts of any human life. Only if we interpreted eros not as aspiration but as the sum total of all desires, momentary or otherwise, would we be forced to ascribe to Plato the view that sexual interest must be abandoned as we progress along the path. According to the interpretation proposed in the above, we need to say only that the "lower" types of desire cannot remain the dominant aspiration in the life of a man who traverses the path described by Plato.

The dissimilarity between C3 and the other two steps of creation suggests that the upper half of the ascent differs from the lower half. Indeed, this much is obvious from a brief glance at the scheme presented earlier. For in this half sequences on a level are not introduced by E-steps, the series within levels do not contain E-steps, and the relations among the R-steps on any given plane are different from the one exhibited by R-steps on the lower two levels. The absence of E-steps might lead one to suppose that when the soul reaches these stages it no longer has passions or aspirations. Such an extraordinary conclusion would be difficult to accept. Bury for one insisted that eros is still at work in the later stages of the ascent, but his account does not explain the absence of E-steps.[10] As a plausible explanation one might suggest that though eros is still at work in the soul in the later stages, it no longer functions as a guide, thus not appearing in the sequence of steps described. No change in over-all aspiration is needed in order to lead the soul from the contemplation of the sciences to the comprehension of Forms. Like Virgil in the "Divine Comedy" eros helps as a guide only until we reach the final stages; there contemplation becomes self-sufficient. This interpretation helps to explain also why Socrates describes eros as "intermediate" and does not bestow upon it the superlatives that other contestants employ. Ironically he concludes that he praised eros as much as he is able to (212B 7–C 3) and suggests that Phaedrus might not consider this a proper hymn of praise. In the scheme that Plato gives in the mouth of Socrates eros is only the "best co-worker of *physis*" (212B 2–4) where "*physis*" clearly refers to reason. This secondary role of eros can be also seen by the fact that the move from the second to the third plane is accomplished without the help of an E-step. R5 effects the transition from mere belief with regard to what is good for man to the appreciation of sciences. In other words, questions about how to justify views about practices and institutions lead to the recognition of the need for sciences and dialectic. Such a recognition is not a matter of a change in general aspirations. These recognitions lead to C3, the creation of philosophy (dialectic), and they together strengthen the soul for the apprehension of Forms.

The lack of parallel between the R-sequences on the lower levels and those on the upper ones can be explained by the nature of the level at which we arrive with R5. The sciences, in contrast with what appeared on the lower levels, do not have particulars as their instances. The instance of bodily beauty is a person, and the instance of spiritual beauty is likewise a person (or his soul). In the case of the sciences, however, the instances of Science are themselves already on the plane of the abstract and general. Thus the movement from R5 to R6 cannot be one of grasping the common element shared by a number of particulars. Given that according to Plato knowledge is always of the general and abstract, the contemplation of the beauty of the sciences should mark the complete turning away from particulars. This is precisely what takes place in R6; thus the "turning toward the wide sea of beauty" and the despising of particular instances. This turn leads to the creation of philosophy, and that again leads to the comprehension of the Form. Thus the relations among the final R-steps show how the relation between knowledge and its instances is conceived differently by Plato from the relation of concrete particulars partaking of characters, and also that the relation between understanding the beauty of sciences is related differently to the comprehension of the Form of Beauty than the comprehension of bodily beauty is related either to the comprehension of the beauty of the next level or to the comprehension of the Form of Beauty.

As a final comment we may add that the fourfold division of levels in this passage has its analogue in the "Divided Line" of the *Republic*; there is no one-to-one correspondence between the levels, but the upper halves are more similar than the respective lower halves.

Having dealt with the nature of the process, let us consider the nature of its object. Textual evidence indicates that there is only one Form, the Form of Beauty, involved in the ascent, and thus what one comprehends on the lower levels are not Forms, but other sorts of unities. The evidence includes the fact that—as Robin observed[11]—whereas the ascent is gradual, the final vision comes suddenly (210E 4), and that only in connection with this final vision are we given a description of the object such that this description coincides roughly with accounts of Forms given in other dialogues. From this we may infer that the dialogue cannot be interpreted in such a way as to construe each of the objects perceived—bodily beauty, spiritual beauty, and intellectual beauty—as Forms, with Beauty as a generic Form presiding over these, making them subordinate in a way similar to that in which specific Forms are ordered under others in the "method of division" of the later dialogues. By ruling out this latter interpretation we reach two conclusions that shed light on the Theory of Forms. One of these is that according to Plato not every predicate expression stands for a Form, and the other is that the mere comprehension of a common element among a plurality of particulars is not necessarily the comprehension of a Form. Furthermore, the point just made shows that the initial comprehension of the more specific types of beauty cannot be "knowledge," in the strict Platonic sense; since it does not involve the grasping of a Form, it must be provisional understanding, to be made complete and adequate only when the different kinds of beauty are seen in the light of their relation to the Form of Beauty. To see the types in this manner is the aim of dialectic.

What Plato says about the Form of Beauty suggests that it is a distinct entity. It is—as we saw above—comprehended suddenly, at the end of the ascent, its grasp is said to be that for the sake of which all previous efforts were made (210E 5–6), and it is that of which all other beautiful things partake (211B 2–3). This matter of participation may show the Form to have certain relations to the participants that modify its distinctness. If one were to interpret participation as analogous to the relation between an object and its image, then perhaps the claim of participation and the claim of total distinctness could be reconciled. Textual evidence, however, rules out this interpretation, for at 211B 3–5 Plato says that in spite of things partaking of it the form suffers no increase or decrease. If Plato meant by "participation" "resembling as image resembles the object," then this remark would be needless, and indeed senseless. The remark makes sense only if we construe the relation as that between entities and one of their common elements. Thus the considerations adduced so far indicate that the Form of Beauty is conceived by Plato both as a common denominator and a distinct entity. There is no reason why these two aspects of the Form should conflict with each other, provided that the relation between the Form and the species that are subordinate to it is properly understood. The Form is the only entity that is beautiful without qualification; i.e., the only entity to which "beautiful" applies descriptively and without any added modification. Everything else is beautiful in some way, some respect, or in some place and time. As an element in a series of complex attributes the Form of Beauty is a common denominator. As the entity that can be known once one understands the variety of ways in which entities can be beautiful, and that serves as the subject of a number of a priori truths, it is also a distinct entity.

This account of the dual nature of Forms leads to a consideration of the properties that Plato ascribes to the Form in this dialogue. This list (210E 6–211B 4) deserves close scrutiny. The properties should be classified into three groups: (a) necessary but not sufficient conditions for being a Form; (b) sufficient conditions; and (c) individuating properties. In other words, some characteristics may be such that all Forms but not only Forms have it, while others may be Form-making characteristics; finally there ought to be a property, or set of properties, that only the Form of Beauty has, for without such individuating marks the Forms could not have their "unity." Plato could not claim that one knows of each what that Form in particular is.

The characteristics of being everlasting and not being subject to becoming or perishing are necessary conditions for being a Form. But if we take into consideration the proofs of immortality from the *Phaedo* these properties cannot be regarded as possessed by Forms only. Two other ones, the properties of "being in itself" and having a simple nature, are such that only Forms and all Forms have these. But neither of these serves to individuate Forms; they are true of all Forms collectively, so to say. There are, however, two properties that can be true of the Form of Beauty only, given a certain interpretation. One of these is the property of having all other beautiful entities partake of it. To be sure, as it stands, this property may be shared by a number of Forms, for it may be that there are a number of Forms, e.g., Being, Sameness, etc., of which all beautiful entities partake. If, however, one adds that all other beautiful entities and only these partake, and that they derive their nature of being beautiful from this participation, then the property is unique to the Form of Beauty. The other property is given in a series of complex and mostly negative characterizations. The Form of Beauty is not beautiful in some specific ways, or respects, or times and places, nor is it the beauty of entities like a face, body or science. As it stands, this could be true of any Form, but if one supplies the obvious premise that the entity in question is beautiful without any qualification whatsoever, then it becomes a property that is unique to the Form of Beauty.

Our last remarks as well as our observations about the need to find a property that singles out the Form of Beauty uniquely lead to the supposition that for Plato at the time he wrote the *Symposium* the Forms are self-predicational. To say that for Plato the Form of Beauty is self-predicational is to say that the term "beautiful" is used by Plato to apply to this Form with descriptive force. The nature of this descriptive force is to be specified later. To deny the self-predicational nature of the Form of Beauty is to say either that "beautiful" does not apply to this Form at all, or to claim that it is the proper name of the Form. Proper names, in contrast with descriptive terms, do not say anything about their bearers; they do not indicate their natures. To say of Mr. X that he is a father, a doctor, and a good golfer is to describe him; to say that his name is John is not to describe him but merely to name him. Below we shall consider evidence to show that Plato did not think of terms[12] like "beautiful" as only baptizing a Form but as indicating something about its nature.

In surveying the evidence it should be kept in mind that the question to be decided is simply whether Plato is committed to regarding the Form of Beauty as having "beautiful" applied to it with descriptive force. The question is not about the extent, if any, to which Plato was aware of the self-predicational nature of his Forms, and the logical consequences of this feature. The realization of all of the consequences of a metaphysical theory is the most difficult task for a philosopher. It is sufficient to note that Plato was committed to such a view; his gradual realization of all of its consequences is a story not for this paper to tell. In 210E 4–5 Plato describes the object of final vision as "beautiful in nature". That which is beautiful in its nature must have "beautiful" applicable to it with descriptive force. Again, the series of negative descriptions of the Form of Beauty in 211A, i.e., that it is not beautiful in some way, or respect, etc., makes sense only if we assume that Plato thought of the Form as beautiful without any such qualifications. This requires that the Form be described, in some sense, by the term "beautiful." In 211B 2 we read about all the *other* beautiful entities partaking of the Beautiful. The implied contrast clearly requires self-predication. Finally, in 211C 1–2 the many beautiful things are contrasted with "this beautiful" for the sake of which the whole journey was undertaken. Only the most tortuous reading of the Greek will make a proper name out of τοῦ καλοῦ in this context.

Having given conclusive evidence for the self-predicational nature of the Form of Beauty, the exact status of this nature as well as the philosophical motivation for its postulation must be examined. The long series of negative characterizations of the Form, mentioned before, as well as the fact that on account of the nature of the Form all other beautiful things partake of it, suggests that the Form is beautiful in some sense different from the sense in which every other beautiful thing has this term applied to it. Of course, to talk about differences in sense is anachronistic, for though Plato is aware of ambiguity, the concept of difference in senses cannot be found at least in the middle period dialogues. A more accurate way of making the point is to say that according to Plato the Form is beautiful in a way different from all of the ways in which the other beautiful entities have this character. This difference need not be the difference between having "beauty" as a proper name or as a predicate; a more plausible proposal is that "beautiful" applies to both Form and participants with descriptive force, but the respective descriptive forces are different. Indeed, this is the only suggestion that makes sense out of the suggestion that the predicate "beautiful" as applied to the participants is derivative from the application of this term to the Form. For if the function of the term as a general predicate is to be explained as derivative from its functioning as a proper name of an entity of which we can give no other unique characteristics, then this sounds very much like Molière's doctor attempting to explain the power of opium to put people to sleep by the dormitive power of opium.

To claim that a term applies descriptively to abstract and concrete entities without ambiguity is hardly objectionable. There are a number of terms in English, for example the word "dangerous," that have ranges of denotation cutting across the abstract-concrete dichotomy. Another example of this sort, more suitable for our purpose, is the term "word." This term applies both to word-types and word-tokens, the former being abstract the latter concrete. Furthermore, the application to the type is complete in itself, while the application to the tokens is always in need of some supplementation; e.g., "the word 'x' as uttered by *S* on occasion *O*." This example parallels the use of terms designating Forms not only in that it cuts across the abstract-concrete dichotomy, but also in that the applications to the sensible things are always incomplete while the application to the abstract is complete. Such was our earlier account of the use of "beautiful." It must be added that not all general terms could be accounted for on this model; but—as we saw occasion to note earlier—not every general term was taken by Plato at the time of the writing of the *Symposium* to be designating a Form. In addition to the complex ones mentioned before, we may add now simples such as "red," "bitter," etc.—in general secondary qualities associated with one sense only. Certainly all of the Forms mentioned in the *Phaedo* can be given the same analysis as the one proposed here for the *Symposium*. It has been thought from time to time that construing the relation of Form to participant as analogous to that between an object and its reflection the problem of self-predication can be bypassed. That this is not so can be seen from the fact that the relation between object and reflection is that of partial common character and causal connection. Objects and their reflections have properties in common, and so have Forms and participants.

The suggestion that "beautiful" applies to the participants with qualifications and to the Form without qualification must be supplemented by the clause that the Form is necessarily the only entity to which the term in question applies without qualification. Thus the role of "beautiful" as applied to the Form of Beauty is that of specifying a unique property, thereby taking up the role of a definite description. To be sure, it is different from ordinary definite descriptions, since these are made up of many properties and a uniqueness-indicator such as "the" in English. Still, the logical force is the same. "The Beautiful" functions as a definite description and it is equivalent roughly to "the only entity that is beautiful without qualification." How Plato arrived at this characterization is a matter for speculation only. It could be that the double negative (not such that it is not beautiful in some way) had a role in Plato's construal of the Form.

In recent discussions the notion of self-predication fared badly. Those who think that Plato held this view[13] speak of it with regret. Those who deny that this was Plato's view write of it as ". . . puerile confusion."[14] To be sure, the view leads to difficulties, though the exact nature of these is far from clear either to Plato in the later dialogues, or to modern scholars and philosophers. We should note, however, that regardless of these difficulties the notion of self-predication has a vital role in the ontology of the middle period dialogues. For as we saw above, it is the only property ascribed to Forms that will help to individuate these. Every Form *F* is thought of as "the unique F." This characterization by itself does not individuate, for it leaves open the possibility that the same Form is both the unique F and the unique G, where "F" and "G" designate different properties. We saw, however, that Plato also lists simplicity of nature ("*monoeides*") as a property of a Form. Self-predication as explained together with simplicity of nature does yield a way to individuate Forms.

It will be objected, no doubt, that the distinction between Form-making and Form-individuating properties is a modern tool of analysis and nothing even approximating a Greek equivalent can be found in the Platonic texts. It is certainly not part of the thesis of this paper that Plato drew a distinction of this sort. It is claimed, however, that Plato thought of the realm of Forms as conceptually much clearer than the realm of particulars. Such priority entails not only that necessary truths can be asserted of Forms in general, but also that each Form can be understood and seen as distinct not only from all of the participants but also as distinct from all of the other Forms. Most likely Plato thought of the world of Forms as analogous to the world of numbers; and not only do we have a clear conception of what it is to be a number, but we have also clear conceptual tools for telling the numbers apart. All of this is compressed, more or less tacitly, into Plato's phrase that each Form has to be grasped as "one, and in itself." The self-sufficiency of each Form could hardly be understood had Plato not thought that there was a necessary truth to be asserted uniquely of each Form. Thus, far from being a confusion or a useless burden, self-predication plays a crucial role in Plato's conception of the Forms. Once this view is abandoned, the problem of individuating Forms arises again, and this problem—at least in its analogous form as applied to properties in general—continues to haunt philosophers through the ages.

To sum up, in these relatively brief paragraphs that came to be known as the description of the ascent, Plato compresses the outlines of a theory of mind as well as the main theses of his ontology. The two must have seemed to Plato harmonious, and one is tempted to think that for Plato this dual construction as an exciting philosophic edifice must have appeared in a way not unlike the vision of the Beautiful that he ascribes to the soul at the end of its journey toward understanding. If the later dialogues sound a different, more critical and tentative note, at least in the *Symposium* one still sees Plato as a confident constructor of metaphysical theories, to embrace a view of reality and to combine this with a view of the soul and its suggested movement, or "paideia." It would be an irony of history if the Platonic conception of "paideia" were to survive without the metaphysical architectonics that its inventor thought to be indispensable.

NOTES

* This essay is dedicated to the memory of my former colleague, the late Professor Paul Henle of the University of Michigan. His penetrating discussions and kind encouragement as well as his example as a fine philosopher and deep human being have inspired much of my work on Plato.

[1] E.g., Wilamowitz-Moellendorf, Stenzel, Shorey and Grube.

[2] For a contrasting view see R. Hackforth "Plato's *Phaedo*" (Cambridge, 1955), p. 12.

[3] R. G. Bury in his edition of the *Symposium* (p. 125) outlines three interpretations of this phrase, and opts for the reading "beautiful in shape." In the context this seems to make little sense.

[4] The translation here is closer to that of Robin (Bude, ed., p. 68) than the Jowett or Loeb renderings.

[5] Bury, *op. cit.*, pp. xlvi.

[6] G. M. A. Grube, *Plato's Thought* (London, 1935), p. 95.

[7] E. R. Dodds, *The Greeks and the Irrational* (Berkeley, 1951), p. 218.

[8] This was once suggested to me by the late Prof. Paul Henle.

[9] This possibility was suggested to me by Mr. C. C. W. Taylor.

[10] Bury, *op. cit.*

[11] Robin, *op. cit.*, p. 69.

[12] One has to be careful to recognize the meanings of "ὄνομα". It means "term" in general, or "noun" in particular. It does not mean "proper name," though it covers proper names as well.

[13] G. Vlastos, "The Third Man Argument in the *Parmenides*," *PR*, 63 (1954): 319–50.

[14] R. E. Allen, "Participation and Predication in Plato's Middle Dialogues," *PR*, 69 (1960): 148.

MICHAEL J. O'BRIEN

The Unity of the *Laches**

The interpretation of many of Plato's early dialogues is hampered by their apparent inconclusiveness. One pattern which several of them share involves the statement of a problem (e.g., "Can virtue be taught?" or "What is temperance, or courage, or piety?"), the analysis of various suggestions, and the decision, finally, to accept none of them.[1] The conversations have the air of being unplanned, of moving in no predetermined direction and of coming to an end when suggestions have been exhausted. Not surprisingly, there has been no agreement, even in a broad sense, about their meaning. The simplest, and at first the most attractive, hypothesis is to take them for what they seem to be, conversations on themes recollected from Plato's hours with Socrates. John Burnet and A. E. Taylor have argued for this view. Burnet has sketched for us a picture of "the youthful Plato who was a great dramatic genius and whose chief aim was to set before us a picture of Socrates as he was" in dialogues which "do not give us Plato's own philosophy" but which "preserve the memory of the teaching of Socrates."[2]

The notion that the early dialogues are idealized essays in biography by a young man with no original philosophy of his own has often led to their being classified as literature and not philosophy.[3] In apparent support of this classification is the fact that Plato in these dialogues seems to lack the ability or desire to draw together into a conclusion the many scattered suggestions and arguments. Instead he seems content to offer a philosophic potpourri. The disarray of ideas in these works caused Wilamowitz to treat them as literature and biography. He decided that a dialogue like the *Laches*, for example, which does not settle the question it sets out to answer ("What is courage?"), was not written with that theoretical interest in mind but in order to show that Socrates was a brave man and the best teacher of that virtue.[4] It commemorates his courage at the battle of Delium (181B, 189B) and records the

* This is a slightly revised version of a paper presented at the 1962 meeting of the SAGP in Baltimore, Maryland. Reprinted with only slight variation from *Yale Classical Studies*, 18 (1963): 131–47. By permission of the editor, Lawrence Richardson, Jr.

admiration of two distinguished contemporaries for his qualifications as a teacher of the young (200CD). It is a personal tribute by Plato to a brave and wronged friend.

Regarded as philosophy, the *Laches* offers no such clear and explicit conclusion. Its result, in Socrates' own words, is: "We have not found out what courage is" (199E). Those who insist on treating it as philosophy have understandably produced quite irreconcilable versions of its main thesis. Grote summarizes this thesis as follows: "The perfect condition of the Intelligence, is the sole and all sufficient condition of virtue. None can possess one mode of virtue separately." Horneffer, on the contrary, argues that the dialogue is an attack on the Socratic view that virtue is knowledge, though remaining a tribute to Socrates' personal bravery, and Gauss goes so far as to call it "anti-intellectual."[5] Such polar opposition in the interpretation of Plato is not at all uncommon. Its frequent occurrence shows that the fundamental technique of reading the dialogue form still remains to be settled. As Victor Goldschmidt has said, "le dialogue, en tant que *genre littéraire*, reste encore à définir. Nous n'en connaissons avec certitude ni la préhistoire, ni le but, ou les buts . . . ni les lois de composition."[6] What I propose to show is that in one dialogue at least, the *Laches*, some of Plato's "laws of composition" can be discovered. That work is not a literary vignette featuring random philosophic conversation, nor is it a treatise on philosophy spiced with wit and interesting characters. It is a balanced work of art, in which character and action illuminate the thought, and the thought is in turn a judgment on the characters. The cornerstone of its construction is the familiar Greek opposition of λόγος and ἔργον.[7]

There are five adult characters in the *Laches*. Lysimachus, son of Aristides, and Melesias, son of Thucydides, are the undistinguished offspring of famous fathers. With them are Laches and Nicias, Athenian generals during the Peloponnesian War, and Socrates. Lysimachus and Melesias are anxious to find a way of schooling their sons to greater distinction than they themselves have won, perhaps by training in arms, and ask the advice of the two generals. How does one train one's son to καλὰ ἔργα (179CD)? Laches is surprised that Socrates' advice has not been asked. Laches and he fought together at Delium, and Socrates more than proved his mettle (181AB). Nicias knows him too, but rather as the man who recommended a fine teacher of music, Damon, to his son.

Socrates insists that his elders should speak first, and they do. Nicias believes in the value of learning how to handle weapons from a professional instructor like Stesileos; the skill will prove useful in actual fighting, and it may lead the student on to the study of strategy (181D ff.). Laches does not put much stock in theoretical knowledge. He has seen quite a few of these professionals ἐν αὐτῷ τῷ ἔργῳ (183C) and has not been impressed. In fact, he once saw Stesileos make a fool of himself in a battle. Socrates, he repeats, is the man to consult. Socrates points out that they are looking for an expert (τεχνικός) in the care of the soul (185A, E). Now in any art one can judge an expert by the teachers he has had, or, if he has had none, by his ἔργα in that art (185E). Socrates has had no teachers in the art of caring for souls (186C), and he has not yet discovered the art, but no doubt Laches and Nicias, who have spoken out so confidently on the subject, have mastered it (186CD).

Let the λόγος begin, says Lysimachus (187CD). Nicias, who has conversed with Socrates often before, as Laches has not, warns the company that Socrates' partners in conversation are regularly forced to give an account of their past and present way of life. Socrates, moreover, will not let a man go until he is thoroughly tested. There is an ominous hint here that the conversation to come will be in some sense quite personal. Laches is of two minds about discussions (λόγοι, 188C ff.). When a man's ἔργα are in harmony with his λόγοι, when he is truly a man (and not, we may infer, a Stesileos), then Laches is φιλόλογος. Otherwise he is μισόλογος. With Socrates' λόγοι he is not familiar, but he has been well acquainted with his ἔργα since the battle of Delium, and Socrates, if anyone, has earned the right to speak about virtue.

Socrates begins by steering the discussion to general questions. What they really want to know is how to make the boys virtuous, and this requires knowing what virtue is. But since that is too broad an issue, he narrows it down to the question what courage is (190D). Laches offers the first definition with high confidence and spirit: the courageous man is one who holds his place in the ranks and does not run away (190E). But Socrates points out that good tactics often require withdrawal even in infantry warfare, and that what he wanted was a definition of courage, not a single example. Laches then defines it as perseverance or steadfastness (καρτερία) of soul. But steadfastness can be intelligent or foolish, and courage must certainly be the former, since courage, a good, cannot be joined with foolishness, which is harmful. But this definition seems unsatisfactory too. Intelligent perseverance in spending money, if one foresees gain, is not courage. The physician, who intelligently perseveres in treating a patient, is not for that reason courageous. Even in war, soldiers are not considered courageous because they show intelligent steadfastness. It is intelligent to persist in fighting an outnumbered and disadvantageously placed enemy, but if both sides fight on, the enemy is more courageous, though more foolish. If two men fight with equal perseverance, the one who knows less of military art is the more courageous, and the less skillful swimmer needs all the more courage to stay in the water. All these examples seem to prove that courage is foolish perseverance, which a moment ago was called an evil.

They seem defeated. Their ἔργα, says Socrates, are not in harmony with their λόγοι. Anyone who overheard them might say they had a share of courage ἔργῳ but not λόγῳ (193E). Nevertheless, he adds, they should heed their own argument to the point of showing steadfastness, so that courage herself may not mock them for not seeking her out courageously. Socrates turns to Nicias and asks him for a helping hand in the investigation.

Nicias proposes that courage is knowledge of the fearful and the safe in war and in all other matters (194E–195A). Nonsense, says Laches. Physicians know better than laymen what is fearful and what is not in matters of health, farmers know in farming, and every artisan has that knowledge in his own craft. Are doctors, farmers, and artisans all ex officio brave men? No, says Nicias, for each craft has a limited purpose, and what seems fearful with respect to that purpose may not be so in broader perspective. A doctor may not know if his patient is better off alive or dead, and so will not know which is really fearful. Even prophets, who can predict suffering, cannot by their art judge if it is good or bad, to be feared or welcomed. Courage is distinct from any art or profession. On the other hand, it is a knowledge, and the common attribution of courage to animals and children, and in fact to many unreasoning adults, is wrong. They are bold, or daring, or fearless, rather than courageous.

Laches has by now lost patience with the turn of the argument. Ironically, he lacks steadfastness on the unfamiliar terrain of philosophical discussion, and he says he has had enough of questions and answers (196C, 197E). Nicias, with a touch of sarcasm, urges him not to lose heart: the argument is not meant to reflect on *his* courage (197C). Socrates, who has taken over the questioning, begins to treat him now like a lagging comrade whom he will not let run away from the fray. They are the comrades of Delium again, and just as at Delium (*Symposium*, 221AB) Socrates has the clearer grasp of what has to be done.

Socrates has an objection of his own to the definition of Nicias. Courage, presumably, is only one part of virtue among others, like justice and temperance. Nicias has called courage a knowledge of the fearful and the safe, i.e., of future good and evil. But if its object lies entirely in the future, the knowledge or science of courage will differ from all other sciences; it will, in fact, contradict the very notion of science, whose objects are independent of time. There is not one science of medicine to deal with the past, another with the present, another with the future. Courage, the knowledge of future good and evil, must also be knowledge of good and evil in general. But then courage is the whole of virtue, not a part, and that is not what they assumed. The dialogue ends in apparent failure. "Then we have not found out what courage is, Nicias" (199E).

This failure to find even a tentative answer to the question under discussion is what tempts students of philosophy to abandon the dialogue to the literary critics. They would be wrong to do so. There is no disorder or even real inconclusiveness in the philosophy of the *Laches*. That philosophy is not set out explicitly in a conclusion; it is to be found in the interplay of thought and character. The dialogue, as Nicias reminds us (187E–188A), is not only a seminar for ideas, but a testing of the lives and actions (ἔργα) as well as the arguments (λόγοι) of the participants.

First the λόγος. For all their perplexity, the speakers are closer to a definition of courage at the end than they were at the beginning. Socrates has discredited both Laches' final definition and Nicias', but it goes unnoticed that the merit in each corresponds to the fault in the other. Laches' definition, "intelligent steadfastness," is disproved by showing that in some things the more you know the less courageous you are. But the intelligence proved to be the inverse of courage is either technical knowledge, e.g. in warfare or swimming, or the good sense of fighting on when victory is almost assured. When Socrates "proves" to Laches that courage is actually foolish steadfastness, he means foolish in technical skills or in regard to immediate ends like military victory. He overlooks the possibility that there are other forms of intelligence consistent with courage. And he does not challenge the relevance of "steadfastness."

When Nicias defines courage as the knowledge of what is fearful and safe, Laches objects that the craftsman has this knowledge within his craft and is not thereby courageous. This is essentially the same objection that Socrates brought against "intelligent steadfastness" when he proved that the courageous man can be technically ignorant and often has the bad sense to endanger his life. Laches could not answer Socrates, but Nicias does answer Laches. In doing so, he answers by implication Socrates' objection to Laches' definition. Courage, says

Nicias, is the knowledge of what is ultimately fearful; it is beyond technical skill or grasp of immediate ends. But then, as Socrates shows, there is nothing to distinguish courage from virtue in general.

Does the λόγος imply any conclusion? Socrates, let it be noted, has left one thing unchallenged in each definition. Courage remains a kind of steadfastness. On the other hand, it involves knowledge of good and evil, since all virtue does. Laches anticipates Socrates' objection to Nicias' definition (the absence of a distinguishing mark) by calling courage, not intelligence alone, but intelligence joined with perseverance; and Nicias answers the objection to Laches' definition by explaining "knowledge of the fearful and safe" as Laches ought to have explained "intelligent." Plato has brought his readers within sight of a resolution and has stopped short. The λόγος, which has on the surface the appearance of unrehearsed conversation, is actually carefully directed by the author's guiding hand. The definitions of Laches and of Nicias complement each other too well not to suggest conscious contrivance. The dialogue, when it is interrupted, is moving towards a conception of courage which will join knowledge of good and evil with a steadfast quality of soul.[8]

Λόγος in the *Laches* is matched by ἔργον. The participants in a Platonic dialogue are not chosen at random, and for the total meaning of this dialogue what the characters are and do is as important as what they say. Lysimachus and Melesias are men of no distinction in life or in intelligence. They have achieved little, leaving almost no mark on their times (179C), and so they contribute nothing to this discussion either (189CD). Laches and Nicias are men of great distinction in Athens, and each has much to add to the discussion of courage. They are soldiers, and this is appropriate. But the suitability of their personal characters and history to what they say goes further than this. Laches' conception of courage is standing one's ground in battle (190E), or, more generally, steadfastness of soul (192B). He does not immediately see that intelligence has anything to do with it. This is as we might expect. He is a practical soldier who has fought among the hoplites at Delium and who will die in battle at Mantinea (Thucydides 5.74.3). He scorns theoreticians of war, like Stesileos, and sees no absolute need for teachers of any sort (185E), especially sophists (197D6), and Damon in particular (200A). He is hearty and blunt and quick to cry "Nonsense!" (195A6, 196B1); he has a feeling for the colorful and humorous (the instructors in arms tiptoeing around Sparta, 183B); and he is a good raconteur (Stesileos in the sea-fight, 183D ff.). He is out of his depth, however, in intellectual discussion and quickly gives in when it goes against him. He regards the subtleties of argument with suspicion (196B3). But he knows a brave man when he sees one: he is the first to invite Socrates to the discussion, and the first to point out at the end that Socrates is the man to teach courage, not he or Nicias. He is a likeable man, and steadfastness of soul, his notion of courage, is a worthy ideal, but his behavior in the dialogue proves its insufficiency when it is not accompanied by knowledge. He can give no account of courage, though he feels sure he knows what it is (194B), and in his efforts to find out his steadfastness deserts him. He is a coward in argument; his own behavior discredits his notion (at 192B) that the courageous man is merely the steadfast man.

Nicias makes a good contrast to Laches and a good exemplar of his own definition of courage. Less brusque and more at home in intellectual discussion, he has cultural interests too and is happy to have found in Damon a good teacher of music for his son Niceratus (180D). We read elsewhere that Nicias forced this son to learn all of Homer by heart and that Niceratus actually took part in a rhapsodic contest.[9] Even in discussing warfare, Nicias dwells on the refined and the intellectual. A graceful soldier is a better soldier (182CD), and knowledge brings grace. Swordsmanship is a preface to strategy. This in a speech that echoes with the words μάθημα and ἐπιστήμη (as noun or verb eleven times in thirty-five lines). Laches' reply, at 182D6 ff., parodies that repetition with noticeable sarcasm (eight times in the first seven lines). Laches goes on to recall a battle in which Stesileos, the theoretician, got himself into an ungraceful posture (183C ff.), and he avows that the only music he admires is the good old Doric harmony of λόγοι and ἔργα (188D).[10] Nicias, on the other hand, not only reveres knowledge, but he is used to having discussions with Socrates (188B), and he acquits himself fairly well, at least in repelling Laches' objections. But he is vain about his ability in discussion (200B). His definition has succumbed to Socrates' objections, but he is confident that a little thought and some help from Damon will right it again (200B).

To follow some commentators, one could only agree that he is right. If "the perfect condition of the Intelligence, is the sole and all sufficient condition of virtue," as Grote puts it, then we will have to accept Nicias' definition, as Socrates revises it at 199C5–D1 (courage is the knowledge of good and evil). But, apart from the fact that all present balk at this conclusion, there is Nicias himself to consider. Laches' failings as a man are obvious; he is shown here to his worst advantage, in philosophical argument. Laches' behavior is a commentary on the insufficiency of his own definition. What of Nicias? The memory which

Nicias left to posterity was that of an intelligent and extremely prudent man without much force of character who was more than once overborne in matters of policy by stronger-minded rivals and who ended his life in spectacular failure.[11] In 425 he resigned his command to Cleon in the face of criticism of his policy in the Pylos campaign and suffered the chagrin of seeing his rival score an unexpected victory. In 421, with Cleon now dead, Nicias had the satisfaction of seeing Athens and Sparta conclude the peace which goes by his name; but soon after this his pro-Spartan policy was frustrated by Alcibiades, and Athens allied itself with Argos. The event, however, which his name calls to mind before any other is the Sicilian expedition. No one of Plato's contemporaries who read the *Laches* could have dissociated the Nicias of the dialogue from the man who led the Athenian army and navy to utter defeat at Syracuse. Those events took place in 415–413, a few years after the dramatic date of the *Laches*, which falls between Delium (424) and Laches' death at Mantinea (418). Of all the Athenians, Nicias perceived most clearly what was "fearful and safe" about the Sicilian expedition. His speech in the Assembly (Thucydides 6.9–14) is evidence of his prudence at a time when Athens was in the grip of folly and over-confidence. Later, when the expedition had been voted in spite of him and he had been made general with Lamachus and Alcibiades, his proposals for the armament were on a generous and prudent scale. They were designed to discourage Athens' zeal for the venture, or, if that failed, to insure its success (Thucydides 6.24). The long story of the expedition, with its early successes and eventual disaster, is well known to all readers of Thucydides. Nicias, so foresighted in the Assembly, was ineffective in Sicily, the more so after Alcibiades had been forced out of command and Lamachus killed. The last stages of the campaign were a personal failure for him. Defeated before Syracuse, he at first rejected the proposal to retreat: then he gave in. Finally, when all was ready for the abandonment of the siege, the moon was eclipsed, and his superstitious fear made him follow the advice of his soothsayers and delay the retirement for a month. By that time all was lost. At the end, quaking before the moon while the Syracusans made their preparations to destroy his army, he even lost his knowledge of "the fearful and the safe" (Thucydides 7.50).

The irony of Laches, who proposed steadfastness as a definition of courage and then failed to persevere in the argument, needs no point of reference outside the dialogue. The irony of Nicias is the sort possible only for an author who puts historical figures in his fiction. Plato makes

Nicias argue for an intellectual's conception of courage. But he was perhaps the most notorious example in recent Athenian history of the intelligent man who failed, and in the last crucial decisions of his life he fell short of his own definition of the courageous man. No reader in the early part of the fourth century should have missed that. If he did, certain remarks in the dialogue were meant to jog his memory. It is Nicias himself who insists that Socrates is about to submit them to a test of their whole way of life. "I am used to him, and I know that one must endure this from him; moreover, that I myself will suffer this [test] I am well aware" (188A). The argument will not be about the boys but about Laches and Nicias (188B). Nicias does not mind. He wants to go on learning as long as he lives, for he believes, like Solon, that old age will not of itself bring him good sense (188B). Those bitterly significant words are later underlined by some pointed references to soothsaying, Nicias' peculiar weakness. "You're calling the prophets the courageous," says Laches at 195E. Nicias denies it: prophets may not know what is really fearful. Socrates remarks later that prophecy should be the servant of strategy, not the reverse (198E–199A). The comment grows naturally out of the context, but it is also an unmistakable reference to Nicias' superstitious decision to postpone retreat at Syracuse.[12] Finally, Socrates' description of the fully virtuous man is *ad hominem*. He is the man "to whom it will belong, in matters concerning the gods and men alike, not only to be exceedingly cautious regarding the things that are fearful and not fearful, but to produce the good, since he knows the right way of dealing with them" (199DE). Nicias, though reverent and cautious in the extreme, fell short of this ideal. Plato's pen, therefore, wrote ironically at 200B, where Nicias rebukes Laches for "the truly human practice" of "looking not at yourself but at others."

The process of testing (βασανίζειν, 188B) in this dialogue proceeds on two levels, a testing of ideas, a testing of men; in the terms of the dialogue itself, of λόγοι and of ἔργα. The unity of the dialogue lies in the fact that the men not only defend the ideas tested but by their personal history are identified with them. Laches, the bluff soldier, thinks courage is standing one's ground. Nicias, the strategist, thinks it is a knowledge of the fearful and the safe. Both conceptions are relevant to courage, but both are incomplete; and, though both men have courage, both have it incompletely. Laches, according to Alcibiades in the *Symposium* (221AB), did not show Socrates' presence of mind at Delium. Nicias, prudent as he was, was ineffective at Syracuse. Furthermore, steadfastness alone will not even make a man consistently steadfast. Laches proves this by being a laggard in argument. On the other hand, as Nicias showed in later life, even a man's knowledge of what is fearful may desert him in a crisis, if he lacks the firmness of purpose needed to sustain it.

The two men not only match their own conceptions of courage but, in a general sense, Nicias represents λόγος in human affairs and Laches ἔργον. The inadequacy of men who are merely reasonable or merely decisive was not a new idea with Plato. Pericles had already praised Athenians for not regarding discussion (λόγοι) as an impediment to action (ἔργα) and for "daring to act as well as reasoning out their ventures beforehand" (Thucydides 2.40.3). Here, as elsewhere, Plato adopts an old ideal and old terminology and turns it to his own purposes. The *Laches* dramatizes two aspects of courage by contrasting a thoughtful soldier with an active one.

On the level of ideas the dialogue remains incomplete. A satisfactory conception of courage is never formulated, although one may infer that it would draw on the suggestions of Laches and of Nicias.[13] On the level of personalities, however, there is a solution, in the person of Socrates. Socrates has fought bravely at Delium and has matched or surpassed Laches in steadfastness. But he can also examine courage rationally and realizes the importance of knowledge to virtue (194D1–2), like Nicias. More steadfast than Laches in discussion, more clear-sighted than Nicias, and more aware than either of what he lacks in knowledge, he is the truly "musical" man, in the sense in which Laches uses the word (188D). His deeds are in harmony with his words; his character befits the subject on which he speaks. The way he died, as Plato's readers knew, showed not only his steadfastness but his clear knowledge of what in that crisis was fearful—injustice (*Crito* 54C), and what was not—death itself (*Phaedo* 67E, *Apology* 29A ff.). In Socrates the theoretical strands of the dialogue come together and find their practical solution.

Neither Laches nor Nicias is fully worthy as a person of the subject under discussion, as Socrates is. However there is a harmony between the incomplete definitions they offer and their own characters. The unity of the *Laches* rests in this. It is both a piece of dramatic literature and an essay in philosophy, and the purposes of the dramatist and the philosopher are in perfect agreement.

NOTES

[1] So, e.g., the *Laches*, *Charmides*, *Protagoras*, *Meno*, *Euthyphro*.

[2] *Platonism* (Berkeley, 1928), pp. 15, 13, 3.

[3] J. Moreau, in *La Construction de l'idéalisme platonicien* (Paris, 1939), pp. 2 ff., has called attention to the markedly different treatment, in the Budé editions, of the early dialogues and those of Plato's maturity, which alone are judged important as philosophy. The *Protagoras* is "avant tout une très belle œuvre d'art" and an essay in method, but of slight interest philosophically (Platon, *Œuvres complètes*, Vol. 3, Part 1—*Protagoras*, eds. A. Croiset and L. Bodin, Paris, 1923, 3). The *Laches* is "une simple exposition de méthode," like the *Charmides* (ibid, Vol. 2, *Charmides*, *Laches*, ed. A. Croiset, Paris, 1921, 88). The *Hippias Minor* has no distinctively Platonic ideas (ibid, Vol. 1, *Hippias Minor*, ed. M. Croiset, Paris, 1920, 21). Ernst Hoffmann defends a similar notion in "Die literarische Voraussetzungen des Platonverständnisses," *ZPF*, 2 (1947): 465–80. He calls the *Ion*, *Hippias Minor*, *Protagoras*, *Laches*, *Lysis*, and *Charmides* "comedies in prose [and sometimes] pure persiflage" (476).

[4] U. von Wilamowitz-Moellendorf, *Platon* 1 (Berlin, 1920), pp. 186–87.

[5] G. Grote, *Plato and the Other Companions of Sokrates*, 2 (new ed. London, 1885), p. 149; E. Horneffer, *Platon gegen Sokrates* (Leipzig, 1904), pp. 35 ff.; H. Gauss, *Philosophischer Handkommentar zu den Dialogen Platos*, Vols. 1 and 2, *Die Frühdialoge* (Bern, 1954), pp. 91–92. Among those in essential agreement with Grote on this question are E. Zeller, *Philosophie der Griechen*, Part 2, Vol. 1, 4th ed. (Leipzig, 1889), p. 502; H. Raeder *Platons Philosophische Entwickelung* (Leipzig, 1905), p. 210; and C. Ritter, *Platon*, 1 (Munich, 1910), pp. 295–97.

[6] "Sur le problème du 'système' de Platon," *RCSF*, 5 (1950): 173.

[7] The pairing of λόγος and ἔργον as doublet (word and deed) or as antithesis (claim v. fact) was a thoroughly ingrained feature of Greek style before Plato. Cf. Aeschylus, *Prom.* 338; Herodotus 6.38; Sophocles, *Electra* 59–60, 357–58, 625, 1360, *Oed. Tyr.* 517, 864–65, *Oed. Col.* 382–83, 782, 1187–88; Euripides, *Androm.* 265, *Alcestis* 339, *Electra* 893, *Orestes* 287, and fragments 360, 890, 898 [A. Nauck, *Trag. Graec. Frag.*, 2nd ed., (Leipzig, 1889)]; Thucydides 1.128.3, 2.40.1–2, 2.43.2 (among many occurrences). A glance at Ast's *Lexicon Platonicum* confirms that the formula is common in Plato too. Cf. *Phaedo* 100A, *Protagoras* 325D, *Crito* 52D, *Menexenus* 244A, *Gorgias* 461D, *Republic* 382E, 389D, 396A, 492D, 498E, *Phaedrus* 240E, *Timaeus* 19E, *Laws* 679DE, 717D, 769E, 907DE.

[8] This method of reading a Platonic dialogue as a deliberately incomplete but suggestive expression of Plato's thought is well known, though not by any means universally accepted. For example, Paul Shorey, in *The Unity of Plato's Thought* (Chicago, 1903), pp. 14–15, argues that the early dialogues present in dramatic, antithetical form what the *Republic* presents as systematic exposition. W. Jaeger describes the inconclusiveness of the early dialogues as Plato's way of "setting us a riddle . . . the solution [of which] lies within our grasp" [*Paideia*, trans. G. Highet, 2 (New York,

1943), p. 91]. T. Gomperz regards the *Protagoras* as a kind of riddle [*Griechische Denker*, 2, 2nd ed. (Leipzig, 1903), p. 261]. The method could not be thoroughly justified here without a detailed analysis of several other early dialogues. I propose to show only that it works well in the *Laches* and that it is reinforced by the dramatic interplay of character.

9 Xenophon, *Symposium* 3.5; Aristotle, *Rhetoric* III. 11, 1413a.

10 Aristophanes' *Wasps* 959 seems to be a joke about Laches' unmusical tastes.

11 The principal sources for Nicias' life are the generally sympathetic account in Thucydides and the biography by Plutarch. Plutarch draws mainly on Thucydides and on Philistus, the Syracusan historian [cf. G. Busolt, "Plutarchs Nikias und Philistus," *Hermes*, 34 (1899): 280–97]; his judgments on Nicias' character and ability are harsher than those of Thucydides. Nicias, according to Plutarch, was not only childishly cautious and hesitant on the Sicilian campaign (14.2), but he was by nature a coward (2.4); on occasion he had to be forced to fight by his colleagues (21.4). But his cautious nature is attested by Thucydides too (7.48, 7.42–43), who also presents his peace policy in an unfavorable light, as an attempt not to endanger his own good fortune (5.16). His resignation to Cleon in the Pylos debate, says Plutarch, was regarded at Athens, after Cleon's success, as an act of cowardice (8.1). Plutarch also records that blackmailers had great success with him owing to his timidity (4.3). Both Thucydides (7.50) and Plutarch (4.1–2) mention his superstitious nature. Aristophanes refers to his caution, using the word μελλονικιᾶν, "to delay victory like Nicias," at *Birds* 638; and "I will fluster Nicias" is meant to raise a laugh at *Knights* 358. Phrynichus jokes about his timidity in the line "He did not walk with a cringing air (ὑποταγείς) like Nicias" [J. M. Edmonds, *The Fragments of Attic Comedy*, 1 (Leiden, 1957), p. 468, frag. 59]. On the positive side, "intelligence" and "good fortune" are the terms associated by Plutarch with his initial successes in Sicily (18.5), and Thucydides' comment on his virtue is well known (7.86). His policies and character are discussed by A. B. West in "Pericles' Political Heirs," *CP*, 19 (1924): 124 ff., 201 ff., and by G. Reincke under "Nikias" in Pauly-Wissowa. He is severely criticized by R. Cohen in "Quelques Mots sur Nicias," *Mélanges G. Glotz*, 1 (Paris, 1932), pp. 227 ff.

12 Wilamowitz thinks not (1.184).

13 B. Jowett saw this. Cf. *The Dialogues of Plato*, 1 (New York, 1871), p. 70. So did H. Bonitz, whose perceptive comments on the *Laches* are found in his article "Zur Erklärung Platonischer Dialoge," *Hermes*, 5 (1871): 413–42. He repeated them and replied to Zeller's criticism in his *Platonische Studien* (Berlin, 1886), pp. 216 ff.

Postscript (1968): I would now refer the reader to Werner Nagel's article "Zur Darstellungskunst Platons insbesondere im Dialog 'Laches'," *Serta Philologica Aenipontana*, ed. R. von Muth [Innsbrücker Beiträge zur Kulturwissenschaft, 7–8 (Innsbruck, 1962), pp. 119–42], which illustrates the contrast between Nicias and Laches by reference to their speech-patterns, emotional reactions, and ways of arguing. Nagel maintains, as I do, that much of this characterization has a demonstrable historical basis. More recently, Robert G. Hoerber, "Plato's *Laches*," *CP*, 63 (1968): 95–105, has argued that the dialogue embodies an elaborate construction by "doublets" (too elaborate, I think, to be quite convincing), which he finds is intensified by numerous and carefully marked "contrasts." The λόγος-ἔργον theme, as I had defended it, appears in his theory as one of many such contrasts. The *Laches* is also thought by Hoerber to foreshadow in its choice of four main characters the principle of the Divided Line of *Republic* 509D ff., a notion which Erazim V. Kohák had proposed earlier in "The Road to Wisdom: Lessons on Education from Plato's *Laches*," *CJ*, 56 (1960): 123–32.

MARTIN OSTWALD
Swarthmore College and the University of Pennsylvania

The Two States in Plato's *Republic**

RECENT discussions of Plato's *Republic* often take it for granted that Guardians and Philosophers are identical, and that the Philosopher of Books V–VII is nothing but a refined and more highly intellectualized version of the Guardian described in Books II–IV. The purpose of this paper is to take issue with this position by arguing that Plato maintains a clear distinction between Guardians and Philosophers throughout the *Republic* and that his political doctrine in the *Republic* involves not one kind of state but two, which, although they are not mutually exclusive, are still sufficiently distinct from one another to justify our taking Plato at his word when he speaks of them as separate entities, the state of the Guardians and the state of the Philosopher. I should like to examine the nature of these two states and their rulers and try to ascertain Plato's purpose in introducing each.

In a passage which has, as far as I know, not received the attention it deserves in recent discussions of the *Republic*, Plato is quite explicit about the fact that it is two states with which he is concerned. At the opening of Book VIII, Socrates wants to bring the discussion back to the point where the "three waves" had interrupted it. It will be remembered that, after the account of the state of the Guardians, when Socrates was just about to speak of the degenerate states here on earth in their relation to the state of the Guardians (V, 449AB), Polemarchus and Adeimantus made him digress to take up the problems of the equality of women, of the common possession of women and children, and of the Philosopher and his education. The end of Book VII brings with it the end of these "three waves", and the words with which the subject of the degeneration of states is resumed are the following. Socrates asks Glaucon: "Come now, since we have completed this account (*sc.* of the Philosopher), let us remember at what point we digressed, so that we can go back to it." "That is not hard," he replied. "You were talking, just as

* This is a revised version of a paper presented at the 1960 meeting of the SAGP in Hartford, Connecticut.

you are now, as if you had completed your account of the state, and you were saying that you would regard the state which you had been discussing and the man corresponding to it as good. But for all that it seems that you had a state and an individual still more beautiful to talk of . . ."[1] Glaucon's reply indicates that Plato, at this point in the discussion, speaks of two states rather than one, and the reference back to V, 449A leaves no doubt about the nature of these two states: the first is that which had been discussed before V, 449A, i.e. the state of the Guardians, and the individual corresponding to it is the just man; while the second state and individual "still more beautiful" are those discussed in the digression, i.e., the Philosopher and his state of Books V–VII.

Although the differentiation between the two states and their respective rulers is here made most emphatic, there are a number of other passages in the *Republic* to corroborate it. For example, in constructing the state of the Guardians, Socrates had insisted on older men being the rulers and the younger the ruled (III, 412C2–4); but when speaking of the philosophic rulers, he says: "But don't let us forget that while in our former selection we chose old men, that will not be possible in the present selection . . . . All great and recurring hardships are the job of young men."[2] The distinction drawn between the "former selection" and the "present" one again points to a conscious difference between the two states and their rulers.

What, then, is the precise difference between the two? And what exactly is Plato's purpose in introducing each? Let us begin with the Guardian and their state. Even before the foundations for the state of the Guardians are laid, Plato clearly states its purpose: "If we study in our discussion the developing state, we should also see justice and injustice develop in it."[3] If we get here the first hint that the account of the origin of the state, which Plato is about to give, is not meant to be historical, this impression is confirmed at once by the ἀναγκαιοτάτη πόλις which Socrates begins to construct. It consists of only four or five men, each a specialist craftsman; no mention at all is made of any women and children that are to inhabit it. It is hardly necessary to stress the point that Plato was quite aware that women, too, are needed for the establishment of an actual state, and we only have to point to the entirely different account in the *Laws* to show that he knew that division of labor did not stand at the beginning of the history of human society. Accordingly, Plato's purpose in constructing the state in which the Guardians are to be placed is not historical but paradigmatic.[4] He constructs the state not for its own sake, but to discover the principles of justice and injustice in it: it is to exist λόγῳ and not ἔργῳ (cf. V, 473A5–6); and by means of it Plato wants to show step by step what justice is, not how it can be attained. In short, the state of the Guardians is meant, initially at least, to be a model to demonstrate something other than a state.

The truth of this is borne out by the deliberate parallelism between the structure of the completed state and the structure of the soul of the individual, in order that the virtues as social qualities will be shown to be identical with the virtues as private and personal qualities. Moreover, Plato shows so little concern for the practical aspects of the Guardian state that some of the most serious administrative problems posed by it are not faced at all, and many of the proposals made are so difficult of realization as to be completely impracticable. To single out a few points only: though much is said in Book II about the education of the Guardians, we are not told who is to educate them; no attention is given to the problem of enforcing the marriage regulations; and, though the point is made that the state must not grow too large, only the birthrate of the Guardians—the best element in the state—is controlled, so that, as Cornford remarks, they will soon be so outnumbered by the producing class that they will not be permitted to procreate at all, if the total number of citizens is to remain constant. Many more examples could be adduced to demonstrate Plato's lack of concern with the practical side of the state of the Guardians, and it is surely not insignificant that the problems connected with marriage and procreation, which had been brushed aside by Socrates at IV, 423E, are brought back into the discussion only on the insistence of Polemarchus and Adeimantus at V, 449C. But even in dealing with the first two waves, the equality of women and the common possession of women and children, Socrates expresses grave doubts as to the feasibility of his proposals (V, 450C, 456B, 457D), and finally requests his interlocutors merely to assume (θέντες) that the common possession of women and children is possible. In other words, the scheme is proposed as a theoretical program rather than as a plan of action to be implemented in actual practice.

This will suffice to show that the state of the Guardians is not meant to be the statement of a practical political aim. It is rather intended to be a theoretical paradigmatic embodiment of justice, courage, self-control, and wisdom in society, and since these are Essential Forms, which for Plato constitute the only realities, only this is a state worthy of the name, whereas all other states "are very many states, but not a state."[5]

The relation in which this paradigmatic state stands to actual states here on earth and to what is desirable in them is brought out with the utmost clarity as Glaucon's insistent questioning about the practicability of the state of the Guardians brings the third wave of paradox down upon Socrates. Socrates' reply to Glaucon requires a detailed analysis. He begins by re-emphasizing (V, 472B) that the state was constructed to show ". . . what kind of thing justice and injustice are,"[6] and then proceeds to introduce a distinction which will become fundamental for everything that is to follow: "Shall we demand that the just man, too, must in no way differ from justice itself, and that he must in every respect have the same qualities as justice? Or shall we be satisfied if he comes as close as possible to justice and has a larger part in it than any one else?" "Yes," he said. "We shall be satisfied."[7] What we learn here is made still more explicit in the immediate sequel: Socrates differentiates between the ἀνὴρ τελέως δίκαιος, the "perfectly just man", who had been outlined earlier (IV, 443C–444A) and the kind of just man we may encounter in our existence here on earth. Justice itself and the perfectly just man were sought only "as a model,"[8] and the actual existence of such a man is thrown in doubt by the addition of ". . . if he were to come into being":[9] justice and the just man as we meet them in the world around us may come close to, but they never completely attain, the perfection embodied in the model. The same applies to the state of the Guardians as a whole: "we created in our discussion a model of a good state"[10] and here, too, Socrates warns Glaucon, we must not expect to be able to demonstrate that it is possible to govern a state in the way described.[11] Accordingly, it is wrong to expect ever to achieve an exact correspondence between the perfection of thought and the imperfection of action: the best that can be hoped for is an approximation of action to thought, and if that can be brought about, the optimum state must be regarded as possible, but possible within the limitations of the actualities of this world.[12] For the actual states which we encounter in our lives are all badly governed, and what we must look for are one or perhaps two of the least changes by which an approximation to the state of the Guardians can be brought about.[13]

This is the context into which the paradox of the Philosopher Kings is introduced in words carefully chosen to emphasize the difference between their state and the state of the Guardians: "Unless either philosophers will be kings in their states, or those who are now called kings and potentates will engage genuinely and adequately in philosophy; and unless political power and philosophy will coalesce in that the many natures of those who now travel their paths separately in the one direction or in the other will forcibly be precluded from doing so;

there is no possible respite from ills, my dear Glaucon, for states and, I think, not even for mankind; nor will this constitution, which we have gone through in our discussion, ever until such a time grow into the realm of the possible and see the light of the sun."[14] This is the crucial passage in which the relation between the two states is established. The Philosopher is the only hope through which the state of the Guardians can be realized, or rather, in the light of the preceding passage, through which it can be approximated. And yet, the differences between the two states are remarkable. Unlike the state of the Guardians, the state to which Plato introduces us here is not to exist λόγῳ in the realm of thought, but it is a state which may be realized ἔργῳ, a state which can grow εἰς τὸ δυνατόν. Plato does not speak of a Philosopher King arising in *the* πόλις in the singular, as he did in creating the state of the Guardians, but he speaks of αἱ πόλεις, the actual states here on earth which, as he had pointed out previously, are now all badly governed. It is in these corrupt states that the Philosopher Kings are to effect a change, by which these states are to be brought close to the state of the Guardians, though, as we have just learned, actual states can never be identical with the παράδειγμα ἀγαθῆς πόλεως.

This brings us to the question of the precise meaning to be attributed to the term "Philosopher Kings." Plato takes great pains from here on to the end of Book VII to describe the Philosophers as fully as possible. He is, however, not as explicit in explaining what he means by "Kings"; still, the passage we have just been discussing provides us with adequate clues: the Kings he means are those who are called kings and potentates by his contemporaries (οἱ νῦν λεγόμενοι). There is, accordingly, nothing philosophical or intellectual about the Kings. They are monarchical rulers in actual states, and perhaps not even monarchical rulers at that: the vagueness of the term δυνάσται does not seem to preclude the possibility of some kind of oligarchical or aristocratic rule. Plato does not tell us how these kings and potentates are to attain power in the first place; but it is safe to assume that they attain it in the normal constitutional way in which a given state appoints its kings and potentates: in a hereditary monarchy, for example, a king will succeed to the throne by reason of his birth as the son of a royal father; in an elective monarchy he will be chosen by those who, in that state, have the right to vote from among those who are eligible for the office, and so forth. That this is what Plato had in mind is confirmed by the alternative he proposes: either Philosophers become Kings, i.e., a Philosopher succeeds to the throne in the constitutionally accepted way, or those who have already become kings in the normal constitutional course of events turn to Philosophy—not in the sense that they dabble in it, but in that they thoroughly (γνησίως τε καὶ ἱκανῶς) imbue themselves with it.

What Plato advocates is, therefore, not a revolution but a peaceful transition involving the least possible change from an actual state as it is to an actual state which comes as close as possible to the παράδειγμα ἀγαθῆς πόλεως. He is concerned with what is possible, δυνατόν: the Philosophers and Kings who are to rule actual states are not ἄνδρες τελέως δίκαιοι nor are they to be ". . . very precise fashioners of the freedom of the state,"[15] as he had described the Guardians; they are to be the actual rulers of actual states. The reason why a monarchical or aristocratic-oligarchical form of an actual state is chosen for the Philosopher is not explicitly stated here. But there is no doubt that Plato regarded it as easier to effect a change through one man or a few than through many. We see him argue the same thing in *Laws* IV, 709E ff., where he states that a change for the better in the existing order of things can be brought about most effectively by a young, intelligent, and virtuous tyrant.

Furthermore, unlike the Guardians and their state, which can attain the theoretical perfection of which thought is capable, there is in the passage we have been discussing every indication that no such perfection can be achieved by the Philosopher. Without the coalescence of political power and philosophy, Plato says in a phrase which is repeated almost verbatim at VI, 487E and 501E, "there is no respite from ills . . . for states and . . . not even for mankind." There is no assurance that the ills to which actual states are subject will ever cease. All we are promised is that a mitigation of these ills, if possible at all, can come only through the rule of the Philosopher. We are decidedly far from the state of the Guardians and in the world of change and decay in which we now live.

If, then, the purpose of the Philosophers is to bring about that transformation in actual states which will bring them as close as possible to the state of the Guardians, our next question is how that approximation is to be effected. Before Plato tells us that, he prepares the way by making three rather subtle points. The first of these is that at VI, 484B he describes the Philosophers as "guardians." But unlike the Guardians of the paradigmatic πόλις, these Philosopher guardians are to govern the πόλεις, the actual states here on earth: ". . . if they appear capable of guarding the laws and pursuits of states, we must make them guardians."[16] The second point is introduced immediately after this: the Philosophers must have in their soul an ἐναργὲς παράδειγμα, a "clear model," to which they look in order to enact ". . . measures here on earth as regards things beautiful, just, and good,"[17] and they are to do so ὡς οἷόν τε ἀκριβέστατα. That the model in their soul is the state of the Guardians, which embodies all the moral qualities, is shown by a later passage (IX, 591E), when the model is referred to as the "constitution within" the Philosopher (ἡ ἐν αὑτῷ πολιτεία). This means that the state of the Guardians is now internalized to be precisely what Socrates had earlier claimed it was: it is a παράδειγμα which cannot be actualized with the same precision with which the Guardians were to fulfill their task at III, 395C, but only "as precisely as possible." Finally, a point is made at 484D, which is later elaborated at VII, 539E ff.: in order to be guardians of actual states, the Philosophers must have experience (ἐμπειρία) as well as knowledge. This, too, marks them off from the Guardians: general experience in governing of the kind a king has played no part at all in the state of the guardians; the only experience required there was in the Guardians' education for war.

With these qualities, the Philosopher can begin his work of transforming actual states. His first task is to make the state a *tabula rasa* (501A ff.; cf. VII, 540E ff.), and then re-create it in the light of his knowledge of "what is by nature just, self-controlled, and so forth,"[18] and his creation will then be the ἀρίστη πολιτεία. This "best constitution," as Socrates again takes care to point out, is very similar to, but not identical with, the state of the Guardians. It will be like the state of the Guardians in all points but one; for while it had been suggested at IV, 429C that the Guardians are to accept unquestioningly what the lawgiver tells them, in the state of the Philosophers "there will always have to be . . . an element which adheres to the same constitutional principles as those which you, as the lawgiver, had when you enacted the laws."[19] In other words, the Philosophers must perpetuate through education the λόγος on which their constitution is based;[20] for the Guardians it was sufficient to accept what the lawgivers told them.

We have in these statements the clue to answering the question why Plato felt constrained to treat the subject of education twice in the *Republic*. The discussion in Books II–III deals with the education of the Guardians who, as the watch-dogs of the state, have to be trained physically and intellectually for the possession of the virtues: ". . . neither we nor the Guardians whom, we say, we have to educate will be cultivated until we gain knowledge of the Forms of self-control, courage, generosity, magnificence, everything related to them, and their opposites, wherever they occur, and until we perceive them and their images as being present in the things in which they reside, and do not slight them in small matters or in great . . . ."[21] The discussion about the education of the Philosophers, on the other hand, is less descriptive of the virtues than prescriptive about the way by which they are to be acquired. The approach taken from VII, 521C–535A thus becomes primarily practical: we are given in concrete terms a program of education by which, Plato believes, the Philosopher ruler can be created, provided that he has the right kind of disposition to start with.

That the educational program of Book VII is meant for the Philosophers and not for the Guardians is clear beyond reasonable doubt. As if to emphasize the point, it is here (535A and 536C) that Plato speaks of the selection of Guardians at III, 412BC, in which older men were to be chosen as Guardians, as the προτέρα ἐκλογή, which will not do in the case of the Philosophers: here it is the younger men who must be selected. Before the education of the Philosopher is treated in detail, Plato states the goal of that education in a way which shows the relation he wanted to establish between Philosopher and Guardian.

For the discussion of the Essential Form of the Good through the analogy of the sun and the eye, he takes the Guardians as his point of departure. He begins by enumerating again all those qualities which had been mentioned at III, 412C ff. as prerequisites of the Guardians, but soon introduces an important modification. Though he had required, at II, 375E and 376BC, that some kind of vague philosophical element be present in the Guardians, he had also stated at III, 412E and 413C that they must be constant in their belief (φύλακες τοῦ παρ' αὐτοῖς δόγματος). But now we are told, on the basis of insights gained through the discussion of the Philosopher, that as Guardians in the fullest sense philosophers must be appointed.[22] The difference between this statement and the demand that Philosophers be made Kings or Kings Philosophers is rather remarkable. While in the discussion of existing states Kings and Philosophers are treated equally as rulers, here in the realm of thought the Guardians are not interchangeable with Philosophers. What we find is simply that a further requirement has been added: it is now considered no longer sufficient for the Guardians to have constancy of *belief*, but the best of them must also be philosophers in the sense that they must themselves gain the *knowledge* of the moral entities, which forms the basis of their rule. This is not a shift in Plato's position: Guardians and Philosophers are not now suddenly identified with one another, but we merely get the assertion, elaborating in the case of the Guardians the earlier requirement that they know the Forms of the virtues (III, 402B ff.), that knowledge of the Good is as necessary for the rulers of the paradigmatic state as it is for those of the actual one.[23]

The Allegory of the Cave shows that this is what Plato has in mind. The Guardians are here no longer mentioned, but only the Philosopher. For it is from the Cave, i.e., from our actual world, that the Philosopher proceeds on the upward path toward the world of the Essential Forms, and once he has seen them in all their purity, he must be compelled to return to the Cave to care for and watch over its denizens: "Observe, then, Glaucon, I said, that we shall do no wrong to the philosophers among us, but what we shall tell them is just when we compel them to care for the others and be their guardians."[24]

With the program of education, Plato's treatment of the Philosopher as ruler reaches its end, marked as such formally by the return, at the opening of Book VIII, to the discussion which had been interrupted at 449A ff. by the "three waves" and which we cited earlier in this paper. Socrates now proceeds to measure existing constitutions and the individuals dominating each against the paradigmatic construct of the state of the Guardians. While this part of the *Republic* is relevant for our purposes only in that it indicates that Plato is here, as he was in the ἀναγκαιοτάτη πόλις, not concerned with describing an historical development, but with measuring existing actual constitutions against his paradigm, there is in the sequel a passage which throws an important light on the problem of the degree of practicability which Plato himself attributed to his proposals in the *Republic*. As a final answer to Thrasymachus' contention that justice is not profitable, Socrates, in proving the opposite, reaffirms the paradigmatic nature of the state of the Guardians. The just man neglects the honors and distinctions of this world and instead "looks at the constitution within him, being on his guard not to upset anything there either by the abundance or the lack of his possessions."[25] That this "constitution within him" is the state of the Guardians becomes clear in the subsequent interchange between Socrates and Glaucon: " 'Surely,' he said, 'if a man cares for such things, he will not be willing to engage in politics.' 'By the dog,' I replied, 'in his own state he will, though perhaps not in his country, barring some divine chance.' 'I understand,' he retorted. 'You mean the state we have now been founding, the state which is established in the realm of discourse, since I believe that it exists nowhere on earth.' 'No,' I said, 'but perhaps it is set up as a model in heaven, which anyone who wants to may see, and seeing it found one in himself. Whether it exists anywhere or will exist makes no difference. For he can engage in the politics of this state, but of none other.' "[26] The distinction between the just man's "own state" and his "country," the fact that the state under discussion exists only "in the realm of discourse," and that it is called a "model," all point to the conclusion that the state of the Guardians is meant here, that its actual existence and non-existence in our world is irrelevant, and that Plato nowhere meant to suggest the possibility of its actual existence.

But is that also true of the state of the Philosopher, which, if any state can, will come close to it? In the passage just quoted Socrates reveals a glimmer of hope that "some divine chance" may make the just man engage in the political life of his country. That this glimmer presents for Plato a genuine hope is shown by his formulation earlier in the work as to how the ἀρίστη πολιτεία of the Philosopher may be realized: "If men endowed with the highest gifts for philosophy are ever constrained to take care of a state, if they ever have been so constrained in the infinity of time past, or are so constrained at the present in some foreign place, far beyond our sight, or if they will ever be so constrained; then we are ready to argue that the constitution we have described has come into being, exists, and will exist, when this Muse (sc. philosophy) will hold power over the state. It is neither impossible, nor is what we are saying impossible. That it is difficult we agree."[27] Unlike the state of the Guardians which remains "set up as a model in heaven," there is, in Plato's view in the *Republic*, the faint hope that the state of the Philosopher may be possible.

NOTES

[1] VIII, 543C: ἀλλ' ἄγ', ἐπειδὴ τοῦτ' ἀπετελέσαμεν, ἀναμνησθῶμεν πόθεν δεῦρο ἐξετραπόμεθα, ἵνα πάλιν τὴν αὐτὴν ἴωμεν.—Οὐ χαλεπόν, ἔφη. σχεδὸν γάρ, καθάπερ νῦν, ὡς διεληλυθὼς περὶ τῆς πόλεως τοὺς λόγους ἐποιοῦ, λέγων ὡς ἀγαθὴν μὲν τὴν τοιαύτην, οἵαν τότε διῆλθες, τιθείης πόλιν, καὶ ἄνδρα τὸν ἐκείνῃ ὅμοιον, καὶ ταῦτα, ὡς ἔοικας, καλλίω ἔτι ἔχων εἰπεῖν πόλιν τε καὶ ἄνδρα.

[2] VII, 536C–D: τόδε δὲ μὴ ἐπιλανθανώμεθα, ὅτι ἐν μὲν τῇ προτέρᾳ ἐκλογῇ πρεσβύτας ἐξελέγομεν, ἐν δὲ ταύτῃ οὐκ ἐγχωρήσει . . . νέων δὲ πάντες οἱ μεγάλοι καὶ οἱ πολλοὶ πόνοι.

[3] II, 369A 5–7: εἰ γιγνομένην πόλιν θεασαίμεθα λόγῳ, καὶ τὴν δικαιοσύνην αὐτῆς ἴδοιμεν ἂν γιγνομένην καὶ τὴν ἀδικίαν.

[4] The state of the Guardians is usually referred to as Plato's "ideal" state. Since in modern usage "ideal" is the opposite of "real," I think this term should be avoided in discussions of Plato, for whom "realities" lie only in the realm of thought. Moreover, if we equate "ideal" with "existing as a perfect exemplar" (*Webster's Third New International Dictionary*, 1966 ed.), the term would not be applicable to the state of the Guardians, because at VIII, 543D–544A1 the state of the Philosophers is described as καλλίων ἔτι.

[5] IV, 422E: . . . εἰσὶ πάμπολλαι ἀλλ' οὐ πόλις.

[6] V, 472B: δικαιοσύνην οἷόν ἐστι καὶ ἀδικίαν.

[7] V, 472B7–C2: ἆρα καὶ ἄνδρα τὸν δίκαιον ἀξιώσομεν μηδὲν δεῖν αὐτῆς ἐκείνης διαφέρειν, ἀλλὰ πανταχῇ τοιοῦτον εἶναι οἷον δικαιοσύνη ἐστίν; ἢ ἀγαπήσομεν ἐὰν ὅτι ἐγγύτατα αὐτῆς ᾖ καὶ πλεῖστα τῶν ἄλλων ἐκείνης μετέχῃ;

[8] V, 472C4: παραδείγματος ἕνεκα.

[9] Ibid: εἰ γένοιτο.

[10] V, 472DE: παράδειγμα ἐποιοῦμεν λόγῳ ἀγαθῆς πόλεως.

[11] V, 472E: . . . ἐὰν μὴ ἔχωμεν ἀποδεῖξαι ὡς δυνατὸν οὕτω πόλιν οἰκῆσαι ὡς ἐλέγετο.

[12] V, 473AB: Τοῦτο μὲν δὴ μὴ ἀνάγκαζέ με, οἷα τῷ λόγῳ διήλθομεν, τοιαῦτα παντάπασι καὶ τῷ ἔργῳ δεῖν γιγνόμενα ⟨ἂν⟩ ἀποφαίνειν· ἀλλ', ἐὰν οἷοί τε γενώμεθα εὑρεῖν ὡς ἂν ἐγγύτατα τῶν εἰρημένων πόλις οἰκήσειεν, φάναι ἡμᾶς ἐξηυρηκέναι ὡς δυνατὰ ταῦτα γίγνεσθαι ἃ σὺ ἐπιτάττεις.

[13] V, 473B: τίνος ἂν σμικροτάτου μεταβαλόντος ἔλθοι εἰς τοῦτον τὸν τρόπον τῆς πολιτείας πόλις.

[14] V, 473C–E: 'Εὰν μή, ἦν δ' ἐγώ, ἢ οἱ φιλόσοφοι βασιλεύσωσιν ἐν ταῖς πόλεσιν ἢ οἱ βασιλῆς τε νῦν λεγόμενοι καὶ δυνάσται φιλοσοφήσωσι γνησίως τε καὶ ἱκανῶς, καὶ τοῦτο εἰς ταὐτὸν συμπέσῃ, δύναμίς τε πολιτικὴ καὶ φιλοσοφία, τῶν δὲ νῦν πορευομένων χωρὶς ἐφ' ἑκάτερον αἱ πολλαὶ φύσεις ἐξ ἀνάγκης ἀποκλεισθῶσιν, οὐκ ἔστι κακῶν παῦλα, ὦ φίλε Γλαύκων, ταῖς πόλεσι, δοκῶ δ' οὐδὲ τῷ ἀνθρωπίνῳ γένει, οὐδὲ αὕτη ἡ πολιτεία μή ποτε πρότερον φυῇ τε εἰς τὸ δυνατὸν καὶ φῶς ἡλίου ἴδῃ, ἣν νῦν λόγῳ διεληλύθαμεν.

[15] III, 395C1: . . . δημιουργοὺς ἐλευθερίας τῆς πόλεως πάνυ ἀκριβεῖς.

[16] VI, 484B: 'Οπότεροι ἄν, ἦν δ' ἐγώ, δυνατοὶ φαίνωνται φυλάξαι νόμους τε καὶ ἐπιτηδεύματα πόλεων, τούτους καθιστάναι φύλακας.

[17] VI, 484D: τὰ ἐνθάδε νόμιμα καλῶν πέρι καὶ δικαίων καὶ ἀγαθῶν.

[18] VI, 501B2: πρός τε τὸ φύσει δίκαιον καὶ καλὸν καὶ σῶφρον καὶ πάντα τὰ τοιαῦτα.

[19] VI, 497CD: . . . δεήσοι τι ἀεὶ ἐνεῖναι ἐν τῇ πόλει λόγον ἔχον τῆς πολιτείας τὸν αὐτὸν ὅνπερ καὶ σὺ ὁ νομοθέτης ἔχων τοὺς νόμους ἐτίθεις.

[20] VI, 497D8: Τίνα τρόπον μεταχειριζομένη πόλις φιλοσοφίαν οὐ διολεῖται.

[21] III, 402BC: οὐδὲ μουσικοὶ πρότερον ἐσόμεθα, οὔτε αὐτοὶ οὔτε οὓς φαμεν ἡμῖν παιδευτέον εἶναι τοὺς φύλακας, πρὶν ἂν τὰ τῆς σωφροσύνης εἴδη καὶ ἀνδρείας καὶ ἐλευθεριότητος καὶ μεγαλοπρεπείας καὶ ὅσα τούτων ἀδελφὰ καὶ τὰ τούτων αὖ ἐναντία πανταχοῦ περιφερόμενα γνωρίζωμεν καὶ ἐνόντα ἐν οἷς ἔνεστιν αἰσθανώμεθα καὶ αὐτὰ καὶ εἰκόνας αὐτῶν, καὶ μήτε ἐν σμικροῖς μήτε ἐν μεγάλοις ἀτιμάζωμεν . . . .

[22] VI, 503B: τοὺς ἀκριβεστάτους φύλακας φιλοσόφους δεῖ καθιστάναι.

[23] Cf. also VII, 543A on the rulers of a good state, i.e., Guardian state as well as Philosopher state: βασιλέας δὲ αὐτῶν εἶναι τοὺς ἐν φιλοσοφίᾳ τε καὶ πρὸς τὸν πόλεμον γεγονότας ἀρίστους.

[24] VII, 520A: Σκέψαι τοίνυν, εἶπον, ὦ Γλαύκων, ὅτι οὐδ' ἀδικήσομεν τοὺς παρ' ἡμῖν φιλοσόφους γιγνομένους, ἀλλὰ δίκαια πρὸς αὐτοὺς ἐροῦμεν, προσαναγκάζοντες τῶν ἄλλων ἐπιμελεῖσθαί τε καὶ φυλάττειν.

[25] IX, 591E: ἀποβλέπων γε . . . πρὸς τὴν ἐν αὐτῷ πολιτείαν, καὶ φυλάττων μή τι παρακινῇ αὐτοῦ τῶν ἐκεῖ διὰ πλῆθος οὐσίας ἢ δι' ὀλιγότητα.

[26] IX, 592AB: Οὐκ ἄρα, ἔφη, τά γε πολιτικὰ ἐθελήσει πράττειν, ἐάνπερ τούτου κήδηται.—Νὴ τὸν κύνα, ἦν δ' ἐγώ, ἔν γε τῇ ἑαυτοῦ πόλει καὶ μάλα, οὐ μέντοι ἴσως ἔν γε τῇ πατρίδι, ἐὰν μὴ θεία τις συμβῇ τύχη.—Μανθάνω, ἔφη· ἐν ᾗ νῦν διήλθομεν οἰκίζοντες πόλει λέγεις, τῇ ἐν λόγοις κειμένῃ, ἐπεὶ γῆς γε οὐδαμοῦ οἶμαι αὐτὴν εἶναι.—Ἀλλ', ἦν δ' ἐγώ, ἐν οὐρανῷ ἴσως παράδειγμα ἀνάκειται τῷ βουλομένῳ ὁρᾶν καὶ ὁρῶντι ἑαυτὸν κατοικίζειν. διαφέρει δὲ οὐδὲν εἴτε που ἔστιν εἴτε ἔσται· τὰ γὰρ ταύτης μόνης ἂν πράξειεν, ἄλλης δὲ οὐδεμιᾶς.

[27] VI, 499CD: Εἰ τοίνυν ἄκροις εἰς φιλοσοφίαν πόλεώς τις ἀνάγκη ἐπιμεληθῆναι ἢ γέγονεν ἐν τῷ ἀπείρῳ τῷ παρεληλυθότι χρόνῳ ἢ καὶ νῦν ἔστιν ἔν τινι βαρβαρικῷ τόπῳ, πόρρω που ἐκτὸς ὄντι τῆς ἡμετέρας ἐπόψεως, ἢ καὶ ἔπειτα γενήσεται, περὶ τούτου ἕτοιμοι τῷ λόγῳ διαμάχεσθαι, ὡς γέγονεν ἡ εἰρημένη πολιτεία καὶ ἔστιν καὶ γενήσεταί γε, ὅταν αὕτη ἡ Μοῦσα πόλεως ἐγκρατὴς γένηται. οὐ γὰρ ἀδύνατος γενέσθαι, οὐδ' ἡμεῖς ἀδύνατα λέγομεν· χαλεπὰ δὲ καὶ παρ' ἡμῶν ὁμολογεῖται.

GEORGE KIMBALL PLOCHMANN
Southern Illinois University

Supporting Themes in the *Symposium**

PLATO's *Symposium* has so much charm but contains so little open debate over concepts that were it to have been his only surviving work, literary critics would seldom have conceded that its author was really a worker in the philosophical vineyard. It is only because Plato wrote a good many of his dialogues in the form of back-and-forth argument that readers have been conditioned to expect dialectic even in the most improbable frameworks. Otherwise they would hardly have glanced within the incisive characterization, the dazzling rhetoric, and the glowing mythology of the *Symposium*—and would accordingly have missed an extraordinarily subtle philosophic structure, a stately dialectical sequence that when laid bare astounds us.

There is a second tendency, opposite to the first, which finds in Plato not much more than a unitary doctrine, a dogma of love, and plays down all the dramatic and poetical touches as being delightful but excrescent. These critics, overly sensitized, perhaps, to the formalities of philosophy, have been hesitant to seek for "Platonic philosophy" in any discourse but that of Socrates, and they continue to think of the half-dozen other speakers as mere attractive foils to the hard going of the theory of ideas and the ladder of aspiration[1] or love.

To put my view bluntly, these critics, both the literary and the philosophical ones, are in their separate ways wrong. Their errors are all the more inexcusable because Plato himself has supplied literally dozens of clues to his double intention to set forth both a doctrine and an embodiment of it—a fusion of philosophy and life. We can go a step further by saying that this very fusion is both a doctrine itself and also a transcript of conditions of life. And Plato's only way of showing this, I think, is to furnish the broadest possible hints that the whole train of discourses,

* Presented in its original form at the 1962 meeting of the SAGP in New York, New York. Reprinted with slight corrections by permission of the *Bucknell Review*, XI (1963): 1–18, where it appears under the title "Hiccups and Hangovers in the *Symposium*."

Phaedrus to Alcibiades, should be taken as integral to the very heart of this doctrine of love, virtue, and knowledge, and that, turn about, the exhibition of the persons in the drama in their respective postures, amours, and stages of inebriety would be no better than pointlessly entertaining, perhaps even degrading (even as the frivolities of Homer's gods are degrading), were it not that the gestures and the discourses were set end to end in an inescapable pattern of asseverations and meanings.

To neglect, then, the multiple clues to the intention of Plato that the dramatic and the philosophic be considered instinct one with another is to miss a good deal on both sides, and to lose hold of the special unity of the dialogue as well. Some of these clues are as trivial as the personal traits of Aristodemus, as outlandish as the hiccups of Aristophanes (surely more significant than any belch in Shakespeare!), or as hammered-in as the repeated references to wine. Relatively few of the studies made on the *Symposium* take it as all of a piece,[2] and especially are the speeches of Aristophanes and Alcibiades treated as extraneous to the ladder of Eros and whatever else is taken as *echt*-Platonism.[3] Hence I propose to re-examine some of the passages that have excited interest largely for their "drama," "satire," "poetic fantasy," and see if these, too, cannot be found to fit nicely into the total scheme. But there is one proviso: I do not wish them to bear more than their just weight, nor overload them so that they cease to be exciting, or funny, or imaginative, as the case may be. The hoped-for result of my study will be, perhaps, to discover that the genius of philosophy and that of literature do not change places, yet are somehow the same; and if this conclusion involves getting rid of certain textbook conceptions of either philosophy or literature, this too will be all to the good.

At the outset, readers are confused about the philosophic purposes as soon as they see that rhetoric and poetic appear to dominate Agathon's party, and that even the plea for giving epideictic speeches on love has a most personal cause—hangovers. The excuse offered by Phaedrus (and Eryximachus) for talking about Eros is a rather incidental one—the poets have been remiss. Moreover, the chief feature of the dialectic in almost all the *other* dialogues lies in the control of meanings of words, and the consequent checking of definitions, by some one master—Socrates, Parmenides, the Eleatic Stranger, Timaeus, Critias, or the Athenian Stranger.[4] In the *Symposium*, on the other hand, there is little attempt (except for a short colloquy between Socrates and Agathon) to alter directly the statements of previous speaker, or affect those whose turns are still to come. It must be, then, to other hints which we must listen if we wish to discover the precise meanings of the terms that Plato would have us carry away: we must partly gather the dialectic from the sequence of characters and incidents of the piece.

It is, on the other hand, just as essential to keep the philosophy in mind if the human relations of the dialogue are to remain clear. A modern reader who failed to perceive the purposes of these for clarifying the connections of philosophy and literature and who came across Socrates for the first time here would think of him as an unaccountably tardy, informal guest with a hollow leg whose speech is elevated, paradoxical, difficult to follow, and who seems to be having a negative effect on a handful of the younger men as a result of having displayed a sneaky puritanism.[5] Without the manifest skill in debate and the uncanny refutations of other Platonic dialogues it is hard to discover just how Plato could hope to achieve the necessity and universality ordinarily demanded for philosophic propositions. Discard the "philosophy," and the moral dignity of *all* the participants vanishes at once. This can be re-established only if we are willing to acknowledge the circularity in the work: the place of debate is taken by the patterns of applause and jocular criticism, drinking, and erotic companionship, by the placing of the guests and their order of speaking. These, I say, point up the doctrine and this *in turn* flashes a new light upon the personal relationships.

The *Symposium* depicts a situation in which encomium rather than analysis or exposition is to be the aim of discourse.[6] Thus the applause after Agathon's talk is universal and prolonged, showing that he fulfills the common ideal of what encomium should be, and that his fanciful ascriptions really gather up a number of earlier threads of discourse and tie these together. The applause for Socrates is fairly general, but the thin-skinned Aristophanes attempts a reply to Socrates' slight correction of love as a blind seeking of another part to reconstitute a whole, regardless of the goodness of this whole. Then Aristophanes and the applause are both halted by shouts, just as Socrates' defense of himself as philosopher is interrupted by shouts in the *Apology*.[7] But the shouts here are not those of a dicast but of a lover, Alcibiades, who later will praise Socrates, and whose irruption stops the applause as a way of hinting, first, that the applauders may have enjoyed the speech for the wrong reasons (let us say rhetorical rather than dialectical reasons),[8] and, second, that what will ensue must be quite a different sort, taking rise from lower, less-taught and less teachable levels of man's nature, rather than the quite carefully instructed contrivances of the earlier speakers. (We remember that the teacher of Phaedrus was Hippias, or maybe

Lysias;[9] of Pausanias, Prodicus;[10] of Eryximachus a number of pre-Socratic thinkers and men of medicine; of Aristophanes, the Muse;[11] of Agathon, Gorgias;[12] and of Socrates, Diotima.) Not one of these men speaks altogether in his own name, though Socrates is the only one wholly to disclaim originality,[13] regardless of how much he professes to know about matters pertaining to Eros.[14] It is accordingly of high importance that Alcibiades be neither a man much instructed nor a man sober enough to exercise traditional restraints, but rather a man of miscellaneous experience who in his puzzled, groping way has divined a little of the real business of philosophy, which is not only to elevate men in words, as Agathon and Socrates had just elevated, but to give men the virtues in fact—in actions. The function of Alcibiades in the dialogue, in this connection, is not so much to praise Socrates before strangers as it is to differentiate him before friends from the sophistic temperament of Agathon, whose speech is quite like that of Socrates in its exaltation and poetic freedom, but unlike it in substance as a statement of what love really means for man.

Secondly, there is the wine, which has given pain to all the other guests (Socrates alone excepted) yet gives pleasure and freedom to Alcibiades, although Agathon cannot pour wisdom into Socrates or anyone else as he can water.[15] Alcibiades can communicate to others his partial insight into the nature of Socrates with the help of this wine. There are, withal, several relations that the participants in the *Symposium* bear to wine—indeed, almost all possible. Wine brings pain to most, regardless of how much pleasure it has brought before—it is a mixed pleasure, according to the *Philebus*.[16] To Socrates it is neither a pleasure nor a pain, nor is it useful or detrimental to promoting his intellectual insights. To Alcibiades, it is allowed to seem an unmixed good, because it permits his telling of the truth. The anonymous heedless ones who break in after Alcibiades, and who seem also to be drunk, put an end to all discourse.

Thirdly, the pattern of lovers and those loved cuts across that of drinkers. Thus Pausanias and Agathon form a pair within the group; Phaedrus is not distinctly paired with someone present, though in two other dialogues it is indicated that he and Eryximachus are lovers; and Socrates, though neither lover nor beloved in the sense intended by the other speakers, has two quite opposite sorts of admirers, Alcibiades and Aristodemus.[17] The former desires actively, while the latter is the typical passive well-wisher, content with a few crumbs of attention and with no hope or need of further satisfactions.[18] (In a way, Aristodemus is as chaste as Socrates, but mere passive chastity is insufficient, in Plato's view, to constitute philosophic virtue. It is at the end of, not apart from, the climb up the great ladder that a man becomes a true lover.) Then there is the extraordinary bond between Socrates and his sublime prophetess: here it is impossible to decide in *ordinary* terms which is the lover and which the beloved; even in *Socratic* terms both seem to be ranged together as common lovers of a truth. Their differences arise from the unsureness of Socrates' step as he is about to enter into the great mysteries of Eros.[19]

What I have been trying to establish by these three examples is this: that the *Symposium* is neither a statement of philosophy with a delightful background, a "drama of ideas" pure and simple, nor is it a drama of persons who happen to be talking theory,[20] but rather it is a new form, which makes the two sorts of drama wholly integral one with another. Many scholars now agree that the highest kind of literature in Plato is philosophy; less often the critics insist that the supreme philosophy is literature. The objection that the *Parmenides* and *Sophist* are, after all, good philosophy and bad literature holds only if one looks to a more popular conception than Plato's of what literature should be. It seems to me that *both* these statements are true as parts of a completer truth: that for Plato *real* philosophy (not the bogus kind that the sophists teach in public or that Dionysius II would like to write) and *real* poetry (not even that of Homer and his great themes of war and human society and the intercourse of men and of gods,[21] but something truer) are precisely the same. I do not suppose this fusion could have been completely written out, even by Plato. But for all his reservations regarding the written word, he endeavored mightily.[22] In his dialogues the movement is from persons to ideas and back to persons; but equally it is from ideas and back to ideas. This, of course, is not all: *which* ideas (I mean here Platonic ideas) are presented in connection with *which* persons, and how they are substantiated or refuted, clarified or obscured, lies deep in the nature of Platonism, and manifests the rhetoricico-dialectical genius of Plato in its uniqueness rather than in its accidental similarities to other writers of dialogue. What this leads to is a reformulation of the connections between personality and that which is known. The person is most properly the way in which perfectly understandable ideas are *in fact* viewed, by reason of the confusions wrought by the senses[23] and the vagaries of popular education; and the ideas, in their turn, are indistinguishable from what the enhanced and instructed mind can apprehend by dialectical refection upon the widest possible variety of the objects of experience. This knowledge must be intimate with the experience. Thus Socrates talks with two poets about the fundamental unity of intellect behind both comedy and tragedy. Even when they are weary and drunk the assertion seems plausible to them as it would not to persons mis-schooled and lacking native talents. For their common outlook upon *poiesis* derives from their having natural gifts beyond the others—had not Agathon, for instance, in spite of his Gorgian conceits, won a prize which neither Phaedrus, nor Pausanias, nor the irretrievably stuffy Eryximachus could ever have taken?

But the dialogue illustrates what I have said still more fully. There are no refutations in the *Symposium*, as we pointed out, except for the passage where Socrates forces upon Agathon an awareness of a possible mean between contrary opposites, politely pretending—or *was* he pretending?—that a similar distinction had been forced upon *him* by Diotima. At any rate, lacking any further recourse to refutation, the participants cannot launch interpretations of poetry either[24] and hence no valuing or disvaluing of poetic stories, except for the silence when there might have been applause. The only way to show where poetry resides is to show how it is incorporated into philosophy, and this is one function of the great speech of Socrates. Nearly everyone *laughs* after the tall tale of Aristophanes, but they all *applaud* after a tale almost as tall when it is told by Socrates. Even the general company can see that a story standing by itself is ludicrous when the dialectic it illustrates is shaky and indeed patently false, whereas a very similar story, exemplifying much more complex relations between parts and wholes of bodies *and* of souls and their progeny, strikes them as praiseworthy. This much of Socrates they do understand. The fact that the dialectic of Socrates is a complete statement of human aspiration is further driven home when, at the very end, he proves to the reposeful poets that their knowledge is fundamentally the same. This does not mean that Aristophanes could assume Agathon's role as a limited poet—indeed in some ways he can more easily change places with Eryximachus, the Chief Medical Officer of the group—but it means rather that the *real* knowledge which is at the bottom of comedy and tragedy, and which has the characters of both, is the poetically enriched dialectic of the philosopher. This next-to-last line of the dialogue makes little sense if we forget that the speech of Socrates, with its being-becoming-non-being triad, is preceded by a passage-at-arms with Agathon, who has a simple diremption of fixed contraries, and is followed by an attempted interruption of Aristophanes, who in his own speech had attempted to show compounds of contraries, in a crude version of the Eleatic Stranger's blending of classes in the *Sophist*.[25] The contributions of Aristophanes and Agathon to the evening had much the same strengths and weaknesses. Moreover, the identification of the two kinds of poetry is clear to anyone who can grasp the long speech of Socrates as a whole, that is, a fusion of the comic and the serious, or at any rate a mean between them. The two men, however, agree to this only half-heartedly. Their grasp is partial.

Let us go on to the famous hiccups. Either the critics have set these aside as a mere literary touch[26] or else they have pointed out that the purpose is get Aristophanes' harangue postponed, so that it could be made to fit the dialectical order of the speeches. It would seem that the first view could now be dismissed as an improbability because so many other "touches" seem to point in philosophical directions, just as the sequences of hands in Leonardo's *Last Supper* indicate the spiritual relationships of the disciples to each other and to Jesus. The second ignores the lack of economy of having two men trade their speaking-order, when they could have sat differently at the outset. I like to think that these hiccups are one of the surest indications in the dialogue that *nothing* is wholly casual and that if we follow them far enough they will give even more weight to the contention that Plato, in his dialectical poetry is composing a work of incredible, if often unappreciated, tidiness. First of all, of course, the hiccups are a disharmony of the diaphragm, which in the *Timaeus* is listed as the point of separation between the respective seats of appetitive and the ambitious parts of the soul.[27] It is the maladjustment of bodily love and ambition which for Aristophanes is the very point in question—Zeus splits four-legged men not because they are lovers but because they are overly ambitious, and he is jealous of his ramparts. This turns men back upon themselves, eliciting their most abject sexuality. Second, if this harmony goes awry, the cure is not so easy—three remedies must be applied. But more important still is the fact that when Aristophanes begs for a prescription or a substituting speech, Eryximachus gives him both. This can only mean that the two speeches, rather than the two men, are somehow transposed, in their subject matter and manner of treatment. Normally, Aristophanes would be expected to talk about love in a very general way, making it a universal and perhaps blind passion; and Eryximachus would then talk about the phylogenesis of love, its possible mutations.

Because it is plainer, we may look at the discourse of Aristophanes first. His strange assortment of limbs and heads is more than likely a parody of the Empedoclean view (reported by Aetius)[28] that the generations of animals and plants do not breed true, but are altered radically from parental to filial; and of the related Empedoclean assumption (reported by Aristotle)[29] that faces without necks sprang up, arms without shoulders, and so on.[30] I do not need to labor the fact that love and strife, which are not contraries anywhere else in the *Symposium*, are related and opposed by Aristophanes, though admittedly he scarcely applies them as Empedocles applies them. Moreover Aristophanes' threefold combinations of like and unlike may stem directly from Empedocles; but that they stem from him alone would be dubious, inasmuch as the like-unlike principles could be taken from Heraclitus and others. But certainly Empedocles was the chief influence upon medical thinkers of the period and his four-phase cosmology is indeed a vast expansion of simple chemical elements, changes, and their causes: a projection of them on a grand scale. Were a poet asked to speak imaginatively on Empedoclean biology and cosmology, taking a physician's place, no doubt this would be his subject matter.

Eryximachus, for his part, makes an equally radical shift away from the materials that a doctor would be expected to deal with. The talk is about physiology not at all, but rather about the arts—music, the mantic art, poetry. And Eryximachus dwells at length upon the extension of the same knowledge throughout earth and heaven; and this it happens, is a point that the real Aristophanes had already made in *The Clouds*.[31] The doctor turns the tables on Aristophanes by advocating the very type of cosmic knowledge which the comic playwright had already disparaged in his play about Socrates; and as he does this he also sets up a vague hierarchy which makes his speech seem structurally the one most nearly akin to that of Socrates with his ladder of love.[32] In sum, the speech of Eryximachus turns the Aristophanic attack on Socrates upside down; the speech of Aristophanes reduces the Empedoclean cosmology of Eryximachus to a relatively puny human scale and shows by implication (when contrasted with the addresses of Agathon and Socrates) that physiology is unable to account for the psychic aspects of Eros. If the *Symposium* is in part about the lover, Socrates, then Aristophanes and Eryximachus nullify the implied attack of the other upon Plato's heroic, daimonic philosopher. The two men, outwardly doctor and patient, deliver speeches that are also related by their diverse transformations of Empedoclean and other sources, and by their quite different direct bearings upon Socrates and his view of Eros. As with Phaedrus and Pausanias, one builds upon the other, but also each has a different relation to Socrates.

This hints at something not often remarked concerning the order of speeches; it is a twofold order. The speakers recline in a circle, so that their discourses must be arranged serially, and if you like cumulatively. This is indicated by the frequent backward references to the distinctions set forth earlier.[33] But the effect of this arrangement taken by itself, would be either total dialectical indigestion or else total cancellation of the positive results of each speaker. (Remember, there is practically no refutation, as there is in *Republic I*, to separate out what is worthwhile from what is trivial or false.) So there must also be a different order, which is indicated not by physical placement at all but rather by the dramatic prominence given to one central personage, Socrates. This is conferred upon him by Apollodorus' opening remarks, by the bath, the cryptic episode under the neighbor's porch, the banter with Agathon, the very length of Socrates' speech, not to mention the ambivalent enthusiasm and jealousy of Alcibiades, and by the final departure and second bath at the end—all these establish the centrality of Socrates, his position at the hub of a dialectical wheel.

Let us look at the serial order first. The patterns of contrary pairs of terms selected by the seven speakers to explicate love are of some interest. Thus Phaedrus speaks of lover and non-lover, though the latter is a shadowy creature indeed, and the former is hard to make out; Pausanias, of the heavenly and popular, to his mind similarly related as are good and bad; Eryximachus divides love into the healthy and the sick, while Aristophanes takes love to be good if it be between like persons, bad if between unlike; for Agathon there is a contrast between the ugly and the beautiful, to be corrected only by Socrates' insistence that these contraries (along with certain others) have intermediates. The contraries in all these pairs are what might be called *ideas* or principles; the two chief opposites in Alcibiades' bibulous eulogy are *persons*—himself and Socrates.[34]

Running side by side with these is a very important discussion of the virtues, which are used throughout to interpret either what love does for man or what man should do for love. These virtues are the same four that occupy Socrates in the *Apology*, in the *Republic*, the *Laches*, and elsewhere. Thus Phaedrus refers only to courage (a bad mark against him, inasmuch as it appears to be the least rational of the virtues, and least implies the other three). For Pausanias, good love, heavenly love, is really the same as temperance, though what is temperate is fixed according to extrinsic standards of custom; where widsom intrudes, it is only as an adventitious education of the beloved. Eryximachus, who quite naturally sees all things in terms of health (harmony) and disease, looks upon the former as a kind of temperance, or, if you like, justice; here wisdom enters in the guise of a rather superficial knowledge of the arts—an "integrated course." Aristophanes, taking justice as the paramount virtue, treats it as a restraint, a holding-back of ambition to supersede the gods; courage now becomes subordinate, but exists as one of the kinds of love, that of man for man. Agathon, the rhapsodic Agathon, tries to say that love is *all* the virtues, or at any rate that love promotes them, but he fails to order them in the right way, because he leaves wisdom as nothing more than the poet's skill. This is soon corrected by Socrates, who points out (in the context of a long account of the virtues) the identity of love and wisdom which is in turn the knowledge of the good and of beauty, and which implies the knowledge of what is everlasting.

Now comes Alcibiades. He is drunk, he has no tricked-out discourses, he will tell the truth. (The point of this is that when he praises Socrates the goodness of the master is to be estimated in terms of a *universally* felt standard, not one taught for special occasions.) It is remarkable now that he puts all four of the virtues in fairly good order: Socrates is said by him to be temperate, courageous, just (he takes no bribes), and finally he has wisdom, as manifested in his persuasive, indeed stunning use of words.[35] But Alcibiades, while he gives a fair description of what it means to be temperate and brave (the two conspicuous virtues of a soldier), is woefully weak on the other two virtues.[36] How, then is his speech internally related to that of Socrates? The relations are indeed very many, and the closeness that Plato intends is hinted at by the inordinate amount of banter between the two men, by their continued sitting next each other, even though they change places; and of course by the contents of their respective discourses, the second of which draws a picture of the life of the true lover, in near-ignorance of the nature of true love. But these are only pointers.[37]

Briefly, his chief function is not unlike that of the chilling description of the degradation of states in Books VIII and IX of the *Republic*. There is a kind of external ambiguity in the culminating account of the best state—it looks as though man states having a temperate populace and a well-trained soldiery would fit the account, and certainly the curriculum, in Book VII, for the philosopher-king is politically a trivial thing unless we are talking abstractly, about an ideal, never-never city. But what Books VIII and IX show is that *no* existing state can be made to fit that description of the best one, that as the discrepancies between them and this best one become ever greater they in fact are worse and worse. There is a similar external ambiguity and abstractness about the speech of Socrates in the *Symposium*; but dialectic as a matter of fact always requires supplements of various kinds to show that it can fit real-life situations, or that ordinary life really differs significantly from the description he gives.[38] Socrates has a little of the weakness of Agathon—his *talk* makes one think of an emotionally charged situation in which we simply keep our eyes glued to something unshakeably wonderful—but not very important in our lives. Alcibiades, at the price of describing successive degradations of himself, shows that the difference between what Socrates is really talking about and what *might* be taken as satisfying that account in the lives of men is of vast import: Socrates cannot live up to Diotima's discipline of love simply by being a *Feinschmecker*, fixing his gaze upon eternal beauty as Max Beerbohm's Oscar Wilde fixes *his* gaze upon a delicate flower, and committing the indiscretions which Athens would have cheerfully tolerated but which in London were enough to land a man in jail. It is noteworthy in this context that Alcibiades, though a frequent hearer of Socrates, is not really a pupil of his, as Theaetetus would have been; and he picks up the plainer features of Socrates' talk, without paying close attention to the rest. Thus he says that Socrates speaks only of packasses and cobblers,[39] which is interesting in that in the speech just finished there was scarcely any reference whatever to anything so homely; the artisans and horses are back in Book I of the *Republic*, where they are used to illustrate the deficiencies of a conception of justice as an art of money-dealing.

I suppose that one ought to say something of Alcibiades' political position, the fact that he was a great tactician on the eve of his first triumph and disgrace, the fact that he came to a bad end; perhaps Plato would have had us see his weaknesses implicit in his speech of the evening, leading to his undoing. But it is really just an accident that Thucydides and Plutarch (among others) have supplied us with details of his life over and above what we learn in the *Symposium*, and that there is scarcely any clear testimony regarding the other participants, even Socrates, beyond what Plato chooses to let us know. According to Plutarch, Alcibiades met his death under a hail of arrows and javelins, but what we know of him at Agathon's party from Plato's portrait is that he was, as they say, stoned. Not only is he drunk, but even sober he is made by Plato to seem the almost totally unphilosophical man.[40] He is not a real philistine, for he admires Socrates, has some eye for statuary, and quotes Aristophanes, all very aptly; but for all that the man is wholly immersed in particulars. It is to the point to say here that Dionysius II, in the Seventh Letter, is another kind of unphilosophical man, and that the two differ in Plato's mind as the dilettante differs from the soldier, as the man who wants to copy doctrines differs from the man who wants to copy deeds, though both waver so that as often as they advance toward philosophic insights they fall away from them too. But both men have a dialectical service to perform, clarification of what philosophy is *not*, and this they do in their several ways. Alcibiades has Thomas Gradgrind's respect for fact, sir, nothing but fact; yet the facts are remarkable, not trivial, and the attitude of Alcibiades, which may be summed up in the phrase, "It beats *me*!" is an indispensable part of the milieu in which a philosopher, the real Socratic kind, the sort that Nietzsche himself speaks of as the Superman, must live and have an impact upon his multifarious companions.[41]

We have already said that Socrates is at the hub of a wheel of discourse and of discourses. Each speaker at the perimeter is related to him in a way differing uniquely from the way in which every other one is related. To explore these ways in detail would take a long time. Distinctions both horizontal (the opposites having the same value) and vertical (the opposites having unequal value), hierarchies, myths—all these dialectical devices are present in the first five speeches, and Socrates takes over from each of them in a new fashion; but they cannot borrow from and improve upon each other. As well as sharing a cumulative, serial relation to the speakers, Socrates is *directly* inclusive and sublative of each of them.

We can read the description of the "greater mysteries" in such a way that its relationships to the other speakers become fairly clear. The obscurities stem from the fact that one cannot merely add speaker to speaker to get Socrates; there must be principles of selection. Had Socrates done nothing more than place them end to end, every reader would have noticed this long ago; but as it is, many students find no dialectical order at all.

Let us assume that Socrates is expounding love in nine stages:[42] (1) we encounter beautiful bodies; (2) love one particular body; (3) discover the similarity of beauty of one body to another; (4) love all beautiful bodies and discount the one; (5) value beauty of souls more than beauty of body; (6) love the beauty in institutions and laws; (7) love sciences; (8) love a single knowledge; (9) contemplate the one. The speech of Phaedrus makes two emphases: these are to be found in the first and fifth of Socrates' steps. Pausanias plays upon the second and sixth, Eryximachus upon the third and seventh. Now comes Aristophanes with his recent hiccups, which betoken a temporary overturn of the order established: he sums up all seven of the steps so far set forth, but in so doing he gives a twist to each one, to make it advocate the opposite of what is intended in words by its original proponent and in fact by Socrates. The love of institutions and laws, to take the sixth rung at random, is intended by Pausanias to be merely a willingness to abide by local customs; by Aristophanes it is twisted into overweaning pride in man to storm the bastions of the heavens, and into Zeus' pride and efforts to keep his divine prerogatives whatever the costs to man.

Agathon now, with his notion of universal beauty as belonging to all, approached through a unitary art, of poetry, reinterprets the fourth step and adds the eighth, but leaves the philosophy of love open at both ends by failing to include either bodily nature or the divine essence. Socrates must straighten out the dialectic again, which he does by adding the last stage, which is no doubt the same One that he introduced in Book VI of the *Republic*.

It now devolves upon Alcibiades to explain what all this means in human terms. He clarifies the discourse of Socrates, chiefly by giving the ladder in what amounts to a reverse order—thus he begins with contemplation of the one, though it is now the one Socrates, and ends with silly flirtatious talk about changing places on the couch. In between he touches upon practically all the rungs of the ladder, but there is a great weakness in his discourse: in order to explain what real love is in concrete terms, he must adopt the most concretely human attitudes of all, and these are philosophically ambiguous. However, this reversal is precisely what Plato would like to include as explanatory of the full meaning of love; we affirm the ladder and then turn it upside down to show its direct application to the human condition, much as old Father Parmenides thought it necessary to deny whatever is said about the one and the others, as well as affirm.[43] I think too that not only do these speakers expound and advocate certain rungs of the ladder, but also they *represent* them. Thus Alcibiades, with his lack of general knowledge and his jealousies over particular persons, stands lower than the others, and his character sets a limit to his dialectic. Aristophanes, too, is jealous, though it is over his ideas and the way they are viewed by others. Socrates can live upon all the rungs with ease, but it requires the speech of Alcibiades, to show this to the other guests, and to the readers of Plato's dialogue. So he interprets love by depicting Socrates, but at the same time—Plato is nothing if not subtle—he all but jettisons all the distinctions and all the rigor by which Socrates had constructed the theory. Small surprise, then, that the only possible conclusion to this is a party of revellers, several hurried departures, and a bath before facing the problems of the next day.

Oh yes. We were talking earlier about hiccups. Why did Aristophanes have them when he had had not a drop to drink that night, and why was Alcibiades free of them, though he was far gone in his cups? This would be a question for Socrates to answer, not Eryximachus. Aristophanes was hiccupping from a surfeit of *speeches* from which Alcibiades had fortuitously stayed away. Would the latter have been able to make head or tail out of the second-hand vapidities of Phaedrus, the confused travel-diary of Pausanias, or the professional sententiousness of Eryximachus? Would *any* man, unless he had a Socrates to set him right, and put him back on the plain path of mules and packasses and reason and inwardly-lived divine poetic philosophy?

NOTES

[1] I use this word here and there, following Professor J. M. E. Moravcsik, whose acute paper on the ladder in Socrates' speech was presented at the Society for Ancient Greek Philosophy in 1961. It was intended by him as a workable translation of *Eros*, and will be used on occasion here. Cf. Francis M. Cornford, "The Doctrine of Eros in Plato's *Symposium*," in *The Unwritten Philosophy and Other Essays* (Cambridge, England, 1950), p. 72: "Just as the word 'making' (*poiesis*) really means creation of any kind . . . so the name of Eros . . . really means 'any and every desire for good things and for happiness.' "

[2] A happy exception to this is Meyer W. Isenberg, who in his *The Order of the Discourses in Plato's Symposium* (privately printed, Chicago, 1940) attempted to find the real dialectic of the speeches. This is a doctoral dissertation, buried so deep that I have found it referred to in very few places, even other dissertations. I differ from Isenberg in many questions of detail, and I miss in his dialectical zeal a sustained interest in the literary side of the work; but his interpretation of Plato's metaphysical point of view seems to me right. Another paper that does excellent justice to the relation of the persons who participate in the religio-philosophical ideas presented is that by John P. Anton, "Some Dionysian References in the Platonic Dialogues" (too modest a title!), in *CJ*, LVIII (1962). R. Hornsby's "Significant Action in the *Symposium*," printed in the same journal in the 1956–57 volume (37–40), approaches a slightly different problem, but with comparable methods. A note, "More on 'Action' in Plato's *Symposium*," was added (200–21) by R. G. Hoerber. I differ from these four men in minor points, but find their conceptions very fruitful.

3 See, for example, G. C. Field, *Plato and His Contemporaries* (London, 1930), p. 154: "There is one other dialogue of importance in which other interests seem to occupy a place at least as important as that occupied by the philosophical interest. And that is the *Symposium*. This also, though to a lesser degree, differs in form from the other dialogues. The serious argument occupies a relatively small place, there is a much greater amount of narrative, and in particular there is the intervention of Alcibiades."

4 For a sketch of some of the principal differences in the ways that the six chief interlocutors manipulate their dialectics, see G. K. Plochmann, "Socrates, the Stranger from Elea, and Some Others," *CP*, XLIX (1954): 223–31.

5 Warner Fite, *The Platonic Legend* (New York, 1934), strings together adjectives and allegations even more damning than these.

6 At this point it should be clear that I do not think of the dialogue as reporting an actual occasion. If there *was* such a party, it probably occurred in 416 B.C., but as I hope to show later, it is unnecessary for our understanding of the function of Alcibiades in the *Symposium* to know that he was just a year away from his expedition to Sicily, or indeed that he ever went to Sicily at all. It would have taken but a stroke of Plato's pen to have hinted at this major event in the life of Alcibiades and his mother city. On the other hand, Aristodemus is represented as having repeated the dialogue to Apollodorus many years later, long after Alcibiades' impulsive duplicity had shown itself publicly. But I still think there is a riskiness in W. Hamilton's conjecture "that one object of the *Symposium* in general and of Alcibiades' speech in particular is to make plain that Socrates was in no way responsible for Alcibiades' betrayal of his country in the Peloponnesian War two years after the dramatic date of the dialogue" [*Plato's Symposium* (Baltimore, 1951), p. 29].

7 E.g., *Apology*, 30B.

8 It is always dangerous to import statements of other dialogues while interpreting some one work, as this must be done with insight equal to what is necessary when keeping to one. But I think it fair to borrow the conclusion of the *Phaedrus*, anyway (270E), that dialectic is like rhetoric, but higher.

9 *Protagoras*, 315C; *Phaedrus*, 228A.

10 *Protagoras*, 315D.

11 *Symposium*, 189B.

12 Ibid, 198C.

13 Ibid, 201D; 212B.

14 Ibid, 177E.

15 Ibid, 175D–E.

16 31B. The limit that the drinkers set upon their portion of wine was dictated by the body primarily, not the mind.

17 I do not count Apollodorus, as he was not present at Agathon's party.

18 The question whether these two men were *really* like this, historically speaking, might be of interest, but it is certainly not the primary one in a philosophico-literary analysis. I do not wish to disintegrate Plato's writings as testimony to leading figures of Athens and other cities; but it

appears reasonable to insist that we reserve judgment upon Plato's "accuracy" until we have exhausted the possible literary and dialectical purposes why these personages should be depicted as they are. My own guess, though, is that Plato had such a rich experience of men in public and private life to call upon as he wrote, that there was little trouble in finding characters to fit his dialectical schemata and at the same time to fit many, though probably not all, the facts.

19 *Symposium*, 210A.

20 F. J. E. Woodbridge, *The Son of Apollo: Themes of Plato* (New York, 1929), passim.

21 *Ion*, 531C.

22 This, by the way, is true in every one of the dialogues, even the driest and seemingly most impersonal of the "late" ones. For the relations between persons and dialectics in the *Parmenides*, see Robert S. Brumbaugh, *Plato on the One* (New Haven, 1961), part I.

23 *Timaeus*, 43B–44D.

24 Poetry is carefully interpreted, for example, in the *Protagoras Republic*, and *Ion*.

25 225E ff.

26 So A. E. Taylor says in *Plato, The Man and His Work* (New York, 1936), p. 216: "Aristophanes, one of the sturdy topers of the party (176B), is held up, when his turn to speak comes, by an accident which is a small joke in itself; the medical man of the group, who also happens to be a sober soul (176C) not able to carry much liquor, gives him professional aid and fills up what would otherwise be a gap in the evening's programme. There is nothing here which calls for a 'serious' explanation."

27 70A.

28 *Aetius* (V, 19, 5).

29 Aristotle, *On the Heavens*, III, 2, 300b 30.

30 Incidentally, Zeus and Apollo, who as gods represent the powers of reason, severally disjoin and rejoin the whole man and his parts. This is exactly similar to the "god" of *Phaedrus*, 266B, whose dialectical method consists of separating and recombining. The use of reason, Aristophanes seems to be saying, at first splits the ambitious sensualist and then reconstitutes him, although he is no longer able fully to gratify either his passions or his ambitions. He is both greater and less than he was before. Note how closely this approximates the unconscious self-portrait of Alcibiades later in the *Symposium*.

31 The parode of this play is really an account of knowledge as it ranges through the cosmos and over things terrestrial. But I do not insist that Eryximachus' list of arts is taken from *The Clouds*.

32 Eryximachus is complimented by Socrates at 193E for his speech in general.

33 Pausanias refers to Phaedrus, Eryximachus to Pausanias, Aristophanes to all earlier ones, Agathon to all, Socrates generally to all and specifically to Agathon. Alcibiades refers not to what Socrates has *said* but to what he *is*.

[34] This is not an unusual sort of dialectical situation in Plato, where Athens and Atlantis, or Zeus and Apollo, are made contraries, though these appear in myths, not in patently historical outlines.

[35] Socrates is shown in a good light in military and private life. In the *Theaetetus*, using similar extrinsic criteria, Socrates sketches the philosopher in ordinary society and public life as something of a fool (173B ff.).

[36] His notion of wisdom derives purely from an emotional response to a great teacher; he knows little about justice—and here I am willing to concede that Plato may have been thinking of the future shortcomings of the real Alcibiades.

[37] At least these pointers help to show that Paul Shorey is wrong when he calls the entrance of Alcibiades an "afterpiece" [*What Plato Said* (Chicago, 1933), p. 196].

[38] There is another correspondence, between the speech of Alcibiades and the closing pages of the *Laws*, 968A ff., where the Athenian and his two comrades, having agreed that their account of legal theory is virtually complete, further agree that it is absolutely necessary that their next move should be the practical one of setting up the actual state they envisage and participating in the councils.

[39] 221E.

[40] Professor Anton, in the paper cited earlier, persuasively argues the dionysiac, poetic, and tragic aspects of Alcibiades' nature. This is almost certainly right, and in stressing his unphilosophical character I have not tried to remove its dark romanticism. Alcibiades could easily have a temperamental affinity to Orphism (or even to the ladder of aspiration) and yet lack both the words for describing it and the reason whose control is needed for its full understanding.

[41] A point commented upon too infrequently is that Diotima, when she was instructing the younger but not youthful Socrates, entertained strong doubts about his being able to enter into "the greater mysteries." Let us take this seriously. The speech of Alcibiades gives a close account of what changes have been wrought in a man who actually *is* able to enter the discipline of Eros-philosophy. But of course his teacher would have entertained doubts regarding the *ultimate* success of her instruction.

[42] 210A–211A. A brief summary which can best be read as seven steps, not nine, is given at 211B–C.

[43] *Parmenides*, 135E–136A.

THOMAS M. ROBINSON
University of Toronto

The Argument for Immortality in Plato's *Phaedrus**

ONE of the most condensed and abstruse arguments for soul's immortality is to be found at *Phaedrus* 245C–246A. It is not even clear whether "soul" here is meant to refer to soul collectively[1] or to individual souls;[2] perhaps it refers to neither, but simply to "soul in all its forms."[3] Certainly the very general form of the argument which follows would lead one to the latter conclusion, though "soul" must still be understood as "rational soul" or perhaps rational *part* of soul if one is to abide by the limiting characteristics outlined in 245C 2–4: "our first step . . . is to discern the nature of soul, *divine and human*, its experiences and its activities." If this description has any meaning at all, the phrase πᾶσα ψυχή can hardly refer to World Soul (as Posidonius seems to have thought[4]), nor can it include the souls of flies (as Harpocration seemed to think[5]). It must be the noetic soul, as Hermias saw,[6] the θεῖόν τι common to gods and men.[7]

Until recent times this argument for soul's immortality seemed to stem from an assertion that it was "eternally moving" (ἀεικίνητος).[8] The discovery of an Oxyrhynchus papyrus, however, which read "*self*-moving" (αὐτοκίνητος)[9] convinced Robin that this reading made much more sense of the argument, and he duly incorporated it into the Budé text.[10] The move has found a number of champions, notably Vollgraff, Bignone, Pasquali, Müller, Ross, and more recently J. L. Ackrill.[11] It is certainly true that with this reading one can reduce a complicated argument to the neater lines of an Aristotelian first-figure syllogism, but this in itself ought perhaps to be grounds for suspicion. As Diano has pointed out, αὐτοκίνητος is a word found nowhere else in Plato;[12] the first incontrovertible instance of its usage is at Aristotle, *Phys.* VIII. 5, 258a 2. Plato tends rather to use phrases like "that which moves itself"

* This is a revised version of a paper presented at the 1966 meeting of the SAGP in Toledo, Ohio. A modified version has appeared in *Apeiron*, II (July, 1968): 12–18. By permission of the editors.

(τὸ αὑτὸ ἑαυτὸ κινοῦν). So it is at least possible that αὐτοκίνητος is the gloss of some commentator interested in reducing Plato's looser arguments to a more terse and respectable logical format. Be this as it may, the original reading ἀεικίνητος ought, I think, to be defended. The diffuse series of arguments will then run as follows:

Introduction (=the argument in a nutshell)

All soul is immortal, because it is ἀεικίνητος, and anything ἀεικίνητον is immortal (245C 5).

The meaning and implications of the word ἀεικίνητος are then brought out in two arguments:

1. (i) To call anything ἀεικίνητον is to call it a αὑτὸ κινοῦν.

(ii) For if it were *not* a αὑτὸ κινοῦν there would be a cessation of life and movement, and conversely, if it *is* a αὑτὸ κινοῦν there can *never* be any cessation from movement, since a αὑτὸ κινοῦν never "breaks contact" with itself.

(iii) Unstated conclusion: αὑτὸ κινοῦν and ἀεικίνητον are one, and presumably immortal.

2. (i) The ἀεικίνητον never had a beginning, for it is a "source of motion" (ἀρχὴ κινήσεως), and ἀρχαί cannot come to be from something else without ceasing to be ἀρχαί.

(ii) *Qua* ἀρχή it is also *ipso facto* indestructible, since "if a first principle were to be destroyed, nothing could come to be out of it, nor could anything bring the principle itself back into existence, since that first principle is needed for anything to come into being."

A third argument links together the results of the first and second arguments, corroborating them with a *per impossibile* consideration for good measure. It runs as follows:

3. (i) ἀρχὴ κινήσεως and αὑτὸ κινοῦν are one and the same (since both are identical with what is eternally in motion).

(ii) From this it follows that there will be no cessation from being and no coming into being.

(iii) If this were *not* the case, the whole universe would sooner or later collapse into immobility.

These results are now applied to the notion of soul itself, and the fourth and final argument runs as follows:

4. (i) It has already been seen that the αὑτὸ κινοῦν is immortal (i.e., by implication at the end of the first argument).

(ii) This will mean that soul, too, is immortal. For body, whose movement is from without, is as such "soulless" (ἄψυχον), whereas soul has as its nature movement which is from within.

(iii) One must therefore conclude that αὐτὸ κινοῦν and soul are one and the same, and that soul will thereby be necessarily without beginning and immortal.

While Hackforth defends the original reading ἀεικίνητος, he can hardly be right in assuming that it is an ἔνδοξον[13] serving as a major premise, since the greater part of the argument is spent in elucidating it and outlining its implications. In Ackrill's words, "it (i.e., the major premise) can perfectly well express a proposition required for the main proof though itself needing to be established by a subordinate proof."[14] This "subordinate proof" in fact follows three stages:

1. The ἀεικίνητον is a αὐτὸ κινοῦν.
2. A αὐτὸ κινοῦν is immortal.
3. Soul is a αὐτὸ κινοῦν and thereby immortal.

In the total argument as I have outlined it, the first two proofs are apodeictic, and each one sufficient of itself to show the immortality of ἀεικίνητον and αὐτὸ κινοῦν. But Plato chooses to stress their cumulative rather than their individual plausibility, and adds what Hermias calls an argument *per impossibile* for good measure.[15]

The argument, as many have pointed out, has much in common with the final argument for immortality in the *Phaedo*.[16] But whereas that of the *Phaedo* sprang from a metaphysic of Plato's own creation, the *Phaedrus* argument is of a more empirical cast, and has its roots deep in the pre-Socratic tradition.[17] It also goes a long way towards solving difficulties presented by the psychology of the *Phaedo*. *There* the soul had been assimilated to the Ideas, and the hiatus between the unmoving intelligible world and that of sensible things subject to motion had meant an inadequate explanation of the soul as we experience it in the world of movement. In the *Phaedo* he had found himself compelled to run in the face of all philosophic tradition, as part of his defence of his new-born metaphysic; the elementary attribute of all living things, movement, was quietly shelved, and the static, homogeneous, unchanging entity whose immortality he was left to prove was recognizable only to himself. Now soul is seen as the source of motion or activity, and a more balanced appreciation of its true nature is possible. This is not to argue, of course, that the notion of movement appears like a bolt from the blue in the *Phaedrus*. It was there by implication in both *Phaedo* and *Republic* when soul was seen as a principle of Life, or bound up with the Idea of Life;[18] unfortunately this notion was allowed to stand on equal terms with others barely compatible with it—such as that of soul's likeness to the static Ideas—and one is led to conclude that Plato was not then fully aware of the implications of what he was asserting.

A much-discussed question is the relationship of this doctrine of soul as source of motion to the problem of the pre-cosmic chaos at *Tim.* 49A ff., and a number of scholars in recent years have used the one to explain the other. For at 53A2 in particular we read how the Receptacle, itself in motion, moves the four "kinds" (γένη) which it has received into itself, thus separating the "unlike" sorts farthest from one another, and bringing "like" kinds close together; so that even in this pre-cosmic world there is *some* sort of organization, some region to which each "kind" gravitates. Before that they are "without plan" (or "without pattern," or "without proportion," ἀλόγως[21]) and "without measure" (ἀμέτρως[22]). It is the action of the Receptacle itself, apparently, which gives them some sort of primitive organization. It is when they are in this latter state—a state qualified as "what one would expect from a thing when θεός is absent from it"[23]—that the Demiurge intervenes. The point at issue is whether the power of motion here expressly attributed to the Receptacle indicates the presence of soul or not. One can begin by saying that in the *Phaedrus* and *Laws* the argumentation is very generalized and schematic: no reference is made to pre-cosmic states, and understandably so, since the context does not demand them.[24] In addition, the reader coming new to the text can be forgiven for assuming that in these two dialogues the movement referred to is that which he sees operating in the world around him, and that the "bodies" in question are those with which he is acquainted in the world of everyday experience: in a word, the movement which is to be found in an (already) organized universe. How far it would apply, if at all, to a pre-cosmos is hard to see. It was argued by Plutarch that it definitely does apply to the pre-cosmos;[25] by most modern scholars, following Proclus, that it applies to that element in the cosmos which talk of a pre-cosmos is meant to symbolize;[26] by Herter that it ought logically to have applied to the pre-cosmos (real or metaphorical) but that it does not appear to do so.[27] Certainly the passage 52E–53C (like 30A3–5) offers no hint of the presence of soul, rational or irrational. While it must be admitted that the *argumentum e silentio* is often a foundation on quicksands, in this particular instance it seems to have more cogency than usual. If the pre-cosmic chaos did possess soul, that soul is part of what the Demiurge "took over"; he did not create it. It will also be an irrational soul, since it does not possess the exclusively rational circular motions with which (rational) World Soul is endowed.[28] These conclusions combined lead one to doubt any thesis that such an irrational soul is to be included within World Soul as outlined in the *Timaeus*, since it is apparently both distinct from it and different in kind from it.[29] If, however, one still accepts the notion of soul as the motive force of the pre-cosmic chaos, though not as "part" of World Soul, one is left with the conclusion that there are or were two distinct psychic forces in the universe, one rational, one irrational. But in the *Politicus* myth Plato rejects the notion of two opposing divinities in the universe,[30] and one could argue that the notion of two opposing "psychic agents" would be open to the same objection. (On the other hand, there is no particular reason why Plato should not have changed his mind; the problem is sufficiently puzzling to give pause to the most confident.) The most basic objection to the theory, however, seems to be as follows: the notion of a soul other than that created by the Demiurge is so crucial in its implications that it seems incredible that Plato should not have given clear indication of its presence. To say that one can "infer" its presence from the evidence of the *Phaedrus* and *Laws* is not enough. For, if Owen and others are right, both *Phaedrus* and *Laws* may well have been written after the *Timaeus*,[31] and if this is the case, one would be engaged in the dubious task of interpreting an earlier dialogue in the light of later ones. But even if, for the sake of argument, one granted that the *Phaedrus* predates the *Timaeus*, it is still far from evident that both are talking about the same thing. In the *Phaedrus*, for example, it is natural to assume that the movement in question is that which obtains among bodies in the fairly organized cosmos known to us by sense experience; to infer that it also applies to the pre-cosmic world where duration is not Time and the bodily (i.e., organized bodies which we can recognize) is as yet non-existent, is less easy. The *Phaedrus* seems to be saying that soul is the cause of all movement in an organized world, a world measurable by Time. In a non-organized world *not* measurable by Time one can wonder whether the movement in question has anything to do with this.[32] At this stage words start to break under the strain. Plato is compelled to give *some* description of the pre-cosmic chaos, and talk of movement in such a world is no more and no less intelligible than phrases like "before this" (πρὸ τούτου) (53A8) in the same passage, when Time has been admitted to be absent. So Herter seems right in saying that the doctrine of *Phaedrus* and *Laws* is not to be applied to the *Timaeus*, but perhaps unjust in saying that logically it ought to have been. Plato, as far as one can see, is dealing in two instances with two completely different types of motion, the one accepted and universally admitted, and operating in an organized world of temporal succession, the other a *pis aller* trying to describe a reality in every sense different. If this analysis is correct, there seems no reason to reproach Plato here with lack of logic, though on points of clarity he may leave a lot to be desired.

NOTES

[1] A.-J. Festugière, "Platon et l'Orient," *RP*, 3 (1947): 21. Like Posidonius, he takes the argument to refer to World Soul.

[2] P. Frutiger, *Les Mythes de Platon* (Paris, 1930), pp. 130–34.

[3] J. B. Skemp, *The Theory of Motion in Plato's Later Dialogues* (Cambridge, 1942), p. 3, n. 1, and A.-J. Festugière, *REG*, 59/60 (1946–47): 496.

[4] Hermias, *Commentary*, ed. P. Couvreur (Paris, 1901), *ad loc.*

[5] Ibid.

[6] Ibid.

[7] *Timaeus* 41C 7, 69C 3.

[8] 245C 5.

[9] *Ox. Pap.* 1016.

[10] See n. 11.

[11] For the references and comment (both on these and on L. Robin) see C. Diano, *PP*, 2 (1947): 189–92. For J. L. Ackrill's comment see *Mind*, 62 (1953): 278.

[12] Diano, *art. cit.*, 190 ff. For a number of recent comments on the subject see H. Cherniss, "Plato (1950–57)," *Lustrum*, 4–5 (1959), Band 4, p. 137. The most telling criticism of Robin's arguments for αὐτοκίνητος is that of Diano, followed by W. J. Verdenius, "Notes on Plato's *Phaedrus*," *Mn*, IV (1955): 267. Robin has made the opening lines into an Aristotelian syllogism, taking δέ at C 6 as adversative, and δή at C 7 as consecutive (see his translation *ad loc.*, Budé edition). Diano points out how δέ can equally well be progressive, and δή emphatic, thereby changing the character of the argument considerably. At C5 the words τὸ γὰρ ἀεικίνητον ἀθάνατον are really a definition, as Diano sees (191). As such, it is the argument's conclusion, rather than its starting-point. It gains by being placed startlingly at the beginning, in the manner of a textbook definition; what follows is an *explicatio* and *probatio* of what it contained succinctly.

[13] R. Hackforth (trans.), Plato's *Phaedrus* (Cambridge, 1952), p. 65.

[14] *Art. cit.*, p. 278.

[15] *Op. cit.*, p. 103. 3 ff.

[16] On the affinities between the two arguments see Hackforth, *op. cit.*, p. 68, who refers to Skemp, Frutiger and Bury. Add H. Cherniss, *Aristotle's Criticism of Plato and the Academy*, I (Baltimore, 1944), pp. 435–38, and H. Cherniss, "The Sources of Evil According to Plato," *PAPS*, 98 (1954): 208. These scholars take it for granted that Plato got his idea of psychic movement from the observation of living things (e.g., Hackforth, *op. cit.*, p. 68, and Cherniss, *op. cit.*, pp. 435–38). Festugière, however, has argued

that he took it from "la découverte purement grecque de la régularité des mouvements célestes" (*art. cit.*, 21). In this he is followed by V. Martin, "Sur la condamnation des athées par Platon au Xe Livre des *Lois*," *SP*, XI (1951): 116, who also allows some cogency to the accepted explanation (117). If this guess is correct, the line of reasoning seems to be as follows:

(a) the circular motion of the heavenly bodies manifests the operation of intelligence (νοῦς) (*Timaeus* passim).

(b) intelligence cannot arise apart from soul (*Timaeus* 30B3; *Sophist* 249A4–8).

(c) soul, with intelligence, is consequently responsible for the movement of heavenly bodies.

(d) by analogy, the same reasoning will be applicable to *all* noetic souls, celestial or otherwise.

The strength of this argument, if it genuinely represents Plato's thought, is that it accounts for the motive power of the *noetic* soul (see nn. 6 and 7 of this paper)—i.e., the *only* soul apparently in question in the *Phaedrus* argument. In the *Laws*, however, the soul which is the source of movement is something much wider than the noetic soul: it is in itself neutral, only taking on ethical colour when seen as νοῦν προσλαβοῦσα or ἀνοίᾳ συγγενομένη. This seems to lay stress on the nature of soul as a vital principle, the *sine qua non* of all activity, good or bad (V. Martin, *art. cit.*, 120), rather than soul as essentially characterized by intelligence and "care" (ἐπιμέλεια) (the *Phaedrus* position), and here Festugière's explanation hardly fits.

[17] For a study of the doctrine of movement in Empedocles, Alcmaeon and Pythagoreans see Skemp, *op. cit.* [His views on Alcmaeon are criticized by Festugière, *REG*, 58 (1945), 59–65]. H. C. Baldry, ["Embryological Analogies in pre-Socratic Cosmogony," *CQ* , XXVI (1932): 27–34] has shown, I think convincingly, that Anaximander saw the world as a living creature, in many ways like a foetus. For an account of soul as source of motion in Alcmaeon, Anaxagoras and Diogenes of Apollonia, see A. Diès, *Autour de Platon II* (Paris, 1927), p. 536. For Aristotle's views on soul as a principle of motion among pre-Socratic thinkers, see *De An.* 403b 24 ff., and compare *Phys.* VIII. 9, 264b 17–266a 5.

[18] Cherniss seems to me to go beyond the evidence when, in seeing a connection between the final proof of the *Phaedo* and that in the *Phaedrus*, he identifies the "idea of life" with the "idea of motion" (*op. cit.*, pp. 435–38). Compare H. Cherniss, *Gnomon*, 22 (1955): 208, where he makes the point that the notion of self-motion is to be found as early as *Charmides* 168E. To have a notion, however, is not necessarily to see its implications. If, at the time when he wrote the *Phaedo*, Plato really did see all the implications of the notion of the "Idea of Life," it is hard to think that he would have painted the very static portrait of ψυχή that he did. For a different viewpoint see G. Müller, *Studien zu den platonischen Nomoi* (München, 1951), pp. 79–80.

[19] *Phaedo* 80B1 ff.

[20] Skemp, *op. cit.*, pp. 77–78, and Cherniss, *art. cit.*, p. 25. Both use the same notions of "first order" (πρωτουργός) and "second order" (δευτερουργός) movement at *Laws* 897A4–5 to prove rather different things. For Skemp,

the "second order" movements are the "necessary conditions" (συναίτια) of the *Timaeus* and *Phaedo*; that is, they are the purely mechanical *sine quibus non* of the (psychic) actions of Intelligence and Necessity. In this way the *Laws* is used to bolster a view of soul, rational or irrational, as the direct (πρωτουργός) cause of all movement. For Cherniss, (rational) soul is the *indirect* (though ultimate) cause of all movement: this is based on his assumption that the "first order" and "second order" movements of *Laws* 897A4–5 stand for "primary" and "secondary" causation respectively, and that they find their exact parallel at *Tim.* 46E in the causes:

(a) "which work with intelligence to produce what is good and desirable" and

(b) "which, being destitute of reason, produce their sundry effects at random and without order."

On his analysis, (b) are the side-effects of (a), and, while serving no directly rational end, find their *fons et origo* in rational soul all the same. The point to notice is that soul is taken to be rational; Cherniss will not concede that there is an irrational World Soul (Skemp) or part of World Soul [F. M. Cornford, *Plato's Cosmology* (London, 1937), p. 208] represented by Necessity (Skemp) or by the Different (Cornford). See also H. Herter, "Bewegung der Materie bei Platon," *RhM*, N.F. 100 (1957): 332.

21 53A 8.

22 Ibid.

23 53B 3–4.

24 See G. Vlastos, "The Disorderly Motion in the *Timaeus*," *CQ*, XXXIII (1939): 78.

25 *De an. procreat. in Tim.* 1016C–D.

26 Proclus *In Tim.* 323B (Diehl III, 273/31); J. Moreau, *L'Ame du Monde de Platon aux Stoiciens* (Paris, 1939), pp. 25 ff., 39 ff.; W. F. R. Hardie, *A Study in Plato* (Oxford, 1936), p. 152; A. E. Taylor, *A Commentary on Plato's Timaeus* (Oxford, 1928), pp. 115 ff., 390 f.; F. M. Cornford, *op. cit.*, p. 207.

27 H. Herter, *art. cit.*, pp. 343, n. 55, and 346.

28 Several scholars have taken it for granted that the Circle of the Different in World Soul is or represents irrationality. See L. Robin, *Platon* (Paris, 1935), p. 328; F. M. Cornford, *op. cit.*, pp. 76, 96, 118–19, 144, n. 2, and 208; A. D. Winspear, *The Genesis of Plato's Thought* (New York, 1956), p. 332, and G. Morrow, "Necessity and Persuasion in Plato's *Timaeus*," *PR*, LIX (1950): 162–63. But there is no indication in the text that the composition of the one Circle is in any way different from that of the other. True, both have different provinces, different spheres of influence. The Circle of the Same has to do with the eternally stable world of the Ideas, a world only penetrated by pure intelligence, while that of the Different deals with the sub-rational world of sense-experience. But it still approaches the world of sense in the most rational manner compatible with that exiguous amount of reality which such a world enjoys, and compatible with such a world's inherent inability to be fully comprehended by rational analysis. Given the nature of the subject-matter, the Circle of the Different will never

come to conclusions other than δόξαι and πίστεις, but its *rational* activity is made clear by the way it can guarantee that any such δόξαι and πίστεις will be factually correct. See J. B. Skemp, *op. cit.*, pp. 208–09, n. 5, and J. Gould, *The Development of Plato's Ethics* (Cambridge, 1955), p. 199.

[29] No doubt this is one reason why Aristotle (*Metaph.* Λ 6, 1072a 1–2) says that Plato's αὐτὸ ἑαυτὸ κινοῦν is only ἐνίοτε ἀρχήν; as he goes on to say, ὕστερον γὰρ καὶ ἅμα τῷ οὐρανῷ ἡ ψυχή, ὡς φησίν. See Herter, *art. cit.*, 329, n. 6, and A. Rivaud, *Le problème du devenir et la notion de la matière dans la philosophie grecque depuis les origines jusqu'à Théophraste* (Paris, 1906), p. 337. T. Gould, [*Platonic Love* (London, 1963), p. 29] suggests that the pre-cosmos is described as in chaotic motion to make the most complete contrast with the static permanence of the Ideas, where Intelligence is supremely manifest.

[30] 270A 1–2.

[31] For the arguments, see G. E. L. Owen, "The Place of the *Timaeus* in Plato's Dialogues," *CQ*, N.S. 3 (1953): 79–95. He is followed by J. Gould, *op. cit.*, p. 202, n. 3; D. W. Hamlyn, "The Communion of Forms and the Development of Plato's Logic," *PQ*, V (1955): 290, n. 3; D. A. Rees, "Bipartition of the Soul in the Early Academy," *JHS*, 77, Part I (1957): 113, n. 29; and C. Strang, "Plato and the Third Man," *PAS*, Supplem. XXXVII (1963): 147–64. W. G. Runciman, [*Plato's Later Epistemology* (Cambridge, 1962), p. 4] while still somewhat diffident, feels that Owen has at any rate tested the accepted dating of the *Timaeus*. For extended criticisms of Owen's view, see H. Cherniss, "The Relationship of the *Timaeus* to Plato's Later Dialogues," *AJP*, LXXVIII (1957): 225–66, and J. Rist, "The Order of the Later Dialogues of Plato," *Phx*, XIV (1960), 207–21. See also the postscript in J. B. Skemp's edition of the *Politicus*. For a startling piece of statistical evidence in favour of Owen's thesis, see D. R. Cox and L. Brandwood, "On a Discriminatory Problem Connected with the Works of Plato, *JRSS*, Series B, 21 (1959): 195–200.

[32] Cornford (*op. cit.*, p. 205) finds "bodily changes" in the pre-cosmic chaos, and so argues (from the *Phaedrus* and *Laws* X) to the presence in it of an (irrational) soul. In this he seems to stress the wrong alternatives in the two ambiguous terms "change" and "bodily" which Plato is using. It is true that the Demiurge is said to "take over" all that is *visible* (30A3–4), but one need hardly conclude, with Proclus, that the bodily must therefore be present in the pre-cosmic chaos, if only in some minimal way. (See Cornford, *op. cit.*, p. 205.) Plato himself only talks about ἴχνη and δυνάμεις, and there is no reason to think they necessarily obey the same rules as organised bodies (52E–53B). The word "visible" is probably used loosely for "non-spiritual" or "non-psychic," in much the same way as in the *Phaedo* soul is called ἀειδές.

THOMAS G. ROSENMEYER
University of California at Berkeley

Plato's Hypothesis and the Upward Path*

RICHARD ROBINSON, in his stimulating and searching book on *Plato's Earlier Dialectic*, has a section entitled "Hypothesizing a Higher Hypothesis."[1] Like other recent scholars, he takes it for granted that in Plato's scheme of hypothetical reasoning as developed in the *Phaedo* and the *Republic*, the more general hypothesis, the hypothesis bordering more closely upon the ἀνυπόθετον, is the higher hypothesis. That is to say, in a deductive system, as the Latin base of the term indicates, the premises are thought of as located higher than the conclusions. In this, Robinson follows not only what he conceives to be Plato's own hints, but also the usage of Aristotle: "By 'upward' I mean the ascent to the more universal, by 'downward' the descent to the more particular."[2] In this footnote on terminology, Aristotle is talking about κατηγορίαι, predicates in syllogistic reasoning. It might at first be supposed that ἄνω and κάτω are references to the purely formal structure of the syllogism itself rather than to the structure of the reality signified by the terms of the syllogism.[3] But other passages make sufficiently clear that the reference is indeed to higher and lower Being.[4] For Aristotle, the movement of the syllogism is downward because we demonstrate certain conclusions from certain assumptions—often, paradoxically, called κείμενα—of a more universal character. τὸ ἄνωθεν is a regular term for the superordinate genus.[5] In his discussion of Plato, also, τὰ ἄνω and τὰ κάτω always refer to genus and species.[6] It is not surprising, therefore, that Aristotle's logical terminology is generally thought to be based on Plato's. The facts, however, do not entirely bear out this view. In this paper I shall attempt to show that Aristotle's logical terminology, ontologically conditioned or determined as it obviously is, contrasts with that of Plato, who, on the whole, with perhaps one or two exceptions, was

* Presented at the 1958 meeting of the SAGP held in conjunction with the Pacific Coast Division of the American Philological Association in Claremont, California. Reprinted from the *American Journal of Philology*, LXXXI, 4 (1960): 393–407. By permission of the Johns Hopkins Press.

very careful not to introduce unwarranted ontological perspectives into matters of logic.[7]

To begin with, it will be convenient to note the implications of Platonic diaeresis. It is true that this operation of Platonic dialectic is not the same as the logical progress from premise to inference. Genus and species are ontological rather than logical terms. And yet it may be assumed that if Plato's logic anticipated the Aristotelian distinction between the higher and the lower, the same topographical perspective should also be apparent in the area studied by diaeresis. It will be all the more striking, then, if we can show that diaeresis does not make provision for a vertical hierarchy of Being, or, at least, that Plato's discussion does not suggest that such a hierarchy is reflected in the diaeretic procedure so as to shape it in its image.

Modern discussions of Plato's analysis via division and collection often refer to higher or superordinate and lower or subordinate γένη. μέγιστα γένη is sometimes rendered as "highest forms."[8] And elegant stemmata are devised, spreading from the top of the page to the bottom, to reproduce the upward or downward movement of the dialectical process. But if we look closely at the relevant passages, both at those where Plato practices the technique of division and collection, and at those in which he states his method, we find that the directional implications of the process are either indifferent or horizontal. That is to say, to the extent that Plato conceives the diaeretic procedure as moving, it moves on one plane or level.

Here is a listing of the principal passages in question, with the key words, the topographical orientation implied, and occasional further comment.

Phaedrus 265D–266C: diaeresis operates by dividing the entity to be analyzed into a left (ἐπ' ἀριστερὰ τεμνόμενος) and a right part (εἰς τὰ ἐν δεξιᾷ). Orientation: not vertical. Hence such terms as "sub-form" and "infima species" should be eliminated from the discussion of diaeresis passages.

Sophist 253: analysis consists of showing which γένη associate with one another and which do not (. . . ποῖα . . . συμφωνεῖ . . . ποῖα . . . οὐ δέχεται) and which γένη have another "stretched through" them (διατεταμένην) so as to contain them (περιεχομένας). Orientation: indifferent.[9]

Politicus 262A–263B: analysis should operate by cutting through the middle (διὰ μέσον . . . ἰέναι τέμνοντας). Orientation: inconclusive.

Politicus 268C: analysis involves disengaging the item to be isolated from connected and related γένη "poured around" it (περικεχυμένους αὐτῷ). Orientation: indifferent.

Politicus 275E: the choice of the proper inclusive concept will allow us to "wrap up" (περικαλύπτειν) one species along with the others with which it constitutes a genus. Orientation: indifferent.

Politicus 285A–C: analysis requires orderly procedure, especially the grouping of separate elements into the one comprehensive genus to which they belong (τὰ οἰκεῖα . . . ἕρξας . . . περιβάληται). Orientation: indifferent.

Philebus 16D–18D: the analogy of grammatical and musical analysis shows that philosophical analysis must interpose various stages between the conception of the one and the conception of the infinite number containing the one (μίαν ἰδέαν περὶ παντὸς . . . ἐνοῦσαν). Orientation: indifferent.

Sophist 265E–266A: In a progressive division of a γένος into 2, 4, 8, etc., parts, the division is made alternately by drawing a vertical line (κατὰ πλάτος) and a horizontal line (κατὰ μῆκος). Orientation: indifferent.

Sophist 235B–C: the sophist is pictured as caught in an enclosure which contains, as the area to be investigated, the art of image-making. If we divide this area, and descend into it (καταβάντας), we may either find our quarry right away, or we may have to do some further dividing until we find him in the place where he lies hidden (δύηται; cf. καταπέφευγεν, 236D3). The imagery is taken from the method of flushing out game, and though the situation is not completely clear—why should one division, i.e., one flushing, not uncover whatever is to be found?—the terms καταβάντας, i.e., proceed deep into the woods, and δύηται, i.e., cower, should not be regarded as evidence for a vertical arrangement of classification. See also below, note 20. In the sequel, when Plato gives up the hunting imagery, there is no further mention of καταβαίνειν.

Other references could be added, but the result would be the same, namely that logical implication is regarded by Plato not as subsumption but either as containment—that is to say the genus envelops the species, or as division—that is, the species constitutes the right or left half of the genus. The movement experienced in the transition from genus to species or, in the case of collection, from species to genus is not in a single instance characterized as a descent from or an ascent to the genus.

One possible answer to this would be that the εἴδη may not be organized in a vertical hierarchy, but that the Ideas of Plato's middle dialogues are, and that such terms as ὑπόθεσις, ἀρχή, and ἐπαγωγή, with their well-known connotations, speak palpably for a vertical perspective. ἐπαγωγή may be dispensed with out of hand. Even Robinson, who insists that Plato practices ἐπαγωγή, admits that he is not aware of it as a logical procedure, and has in fact no term for it. Does Plato use induction? The boundary line separating induction from analogy is of course tenuous. But "all that business about cobblers and cleaners and cooks and doctors," as Callicles calls it, suggests that when Plato refers to practical reality, he appeals to some sort of intuition rather than the powers of reasoning. However that may be, Plato does not use the term ἐπαγωγή, and that relieves us of the need to discuss it.

As for ὑπόθεσις and its near-equivalent ἀρχή, the situation is very complex. Robinson himself has done much to shed light on the obscure standing of hypothesis in Plato. According to him, the case is the reverse of that obtaining in the matter of induction: "Plato discussed but rarely used the hypothetical method." Since, therefore, we have Plato's methodology but little of his application, obscurities and even inconsistencies in the former leave matters somewhat doubtful. This much, however, is clear. A hypothesis is something posited—cf. Aristotle's κείμενον—as a preliminary assumption, as a basis[10] for further logical operations which may either analyze the assumption itself or depend on it for the analysis of other assumptions. Normally the latter is the case, i.e., the hypothesis is a premise rather than a demonstrand.[11] Broadly speaking, then, "hypothesizing is positing with a view to future action." Often the assumption which forms the point of departure for further investigation is a κοινὸν ἀξιώμενον, a statement tacitly assumed to be true by all.

The important question which now arises is this: does the ὑπό-part of the word ὑπόθεσις signify that this basic assumption is conceived of as lying under and thus supporting the logical edifice constructed from it? Let us call this the U- (=under) perspective, to contrast with the A- (=above) perspective whereby the assumption is conceived of as lying above the conclusion. Now, on the face of it, it would seem likely that the ὑπό points to a U-perspective. But according to Robinson and most Platonists that cannot be, for a hypothesis to be useful must refer to a higher reality than the propositions deduced from it. Hence Plato's hypothesis, like Aristotle's premise, and equally paradoxically so, must be pictured as vaulting above the conclusions and deductions which are suspended below it.

To render this unlikely notion palatable, Robinson undertakes, in the wake of Burnet,[12] to demonstrate that the first sense of hypothesis was intellectual, not architectural or physical in any way.[13] His reasoning is that if the word had ever "borne some such sense as 'physical foundation,' Plato would hardly have written the phrase ἄλλην αὖ ὑπόθεσιν ὑποθέμενος ἥτις τῶν ἄνωθεν βελτίστη φαίνοιτο (*Phaedo* 101D); for it would have carried the absurd suggestion of 'placing as base whatever base seemed best of those above'!" As we shall see later, Robinson's interpretation of the *Phaedo* passage, though commonly accepted, is not the only possible one. At *Republic* 511B, where Plato does understand hypothesis in the sense of a physical stepping stone—ἀλλὰ τῷ ὄντι ὑποθέσεις, οἷον ἐπιβάσεις τε καὶ ὁρμάς—Burnet and Robinson suspect a pun. But even granted that Plato is speaking humorously here, the passage proves that he felt the ὑπό-part of the term strongly enough to allow his conception of logical procedure, at this point, to be guided by it or at least to make allowance for it.

Though there is no uncontested case of Plato using ὑπόθεσις in the sense of "foundation," other writers supply us with the required supplementary information. Closest to that of Plato is, perhaps, the usage of the Hippocratic writers. For instance, the writer *On Ancient Medicine* (chs. 1, 13, 15) uses ὑπόθεσις to refer to one of the opposites—τὸ θερμόν and τὸ ψυχρόν, etc.—alleged to determine health, as well as to the assumption of the operation of such an opposite. The spatial perspective is not entirely clear, but it cannot be doubted that these opposites should be ranged closely with the Empedoclean ῥιζώματα, and as ῥιζώματα they would of course realize their ὑπό-function to the fullest.

Other writers who capitalize on the ὑπό-force of the word ὑπόθεσις are Aeschines (3, 76) and Polybius (XV, 35, 2). But our clearest evidence for the dynamic implications of ὑπόθεσις occurs in a popular text, and a simile, to boot—Demosthenes, II, 10, 5: "Just as the foundations of a house and a ship and other such structures must be very strong, so the ἀρχαί and ὑποθέσεις of actions ought to be true and just." Here there can be no doubt; a hypothesis is analogous to the foundation of a house, not to its roof. And this, I suggest, was the natural significance of the word ὑπόθεσις, before its meaning was obscured in a manner to be described directly: a foundation upon which to erect a superstructure of some sort, a broad basis on which things of lesser extent but greater concreteness are supported.[14]

Logical progression, therefore, naturally leads from the hypothesis below to the inferences above. But there is another way of looking at logical progression. It may be pictured as leading forward horizontally from the start to the finish of a sentence or argument. This perspective is well illustrated by the usage of Xenophon, *Memorabilia* IV, 6, 13: ἐπὶ τὴν ὑπόθεσιν ἐπανῆγεν ἂν πάντα τὸν λόγον ὧδε. The understanding is that the hypothesis, the subject or foundation of the discussion, had been voiced, or should have been voiced, at the beginning of the conversation. A "getting down to the fundamentals" is, therefore, a "going back" to the beginning. Here the horizontal advance of the discussion has imposed its stamp on the topography of ὑπόθεσις. In most cases it is a relatively simple matter to distinguish between this perspective and the perspective which mirrors the structural concept outlined above.

After these few preliminary remarks, we must now turn to some of the passages in which Plato exemplifies his understanding of ὑπόθεσις. Again our list is representative rather than exhaustive. As before, I shall state the references, cite crucial words, and indicate the contribution of the passage to the subject under discussion. The actual word ὑπόθεσις does not occur in all of the passages cited. Sometimes ἀρχή takes its place, sometimes there is no technical term to be found. Not all of the passages describe what we would term a logical procedure. But the process envisaged is always the same: the movement from general assumption to specific conclusion. It is this movement which according to the usual interpretation should be a movement ἄνωθεν κάτω.

Gorgias 454C 2ff.: . . . ἵνα . . . σὺ τὰ σαυτοῦ κατὰ τὴν ὑπόθεσιν . . . περαίνῃς. The perspective is undetermined.

Charmides 171D 2–3: . . . ὃ ἐφ ἀρχῆς ὑπετιθέμεθα . . . Perspective undetermined.

Protagoras 339D 2–4: . . . πρῶτον . . . ὑπέθετο . . . , ὀλίγον δὲ . . . εἰς τὸ πρόσθεν προελθών . . . Perspective horizontal.

Crito 48E 5 and 49D 6: ἀρχή and ἄρχομαι are used of the hypothesis (here not so called) from which further statements are inferred. ἀρχή is seen as the beginning of a ὁδός. Perspective undetermined.

Cratylus 428D 5–8: δεῖ . . . θαμὰ μεταστρέφεσθαι ἐπὶ τὰ προειρημένα, καὶ πειρᾶσθαι . . . βλέπειν ἅμα πρόσσω καὶ ὀπίσσω. "Looking backward" refers to revising prior agreements, "looking forward" to inferring or deducing results. Perspective horizontal.

Cratylus 436D 4–7: δεῖ δὴ περὶ τῆς ἀρχῆς . . . τὸν πολὺν λόγον εἶναι καὶ τὴν πολλὴν σκέψιν εἴτε ὀρθῶς εἴτε μὴ ὑπόκειται· ἐκείνης δὲ ἐξετασθείσης ἱκανῶς, τὰ λοιπὰ φαίνεσθαι ἐκείνῃ ἑπόμενα. Perspective undetermined.

Meno 86E 3 ff.: . . . ἐφ' υποθέσεως αὐτὸ σκοπεῖσθαι, εἴτε διδακτόν ἐστιν εἴτε ὁπωσοῦν. In this interesting passage which features a number of hypotheses in action, with the result that all of them are either demonstrated or refuted or both, the perspective is undetermined throughout.

Parmenides 128D 5–6: . . . ἔτι γελοιότερα πάσχοι ἂν αὐτῶν ἡ ὑπόθεσις εἰ πολλά ἐστιν, ἢ ἡ τοῦ ἓν εἶναι, εἴ τις ἱκανῶς ἐπεξίοι. Perspective undetermined.

Parmenides 135E9–136A2: . . . μὴ μόνον εἰ ἔστιν ἕκαστον ὑποτιθέμενον σκοπεῖν τὰ συμβαίνοντα ἐκ τῆς ὑποθέσεως, ἀλλὰ καὶ εἰ μὴ ἔστι τὸ αὐτὸ τοῦτο ὑποτίθεσθαι . . . Perspective undetermined.[15]

Timaeus 61D 3–4: ὑποθετέον δὴ πρότερον θάτερα, τὰ δ'ὑποτεθέντα ἐπάνιμεν αὖθις. Perspective probably horizontal.

Timaeus 53D 4–7: ταύτην δὲ πυρὸς ἀρχὴν . . . ὑποτιθέμεθα κατὰ τὸν μετ' ἀνάγκης εἰκότα λόγον πορευόμενοι. τὰς δ' ἔτι τούτων ἀρχὰς ἄνωθεν θεὸς οἶδεν . . . This last sentence poses a problem on which neither Taylor nor Cornford comments. The question is whether ἄνωθεν goes with the preceding words, and is to be construed with ἔτι, or whether τὰς δ' ἔτι τούτων ἀρχάς forms a self-contained unit, as Archer-Hind certainly understood it, in which case ἄνωθεν signifies the position from which the god exercises his knowledge. If the latter interpretation is adopted, as I suspect it should be, ἄνωθεν . . . οἶδε would be parallel to such an expression as *Theaetetus* 175D 3 βλέπων . . . ἄνωθεν. Translators who have favored the former interpretation have usually ended up blunting the force of ἄνωθεν and substituting innocuous terms like "remote" or "principal." Hence, probably, perspective undetermined.

Laws 812A 4–5: κατὰ μὲν τὴν ὑπόθεσιν, ὦ ξένε, ἔμοιγε οὐ φαινόμεθα ἐκτὸς πορεύεσθαι τῶν ὑποτεθέντων λόγων . . . Perspective undetermined.

Phaedo 100A3–101E3: ἀλλ' οὖν δὴ ταύτῃ γε ὥρμησα, καὶ ὑποθέμενος . . . ἃ μὲν ἄν μοι δοκῇ τούτῳ συμφωνεῖν τίθημι ὡς ἀληθῆ ὄντα . . . 101D 3: εἰ δέ τις αὐτῆς τῆς ὑποθέσεως ἔχοιτο, χαίρειν ἐῴης ἄν . . . ἕως ἂν τὰ ἀπ' ἐκείνης ὁρμηθέντα σκέψαιο . . . ἐπειδὴ δὲ ἐκείνης αὐτῆς δέοι σε διδόναι λόγον, ὡσαύτως ἂν διδοίης, ἄλλην αὖ ὑπόθεσιν ὑποθέμενος ἥτις τῶν ἄνωθεν βελτίστη φαίνοιτο, ἕως ἐπί τι ἱκανὸν ἔλθοις . . . We should note that this last passage, as so many others dealing with hypothesis, employs a verb of motion or progression, in this case ὁρμάω and ὁρμάομαι. The usual sense of the word is "to move forward," in a horizontal direction. The direction may occasionally be vertical; but in that case it is likely to be upward rather than downward, for the simple reason that the word denotes willed rather than automatic motion. And yet in this passage ὁρμάομαι has been interpreted as downward motion, the reason being that hypothesis in the *Phaedo* is clearly associated with the Ideas, and the Ideas are highest. However, the argument is not from Ideas to sensibles and back but, according to Socrates, from Ideas to Ideas; and there is no evidence to indicate, at least in this passage, that one Idea is higher than another. Thus the more comprehensive or basic hypothesis should not be pictured as lying above a hypothesis entailed by it or generated by it. Plato avoids the use of such a phrase as ἐκ δύο ὑποθέσεων ἤρτηται[16] or a similar verb of suspension in connexion with the hypothesis method. But we can go further than that, and suggest that in the *Phaedo* Plato seems to conceive of the premise as lying below the conclusion, that is to say, Plato adopts the U-perspective. This emerges from the words: ἄλλην αὖ ὑπόθεσιν ὑποθέμενος ἥτις τῶν ἄνωθεν βελτίστη φαίνοιτο . . .[17]

Plato's language here points to the notion of an inverted pyramid, with the more comprehensive hypothesis lying at the bottom, and the ὁρμηθέντα radiating upward from each hypothesis. τὰ ἄνωθεν is merely another way of saying τὰ ὁρμηθέντα. We translate as follows: "placing below hypothesis X another hypothesis Y which would seem to be the best (hypothesis) of the (propositions) above it," that is, which would account best for X and other statements on the same level. Usually the genitive τῶν ἄνωθεν is explained as a partitive genitive. It is, however, equally possible to take it as an objective genitive, referring to the conclusions generated by the premise. (Cf. the Aristotelian parallel given above, note 17.) The word βελτίστη in the sense of "most effective" may seem unusual, but the functional connotation of ἀγαθός is well known. The phrase as it stands may appear awkward, but the stylistic difficulties seem to me less decisive than the difficulties of interpretation which result from the traditional assumption of a "higher hypothesis." To imply, as one would have to on the old assumption, that there are many hypotheses of a more universal character, any of which might be relevant to the argument, is to render the method itself almost unworkable. The plural τῶν makes better sense if it can be supposed to refer to the several conclusions inferrable from a particular premise chosen with the assistance of common sense and synoptic experience.[18]

Theaetetus 156A 3–5: ἀρχὴ δέ, ἐξ ἧς καὶ ἃ νυνδὴ ἐλέγομεν πάντα ἤρτηται, ἥδε αὐτῶν, ὡς τὸ πᾶν κίνησις ἦν καὶ ἄλλο παρὰ τοῦτο οὐδὲν . . . This, at long last, is an unmistakable instance of the A-perspective, characterized by the use of the verb ἀρτάω (cf. above, note 14). The proposition "motion is all" is here said to be the premise from which all earlier arguments are "suspended," as a piece of metal is suspended from another piece of metal that is magnetized (*Ion* 533E 2), or as the human world is suspended from the world of the gods (*Laws* 631B 8), or as certain kinds of human behavior are suspended from, i.e., dominated by, certain physical, psychological or moral causes (*Laws* 782D 11; 884A 5). It may, of course, be objected that ἀρτάω does not always or necessarily indicate vertical dependence. Yet the presumption, as in the passages in the *Laws*, is in favor of influence from above, from the inscrutable realm of Hesiodic or Euripidean forces controlling man. In the *Theaetetus* passage various statements are felt to be quite literally suspended from a superior premise, perhaps by analogy with the notion of the fluxists that "motion rules supreme." It should be mentioned that in this particular case the premise is one with which Plato would not agree; that, in fact, it is the sort of physical or meteorological assumption which Socrates occasionally makes fun of by regarding it as "meteoric" itself (*Republic* 489C 6). May we say that it is this which caused Plato to use the verb ἀρτάω in the present case, in order to underscore the insubstantiality and perhaps the topsy-turvy quality of the proposition contained in the premise? But whatever the reason, the passage does give us one instance in which an ἀρχή (not a ὑπόθεσις!) is said to be located higher than the propositions derived from it.

If we now draw the balance of the passages we have discussed, it appears that most of them do not tell us anything about the direction of the activity prompted by hypothesis. Two, perhaps three, instances favor the horizontal perspective; here the eye focusses on the progress of the operation rather than on the mutual relations between the terms of the operation. One passage speaks for the U-perspective; here the etymological meaning of ὑπόθεσις seems to rise more fully to the consciousness. And finally there is one tolerably clear piece of evidence for the A-perspective.

It now remains to investigate some passages from the *Republic*, particularly from the section containing the allegory of the Cave and the diagram of the Divided Line. These passages have been reserved for the final part of our discussion because they appear, at first glance, to occasion the greatest difficulty. It is only natural, given the perspectival connotations of Cave and Line, that the Platonic distinction between "up" and "down" should here find its most marked expression. We should, however, remember that this perspective refers to the distinction between levels of reality, or rather between reality and the various kinds of non-real, and to the distinction between the correlate mental activities, such as knowledge and belief. The method of hypothetical reasoning, on the other hand, functions on only one level of mental activity, and is concerned with only one level of reality, viz., the Ideas (511C 1–2), whether these Ideas be visualized in their pure state, as in dialectic, or less purely, as in mathematics and other sciences (510B 4 ff.).

First, a preliminary passage, *Republic* 437A 6–9: . . . ὑποθέμενοι . . . εἰς τὸ πρόσθεν προίομεν, ὁμολογήσαντες, ἐάν ποτε ἄλλῃ φανῇ ταῦτα ἢ ταύτῃ, πάντα ἡμῖν τὰ ἀπὸ τούτου συμβαίνοντα λελυμένα ἔσεσθαι. In this concise description of argument on the basis of postulates, the perspective is horizontal, or at best undetermined. What makes the passage important is the fact that the quotations to be studied directly refer by and large to just such reasoning as is contemplated here, in language very similar to the terms used here.

Republic 533C 7–D 3: . . . ἡ διαλεκτικὴ μέθοδος μόνη ταύτῃ πορεύεται, τὰς ὑποθέσεις ἀναιροῦσα, ἐπ' αὐτὴν τὴν ἀρχὴν ἵνα βεβαιώσηται, καὶ τῷ ὄντι ἐν βορβόρῳ βαρβαρικῷ τινι τὸ τῆς ψυχῆς ὄμμα κατορωρυγμένον ἠρέμα ἕλκει καὶ ἀνάγει ἄνω . . . The perspective of the operation itself is undetermined. The effect of the operation is to turn the mind upward from the swamp of Becoming to the exalted status of Reality. Analogously, the activity of dialectic is seen to lie at the top of the hierarchy of sciences, 534E 2–4: . . . δοκεῖ . . . ὥσπερ θριγκὸς τοῖς μαθήμασιν ἡ διαλεκτικὴ ἡμῖν ἐπάνω κεῖσθαι, καὶ οὐκέτ' ἄλλο τούτου μάθημα ἀνωτέρω ὀρθῶς ἂν ἐπιτίθεσθαι . . .[19]

Republic 510B 5–9: . . . ψυχὴ ζητεῖν ἀναγκάζεται ἐξ ὑποθέσεων, οὐκ ἐπ' ἀρχὴν πορευομένη ἀλλ' ἐπὶ τὴν τελευτήν, τὸ δ' αὖ ἕτερον—τὸ ἐπ' ἀρχὴν ἀνυπόθετον—ἐξ ὑποθέσεως ἰοῦσα . . . τὴν μέθοδον ποιουμένη. Perspective undetermined. ἀρχή and τελευτή, πορεύεσθαι and μέθοδον ποιεῖσθαι are relative opposites but not absolutely fixed topographically. Cf. 510D 1–3: ἐκ τούτων ἀρχόμενοι τὰ λοιπὰ ἤδη διεξιόντες τελευτῶσιν . . . ἐπὶ τοῦτο οὗ ἂν ἐπὶ σκέψιν ὁρμήσωσι.

Republic 511A 3–7: . . . ὑποθέσεσι δ' ἀναγκαζομένην ψυχὴν χρῆσθαι . . . οὐκ ἐπ' ἀρχὴν ἰοῦσαν, ὡς οὐ δυναμένην τῶν ὑποθέσεων ἀνωτέρω ἐκβαίνειν, εἰκόσι δὲ χρωμένην αὐτοῖς τοῖς ὑπὸ τῶν κάτω ἀπεικασθεῖσιν . . . For this analysis of non-dialectic hypothetical argument, cf. above, 510B 5–9. There is, however, one difference between this statement and other statements we have discussed: ἀρχή is now distinguished from ὑπόθεσις; it is equated with the ἀνυπόθετον. Mathematical demonstration is contrasted with the genuine dialectical method which leads to the ἀνυπόθετον and which is outlined in 511B 3 ff. Mathematical reasoning functions on the second highest level of mental activity. Compared with pure dialectic, it is a swamp which does not permit a man to get his head free. That is to say, in the hierarchy of the sciences mathematics is so far below dialectic that it might as well be thought to be located in the quagmire of belief. There is no transfer or transition possible between mathematical and dialectical reasoning. "To get above the (mathematical) hypotheses" is tantamount to entering an entirely different arena of logical endeavor.

Republic 511B 5–8: τὰς ὑποθέσεις ποιούμενος οὐκ ἀρχὰς ἀλλὰ τῷ ὄντι ὑποθέσεις οἷον ἐπιβάσεις τε καὶ ὁρμάς, ἵνα μέχρι τοῦ ἀνυποθέτου ἐπὶ τὴν τοῦ παντὸς ἀρχὴν ἰών . . . πάλιν αὖ . . . ἐπὶ τελευτὴν καταβαίνῃ . . . The key expressions are: . . . ἐπὶ τὴν . . . ἀρχὴν ἰών . . . ἐπὶ τελευτὴν καταβαίνῃ. Cf. 511C 8–9:

. . . διὰ δὲ τὸ μὴ ἐπ' ἀρχὴν ἀνελθόντες σκοπεῖν. The mental activity described is that of dialectic, as contrasted with that of mathematics and the inferior sciences. It is difficult to decide whether the words, and especially the prepositions employed in the compound verbs, refer to a vertical or a horizontal perspective. The horizontal or "progress of argument" significance of ἀνὰ- and κατὰ-compounds is well known and has already been instanced.[20] τελευτή refers to the end of the supreme deductive argument, just as ἀρχή refers to its beginning, or to the end of the ensuing synthesis. What complicates the situation is the image, probably humorous, of the stepping stones which seem to indicate an "up" and "down" orientation. And yet, if that were Plato's conscious intention, he might well have spoken of higher and lower hypotheses, or he might have detailed the location of the ἀρχή vis-à-vis the other "steps" in the logical process. This he does not do. For the rest, the language does not differ significantly from the language of the other passages in the *Republic* which we have discussed. The best we can say, therefore, is that for one moment there is promise of a vertical perspective coming out into the open, only to be silenced immediately by what is probably a vague assumption of horizontal procedure. Whether the vertical perspective lurking under the surface would have been a U-perspective, as is suggested by the image of the stepping stones, or an A-perspective, as the alternative meaning of the prepositions may indicate, is impossible to say. But this very uncertainty should help to drive home the point that Plato is not in this context interested in establishing an unambiguous vertical perspective.

To repeat, when Plato, in his analysis of the Divided Line and Cave, talks about hypothesis, ἀρχή, τελευτή, etc., his language is usually noncommittal on the score of perspective. Where he does speak of "up" and "down" he is ranking scientific hypotheses in the second highest division, below those of dialectic. Once, 511B 5 ff., the ontological and epistemological context does, on one interpretation, seem to color the logical perspective, and he appears to believe that those hypotheses which bring a man closer to the ἀνυπόθετον are seen as higher than more mediate hypotheses. But we have shown that the language need not carry this meaning, and that the similar phrasing of other passages speaks against the adoption of this interpretation.

In only one of all the passages we have studied, *Theaetetus* 156A 3–5, does Plato speak as if certain propositions based on a universal premise were thought of as suspended below it. But there Plato is not arguing in his own person or giving rules for a tidy logical procedure, but exposing and transfixing the mistaken assumptions of Protagoras and the fluxists. Nevertheless, this passage, in combination with *Phaedo* 101D3 ff. (U-perspective) and *Republic* 511B 5–8 (inconclusive perspective), serves to confirm our suspicion that Plato's logical terminology is not shaped by a consistent (and irrelevant) metaphysical topography. We conclude, therefore, that the evidence for Plato systematically regarding the argument by hypothesis as leading downward from premise to inference is nil. It may be wondered why Plato was misunderstood so soon, notably by Aristotle. One explanation may be that Plato provides few examples of the technique in action. Another may be that Plato's followers regarded him as a metaphysician first and last, and could not separate his logic from his ontology. The problem calls for a close investigation.

NOTES

1 R. Robinson, *Plato's Earlier Dialectic*[2] (Oxford, 1953), p. 136, ch. 9, 4.

2 *An. Post.* I. 20, 82a 23, tr. G. R. G. Mure: λέγω δ' ἄνω μὲν τὴν ἐπὶ τὸ καθόλου μᾶλλον, κάτω δὲ τὴν ἐπὶ τὸ κατὰ μέρος.

3 See especially *An. Pr.* II. 17, 65b 23: τοῦτο γὰρ ἐγχωρεῖ γενέσθαι καὶ ἐπὶ τὸ ἄνω καὶ ἐπὶ τὸ κάτω λαμβάνοντι τὸ συνεχές . . . .

4 Cf. the passage just preceding the footnote on terminology, *An. Post* I. 19, 81b 38: ἆρα ἐνδέχεται ἀρξαμένῳ ἀπὸ τοιούτου ὃ μηδενὶ ὑπάρχει ἑτέρῳ ἀλλ' ἄλλο ἐκείνῳ, ἐπὶ τὸ ἄνω εἰς ἄπειρον ἰέναι, θάτερον δὲ ἀρξάμενον . . . ὃ αὐτὸ μὲν ἄλλου, ἐκείνου δὲ μηδὲν κατηγορεῖται, ἐπὶ τὸ κάτω σκοπεῖν εἰ ἐνδέχεται εἰς ἄπειρον ἰέναι.

5 *An. Post.* II. 13, 97a 33.

6 *Metaph.* A 9, 992a 18.

7 I wish to thank Professors J. B. Skemp, D. J. Allan, L. Edelstein, and G. Vlastos for reading the manuscript and suggesting various improvements. My gratitude should not, however, imply that they approve the thesis of this paper.

8 C. Ritter, "Platons Logik," *Phil*, LXXV (1919): 1 ff., and *passim*.

9 That "subsumption" is regularly visualized by Plato as containment appears also from such passages as *Gorgias* 464A ff., and *Theaetetus* 205D 4: . . . εἰς ταὐτὸν ἐμπέπτωκεν ἡ συλλαβὴ εἶδος ἐκείνῳ [sc. τῷ στοιχείῳ] εἴπερ . . .

10 The word is Robinson's, *op. cit.*, p. 95.

11 Ibid., 112.

12 J. Burnet, ed., *Plato's Euthyphro*, etc. (Oxford, 1924), p. 51.

13 Robinson, *op. cit.*, pp. 68, 98.

14 It may be asked how the notion of "dependence" is naturally expressed in Greek. The word "dependence" itself, of course, betrays an A-perspective; here the more solid or more substantial matter is pictured at the top. In Greek also this perspective is utilized for the notion of dependence and vital connexion, chiefly through the verb ἀρτάω and its compounds

ἀναρτάω and ἐξαρτάω. Herodotus, for example, uses them frequently in this sense. But more or less the same conception may be expressed via the verb κεῖμαι in combination with the preposition ἐν; and there the perspective is the opposite. Thus the linguistic data bearing on the notion of dependence are inconclusive on the score of perspective.

[15] In this passage, ὑπόθεσις has come to mean little more than πρότασις; this becomes clear from the fact that in the sequel the various hypotheses are εἰ-clauses.—Robinson, *op. cit.*, pp. 278–80, indicates the ways in which hypothesis in the *Parmenides* differs from the hypothetical method in the *Republic.* One difference on which he comments, with apparent surprise: "There is almost no trace in the *Parm.* of the upward path of the *Rep.*" Incorrect; there is no trace whatever. Furthermore, as we shall see later, there probably is no upward path in the *Republic* either.

[16] Olympiod. in *Phaed.* 188, line 3, Norvin.

[17] The combination of ὑπόθεσις or ἀρχή with the genitive, so familiar in ontological contexts (example: *Timaeus* 53D4, as above), recurs in Aristotle's terminology: *Metaph.* Δ 1, 1013a 16: τῶν ἀποδείξεων αἱ ὑποθέσεις. Compare also 1013b 20 and *Phys.* II. 3, 195a 18: αἱ ὑποθέσεις τοῦ συμπεράσματος, where however αἰτία is understood.

[18] R. S. Bluck, in *Phr*, II (1957): 26, asks what Plato could have meant by the "higher" hypothesis that is to be substituted for the hypothesis that turned out to be unsatisfactory. He believes that Plato is here thinking of the Form of the Good, i.e., the teleological cause. He shrugs off the stubborn fact that Socrates had announced he was going to undertake a δεύτερος πλοῦς. On rejecting the translation "higher hypothesis" the difficulty resolves itself.

[19] F. M. Cornford's translation of *Republic* 510B 4 ff. and 533C 7 ff. freely interpolates "up" and "down" (cf. also his "highest" for μέγιστον 505A 2), instead of reproducing the inconclusive perspective of the text. H. D. P. Lee has managed to do this admirably.

[20] Cf. ἐπανῆγεν, Xenophon, *Memorabilia*, IV, 6, 13, cited above, p. 358; also the use of ἐπανέρχομαι and ἐπάνειμι, Plato, *Parmenides*, 142B 1–2, and the parallel use of ἄνω and κάτω to refer to the limits of the race course, Plato, *Republic*, 613B 11–12. Cf. further O. Becker, *Das Bild des Weges*, *Hermes Einzelschriften* IV (1937): index, s.v. καταβαίνω, and *LSJ*, s.v. ἀνέρχομαι, II.2.

ROSAMOND KENT SPRAGUE
University of South Carolina

Reply to Dr. Levinson*

LET me say at the outset that I am in fundamental agreement with the main points of Professor Levinson's enlightening summary[1] of Plato's contributions to logic and the philosophy of language. He has demonstrated clearly and well the extent to which Plato's contributions were negative and the extent to which they were positive. Plato rejected, for instance, the study of etymology and of synonymic as guides to the nature of reality; he disparaged, although with some reservations, the use of the written as opposed to the spoken word, and he waged war upon the empty verbal antics of the sophists and eristics, in particular upon the fallacy which results in the denial of false statement.[2] On the positive side we have Plato's awareness of both the power of words and of their limitations, as shown in his attitude toward definitions, toward the ambiguities present in common speech, and toward the problem of a technical vocabulary. I am also in agreement with Professor Levinson's view that the results of the *Cratylus* are substantiated by the rest of Plato's writings on the topic of language, and shall therefore confine myself to this one dialogue, raising two major topics for discussion.

My first topic may be stated in the form of a question: was Plato's main purpose in the *Cratylus* to put forward a philosophy of language, or was it rather to demonstrate, by means of the rejection of current linguistic theories, the necessity for the theory of Forms? My own view would be that the theory of language is, in the long run, subordinate to the theory of Forms in the *Cratylus*, in spite of the fact that language does, statistically at least, play the more prominent part. I do not by any means intend to suggest that Professor Levinson is unaware of the importance of the ideal name as the model for the law-maker in the *Cratylus*, or that he would not agree that the outcome of the dialogue is the recommendation that "the Forms must be sought and somehow found"; he in fact takes both these points into account. However, because he is immediately concerned to demonstrate Plato's belief in the "potential

* Presented at the 1955 meeting of the SAGP in Boston, Massachusetts.

dignity" of language, it seems to me that he has, perhaps necessarily, underplayed the relationship of linguistic problems to the problems of metaphysics.

Let me then mention two points in the *Cratylus* at which Plato seems to me to show clearly that the theory of Forms is uppermost in his mind in this dialogue.

1) The immediate reaction of Socrates to the convention theory put forward by Hermogenes at the opening of the dialogue is to demonstrate (386A ff.) that such a theory will lead either to the relativism of Protagoras, a relativism which extends to things, not simply to words, or to the universal predication theory of Euthydemus, which would result in a similar relativism, also among things, not words. This demonstration paves the way for Socrates to say at 386D:

> Then if neither all things belong equally to all men at the same time and perpetually nor each thing to each man individually, it is clear that things have some fixed reality of their own, not in relation to us nor caused by us; they do not vary, swaying one way and another in accordance with our fancy, but exist of themselves in relation to their own reality imposed by nature.[3]

In other words, Socrates has rejected the relativism implied by the convention theory in such a way as to make the theory of Forms appear to be the inevitable alternative. He then goes on to develop the comparison of the ideal shuttle with the ideal name, and the accompanying comparisons between the carpenter and the law-giver, the weaver and the dialectician. These comparisons, which Hermogenes readily accepts, prepare the way for Socrates' explanation of the state of affairs which gave rise to the convention theory in the first place, that is, of the fact that the same object may receive different names in different countries. So Socrates at 389D:

> And if different law-givers do not embody [the object] in the same syllables, we must not forget this ideal name on that account; for different smiths do not embody the same form in the same iron, though making the same instrument for the same purpose, but so long as they reproduce the same ideal, though it be in different iron, still the instrument is as it should be, whether it be made here or in foreign lands, is it not?

Plato has thus succeeded in disposing of the convention theory before the discussion of etymologies even begins (392A) and he has done so by inducing Hermogenes to accept the theory of Forms.

2) The natural rightness theory advanced by Cratylus is defeated in a very similar manner. We should notice first that Cratylus is not allowed

by Plato to present his own version of the theory. Hermogenes gives us a description of it as the dialogue begins, and there are two or three summaries of it (not always quite accurate) by Socrates. Cratylus' function in the dialogue is therefore very nearly restricted to his attempts to prevent Socrates from establishing the point that there are degrees of rightness among names, e.g., at 429B ff. Whenever he is effectively countered he subsides, but only to return to the attack later on in a totally unrepentant mood. Cratylus is, of course, perfectly correct in perceiving that his theory stands or falls on this one issue. If he is to succeed in maintaining his position, he must insist that any name which does not possess complete natural rightness is simply not a name at all. The basis of his argument is perfectly clear; it is the familiar Parmenidean argument about the unreality of not-being which, in turn, had given rise to the sophistic denial of the possibility of false statement. Plato of course disposed of this fallacy once and for all when he pointed out in the *Sophist* (256E ff.) that not-being can perfectly well exist since it is simply other than being, not its opposite. However, he could make this assertion only within the framework of the theory of Forms, since the assertion depends ultimately on the communion of classes. Similarly in the *Cratylus*, Socrates shows (438C ff.) that it is not even possible to tell which names are really names and which are not except through an appeal to something else, that is, to the realities in accordance with which the names were fashioned. But he is not really entertaining the possibility that some names might not be names at all; once he has established the point that a name imitates an object with reference to the ideal in which the object participates, he has really also established the point that the imitation may be good or bad. In other words, his analysis of being is already more complex than that of Cratylus, and Cratylus cannot continue to maintain the natural rightness theory when he has once made concessions to the theory of Forms.

The second topic which I should like to raise for discussion concerns a principle which Plato appears to me to use in the dialogue but which I have never seen specifically identified and defined; it might be called the principle of the "atomicity" of language. It is assumed by Plato, in the course of the dialogue, that language is constructed in a hierarchical manner. The letter is the basic unanalyzable element. Syllables are constructed from letters, names from syllables, sentences from names, and connected speech from sentences. Whatever is predicated of any single member of the hierarchy spreads, by a kind of infection as it were, to all the other members. If letters, for instance, represent objects by means of likeness, so does speech in general, or if a name is inappropriate, its letters and syllables were so too. As employed by Plato, this principle of atomicity is an extremely useful device which can be turned to account in a variety of contexts. I shall mention, very briefly, several passages in which it occurs.

1) At 385B ff., Socrates gains from Hermogenes the admission that, if there is true and false speech, there must also be true and false names, since if speech as a whole is true or false, its parts are true or false also. The fact that an individual name may be true or false will prove to be of considerable importance in the dialogue, since it will be necessary to Plato's demonstration, culminating at 390D, that the giving of names is a highly skilled matter calling for the combined arts of the law-giver and dialectician. It will also, as Professor Levinson has pointed out, be an essential element in the defeat of Cratylus' assertion that there are no names except true names. Plato has shown that there can be false names as well, and, consequently, that there can be false speaking.

2) At 421E, Socrates points out to Hermogenes that questions about the etymologies of names will never come to an end unless some elements are reached which are no longer capable of being explained in terms of other names. These will need to be investigated by some other method. When this other method is discovered (and we can guess what it will be) all names will be affected by it, since, as Socrates says at 422C

> . . . there is but one principle of correctness in all names, the earliest as well as the latest, and . . . none of them is any more a name than the rest.

In other words, this is a case in which whatever is true of the elements of names is true of names also. Therefore it is by studying these basic elements that one reaches conclusions concerning language as a whole.

3) At 432A ff., the principle of atomicity is employed by Plato with a view to establishing the point that some names may be more right than others. Socrates points out, to Cratylus this time, that a name should by no means possess all the qualities of the thing named; if it did, the two would be indistinguishable, just as an imitation Cratylus which possessed all the qualities of the real one would be a second Cratylus and not an imitation at all. By means of this illustration he persuades Cratylus, temporarily at least, that a name may be correctly given and still contain some incorrect letters. And, he goes on,

> . . . if a letter, then grant that also a noun in a clause, and if a noun, then also a clause in a sentence may be employed which is not

> appropriate to the things in question, and the thing may be none the less named and described, so long as the intrinsic quality of the thing named is retained . . . [It will be named] well, when it has all the proper letters, badly when it has only a few of them.

Thus, by getting Cratylus to allow some incorrectness in the basic relationship between things and the letters which imitate them, Socrates has forced him to admit some degree of incorrectness in names. "Otherwise," he says, "he [Cratylus] must look for some other principle of correctness in names, and must allow that a name is the representation of a thing in syllables and letters." (We have seen already that if there is one point Cratylus cannot afford to admit, it is the possibility that some names might be incorrect.)

4) The principle of atomicity is also useful in connection with the classification of parts of speech (424 C ff.) and

5) as a means (436B ff.) of urging the utmost care in establishing the earliest names, since any initial error, even if small, will affect the validity of later names which are based upon them.

In view of the fact that the principle of atomicity is intimately bound up with a number of basic issues in the *Cratylus*, I would like to ask Professor Levinson whether, assuming that he agrees with me that Plato did in fact employ such a principle, he regards its use as a positive contribution either to logic or to the philosophy of language. I should also like to hear his comments on the relation of this principle to the historical origin of language. Does Plato, for instance, regard the letter as temporally prior to the other parts of language or only as logically prior? In view of Professor Levinson' interesting observation on p. 261 that "the ideal Nomothete can best be understood as the fusion of the everyday actuality of past law-givers with an ideal," he probably has some decided opinions on this point.

The topics I have suggested for discussion, both by Professor Levinson and by the other members of the *Society*, therefore fall into two groups: those just mentioned concerning the atomicity of language, and the more general questions raised earlier concerning the relation, in the *Cratylus*, of the philosophy of language to the theory of Forms.

NOTES

[1] Cf. "Language, Plato and Logic" in this volume [ed.].

[2] I have since written on this topic in *Plato's Use of Fallacy*, (London, 1962), Chapter III.

[3] All quotations from the *Cratylus* are from the translation by H. N. Fowler in the Loeb edition.

LEONARDO TARÁN
Columbia University

The Creation Myth in Plato's *Timaeus**

THE purpose of this paper is to discuss the question whether the creation myth in Plato's *Timaeus* is to be taken literally or not. My reason for reopening the discussion is the recent publication by Professor Vlastos of a paper entitled "Creation in the *Timaeus*: is it a Fiction?"[1] In this paper Vlastos tries to answer the arguments that Professor Cherniss[2] gave in favor of the metaphorical interpretation, in the course of which arguments he attacked Vlastos' earlier article "The Disorderly Motion in the *Timaeus*."[3] My reason for concentrating on Vlastos' papers is that his is the most recent and most complete statement of the question among those who consider that the creation of the world was meant by Plato literally.[4] Since Cherniss' discussion is the latest, most complete and coherent presentation of the metaphorical interpretation of the *Timaeus*, I shall take my point of departure from his treatment of the question, though here and there I shall refer to earlier discussions.[5]

The interpretation of the creation myth in the *Timaeus* is intimately connected with the problem of the origin of evil in Plato; since I believe, however, that it is necessary to elucidate first the former problem, I will not enter here into a systematic discussion of the latter.[6]

In the *Timaeus*, the myth of the creation of the world is part of another and larger myth: that of the victory of ancient Athens over Atlantis. The latter is brought about by Critias' desire to requite Socrates for the conversation held "yesterday", in the course of which Socrates had shown the nature of the ideal state.[7] The purpose of the story of Atlantis is to identify the ideal state with ancient Athens and thereby satisfy Socrates' desire to see his ideal society in action, so to say.[8] But before this can be treated in full,[9] it is necessary that Timaeus, an eminent philosopher, astronomer, and physicist,[10] should tell first the story that starts with the birth of the universe and ends with the nature of man.[11]

* This is a revised version of a paper presented at the 1966 meeting of the SAGP in Toledo, Ohio.

It seems, then, that the purpose of the creation myth is to give an account of the nature of man and of the universe to serve as the background for another mythical account, the purpose of which will be to show that the ideal state is superior and ultimately more powerful than an adversary which has greater material resources and skill but is morally inferior.[12] That the purpose of the creation myth is to give a *systematic* account of the nature of man and the world rather than a chronological report of how the world came into being, is, I think, undeniable; this systematic character of Timaeus' exposition can be seen even in the three main divisions of his discourse. There is first a prelude (27C–29D)[13] in which the nature and the limits of the exposition are set down.[14] Timaeus deals then with the work of the Demiurge and of the created gods (29D–47E) which constitutes the work of Reason in the universe. At 47E ff., however, he declares the need to begin all over again and introduces the third factor, the receptacle; this is done in order to describe what comes about of Necessity (47E–69A). We hear now of things that the Demiurge had done *before* some of those described in 29D–47E.[15] In the third and last part of the myth (69A–92C), after recapitulating the two previous sections, Timaeus explains the creation of those things which are a result of the cooperation of Reason and Necessity. There is, I think, a plausible reason for Plato's choice of this order of narration;[16] at present it is sufficient to notice that Plato gives a systematic account of, and is interested in, the two causes which are at work in the universe, and that to give this systematic account he decided to do away with the chronological order, placing "first" what was chronologically "second."

The systematic character of the creation myth in the *Timaeus*, with the consequent abandonment of the chronological order of creation, is sufficient to place it in a different category from other creation myths. By itself, however, the systematic character of the narrative does not yet imply that the creation of the world was not meant by Plato to be taken literally. But if we discover indications, in the *Timaeus* itself, that the creation was not meant to be taken literally, then we would be entitled to concluding that Plato purposely chose the form of a creation myth in order to give a systematic account of the nature of man and of the universe.[17] In that case, we should not put special emphasis, for example, on the fact that Plato speaks of a precosmical state of things or talks as if the universe was really created by the Demiurge; for Plato was a great artist, and once he had decided to explain the nature of the universe in the form of a genetic myth, he was naturally going to do whatever seemed necessary to preserve the likelihood of the creation myth.[18] What I mean to say is that the burden of the proof lies with those who claim that Plato did not intend the creation of the universe to be taken literally; but if we find as much as one clear indication in the *Timaeus* itself that Plato is warning the reader not to take the chronological account literally, or that he is pointing out a contradiction which would disappear if the creation is interpreted metaphorically, then we would be entitled to interpret the chronological account as a means used by Plato to analyze the different factors and causes acting in the universe as it is. It is neither impossible not unlikely that Plato may have decided to explain his conception of the universe through a creation myth;[19] that much, I think, should be granted by those who interpret the *Timaeus* literally. The discussion should, then, be centered on the arguments given to show the metaphorical character of the cosmogony.

I

Though the order of creation is not followed in the narrative, it is legitimate to put together all that is said about it in the myth and thereby reconstruct the temporal order of creation. If, in doing this, we find contradictions, contradictions that could only be removed by a different order of narration which would entail a modification of Plato's account of a part of the universe, then it would be legitimate to conclude that Plato did not mean the creation to be taken literally, unless there were strong reasons to believe that he was unaware of the contradictions that the true chronological order of creation would introduce. In fact, one sufficiently decisive argument in favor of the metaphorical interpretation is the contradictions which would be patent if the true chronological order were followed in the account of the creation of the body and the soul of the universe. This argument is not based, as Professor Vlastos thinks,[20] only on the fact that the order of exposition does not follow the chronological order of "creation." If this were the same case as when a historian narrates in the order C, A, B, three facts that chronologically had the order A, B, C, Vlastos would be right in considering that this is not a valid argument to prove that the account of the creation of the body and the soul of the universe should not be taken literally. But if Plato himself calls attention to the fact that the order of creation is not the order followed in the narrative, and if we are able to show that, had he followed in the narrative the mythical order of creation, this would introduce contradictions which a different order of narration from the one chosen could not remove without changing the *content* of the account, then we would be right in contending that this proves the metaphorical character of the creation myth.[21]

Plato describes first the creation of the body of the universe[22] and after this the creation of its soul.[23] But, before starting to describe the creation of the soul, Timaeus explains that though in the narrative body is dealt with first and soul second, soul is really prior to body in birth and excellence, the reason being that soul must be *prior* to body if it is to rule it.[24] The reversal of the "chronological" order of creation is said to be due to the fact that "there is in us too much of the casual and random, which shows itself in our speech."[25] This "casual and random" must be understood in the light of those "secondary causes" referred to in 46E 1–6.[26] But it is clear that Plato could not have meant this explanation of the reversal suffered by the mythical order in the narrative to be taken literally, for he is himself warning us that the chronological order has been reversed and, consequently, he could have modified the order of narration if he had so wished. The reversal and the warning look, then, like a conscious device to call attention to the fact that "prior" and "posterior," or "older" and "younger," should not be taken in the temporal sense.[27] Moreover, when we read the paragraph devoted to the creation of the soul we see one reason at least for the order chosen by Plato in his narrative. In 35A 1–8, the soul is constructed as intermediate between the ideas and body, and as an intermediate it presupposes the extremes between which it is an intermediate;[28] from this it follows that soul cannot really be temporally prior to body.[29] Consequently, if the account of the structure of soul and body given in *Timaeus* 31B–35A is serious Platonic doctrine, soul and body must be contemporaneous (see also note 47); and, since soul is said to be "prior" and "older" than body, it follows that these words must refer to ontological and not to chronological priority.[30] Had Plato followed the mythical order of creation in his narrative he would have been forced to modify his account of the creation of the soul; the implications of the order of narration here are, then, intimately connected with the content of Timaeus' discourse and cannot be compared to the method of a historian when he chooses to give flashbacks to illuminate a later event.

II

There is in the *Timaeus* another device by which Plato probably meant to indicate that the creation of the soul and the body of the universe should not be interpreted literally. This device consists in the omission, which must have been conscious as we shall see, of a factor which, if openly mentioned, would destroy the likelihood of the creation myth. Both in the *Phaedrus* and in the *Laws* Plato maintains that the soul is self-motion and the source of all other motion.[31] I do not wish to discuss in this paper the argument that the soul as self-motion must be eternal; but even if Vlastos were right in his interpretation that in the *Laws* soul is a "created" entity, still even there the essence of the soul is said to be self-motion and because of this the soul is declared to be the source of *all* motion.[32] In the *Timaeus* there are several references to this notion that the soul is self-motion;[33] yet it is never openly stated that this is the essence of the soul and, significantly enough, all reference to self-motion is omitted from the *psychogonia*, the place where we would naturally expect Plato to mention it. I submit that the reason for this omission must be that, if self-motion were openly stated to be the essence of the soul, this statement would destroy any likelihood that the creation myth could have. Vlastos for his part asserts that there is no contradiction in the fact that self-moving souls should be created; but if this were the case, *why* did Plato omit all reference to self-motion in the *psychogonia*?

Professor Vlastos, if I understand him correctly, would say that there is no omission at all; for in answer to another argument, that it is contradictory to have a soul create all the other souls,[34] he maintains that we should distinguish between: (A) the Craftsman generates self-moving souls, and (B) he generates the self-motions of self-moving souls. Vlastos thinks that the *Timaeus* refers to the first alternative, not to the second. His argument is: "*B* is obviously self-contradictory, since the very description of the motion of a given soul as a 'self-motion' entails, in Plato's scheme, that it is caused by just that soul and by no other individual in the universe—hence, *a fortiori*, not by the Demiurge. But *B* is never mooted in the *Timaeus*, where the Craftsman creates souls and leaves them alone to do their own self-moving for ever after. How then could *A*, once it is clearly distinguished from *B*, involve a contradiction? What is there to keep the Demiurge (assuming he has the wonderful powers of world-creation) from creating entities that have the power of self-moving and, once created, go on to exercise this power to their heart's content?"[35]

But where does Vlastos find evidence for statement *A*? It is never said in the *Timaeus* that the Demiurge created a soul, or souls, and that afterwards they start to do their own self-moving. This is, then, an inference on the part of Vlastos, an inference prompted by the fact that the relation of the soul to self-motion is never openly stated, as we said.[36]

Plato, however, means that the soul *is identical* with self-motion, not that it has the power of self-motion, as Vlastos says.[37] But even apart from this, there are passages in the *Timaeus* which definitely point to *B* in regard to the world-soul and, *a fortiori*, for all souls. The first such reference occurs in the passage that we discussed in the previous section, i.e., *Timaeus* 31B–35A. After describing the creation of the body of the universe, and after explaining why the Demiurge gave to it a spherical shape with neither eyes nor ears, neither hands nor feet, Timaeus says that the Demiurge *imparted* movement to the body of the universe, "that one of the seven which above all belongs to reason and intelligence."[38] But this motion imparted to the universe must be the motion of the world-soul[39] which, as we are told almost immediately,[40] was created *before* the body of the universe. Moreover, whereas in the *psychogonia*[41] there is no mention at all of self-motion or of any other motion that is proper to the soul, in 36C–E the Demiurge, after "splitting" the soul into the circle of the Same and the circle of the Different, does the following things: he "enveloped" the circles with the motion that is carried around uniformly in the same place,[42] he "made" one the outer and the other the inner circle,[43] he *caused* the circle of the Same *to move* to the right and the circle of the Different to the left,[44] he *gave supremacy* to the revolution of the Same,[45] and the soul being inwoven with the universe and enveloping it on the outside "revolving within its own limit, made a divine beginning of ceaseless and intelligent life for all time."[46] All these actions of the Demiurge are incompatible with the voluntary self-motion of soul.[47]

It follows, then, that if the Demiurge really created the soul of the universe he started also its self-motion. But why did Plato not say so openly? Because, I think, it is self-contradictory to state that the Demiurge started the self-motion of the soul, as Vlastos himself recognizes. On the other hand, Plato could not suppress *all* reference to self-motion, since this would falsify his teleological conception of man and of the universe.[48] We are now able to discover one more reason for Plato's decision to relate first the creation of body; had he done otherwise he would have faced two alternatives which he could not accept: (a) either to state openly that the Demiurge started the self-motion of the world-soul, or (b) that he created a soul, attached it to a body created afterwards, and that after this the soul, by its own power, started its never-ending motion. The second alternative is Vlastos' interpretation; but the fact that Plato did not choose it and that he preferred instead to have the Demiurge "envelop" the soul with motion and impart motion to the body of the universe, a motion that is the movement given to the universe by its soul, shows that Plato, by calling attention to the reversal in the narrative of the chronological order of creation (with the explanation that soul must be "older" than body if it is to govern it, i.e., *move it*), meant to suggest to the reader that the creation should not be taken literally.

Plato was not trying to deceive his reader; he chose a genetic myth over a direct analysis of the causes at work in the universe[49] and, once he had chosen this form of exposition, he had to preserve the likelihood of the *mise-en-scène*. To reach the conclusion that the creation of the universe should not be taken literally, it is not necessary that the reader be acquainted with the *Phaedrus*[50] and the *Laws;* for the notion that soul is self-motion is implied in the *Timaeus*, as is also the notion that the world-soul moves the universe. And, finally, the *Timaeus* states unambiguously that soul is primary causation as opposed to the secondary or "necessary" causes.[51] If Plato never openly states in the *Timaeus* that the soul as self-motion is the ultimate source of *all* motion, it is not openly to contradict what he said about the precosmical chaos,[52] which is the symbol of the "necessary" causes, even as the Demiurge is the symbol of the intelligent causation of the self-moving soul. (See further section VI of this paper.)

III

Plato declares that time and the universe came into being simultaneously, that no time existed before the universe and that none would exist if the universe were ever destroyed.[53] Yet events are described which took place *before* the creation of time. This looks like a contradiction, a contradiction of which Plato must have been aware, since he emphatically asserts several times that time and the universe are contemporaneous. These assertions must be interpreted as a device to call the reader's attention to the fact that, as there was no time when the universe did not exist, neither the universe nor time ever came into being.

Vlastos, however, asserts that Plato, in *Timaeus* 37D–38A, speaks only of a time (U) which can be defined as *uniform and measurable time-flow*, and he maintains that this is different from saying that the Demiurge introduced temporal succession, or time-flow as such, into the world. The latter Vlastos calls time (S) and defines as *irreversible temporal succession*. Vlastos maintains that this distinction would eliminate the contradiction mentioned above and, although he admits that

Plato did not make this distinction, he asserts that what Plato says about time in the *Timaeus* shows that *he did not deny* the proposition that time (S) is instantiable in the absence of time (U).[54] He then goes on to say: "Nor is there any evidence that he (sc. Plato) had made the analysis that would have enabled him to do this by revealing how time (U) was both different from, yet related to, time (S). He is perfectly capable, certainly, of thinking and speaking of time in other contexts in terms of the past/present/future distinction without specific reference to measurable time-flow: he does so in the *Parmenides* (151E–157B). But there is no indication there, or anywhere else, that he saw precisely how these two concepts are related. *We would do well to keep in mind that no one in antiquity succeeded in seeing this—not Aristotle, for example, who wrote more extensively on time, with greater analytical thoroughness, and with knowledge of what Plato had already contributed to the partial exploration of this difficult concept.*"[55]

I have italicized the last part of the quotation because I wish to emphasize that the distinction that Vlastos thinks so difficult to make was indeed made in antiquity; and I think that such a distinction would have been made by Plato if he meant even to leave open the possibility of a precosmic time. At any rate, the distinction between a precosmic time and a cosmic, "ordered," time is made, among others, by the Epicurean Velleius in Cicero's *De Natura Deorum* and, interestingly enough, the distinction is made in a passage where Plato's *Timaeus* is being criticized.[56] Moreover, Aristotle himself must have been aware of such a distinction, since he reports that whereas Plato held that both time and the world were created, all his predecessors held that the universe was generated, leaving time as ungenerated.[57] Whether or not Aristotle is accurate here in his report, there can be no question that he must have been aware of the distinction between precosmic and cosmic time. Moreover, even if Plato could not make such a distinction, if he really meant the creation to be taken literally, he would, like some of the Presocratics at least, have left time as ungenerated. His emphatic assertions that time and the universe were generated together, that God created the heavenly bodies, in order that time may come into being,[58] and that ἦν and ἔσται "became forms of time,"[59] can only be interpreted as his way of indicating to the reader that *there was no time* when the universe did not exist, i.e., the universe must have existed always.[60] These expressions, in the absence of any indication to the contrary, imply a denial of the possibility of time (S) or precosmic time;[61] unless we are willing to admit that Plato was unaware of the contradiction that his statements about time imply. A very unlikely prospect, I think; the more so, if we consider that these expressions were interpreted as contradictions in antiquity, both by those who, interpreting the *Timaeus* literally, attacked Plato,[62] and by those who, considering that these statements imply a contradiction (namely, "there was a time when time was not"),[63] considered that Plato tried to indicate that the creation of the world should not be taken literally. Neither Plato nor Aristotle explicitly distinguish a cosmic from a precosmic time because, believing that the cosmos is eternal, they *did not need* to make such a distinction.[64]

IV

After creating soul, the body of the universe, the heavenly bodies, and the gods of traditional mythology, the Demiurge passes on the task of creating the other three kinds of living beings to the created gods.[65] It is then said of the Demiurge: καὶ ὁ μὲν δὴ ἅπαντα ταῦτα διατάξας ἔμενεν ἐν τῷ ἑαυτοῦ κατὰ τρόπον ἤθει.[66] This is a reference to the doctrine that God is unchangeable; and Proclus already noticed that to be always in the same state in relation to the world the Demiurge must create always, if he creates at all (i.e., the universe must be eternal).[67] If the Demiurge created the universe at a certain time and then ceased creating, his relation to the universe must have changed.[68] This doctrine that God is unchangeable is explicitly stated and explained in the *Republic*[69] and is in agreement with Plato's conception of the divine as expressed in other dialogues.

Vlastos, however, says that "the constancy of God's ἦθος would comport with any amount of world-making, provided only his behavior as Craftsman remains consistent with his character as god. In *Republic* 381C the point of the statement that 'it is impossible for a god to wish to change himself but, as is only right, each of them being as fair and excelent as it is possible to be, abides for ever in his own character,' is not that god does not act at all, but that he does not act in undignified and wicked ways: he does not lie, masquerade, etc., like the Homeric deities; he never causes evil, only good (379B–380C). Since the world-creation is an act of supreme beneficence (30A–B), it would imply no shift of nature or character in this 'best of causes' (29A), but rather a fitting expression of it."[70]

But what Vlastos quotes from the *Republic* is only 381C 7–9, and these lines are only the conclusion of the argument that shows that God must be unchangeable. Granting that in the *Republic* it is Plato's purpose to show that God cannot wish to lie, masquerade, etc., *how* is this proved? It is proved by a general argument the import of which is to establish that God, *if he changes at all, must change for the worse*, since he is as good and beautiful as possible.[71] This same doctrine is echoed in the *Timaeus*.[72] If the Demiurge really created the world because he wanted everything to be as good as possible, since there is no φθόνος in the divine,[73] then, why, if this act of creation is good, did the Demiurge create the world at one time rather than at another? If God is good and always possessed this power of creation, why did he allow the precosmic chaos to exist for some time before he decided to bring order into it?[74] If the creation is interpreted literally, it would imply that a change took place in the divine ἦθος from worse to better, a notion incompatible with what is said in the *Timaeus* about the Demiurge.

The notion of a god starting the creation of the world at a certain point in time presupposes a divinity powerful enough to create his own values; but such a thing is incompatible with Plato's conception of the divine. For Plato God, or a god, is soul[75] and as such it must be subordinated to the ideas. In the *Euthyphro*, undoubtedly an early work, it is said that the holy is loved by the gods because it is holy and not that it is holy because it is loved by the gods.[76] In the *Laws*, his last work, Plato asserts that there are θεῖαι ἀνάγκαι which bind even the gods and against which the gods do not, and never will, fight;[77] in fact, it is a condition for the existence of the divine the knowledge and practice of these θεῖαι ἀνάγκαι.[78] The same thing is meant in the *Phaedrus* when the life of the gods is described in mythical terms as the contemplation by *NOUS* of the ὑπερουράνιος τόπος,[79] a contemplation that must be eternal,[80] since it is "contact" with, or "closeness" to, the ideas that makes a god divine.[81] Only man searches and seeks wisdom, only man can be a φιλόσοφος; a god does not need to search, for he is already wise, as we are told in the *Symposium* (204A). Even the heavenly bodies are considered to be divine because their revolutions are regular (*Timaeus*, *Laws*), and this is considered the proof that they are alive and that their movement is voluntary. The nature of the Platonic god being what it is, he could not start capriciously to create the world because this work of creation is good. If he creates, he must create always; and, since this is incompatible with what is expressed in *Timaeus* 42E 5–6, we must interpret the Demiurge as a mythical figure and as a symbol of the causes ὅσαι μετὰ νοῦ καλῶν καὶ ἀγαθῶν δημιουργοί.[82] If the Demiurge is mythical and is a symbol of intelligent causation, this would explain why the distinction between "God," "the God," and "the gods" is not maintained[83] after the created gods are introduced at 41A–D.

The use of the figure of the Demiurge is not restricted to the *Timaeus*; we find it also in the *Sophist*[84] and in the *Politicus*[85] (in the latter we also find the precosmic, disorderly motion).[86] It cannot be a development in Plato's "later" works, since we find it even in the *Republic*,[87] where it is said that the Demiurge fashioned the heaven and all that it contains in the best possible manner (οὕτω συνεστάναι τῷ τοῦ οὐρανοῦ δημιουργῷ αὐτόν τε καὶ τὰ ἐν αὐτῷ).[88] And even in the early dialogues δημιουργός is personified and applied to Rhetoric and to other τέχναι.[89] Aristotle himself, who certainly considered the cosmos to be ungenerated and imperishable, said that God made coming to be perpetual as the closest approximation to real being that is possible for sensible existence.[90] It is also to be noticed that Aristotle, who interpreted the *Timaeus* literally, pays no attention to the Demiurge.[91]

V

Have I not forgotten, however, what may be in fact the most important argument to assert that according to Plato the universe came into being? Is it not decisive that Plato himself says that the cosmos γέγονεν?[92] Such has always been the claim of those interpreters who take the creation of the world in the *Timaeus* literally. Moreover, Hackforth,[93] followed by Vlastos,[94] argues that the sentence in which Plato asserts that the universe has been generated, having started from an ἀρχή,[95] is demonstrated[96] from premises which express serious metaphysical doctrine, with no metaphorical or mythological language at all. The premises by which it is proved that the cosmos came into being are, according to Vlastos,[97] two: (1) it is corporeal and as such it is an object of sense perception and belief, while (2) all such objects are in process of becoming and have been generated.

Zeller,[98] followed by Cherniss,[99] had objected to (2) on the ground that, if all that is visible must have come into being, this must also be true of the precosmical chaos; the latter is said to exist before the universe was created and as such it is said to have been visible.[100] Vlastos maintains that "Plato's cursory reference to the primal chaos in 30A as 'all that was visible' is one of the most obscure of his remarks about that all too obscure subject" and that it is contradicted by the assertion in 31B 5, that nothing is visible unless it has fire in it, "but chaos had only an inchoate antecedent of fire which did not have the nature of fire, but only 'certain traces' of it (53B 2). How and in what sense this would or could be 'visible' Plato does not explain." Consequently, according to Vlastos, this very silence would be enough for Plato to escape Zeller's charge of contradiction, or at the very least it would not be a glaring contradiction, but, at best, an unexplained obscurity. Moreover, if Zeller's charge would be valid, "it would put Plato in the position of palming off on his readers falsehoods in the major premise and conclusion of our syllogism. Believing that it is quite false that all objects of sense-perception and belief are generated, and also false that the world was generated, Plato would be making his mouthpiece, Timaeus, assert the first and join it to a true premise to engender a false conclusion."[101]

I do think, however, that Zeller's argument is valid; for it is a fact that Plato calls the precosmic chaos "visible" and, whatever may be the obscurities of Plato's conception of the precosmic chaos, if it is "visible," the reasoning of 28B 7–C 3 would apply also to it. After all Plato might very well not give this information if it introduces a contradiction; or must one suppose that, even granting that Plato wrote that the precosmic chaos is visible inadvertently or without being able to see "clearly" the contradictions of such an obscure notion, he never re-read the *Timaeus* carefully before publication? If he wrote that the precosmic chaos is "visible" it must have been with full awareness of the implications that this entails in relation to the reasoning employed in 28B 7–C 3. We must assume that he called the chaos "visible" in order to make it clear that it was sensible. Fortunately, there is more evidence to support Zeller's thesis. Let us start by interpreting literally 28A–C as Hackforth and Vlastos do. From 28A 4–6 and B 7–C 3 we may conclude that γένεσις or anything that is a γιγνόμενον must ὑπ' αἰτίου τινὸς ἐξ ἀνάγκης γενέσθαι. Now in 29D 7–E 1 it is said that God is the cause of *genesis* and of the universe. This *genesis* can be understood only as cosmic *genesis*, of which the Demiurge is the "father"; this is in agreement with the reasoning in 28A–C. But later on it is said that Being, space, and *genesis* existed even before the generation of the universe.[102] There can be no question that this *genesis*, according to the reasoning in 28A–C must have been "created" or must necessarily have a cause; but this would contradict the whole system of the *Timaeus*. Consequently, what Plato says about the precosmical chaos being "visible" and what he says about *genesis* introduces contradictions into the *Timaeus*. Is Plato, then, palming off falsehoods on his readers? I do not think so. My reason for this belief is that I consider that to judge any part of a Platonic work we should first read the whole of it; after all, Plato is not writing a treatise on mathematics or on logic. Many times Plato's works end in aporiae or contradictions and it seems to me that he leaves it to the reader to deduce by himself the implications of what is said *literally* in the work. The reasoning in 28A–C is, I think, correct. If we read the *Timaeus* and we find in it contradictions of which Plato was conscious and which seem to have been purposely included to call the reader's attention to them, is it so strange to conclude that Plato is thereby indicating to the reader that the creation of the world should not be interpreted literally? If, after reaching this conclusion, we come back to 28A–C we would naturally conclude that when Plato says that the universe "came into being" he meant only that it is "process," i.e., that the universe is always in the process of coming into being. There is no question that *genesis* and its derivatives *can* have this meaning, and they were so interpreted by some in antiquity, in relation to this passage of the *Timaeus*.[103] Plato's point is, then, that the universe being a γενητόν must have a cause and that this cause is νοῦς and consequently soul. On the surface Plato seems to mean γέγονεν in the sense of something that came into being, not having existed previously; and this is only natural if he chose a genetic myth to explain the nature of the universe, a genetic myth with which Plato tried to illustrate by means of temporal succession the ontological structure of man and the universe.[104]

We may now also give an explanation for the systematic order of the *Timaeus*. Had Plato chosen to give a purely chronological account of the creation of the world, this would have falsified his teleological conception of the universe; had he introduced the third factor from the very beginning, it would have contradicted his purpose of showing that the causation of soul is "primary," for it would have been obvious that the Demiurge is limited by the precosmic chaos. Plato, then, chose the order of narration that would best exemplify his notion that soul is primary causation and that soul is "prior" to body. This being so, according to 46D–E, soul must be the ultimate source of *all* motion. The importance that Plato attributed to this notion can be seen in the *Phaedrus* and in the tenth book of the *Laws*; a teleological explanation of the universe in which soul would be shown to be the master of body is, after all, the desiderata of Socrates even in the *Phaedo*. Nobody succeeded so well in fulfilling this programme as Plato himself in the *Timaeus*.[105]

VI

In analyzing the account of motion in the "created" universe given by Timaeus, we shall find a confirmation of the metaphorical character of the creation myth; for if the interpretation given in the preceding pages is correct, then even in the *Timaeus* Plato holds that soul is the ultimate source of all motion;[106] and the Demiurge and the precosmic chaos are merely symbols representing two factors or "causes" which are always at work in the universe, *NOUS* and *Necessity*, the latter depending ultimately on the former. If, on the other hand, those critics who interpret literally the cosmogony of the *Timaeus* are right, we should see the precosmic chaos as an autonomous cause not only before the creation of the cosmos but also after it.

It has indeed been maintained that Plato attributes spontaneous disorderly motion to "matter,"[107] a motion which is not and cannot be due even indirectly to the action of God, and that this does in fact contradict the doctrine that soul is ultimately the cause of all motion, a doctrine that Plato maintains both in the *Phaedrus* and in the *Laws*.[108] If this interpretation is correct, Plato when he wrote the *Timaeus* would in fact have made of matter a self-mover.

According to the *Timaeus* the universe is the result or effect of two causes, *NOUS* and *Necessity* (or the "Errant Cause").[109] Plato maintains that the causation of soul is primary, in fact that only soul is truly a cause, because only soul possesses *NOUS*, i.e., intelligence and purpose. The rest are not properly causes but accessory or auxiliary causes (συναιτία), precisely because such things as "cooling," "heating," etc., though mistakenly considered by most people to be causes, "are incapable of any plan or intelligence for any purpose." Making a concession to ordinary usage Plato later calls them "causes," causes pertaining to things which, being set in motion by others, of necessity set yet others in motion and, being destitute of wisdom (i.e., of purpose), "produce their sundry effects at random and without order."[110] It is this kind of motion that according to the myth precosmic "matter" has. But according to the economy of the *Timaeus* the cause of the disorderly motions in the created universe must be that part of the spontaneous motions of precosmic matter that the Demiurge could not subordinate to his will, for it is clear that Plato does not admit any causes other than *NOUS* and *Necessity*; and it is because he wishes to explain the "creation" of the universe as a result of these two causes that he brings in the "Errant Cause" into his account and establishes "in what manner its nature is to cause motion."[111] To this end he subsequently introduces the "receptacle" (or space) and finally in 57D 7–58C 4 explains how the "Errant Cause" causes motion. It is necessary to determine whether or not the "Errant Cause" is an autonomous factor in the universe. If it is not, the precosmic chaos could only have been meant by Plato to be taken as a symbol of the disordered motions of "matter" which are indirectly caused by the soul. In other words, if the secondary motions caused by the "Errant Cause" have their ultimate source in the world-soul, chaos cannot be in constant motion "for purely mechanical reasons."[112]

The first statement about the precosmic chaos at 30A 2–6 describes the state of "matter" before the creation of the universe, but it is only at 52D 4 ff. that a more complete description of chaos is given and it is only there and also at 57D 7–58C 4 that the account of motion and of the role of the "Errant Cause" in it is finally completed. In 52D 2–4 resuming what went on in the previous pages, Timaeus states that Being (i.e., the ideas), space, and *genesis* existed before the universe came into being. He then (52D 4–53C 3) describes the precosmic state of affairs. The receptacle had the characters of what will later become earth, water, air, and fire; since the powers of these were neither alike nor evenly balanced, there was no equilibrium, but the receptacle was being moved by these things, and it at its turn moved them. This state of affairs is described as a σεισμός. Even in this chaos, however, there is a certain differentiation, for the reflections of the ideas in the receptacle must be what produces the "vestiges" (ἴχνη) of the four elements.

What is of particular importance is the notion that the receptacle in moving the particles was sorting out from one another the four kinds and that each kind came to have a different region "even before the ordered whole consisting of them came to be."[113] This account, if taken literally, implies that the effect of the receptacle on the particles should have been the complete separation of the four kinds of particles into four separate, homogeneous masses; and the consequence of this complete separation would have been the cessation of the disorderly motion of precosmic "matter." Why the four kinds were not completely sorted out from one another, Plato does not immediately explain. But this is not an idle question, nor one that the modern interpreter merely imposes on the *Timaeus*, for it is a question that Plato himself raises a few pages later, and one to which he provides an answer. The importance of this answer is that it is given not in the context of the precosmic state of affairs but in that of the created universe.[114]

The purpose of *Timaeus* 57D 7–58C 4 is to examine the manner and the conditions in which motion and rest arise; to this end Timaeus assumes what has been said previously about motion,[115] and he presently adds a point concerned only with physical motion: there is no motion in a state of homogeneity, for motion, presupposing both a mover and something which is moved, can exist only in a state of heterogeneity.[116]

A cause of heterogeneity is inequality, and, Timaeus adds, the origin of inequality has already been described.[117] This is clearly a reference to 52D 4–53C 3 where the "powers" or the "characters" in the receptacle were described as being neither alike nor evenly balanced.[118] "But we have not explained," says Timaeus, "how it is that the several bodies have not been completely separated apart in their kinds and so ceased to pass through one another and to change their place. We must, then, resume our explanation as follows."[119] It is apparent, then, according to 52D–53C and 57D–58C, that the precosmic chaos did not possess self-sustained motion, since, under the conditions described in these two passages, *the disorderly motions of precosmic "matter" would have come to an end as a result of the very effects that these motions produced on the "receptacle."*

Timaeus next explains how heterogeneity is preserved,[120] and it is clear that the necessary condition for its preservation is the fact that the revolution of the whole universe encloses all the corpuscles in a plenum where there is no void.[121] But this revolution, which is caused by the world-soul[122] and which pervades the whole sphere,[123] also moves the corpuscles of matter and thereby causes them to move one another with secondary, induced motion precisely because they are heterogeneous and of different size. The indirect effect of the revolution caused by the world-soul would have been to separate the four kinds of corpuscles into four homogeneous regions,[124] but because the revolution of the universe at the same time confines all the particles in a plenum where there is no void, there will always be, to some extent, contact of heterogeneous corpuscles, since corpuscles of the same kind leave gaps in their texture, the largest particles leaving the largest gaps, the smallest the least, "so the coming-together involved in the condensing process thrusts the smallest bodies together into interstices between the largest ones. Accordingly, when the small are set alongside the large, and the lesser disintegrate the larger, while the larger cause the lesser to combine, all are changing the direction of their movement, this way and that, towards their own regions; for each, in changing its size, changes also the situation of its region. In this way, then, and by these means there is a perpetual safeguard for the occurrence of that heterogeneity which provides that the perpetual motion of these bodies is and shall be without cessation."[125] It is clear, then, that the created universe is the necessary condition for the continuity of the process of generation,[126] and it also follows that the ultimate cause of the random motions of "matter" is the revolution of the world-soul. Therefore, the description of precosmic chaos given at 52D 4–53C 3 could not have been meant by Plato to be taken literally, since he makes it clear at 58A 2–4 that the explanation of the continuity of process given in 57D 7–58C 4 applies to the precosmic chaos too.

The implication, then, of *Timaeus* 46C 7–E 6 and 57D 7–58C 4 is that soul is the source of all motion. And these passages also show that matter has no inherent or spontaneous motion of its own,[127] that there is no attraction of like to like nor any other purely mechanical cause of motion or change;[128] that there is no need, moreover, to postulate either an evil world-soul (of which there are no traces in the *Timaeus* or anywhere else in Plato)[129] nor an irrational element in the world-soul[130] in order to explain disorderly motion in the universe. In fact, the theory of motion presented in the *Timaeus* is essentially the same as that of the *Laws*.[131]

VII

We possess the complete text of the *Timaeus* and are entitled to interpret it ourselves. It may therefore be argued that the testimony of Plato's contemporaries cannot be decisive; but even so, since Plato's contemporaries were apparently already divided *vis-à-vis* the interpretation of the creation myth, it would be profitable to discover the reasons that caused them to hold their opposite interpretations.

Aristotle interpreted the creation in the *Timaeus* literally, and Professor Vlastos argues that "if we are to discount Aristotle's testimony we must charge him with deliberate misrepresentation. It is hard to believe that Aristotle, with all the limitations of his subtle and unimaginative mind, was capable of quite that."[132] Aristotle's testimony, however, is more complex than we might think at first. It is out of question that he did interpret the creation myth literally;[133] but it is also significant that he did not attach any importance to the figure of the Demiurge[134] and that he himself used the image of the creating god in a purely metaphorical sense.[135] But if the Demiurge is a purely mythical figure, the whole machinery of the myth must be given up.[136] Aristotle is not interested in the literary question of the interpretation of the myth *per se*; he is a philosopher who discovers inconsistencies in his predecessors' views on time, motion, the eternity of the universe, etc.; and when a philosopher is trying to vindicate his own originality, as Aristotle does when he claims that he is the first to maintain that the universe is ungenerated,[137] we should not be shocked when he misrepresents the views of his predecessors. If Aristotle could take literally, and thereby misinterpret, the myth of the progressive degeneration of the four inferior constitutions in the *Republic*[138] and if he could attack Plato for failing to recognize the relative nature of non-being,[139] I cannot see why we should attach the special value of an historical testimony to his literal interpretation of the *Timaeus*.

The testimony of Aristotle conflicts, moreover, with that of his contemporaries who were members of the Academy and who thought that in the *Timaeus* the creation of the world should be interpreted metaphorically. Since both parties to the dispute cannot be right, there is no obvious reason why Aristotle's testimony or interpretation should be more trustworthy than that of Speusippus or Xenocrates. We possess but meagre fragments of their works, and they may have been better or worse philosophers than Aristotle, but since they too were Plato's contemporaries, their testimony has as much value as that of Aristotle.

Speusippus,[140] Xenocrates,[141] Crantor[142] (and perhaps also Heraclides Ponticus)[143] denied that the creation of the world was meant by Plato literally. Speusippus and Xenocrates explained that the creation was διδασκαλίας χάριν, and compared Plato's procedure to the figures drawn by the mathematicians. Aristotle himself reports this defense,[144] which was meant to be an interpretation of Plato's *Timaeus*,[145] and against it he argues that the analogy with the construction of a geometrical figure is a false one, for in the latter case the simultaneous existence of the parts of a geometrical construction does not involve a contradiction, whereas in the construction of the universe a process must take place between the original state of disorder and that of order, since the latter is said to arise from the former and, being contrary states, they could not exist simultaneously.[146] But Aristotle's rejoinder begs the point at issue when he assumes that the production of order from disorder was meant literally.[147] Aristotle, moreover, neglects the fact that according to the *Timaeus*, the universe is, at any given moment, a mixture of order and disorder, which are the respective results of *NOUS* and *Necessity*;[148] and, furthermore, even if Aristotle's refutation of the analogy were correct, he still has not refuted the defense in so far as it is a defense of Plato's *intention* in the *Timaeus*.

Be that as it may, it is significant that when Aristotle tries to refute the advocates of the metaphorical interpretation he does not appeal to Plato's intention, but rather attempts to show that the defense involves a contradiction; that his rejoinder implies, as we said, a misinterpretation of the *Timaeus* should make us sceptics as to the trustworthiness of Aristotle's "testimony." And it is even more significant that Theophrastus, before he uses Aristotle's rejoinder against the partisans of the metaphorical interpretation, admits that Plato possibly called the universe "generated" σαφηνείας χάριν, ὡς καὶ τοῖς διαγράμμασι παρακολουθοῦμεν γινομένοις.[149] Thus to the unanimous testimony of the Academy we can add that of Theophrastus, the disciple and successor of Aristotle, who at one time was himself a member of the Academy.[150]

While Xenocrates established himself as the official interpreter of Plato, it is important to note that Speusippus, who did not attempt a systematic interpretation of Plato in order to discover in it his own philosophical system (as Xenocrates did) and who saw difficulties in Plato's theory of ideas which he therefore abandoned,[151] is also said to have interpreted the creation myth metaphorically.[152]

VIII

In his article, "The Disorderly Motion in the *Timaeus*," Professor Vlastos maintains that the myth of the *Timaeus* stands apart from all the other Platonic myths in that in it Plato uses none of the devices by means of which in his other works he disavows the scientific seriousness of major features of their accounts.[153] That the creation myth of the *Timaeus* is unique I readily concede; but even if Vlastos were right as to the absence of formal mythical devices from the *Timaeus* this absence would still not prove that Plato meant the creation to have taken place in time. For Plato might have considered that the indications given in the account of "creation" itself, especially his calling attention to the reversal in the narrative of the chronological order of creation and the very explanation offered as the cause of this reversal, are a warning against a literal interpretation of the creation of the body and the soul of the universe. (See sections I and II *supra.*)

Vlastos appears to think that the typical Platonic myth is mythological, but that there is nothing mythological in Timaeus' discourse. The absence of mythology does not in any case validate the literal interpretation of a Platonic dialogue or of a passage in it. Thus in the tenth book of the *Republic* god is represented as the "creator" of ideas, and though this passage is not mythical and though in it no literary devices, mythological or otherwise, are employed as an indication that this "god" should not be taken literally, the passage should be, and is most often, interpreted in a non-literal sense.[154]

As it is, however, there are some formal, mythical elements in the *Timaeus*. For one thing, the language is highly metaphorical, and no interpreter, as literal minded as he may be, can accept everything in the

Timaeus at its face value.[155] But even apart from that, Timaeus' discourse is only part of a larger myth, that of the war between Athens and Atlantis;[156] and this subordination of the creation myth as a whole to a purely mythological myth is surely an indication that Timaeus' discourse should not be taken as a strictly historical account.[157] This point may not be so ostensible because Plato did not complete the trilogy (in fact he probably did not even complete the *Critias*) of which the *Timaeus* was to be but the first work. But we should not forget, as Cornford has pointed out,[158] that the unfinished state of the trilogy gives the *Timaeus* a prominence it would not have had in the completed design. In any case the creation myth is "framed" by the myth of Atlantis, as we can see from the *résumé* of that myth given in the *Timaeus* itself and from the beginning of the *Critias*.[159]

Modern readers will always feel somewhat puzzled by Plato's choice of a creation myth to represent the actual working of the universe. But we must consider that whereas we accept as a matter of fact purely mechanistic accounts of causation, Plato's conception of causality is teleological, and this can best be exemplified by "constructing" the universe as the conscious design of an artisan. Even more significant is the fact that whereas our Judeo-Christian upbringing causes us to focus attention on the "creating god," Plato must have considered that a literal interpretation of his figure of the Demiurge was highly unlikely. Witness the fact that Aristotle, who interpreted the *Timaeus* literally, paid no attention to the Demiurge[160] and used himself the image of the "creating god," even though he also asserted that the universe is ungenerated.[161] The "creating god" is absent from Greek cosmogonical thought,[162] and those philosophers, among Plato's predecessors, who postulated a beginning for the universe thought that the universe was generated by purely mechanical and blind causes.[163] There are good grounds, then, for believing that Plato could have taken almost for granted that the figure of the Demiurge was not going to be taken literally. If the Demiurge, however, is mythical, so is the creation of the world itself.[164] But once Plato had decided to present his account of the universe in the shape of a creation myth,[165] he had to preserve the likelihood of his story. Thus he could not state openly that the creation was merely "for the sake of explanation," and any good writer of tales would do the same thing, for the open and unambiguous explanation of the purpose of a literary device deprives the work itself of interest.

I am aware that the indications, present in the *Timaeus* itself, that have been used in support of the metaphorical interpretation, will be rejected by more literal-minded readers who will always maintain that, whatever contradictions we may find in the *Timaeus*, Plato must have believed that the universe was created, since this is what he says. What Plato says and what he means, however, may be two different things. But this point cannot be settled by discussion, for what is in question is how one reads Plato, how one conceives Plato's role as a writer and as a thinker. The problems we face in interpreting the *Timaeus* are similar to those we encounter when we approach Plato's other works: the relation between form and content is one of the main sources of the irreducibly different conceptions of Platonism.

But the issues presented in this paper, in so far as they bear on the interpretation of individual passages in the *Timaeus* and on the arguments advanced by both sides in this controversy, can be discussed and can at least be clarified by the use of argument. The larger issue of the creation myth itself will probably never be settled to the satisfaction of all scholars. After all, even the story of Atlantis, despite its purely mythological framework and despite Plato's indications that it is only a creation of his mind, so fires the imagination of its readers that they are endlessly searching and "discovering" the lost island. It all is, in a sense, a tribute to the powers of Plato as a writer and as a thinker; and of him in both capacities, which today for us can only be one and the same, we can say what he himself said of his teacher: ἀνὴρ ἄριστος καὶ ἄλλως φρονιμώτατος καὶ δικαιότατος.

NOTES

[1] This essay has been published in *Studies in Plato's Metaphysics*, edited by R. E. Allen (London, 1965), pp. 401–19. Hereafter I shall refer to this essay as Vlastos, *Creation*.

[2] Cf. H. Cherniss, *Aristotle's Criticism of Plato and the Academy*, vol. I (Baltimore, 1944), pp. 421–31; cf. also nn. 314, 349, 382, 385. Hereafter I cite this work as Cherniss, I.

[3] Originally published in *CQ*, XXXIII (1939): 71–83. The article is now reprinted in *Studies in Plato's Metaphysics*, pp. 379–99. Since Vlastos has introduced some changes, I shall quote this paper from the *Studies* and will refer to it as Vlastos, *Disorderly Motion*.

[4] Hackforth's article "Plato's Cosmogony (*Timaeus* 27D ff.)," *CQ*, N.S. IX (1959): 17–22, the main argument of which has been accepted by Vlastos (*Creation*, pp. 402–05), will be discussed in section V. For other interpreters who have recently argued for a literal interpretation of the *Timaeus*, cf. section VI of this paper.

[5] For references to the more important earlier publications, cf. Cherniss, I, n. 357.

[6] These publications are referred to and criticized by Cherniss in his article "The Sources of Evil According to Plato," *PAPS*, 98 (1954): 23–30. For publications later than 1954, cf. those mentioned by Vlastos, *Creation*, p. 402, n. 1.

[7] Cf. *Timaeus* 20D–26D.

[8] Cf. *Timaeus* 19D–20C, 26C–D, 27A–B; *Critias* 110C–D. Cf. Cornford, *Plato's Cosmology* (London, 1937), pp. 2–8.

[9] A summary is given in *Timaeus* 20D–25D.

[10] Cf. *Timaeus* 20A and 27A.

[11] Cf. *Timaeus* 27A 5–6.

[12] Cf. Taylor, *Plato: Timaeus and Critias*, translated into English with introductions and notes on the text (London, 1929), p. 104. Cf. also Taylor, *A Commentary on Plato's Timaeus* (Oxford, 1928), pp. 50–51.

[13] Cf. *Timaeus* 29D 5, τὸ μὲν οὖν προοίμιον κτλ.

[14] On this, cf. section V.

[15] Such is the "generation" of fire, air, water, and earth, out of which the Demiurge was said to have created the body of the universe.

[16] Cf. section V.

[17] Cf. sections I, II, III, and IV.

[18] I mention this in view of Hackforth's argument, accepted by Vlastos, that in *Timaeus* 27D 5–28C 3 an argument is given which, being philosophically correct, would imply, if the creation was not meant literally, that Plato was deceiving his reader. I deal with this problem in section V.

[19] He had used this device in the account of the four inferior constitutions in the *Republic* (545C–576B).

[20] Cf. Vlastos, *Creation*, 406.

[21] This is in fact the way in which the argument is presented by the partisans of the metaphorical interpretation; cf., e.g., Cherniss, I, pp. 424–25.

[22] *Timaeus* 31B 4 ff.

[23] *Timaeus* 35A 1 ff.

[24] *Timaeus* 34B 10–35A 1.

[25] *Timaeus* 34C 2–4, ἀλλά πως ἡμεῖς πολὺ μετέχοντες τοῦ προστυχόντος τε καὶ εἰκῇ ταύτῃ πῃ καὶ λέγομεν. I have given in the text above Cornford's translation (*Plato's Cosmology*, p. 59); my translations of the *Timaeus* all come from this work.

[26] Cf. Cornford, *op. cit.*, 59, n. 1.

[27] The notion that soul rules and is the master of body is good Platonic doctrine (cf., e.g., *Gorgias* 465C–D; *Phaedo* 79E–80A, 94E; *Laws* 892A, 896B–C, etc.); but this notion does not require that soul be temporally "prior" to body. This is implied in the *Timaeus* itself (cf. nn. 29 and 30). That Plato could use "prior" and "posterior" in a logical and ontological sense is shown also by Aristotle, *Metaphysics* 1019a 1–4; though this passage is not a specific allusion to *Timaeus* 34B–C, as Apelt [*Beiträge zur Geschichte der griechischen Philosophie* (Leipzig, 1891), pp. 226 ff., especially p. 228] thought, the distinction is here employed (cf. also *Laws* 892C and 896C). Cf. Mondolfo, *L'Infinito nel pensiero dell' antichità classica*[2] (Firenze, 1956), p. 109, n. and Cherniss, I, n. 33.

[28] Even the description of the middle element as a "mixture" of the two extremes is present in the *psychogonia* (cf. *Timaeus* 35A 3–4, τρίτον ἐξ ἀμφοῖν ἐν μέσῳ συνεκεράσατο οὐσίας εἶδος). Cf. Cherniss, I, n. 33, last paragraph, and the references there given. For the interpretation of *Timaeus* 35A–B, cf. Grube, *CP*, 27 (1932): 80–82.

[29] The soul must be intermediate between the ideas and the body of the universe (cf. *Timaeus* 35A 2–3, καὶ τῆς αὖ περὶ τὰ σώματα γιγνομένης μεριστῆς; 5–6, τοῦ τε ἀμεροῦς αὐτῶν καὶ τοῦ κατὰ τὰ σώματα μεριστοῦ); before the creation of the body of the universe there can be no bodies. If the soul were intermediate between the ideas and the precosmic chaos (but cf. n. 30), then: *either* the soul would possess disorderly motion (but there is no mention in the *Timaeus* of disorderly motion in the soul, and, moreover, disturbance by sensation is introduced later [43A–44B] and sensation is the result of the incarnation of particular souls [42A] and of the rectilinear motion of vision [45C]; cf. Cherniss, I, n. 315), *or*, if the "substraction" of the six motions in 34A is interpreted to mean that the Demiurge did not need to impart motion to the body of the universe (but Plato says specifically that he did: 34A 1, ἀπένειμεν; cf. section II), the mere substraction of the six wandering motions being sufficient to start the motion of the universe (as Vlastos once maintained: *Disorderly Motion*, p. 396), this would imply that the intelligent motion of the soul was already present in the precosmic chaos (cf. Cherniss, I, n. 364).

[30] If we insist both in interpreting "older" and "younger" in the chronological sense and in the literal interpretation of the *Timaeus*, contradictions appear when we consider the relation of the Demiurge to the precosmic chaos. Both are uncreated; yet the Demiurge, if not mythical, must be a soul (cf. n. 34), and as a soul he must be "prior" to body or sensible existence and, at the same time, intermediate between sensible existence and the ideas. (If he is a soul, he must be constituted in the same way as that described in 35A, even assuming for the sake of the argument that the reference to sensible existence there is to the precosmic chaos [but cf. n. 29].) At any rate, the Demiurge, as soul, governs the precosmic chaos and imposes on it a certain order; yet the Demiurge cannot be temporally "prior" to the precosmic chaos; if it were, the Demiurge must have created it, but such a notion is incompatible with the *Timaeus*. (For another contradiction if the Demiurge and chaos are taken literally, cf. section V.)

[31] Cf. *Phaedrus* 245C–246A; *Laws* 895A–896B. Vlastos now admits that in the *Laws* soul is the source of *all* motion (*Disorderly Motion*, 396, n. 4), whereas he previously tried to reconcile the *Laws* with a literal interpretation of the *Timaeus* (cf. *op. cit.*, pp. 397–99). On the source of motion in the *Timaeus* and in the *Laws*, cf. section VI *infra*.

[32] Cf. *Laws* 895A–B, 896A–B.

[33] Cf. *Timaeus* 37B 5, 77C 4–5, 89A 1–3. The doctrine is also implied in *Timaeus* 46D–E, where the causality of *NOUS*, and consequently of the soul (cf., n. 34), is declared to be primary. Yet, since T. M. Robinson (*AJP*, 88 [1967]: 59) still writes as if it were a matter of fact that in the *Timaeus* no

"self-movement of *any* ψυχή is mentioned," I may repeat here what Cherniss said in *PAPS*, 98 (1954): 26, n. 24, namely, that *Timaeus* 37B 5 (ἐν τῷ κινουμένῳ ὑφ' αὑτοῦ) refers to the soul, as 37C 3–5 (τούτω δὲ ἐν ᾧ τῶν ὄντων ἐγγίγνεσθον, ἄν ποτέ τις αὐτὸ ἄλλο πλὴν ψυχὴν εἴπῃ, πᾶν μᾶλλον ἢ τἀληθὲς ἐρεῖ) shows. And the general implication of this passage for the conception of the soul as self-motion would hold even if Cornford's interpretation of 37B 5 (cf. *Plato's Cosmology*, p. 95, n. 2) were correct, which I do not think it is.

[34] The Demiurge, if not mythical, must be a soul, since his work is that of *NOUS* (47E 3–4) and *NOUS* exists only in soul (30B 3, νοῦν δ' αὖ χωρὶς ψυχῆς ἀδύνατον παραγενέσθαι τῳ, 46D 5–6, τῶν γὰρ ὄντων ᾧ νοῦν μόνῳ κτᾶσθαι προσήκει, λεκτέον ψυχήν). Cf. Cherniss, I, pp. 425, 437–38, and 606–07 with his references to the *Sophist*, *Philebus*, and *Republic*. This is accepted by Vlastos. What is said about the creation of the soul in 34B–35A (cf. nn. 28, 29, 30) shows that it is inconsistent to have the Demiurge create all the other souls. Moreover, whether the soul is "generated" or "ungenerated" cannot be an accidental characteristic of it if the soul is self-motion (cf. below this same section); consequently, if all the other souls were created by the Demiurge, this would introduce a contradiction in Plato's conception of the soul.

[35] Cf. Vlastos, *Creation*, p. 416.

[36] This is why Cherniss, I, p. 428, said that the passages quoted in n. 33 are hints or veiled reminders of self-motion. These texts presuppose the notion of self-motion, but they do not discuss it nor do they state openly that this is the essence of the soul. But if the soul is self-motion and if its causality is "primary" (cf. 46D–E), then, it follows that soul is the source of *all* motion, and consequently the precosmical chaos cannot have been meant by Plato to be taken literally. This is why Plato avoided stating openly the identity of soul with self-motion, while at the same time giving enough indications that this is his conception.

[37] This is precisely the point raised by the criticism of Aristotle which Xenocrates tried to answer (fragment 68 [Heinze]); but in doing so Xenocrates, as well as Aristotle, did not take into consideration the fact that Plato declared that the source of *all* motion must be self-motion, because motion cannot be analyzed into factors which are not motion (cf. Cherniss, I, pp. 412–13 and n. 366). This is why Plato, to "explain" motion, postulated the existence of a non-physical self-motion: the soul.

[38] Cf. *Timaeus* 34A 1–5 (*n.b.* A 1, ἀπένειμεν, A 2–3, τῶν ἑπτὰ τὴν περὶ νοῦν καὶ φρόνησιν μάλιστα οὖσαν).

[39] Since it is the soul that moves the body of the universe and the soul that possesses the "movement" proper to *NOUS*. (Cf. also 36E, 37A–C, 39C, 40A, 77B–C, 90C–D.) Cf. also n. 29.

[40] *Timaeus* 34B 10–35A 1.

[41] *Timaeus* 35A–36B.

[42] *Timaeus* 36C 2–3, καὶ τῇ κατὰ ταὐτὰ ἐν ταὐτῷ περιαγομένῃ κινήσει πέριξ αὐτὰς ἔλαβεν. However one translates ἔλαβεν πέριξ, one is forced to conclude that either the Demiurge places the soul into a pre-existing motion and,

therefore, the world-soul has no power to move itself, or that the Demiurge imparts motion to the self-moving soul. The third possibility is that the creation of the soul was not meant to be taken literally (cf. also n. 47).

43 *Timaeus* 36C 3–4, καὶ τὸν μὲν ἔξω, τὸν δ' ἐντὸς ἐποιεῖτο τῶν κύκλων.

44 *Timaeus* 36C 5–7, τὴν μὲν δὴ ταὐτοῦ κατὰ πλευρὰν ἐπὶ δεξιὰ περιήγαγεν, τὴν δὲ θατέρου κατὰ διάμετρον ἐπ' ἀριστερά; cf. also the "splitting" of the circle of the Different into seven circles having different speeds (36D).

45 *Timaeus* 36C 7–D 1, κράτος δ' ἔδωκεν τῇ ταὐτοῦ καὶ ὁμοίου περιφορᾷ.

46 *Timaeus* 36E 2–5; that is, the soul, having been placed into its motion, is moving and, once it is interwoven with the body of the universe, makes a beginning of ceaseless and intelligent life (i.e., the life of the universe, a living creature composed of soul and body; cf. 30B 1–C 1 and 34B 8–9).

47 It is interesting to compare 34B 3–9 with 36D 8–E 5. In the first passage the Demiurge sets the soul in the body, while in the second he fashions the body within the soul. These two parallel accounts show that the fashioning of soul and body are contemporary and cannot have been meant literally, since the Demiurge "created" first the soul and then the body of the universe. This double account, when set against the warning given in 34B 10–35A 1, leads to the conclusion that this passage, calling attention to the reversal in the narrative of the mythical order of creation, is a hint to the reader not to take the creation literally.

48 After all Plato's purpose is to isolate and show the work of the two "efficient" causes in the universe (cf. especially 46D–E and 69A–B).

49 Cf. Cornford, *Plato's Cosmology*, p. 31, "There are two senses in which the *Timaeus* is a 'myth' or 'story' (μῦθος). One we have already considered: no account of the material world can ever amount to an exact and self-consistent statement of unchangeable truth. In the second place, the cosmology is cast in the form of a cosmogony, a 'story' of events spread out in time. Plato chooses to describe the universe, not by taking it to pieces in an analysis, but by constructing it and making it grow under our eyes. Earlier cosmogonies had been of the evolutionary type, suggesting a birth and growth of the world, due to some spontaneous force of life in Nature, or, as in Atomism, to the blind and undesigned collision of lifeless atoms. Such a story was, to Plato, very far from being like the truth. So he introduced, for the first time in Greek philosophy, the alternative scheme of creation by a divine artificer, according to which the world is like a work of art designed with a purpose. The Demiurge is a necessary part of the machinery, if the rational order of the universe is to be pictured as a process of creation in time. But the important point is that, no matter whether you prefer to analyze the world or to construct it piece by piece, the account can never be more than 'likely,' because of the changing nature of its object; it can never be revised and amended into exact truth." Cf. also section V.

50 There is a striking reminiscence of the *Phaedrus* in 41E ff. (cf. Cornford, *Plato's Cosmology*, p. 144). Though we cannot assume that Plato considers that the reader of the *Timaeus* knows the *Phaedrus*, this reminiscence may help us to understand what was in Plato's mind.

[51] Cf. *Timaeus* 46D–E: primary causation is that of *NOUS*, but *NOUS* can only exist in a soul (cf. n. 34).

[52] I.e., that it was in disordered motion (cf. 30A, 52D ff.).

[53] Cf. especially, *Timaeus* 37C–38C.

[54] Vlastos, *Creation*, pp. 410–11.

[55] Vlastos, *op. cit.*, p. 413.

[56] Cf. Cicero, *De Natura Deorum* I. 9.21: . . . *saecla nunc dico non ea quae dierum noctiumque numero annuis cursibus conficiuntur; nam fateor ea sine mundi conversione effici non potuisse; sed fuit quaedam ab infinito tempore aeternitas, quam nulla circumscriptio temporum metiebatur, spatio tamen qualis ea fuerit intellegi potest, quod ne in cogitationem quidem cadit ut fuerit tempus aliquod nullum cum tempus esset* (and cf. Pease's note on *intellegi potest* in his *M. Tulli Ciceronis De Natura Deorum*, vol. I [Cambridge, Mass., 1955], p. 191). *Why* an Epicurean would distinguish a precosmic from a cosmic time is, I think, intelligible. Cf. also Proclus, *In Timaeum*, vol. III, p. 37, 12–13 (Diehl): λέγουσιν οἱ περὶ 'Αττικόν, ὅτι χρόνος μὲν ἦν καὶ πρὸ οὐρανοῦ γενέσεως, τεταγμένος δὲ χρόνος οὐκ ἦν.

[57] *De Caelo* I. 10, 279b 12–13: All say that the world has come into being, and some maintain that, having come into being, it is imperishable; in 280a 28–32 the *Timaeus* is cited for this notion. *Physics* VIII. 1, 251b 14 ff.: all agree that time is ungenerated, except Plato who generates it, since he makes it contemporaneous with the universe which has been generated.

[58] Cf. *Timaeus* 38C 4, ἵνα γεννηθῇ χρόνος.

[59] Cf. *Timaeus* 37E 3–38A 2. Vlastos (*Creation*, pp. 411–12) denies that Plato's statement implies that ἦν and ἔσται can *only* be predicated of motion that proceeds in time. He says: "To say that F and G come into existence as attributes of *x* when *x* comes into existence is uninformative as to any prior instantiation of F and G." But what Plato says about time and its "parts" *is not* a case of accidental predication as Vlastos' example is. Plato says (a) time did not exist before the universe came into being; (b) ἦν and ἔσται are parts of time; the logical conclusion is that ἦν and ἔσται did not exist before time and the universe were generated. This is precisely the place where Plato would have differentiated a precosmic from a cosmic time, if he had so wished; since he did not, we can only understand him as saying that there *was* a time when time was not; since this is a contradiction we must assume either that he did not see it or that he purposely insisted on it several times to call attention to the fact that the creation should not be taken literally. I can say "green and blue became predicates of grass and the sea when the latter came into being," and to this Vlastos' example would apply; but if I say "green and blue became predicates (or 'parts') of color when color was created," I must mean that there was no instance of green and blue before color was created.

[60] As Plato himself implies in *Timaeus* 37D 7 when he says that the Demiurge made of time an "eternal image" (αἰώνιον εἰκόνα) that the universe may imitate more closely the model which is itself eternal (37D 3, ἡ μὲν οὖν τοῦ ζῴου φύσις ἐτύγχανεν οὖσα αἰώνιος). Since the word αἰώνιος is applied to the model and to the copy, it cannot mean in the case of the latter only

imperishability: there must be something common to the model and the copy in order that both may be said to be αἰώνιος. And *Timaeus* 37C 6–38B 5 implies the answer: both model and copy are αἰώνιος, but whereas the former is eternal and atemporal, the latter possesses the eternity of infinite duration. This explicit contradiction of the creation myth should be given its full value and should be interpreted, I submit, as another indication given to the reader not to take the creation literally. (Against Cornford's suggestion to read ἀέναον εἰκόνα in 37D 7 [*Plato's Cosmology*, p. 98, n. 1], cf. Cherniss, I, n. 350.)

We may add that for Aristotle, too, the eternity of the universe implied that of γένεσις which he declares to be the closest approximation to the eternity of οὐσία. Cf. Aristotle, *De Generatione et Corruptione*, II. 10, 336b 25–337a 7.

61 I see no reason why Plato should specifically distinguish time (U) from time (S) only to deny that the latter exists. The assertion that the Demiurge generated time contemporaneously with the universe "in order that, as they were brought into being together, so they may be dissolved together, if ever their dissolution should come to pass" (38B), is a tacit denial of the possibility of a time (S).

62 So Aristotle and Eudemus. The latter said that Plato's definition of time (which he misinterpreted in the same way Aristotle did [cf. Cherniss, I, pp. 417 f., and n. 348]) is inconsistent with the existence of a precosmic motion since all motion is in time (Simplicius, *Phys.*, p. 702, 24–29= Eudemus, fr. 46 [Spengel]=fr. 82 b. [Wehrli]). For Aristotle's criticism, cf. n. 64.

63 Cf., for example, Proclus, *ap.* Philoponus, *De Aeternitate Mundi*, pp. 103, 1–104, 3 (Rabe).

64 Consequently, had Plato meant the creation of time to be taken literally, Aristotle's criticism (*Physics*, VIII. 1, 251b 19 ff.), that time must be unlimited because it implies the instant which is the limit between past and future time, would be valid. Vlastos (*Creation*, p. 413 and n. 1) denies that there is a logical reason why time must extend infinitely into the past, and asserts that "if it did not, one 'now' (the first) would have no 'before.'" We must take into consideration, however, that Plato himself was aware of the definition of "now" as the limit between past and future, since he uses it in the *Parmenides* (152B–E). At any rate, the notion of a first "now" which would have no "before" presupposes the existence of a creator, a notion to which Aristotle would not subscribe (therefore, his criticism is valid at least from his own point of view), which he does not attribute to Plato, and which is incompatible with Plato's conception of the divine (cf. section IV).

65 *Timaeus* 41A 3 ff.

66 *Timaeus* 42E 5–6.

67 Cf. Proclus, *In Timaeum*, vol. I, p. 288, 14–27 (Diehl).

68 Cf. Proclus, *op. cit.*; Cherniss, I, p. 425.

69 *Republic* 381B–C.

70 Vlastos, *Creation*, p. 406.

[71] Cf. *Republic* 381B 8–C 10 (*n.b.* B 10–C 9. Πότερον οὖν ἐπὶ τὸ βέλτιόν τε καὶ κάλλιον μεταβάλλει ἑαυτὸν ἢ ἐπὶ τὸ χεῖρον καὶ τὸ αἴσχιον ἑαυτοῦ;—'Ανάγκη, ἔφη, ἐπὶ τὸ χεῖρον, εἴπερ ἀλλοιοῦται· οὐ γάρ που ἐνδεᾶ γε φήσομεν τὸν θεὸν κάλλους, ἢ ἀρετῆς εἶναι . . . — 'Αδύνατον ἄρα, ἔφην, καὶ θεῷ ἐθέλειν αὑτὸν ἀλλοιοῦν, ἀλλ' ὡς ἔοικε, κάλλιστος καὶ ἄριστος ὢν εἰς τὸ δυνατὸν ἕκαστος αὐτῶν μένει ἀεὶ ἁπλῶς ἐν τῇ αὑτοῦ μορφῇ). This passage of the *Republic*, then, states unambiguously that God is unchangeable. Cf. Aristotle, *Metaphysics*, Λ. 9, 1074b 25–27.

[72] Cf. *Timaeus* 42E 5–6. God is the best of causes and his work is good, cf. 28A 6–B 1, 29A 2–6, 29E–30B, etc.

[73] *Timaeus* 29E 1–3, ἀγαθὸς ἦν, ἀγαθῷ δὲ οὐδεὶς περὶ οὐδενὸς οὐδέποτε ἐγγίγνεται φθόνος· τούτου δ' ἐκτὸς ὢν πάντα ὅτι μάλιστα ἐβουλήθη γενέσθαι παραπλήσια ἑαυτῷ; cf. *Phaedrus* 247A; cf. Aristotle, *Metaphysics* A 2, 983a 2–4.

[74] Cf. Cicero, *De Natura Deorum* I. 9. 21: *ab utroque autem sciscitor cur mundi aedificatores repente exstiterint, innumerabilia saecla dormierint;* cf. Lucretius V. 168–73; the criticism, probably also of Epicurean origin, of Anaxagoras and Plato in Aetius I 7, 5–9 (=Diels, *Doxographi Graeci*, pp. 299–301); and cf. especially Proclus, *In Timaeum*, vol. I, p. 288, 17–27 (Diehl). This kind of argument is at least as old as Parmenides (cf. *Parmenides* 28B 8, 9–10, τί δ' ἄν μιν καὶ χρέος ὦρσεν ὕστερον ἢ πρόσθεν, τοῦ μηδενὸς ἀρξάμενον, φῦν; and cf. my *Parmenides* [Princeton, 1965], pp. 102 f.).,

[75] Cf. above n. 34.

[76] Cf. *Euthyphro* 10A–11A.

[77] *Laws* 818A–E.

[78] Cf. *Laws* 818B 9–C 3 for the interpretation of which see Cherniss, I, pp. 608–609.

[79] *Phaedrus* 247D–E.

[80] Cf. Hackforth, *Plato's Phaedrus* (Cambridge, 1952), p. 78, n. 1, and p. 80.

[81] *Phaedrus* 249C 5–6.

[82] *Timaeus* 46E 4.

[83] Cf. Grube, *Plato's Thought* (London, 1935), p. 169; Cornford, *Plato's Cosmology*, pp. 38 and 280.

[84] *Sophist* 265B–E.

[85] *Politicus* 270A, 273A–C.

[86] *Politicus* 273B–D.

[87] Cf. *Republic* 507C 6–8, 529D–530B (cf. also 532C 1 with Shorey, *Plato, The Republic*, vol. II, p. 199, n. b).

[88] *Republic* 530A 5–7.

[89] Cf. *Gorgias* 453A 2 and E 4–5 where Rhetoric is said to be πειθοῦς δημιουργός; cf. also 454A–E; *Charmides* 174E–175A; *Symposium* 188D; *Euthydemus* 292D.

[90] Cf. *De Generatione et Corruptione* II. 10, 336b 27–34. That this passage of Aristotle's is related to the *Timaeus* has been recognized by some scholars (cf. Cherniss, I, n. 352 with references). But however this may be, the passage clearly shows that Aristotle, too, could use the image of the

creator to make clear to his readers his teleological conception of the universe, and that he could do so though he does not even cast his thought into a creation myth, as Plato did.

91 Cf. Cherniss, I, pp. 609 ff. Cf. also the previous note, and n. 160 *infra*.

92 *Timaeus* 28B 7.

93 Hackforth, *CQ*, N.S. IX (1959): 18 f.

94 Vlastos, *Creation*, pp. 402–05.

95 *Timaeus* 28B 6–7.

96 *Timaeus* 28B 4–C 2.

97 Vlastos, *Creation*, p. 402.

98 Cf. Zeller, *Die Philosophie der Griechen*, II, i^5 (Leipzig, 1922), p. 793. The point had already been raised by Proclus, *In Timaeum*, vol. I, pp. 283, 27–285, 7 (Diehl).

99 Cf. Cherniss, I, n. 361.

100 *Timaeus* 30A 3.

101 Cf. Vlastos, *Creation*, pp. 403–05.

102 Cf. *Timaeus* 52D 3–4, ὄν τε καὶ χώραν καὶ γένεσιν εἶναι, τρία τριχῇ, καὶ πρὶν οὐρανὸν γενέσθαι.

103 Cf. Cornford, *Plato's Cosmology*, pp. 24–26; Alcinous, *Epitome* XIV, 3 (Louis); Taurus, *ap.* Philoponus, *De Aeternitate Mundi*, pp. 145, 8–147, 13 (Rabe); Proclus, *In Timaeum*, vol. I, pp. 290, 13–291, 12 (Diehl); Asclepius, *In Nicomachi Isagogen* I γ, 68–79 (Tarán). For this meaning of γένεσις and γίγνεσθαι cf. also Aristotle, *De Generatione et Corruptione* II. 10, 336b 25–34. The interpretation of line 34 does not affect my argument, though I prefer to retain the words καὶ τὴν γένεσιν; cf. W. J. Verdenius and J. H. Waszink, *Aristotle On Coming-to Be and Passing-Away. Some Comments* [second edition revised and enlarged (Leiden, 1966)], p. 67; *contra* F. Solmsen, *Aristotle's System of the Physical World. A Comparison with his Predecessors.* (Ithaca, New York, 1960), p. 386, n. 28.

104 Solmsen (*Aristotle's System of the Physical World*, p. 51), while recognizing that "there are definite reasons why Plato's cosmos should have no temporal beginning," says that "we have no right to give them more weight than did Plato himself and to set aside his unequivocal and emphatic statement that the Cosmos 'has come into being.' . . . The arguments for the eternity of the Cosmos become decisive only with his pupils." Solmsen (*op. cit.*, p. 50, n. 114) appears to think that Plato himself gives a warning against going beyond the myth when he says τὸν εἰκότα μῦθον ἀποδεχομένους πρέπει τούτου μηδὲν ἔτι πέρα ζητεῖν (29D 2–3). I have given my reasons against such an interpretation of γέγονεν in 28B 7. I would like to add that the fact that the mythical form may be intimately connected with a subject does not mean that we cannot derive conclusions that go beyond the myth. Moreover, we should distinguish in the *Timaeus* two things which could be εἰκός: on the one hand we have the mythical account of creation, on the other the *content* of Timaeus' discourse about the physical world. Now 29D 2–3 is Timaeus' conclusion from the fact that his discourse is about the universe which is a physical object and about which there can be only an εἰκὼς λόγος

or μῦθος (cf. 29B 3–D 3). An examination of the different passages where Plato uses these expressions will show that it is the content of the physical doctrines propounded by Timaeus that is declared to be "likely," or as "likely" as any other, *not* the creation myth itself. (See also Cornford's remarks cited in n. 49 *supra.*) Finally, that Plato was interested in the question whether the universe had a beginning or not is shown by the *Timaeus* itself [cf. 27C 5, ᾗ γέγονεν ἢ καὶ ἀγενές ἐστιν, with Shorey's comment in *AJP*, X (1889): 47–48]. For some plausible reasons why Plato adopted the mythical account for the *Timaeus*, cf. Friedlander, *Platon*, I[3] (Berlin, 1964), pp. 211–12=*Plato*, vol. I (New York, 1958), p. 200. Cf. also in the English edition, p. 248, a passage which has apparently been omitted from the last German edition.

105 Cf. especially 46D–E.

106 As he did in the *Phaedrus* and in the *Laws*, cf. n. 31 *supra.*

107 I employ the term "matter" fully conscious that it is a notion foreign to Plato, and I use it because it is often employed in analyses of the *Timaeus*. But I take it as a mere synonym for "phenomenal" or "sensible" existence.

108 Cf., e.g., Vlastos, *Disorderly Motion*, esp. pp. 395 ff., Festugière, *La révélation d'Hermes Trismégiste.* II. *Le dieu cosmique* (Paris, 1949), pp. 110 ff., Festugière, *La révélation* . . . III. *Le doctrines de l'âme* (Paris, 1953), pp. xii–xiv, H. Herter, "Bewegung der Materie bei Platon," *RhM*, 100 (1957): 327–47, M. Untersteiner, *Aristotele, Della Filosofia* (Roma, 1963), pp. 112–13. I am, of course, aware that it is possible to interpret the cosmogony of the *Timaeus* metaphorically and at the same time consider that Plato nevertheless attributed spontaneous disordered motions to matter, as for example Festugière does. I believe, however, that *Timaeus* 57D 7–58C 4 refutes both positions at once. See also n. 131, *infra.*

109 Cf. *Timaeus* 46C 7 ff., 47E 3 ff., etc.

110 Cf. *Timaeus* 46C 7–E 6.

111 Cf. *Timaeus* 47E 3–48A 7. For the correct interpretation of 48A 5–7, especially of ᾗ φέρειν πέφυκεν, cf. Shorey, *CP*, 23 (1928): 356; Cornford, *Plato's Cosmology*, p. 160, n. 2.

112 Cf. Vlastos, *Disorderly Motion*, p. 396.

113 Cf. *Timaeus* 52E 5–53A 7; see also 57B 7–C 6.

114 Cf. *Timaeus* 57D 7–58C 4, especially 58A 2–4, and what follows below in the text. This refutes, I think, Vlastos' conception of chaos (cf. *Disorderly Motion*, p. 396) as something which is in constant motion for purely mechanical reasons, so that the Demiurge "never has to think of starting motion, but only to keep it going." The important point, however, is that the conditions attributed to chaos in 52D 4 ff. entail that chaos cannot be in *constant* motion for purely mechanical reasons, since motion would have come to an end with the complete sorting out of the four kinds into four separate homogeneous masses.

115 Cf. *Timaeus* 57E 1–2, τὰ μὲν οὖν ἤδη περὶ αὐτῶν εἴρηται, πρὸς δ' ἐκείνοις ἔτι τάδε, κτλ. This must refer to everything that was previously said about motion, including the revolution of the world-soul, cf. Cherniss, I, pp. 449 and 450.

116 Cf. *Timaeus* 57E 2–58A 1. But this principle was already implied and used to explain the transformation of one kind of corpuscle into another, cf. *Timaeus* 56C–57C and *n.b.* 57A 3–B 7.

117 Cf. *Timaeus* 58A 1–2, αἰτία δὲ ἀνισότης αὖ τῆς ἀνωμάλου φύσεως. ἀνισότητος δὲ γένεσιν μὲν διεληλύθαμεν.

118 Cf. *Timaeus* 52E 1–3.

119 *Timaeus* 58A 2–4.

120 *Timaeus* 58C 2–4, οὕτω δὴ διὰ ταῦτά τε ἡ τῆς ἀνωμαλότητος διασῳζομένη γένεσις ἀεὶ τὴν ἀεὶ κίνησιν τούτων οὖσαν ἐσομένην τε ἐνδελεχῶς παρέχεται.

121 Cf. *Timaeus* 58A 4 ff. and *n.b.* A 7–B 2, σφίγγει πάντα καὶ κενὴν χώραν οὐδεμίαν ἐᾷ λείπεσθαι. διὸ δὴ πῦρ μὲν εἰς ἅπαντα διελήλυθε μάλιστα, ἀὴρ δὲ δεύτερον, κτλ. The διό shows that the reason for the penetration of the different kinds of particles into the spaces left by the others is due to the fact that they are all confined inside a rotating universe where there is no void.

122 In 58A 4–5 ἡ τοῦ παντὸς περίοδος means "the revolution of the whole universe," as *Timaeus* 34A 6–7 proves; so Cherniss, I, p. 449 and n. 392. See also *Laws* 897B 7–8 with C 4–5 which also shows that περίοδος = revolution.

123 Cf. *Timaeus* 34A 8–B 9, 36D 8–E 5; Cornford, *Plato's Cosmology*, pp. 58, 93.

124 This is to say that the direct cause of the separation of the different kinds of corpuscles is the secondary motions of the receptacle, and of the corpuscles themselves, cf. *Timaeus* 53A, 57B 5–6, 57B 7–C 6; but 58A 4 ff. makes it clear that these secondary motions are not inherent in the precosmic chaos but are indirectly caused by the world-soul. It is these secondary motions and the characteristics of the four kinds of corpuscles as described in 55E–56A that explain the formation of the four regions in the universe (starting from the center): those of earth, water, air, and fire. Cf. Cherniss, I, n. 393.

125 *Timaeus* 58B 4–C 4.

126 This would be true even if ἡ . . . περίοδος in 58A 4–5 would mean only "circumference" and not "revolution" (but cf. n. 122 *supra*). And this being the case, it is clear that the precosmic chaos lacked the necessary conditions to insure the continuous existence of heterogeneity and consequently of motion, cf. 57E 2–58A 4. It could not have been the act of creation that prevented the complete separation of the masses of the four simple bodies from one another, because, if taken literally, the precosmic state of affairs had existed for an infinite time before the moment of creation.

127 *Timaeus* 58A 2–4, when taken together with 52E–53B, shows that Plato must have been conscious of the contradiction of attributing spontaneous motion to the precosmic chaos, since this motion could only be sustained with the creation of the universe.

128 We have seen that Plato explains the sorting out of the different corpuscles as the effect of their secondary motions upon one another, and that this secondary motion is indirectly caused by the world-soul. Moreover, Plato expressly denies the existence of the attraction of like by like (cf.

Timaeus 80C with Cherniss, I, p. 387, n.) and explains physical motion by the principle of circular thrust (περίωσις), which implies that there is no void and that ultimately purely physical mechanical motion depends on the revolution of the whole universe. In fact the principle of circular thrust, which Plato uses in the *Timaeus* to explain such physical phenomena as the movements of projectiles, thunderbolts, etc., by itself proves that in 58A 4–5 ἡ τοῦ παντὸς περίοδος means "the revolution of the whole."

129 Cf. Cherniss, *PAPS*, 98 (1954): 26 and nn. 27 and 29.

130 Cf. Cherniss, I, pp. 447 f., and *PAPS*, 98 (1954): 26 and nn. 26 and 28.

131 Cf. *Timaeus* 46C 4–E 6, 57D 7–58C 4, *Laws* 894E–896A. In a paper entitled "Causation in the *Timaeus* and *Laws* X," *Eranos* 65 (1967): 25–38, H. J. Easterling also maintains that the doctrine of the *Timaeus* concerning causation is consistent with that of *Laws* X, but he does so on the assumption that the disordered motions of the *Timaeus* and the secondary motions of the *Laws* are independent from the soul though subservient to it. Easterling thinks that his interpretation holds whether one interprets the *Timaeus* literally or not, that "there is no hint in the *Timaeus* that ψυχή is in any way responsible for the pre-cosmic motion" (30), and that whereas "in the created universe ψυχή causes motion by acting upon disequilibrium (57D–58A)" before the creation of soul "Plato describes motion as taking place because of disequilibrium alone (52D–E)" (38). As for the *Laws*, citing 896E–897A, Easterling places special emphasis on the meaning of παραλαμβάνουσαι "to put to work" something already in existence, and concludes that in the created universe the physical effects are the result of soul making use of physical motions already in existence (37). But, even apart from the question of the metaphorical interpretation of the *Timaeus* which, I believe, is fatal to Easterling's interpretation, 57D 7–58C 4 shows not only that the soul causes motion by acting upon disequilibrium, but that the rotatory motion caused by the world-soul (one should notice that Easterling accepts Cherniss' interpretation of this passage) is the cause of the preservation of disequilibrium; and since 58A 2–4, with its backward reference to 52D–53C, shows that the motion of the precosmic chaos is not self-subsistent (cf. the text above), it seems clear that Plato could not attribute spontaneous motion to matter and that he implies that soul is the ultimate source of all motion (were it not for the rotation of the universe caused by the world-soul everything would come to a standstill in the created universe as well as in the precosmic chaos). Because of the myth of creation Plato cannot openly say in the *Timaeus* that soul is the source of all motion, as he does say in the *Laws*; but he does say in 46D–E that secondary causes belong to those things which being set in motion by others move yet other things with random motions. This is to say that the secondary causes do not possess self-motion and owe their motion to the soul, and this is essentially the same thing said in *Laws* 896B 4–8, ἡ δι' ἕτερον ἐν ἄλλῳ γιγνομένη κίνησις, αὐτὸ δὲ ἐν αὑτῷ μηδέποτε παρέχουσα κινεῖσθαι μηδέν, δευτέρα τε, καὶ ὁπόσων ἀριθμῶν βούλοιτο ἂν τις ἀριθμεῖν αὐτὴν πολλοστήν, τοσούτων, σώματος οὖσα ὄντως ἀψύχου μεταβολή. Nor

is there any need to speculate on what would happen in a universe without soul, for Plato says in 895A 5–B 7 that if everything were at a standstill motion could be started only by a self-mover, and this self-mover (identified with the soul in 895C–896A) would then move that kind of movers which being moved, or changed, by another moves yet others and has therefore secondary motion (τὴν δὲ ἀλλοιουμένην ὑφ' ἑτέρου κινοῦσαν δὲ ἕτερα, δεύτεραν). These two passages, among others, show that in the *Laws* Plato maintains openly and unambiguously that without soul there would be no motion at all. But soul produces the secondary motions and then tries to control them; consequently there is nothing strange in Plato's use of παραλαμβάνειν to refer to the action of the Demiurge or of soul on the secondary motions. Since Plato believed that the universe is eternal (soul being identical with self-motion cannot have been created), the secondary motions are a constant factor in the universe. Ultimately each secondary motion is caused by soul; but as a whole class of causes the secondary motions may be treated as subservient to soul and at the same time as producers of disordered motions, which disordered motions are further and further deprived of purpose unless they are brought again under the direct "control" of soul. I conclude, then, that both the *Timaeus* and the *Laws* preserve the doctrine of the *Phaedrus* that soul being identical with self-motion is the ultimate source of all motion. The apparent divergencies among these three works are due to their different dramatic settings and to the specific purpose of each one. For the relative chronology *Phaedrus*, *Timaeus*, *Laws*, cf. Cherniss, "The Relation of the *Timaeus* to Plato's Later Dialogues," *AJP*, 78 (1957): 225–66, reprinted in Allen, *Studies in Plato's Metaphysics*, pp. 339–78.

132 Vlastos, *Disorderly Motion*, p. 385.

133 Cf. Cherniss, I, pp. 414 ff., Vlastos, *Disorderly Motion*, p. 384.

134 Cf. Cherniss, I, pp. 609 f. and n. 160 *infra*.

135 Cf. section IV *sub fin.* with n. 90 *supra*.

136 That the Demiurge and the "created gods" are a symbol of intelligent causation is suggested even by the fact that Plato often uses both expressions interchangeably, cf. section IV and the references in n. 83 *supra*.

137 Cf. *De Caelo* 279b 4–283b 22 and *n.b.* 279b 12–13.

138 Cf. Plato, *Republic* 545C–576B and Aristotle, *Politics*, V. 12, 1316a 1-b 27; Cherniss, I, n. 358 and the references there given.

139 Cf. Aristotle, *Metaphysics* N 2, 1088b 35 ff. with Cherniss, I, pp. 92–93. Aristotle thinks that the difficulties in which the Platonists involved themselves in identifying matter with non-being were caused by their desire to prove that absolute non-being is real, the point that Plato specifically denies in the *Sophist* (238C, 258E); yet, as Cherniss points out, it is to the *Sophist* that Aristotle is referring in *Metaphysics* N 2, 1088b 35–1089a 6. Cf. also Ross *ad loc.*

140 For Speusippus' interpretation, cf. n. 152 *infra*.

141 Cf. Xenocrates, frag. 54 (Heinze).

142 Cf. Plutarch, *De Anim. Procr.* 1013A–B, Proclus, *In Timaeum*, vol. I, p. 277, 8–10 (Diehl).

143 We find in Aetius II, 4, 1 and 3 (=Diels, *Doxographi Graeci*,

pp. 330, 331) two statements to the effect that Pythagoras and Heraclitus considered the world to be generated not in time ἀλλὰ κατ' ἐπίνοιαν. Gigon, *Untersuchungen zu Heraklit* (Leipzig 1935), pp. 61–62 thinks that this information comes from Heraclides Ponticus, and if this is so Heraclides must have interpreted the *Timaeus* metaphorically and extended this interpretation to Pythagoras and Heraclitus (cf. Cherniss, I, n. 356). But I think it is more likely that in the second passage Heraclitus is a mistake for Heraclides, as Cherniss suggests, for the doxographers confused sometimes the names Heraclitus and Heraclides (cf. Aetius II 25, 13 = Diels, *Doxographi Graeci*, p. 356; Aetius III 17, 1 = Diels, *Doxographi Graeci*, p. 382). To this we may add that Proclus, *In Timaeum*, vol. I, p. 290, 3–17 (Diehl) mentions two metaphorical interpretations of the *Timaeus*: the first maintains that Plato "generated" the universe κατ' ἐπίνοιαν μόνην, the second σαφηνείας ἕνεκα διδασκαλικῆς. Proclus does not mention the names of the authors of either theory, but just as the latter is the interpretation of Speusippus and Xenocrates, so it is likely that the former (κατ' ἐπίνοιαν) is that of Heraclides Ponticus. We possess evidence that Heraclides "interpreted" the *Timaeus* and that he tried to read into it his own doctrines, cf. Cherniss, I, pp. 545–57.

144 Cf. *De Caelo* I. 10, 279b 32–280a 2.

145 Thus *De Caelo* I. 10, 280a 6–7 is a reference to *Timaeus* 30A 5, and notice also in 279b 32–33 (where line 33, the universe is indestructible but generated, must be a reference to the *Timaeus*) the word βοήθειαν.

146 Cf. *De Caelo* I. 10, 280a 2–10.

147 Cf. Cherniss, I, pp. 421–22.

148 Cf. *Timaeus* 46C 7–E 6, 47E 3–48B 3, 57D 7–58C 4, 68E 1–69B 2 and section VI *supra*. Cf. also Simplicius, *De Caelo*, pp. 306, 16–307, 11 (Heiberg).

149 Cf. Theophrastus, frag. 29 (Wimmer) = *Phys. Opinion.* fr. 11 (Diels, *Doxographi Graeci*, pp. 485, 20–486, 1). Cf. also frag. 28 (Wimmer) and the rest of Diels' frag. 11.

150 Cf. Diogenes Laertius V, 36; Regenbogen *s.v.* "Theophrastos von Eresos," *R.E.* Suppl. VII (1940): col. 1358.

151 Cf. Cherniss, *The Riddle of the Early Academy* (Berkeley, 1945), pp. 38–43.

152 Cf. the *scholion* in *Cod. Paris. Gr.* 1853 (p. 489A 9–12 [Brandis]), ὁ Ξενοκράτης καὶ ὁ Σπεύσιππος ἐπιχειροῦντες βοηθῆσαι τῷ Πλάτωνι ἔλεγον ὅτι οὐ γενητὸν τὸν κόσμον ὁ Πλάτων ἐδόξαζεν ἀλλὰ ἀγένητον, χάριν δὲ διδασκαλίας καὶ τοῦ γνωρίσαι καὶ παραστῆσαι αὐτὸ ἀκριβέστερον ἔλεγε τοῦτον γενητόν. Vlastos, *Disorderly Motion*, p. 383, n. 2, apparently would question the attribution of the metaphorical interpretation to Speusippus: "The textual authority . . . is frail: the *scholion* in the Parisian MS of the *De Caelo*; no mention of Speusippus in Plutarch, Proclus, or Simplicius." What this scholiast reports about Xenocrates, however, is correct, and he probably had a good authority for his report on Speusippus too. There is, moreover, more indirect evidence: Aristotle attacks those who maintain that numbers are "separated" and "eternal" and yet speak of the "generation" of numbers

τοῦ θεωρεῖν ἕνεκα, and concludes that what these thinkers say about the "generation" of the even shows clearly that οὐ τοῦ θεωρῆσαι ἕνεκεν ποιοῦσι τὴν γένεσιν τῶν ἀριθμῶν (cf. *Metaphysics* N 3, 1091a 12–13 and 23–29). This criticism of the "generation" of numbers is to be connected with Aristotle's attack on the metaphorical interpretation of the generation of the universe, as the Pseudo-Alexander saw; and as the position attacked by Aristotle in the *Metaphysics* is both that of Xenocrates and that of Speusippus, so it is likely that in the *De Caelo* he has both of them also in mind, though he mentions neither by name in either passage. [For the evidence and an analysis of it, cf. P. Lang, *De Speusippi Academici Scriptis Accedunt Fragmenta* (Bonn, 1911), pp. 30–32]. Thus the *scholion* in the *Parisinus* provides us with valuable information that we should not dismiss without good reasons.

[153] Cf. Vlastos, *Disorderly Motion*, pp. 380–83, esp. 380.

[154] Cf. *Republic* 595C–597E; see Frutiger, *Les Mythes de Platon* (Paris 1930), pp. 105–06; Cherniss, "On Plato's *Republic* X 597 B," *AJP*, 53 (1932): 233–42.

[155] Cf., e.g., 69A 6–7: the kinds of causes are "the materials for our building"; the names applied to God—Demiurge, ὁ τεκταινόμενος (28C 6), ὁ συνιστάς (29E 1), etc.; the Demiurge fits the heavenly bodies into their motions (instead of starting their motions), cf. 38C, 40A, see section II *supra*; in the third part of the dialogue (69A ff.) the distinction between god and the "created gods" is ignored, cf. n. 83 *supra* for references. Even more important: if the "creation" is taken literally, the language used by Plato would suggest that the motion of soul is locomotion (and the myth forces Timaeus to speak as if it were; cf., e.g., 47B–C, 90C–D), whereas the "motions" of soul are psychical (cf. 37A–C; Cherniss, I, pp. 402–05, esp. n. 331); consequently, axial rotation is only a symbol of the psychical self-motion of soul.

[156] See the introductory remarks to this paper and nn. 7, 8, 9, 12 *supra*.

[157] Similarly, the "generation" of the minimal city in *Republic* 369B ff. is not to be interpreted "historically," though Aristotle apparently did interpret it so, cf. *Politics* IV. 4, 1291a 10–33; cf. Frutiger, *Les Mythes de Platon*, pp. 49–52.

[158] Cornford, *Plato's Cosmology*, p. 20.

[159] Cf. the references in nn. 8 and 9 *supra*.

[160] Cf. Cherniss, I, pp. 609 f. We should notice that in *De Caelo* I. 10, 279b 17–31 Aristotle is arguing against the view that the Universe can be both "generated" and everlasting. Here, if anywhere, Aristotle should have said something about the Demiurge, since in the *Timaeus* (41A–B) the Demiurge declares that the created gods and by implication the universe (cf. also 37C–D) will be everlasting, since this is *his will*, but tacitly admitting that, as Aristotle says, anything generated will perish. One would have expected Aristotle, had he taken the figure of the Demiurge literally, to deny that even a god would have the power to make everlasting something that came into being. That Plato himself considered the statement of 41A–B only as part of the mythical *mise-en-scène*, is shown by the fact that he gave

another reason why the universe is everlasting: in 32C–33B the Demiurge is said to have included the whole of the four simple bodies into the making of a single universe, that it might be free from age and sickness, i.e., that it might be everlasting.

[161] Cf. nn. 90 and 137 *supra*.

[162] The "creator" is absent from Greek pre-philosophical cosmogonies (Hesiod, Epimenides, Pherecydes, etc.) and from the cosmogonies of the Presocratics. Neither Empedocles' Love and Hate, nor Anaxagoras' *NOUS* can be compared to a creating god. In the "cosmogony" described in the second part of Parmenides' poem there is a δαίμων ἣ πάντα κυβερνᾷ (28B 12, 3); she is not a "creating" god, but only the cause of union and birth, perhaps the traditional god that governs all things; her "creation" of Eros in 28B 13 is a "mental" act (μητίσατο), see my *Parmenides*, pp. 247–50. W. Burkert, *Phr*, XIV (1969) 3, n. 7, would compare 28B 13 with the *Derveni Papyrus*, col. 19,4 (cf. Kapsomenos, *Arch. Deltion* XIX [1964]: 24), where ἐμήσατο is used according to Burkert of the "Schöpfungsakt des Zeus, vgl. Orph. Fr. 91." But even if "Orpheus" had written (ἐ)μήσατο (cf. Burkert, *Antike und Abendland* XIV [1968]: 96, n. 6), this verb is always used in reference to a mental act of planning or contriving, and not to real "creationism." Moreover, it is not certain that "Orpheus" wrote (ἐ)μήσατο because *Orph. Frag.* 91 (Kern) is late and not directly related to the content of col. 19,4 of the *Derveni Papyrus*, and also because in the latter ἐμήσατο may be only the commentator's rendering or interpretation of what he saw in his text of "Orpheus."

[163] It is against them that Plato reacts in Book X of the *Laws* and also in the *Timaeus* itself as 46C 7–D 4 shows.

[164] For the Demiurge as a mythical figure, cf. Cornford, *Plato's Cosmology*, pp. 34–39. The Demiurge is neither identical with the idea of Good nor with the world-soul, cf. Cherniss, I, pp. 603–10.

[165] Since "physics" for Plato can only be a likely story, it was preferable for him to present the working of the universe as the construction of a machine by an artisan, rather than to offer a direct analysis of the universe which would have forced him to make many arbitrary assumptions. Presenting it as a story has the advantage of passing over those unexplained assumptions and seeming less arbitrary: either you accept the story as "saving the phenomena" or not.

KURT von FRITZ
University of Munich

The Philosophical Passage in the Seventh Platonic Letter and the Problem of Plato's "Esoteric" Philosophy*

In recent years the problems concerning the seventh of the letters that have been handed down to us under the name of Plato and especially concerning the philosophic passage that it contains have once again become the object of a very lively discussion. Within the last few decades most competent scholars had finally become convinced by the arguments in favor of the authenticity of the letter. The new controversy, that has sprung up only recently, appears to move in two opposite directions. On the one hand the authenticity either of the letter as a whole or of the philosophic passage has been attacked by new arguments. On the other hand, the very same passage, acknowledged as indubitably authentic, has been taken as an incontestable testimony for the existence of an "esoteric" doctrine, not contained in Plato's dialogues, but communicated by him orally, either to a selected group of students, or perhaps also, to some extent, to the audience of his public lectures. It was then considered a most important task of modern scholarship to reconstruct this "esoteric" doctrine from various sources and testimonies, direct and indirect.

The question of the authenticity of the *Seventh Letter* as a whole, it seems to me, is very closely connected with the problem of Plato's attempt to take an active part in politics and to apply his political theories in practice. This problem, however, can be solved only with the help of a careful analysis of the testimonies of the historians, Plutarch, Diodorus, and Cornelius Nepos, a task which has hardly ever been tackled in real earnest up to the present.[1] It must therefore be left for another occasion.[2] In this paper I shall concern myself exclusively with the so-called philosophic passage in the context of recent discussion.

* Presented at the 1965 meeting of the SAGP in Providence, Rhode Island.

A most important question discussed within the "philosophic passage" concerns the inherent weakness of every written statement of things that require *understanding*, i.e., which are not capable of being expressed in ordinary language with the unambiguous precision of a mathematical formula. This weakness springs from the fact that in all such statements the possibility of misunderstandings and of objections based on such misunderstandings is infinite and that, therefore, a written statement can deal expressly only with part of these possible misunderstandings but is incapable of clearing up all of them, so that, if this is to be done, someone has, as Plato expresses it, "to come to its help." This then is the advantage of a spoken dialogue—that every misunderstanding of a statement by the interlocutor can be cleared up right away and every objection to the statement arising from such misunderstanding can be refuted as it occurs, whereas in a written account it is impossible to foresee in what particular way the individual *reader* may misunderstand what is said.

Some of the objections raised against the authenticity of the *Seventh Letter* have taken their starting point exactly from these observations on the weakness of written communication. Their authors have tried to show that these observations are un-Platonic and originated in misunderstandings of authentic utterances of Plato in some of his dialogues. To me, the very opposite appears to be true, namely that these objections and, in general, most of the arguments commonly set forth against the authenticity of the philosophic passage present in fact a prime illustration of what the author of the letter says about the inevitable weaknesses of every written account of certain things. If this should be true, the most urgent task is obviously to "come to the help" of the "logos" of the *Seventh Letter*, i.e., to interpret it most carefully with a view to the objections raised, and thus to clear away, so far as possible, the whole complex of misunderstandings that have recently arisen concerning it—though, if what the author of the letter says is true, it will inevitably remain possible that, after these objections have been refuted, new misunderstandings and new objections based on them may arise in the future. It is only when this task of interpretation is discharged as far as possible that an answer can be given to the further question, whether the text, correctly understood and assuming that Plato is its author, can be considered as a testimony in favor of the existence of an "esoteric doctrine" which can still be reconstructed to a considerable degree, as some younger German authors have recently tried to prove.

The philosophic passage is connected with and follows upon a discussion of the claim of the younger Dionysius to be in possession of true philosophical insight, and of a report according to which the young tyrant had written a philosophical work in which he had compiled and made public, as his own wisdom, all sorts of things that he had heard either from Plato himself or at second hand concerning the latter's philosophy.[3] At this point the author of the letter mentions also the weaknesses of the written word in general, pointing out that if anyone was capable of expressing his (Plato's) deepest thought adequately in writing it would be Plato himself, not a young man, who knew of them only at second hand.

This passage has recently been used in an attempt to show that the letter cannot be genuine.[4] But, as presently will be shown, the objection is based on a flagrant misinterpretation of what the letter actually says. According to this interpretation the letter says that "an unphilosophical man (the younger Dionysius) recognizes the worth of philosophy but also his own incapacity for it, yet out of wickedness gives himself the appearance of understanding." If this was what the letter said, the objections raised against its authenticity would be quite convincing. For this does contradict the philosophy of Plato and Socrates, according to which wickedness and bad conduct arise from ignorance. It is quite true that "the Platonic view would have been to give *lack* of knowledge of the worth of philosophy, not knowledge of it (much less, one might add, the insight into one's own imperfections), as the ground of wickedness." But the *Seventh Letter* says in fact nothing of the kind. What it actually says is that Dionysius had written a "philosophical" work *out of evil ambitions*, because he coveted the fame of being an initiate in philosophy.[5] The "knowledge of the worth of philosophy" therefore is not a knowledge of its true worth, but, so to speak, of its market value. So far, then, no contradiction to Plato's philosophy is to be found.

Still more flagrant, however, is the misinterpretation of the second part of the passage:[6] ἡ μὲν δὴ πεῖρα αὕτη γίγνεται ἡ σαφὴς καὶ ἀσφαλεστάτη πρὸς τοὺς τρυφῶντάς τε καὶ ἀδυνάτους διαπονεῖν, ὡς μηδέποτε βαλεῖν ἐν αἰτίᾳ τὸν δεικνύντα, ἀλλ' αὐτὸν αὑτόν, μὴ δυνάμενον πάντα τὰ πρόσφορα ἐπιτηδεύειν τῷ πράγματι. This passage is interpreted by G. Müller[7] in the following way: "they (the τρυφῶντες) seek the blame in themselves and in their inability, not in the object or the teacher," with the ironical comment—"most amazing in unphilosophical natures." In fact the statement would be most astounding in any case, no matter whether Plato or someone else had written the letter, if it was actually made. It is however obvious and corresponds to the rules of Greek grammar that in the sentence quoted the clause beginning with ὥστε expresses the logical and objective *consequence* of the "πεῖρα," *not* that which the τρυφῶντες actually do. This is also the way in which the sentence in question has always been understood by the most competent translators of all nations: cf. *Plato's Briefe, übersetzt von Otto Apelt* (Leipzig, 1921), p. 71—"So geprüft *können sie* die Schuld nie auf den Führer schieben sondern nur auf sich selbst und ihre Unfähigkeit, alles für die Erfüllung der Aufgabe Erforderliche zu leisten"; E. Howald, *Die echten Briefe Platons* (Zürich, 1951), p. 105—"Das ist also die ganz sichere . . . Probe . . . arbeitsuntüchtigen Menschen gegenüber, bei der sie nie die Schuld auf den Führer werfen *können*, sondern sich selbst zuschreiben *müssen*, wenn sie nicht imstande sind" etc.; *Platon, Œuvres complètes* (Edition Budé, tome XIII, 1: texte établie et traduit par J. Souilhé), p. 50—"Voilà une expérience claire et infaillible, quand il s'agit de gens de plaisirs et incapable d'effort: ils *n'ont pas à accuser* leur maître, mais eux-mêmes, s'ils ne peuvent pratiquer," etc. What the letter actually says then is that the τρυφῶντες *have to* blame themselves and *cannot* (*rightly*) *blame* it on their teacher if they do not understand what he says, and not at all that they actually seek the blame in themselves. G. Müller's objection to the letter therefore is made possible only through a flagrant mistranslation of what it says.

What follows presents at least a somewhat more difficult problem. This is the assertion of the author of the *Seventh Letter* that the deepest meaning of Platonic philosophy can be fully communicated neither by the written nor by the spoken word, and that even so far as its meaning *can* be communicated, this communication is limited to a restricted circle. The question of the meaning of this limitation will have to be discussed later when we shall come to the problem of Plato's so-called "esoteric doctrine." The problem of the essential incommunicability of the deeepest meaning of Plato's philosophy has been discussed *ad infinitum*. It is indeed a most fundamental problem and has to be taken up again for its own sake, and not only in order to meet an objection to the authenticity of the *Seventh Letter*.

According to a famous passage of Plato's *Phaedrus*,[8] the weakness of the written word is caused by the fact that it always says only what it says but cannot answer questions which are put to it, in order to obtain a more perfect insight into the meaning of what has been said. It cannot cope with objections and therefore stands in constant need of someone, preferably the author himself, who "comes to its help." According to G. Müller's[9] interpretation, this passage means that only what is written is "weak and superficial," but that, in contrast, the truth can very well be expressed in oral conversation if this conversation proceeds according to strict method. When, therefore, it is said in the *Seventh Letter*,[10] that the essence of the matter is incommunicable *both* in writing and through oral conversation, this is in flagrant contradiction with what Plato says in the *Phaedrus*.

However, in order to see whether this argument, which at first sight has a certain plausibility, is cogent, it is necessary to determine exactly the cause of the inadequacy of the written word. As has been pointed out it consists in its incapability of answering questions in further explanation of its meaning. But if the weakness of the written word lies in its being written, not in the personal incapacity of its author for correct expression, this means obviously that even the most capable author cannot find a formulation of his ideas so perfect that it excludes misunderstanding. The advantage of oral over written communication, as the *Phaedrus* quite correctly shows, lies in this, that the teacher can try again and again to clear up the misunderstandings of his interlocutor and to meet objections raised because of them. But, because of the inherent imperfections of human language, there is no *certain* way of avoiding ever renewed misunderstandings even in oral communication. The *Seventh Letter*, therefore, merely draws the ultimate consequence of what is said in the *Phaedrus*. There is no contradiction between the letter and the dialogue.

It is necessary to be quite clear on this point in order to understand correctly what the *Seventh Letter* says[11] about a "spark that must jump across" (from the teacher to the student) "and kindle a light that thenceforth nourishes itself." This passage was misunderstood as far back as late antiquity as if some kind of mystical illumination were meant. Porphyry, for instance, in a famous passage of his life of Plotinus,[12] says that while the great Plotinus succeeded four times in his life-time in seeing this light, he (Porphyry) accomplished this only once, in his sixty-eighth year. Among the Neo-Platonists this misunderstanding sprang from their own inclination to mysticism. Among the moderns, who continually commit the same error, it arises, on the contrary, from modern scientism and positivism. The positivists with their senseless assertion that every statement that cannot be "verified" in a very specific fashion is "meaningless" have produced such a blindness with regard to the commonest types of cognition that they are no longer capable of seeing what is directly before their eyes.

In fact what is pointed to in this passage of the *Seventh Letter* is nothing but the highest stage of something which at lower stages occurs every day and everywhere. It is a cognition very different from the transmission of mathematical formulae or the communication of bare facts, a kind of cognition that is achieved in the understanding of a work of art (including literature), of historical works or of philosophical ideas—in other words, in all those cases in which understanding is achieved through interpretation. It would not be necessary to interpret a Greek tragedy again and again, if what can be said about it could be said, either in writing or orally, completely once and for all. Everyone who has given an interpretative lecture which was worth the effort will occasionally have the experience that later, for instance at an examination, some sentences that he has said are served up to him again completely out of their context and that every question which goes beyond what was actually said in the lecture reveals the complete lack of understanding on the part of the student. But he will also have experienced a great joy when he has seen how a spark has jumped across and a light has been kindled that continues to burn independently and enables the student to apply, to enlarge, to amplify on his own what the teacher has said. What the *Seventh Letter* says about the necessity of living for a long period of time with certain subjects is also quite correct. It is just what Lichtenberg means when he says that though one may read Tacitus as a young man and admire him as a great writer, it is not until old age, when one has acquired a wider knowledge of human life, that, re-reading his work, one realizes how great a writer he is. The philosophical insight, of which the *Seventh Letter* speaks, is, to be sure, of a still higher kind. But in principle the difficulty of the transmission of true insight from one person to another, whether by writing or orally, is just the same in one case as in the other. What the *Seventh Letter* says about the spark that must jump over, and the light that must be kindled, has nothing whatever to do with mystical contemplation or with dialectical "dervish-dances," as many modern interpreters of the passage believe. Far, therefore, from contradicting what is said in the *Phaedrus*, the *Seventh Letter* complements it very suitably—a fact which at least proves the intelligence of its author.

The discussion of the difficulties of written or spoken communication is followed by the famous passage on what—not quite appropriately—has been called "the gradation of knowledge." At this point G. Müller, whose objections to the authenticity of the *Seventh Letter* we have discussed so far, acquires an ally in W. Bröcker,[13] who accepts the authenticity of the *Seventh Letter* as a whole, including the passages just interpreted, but finds a great part of the ensuing theory of the acquisition of knowledge to be contradictory of true Platonic philosophy and therefore considers it as an interpolation. Again, then, the question must be asked whether it is possible to "come to the aid" of the *Seventh Letter*.

The process that leads to real knowledge of an object, according to this passage, begins with the *word* (ὄνομα) which signifies the object and passes through: (1) its definition (λόγος); (2) its image in space and time; and (3) its epistemological apprehension, to the object itself. All this is illustrated by the example of a circle. The ὄνομα is the word "κύκλος" or "circle," the definition is "a curve in a plane, all of whose points have equal distance from a point in the center," the image is the figure of a circle drawn on a tablet. With the fourth stage a difficulty comes in which is not, as in nearly all other cases, merely the consequence of false interpretation but, as will be shown presently, the result of the intricacies of the process involved. Of the fourth stage it is said[14] that it comprises knowledge (ἐπιστήμη), insight or apprehension (νοῦς), and true or right opinion (ἀληθὴς δόξα) "in reference to these," namely the first three stages and the fifth; in other words, correct knowledge in regard to the signification of the word and the definition, the true nature of the drawn figure, and finally in regard to the "circle itself"—i.e., what Plato calls the idea of the circle.

These three variations of the fourth stage (ἐπιστήμη, νοῦς, and ἀληθὴς δόξα) have this much in common—that they are not incorporated in sound (like ὄνομα and λόγος) and not in corporeal forms (like the circle drawn on a tablet) but exist exclusively in the soul. But what exists in the soul is not identical with the nature of the circle itself (i.e., what Plato calls elsewhere ὁ κύκλος αὐτός or the idea of the circle). These statements are followed by the assertion that whoever does not succeed in some way in grasping all of the first four will never completely share in the knowledge (ἐπιστήμη) of the fifth. This formulation presents a real difficulty, which has also been seized upon by G. Müller,[15] viz., that ἐπιστήμη belongs to the first four, so that it appears a senseless truism to say that without it one cannot share in the knowledge (ἐπιστήμη) of the fifth. Now in so far as the difficulty is caused by the repetition of the word ἐπιστήμη it could be easily removed by cutting out the last "ἐπιστήμης" and reading instead: "will never share in the fifth." But this makes the real difficulty only more apparent. For how can one share in the fifth, i.e., in the idea itself, in the sense meant here, unless epistemologically? On the other hand, the idea, for its part, according to Plato, can never completely enter the soul. What is in the soul is always only a greater or lesser approximation, a stronger or weaker condition of being, so to speak, trained on the idea as on a target. To this extent it is quite correct to say that one can never attain the highest possible knowledge of the idea simply by means of the word which signifies the idea plus its definition plus its corporeal image without the soul's fixed attention on the idea, which in its weaker form is called ἀληθὴς δόξα and in its stronger form ἐπιστήμη. The difficulty one encounters here is quite analogous to the difficulty with which Plato is grappling everywhere in his late dialogues, especially in the *Parmenides*: the difficulty of finding a word that expresses exactly the relation between ideas and *things*. For lack of a better expression he often uses the word μετέχειν, which, literally translated, means "to participate in" or "to share in." The expression appears adequate in as much as every individual man "shares in" the idea of man, but is only an imperfect incorporation of the idea of man. Yet, in another sense, not just *part* of the idea of man but the whole idea of man is somehow present in each individual man: hence the expression "participate in" seems not quite correct. This impossibility of finding an expression that expresses the relation of ideas and things with absolute precision has also caused many misunderstandings, which in their turn gave occasion to objections to the theory of ideas as such.[16] This fact is a very good illustration of the difficulty, so strongly emphasized in the *Seventh Letter*, of expressing certain things adequately in words. But to emphasize this difficulty is quite Platonic.

The next objections raised in the articles of Müller and Bröcker (who starts at this point) rest chiefly once again on incorrect interpretation of the text; and it is interesting to see that, though they have also a good deal in common, they are also in part mutually contradictory. This section of the *Seventh Letter* begins with a statement of the deficiencies of the first stage, the ὄνομα.[17] These deficiencies make it difficult to communicate knowledge because of the weakness of any expression in speech (διὰ τὸ ἀσθενὲς τῶν λόγων). For the words designating things have no foundation in the nature of the things designated but are arbitrarily formed, as follows also from the fact that, if one wishes, one can interchange the signs. The same holds of course good of the λόγος, i.e., the definition of a thing or, in fact, of any kind of speech that tries to designate the nature of a thing, since all speech is made up of ὀνόματα (designations of objects) and ῥήματα (other kinds of words),[18] all of which are arbitrarily formed or chosen. Furthermore, the image in space and time (for instance, the circle made by a draughtsman or a turner) is full of what is quite contrary to the fifth (the idea of the circle), the circumference of the latter being strictly one-dimensional, which the circumference of the drawn circle, that inevitably has a certain breadth, is obviously not, the ideal circle being absolutely equally curved in all its parts, which the drawn circle is not, etc. Finally all three "stages" share the defect that all of them reveal mere qualities (τὸ ποιόν τι) of the object just as much as its being (τὸ ὄν), which causes further confusion. For this reason communication (of insight into ideas) through speech is so difficult, that it may seem better to give up the attempt, except with those who are capable of grasping the true essence of things even through such imperfect instruments (sc. such people, however, can be selected for oral conversation only, since what is written is available to everyone).

Against these statements of the *Seventh Letter* a whole storm of objections has been raised. Bröcker,[19] in contrast to Müller, maintains the authenticity of the preceding sections concerning the stages of approximation to true knowledge. That the passage which follows is an interpolation, is in his opinion proven "by the sudden change in the use of the word λόγος," which previously meant "definition," but now suddenly appears to mean "speech in general." But this transition from one meaning to the other is wholly legitimate. For the definition shares the weakness of the individual word, since it is made up of words. The same is obviously true of every other kind of speech. What is strange about this? The only apparent difficulty arises from the fact that the word λόγος with Plato can signify not only speech in general *but also* "definition": a very good illustration for the defective "stability" and precision of verbal signification of which the *Seventh Letter* speaks in this passage. Furthermore, Bröcker believes that what is said in this passage has nothing to do with the inexpressibility discussed in the preceding parts of the letter. For this, Bröcker remarks, "is as little to be overcome in the silent conversation of the soul (with itself) as in spoken utterance." But what Bröcker says here is quite incorrect or at least expressed in an entirely misleading fashion. If "as little" means that even in the silent conversation of the soul with itself the object (the transcendent idea) is not wholly apprehended, then one can agree. But—and this aspect is completely neglected in Bröcker's observation—there still remains the most essential distinction that in this conversation with itself the soul is directed towards the object and knows what the word it uses is meant to designate or to point at (in the particular case in question whether the word λόγος means "definition" or "speech in general"), while the reader of a dialogue or treatise in which the word is used may understand one meaning instead of the other and be thereby misled.

While Bröcker's objection is based on the view that the lonely conversation of the soul with itself overcomes inexpressibility "as little" as the spoken word, Müller, on the contrary, "becomes indignant"[20] at the thought "that the 'logos' can be 'pushed' into the (totally inferior) sphere of mere sound," whereby, in his opinion, "a foundation-pillar of Platonic philosophy is shattered." Quite contrary to Bröcker, he is also shocked by this "discrediting of knowledge within the soul." And yet, Müller says, according to *Sophist* 263, thought and speech are the same, except that speech within the soul, which proceeds without sound, is called διάνοια, while that which proceeds from the mouth is called λόγος (in the narrower sense). If "logos" is unreliable, dialectic and the theory of ideas become untenable. Such scepticism as is expressed in this passage of the *Seventh Letter*, in Müller's opinion, "is without example and without place in Plato's philosophy."

The reason why Bröcker and Müller are able to raise completely opposite objections against the very same passage of the *Seventh Letter* is of course the same as always: that in both cases the argument is imprecise because of the ambiguity of the words used. In Müller's case this is still more easy to show than in Bröcker's. If one were to use against his objections the same method of argument that he himself uses, one need merely point out that in the very passage from the *Sophist*, that Müller quotes, the subject of the sentence is ψευδεῖς λόγοι, i.e., "false logoi" and that this means both kinds of logoi, the silent ones within the soul as well as those in spoken utterance. Therefore, dialectic and the theory of ideas, according to the *Sophist*, are untenable. Since both are Platonic, the *Sophist* cannot be a work of Plato. Of course, this argument is sheer sophistry. But it differs in no way from an argument which draws inferences concerning the untenability of the theory of ideas from the possibility of misunderstanding the spoken word (λόγος). It is in fact exactly the purpose of living dialectic, which is realized only in speech and not in writing, to direct the vision of the interlocutor towards the ideas by incessant correction of the imperfections of the spoken logos, and of the errors and misunderstandings that arise from these.

Bröcker's next objection is directed against what the letter says[21] about the ποιόν and its relation to the ὄν. This time the objection does not even proceed from the ambiguity of the meaning of the written word, but simply from an incorrect rendering of the text. For a whole page Bröcker attacks the view[22] that name, definition, image, and "knowledge" offer *only* the ποιόν of the object and not also the ὄν. He is perfectly right in refuting this view. But not a word of it is said in the *Seventh Letter*. In fact the *Seventh Letter* says something quite different, almost the opposite,[23] viz., that all four of them seek to give the ποιόν *no less than* the ὄν, which clearly implies that they also seek to point to the ὄν. It explicitly states that the confusion arises from the fact that when the soul seeks *exclusively* the ὄν it is continually offered the ποιόν (of course, because the ποιόν and the ὄν are not properly distinguished, as follows from what had been said just before, and *not* because the ὄν was not also included in the intention of the first four). This is continually shown in Plato's early dialogues, when the interlocutors who are asked by Socrates what rhetoric is, or bravery, or the ὅσιον, or something else, always answer first with a ποιόν, as for instance "something very wonderful" or the like, instead of answering the question about the ὄν. The answer to the question *what* (τί) the object really is, then, always turns out to be very difficult to find because of the ἀσθενὲς τῶν λόγων mentioned in the *Seventh Letter*. Once again, therefore, we find that what the *Seventh Letter* says is thoroughly Platonic unless by so-called "interpretation" one replaces it by something that the *Seventh Letter* does not say.

"But," we are now asked in turn by G. Müller,[24] "why should the weakness of λόγος affect or be responsible for the inadequacy of images (the drawn circle) or even of the epistemological act in the soul (or the reverse)?" Again Müller's formulation does not render quite precisely what the *Seventh Letter* says. It is true that, according to the *Seventh Letter*, the individual inadequacies of the several means of acquiring and communicating knowledge are not completely independent of one another, but that there is a certain interconnection and relation between them. What this relation is, is in fact not very difficult to see. The ὄνομα, according to Müller, is at most uncertain because it can signify different things, but has absolutely nothing to do with the imperfection of the drawn circle. Really nothing? Protagoras, as is very well known, attacked the mathematical definition of tangents, according to which a tangent touches the circle at only one point. Obviously for him the word "circle" or κύκλος signified the drawn circle and not the ideal mathematical circle, and led him to ascribe to the circle of the mathematicians (which he did not recognize as really existing) properties (ποιά) which pertain only to the drawn circle.

Modern mathematicians still encounter the same difficulty, though at a higher level, precisely in regard to the definitions of geometrical objects—to which in Müller's opinion the statements of the *Seventh*

Letter can find no application whatsoever. Hilbert said once he would prefer never to speak of straight lines, angles, circles, polygons and the like but instead to use other, arbitrarily chosen(!!) names or designations. His purpose was to prevent anyone from being misled by looking at these objects (or their representatives on paper: the drawn angles, etc.) so as to make assumptions about them other than or beyond those explicitly stated in the axioms or demonstrated in the proofs based on these axioms. Here then, just as in the *Seventh Letter*, the fear is expressed that the inadequacies and inaccuracies of sense perception might be introduced into strict mathematical theory *by means of the designations of the mathematical objects in every day language*. To be sure, a hypothetical remedy to this was discovered by him precisely in that arbitrariness of nomenclature which the *Seventh Letter* marks out as a reason for the "instability" of names. But that this hypothetical remedy is no real remedy is shown by the fact that Hilbert did not actually use it, but continued to use the terms: straight line, angle, circle, polygon, etc. For it is easy to see that the mere choice of different terms would not prevent the confusion of perceptual with mathematical objects.

An analogous difficulty arises in modern mathematics in regard to definition (Plato's λόγος in the narrower sense). This difficulty has induced modern mathematicians to replace definitions (in the ordinary and Platonic sense of the word) of certain basic mathematical concepts or objects by so-called implicit definitions—which means that instead of a definition of the concept, a series of axioms, in which the concept occurs, is set up, and it is then claimed that through this set of axioms the concept is "implicitly defined." The same difficulty of defining objects accurately and sufficiently has also led to the attempt to convert everything into pure calculation, i.e., to a process of deriving relations of mathematical objects (to one another) from other relations previously stated and so forth, while the terms of the calculations, which originally signify objects that can enter into such relations to one another, are, so far as possible and in the ideal case, completely emptied of their content—precisely because of the inherent difficulty of an accurate designation of the objects represented by the terms (with their full content). The author of the *Seventh Letter* has thus implicitly anticipated a problem that has been radically revealed for the first time by modern scientism and with which modern science is still struggling. In the same way Plato in his *Theaetetus* has anticipated epistemological problems and their possible solutions of which nobody else at his time had been fully aware and which began to be really discussed in a still rather imperfect way in the Hellenistic age and with greater clarity and consistency only by the empiricists of the 17th and 18th centuries. In fact he tried to point out the deficiencies and imperfections of theories which were fully elaborated only 2000 years after his time.

The enormously compressed presentation in the *Seventh Letter*, to be sure, leaves no room for detailed explanation of the problems—nor for the discussion of various possible attempts at their solution—to be compared with the way in which the problems of a sensualist theory of knowledge are handled in the *Theaetetus*. But it is clear that the author would not be in agreement with that sort of modern scientism which is not content to create or adopt a method that yields very good results within certain limited areas of inquiry but declares dogmatically that there is no other method leading to true knowledge and that everything that cannot be unequivocally formulated and "verified" in a narrowly circumscribed manner is meaningless.[25] On the basis of the principles set down by the author of the *Seventh Letter* there would be no objection to the validity of the methods of modern scientism within a limited sphere. This, too, is quite in agreement with Plato, who, at the end of the *Republic* Bk VI, acknowledges the validity of the methods of the mathematicians, who take certain basic assumptions, whose validity they take for granted, as their starting point and from there move on to their theorems—though he insists that this method has to be supplemented by the method of the dialectician and philosopher, who inquires into the validity of the basic assumptions by trying to connect them with and derive them from an ἀνυπόθετος ἀρχή, and that this method of the dialectic philosopher is in a certain way the higher one.[26] The author of the *Seventh Letter* is, however, aware, just as Plato is in the *Republic*, that the most important knowledge of man *as man* is not the knowledge of the scientists and of the mathematicians and cannot be set down in fixed and unmisunderstandable formulae, as the knowledge of the mathematicians can, and realizes the difficulty of the communication of this kind of knowledge and insight. This inherent and unavoidable difficulty in the communication of such knowledge is the reason why the theoreticians of scientism theoretically do not acknowledge this knowledge as knowledge and pretend that it is void of content and that its expression in language is meaningless—though in actual fact they cannot for an hour of their waking life do without this kind of knowledge and its ever so imperfect communication.[27] Thus, the arguments of the *Seventh Letter* are thoroughly Platonic. Not only this, but they are also extremely worthy of consideration, especially in a time which, through positivistic and scientistic theories, has allowed itself to become totally blind to the most everyday and most indispensable processes of acquiring knowledge—viz., those which cannot without loss be transmitted from one person to another or committed to paper by means of signs or symbols of absolutely fixed meaning, but require the "jump of the spark."

What has been said so far is perhaps sufficient to explain the most essential meaning of the arguments used in the philosophic passage of the *Seventh Letter*. But it is still necessary to counter the further objections that Müller and Bröcker have advanced. All the more so since they present a wonderful illustration of the helplessness of the written *logos*, unless someone comes to its aid. They also show very clearly what results when, instead of trying to ascertain from the context exactly what meaning the words (ὀνόματα) have in the particular place in which they occur, one takes the words in any one of the various meanings they may have in different contexts and proceeds from there.

At the end of the argument in the *Seventh Letter*,[28] as we have seen,[29] it is stated that, whenever the soul tries to grasp the "what" (τί) of a thing, the various instruments of knowledge and of its communication (word, definition, image, and the inaccurate representation that these summon forth in the soul) present it also (and in a way preferentially) with a ποιόν τι. In consequence, what is said or shown becomes easily refutable, so that the soul cannot see its object clearly and becomes utterly confused. Against this Bröcker raises the following objection:[30]

> In truth and also according to an opinion frequently expressed in Plato's dialogues one can refute nothing but propositions and opinions, and not all of these, but only false ones. Our passage, however, speaks of a refutation of the four: namely: name (ὄνομα) definition, image, and knowledge (true opinion: ἀληθὴς δόξα). The only one of these which can be possibly refuted is λόγος or definition if it (as often in Plato's dialogues) is understood as an assertion of what meaning is usually linked with a certain name. But one cannot refute either names or images or true opinions. The refutation of an argument can be undertaken by argument, i.e., by means of other propositions. In some cases it can also be done through a *demonstratio ad oculos.* In this way one can say that the Eleatic doctrine of the impossibility of motion is refuted by a *demonstratio ad oculos* (that motion actually occurs). But not every proposition is refutable because of this—not by a long shot, not even every false proposition.

All of this is completely correct as far as the principles brought in are concerned. But it does not concern the text, because the text does not say what is imputed to it. In the first place, as the wording of the passage clearly shows, it is a question of the refutability not of the four as such, but naturally of the propositions that can be based on them. In the second place the word εὐέλεγκτος is not correctly interpreted. This latter fact would be difficult to prove—which is again an example of the helplessness of the written *logos* whenever the author cannot come to its aid in person, for any other interpreter may be accused of having given the text a meaning that the author did not intend—if there were not fortunately an exactly parallel passage incapable of misconstruction in the *Theaetetus*,[31] so that Plato himself can be called to our assistance.

The problem treated in the *Theaetetus* is not the same as in the *Seventh Letter*, or at least it is seen from an entirely different angle. What is discussed there is the assertion that all knowledge is perception, and that perception is always in flux, always in a process of change. Thus it is said, knowledge can never be fixed, but everything is simply what it appears to the perceiver at any given moment. Upon this there follows the sentence which is of crucial importance for the interpretation of the *Seventh Letter*: "If, therefore, anyone wishes to fix it (i.e., the object of perception and knowledge) through speech he is εὐέλεγκτος." By this sentence any opinion that is more than the statement of a fleeting perception is designated as εὐέλεγκτος: as easily refutable. Now it is obvious and in accordance with Bröcker's own conviction that Plato acknowledged the validity not only of opinions characterized as statements of momentary perceptions, but certainly also of opinions which, as he says, "stabilize knowledge," i.e., concern lasting truth. If therefore he says that any opinion of the latter kind is εὐέλεγκτος, "easily refutable," he obviously speaks not of true but of *apparent* refutation: refutations like Protagoras' refutation of the mathematical definition of a tangent, for this definition can be easily refuted by pointing out that any (drawn) tangent touches a (drawn) circle in more than one point. But for the mathematician and for Plato this is not a valid refutation.

The argument in the *Seventh Letter* is exactly the same. For good measure this is expressly stated at the end when it is said[32] that when the aim (of the philosopher as teacher) is to reveal, as far as possible, "the fifth," i.e., the final object of knowledge, the idea, then anyone can easily make it appear in the eyes of the audience *as if* he who is trying to make it (the fifth, the idea) accessible to their knowledge (by word or by writing or by answers he gives to their questions) understood nothing of what he is trying to explain; but if this happens, they (the audience) fail to see that it is not the "soul" of the philosopher that is convicted of error (refuted) but the nature of the four preliminary stages of inquiry, which are shown up as inferior. In this passage then it is expressly stated that it is not a question of real refutation of the actual knowledge of or insight into the idea, a knowledge that exists in the soul of the philosopher who tries to transmit his own insight to his audience, but of an *apparent* refutation in the eyes of the audience (who is misled by the false objections raised by one of its members). If then at the end of this part of the exposition the *Seventh Letter* seems to speak of a "refutation" of the four stages, instead of speaking—as it had done up to this point—of a refutation of the *opinions* pronounced on the strength of them, it should not be necessary to point out that in this connection the word ἐλέγχειν has a slightly different shade of meaning (for which reason I have translated it in one place by "to convict of error" and in another place by "to show up" instead of "to refute"). But this different meaning of the word is quite old. It can, for instance, be established quite clearly in the old proverb χρυσὸς κλῃῖδας ἐλέγχει, which does not mean "gold refutes the locks" but "overcomes the locks," "makes them come to naught," "shows them up as futile," because with gold one can manage to pass through otherwise locked doors.[33] Thus the deficiencies of the first four stages of the approach to knowledge or insight are *shown up* by pointing out that it is these deficiencies that make it possible to raise false objections leading to *apparent but false* refutations. The "refutations" of the authenticity of the *Seventh Letter* by Bröcker and Müller (whose objections at this particular point are not substantially different from those of Bröcker) are exactly of this type. They therefore present an excellent illustration of what the author of the *Seventh Letter* describes when he speaks of the *apparent* εὐέλεγκτον of Platonic *logoi.*

Müller, however, tries to carry his "refutation" of the text still a step further. This continuation of his argument is most revealing.

> Our perplexity," he says,[34] "has not yet reached its highest point. It does so when we read (343E): 'But the passage through all these (four stages), as we ascend and descend in turn from stage to stage can occasionally in the end generate knowledge issuing from a man of high natural accomplishments in a man of high natural accomplishments.' Here we have before us a completely debased dialectic: ascent from name via definition and image to a psychic act of knowledge, descent from this via image and definition to the name. This can only be called a caricature of the classic description in the *Republic* 511B of the ascent from 'hypotheses' to 'that which is without hypothesis' and to the 'source of the Universe,' and of the corresponding descent 'in which one makes no use at all of the perceptible but only of the Ideas themselves and ends with

Ideas.' How in the world is the *eidos* to be recognized by the fine-natured soul through ascent and descent along the steps of a ladder of knowledge so fragile?

The answer to this argument is that the *Seventh Letter* speaks—unlike the passage of the *Republic* quoted by Müller—not of different types of knowledge and of the approach to knowledge, but of the *communication* of knowledge. It is difficult to see how the communication of knowledge (if we exclude logical and mathematical calculations transmitted by formulae expressed in symbols) is to take place unless by means of words, speech (including definitions) made up of words, and possibly reference to models in time and space like the illustrations in geometry books. The fragility of this means of the communication of knowledge caused by the ambiguity of words, and of the speech consisting of words as well as by the inaccuracy of material images, is well known and demonstrated not only by the modern efforts to create meta-languages and to combat the errors caused by material models[35] but also, though quite involuntarily, by the errors of interpretation committed by Müller and Bröcker.

It would be sad if it were entirely impossible to arrive at true knowledge with the help of these fragile instruments. For they are the only instruments we possess. It is, however, *not* impossible to transmit knowledge by means of them, and this transmission occurs, when it occurs, exactly in the manner described by the *Seventh Letter*: namely whenever one tries, through careful consideration of the whole context, in which a word or a statement occurs, not to be led astray by the ambiguity of the words used but to get into one's field of vision exactly that object and that combination of objects, on which the author himself has fixed his attention, and if—after having "ascended" to these objects from the words in their context—one then descends again and, on the strength of the acquired insight into the object, tries to determine the exact shade of the meaning of the words used in the statement or the communication. In fact this is the method of all true interpretation. It is also what I have tried to practice continually in this chapter, not with reference to the highest knowledge of the "source of the universe" but quite modestly with reference to what the author of the *Seventh Letter* wishes to say. This attempt, to be sure, is once more of necessity composed in words and—what is worse—laid down in writing. If I have succeeded, as I hope to have done, in clearly refuting the refuters, there remains nevertheless, as Plato has pointed out, the inexhaustible possibility of new misunderstandings and of new objections arising from such misunderstanding. One can only hope that in answer to such future objections someone will come to the aid of the *logos* of the author of the *Seventh Letter*.

Insofar as this discussion of the objections raised against the philosophic passage in the *Seventh Letter* has yielded a result, it seems to me to be this: that the author of this section is not only an outstanding Platonist, but an extremely good philosopher, a philosopher, I am inclined to say, as distinguished as Plato himself. Since this, after all, is something very rare and since nothing remarkable is otherwise known about the author of the *Seventh Letter*, if he is not Plato, this seems to me to argue very strongly in favor of identifying the author with Plato.

It is, however, perhaps advisable to conclude with a few observations concerning the method of such inquiries into the authenticity of philosophical works, both in general and with special reference to Plato. It belongs to the basic character of Platonic philosophy or rather of Platonic philosophizing to look at an object constantly from new angles; for this is the only way in which one can hope to get as full a view as possible of an object, which, according to Plato's own statement, in its totality can never be expressed adequately in words. For this reason it cannot be expected that Plato will again and again say exactly the same thing about the same subject. This is not at variance with a remark made by Socrates in some of Plato's early dialogues that he not only always says the same thing but that he always says the same thing about the same thing, for even "saying the same thing" may have various meanings. With Socrates this is his answer to the reproach that he always comes back to the same principles. But this did not prevent Socrates any more than Plato from approaching them from different angles. There is then no sense in expecting that the degrees of knowledge at the end of the sixth book of the *Republic* must be the same as in the *Seventh Letter*, where the problem is mainly that of communication, but one must ask whether what is said is meaningful and correct in the context in which it occurs. Thus the method which is often praised as particularly scholarly or scientific, to ask only what a philosopher meant, may fail if the question is not asked whether what he is supposed to have meant is true or *at least understandable as an attempt to explain the world in which we still live*. Even if this attempt was made in terms familiar to the time in which the philosopher lived, philosophical and philological interpretation cannot, in a philosophical text, be separated from each other.

After having tried to prove the authenticity of the *Seventh Letter* so far as the authenticity of any literary work can be really proved and, above all, to defend its most important philosophical passages against misinterpretations, we may then proceed to the question whether or how far these passages, together with other evidence, support the thesis, recently so energetically defended, that there existed an esoteric or secret doctrine which Plato deliberately withheld from the general public and which he therefore did not reveal in his published dialogues. H. J. Krämer,[36] who was the first in recent times to renew this thesis, has certainly done an important service to classical scholarship by pointing out that in one passage of the *Seventh Letter*[37] the statement is actually made that only very few people are able to profit from a discussion of certain things of a very high order and that these few are able to find the truth about them with the help of a very slight suggestion, while all others (who are witnesses of or participate in such a discussion) are either filled with unwarranted contempt which in no way befits its object (because they do not see what it is really about) or with an exaggerated and inflated expectation (of some kind of superhuman wisdom), as though they had learned something wonderful (while in actual fact they have only learned to use high-sounding words).

However, before we draw far reaching conclusions from this passage concerning an esoteric doctrine of Plato's or try to find some connection with the dark and difficult indirect tradition about Plato's lecture περὶ τοῦ ἀγαθοῦ or about his doctrine concerning the "Great and Small" it will perhaps be wise to ask whether we cannot bring the passage in connection with some better known facts of Plato's life. Having done this, we may then again ask the question whether these well known facts confirm the Platonic character of what is said in the *Seventh Letter* or are apt to stir up new doubts in spite of what we have tried to show in the preceding chapters.

In this respect it is perhaps not quite irrelevant, that Socrates, according to the testimony of all his disciples, conversed at all times and in all places—in the marketplace, in the gymnasia, in the homes of friends and acquaintances—with everyone who wished to engage in conversation with him, on any and every subject, while nothing of the kind is reported of Plato. On the contrary, as everybody knows, on the return from his first longer sojourn abroad he founded the Academy, i.e., he bought a house with a garden outside the city where he met and in part lived with a group of older and younger men whom he himself had selected in order to engage with them in philosophical discussion and conversation with the aim of making them true philosophers and potential statesmen as well. This would appear in perfect agreement with what the *Seventh Letter* says about the many and the few.

There are other differences between Socrates and Plato that can be put in relation to what is said in the *Seventh Letter*, though Socrates and Plato have, of course, also a good deal in common. Socrates, like Plato, did not escape the fate of being despised for his philosophic activity. A pre-Platonic witness to this is the *Clouds* of Aristophanes. In the *Gorgias*, one of Plato's earlier dialogues, Socrates' declaration that it is better to suffer wrong than to commit wrong as well as the arguments by which he supports this view are called nonsense, φλυαρία, by his interlocutor Kallikles.[38] But Socrates appears completely immune to contempt and insult. He simply continues to insist that his interlocutor should listen to his arguments. In this respect too Plato appears to have been somewhat different from Socrates.

In regard to the second possible effect of philosophical teaching on the πολλοί, mentioned in the *Seventh Letter*, the difference between Socrates and Plato appears to have been still greater. What one could learn by watching Socrates was his dialectical method. The young men who listened to him did this, as countless witnesses attest, in large measure; and naturally they did not use his method always strictly in the Socratic way, much less with a truely Socratic purpose. It seemed great fun to them to embarrass dignified politicians by asking them tricky questions, and this was perhaps not the least important reason for Socrates' indictment on a charge of corrupting the youth. A priceless illustration of this is the conversation, reported by Xenophon,[39] between Alcibiades and his famous uncle Pericles, who was, to be sure, too superior a man to feel offended by his nephew's tricks. But the end of the conversation, in the course of which Alcibiades has "refuted" one after another of Pericles' arguments is noteworthy. "When I was a young man," says Pericles, "I liked to engage in this kind of intellectual sport; but now I have more serious things to attend to." "O Pericles," answers fresh young Alcibiades, "I wish I had known you when you were a young man." Thus it was obviously possible to misuse Socratic philosophy or rather the Socratic method. But this was not the kind of misuse of philosophical teaching that the author of the *Seventh Letter* has in mind in the passage quoted.

Socrates, it is true, made statements and used dialectical arguments, which most men found rather unusual and paradoxical. But if we do not, with A. E. Taylor, consider everything, even in Plato's late dialogues, a representation of genuinely Socratic philosophy, in the sense of the historical Socrates, there is no indication whatsoever that Socrates ever made use of words, terms, expressions other than those of everyday colloquial attic speech. That he had no Theory of Ideas is proved by the vehement protests of other disciples of Socrates, Antisthenes for example,[40] against this Platonic doctrine. Certainly Socrates did not talk about ideal numbers or about such strange concepts as that of the "Great and Small." But it is these doctrines and these terms that can most easily be misused in the way described in the *Seventh Letter*: by using them on any and every occasion in order to give oneself the air of being in the possession of some amazing wisdom not accessible to ordinary people. There are today, even in the U.S.A., learned blue-stockings who are fond of talking in this way of the ΝΟΥΣ and similar things.

There can then hardly be any doubt that what the *Seventh Letter* says about the πολλοί and the ὀλίγοι is quite Platonic. It shows that Plato believed that only few could fully understand his philosophy. But does this prove that he had a "secret doctrine" that he communicated only to a few and withheld from the general public?

The problem of philosophic communication has three aspects: the aspect of "how," the aspect of "what," and the aspect of "to whom." With regard to the first aspect the *Seventh Letter* says that written communication is the poorest and most insecure since the written *logos* cannot defend itself. Thus oral communication obviously has the advantage over it. This is what Socrates practiced, since he never wrote anything but always talked with everyone. Plato, with his written dialogues, obviously tried to effect a compromise, since these, so far as possible, attempt to preserve the character of living discussion, where new objections are continually raised and, through their refutation, the problem or the object is constantly brought into a new perspective. These written dialogues, on the other hand, can never *completely* overcome the deficiencies of the written word, since nobody can possibly foresee all possible objections and misunderstandings and so refute them. In regard to the "what," the Platonic dialogues can be divided into two main groups: those in which there is no trace of the theory of ideas and in which no words occur not used in colloquial speech, and those in which either the one or the other or both are found. As for the "to whom," the dialogues, since they were published, were accessible to the general public. The oral discussions in the Academy, of course, were not. But the question is whether there were other philosophic utterances of Plato that were not generally accessible, and whether the oral discussions in the Academy could be reported and talked about freely or were deliberately kept secret. Only if this was the case can one really speak of a "Geheimlehre." There are, of course, various possible combinations of "how," "what," and "to whom," that have to be taken into consideration if a clear and definite result is to be obtained.

Since, as everybody knows and is generally acknowledged, some of Plato's dialogues adhere more closely to what is known as the method of the historical Socrates, others less so, it is advisable to begin with one group, instead of lumping everything together as H. J. Krämer does.[41] For only in this way is it possible to determine whether a tendency towards what may be called esotericism can be observed in both groups or only in one of them or in neither.

Krämer begins his discussion with the statement:[42] "Nearly all the great dialogues . . . have the common characteristic that the chief speaker . . . before or immediately at the climax of the conversation explains, in approximately similar terms, that he must pass over in silence the question of the real essence of the object discussed and that he will perhaps come back to it on another occasion." In this description of the character of certain Platonic dialogues the question of esotericism is from the beginning prejudiced by the choice of an entirely unsuitable expression. Nowhere in the passages quoted by Krämer is there any mention of "passing something over in silence." What does happen is that at the end of the dialogues certain important problems remain unsolved and the suggestion is made to continue the *discussion* at another occasion. A discussion is certainly something different from a ready made solution. Krämer's assertion[43] that the reference to further discussion is a mere pretext, i.e., a formula, that really means that the real and important results are only to be communicated to a circle of initiates is therefore without foundation. On the other hand, the question must certainly be asked *why* the main problem is not definitely solved and why reference is made to further discussion.

Let us then take an example. Plato's dialogue *Protagoras* ends with the statement[44] that the interlocutors have arrived at a quite paradoxical result. Protagoras has maintained that ἀρετή can be taught but has questioned that it is an ἐπιστήμη, i.e., that it rests exclusively on knowledge or on true insight. Socrates has tried to prove and, if we acknowledge the validity of his arguments, has proved that ἀρετή rests exclusively on ἐπιστήμη, but has questioned that it can be taught. Yet if it is an ἐπιστήμη it ought to be teachable. If, on the other hand, it is not, how should something be taught that is neither learning nor knowledge? Both interlocutors appear to have contradicted not only each other but themselves. The discussion of this difficulty and the attempt to find a solution are put off for another time.

Now the paradox with which the dialogue ends is capable of theoretical solution on the basis of fundamental Socratic-Platonic assumptions discussed in the *Seventh Letter*. We have only to remember what has been said about the difficulty of communicating certain types of knowledge which, unlike the knowledge of facts and mathematical formulae, cannot be transmitted from one person to another simply by unambiguous words or symbols, but which require a "spark" to jump over, in order to see that according to this conception Socrates is right with both his assertions: that ἀρετή is an ἐπιστήμη, and also that it cannot be "taught" in the usual sense of this word: in the way, for instance, in which the three "r's" are taught in school. But are we really to believe that Plato whispered this secret into the ears of his adepts while he carefully kept it concealed from the readers of his dialogues?

It has long been observed that the dialogue *Laches* is closely related to the *Protagoras*. The *Laches*, like the *Protagoras*, closes with an unsolved problem. Nicias had defined ἀνδρεία, manliness,[45] as the knowledge of what is rightly to be feared and what is not. But at the end of the discussion the conclusion is reached that he who has this knowledge must inevitably at the same time possess a knowledge that goes far beyond the knowledge that appears to be required for the possession of ἀνδρεία: a knowledge, in fact, that could serve as basis for any and every ἀρετή. The definition proposed by Nicias therefore appears to be a definition not of ἀνδρεία, a "part" of ἀρετή, but of ἀρετή as a whole.[46]

In this case the problem that remains unsolved at the end of the *Laches* is clearly solved in the *Protagoras*. In this dialogue it is not Nicias, but Socrates himself, who tries to prove that ἀνδρεία is the knowledge of what should be feared and what can and should be faced fearlessly.[47] But at the same time Socrates has defended the thesis that ἀρετή is a unity[48] and that hence nobody can be in the possession of true ἀνδρεία without possessing ἀρετή in all its aspects. If this thesis is accepted, the difficulty at the end of the *Laches* disappears completely. For then he who possesses ἀνδρεία must by necessity be in possession of ἀρετή as a whole and it follows that the knowledge constituting ἀνδρεία must also be the basis for the possession of ἀρετή as a whole, and that this must also find its expression in the definition of manliness.

In these cases, then, it is obvious, that in fact a sort of game of intellectual hide-and-seek is played in the two dialogues. But does this mean that Plato reserved for oral or written communication to the initiates the booklet with the solutions of the *aporiai* with which the individual dialogues end? And what does it mean that in the *Laches* Nicias defends a thesis that is attested[49] not only by the *Protagoras* but also by indirect tradition as a thesis of the historical Socrates, and that this very thesis in the *Laches* is "refuted" by Socrates, its author—a situation which has its exact parallel in Plato's *Charmides*, where Critias is refuted by Socrates while defending a thesis of the historical Socrates, which in the dialogue itself is introduced as Socratic. The Socratic proposition concerning ἀνδρεία is, so to speak, an existential proposition. It means nothing at all to have accepted it in theory. But to know in a concrete situation whether one should be afraid of the harm which the thirty tyrants can do to one's life and limb or should be more afraid of becoming their instrument in the arrest and execution of an innocent person, like Leon of Salamis—*that* is what really matters—and modern parallels should not be difficult to find. Of this sort of existential knowledge the uneducated Laches, who has met Socrates as a soldier[50] but has no inkling of Socratic philosophy and designates as rubbish[51] the Socratic definition of ἀνδρεία, in the mouth of his cogeneral Nicias, possesses more than the educated Nicias who has heard something of (παρήκουε, as it is called in the *Seventh Letter*) the Socratic definition of ἀνδρεία and theoretically has made it his own, but later in the Sicilian expedition was intimidated by an eclipse of the moon and refrained from breaking off the campaign when he saw that it had become hopeless, because he was afraid of being condemned to death by the Athenians if he should disappoint their exaggerated hopes. According to the Socratic definition of virtue, he should have been more afraid of becoming guilty of the destruction of the Athenian army than of being unjustly condemned to death by an Athenian law court. It appears, moreover, that this is hinted at in the dialogue[52]—though, of course, indirectly, since the fictitious time of the dialogue is earlier than the Sicilian expedition, so that the latter could not have been mentioned directly. It is, however, noteworthy that the Nicias of the dialogue appears to have an inkling—though again only in theory—of what may be called the existential implications of Socrates' definition, as is shown by the scraps from Plato's *Gorgias* contained in his defence of Socrates' thesis.[53] But it is not with him a knowledge that he applied in his actions. This is also the reason why ultimately he is found wanting in his theoretical insight. All this is shown in a very subtle and at times rather amusing fashion in the dialogue *Laches*.

But what then is the meaning and purpose of the *aporiai* that are apparently left unsolved at the end of the *Protagoras*, of the *Laches*, of the *Charmides*, and of similar Socratic dialogues of Plato? Certainly not that the "correct solutions" of the *aporiai* were to be communicated to a circle of initiates but carefully concealed from the rest of the readers of the dialogues. As has been shown, it would not have benefited Nicias at all if he had learned the solution of the *aporia*, which becomes quite easy on the basis of the thesis of the essential unity of all ἀρεταί, including ἀνδρεία, or if this solution had been communicated to him as to an initiate in secret instruction. Such secret instruction would not have brought him one step nearer to the existential insight into what is really δεινόν (namely to do wrong) and what in comparison is θαρραλέον (namely to have to face death), an existential insight that finds its true expression not in what a man says but in how he acts. The purpose of such *aporiai* then can only be to leave, through the paradoxical nature of the results, a sting in the soul of the reader that is meant to impel him to reflect seriously about what the real issue is in regard to true insight into δεινόν and θαρραλέον, and whether he possesses in truth such knowledge. And, indeed, as many disciples of Socrates, widely differing from one another in other respects, have testified[54] it was characteristic of Socrates that he used to leave such a sting in the soul of his interlocutors and of his listeners. Since this effect, according to Plato's opinion, could be achieved much better through oral conversation than through the written word, even a written dialogue, there can be no doubt that Plato, if he wished to imitate his master Socrates in his most essential activity, must have conducted such oral discussions, if not in the marketplace nor in the gymnasia, as Socrates had done, at least with his students in the Academy. That he actually did so, is attested by a quite irreproachable witness, the conservative historian Theopompus,[55] who violently disapproved of this method because he felt that it was not good to *discuss* with young people what is good and what is bad instead of telling them in no uncertain terms how a decent man has to behave. In this type of Socratic conversation the result was not a nicely formulated "word of the great leader" that one could confidently take home, but something to think about.[56] It follows that this type of discussion certainly has nothing whatever to do with definitely formulated esoteric teaching, concealed from the general public but communicated to the selected few.

It is the fundamental weakness of Krämer's arguments that he arrives at his conclusions by means of that very ambiguity of words which plays such an important role in the *Seventh Letter* and has been further analysed in the first part of the present study. Thus Krämer "proves"[57] again and again, that Plato throughout his life was engaged in oral teaching—which needs no proof at all if "oral teaching" means oral discussion—but then this "oral teaching" is identified with the communication of definitely formulated doctrines[58] which were carefully concealed from the general public, which obviously is a totally different thing. On the other hand, one has to admit that Plato in a great many of his dialogues did present and discuss theories and doctrines of a character quite different from what the historic Socrates used to discuss and what forms the essential content of Plato's Socratic (in the narrower sense) dialogues. But in regard to these dialogues also a very careful analysis is required before any conclusions can be drawn concerning the existence of an "esoteric" doctrine of Plato.

In this latter group of dialogues too we are not infrequently left with *aporiai* at the end, and here too the prospect of a continuation of the discussion on some future occasion is often held out. The *aporiai* at the end of *these* dialogues, in which often very abstract problems are discussed, to be sure, are obviously not intended to put a sting in the soul of the reader in order to goad him on to correct action: in so far as one can say that they leave a sting in soul of the reader, it is not a sting of moral self-examination, but rather supposed to drive them on to further purely intellectual activity in regard to the problem or problems broached. But this very fact shows that it would have served no sensible purpose to keep possible insights of a still loftier kind from the readers of these dialogues. And who could the adepts have been for whom these supreme insights were reserved, since in fact most of the dialogues of this group anyway tax the intelligence of their readers to the utmost? Eudoxos of Cnidos, who was one of the greatest mathematicians of all times but who did not understand Plato's Theory of Ideas, as his attempts to explain it to young members of the Academy in Plato's absence very clearly shows.[59] Or Aristotle, who remained sceptical in regard to the Theory of Ideas all through his life? Or Speusippus and Xenocrates, who do not give the impression, from the evidence of the preserved fragments of their works, of having belonged among the greatest philosophical geniuses? Or Heracleides Ponticus, whose works rather give rise to the suspicion that it was not quite beyond his capabilities and inclination to put on an air of profound wisdom by means of gleanings from Platonic philosophy that he had not entirely understood? Or to some other adepts of Plato who were far greater philosophic geniuses than the men just mentioned, but left no trace whatsoever in ancient tradition? Finally, when it is said that Plato concealed his deepest insights, or "passed them over in silence," because he was afraid of the "outcry of the Boeotians," there is quite enough material in Plato's late dialogues to stimulate the Boeotians to such activity, and there is also evidence to show that even among the disciples of Socrates there were some Boeotians, as for instance Antisthenes, who did raise such an outcry.

Above all, however, Krämer's conclusion from what is said in the *Seventh Letter* concerning the superiority of oral over written communication—to wit, that there must have been esoteric oral communication of Plato reserved for particular initiates—is clearly false. In the first place it would be of no earthly interest to us, except perhaps that of idle curiosity, to know that Plato made such communications to some initiates, as long as we did not know what they were about. If such an assumption is to arouse any interest on our part, the assumption must be made that they were not to be kept entirely secret but to some extent have been preserved, which can hardly have been done except in written form. Thus Krämer, in order to show that his discovery is of value to us, is compelled to state[60] that Plato's highest esoteric doctrines were transmitted throughout the centuries not only orally but at least partly in writing. Now, it is self-evident that whatever can be said can also be written, since we have and the Greeks had enough letters in their alphabets to express unequivocally all the phonemes that are essential for the identification of a spoken word. The superiority of oral over written communication lies in this *alone*: that the speaker, engaged in discussion, can meet instantly all the particular difficulties of comprehension that his interlocutor reveals at any given moment, while the author of a written work, not having his readers before him, is unable to do so. From this it follows that for Plato the composition of dialogues was the most appropriate, indeed the only appropriate, form of *written* communication, since in a written dialogue the greatest effort can be made to compensate for the unavoidable deficiency of written communication by anticipating and explaining or countering misunderstandings as far as possible. Hence the analogy of the difference between *Akousmatikoi* and *Mathematikoi* among the Pythagoreans, with the difference between the published dialogues and the secret doctrine of Plato, that Gaiser believes to have discovered,[61] is completely false. For the Pythagorean *Akousmata*, in contrast to Plato's published dialogues, consisted in *dogmatic* pronouncements and rules to which the *Akousmatikoi* were to adhere *without* asking questions and without a discussion (αὐτὸς ἔφα).[62]

But not all of Krämer's results are completely wrong. Thus, having discarded the unfortunate idea of secret doctrine, which in the dialogues was deliberately passed over in silence and reserved for a circle of initiates, we may, without prejudice, return to the question of whether it is likely that Plato in his oral discussions with the members of the Academy —or perhaps even in public lectures, which can hardly have had the purpose to deal with theories that Plato wished to keep secret—touched problems and set forth theories that are not found in his published dialogues. Since the dialogues composed and published in writing seek to consider and, as far as possible, to meet the most important possible misunderstandings and objections, they are naturally rather lengthy. For this reason they in each case take into consideration only one of several interrelated problems. Thus the *Theaetetus* tries to show the difficulties into which an empiricist theory of knowledge falls when it attempts to do without the Theory of Ideas. The *Parmenides* deals with the difficulties which spring up for the Theory of Ideas from the imperfect concept of μέθεξις, a concept or word, which nevertheless is very difficult to replace by a better one, since, because of the imperfection of our language, the choice of a different term will create other difficulties no less great. The *Sophistes* tries to dispose of the logical difficulties that arise from the arguments used by the Eleatics and that must be removed if the Theory of Ideas is to be defended against objections which had been brought up in a great variety of guises by representatives of eristic dialectics both in the time of Socrates and in Plato's own time. All these problems are interrelated and interconnected. All the dialogues mentioned deal, so to speak, with the negative aspects of the epistemological problem. They should have been supplemented by an attempt at a more positive solution of the epistemological problem. We know through Plato himself that he planned to give such a positive supplement in a dialogue with the title *Philosophus*.[63] But this dialogue was never finished nor published. In the same way the *Timaeus* is connected with unfinished and unpublished dialogues. No one can know how many dialogues Plato would have composed if he had lived for another decade. But it is obvious that even then he could not have written down in dialogues "everything" that came to his mind regarding the problems with which he concerned himself in the last years of his life.

Since there is no indication whatsoever that Plato ever ceased to discuss his philosophical ideas within the Academy, it can be considered quite certain that in these discussions problems and theories were brought up that are not contained in the dialogues that were published in Plato's lifetime and that have come down to us. Since, furthermore, a dialogue like the *Timaeus* deals with subject matter partly very far removed from anything that is discussed in any other dialogue of Plato, it is at least not improbable that Plato in his oral discussions in the Academy not only extended and elaborated further what he had discussed in the published dialogue but also may have brought up entirely new subject matter. In all this Krämer is perfectly right, if only we leave aside the unfortunate notion that Plato tried to conceal all this carefully from the general public. But to get rid of this notion is rather important—not because it is so very important in itself, though it is perhaps not quite irrelevant for the evaluation of Plato as a person to be aware he did not shroud himself in mystery—but above all in order to re-establish the proper order of precedence for the understanding of Plato's philosophy.

If we believe that Plato refrained consciously from including the innermost meaning of his philosophy in his dialogues and made it accessible only to a carefully selected circle of initiates, then it must seem as if the few allusions, mostly quite obscure and very difficult to understand, to Plato's lecture περὶ τοῦ ἀγαθοῦ—which, by the way, is supposed to have been a *public* lecture, not a lecture for the selected few—were the most important testimony that we possess concerning Plato's philosophy. But even if Plato should not have found the time before his death, or should not have felt himself in a position (not more than this can be conceded) to elaborate some of his most important thoughts adequately in a written dialogue, an incomparably more important fact is to be set against this: that in the dialogues we possess extensive and interrelated pieces of Platonic philosophy in that form of presentation which Plato must have considered the most adequate for the communication of his philosophy, since he used it exclusively right to the end of his life. Of the lecture περὶ τοῦ ἀγαθοῦ and possible other pieces of Plato's philosophy not contained in the dialogues we have nothing but fragments torn from their context and transmitted to us by students who admittedly found them most difficult to understand and consequently may have misunderstood them.

Krämer treats the claim that all of Plato's philosophy is contained in the dialogues as the "traditional" interpretation and, assuming a rather superior tone, sets against this claim his new discovery of the significance of Plato's "esoteric" doctrine. But the claim that "all of Plato's philosophy" is contained in the dialogues can naturally only mean that the whole of Platonic philosophy *of which we have an adequate knowledge* is contained in the dialogues. For who could be so foolish as to claim that Plato never had a philosophical thought that he has not set down in the published dialogues? Here we meet again with arguments based on the ambiguity of words which is so impressively discussed in the *Seventh Letter.* The statement that the whole of Plato's philosophy so far as it is possible for us to have an adequate knowledge of it is contained in the dialogues is, if not absolutely, yet nearly correct. How misleading the arguments are by which Krämer tries to prove the opposite will be shown by the following analysis.

"The dialogues are," says Krämer,[64] "since they are written, inferior to the spoken word." "They cannot, therefore, replace . . . the proper teaching." And further on:[65] "that the higher subjects cannot fit into the dialogues is, therefore, self-evident. Because all the deeper prerequisites for a full understanding are lacking (sc. in a written dialogue), they would be liable to be misunderstood and misinterpreted." Nonetheless, in Krämer's opinion, what we possess *in written form* in fragments torn from the context in indirect tradition is capable of giving us the most profound insight into Plato's innermost thought. The contradiction could hardly be more obvious. The supposition made, however, is clearly this: that Krämer and his friends have the intellectual capacity of the selected few of Plato's Academy and therewith the prerequisites of true understanding in such a degree that they are not in need of Plato's oral teaching but can grasp the innermost meaning of his philosophy even on the basis of the few scraps of his oral teaching that have been transmitted to us by indirect tradition. So far so good. But then these young adepts are not content to transmit their insight to others by oral teaching, the only way in which according to their own theory it can be transmitted properly, nor even in written dialogues, but in written theoretical treatises. Obviously, then, they believe that it can be transmitted in this way. But if a young German philologist is able to transmit an adequate insight into Plato's "highest subjects" by means of the written word, should we not suppose that Plato himself must have been able to do the same?

It is most unfortunate that Krämer, by such self-contradictory arguments and statements, leads his readers away from a road, which, if followed in the proper direction, may still lead to very valuable results. It is quite true that it is possible to draw from most of Plato's dialogues inferences that are not expressly stated by Plato. It is obvious that Plato not only in his old age but throughout his life, must have had thoughts and most likely have said a good deal about them in oral discussion which has not found its way into the dialogues. It is further true that between the various dialogues connections can be drawn that Plato did not expressly work out—in part intentionally, as we have seen in the case of the *Laches* and the *Protagoras*, in part unintentionally, because Plato did not find the time before his death to fill in the gaps. It is a thoroughly legitimate enterprise and, if undertaken with the requisite penetration, may lead to very fruitful results, to make the attempt to fill in the gaps left between Plato's dialogues. Undoubtedly Plato himself tried to incite the readers of his dialogues to do just this. It is likewise legitimate to use what the indirect tradition has to say about Plato's lectures and other oral communications as a supplement to the dialogues, *if this is done with extreme caution.* But it is not difficult to see that even if Krämer were right with his views concerning the esoteric Plato, all modern research must begin with the dialogues and, in case of doubt, must give preference to these, since *we*, even supposing that we belong to those whom Plato would have admitted to the circle of the selected few, can no longer participate in oral discussions conducted by Plato personally, but at best possess a few written scraps of these conversations torn from their context.

In addition, it is perhaps advisable to test the likelihood that Plato's recent adepts would, without further training, be admitted to the supposed circle of his selected few by means of a test case, which Krämer himself towards the end of his book[66] designates as such: namely the designation of the Idea of the Good as ἐπέκεινα οὐσίας, as "beyond being" which is found at the very center of Plato's extensive explanation of his Theory of Ideas and its various implications in the *Republic.*[67] Krämer, in discussing this passage, begins with the assertion[68] that all those who tried to explain Plato's philosophy down to the present day "have dragged the philosophic half-nonsense of the Idea of the Good, which is supposed to give to things being and the possibility of becoming objects of knowledge[!] and to persons seeking knowledge the possibility of knowledge and insight[!][69] through countless commentaries of Plato, merely paraphrasing the passage" (sc. but never making an attempt at a sensible explanation). In truth, however, he says, a problem of the first magnitude is hidden behind this apparently nonsensical statement. This philosophical problem of the first magnitude is then explained in the following way:[70]

> The way in which the ἰδέα τοῦ ἀγαθοῦ gives being to the εἴδη—it is a question only of these—but remains itself ἐπέκεινα τῆς οὐσίας, above every particular being, shows that it is here primarily a question of an ontological, not of an axiological, problem and that the ἰδέα τοῦ ἀγαθοῦ is a principle of being. The relation is really understandable only if 'being' [Seiendheit] and principle are related to each other in regard to their content and are defined the first as 'being one,' the second as 'One'." And further on: "The

> possibility of being known, or more correctly, the *not being removed from the possibility of being known* [Unentzogenheit] is an essential property of being, as is shown by the distinctions at the end of the fifth book. It is best understood as that accessibility [Erschlossenheit] of that which is, which makes the One accessible as the ground [or cause?] of being [Seinsgrund] out of the μὴ ὄν, the absolutely indeterminate [dem schlechthin Unbegrenzten], inasmuch the One determines that which is by limiting it.

Here we have again in a nutshell the same conglomeration of statements which, if correctly understood, are correct and even important, with lack of clarity and confusion, which is so characteristic of Krämer's book. First of all, looked at from the outside and as an illustration of Plato's supposed secrecy in regard to his "highest" insights[71] the procedure of Plato, author of the *Republic*, as man and philosopher appears totally incomprehensible, if he has *stated in writing* a doctrine so central as that stated in the passage quoted, but is supposed to have purposely concealed its real meaning from the readers of the dialogue and to have formulated it in such a way that what he actually says is "half-nonsense." For what purpose and for whom did he then pronounce it? Moreover, it appears somewhat strange to style as "half-nonsense" the statement that the Idea of the Good gives to things their being and the possibility of being known, and to the person seeking knowledge the possibility of knowing—this statement, mark you, and not its modern interpretations, since, precisely in regard to this statement, Krämer complains that it has always been merely paraphrased and not explained—a statement therefore made by Plato precisely in this form. Or is this again the specifically Platonic procedure of purposely feeding "half-nonsense" to his readers in order to be able to whisper his true opinions into the ears of the selected few?

The explanation of the true meaning of Plato's statement that Kramer tries to give contains indeed some truth—though in a rather indigestible form—besides untruth but, insofar as it is correct, derives not from Plato's secret teaching as known from indirect tradition, but from Plato's *Republic*. This explanation, moreover, could have been made much more correct, much more precise, and much less complicated, if Krämer, instead of ascending to the most nebulous heights of abstraction, had asked the very simple question, whether what Plato says does not make very good sense when applied to the world in which we are still living.

Krämer expresses the opinion that it is much easier to understand the role of the Idea of the Good as a "principle of being" than as "a principle of knowledge." To me the very opposite appears to be true, namely that the concept of the Idea of the Good as principle of being can be best made clear by starting from its role as principle of knowledge. But be that as it may. Regardless of the demand, so generally made to-day, for the dissociation of science from value-judgements—a demand which within certain limits is perfectly justified but when extended beyond these limits reveals a total lack of insight into the most fundamental conditions of all knowledge—it seems self-evident to me that without incessant distinction between what is good or better from what is less good or bad no acquisition of knowledge is possible. It begins with the preference for what is true to what is false, without which any acquisition of knowledge ceases. For, even he who thinks that the untruth (believed by others) is better for him does not wish to deceive himself, and even he who prefers pleasant illusions to the unpleasant truth should like to know *truly* whether the illusions will really make him happy. Furthermore it is not possible to work sensibly in the field of mathematics without preferring neater (or more elegant) solutions to less neat ones, or within the former group the shorter solutions to the longer ones, those which with one stroke solve a whole host of mathematical problems to those which solve only one very special case. Or to select purposely a most trivial example from a totally different realm: even the famous experiments with rats in which the unfortunate rats smell a piece of cheese and become neurotic, when for all their trouble they cannot find it in the maze, become meaningless and cease to be experiments if we take away the piece of cheese which in this case represents the "Good." More generally: even that science which in the narrower sense has completely freed itself from value-judgements is forced constantly to lay stress on what appears more important for its purposes, which for this reason is preferred, thus "better," if it wishes to accomplish anything that is meaningful. Even those who prefer the absurd theatre to the traditional one *prefer* it and by preferring it in some way express the opinion that it is *better* than the traditional one, implying in fact that, in its absurdity, it makes really in some way better sense. To sum up: the world in general remains a chaos incapable of comprehension if emphasis is not laid everywhere on a pattern, preferred to that which lacks pattern. This is exactly the point where the Idea of the Good as the basis of all knowledge becomes likewise the ground or basis of all "being":[72] being not in the sense of "existence" but of "being something" which is the meaning of the word οὐσία. Insofar as the Idea of the Good has a real and necessary relation to pattern as opposed to lack of pattern and chaos, it is, as Krämer quite correctly says, *first of all* the ground of being of the εἴδη, but certainly not, as Krämer also says, of the εἴδη *only*, but *also* of the objects in time and space insofar as they have pattern as identifiable objects and thus, in Plato's terminology, "participate" in the Ideas. On the other hand, the expression ἐπέκεινα τῆς οὐσίας means not only, as Krämer interprets, "above every particular being," but also beyond all other ideas, since it is the basis of the possibility of there being ideas.

This relation of the Idea of the Good to the principle of order and to pattern—which as a closed and completed pattern must in some way constitute a unity of everything it contains—may then perhaps be described with Krämer's words, quoted above: "The relation is really understandable only if 'Seiendheit' [literally: beinghood] and principle are related to each other in regard to their content and are defined the first as 'being one,' the second as 'One.' But I doubt whether such high-sounding abstract formulations lead to a better understanding of what Plato had in mind than an attempt to relate his statement to the world in which we still live and to find out whether it does not make very good sense when applied to this world. That formulations like those preferred by Krämer do not lead to a precise understanding of what Plato meant to say is, it seems to me, proven by the fact that the first sentence of Krämer's interpretation quoted above contains at least two statements, which, in regard to a most essential point, are not quite correct: (1) that the ἰδέα τοῦ ἀγαθοῦ gives "being" only to the εἴδη and not also to the objects in space and time as well, insofar as they are recognizable and identifiable objects, or in Plato's terms participate in the ideas; and (2) that it is a question primarily of an ontological and not of an axiological relation, since in fact both are inseparably connected with each other, and the first would not exist without the second.

With this test case I wish to close my observations. Krämer's book points to a very important road of inquiry, one all too much neglected for many decades: the road of an interpretation of Plato's dialogues, which is not content with remaining within the compass of each individual dialogue, but tries to transcend it, since the dialogues everywhere imply more than is expressly elaborated within them, and also attempts to fill in the gaps left by Plato between the dialogues. This is, to an even higher degree, the case with the book of Krämer's friend and follower Konrad Gaiser,[73] who right at the beginning of his work tones down Krämer's theses, even though he still retains too many of them.[74] It is a great pity that Krämer by his thesis of a Platonic "secret doctrine" has led away his readers and his critics from this most promising road and lured them into the battle field of a completely sterile discussion over the existence or non-existence of this "secret doctrine."

It is quite true that Plato was more "esoteric" than Socrates had been. But it is wrong to draw the line between the dialogues on the one hand and Plato's oral discussions in the Academy and his public(!) lecture περὶ τοῦ ἀγαθοῦ on the other. This division, as I hope to have shown, leads to the absurdest consequences. But a distinction can rightly be made, as in a way it has been made for a long time, between those Platonic dialogues which try to mirror the method of the historical Socrates, who used to converse with everyone in every place, and those which mirror the "esoteric" conversations as Plato conducted them with his ὀλίγοι in the recesses of the Academy. In this function the latter can be supplemented by what we know of these oral conversations through indirect tradition. I should be happy if the present paper could induce scholars to give up the fruitless quarrel concerning Plato's "secret doctrine" and to turn instead to the real and most interesting problems of interpretation which have been posed anew by the works of Krämer and Gaiser.[75]

NOTES

[1] The problem has been dealt with in part in an excellent fashion, as far as the adventures of Plato's friend Dion in Syracuse are concerned [H. Berve, "Dion," *AWL*, X (1956)], but nobody so far had dealt with it seriously as far as Plato's involvement in these adventures is concerned.

[2] In the meantime I have tried to tackle these problems in my *Platon in Sizilien und das Problem der Philosophenherrschaft* (Berlin, 1968). Concerning the general weakness of the arguments with which L. Edelstein in his book *Plato's Seventh Letter* (Leiden, 1966) tries to prove that the author of the letter is not Plato, cf. the excellent review of the book by F. Solmsen in *Gnomon* 41 (1969): 29–34.

[3] Plato, *Ep.* VII 341D ff.

[4] Gerhard Müller, "Die Philosophie im pseudoplatonischen 7. Brief," *AP*, III (1949–50): 251 ff.

[5] *Ep.* VII 344A.

[6] *Ep.* VII 341A.

[7] See *supra* n. 2.

[8] At 275D.

[9] *Op. cit.*, 253–54.

[10] *Ep.* VII 341B–D.

[11] *Ep.* VII 341C–D.

[12] Porphyrius, *Vita Plotini* 23.

[13] Walter Bröcker, "Der philosophische Exkurs in Platons siebentem Brief," *Hermes* XCL (1963): 416 ff.

[14] *Ep.* VII 342C.

[15] *Op. cit.* (n. 4), 234.

[16] Naturally, the way in which the soul participates (μετέχει) in the idea by perceiving it is quite different from the "participation" (μετέχειν) of an individual thing in the idea or ideas to which it is related. But the difficulty of designating or describing this μετέχειν is exactly the same in both cases. For a discussion of the difficulties inherent in determining exactly the μετέχειν of things in ideas, cf. especially the first part of Plato's *Parmenides*.

[17] *Ep.* VII 342E–343B.

[18] With Plato, as is well known, begins the first distinction of different types of words in grammar. According to this distinction the word ὄνομα designates both what we now call "nouns" or "substantives" and what we now call "adjectives." All other types of words are lumped together under the one designation of ῥῆμα, while in later Greek grammar, as is well known, ῥῆμα designates exclusively the verb. See H. Steinthal, *Geschichte der Sprachwissenschaft bei den Griechen und Römern*, I, 2nd ed. (1890), pp. 137 ff.

[19] *Op. cit.* (n. 13), 420–21.

[20] Müller, *loc. cit.*, actually uses the corresponding German expression "sich entrüsten."

[21] *Ep.* VII 342E: πρὸς γὰρ τούτοις ταῦτα οὐχ ἧττον ἐπιχειρεῖ τὸ ποῖόν τι περὶ ἕκαστον δηλοῦν ἢ τὸ ὂν ἑκάστου διὰ τὸ τῶν λόγων ἀσθενές.

[22] *Op. cit.*, 422–23.

[23] See n. 21.

[24] *Op. cit.*, 256.

[25] Cf. in regard to this problem above all the excellent essay of Eric Weil, "The Meaning of Meaninglessness," *Da*, 94 (1965): 171 ff; and, for supplement, my remarks in *GGA*, 213 (1959): 4–34.

[26] For a more detailed discussion of this problem, cf. K. v. Fritz, *Platon, Theaetet und die antike Mathematik* (München, 1969), p. 60 ff. and p. 100 ff.

[27] It should not be necessary—but because of the confusion and superficial argumentation prevailing nearly everywhere in our days—it is perhaps necessary to emphasize once more, that the kind of knowledge of which I am speaking here and which is indispensable to us at every moment in our daily life is not identical with the kind of knowledge of which the author of the *Seventh Letter* speaks when he says that a sensible man will not try to communicate certain insights through writing. There is, however, a certain analogy between the two types of knowledge insofar as many of the insights indispensable to us in every day life are neither capable of unmistakable formulation nor verifiable by the methods of scientism (which is the reason why misunderstandings between individuals and groups of individuals continually occur).

[28] *Ep.* VII 343B–C.

[29] See *supra* p. 418.

[30] *Op. cit.*, 423.

[31] *Theaetetus* 157B.

[32] *Ep.* VII 343D.

[33] In an article published some time after the completion of the present

one, with the title "Nachtrag zum philosophischen Exkurs in Platons siebtem Brief," *Hermes* 93 (1965): 132, Bröcker tried to show that the author of the *Seventh Letter* has misunderstood the passage of Plato's *Theaetetus* discussed above. He concludes, of course, that this misunderstanding proves that Plato cannot be the author of this passage of the *Seventh Letter*. The misunderstanding in his opinion consists in the statement (made in the *Seventh Letter*) that a statement that has been refuted according to the rules of formal logic can nevertheless be true (which is of course wrong), while in the *Theaetetus*, he says, it is correctly stated that a statement that has not been refuted can nevertheless be false.

Again, however, the objection is based on a flagrantly false interpretation of what the *Seventh Letter* says. Not a word is said in the *Seventh Letter* of a statement refuted according to the rules of formal logic. What the *Seventh Letter* says is that the four stages of the approach to the ultimate object of knowledge are "convicted of imperfection" or shown up to be imperfect (εὐέλεγκτοι: see the inquiry into the various meanings of this Greek word above). But what the philosopher who tries to communicate his insight by the spoken or the written word *means*, what he intends to communicate, what he has in the focus of his mental vision, is *not* refuted. What is "refuted" is merely the imperfect expression of what he wants to convey, an imperfection of expression caused by the imperfect nature of the four instruments of the acquisition and communication of knowledge. This imperfection is the reason why that part of the audience which consists *not* of true philosophers receives the *impression as if* what the philosopher says had been refuted. What the *Seventh Letter* says then, is *not*, as Bröcker believes, that a statement which has been actually refuted, according to the rules of formal logic, can nevertheless be true (which would be nonsense), but that what a philosopher *means* to say can be true in spite of the fact that it has been *seemingly* refuted, because of the imperfection of the language in which it has been expressed. It should be hardly necessary to point again to the example of the "refutation" of the mathematical definition of the tangent by Protagoras. Other examples abound both in Plato's dialogues, where they are deliberately brought in in order to illustrate the fallacy, and, quite against the intention of the authors, in many modern interpretations of the *Seventh Letter*.

34 *Op. cit.*, 257.

35 Cf. the statement of D. Hilbert, quoted above, p. 419.

36 Hans Joachim Krämer, *Arete bei Platon und Aristoteles: Zum Wesen der platonischen Ontologie* (Heidelberg, 1959), especially chapter IV, "Das Problem des esoterischen Platon" (pp. 380–486); cf. also by the same author: "Retraktationen zum Problem des esoterischen Platon," *MH*, 21 (1964): 137–67.

37 *Ep.* VII 341E.

38 *Gorgias* 489B; cf. also 489C; 497A–B, etc.

39 Xenophon, *Memorabilia* I, 2, 40 ff.

40 *Antisthenis Fragmenta*, ed. Fernanda Decleva Caizzi (Varese-Milano, 1966); 50*A–C*=*Antisthenis Fragmenta*, ed. Winckelmann, XIII, 3 (p. 34).

[41] As is generally known, it has long been supposed, on the basis of very convincing evidence, that those dialogues which are close to the method of the historical Socrates—as it is revealed through the Socratic dialogues of other disciples of Socrates—are earlier than those in which this Socratic method has been more and more abandoned. This is called into doubt by Krämer. Though personally I hold it for certain that the *communis opinio* concerning the general chronology of the two groups is correct, I have in the present context refrained from making any assumptions concerning the relative chronology of the dialogues. The difference of the two types of dialogues in character and method is so obvious that it cannot be doubted.

[42] *Op. cit.*, p. 389.

[43] *Op. cit.*, p. 392.

[44] *Protagoras* 361A ff.

[45] *Laches* 194E.

[46] *Laches* 199E.

[47] *Protagoras* 360D.

[48] *Protagoras* 349B ff., especially 359A ff.

[49] For good measure Nicias himself says in the *Laches* (194D f.) that he has often heard the thesis from Socrates.

[50] *Laches* 181B.

[51] *Laches* 195A.

[52] *Laches* 195E: what is said about μάντεις in this passage appears to hint at the μάντις (an ill-advised μάντις according to the historian Philochoros, who had been a μάντις himself), who confirmed Nicias in his foolish superstition concerning the meaning of an eclipse of the moon.

[53] Compare *Laches* 195C–D with *Gorgias* 511B–C ff.

[54] Cf. the fragment from a work of Phaidon of Elis in Seneca, *Epistulae Morales* 94, 41 and the fragments of the dialogue *Alcibiades* by Aeschines of Sphettos. There are, in addition, various more or less indirect allusions to this effect of Socrates' teaching in Xenophon's *Memorabilia*.

[55] F. Jacoby, *Die Fragmente der Griechischen Historiker*, 115F, 275.

[56] Concerning the true task of philosophy and the Socratic method, cf. also the excellent article by Eric Weil, "Sorge um die Philosophie—Sorge der Philosophie," *Die Zukunft der Philosophie* (Olten and Freiburg, 1968), pp. 222–38.

[57] *Op. cit.*, pp. 400 and 403; see also "Retraktationen," p. 145.

[58] *Op. cit.*, pp. 395 and 399.

[59] See K. v. Fritz, "Die Ideenlehre des Eudoxos von Knidos und ihr Verhältnis zur platonischen Ideenlehre," *Phil.*, 82 (1927): 1 ff.

[60] All the arguments in Krämer's two treatises (cf. above, n. 36), especially *Arete*, pp. 458 ff., go incessantly back and forth between the two contradictory statements: (a) that the "highest things," i.e., Plato's own esoteric doctrine, cannot be presented in his published dialogues because they cannot be adequately expressed in writing; and (b) that Plato's secret doctrine concerns "extremely precise subjects, namely the One and the 'Indeterminate Duality' as ultimate principles of Being." But if we are to have a precise knowledge of Plato's views concerning these "extremely

precise subjects," it would appear that this doctrine or these views must have come down to us by necessity in writing, if not through written works of Plato, then through written works of other authors, presumably Plato's listeners. But if these listeners of Plato were able to transmit Plato's doctrine "with complete precision" through writing, Plato after all should also have been in a position to do so. It certainly does no great honor to the admired Plato to make the assumption that he could not include his most important doctrines in his written dialogues because he was unable to express them adequately in writing, but that his disciples as well as Krämer and his friends were perfectly able to do so.

[61] Konrad Gaiser, *Platons ungeschriebene Lehre* (Stuttgart, 1963), p. 3.

[62] See also K. v. Fritz, "Mathematiker und Akusmatiker bei den alten Pythagoreern," *SBAW*, XI (1960).

[63] Cf. *Sophistes* 254A.

[64] *Op. cit.*, p. 463.

[65] *Op. cit.*, p. 464.

[66] *Op. cit.*, pp. 473 ff.

[67] Plato, *Republic* 509B.

[68] *Op. cit.*, p. 473.

[69] The exclamation marks are Krämer's.

[70] *Op. cit.*, p. 474.

[71] Krämer uses the word "Geheimlehre."

[72] What is said here about the Idea of the Good, i.e., of the principle of distinction between a better and a worse as presupposition of all acquisition of knowledge, does not presuppose the Theory of Ideas in its Platonic form with all its consequences but can, to a certain degree, be transposed into terms of, for instance, Aristotelian or Kantian philosophy, both of whom did not accept the Theory of Ideas as it had been worked out by Plato. But it shows that Plato's Theory of Ideas and specifically what he says about the role of the Idea of the Good is not, as the representatives of modern scientism and positivism believe, a pure chimera, but is connected with fundamental conditions of the process of the acquisition of knowledge, conditions that anyone who looks at this process without prejudice must discover unless he has become blinded to everyday experience by a one-sided modern theory.

[73] See *supra*, n. 61.

[74] Though Gaiser adheres to Krämer's notion of an esoteric teaching of Plato's, he has in practice given up the sharp separation between the "merely propaedeutic" discussion of all of Plato's dialogues and the "secret doctrine" transmitted to us only through indirect tradition, which is so characteristic for Krämer, and concedes everywhere in his studies a dominating role to the dialogues.

Much more important for him is the question whether or how far Plato had a philosophic system, and if so, how far this system is capable of being reconstructed. But here, too, it seems to me, the danger arises that a worthwhile endeavor of interpretation and reconstruction is impeded by a sterile discussion of abstract questions which, insofar as they admit of solution, can only be answered by the concrete interpretation itself. Is there much sense in quarreling over the question of whether Plato had a philosophic system or whether he did not? Obviously the various problems posed in his various dialogues and his attempts to solve them are in some way related to one another. The totality of these interconnections then, in a way, forms what may be called a "system," and it is a very legitimate enterprise to try to reconstruct as far as possible the totality of these interconnections. On the other hand, it appears to me just as obvious that Plato did not have a closed philosophic system of the kind of, for instance, Schopenhauer, where, after it had once been sketched in its outline, every newly discovered or newly treated problem had merely to be assigned its proper place within the whole. Gaiser himself (*op. cit.*, p. 9) is aware of this, when he says, that "Plato did not aim at a closed and rigid system of theorems." Evidently, then, it is a question of more or less, so that it makes no sense to fight over it in the abstract instead of taking up every concrete and individual problem as it presents itself in the course of the attempt to bring together all traceable interconnections.

[75] A continuation of the discussion concerning the problem of Plato's esotericism and the related questions within the present article will be found in the following articles published after the German version of the present paper had been distributed in the USA: 1. Hans-Georg Gadamer, "Dialektik und Sophistik im VII. platonischen Brief," *SHAW* (1965) [=Gadamer, *Platos dialektische Ethik und andere Studien zur platonischen Philosophie* (Hamburg, 1968), pp. 223–47]; 2. Klaus Oehler, "Der entmythologisierte Platon," *ZPF*, 19 (1965): 393–420; 3. Kurt v. Fritz, "Zur Frage der 'esoterischen' Philosophie Platons," *AGP*, 49 (1967): 255–68; 4. "Idee und Zahl: Studien zur platonischen Philosophie, von Hans-Georg Gadamer, Konrad Gaiser, Hermann Gundert, Hans-Joachim Krämer und Helmut Kuhn," *Abhandlungen d. Heidelberg. Akad. phil.-hist. Klasse* (1968), especially Helmut Kuhn, "Platon und die Grenze philosophischer Mitteilung," 151–73; 5. Margarita Isnardi Parente, "Per l'interpretazione dell'excursus filosofico della VII epistula Platonica," *PP*, XIX (1964): 241–90; 6. Rainer Marten, "Denkbarkeit und Mitteilbarkeit des Ineffabile: Ein Problem der Platonauslegung" in "Die Philosophie und die Wissenschaften," *Simon Moser zum 65. Geburtstag* (Meisenheim, 1967).

ARISTOTLE

THOMAS GOULD
University of Texas

The Metaphysical Foundations for Aristotle's Ethics*

STUDENTS of Aristotle down through the centuries have frequently tried to discern the four "causes" in Aristotle's treatment of various problems. This is an understandable, perhaps even an inevitable procedure, for Aristotle himself discusses his theory of causes in several very different contexts—analytics, physics and biology. Even scholars who doubt that Aristotle was a meticulously careful system-builder usually admit that he probably had a unified approach to causation. At least there is a *prima facie* case for assuming that Aristotle remained faithful to his doctrine of the best kinds of explanation.

Science progresses by finding causes, according to Aristotle, but by "causes" he meant the middle terms which explain a conclusion (*Post. An.* I ch. 11). There appear to be in fact only four kinds of middle terms. The middle term explaining why Socrates must die someday is Man (formal); that which explains why he took walks after dinner is In Order to Digest (final); that which explains why he was brought into court was Meletus (efficient); and that which explains why he died when he did was Hemlock (material). But as there is one best kind of syllogism, the first, which has a substance as its middle term, so is there one best kind of "cause": Forms, such as Man. And as it turns out (*Physics* II), Form is a cause as a good being striven for, so formal and final causes become one; and in cases of actions requiring human agents, they are one with the efficient cause also. (How explain the house? A housebuilder. Why did he do it? The Form House informed his intelligence. How did that lead him to build? The Form includes a function, why someone would want a house.) Even the material cause is partly implied in the others: given the Form and function of House it cannot be built out of air. If it is decided, therefore, that we should look for Aristotle's

* A revised paper originally presented at the 1958 meeting of the SAGP in Cincinnati, Ohio.

doctrine of causation in some work, we must do more than merely discern each separate kind: we must show how Form is the ultimate cause as a good being striven for.

At *Physics* I. 9 Aristotle sets this theory of explanation against Plato's. It was Plato who first worked out the suggestion that Form is good and causes order in the world as a pattern striven for. But Plato concluded that there was also random motion in the world, motion directed toward no particular good.[1] Aristotle, on the other hand, asserted that the only other thing in the universe besides Form, the substratum, by its nature strove toward Form and did not introduce any motions of its own.[2] He was thus able to eliminate the Demiurge, the World-Psyche and the self-moving psyches of plants and animals. Aristotle's universe is neater than Plato's; and the result of his innovation is greater precision in many fields: ontology, cosmology, and the laws of scientific investigation.

Ethics, on the other hand, as well as politics, rhetoric, and poetics, all the areas where success and failure in purely human endeavors are investigated, present a greater challenge for Aristotle than for Plato. Aristotle created a new problem: if there is not a single motion in the universe which is not caused by a good striven for, then why do we treat the strivings of men differently from the strivings of rocks, trees, and horses? What is it that enables us to say of men alone (and of those animals which are able to learn) that some of their strivings are good and some bad? Did Aristotle even try to fit his treatment of Ethics into his general metaphysical program?

Let us suppose, as a hypothesis, that he did try. What light might that throw on the genesis of his ethical theory? Aristotle's first point is that there is a plainly observable difference between the striving of a man to secure his well-being and the striving of a stone to be at the center of the world: a man can always be trained to strive for something else (even, presumably, his own pain or extinction) but a stone can never ever be trained to tend in any direction but "down" (*Nic. Eth.* II 1). The crucial difference between an intelligent and a blind act is that the first might have been different had the past experiences of the agent been different, while the latter could have been different only if the other entities involved in the event itself had been differently disposed. Both the man in choosing a job and the stone in falling from a ledge are seeking their fulfillment, their true well-being. (A man's end, *eudaimonia*, as opposed to the means for achieving it, is aimed at by him as inevitably as the center of the world is aimed at by the stone—*Nic. Eth.* III. 4 etc.)

There may be obstacles in the way of each. But the man has the ability to make inferences from past experience and thus circumvent some of the obstacles;[3] the stone has no such ability, and so is completely at the mercy of the obstacles. Here we discover something peculiar: the stone could never make an error about its true well-being; that is, whenever it was carried in the opposite direction, it was not its fault. There was nothing it could have done which would have had better results. It kept right on pressing downward with complete fidelity. The man, on the other hand, may be making a ghastly error that will lead directly to his doom. Intelligence apparently means the ability to make a mistake (*Metaph.* Θ 2 and 5).

But here is the difficulty. If every motion in the universe is caused by a good striven for, if there is no such thing as a purely random motion, then what account can be given of the act of an intelligent agent when he is acting with less than perfect efficiency toward his true well-being? Like Plato, Aristotle saw that the key to destructive decisions lay in our tendency to follow desires and appetites too uncritically. But if only that decision is truly rational which leads toward our true well-being,[4] then those desires and appetites which tend to lead us in any other direction must be absolutely irrational; but if irrational and not leading toward a true good, are they then the only exception to the rule that all motions are caused by goods striven for? Or if the uncriticized desires and passions are considered natural, like the weight of a stone, the anger of a lion, or the upward thrust of a plant, then is the rational will which goes contrary to some appetite the only unnatural and so in a sense the only irrational thing in the universe?

Suppose we did not have Aristotle's writings on ethics. What should we suppose he would do with this problem? Should we not expect him to do exactly what he did? First, he makes the most of the fact that there is no specific tendency in a man, *qua* man, which cannot be trained out of him (except, presumably, growth into the shape of man). Man can always be trained to desire the very opposite. This, after all, is a real difference between man and the stone, the zinnia, and the bee. The only thing you can count on is that he will strive for whatever appears to him to be his true well-being. No specific action is "natural" to him *qua* man as weight is to a stone. This means that a man's desires, passions, and appetites are not on the same footing as the desires manifested in the non-intelligent entities about him. Or rather, since it is inevitable that man will seek his own true well-being (however bizarre and self-destructive may be the means chosen by some men) only those desires which are truly consistent with his actual well-being are completely natural.

What, then, is the status of the desire which he ought to refuse to indulge? Plato, like Socrates believed that a man always pursues an apparent good. An irrational desire, then, was a desire for an illusory good. Later, however, he came to lay much stress on the definition of psyche as self-generating motion. This suggested that an irrational act by a psyche might be entirely random energy, not necessarily directed toward any goal, real or illusory. (This manner of talking actually appears only in *Laws* X, but it is latent in the *Timaeus* and even the *Phaedrus*.) A depraved appetite, then, according to Plato's later thought, need not be directed toward a goal at all; it is arbitrary, incomprehensible energy. First, as we have seen, Aristotle rejected radical "irrationality" in this sense by denying random energy anywhere in the universe. Then, in order to be consistent, he had to modify even the earlier, Socratic idea that an "irrational" man is motivated by an illusory good. He can use this kind of language occasionally (as at *Nic. Eth.* III 4), but he must contend that at a deeper level even the "irrational" man is motivated by genuine good. This follows necessarily if formal-final causes are actually the only causes of motion in the universe. All actions, whether "rational" or "irrational" are really rational in that they are called forth by goals—real goals. An "irrational" act is a move which, however real the goal which inspired it, is inefficient for the fulfillment of the ultimate goal, the complete development of the human psyche, the realization of the Form "what it is to be a Man."

Thus no action, whether stupid or intelligent, is random and radically irrational, as all are equally determined by real goals, Forms being striven for. But then we ask, how is it that a man may be faced with a goal which is real, and therefore truly good, which, however, he had better reject? How can it be a real good if to pursue it is bad? This would seem to be a grave problem for a teleologist who insists that the universe has but one kind of causation. Aristotle offers an ingenious, if not entirely convincing, solution. No man is ever actually faced with a single real goal suggesting an immediate course of action contrary to his ultimate goal. What happens is rather that he is inevitably faced with pairs of (practically, not necessarily logically) incompatible goals.

Aristotle asserts that a man is never ever faced with only one real goal which it would be ultimately harmful for him to pursue. There must at all times be at least one other goal, equally real, demanding a course of action which is (in practice, at least) incompatible with the first. Thus, if it is to a man's ultimate harm to run away from battle to save his skin, we must assume that there is another goal, however weakly he is aware of it, which bids him run head-long into fire. We need not picture these conflicting pulls as arranged horizontally, as it were, pulling a man simultaneously this way and that. All we need assume is that for every immediate goal which must be rejected, there is another goal or set of goals, however remote or general, which demand the opposite action of us at that moment. Rationality, then, will be some kind of compromise between them.

Notice: it will still be possible to say that the man, no less than the stone, inevitably follows the most compelling course, the one that seems at the moment to lead to his fulfillment. The passion which a man follows may not be the strongest in the sense that it is the most clamorous and painful, but it is the most compelling in some sense or he would not obey it (*Nic. Eth.* VIII. 2 and III. 4–5). As in Plato, a rational move is not made by removing passion; it is the result of the triumph of the passion for true well-being.

Aristotle was obviously impressed by Plato's discovery that any appetite, when often indulged, grows more and more demanding. There is a kind of autonomy in an appetite, once a habit is formed. In Plato's system, this presented no special problem. A depraved desire was merely a senseless activity of the irrational psyche.[5] In Aristotle's system, however, this phenomenon offered a threat to his analysis of the nature of all motion as inevitably aimed toward a true good. Even in the case of the philosophic man who sees that he must sacrifice a real immediate gain for an ultimately greater gain of the whole man, there is something unsatisfactory about calling his rejected appetite good-directed while maintaining that he was right not to follow it. And what about the child or the non-philosophic man? It is obviously not true that a man can never learn to make good decisions unless he perceives correctly the true end of Man. A man with little philosophic insight may still come to be consistently good in all his decisions. Here Aristotle falls back on his criterion for distinguishing the man from the stone: the existence of any tendency in a man, he apparently assumes, is in itself proof that the opposite tendency could be trained into him. If we translate that into the terms of Aristotle's metaphysics, whenever we find that a man unthinkingly pursues one Form, we must conclude that there is another Form or combination of Forms which, if he were properly aware of them, would pull him in the opposite direction at that moment. But since both Forms or sets of Forms are equally good, the man cannot ignore either. Neither, then, can represent his most efficient course of action. The right course, the course directly toward his true fulfillment, whenever that is opposed by any other tendency within him, must invariably be a mean between extremes.[6]

The human psyche is aware of things which it needs on several levels simultaneously. All of the objects pursued by all of the functions of the psyche are genuine goods—Forms or combinations of Forms. Unfortunately, however, repeated satisfaction of any particular desire always has the effect of making that desire grow, and upsetting its balance with the opposite desire. This imbalance in turn leads to failure and pain. Man needs his intelligence, then, to infer from his past experiences which of his tendencies are inefficient and which of his weaker drives must be strengthened. If he is not the philosophic type himself, he may borrow intelligence from his elders or from the laws of a well-ordered state.[7] Aristotle assumes that a case can be made for the supremacy of the life of action which is not dependent on the man's own intellectual activities for its success. Nevertheless, since intelligence—somebody's intelligence—is the key to man's natural fulfillment, it is hardly surprising that Aristotle decides, after careful consideration, that that man is happiest who spends a large part of his time in this crucial and most typical activity—intellection. Furthermore, intelligent activity for Aristotle meant uncovering causes, and, as for Plato, for Aristotle this meant discovering the Forms which are striven for. Ultimately this meant the investigation of how things are caused at all, that is, how all Forms cause motions by being goods striven for—how some particular Forms are more powerful, therefore better, than others, with one ultimately good Form which causes motion everywhere. Intelligence, then, should eventually take a man beyond any immediate training of his appetites to a contemplation of excellence and beauty in the universe as a whole. Since the good life, even for the unthinking, is based on this vision, then this contemplation is obviously not unnatural for man, as it might be for another species;[8] thus the peculiar pleasure of contemplation, although open only to a few, is nevertheless the highest kind of human success, Aristotle decides.

In addition to the infamous theory of moral excellence as a mean between extremes, there is really only one other feature of Aristotle's ethical theory that is strikingly different from that of his teacher: the denial that knowledge of the Form of the Good is needed for knowledge of moral excellence.

Aristotle admits that there is one thing the reality of which is its excellence[9]—referring surely to his ultimate unmoved mover which turns the universe by being a good which all things desire. What he objects to is the confusion of metaphysics and politics in the *Republic*. That is not the way we get anywhere, he says. The botanist looks for the excellence peculiar to the oak tree or the elm, the shoemaker for the excellence peculiar to shoes, and the political philosopher for the excellence peculiar to man.[10] Now it is a little difficult to see how Plato could object to this, and we begin to wonder if Aristotle isn't knocking at a straw man. But once more we must remember Aristotle's metaphysical program. The excellence of the ultimate mover which inspires the whole universe, is, according to Aristotle, the assurance of a perpetual survival of the Forms from parent to off-spring—a great work, inasmuch as the cessation of motion in the sensible world would also mean the disappearance of the immanent Form.[11] But we cannot really learn anything about the excellence which makes the lesser Forms goals striven for by us and by nature merely by contemplating the ultimate mover. For Plato, the excellence of all Forms was due to their participation in the highest Form. Aristotle, on the other hand, emphasized the fact that the Forms pulled substratum in various directions, sometimes at cross-purposes, although on the whole "toward one" (*Metaph.* Λ10). That is, the forms were organized in a hierarchy, and that accounted for order in the universe; but one had to investigate the Forms separately, and could not learn much about the good which pulls man or oak tree by investigating the good which turns the world. Aristotle had a new role for the ultimate mover. It was the good *par excellence* only because without it the lesser Forms, being immanent, would cease to exist. Thus, while the Form of the Good might provide the ultimate inspiring object for the contemplative life, it could provide little insight for the investigation of the morally good in daily life.

It is possible, then, to give a fairly complete account of Aristotle's innovations in ethics as moves necessitated by his innovations in metaphysics. How plausible is this analysis? First, did Aristotle actually maintain that every human urge was called forth by a Form? Secondly, if he did, why does he not talk in these terms more clearly? Why is it that this all important fact escapes the notice of most readers of the *Nicomachean Ethics*? What may be said for the more usual accounts of the genesis of the theory of excellence as the mean between extremes?

In answer to the first question we may reply: (1) Aristotle nowhere denies what he works out in the *Physics* and the *Metaphysics*, that all of the motions of the world can be reduced to formal-final causes; (2) he frequently uses such things as Ball, House, and Health as examples of Forms which cause activities as ends pursued,[12] examples, that is, from human striving; and (3) the only difference which he specifies between Forms in nature and Forms which cause human activity is that the former are from the first embedded in the particular substratum which will eventually display them while the latter cause motion first of all in a separate agent.[13] He never for a minute contemplates the possibility that the carpenter himself creates the Form House or the doctor the Form Health. How could he? These Forms presumably have the same kind of sequential immortality guaranteed to Oak Tree and Man. The only difference is that instead of a house automatically informing a new piece of substratum with its Form, some man, presumably by seeing another house (in nature or built by another man),[14] becomes informed temporarily by the Form House—that is, he is inspired by the "good" of a house. But what about the more basic moral and intellectual activities of man; are they also, like these more trivial manual activities, called forth by Forms? That this is so is proved, I believe, by the assumption in the *Politics* that there is one best constitution which all men are fumbling for, in the *Rhetoric* that there are a few basic patterns for speakers which all orators are striving toward, and in the *Poetics* that there is an ideal tragedy which all serious poets have tried to produce. This last is particularly illuminating. Aristotle's and Plato's analyses of what poetry is and how it affects listeners are surprisingly similar;[15] but Aristotle thought it was urgent to prove that tragedy (1) was a permanent activity of all mankind, and not merely a recent and an Athenian occupation,[16] and (2) that men pursued it because there was a genuine good achieved by it.[17] Why did he feel this was necessary? Presumably in order to prove that this, like all activities, was caused by a genuine Form.[18]

Our second problem was this: why is Aristotle so reticent about telling us what he is doing—so reticent, indeed, that most readers quite miss the point? In the first place, Aristotle was an honest man. He would hardly be satisfied with an explanation of moral activity which, however closely it followed from his metaphysical program, did not make good sense when applied to our ordinary experiences. It is no wonder, then, that the great bulk of the *Ethics* is devoted to more or less common sense analyses of universal human problems. Aristotle's ethics seem more compelling to us than, say, Aquinas' or Spinoza's, largely because he refuses to present it as a logical deduction from his metaphysics, but rather as an honest appraisal of what we all feel. Secondly Aristotle wants to check and support his theory by showing how it coincides with what has always been thought about the subject. This is important for him because philosophy like all other activities must be inspired ultimately by a single Reality. (Is not Aristotle forever arguing that all his predecessors were groping in their inadequate way for a single truth, discovered at last by himself?) And so it is neither surprising nor upsetting to find that Aristotle clearly recalls general Greek truisms,[19] the medical writers,[20] Plato,[21] and his own physics and psychology[22] in the language and arguments he uses in discussing moral excellence as invariably a mean between extremes. We may go further: it is reasonable to suppose that Aristotle would not so readily have seized this particular solution to his metaphysical problem had there not already been this habit of mind among his predecessors. But to suppose that we have adequately understood Aristotle's moral philosophy when we have traced it to these older features in Greek thought is surely a mistake.

NOTES

[1] Random motion in Plato includes: (1) the distracting passions in the lower functions of the human psyche, (2) the "Wandering Cause" in the *Timaeus*, and (3) the "bad kind of psyche" in *Laws* X, which is probably meant to include both (1) and (2).

[2] *Metaph.* Θ 10 and *Metaph.* N 4.

[3] The nature of the crucial difference between an intelligent and a non-intelligent reaction to a situation is most acutely worked out in *De memoria et reminiscentia.* A steel spring might in a sense "learn" from its past experiences, but it cannot infer from a mechanical "memory" that it has experienced something similar before and then deliberately revived that memory.

[4] This definition of "rational" which underlies all of Plato's as well as all of Aristotle's discussions, appears for the first time in Socrates' "autobiography," *Phaedo* 97–98. Cf. also Diogenes of Apollonia, fr. 3 (Diels-Kranz[6], 64B 3).

[5] Sometimes Plato, too, speaks as though each of the three functions of the human psyche had a legitimate goal, but he more typically treats the lower appetites as always dangerous, even in the good man. Cf. *Republic* IX on the savage element which sometimes awakens only during sleep, or the *Phaedrus* myth, where the black horse is depicted as incorrigible, even when in view of heaven. On the other hand cf. passages such as *Republic* IX 586E–587A.

[6] At *Nic. Eth.* II. 6, 1107a 7–27 Aristotle points out (1) that human excellence is an extreme in goodness, and (2) that there is, of course, no virtuous mean with regard to a vice like envy (φθόνος). If read carefully, this passage is seen to be in no way contradictory to the definition, κατὰ μὲν τὴν οὐσίαν καὶ τὸν λόγον τὸν τὸ τί ἦν εἶναι λέγοντα μεσότης ἐστὶν ἡ ἀρετή (1107a 6–7). A bad passion or action will still inevitably be caused by an excess or

deficiency; it is just that while some words refer to passions or actions which are sometimes good, sometimes bad, others are already defined as passions felt under conditions which make them wrong. Incidentally, this passage shows fairly clearly that Aristotle did not arrive at his doctrine of the mean by examining ordinary language.

[7] *Nic. Eth.* X. 9. Cf. *Republic* IX 590–91.

[8] Nature in Aristotle works blindly toward the same universal harmony that the speculative philosopher discovers and is drawn toward. Aristotle no less than Plato was impressed by the essential identity between the procedure of an artist and the process manifested in rocks and trees and animals. But whereas Plato concluded that Nature was intelligent (possessed conscious forethought) Aristotle concluded that even the artist was drawn on blindly. Cf. *Phys.* II. 8 and *Nic. Eth.* III. 4–5.

[9] As he puts it, there is such a thing as "good" in the category of substance, namely God or intelligence: καὶ γὰρ ἐν τῷ τί λέγεται, οἷον ὁ θεὸς καὶ ὁ νοῦς, *Nic. Eth.* I. 5, 1096a 24–25. The second καὶ might be translated "i.e.": cf. *Metaph.* Λ 9.

[10] *Nic. Eth.* I. 6. Cf. the not dissimilar argument at *Republic* IV 438A–439A.

[11] *De gen. et corr.* II. 10, 336b 25–337a 2, *De An.* II. 4, 415a 26–b7, *De gen. An.* II. 1, 731b 31—35.

[12] Above all in *Metaph.* Z.

[13] *Phys.* II. 1, *De part. An.* I. 1, *Metaph.* Z 8. In the latter chapter it is made clear that the artist does not create the Form: Z 8, 1033b 5, ff.

[14] This, presumably, is implied in Aristotle's notion, shared with other Socratics and probably Sophists as well, that "art imitates nature" (*Phys.* II. 2, 194a 21). Cf. *Meteor.* IV. 381b 6–7, *Polit.* VII. 17, 1337a 2, *Protrepticus* fr. 13 (Ross).

[15] Both conclude that its essential nature is to imitate, and that its most important effect on the listener is to call up latent appetites, especially pity. See the first half of *Republic* X. (Notice τὸ ἐλεεινόν, 606B 8, C 5). Aristotle obviously did not make any attempt to investigate poetry all over again, starting from scratch. We should not allow our special interest in the *Poetics* to blind us to the probability that Aristotle thought of poetry as only one minor problem in his grand scheme.

[16] This is obvious not only in his attempt to show that the function of the epic is identical with that of tragedy (*Poetics* 1462b 13–14) but also in his attempt to show how every child automatically creates "tragic" imitation for himself (*Poetics* ch. 4).

[17] This, of course, is the true origin of the theory of *katharsis*. The question of whether it is primarily medical or religious *katharsis* which gave Aristotle the idea is of secondary importance.

[18] That every τέχνη has a good embedded in nature is clearly implied in such passages as *Politics* 1282b 15 and *Nic. Eth.* I. 1, 1094a 1.

[19] Thus Plato sums up the ethical insight of the whole *Republic* as follows (off-hand, and surely meant in no technical sense of τὸ μέσον):

ἀλλὰ γνῷ τὸν μέσον ἀεὶ τῶν τοιούτων βίον αἱρεῖσθαι καὶ φεύγειν τὰ ὑπερβάλλοντα ἑκατέρωσε . . . οὕτω γὰρ εὐδαιμονέστατος γίγνεται ἄνθρωπος. (X 619A5–B1).

[20] See Burnet's editions of the *Ethics*, pp. xxxi–xxxiv and Werner Jaeger, "Aristotle's Use of Medicine as Model of Method in his *Ethics*," *JHS*, LXXVII (1957): 54–61.

[21] See *Gorgias* 507–8, *Republic* I 349–50, *Politicus* 283–87, and *Philebus* 25–26 (*et passim*).

[22] Cf. Burnet, *op. cit.*, pp. 71–73.

JOSEPH OWENS
Pontifical Institute for Medieval Studies, Toronto, Canada

The Universality of the Sensible in the Aristotelian Noetic*

I

As is well enough known, all human cognition originates for Aristotle in sensible things. The closing chapter of the *Posterior Analytics* (II. 19, 100a 1–b 5) and the seventh and eighth chapters of *De Anima*'s third book (431a 1–432a 14) make this role of sensible objects in human intellection indisputably clear. The wording of *De Anima*, however, is that "the soul never thinks without an image" (III. 7, 431a 16–17; Oxford tr.), that "the objects of thought are in the sensible forms" (II. 8, 432a 4–5), that "when the mind is actively aware of anything it is necessarily aware of it along with an image" (a 8–9), and that while concepts are not phantasms they are not had without phantasms (a 14–15). Taken alone, these statements might be compatible with the interpretation that the mind can find in sensible data notions that are wider than the sensible, and see in sensible things an object, such as substance or being, that is more general than either the corporeal or the incorporeal. Such, in fact, is the impression given by Boethius' presentation of the first Aristotelian category. Substance is the highest genus, and is for Boethius divided into the corporeal and the incorporeal as its species.[1] In this sense the category was schematized in the Porphyrian tree and through the centuries has guided the first faltering steps of philosophy students in their initiation into Aristotelian logic. The impression is that just as one sees in man and ox a generic concept universal in regard to both, so in sensible things one sees a concept of substance that is generic in regard to both the corporeal and incorporeal, and accordingly more universal than either.

Is this sound Aristotelian doctrine? If it is, it will have important

* Presented originally under the title "The Universal in *Physics* I, 1" at the 1964 meeting of the SAGP in Boston, Massachusetts. Reprinted from *Mélanges à la mèmoire de monsieur de Koninck* (Quebec, 1968). By permission of les Presses de l'université Laval.

consequences in determining the object of metaphysics. It will allow the human mind to form, through an immediate inspection of sensible things, a concept that is wider than the sensible. It will require no mediating process of judging and reasoning to build a concept that is universal in regard to both the corporeal and incorporeal. Through simple apprehension alone it will furnish a notion capable of serving as an object for the study of what is beyond the sensible. In a word, it will permit the human mind to behold in sensible things a notion that is more universal than the sensible.

Is this situation possible in the Aristotelian noetic? An analysis of a much controverted text in the opening chapter of the *Physics* may throw considerable light upon the topic. The *Physics* begins with a rapid sketch of Aristotle's general concept of scientific knowledge. First, in any scientific discipline to know a thing is to know its principles or elements.[2] Secondly, the natural path of human knowledge is from things that are more knowable for men to things that are more knowable in themselves,[3] and this means proceeding from concretions to the distinct cognition of the principles and elements into which they may be analyzed. These two norms are regarded as applying to all scientific procedure. Here they are but outlined briefly as an introduction to the Aristotelian philosophy of nature.

Up to this point the chapter is recapitulating standard Aristotelianism in quite the expected way. In the Stagirite's general noetic, the origin of human knowledge lies inevitably in sensible things. Accordingly the present chapter of the *Physics* (I. 1, 184a 21–25) is able to state succinctly that sensible composites are the more apparent objects of human cognition, and that from knowledge of them knowledge of their principles is derived. From knowledge of sensible composites, in consequence, all further human knowledge will be obtained in one way or another. The sensible things, however, are concretions. They are composites both in reality and from the viewpoint of the logician. In their own reality they are composites of form and matter (*Phys.* II. 1, 192b 8–193b 18). From the logical viewpoint they are composites of genera and species and subject, or, in the special terminology of the *Categories* (2a 11–19), of secondary substance and primary substance. Their accidents may, for present purposes, be left out of consideration.

So far, then, everything is in order in these two initial assertions of the *Physics*. From the two premises, however, a rather surprising conclusion is drawn: διὸ ἐκ τῶν καθόλου ἐπὶ τὰ καθ'ἕκαστα δεῖ προϊέναι.[4] An unalerted reader would be inclined to understand this in English as:

"Therefore one should proceed from the universals to the individuals." The meaning would in this perspective be that one knows the universal first, and from the universal proceeds to knowledge of individual sensible things. Such an understanding of the sentence, of course, strikes at once a jarring note. Elsewhere Aristotle's noetic regularly sees all human knowledge originating in the individual sensible things. The universal seems only a further and less definite way of considering things that are first known as individual.[5] In the *Posterior Analytics* (I. 2, 72a 4–5) the universal is explicitly described as farthest from sensation, while, in direct contrast, the individuals are closest. Even within a Platonic setting Aristotle maintains that the proponents of the Ideas were actually going from "the things around us" (*Metaph.* A 9, 990b 1—Oxford tr.) to corresponding separate entities of the same name. In an Aristotelian context the notion of going from universals to singulars hardly makes sense. As Tannery noted in his discussion of this passage, towards the end of the nineteenth century, one would expect from all the analogous passages that Aristotle should say just the opposite.[6] The Stagirite should find his point of departure in the particular that is immediately attained in sensation, and proceed to the general or the universal as his goal. The particular things are first known, and in them and through them the universal is reached. One would expect to read: "Therefore we must advance from the particulars to the general." Yet the text clearly states the opposite. It asserts that one should start with the general or universal and proceed to the particulars.

The direction the procedure is to take, accordingly, appears with unmistakable clarity in the text. It is from the universal to the particulars. But what exactly is meant by "universal" and "particulars" in the present setting? Whatever is meant by them respectively, the statement as a whole cannot very well imply against an Aristotelian background that human knowledge starts with non-sensible objects. Procedure from universals, as intellectual abstractions, to concrete sensible things would not be any more acceptable to Aristotle than to Whitehead.[7] The first step in the investigation of the passage, therefore, will be to determine exactly what is meant by "universal" and by "particulars" in its context.

II

To what, then, does "universal" refer in the present passage? In English translations it may appear variously as "generalities" (Oxford tr.), "general character of a thing" (Wheelwright), or "the concrete whole" (Wicksteed). Among the ancient Greek commentators, Philoponus[8] had distinguished its meaning here from the primary sense of "universal," and given it the signification of an indeterminate particular concretion. Among the moderns, Bonitz (*Ind. Arist.*, 357a 16) classed its use in this passage as *alio sensu*, as a meaning other than its ordinary one. But he did not specify the sense or give other instances of the unusual meaning. Ross (*Aristotle's Physics*, p. 457) asserts that in the present passage the term "is not used in its usual Aristotelian meaning." He explains: "The reference must be not to a universal conceived quite clearly in its true nature, but to that stage in knowledge in which an object is known by perception to possess some general characteristic (e.g., to be an animal) before it is known what its specific characteristic is (e.g., whether it is a horse or a cow)." This would mean that the true nature of the universal is specific, while a genus is universal in another and not usual sense of the term.

But in Aristotle does *to katholou* have in fact a number of different significations? It does not seem to be characterized by him anywhere in this way, at least explicitly. It is not listed in Book Δ of the *Metaphysics* among the notions that vary in meaning. It is mentioned there as one of the divergent senses of "whole," namely as containing "many things by being predicated of each, and by all of them . . . being severally one single thing" (Oxford tr. of ὡς πολλὰ περιέχον τῷ κατηγορεῖσθαι καθ' ἑκάστου καὶ ἓν ἅπαντα εἶναι ὡς ἕκαστον—Δ 26, 1023b 30–31). It seems, given the status of one of the definite senses of "whole," as though it itself had only one meaning. The meaning is that of something predicated of a number of instances, something that retains its own self-identity while existing in a number of different things. From a logical viewpoint the universal is regularly described by this capacity to be predicated of subjects. For instance, by "universal" is meant "that which is of such a nature as to be predicated of many subjects, by 'individual' that which is not so predicated" (*Int.* 7, 17a 39–40; Oxford tr.). Examples are given: "Thus 'man' is a universal, 'Callias' an individual" (ibid). From a metaphysical standpoint the presence of the universal in a plurality of things remains its distinguishing mark. The universal is "that which is of such a nature as to belong to a number of things" (ὃ πλείοσιν ὑπάρχειν πέφυκεν—*Metaph.* Z 13, 1038b 11–12). Throughout the Aristotelian corpus the term bears consistently this one meaning. It does not seem to express a notion with many senses. Though it may apply with varying degrees of rigor in physical, mathematical, metaphysical, and ethical contexts respectively, the notion itself seems to remain the same in all its instances.

In particular, the view of John Philoponus that the universal in its primary sense means a determined and articulated nature, for instance man or animal, does not seem to express the notion of the universal that emerges from Aristotle's *Metaphysics*. In Book M (10, 1087a 16–23) the universal, clearly meant in its regular sense, is characterized as indeterminate—τοῦ καθόλου καὶ ἀορίστου. In Book Z (13, 1038b 6–1039a 14) the universal is denied the actuality that would be required to make it something definite in itself. A primary and secondary sense along these lines does not appear in the text of Aristotle. A further meaning of "universal" recognized by the Greek commentators[9] was in regard to a cause upon which other things depended, in the sense that if the cause were done away with, all its effects would thereby vanish. This conception was used to explain how the science of the separate substances was universally the science of all beings. It obtains support from the way Aristotle equates cause with universal in the opening chapters of the *Metaphysics*. But it is hardly applicable in the present context. *To katholou* in the text from the first chapter of the *Physics* is not regarded as functioning in any role of cause, but rather as an effect, as something whose causes or principles or elements are being sought.

Nor does it seem helpful to distinguish from the usual sense of the universal "the other and less frequent sense of 'concrete whole.' "[10] The universal, as first known in the sensible things from which human cognition takes its origin, is always a concrete whole. It is "something composed of this particular formula and this particular matter treated as universal" (*Metaph.* Z 10, 1035b 29–30; Oxford tr.), "the compound of both taken universally" (11, 1037a 6–7). All the universals that are predicated of sensible things will be composites or compounds of that type. In its regularly used sense, accordingly, the universal is a "concrete whole."

Finally, what about Ross's suggestion that "universal" in the present context means a generic nature, instead of the "true nature" of the universal that appears in the specific constitution of things?[11] At one place in the *Metaphysics* (H 1, 1042a 13–15) "universal" is in fact contrasted with genus. There it seems quite clearly taken in the sense of the specific nature in its relation to singulars. But does this imply at all that the generic universals are not universals in the true sense? If the universals were principles, Aristotle (*Metaph.* B 3, 998b 17–19) argues, the highest genera would fill this role. In Mure's translation of the *Posterior Analytics* (II, 19, 100a 16–b 3), accordingly, the specific nature "man" is a "rudimentary universal," while the widest of the generic natures are the "true universals." The translation runs: "for though the act of sense-perception is of the particular, its content is universal—is man, for example, not the man Callias. A fresh stand is made among these rudimentary universals, and the process does not cease until the indivisible concepts, the true universals, are established: e.g., such and such a species of animal is a step towards a further generalization." In a note to the translation Mure states that the highest genera, the categories, are "*par excellence* universal" (n. 2).

Both these translators are sufficiently familiar with the varying moods of the Aristotelian text, so both should be right even when writing verbally opposite statements. Actually, both are right, as far as the positive side of their views enters into question. In the Greek text, the specific and the generic traits are alike called "universal."[12] No adjective is added in either case to distinguish what would be a "rudimentary" universal from a "true" universal. Species and genera both seem regarded as universal in the full sense of the term. In the above text from the *Posterior Analytics*, the specific nature that is perceived in the individual man is the starting point of the process. The next step is the establishing of the genus "animal," and so on in ascending scale until the highest genus is reached. According to this way of regarding the process of cognition, the object is first known in its specific nature and then gradually in its more generic traits. On the other hand, the Greek commentators[13] were inclined to interpret in the opposite direction the process signalized in the opening chapter of the *Physics*. The confused object initially known appeared in its more generic traits, as an object at a distance will first appear as a body, then as something alive, and then as a man. In either case, however, the notion of universality seems to be fully satisfied. Both the generic and the specific natures are predicated of subjects and belong in these subjects as identical with each of them.

What, then, is the exact sense of "universal" in the opening passage of the *Physics*? The context describes it as a "whole," a whole that contains a number of things as its parts. In it the parts are confused (συγκεχυμένα). What are these parts? Whatever they are, they will function as the καθ' ἕκαστα towards which the process of knowledge advances. What is meant by parts in this context, accordingly, should provide the key to the meaning of "universal" as it is used in the present passage.

III

The usual meaning of καθ' ἕκαστον and καθ' ἕκαστα throughout the Aristotelian corpus is the singular sensible thing, or the particular event. In the *Categories* (2a 34–b 5) it is the logically primary substance, the individual that is predicated of nothing else while all the rest are predicated of it. In the *Metaphysics* (A 1, 981a 15–24) it is the singular thing that one encounters in sensible experience, the particular compound that is brought into being or destroyed in the visible and tangible world. In the *Nicomachean Ethics* (VI. 8–9, 1142a 14–1143b 5) it is the variable fact about which one may deliberate and with which moral life is concerned. This regular use of the term in logical, metaphysical, and ethical contexts is too familiar to readers of the Aristotelian treatises to require the citation of any more detailed instances.

The term, however, is also used at times to signify the different species of which a generic nature is predicated. In the *Posterior Analytics* (I. 5, 74a 25–30) it means the equilateral, scalene, and isosceles types that exhibit the general nature of a triangle. In a word, it stands for the different species of triangle.[14] It expresses something that is universal as a species, and not just a singular thing. It is meant in this sense when Aristotle (*An. Post.* II. 13, 97b 28) says that the καθ' ἕκαστον is more easily defined than the universal. In the meaning of an individual sensible thing it would not be definable at all (*Metaph.* Z 10, 1036a 2–5). The conclusion drawn is that one should proceed from the particulars to the universal.[15] In wording, this is just the opposite of the sentence in the opening chapter of the *Physics*. But the "particulars" from which the procedure here commences are clearly enough the lowest species. From them one goes on to the genera.

This use of the term shows that it may mean something universal. The term is therefore not restricted to the singular individual. In the opening chapter of the *Physics*, accordingly, there need be no absolute requirement for it to mean the particular sensible things. With this inhibition removed, one may approach the illustrations brought forward by Aristotle to clarify its meaning in the present context. The illustrations used (*Phys.* I. 1, 184b 10–14) are two. The first is that of a word compared with a definition. The word "circle," for instance, signifies an undifferentiated whole. The definition, on the other hand, divides the whole into its particular components (διαιρεῖ εἰς τὰ καθ' ἕκαστα—b 12). The second illustration is that children first call all men fathers and women mothers, but later distinguish the one from the other.

What does the first of these illustrations establish? The particular components into which the definition expressly divides its objects are clearly enough the genus and the specific differentia. In the case of a circle these would be "plane figure" and "with every point on its circumference equidistant from a given point."[16] The genus and the differentia are the καθ' ἕκαστα that the definition distinguishes separately in the whole signified by the word "circle."[17] The two aspects are fused together in the object expressed by the single word. They are divided from each other and expressed in separate notions by the definition. They are both contained in a confused manner in the one notion "circle," as expressed by the single word. The notion "circle" is immediately accessible to people in general.[18] It can serve as a starting point. The mathematical definition of a circle is not immediately known. But it can be reached through a study of what is known under the notion "circle." In this way one proceeds from what is meant by the word to the components that are expressed in distinct fashion by the definition.

Does the illustration, interpreted in what seems its obvious meaning, serve the purpose for which it was introduced? The overall purpose is to explain that natural philosophy, like any other science, has to proceed from what is more knowable in respect of human cognition to principles and causes and elements that are more knowable in themselves but are not immediately knowable to men. In natural philosophy these are found to be the entirely formless matter and the first form received by it. The matter and the form are contained in the sensible things that human cognition first attains. They are fused together physically in the sensible thing, just as in the logical order genus and differentia are fused together in the definition. From a study of the originally known concrete whole they are reached and expressed in separate notions through the procedure of natural philosophy. Just as the form is the actuation of the matter, moreover, so is the differentia the actuation of the genus (*Metaph.* H 6, 1045a 23–35). The analysis of definition into genus and differentia is in fact used in the *Metaphysics* (Z 12, 1037b 8–1038a 35) as an approach to the study of the composition of matter and form in sensible substances, and the problem dealt with in their regard is characterized (b 9–10) as helpful for the inquiries about substance. In the meaning of a concrete whole analyzed into its logical elements, therefore, the illustration of the word and the definition is quite what should be expected in Aristotle as an approach to the analysis of a physical whole into elements or principles or causes.

When a parallel passage has been found that seems to settle the question, however, it may still have to face objections from leading authorities. Ross (*Aristotle's Physics*, pp. 457–58), in fact, states that the present interpretation "seems impossible." Ross (p. 457), as already noted, identifies the "universal" in this context as generic knowledge, for instance the knowledge of something as an "animal." The procedure, then, would be from the general characteristic as the starting point to the specific traits as the principles or elements, for example, from "animal" to "horse" or "cow." In this understanding of the procedure, the genus cannot be one of the elements reached by the scientific inquiry. As the starting point, it would be expressly contrasted with the elements that are reached as a goal. Hence, from Ross's viewpoint, it seems impossible for the elements in the illustration to be the genus and the differentia that make up the definition.

What alternative does Ross offer? He acknowledges (ibid) that the analysis of a genus into its species will not do here. But, he claims, the distinguishing of the various senses of an ambiguous term will serve the present purpose, and will provide the only interpretation able "to illustrate, even remotely, what it is put forward as illustrating, viz., the transition from the recognition of the generic nature of an object to the recognition of its specific nature" (p. 458). "Circle" in Aristotle is in fact an ambiguous term. Besides a geometrical circle it is also used for an epic cycle (*An. Post.* I. 12, 77b 33), and had still other meanings in everyday speech. Tannery's (*art. cit.*, p. 471, n. 5) suggestion that the καθ' ἕκαστα distinguished by the definition are the circumference of the circle and surface limited by the circumference, both referred to indifferently in Greek mathematics by the word "circle," seems to be in essentials the same as that of Ross.

No one need question the admission that this interpretation is indeed remote. But does any immediate problem about the ambiguous use of terms really enter the consideration here? Where such a problem has an essential bearing upon his theme, Aristotle is usually not slow in bringing it to the fore. That he should use definition to illustrate his point, and without any warning understand by it solely the definition of ambiguous terms, does seem farfetched. It is not paralleled in Aristotle's use of the analysis of definition in the *Metaphysics* (Z 12) as an approach to the analysis of sensible things into matter and form. Moreover, the definition of an ambiguous term, insofar as it can have a definition, does not in fact distinguish its various senses, any more than the definition of a genus distinguishes its various species. A definition of "healthy," or "medical," or "good," would merely provide a vague description that could extend to all the various senses. It would not distinguish the meaning that "healthy" has when applied to food from the meaning it has when applied to color. One may reject, correctly, the possibility of interpreting the illustration in the sense of the division of a genus into its species; but by the same token a division into the various meanings of an ambiguous term becomes inapplicable.

The second illustration is that children at first call all men fathers and all women mothers, and only later distinguish other men from their fathers and other women from their mothers. The relation between these respective people parallels the relation between the components of a definition in the first illustration. "Man" and "woman" are more general, "father" and "mother" are more specific. Does the illustration mean, however, that a child commences with a specific knowledge of his father as father, and wrongly applies that knowledge in its fullness to men in general? Fourth-century Greek children may have been precocious. But to endow their first impressions with full specific knowledge of what it means to be a father, is rather overdoing things. Does the illustration mean, then, that they first have the general impression "man" and express this incorrectly by the word "father," getting only later the specific notion to which the word "father" is restricted?

In the rout simile at the end of the *Posterior Analytics* (II. 19, 100b 1–3), the procedure of human knowledge is clearly taken to be from the specific nature "man" through the generic nature "animal" to the still higher genera, until the highest genus of all, the category, is reached. In one of a number of indiscriminate singulars that appear before human sensation the notion "man" is grasped, and then the other singulars are aligned with it one after another until the species is sufficiently established in one's cognition. In a further step, men are viewed in a panorama with horses, cows, dogs, cats, and so on, and in a corresponding way the genus "animal" is reached. Animals are viewed along with plants in a still wider picture, and the notion "something living" is attained as a broader generic nature. The process continues until the highest genus, "substance," is isolated. This is the way the Porphyrian tree has been climbed by generations of students of Aristotelian logic from Boethius on. On the other hand, the familiar illustration used by the Greek commentators[19] went in the opposite direction. In seeing a distant object, one recognized it first as a body. Then on getting closer to it one saw that it was something alive. On still greater proximity one realized that it was a man, and finally that it was the individual Socrates or Alcibiades. The direction was from genera to species and singulars.

Each of the two ways of proceeding seems to have its legitimate place. From the logician's viewpoint, the singulars are first grouped into species, and then the species into genera, until the highest genus is reached. Epistemologically, however, a thing seems known first under the vaguest general notion of "something," and then its distinguishing traits are gradually seen as in the case of the object first perceived at a distance. Which of the two viewpoints is applicable here? Or are both on the same footing, as far as the present illustration is concerned?

The text reads as though "the one and the other" or "each of the two" (ἑκάτερον) into which the originally known confused whole is distinguished must be "men and fathers" or "women and mothers." Neither the more specific notion "fathers" nor the more generic notion "men" seems to be the concrete whole that is first known. They seem represented as concepts distinct from each other, the καθ' ἕκαστα that emerge from a differentiating knowledge of the objects initially grasped through sensation. The starting point is neither the one nor the other as distinct notions, but rather a vague object in which both are fused and neither is differentiated. Whether the child first becomes accustomed to call the vaguely known object "Dad" or "man" or any other name, is beside the point. It is known first as a confused whole, and only later are the concepts of it as "father" and as "man" differentiated.

Interpreted in this way, the second illustration continues to press home the point made by the first. The καθ' ἕκαστα are the distinct generic and specific notions that were not differentiated in the initially known whole. Καθ' ἕκαστα here cannot mean singular sensible things, but universal notions that set up the species and genera. The confusedly known object that serves as the starting point is, however, universal in regard to them all. It contains them by being predicable of each, for each of the components is a "known object" or "something," or whatever one wishes to call the initially grasped whole in all its vagueness. With each of them is it identical, one by one, while remaining a unitary notion in itself. In this way it fully and univocally satisfies the Aristotelian requirements for universality, namely as containing "many things by being predicated of each, and by all of them . . . being severally one single thing" (*Metaph.* Δ 26, 1023b 30–31). The starting point, accordingly, is neither the lowest species nor the highest genus, but an as yet undifferentiated object that is universal to both. It may therefore be referred to simply as "the universal," while the genera, differentiae, and species contained under it may be called without hesitation its καθ' ἕκαστα.

IV

What Aristotle has been saying, then, is that the confused object initially known in sensation is universal in regard to its parts or components, and that from it one proceeds to the distinct knowledge of the components. That is what he says. But what does it mean, philosophically, in the present context? Sometimes one can determine satisfactorily enough what a Greek thinker is saying, and still encounter difficulty in assessing its correct philosophical meaning. In the opening chapter of the *Physics*, what is the exact bearing of the statement that one must proceed from the universals to their distinct components? It is brought forward as an introduction to a natural philosophy that proceeds from concrete sensible things to the matter and form that are the principles or causes or elements of these things. Is it merely a comparison? Does it just mean that as in the case of a universal you analyze a whole into its parts, so in natural philosophy you analyze the initially known sensible concretion into its distinct components?

This may possibly be all the text asserts. The view, however, offers difficulties, plausible as it may appear at first sight. The notion of proceeding from the universal to its components is not introduced as a comparison, but as a consequence. It is introduced by διό—wherefore. *Because* we first know concretions, we have to proceed from universals. Such is the sequence of thought. It seems to mean that the concretions from which the reasoning of natural philosophy commences will somehow remain universal in regard to their principles and elements. Hence would arise the necessity of the elaborate explanation through the examples of the name and the definition, the fathers and mothers and the men and women.

Secondly, the principles reached by the procedure in natural philosophy have to be themselves more knowable than the concretions from which the procedure started. This requirement is stated expressly in the opening chapter of the *Physics*. The principles reached by the procedure are formless matter and its first form. But in itself the matter is unknowable (*Metaph*. Z 10, 1036a 8–9). As a principle for scientific knowledge of sensible things it will have to appear in a way that renders it more knowable than the observable things themselves. This cannot be the way in which it is present in the singular thing, where, taken apart from the form, it manifests no actuality or determination whatsoever.[20] Yet it is knowable by analogy (*Phys*. I. 7, 191a 7–12). As the bronze is to the statue and the wood to the bed, so is it to the substantial actuality of any body. What does this mean? It means that the basic concept upon which the concept of formless matter is elaborated, is the concept of a body, of the concretion originally known in sensation. It is the universal and vague concept of something corporeal. In this way the subject that receives the substantial form is represented as a corporeal substrate with the added negation that it lacks all the determinations given by the categories. The notion is formed by taking the universal concept of "substrate" as seen in things like a bed or a statue, and by adding to that basic concept the privation of any formal characteristic. In this way it remains basically the concept of a body, the concept of the concretion that was first known in sensation. In regard to it the concept of the concretion remains universal. The basic substrate of bodies is conceived as something corporeal. But it itself, as one of the καθ' ἕκαστα that come under this universal, is likewise represented in the status of a universal. As universal it can serve as a principle for scientific knowledge. It can be used universally as a principle for understanding all bodies. From this viewpoint it is more knowable in itself than the bodies it serves to explain, even though those bodies are more knowable to us.

The same considerations hold correspondingly for the formal principle of sensible things. It cannot be represented just in itself. Even though it is contrasted with matter, it has to be represented as something material. As the shape of the statue is related to the bronze and the shape of a bed to the wood, so the intelligible content of a substance is represented in relation to the formless matter that multiplies it in the many individuals of a species. The concept is basically that of shaped or formed body, with the negation of all substrate added as its distinguishing feature. The concept of something corporeal remains basic to it. The notion of the object originally known in sensation functions as a universal in regard to the form as well as the matter, and from an epistemological viewpoint subsumes both under itself.

Viewed in this perspective, *both* the principles that are reached by the analysis of sensible things in natural philosophy come under the object initially known in sensation, as under a universal. Aristotle is saying that the procedure of natural philosophy is from bodies as known universally in ordinary sensation to principles that are conceived and known under further determinations of the original universal concept. One is proceeding from the first known universal to a distinct cognition of notions that come under it but are as yet undifferentiated in it, somewhat as the definition of a circle differentiates the notions signified confusedly by the word "circle" and as children afterwards distinguish the notions of "father" and "man" that were undifferentiated in their earlier concept. What Aristotle has in mind, if the present interpretation is correct, is that the confused object first grasped in sensation remains universal in regard to all further knowledge. The origin of all human knowledge in sensation would mean, then, that all other objects have to be known basically in terms of concrete sensible things, with the necessary refinements and negations added through judgments and the conclusions of reasoning processes. This would safeguard the Aristotelian conception of scientific knowledge from any atomism in the epistemological sense. The ultimate principles reached by the scientific procedure do not have to be given the status of individually known building blocks from which the universe is to be constructed. Rather, any "correspondence theory" of truth that one might wish to attribute to Aristotle[21] would have to refrain carefully from placing a photographic correspondence between the ultimate principles themselves and the concepts by which they are known. The concepts are not at all immediate replicas of them, but are elaborations of the confused object originally known in sensation and contained under it as under a universal.

V

This interpretation gives the "universal" in the opening passage of the *Physics* the regular and univocal meaning that it has elsewhere in Aristotle. It also finds considerable importance in the use of the notion for the explanation of philosophical procedure at the beginning of natural philosophy, an importance that justifies the space given it in the condensed summary of scientific method. As the most pertinent overall result, however, it shows why the mind cannot attain in simple apprehension any concept that is common to corporeal and incorporeal things. The first confused notion for human cognition is that of "something sensible." This functions as a universal in the Aristotelian noetic for all further cognition. It brings under its scope every other concept, including those of incorporeal objects. It is the all-pervading notion that is always basic, and that is elaborated and built upon in one way or another to construct the concepts of formless matter, of substantial form, of accidents, and of spiritual beings. It does not allow any notion that extends beyond the sensible to be seen immediately in the objects directly presented to human cognition. Rather, it requires a process of judgment and reasoning to arrive at concepts of immaterial substance and immaterial being, or at concepts that are common to both the material and immaterial orders. It will help to explain why so many able thinkers in course of Western thought have not been able to recognize any kind of being except the sensible, and why a subject for the science of metaphysics has proven a stumbling block to them throughout the centuries.

In the Aristotelian noetic, then, the subject of metaphysics is not something that is offered immediately to men's intellects. It is something that has to be reached by a difficult reasoning process. For Aristotle himself the reasoning was from sensibly observed motion to the entirely separate or supersensible movents. To take natures found in sensible things and hypostatize them as separate, appeared to him to be the fault of the Platonic procedure and to result in a useless duplication of sensible reality. But even where the subject of metaphysics is held to be common being, as in St Thomas Aquinas, the universality of the sensible in the knowing process is by no means eliminated. Existence, by actuating a nature other than itself, constitutes common being, the subject of metaphysics. This existence is indeed known in every judgment, but not as something that transcends the sensible world. The subject that it constitutes for intellectual consideration does not appear immediately as transcendentally common being. Rather, the notion is of something sensible, and the difficult process of demonstrating a foundation for the judgment that separates substance and being from the sensible still lies ahead. There is here no immediately known concept that escapes the universality that sensible nature exercises in regard to human cognition.

It may seem a bit hazardous to draw these far-reaching conclusions from a lone text of Aristotle. Yet the text occurs in a passage that summarizes Aristotle's overall conception of scientific method. Accordingly it lends itself in full to interpretation through other texts scattered throughout the Aristotelian corpus, in line with Trendelenburg's well-known norm of *Aristoteles ex Aristotele*. The passage itself is not self-explanatory. It caused trouble for the Greek commentators, and has continued to puzzle modern writers. Simplicius, apparently none too satisfied, concluded his own discussion of it with the remark: "If anyone can give a more convincing account of it, let him please do so."[22] The challenge has remained open. If interpreted as above, in the light of the other relevant Aristotelian tenets, it gives a much sharper meaning to the origin of all human cognition in sensible things.

NOTES

1 "Substantia igitur generalissimum genus est; hoc enim de cunctis aliis praedicatur, ac primum hujus species duae sunt, corporeum et incorporeum . . ." Boethius, *In Porphyrium Commentaria*, III; *PL*, LXIV, 103A.

2 *Phys.* I. 1, 184a 10–16. Cf. *An. Post.* I. 2, 71b 19–23; *Metaph.* A 1, 981a 24–b 6; E 1, 1025b 6–7; K 7, 1063b 36–37. A discussion of this theme at greater length may be found in my paper "The Aristotelian Conception of the Sciences," *IPQ*, IV (1964): 200–16.

[3] *Phys.* I. 1, 184a 16–23. Cf. *An. Post.* I. 2, 71b 29–72a 5; *Metaph.* Z 4, 1029b 3–12; *Eth. Nic.* I. 4, 1095b 2–4.

[4] *Phys.* I. 1, 184a 23–24. At *An. Post.* II. 13, 97b 28–29, the assertion is, verbally at least, just the opposite: διὸ δεῖ ἀπὸ τῶν καθ' ἕκαστα ἐπὶ τὰ καθόλου μεταβαίνειν.

[5] *Metaph.* Z 10, 1035b 27–30; 11, 1037a 5–10. In the Aristotelian texts, the one thing seems described as known in two different ways. There does not seem to be any duplication of objects. The universal way of knowing the sensible thing, however, is seen as a duplication by Chung-Hwan Chen, "Universal Concrete, A Typical Aristotelian Duplication of Reality," *Phronesis* IX (1964): 48–57. On the adverbial force of the Aristotelian word "universal," see Kurt von Fritz, *Philosophie und sprachlicher Ausdruck bei Demokrit, Plato und Aristoteles* (Leipzig, etc., 1938), pp. 40, 65.

[6] Paul Tannery, "Sur un point de la méthode d'Aristote," *AGP*, VI (1893): 468. What seems to be the opposite is in fact stated in the text quoted supra, n. 4.

[7] "It is a complete mistake to ask how concrete particular fact can be built up out of universals." Whitehead, *Process and Reality* (New York, 1929), p. 30.

[8] *In Phys.*, 17. 25–18. 3. Cf. 10. 23–11. 24; 13. 1–12.

[9] Alexander, *In Metaph.*, 246. 10–13; 661. 33–39. Asclepius, *In Metaph.*, 232. 4–11. Cf. Simplicius, *In Phys.*, 19. 5–7.

[10] Note to Wicksteed tr., ad loc., in the *Loeb Classical Library.* In the instance from *De Gen. et Corr.* II. 4, 331a 20, brought forward as an illustration, καθόλου seems used in its regular sense.

[11] *Aristotle's Physics*, p. 457. Passage quoted supra.

[12] Cf. ἠρεμήσαντος τοῦ καθόλου (100a 6–7); πρῶτον . . . καθόλου (a 16); and τὰ ἀμερῆ . . . καὶ τὰ καθόλου (b 2).

[13] Simplicius, *In Phys.*, 16. 17–20; Philoponos, 11. 12–18; 19. 16–19. Cf. Themistius, *In Phys.*, 2. 8–9.

[14] At *MM* II. 11, 1211a 18–23 it is found used for notions as wide as those of the constituents of friendship: "the good, and being, and well-being" (Oxford tr.).

[15] Text supra, n. 4.

[16] See Simplicius, *In. Phys.*, 17. 1–5.

[17] Ibid, line 4.

[18] πρόχειρος καὶ τοῖς πολλοῖς—ibid, pp. 16. 34–17.1.

[19] References supra, n. 13.

[20] *Metaph.* Z 3, 1029a 20–25. A further discussion of the process by which the notion of absolutely formless matter is reached may be found in my paper "Matter and Predication in Aristotle," in *The Concept of Matter*, ed. E. McMullin (Notre Dame, 1963), pp.99–113.

[21] E.g., Whitney J. Oates, *Aristotle and the Problem of Value* (Princeton, 1963), pp. 58–59.

[22] Τοῦτο μὲν οὖν εἴ τις δύναιτο καὶ πιθανώτερον ἀπολογιζέσθω—Simplicius, *In Phys.*, 19. 17–18.

ARTHUR L. PECK
Christ's College, Cambridge

Aristotle on Κίνησις*

THIS paper is zetetic rather than expository. The chief question to which I shall be seeking to suggest an answer is, Can we define the field in which Aristotle believed κίνησις to operate? For me personally the importance of this question became apparent from my work on Aristotle's zoological writings, where κίνησις seemed to play a much more important part in his thought than I had previously realized. This in itself was suggestive, for we know how Aristotle, once he has got hold of a valuable idea, tends to make use of it wherever he can, and sometimes, we may feel, where perhaps he ought not, or at any rate where he does so less convincingly. One such idea obviously is that of matter and form, or, stated otherwise, potentiality and actuality. In the latter of these two formulations Aristotle believed he had produced an indispensable instrument for philosophy, one after which his predecessors had been vaguely groping. The application of this principle reaches its apex when he speaks of the active and passive νοῦς; and although, or perhaps because, there are obscurities in his exposition of this subject, we may sometimes wonder whether here Aristotle has not allowed his enthusiasm for a useful principle to run away with him. However, I do not wish to raise this particular point at the moment. I would merely like to remark in passing that, in order to do justice to the observed phenomena, or what he believes to be the observed phenomena, or to the facts of the case, or what he believes to be the facts of the case, Aristotle is willing to throw over a carefully worked-out scheme. There are several instances of this: I will mention here the one which concerns the contrast which I was speaking of, viz, that of potentiality and actuality. These two, which have accompanied each other *pari passu* all through Aristotle's system, from prime unclothed matter and its first rags of form upward, at the highest and final moment part company; potentiality is dropped, and in the Unmoved Mover there is no potentiality at all, but only pure unmixed actuality. It is significant for my question that the

* Presented at the 1963 meeting of the SAGP in Pittsburgh, Pennsylvania.

scene where potentiality disappears is in the *unmoved* Mover. Has κίνησις also been following potentiality all along, and is it too dropped at this point, and not until this point? In other words, is κίνησις as pervasive in Aristotle's system as potentiality is: does it extend over the same field, and reach its limit at the same point?

To begin with, it may be useful to recall some fundamental definitions. In *Metaph.* Δ 11, 1019a 15 f., Aristotle defines the primary and fundamental sense of δύναμις in the following words: δύναμις is ἀρχὴ κινήσεως ἢ μεταβολῆς ἐν ἑτέρῳ ἢ ᾗ ἕτερον (potentiality is a principle or source of movement or change—a principle subsisting either [a] in some other thing than that which is to be affected by the movement or change, or [b] in the thing itself qua other than changeable in that respect). But in fact Aristotle seldom uses δύναμις in this sense, the potentiality of acting, of causing movement or change: it is the complementary sense which he normally employs, the δύναμις of being acted upon; and he describes this as the ἀρχή, in the thing which is acted upon, of a passive change caused either by some other thing or by itself qua other (ἡ ἐν αὐτῷ τῷ πάσχοντι ἀρχὴ μεταβολῆς παθητικῆς ὑπ' ἄλλου ἢ ᾗ ἄλλο). Agreeably to this definition of δύναμις in terms of κίνησις, we find Aristotle defining κίνησις in terms of δύναμις, at *Physics* III. 1, 201a 10 f. Ἡ τοῦ δυνάμει ὄντος ἐντελέχεια, ᾗ τοιοῦτον, κίνησίς ἐστιν (movement is the realizing of that which is potentially X, qua potentially X). For example, to take the case of the type of κίνησις called ἀλλοίωσις, "alteration," or qualitative change, κίνησις is the qualitative altering of a thing which is qualitatively alterable, qua qualitatively alterable. And so with the other modes of potentiality.

In the passage of the *Metaphysics* Aristotle is using κίνησις and μεταβολή as interchangeable terms. But we cannot dismiss κίνησις as a mere synonym for μεταβολή. On the face of it, κίνησις seems to be a more precise term than μεταβολή, perhaps more informative. In some of its departments, as distinguished by Aristotle, this is indeed quite obviously so: for although the change or κίνησις denoted by ἀλλοίωσις, alteration, change of quality, may be somewhat obscure, the change or κίνησις denoted by αὔξησις καὶ φθορά is at any rate observable—change in size or quantity: things wax and wane, swell and subside; and the κίνησις known as φορά, locomotion, is obviously and patently "movement" even in our own normal sense of the word.

But perhaps this does not get us very far. It is not at first sight obvious what these various modes of κίνησις have in common: alteration, growth and diminution, movement from one place to another. They are, of course, as Aristotle points out, all based on locomotion; and this may be pertinent towards formulating an answer to the question I raised at the beginning. But I do not feel that I am yet in a position to estimate clearly the contribution which this consideration may have to make.

Perhaps before passing on we should note that sometimes Aristotle adds a fourth department of κίνησις in addition to the κινήσεις which affect already existing things, that is to say κίνησις which concerns οὐσία itself: this has two complementary divisions: (a) γένεσις, which is change from non-existent to existent, and (b) φθορά, change from existent to non-existent.

Now it would no doubt be inexact to say that every κίνησις is concerned with the realization of a form. It is certainly true of some κινήσεις, for instance γένεσις: this is the realization of a form in matter which is capable of receiving and exhibiting that form. And there can be no doubt that in a great many cases the connexion between form and κίνησις is very close. After all, is not the Greek for the efficient cause ὅθεν ἡ ἀρχὴ τῆς κινήσεως—that whence comes the source of the movement? And, says Aristotle, (*Phys.* 202a 9) the thing which causes the movement will always bring with it some form (maybe some οὐσία, maybe some quality, maybe some quantity—thus naming three of the modes of κίνησις just mentioned), which will be a "principle" and a cause of movement. In other words, every such κίνησις will be informed, determined, characterized in a definite way, so as to produce as a result a thing which has a certain οὐσία, or a certain quality or quantity. Thus the agent, or the efficient cause, will set up in the matter a movement of a definite and specific kind, which will result in the matter which is potentially X becoming X in actuality, i.e. in acquiring the form to which the specific movement was proper. And this result is brought about generally by the use of an intermediary, an instrument (ὄργανον), to which the agent or efficient cause imparts the movement for transmission.

To take an illustration. How is a table made? Certain appropriate matter, in this case wood, is required, which is capable of being fashioned into a table, i.e., which is potentially a table. An efficient cause is required, in this case, a carpenter. In his soul the carpenter apprehends the form "table." He then imparts to his hands, and they in turn to his tools, the κινήσεις proper to the form "table," and in this way the matter, the wood, becomes actually the table which to begin with it was potentially. If the carpenter had moved his hands and his tools with the κινήσεις proper to the form "piano" the wood would not have been made into a table.

This is, of course, a simple case, and we can almost see what is going on, although without a slow-motion film it would be difficult to analyse and record the details of the κινήσεις. When we go on to examine an example of biological γένεσις, we find the pattern is precisely the same, although there are modifications and complications, and the precise character of the κινήσεις involved is much more difficult to envisage. In the first place, the efficient cause here is different from the efficient cause in the case of the carpenter and the table in one important respect: in biological γένεσις, the efficient cause, i.e., the male parent, itself exhibits the form which is to be transmitted; in the former case the carpenter was not himself a table, but in this case the dog is himself a dog. But as far as our present enquiry is concerned that is a minor modification; otherwise the general pattern of the scheme is the same. We find the same transmission of the appropriate κινήσεις through the intermediary of a tool or instrument. "It is probable," says Aristotle (*De Gen. An.* V, 789b 8), "that Nature makes the majority of her productions by means of πνεῦμα used as an instrument." And he explictly draws the parallel between this and the craftsman. "Πνεῦμα serves many uses in the things constructed by Nature, just as certain objects do in the arts and crafts, e.g. the hammer and anvil of the smith" (*ibid.*). We thus have the κινήσεις proper to the form "dog" transmitted by the πνεῦμα contained in the γονή of the male parent to the matter provided by the female parent, and these κινήσεις which are proper to the form "dog" fashion the matter which is potentially a dog into what is actually a dog.

But this, although an interesting and important example of the working of κινήσεις proper to a form, is really only an extended application of a principle which is operative all the time in living creatures. The production of a new living creature is only an extension of the maintenance of an already existing one. Except in a rudimentary and superficial way, tables and pianos do not require continuous maintenance. There is, of course, such a thing as wear and tear, and occasionally pianos have to be tuned, but this is child's play compared with the maintenance of a living organism from day to day and from hour to hour. Once made, the table or the piano is there: the efficient cause has done its work, the κινήσεις have been transmitted, and the matter has acquired the intended form. Not so the living body. It must continually be kept going, and kept going *as such*. In other words, its form must be continually maintained. And to do this the appropriate κινήσεις must be continually supplied. Where do they come from, and how are they distributed throughout the body of the living organism?

The first answer to this question is, "From the heart." For Aristotle, the heart was the first part of the embryo to be formed; and in the developed animal the heart was the seat of soul, and soul is the "form" of the animal. The heart is also important as containing vital heat: this will concern us again later on. I here omit a number of details which are irrelevant for our present purpose, and say at once that an important function of the heart is to "concoct," by means of heat, the nourishment taken by the body—to concoct it into its ultimate state, the ἐσχάτη τροφή, viz, blood. But Aristotle does not leave the matter there. He distinguishes two grades of nourishment, according to the functions they perform. The business of the lower-grade nourishment is to bring about increase of bulk (*De Gen. An.* 744b 33 ff.), and is therefore described as αὐξητικόν (note: this itself involves a κίνησις, as we have seen); the business of the higher-grade nourishment is to provide the whole organism and its parts with *being* (τὸ εἶναι), and this nourishment is described as θρεπτικόν (not a very satisfactory term, but Aristotle's meaning is perfectly clear). At *De Anima* II. 4, 416b 11 ff., Aristotle again tells us that this higher-grade nourishment maintains the organism's being. In other words, it is concerned with the maintenance of the *form* or specific character of the organism. It is also, says Aristotle, "productive of generation"; i.e., it is concerned with the provision of "being" for another creature similar to the original organism. (We may perhaps notice here that the description θρεπτικόν is not inappropriate from Aristotle's point of view, since the lowest grade of soul is both γεννητικόν and θρεπτικόν.)

This maintenance, then, is effected by the blood: how? As we should expect, by the transmission from the heart, the seat of the "form," of the κινήσεις proper to that form. As the heart concocts, by means of heat, the nourishment into blood, which is its ultimate stage or state, the heart *pneumatizes* the blood; that is what its pulsation indicates: it is a phenomenon similar to that of boiling water in a vessel, when we see bubbles rising up in the liquid: the heart charges the blood with πνεῦμα, and, by means of this πνεῦμα which is carried in the blood, the heart transmits the appropriate κινήσεις to all parts of the body, thereby maintaining its being as such. This πνεῦμα, of course, is not the breath which is breathed in from outside, but is *connate* (σύμφυτον), there from the start. It is important, as Aristotle himself insists, to distinguish it clearly from πνεῦμα breathed in from outside.

There are other functions which the σύμφυτον πνεῦμα has to perform besides acting as the instrument of soul for the maintenance of the living organism's being. It is also the instrument which soul uses in its appetitive aspect (ὀρεκτικὴ ψυχή) for *moving* the limbs of the body. Here, too, ἀλλοίωσις (another mode of κίνησις) is involved; but we cannot now examine the details of this. In addition, this πνεῦμα is the vehicle for κινήσεις received from outside, through the senses: i.e., it not only conveys *from* the heart the κινήσεις of form to the various parts of the body and also to the matter out of which an embryo is to be fashioned, but it conveys *to* the heart κινήσεις received by the sense-organs, κινήσεις set up by some exterior object, which κινήσεις in their turn are appropriate to, and emanate from, some specific form; and that, in fact, is what is meant by saying that in sensation we apprehend a thing's form without its matter—we receive the κινήσεις proper to the form. That is how the soul is "informed" and in a sense becomes that which it perceives.

We must now consider what happens between the sensible object and the sense-organ of the living creature. In a way, the pattern is very much the same as it is in the case of the carpenter making the table. I will take the most interesting and most complicated example, the case of sight, i.e., the apprehension of a coloured sense-object. Just as in the other case we had (1) the carpenter, or rather, the form as apprehended by the carpenter, (2) the instrument, and (3) the matter, so here we have (1) the colour, (2) a medium, and (3) the πνεῦμα in the eye. Colour is "that which has the power to set in movement that which is actually transparent," and the latter acts as the medium. Examples of transparent media are air, water, and certain solids. Their transparency is due not to themselves, but to the fact that they contain a certain substance which is also found in "the eternal substance of the upper cosmos"—in other words, in the αἰθήρ, the fifth element. This substance can be actualized, and its actualization is what we call light. This actualization is brought about by the agency of Fire or something of a similar kind as the substance of the upper cosmos. When this substance in the medium, therefore, has been actualized by light, it can be set in movement by colour, and in that way can transmit the κινήσεις proper to whatever colour is involved. This takes us as far as the eye. Obviously there must be light in the eye as well as in the external medium, so the eye will have to be transparent; so the eye, or rather the pupil of the eye, is made of water. Thus both the external medium and the internal constituent of the pupil are transparent. And it is the movement of this watery part, not qua fluid, but qua transparent, which constitutes sight. It is capable of picking up the κινήσεις which have been conveyed by the external medium. These κινήσεις now have to be transmitted to the heart. This is done by means of certain πόροι, passages, which connect the eyes with the φλέβες round the brain; and as these φλέβες (because they contain blood) contain σύμφυτον πνεῦμα, we have here an internal medium capable of transmitting the κινήσεις along the final stage of their journey, to the heart.

We notice here that right from the coloured object to the heart there is a substance—either the stuff in the transparent medium outside, or the σύμφυτον πνεῦμα within the organism, both of which are in some way analogous to the αἰθήρ—capable of transmitting the κινήσεις appropriate to form. What precisely these κινήσεις are Aristotle does not tell us; but he must have conceived them to be in some way comparable with the κινήσεις set up in the tools of the carpenter and the smith, though of course the stuff in which they are conveyed is of much greater fineness and subtlety than the metal which is used for these craftsmen's operations.

Up to now I have been speaking of forms which for their realization require matter which is already in a fairly advanced state of "information." This is obviously true of the form of a living organism, which requires very highly informed "matter"—indeed, it requires matter which is already informed by the lower grades of soul. But there are many degrees of information or, to put it in another way, many degrees of matter, and one question which arises is how far down can we trace this association of κίνησις with form?

I do not intend now to deal exhaustively with that mode of κίνησις known as locomotion, fundamental as that may be; though a few observations on the subject may be useful. It is well known that according to Aristotle the four so-called elements each have their proper place in the universe. They are not, of course, elements in the proper sense according to Aristotle, but that does not concern us here. The proper place for Fire is at the circumference, for Earth at the centre, for Air and Water in between, Air next to Fire, Water next to Earth. This means, for Aristotle, that to be in those places is part of their "form." If they are not in those places, their form has not been completely realized, their potentiality has not been completely actualized, their τέλος has not been attained. Hence, if they are not in those places, or have been shifted from them forcibly, they will naturally try to get to them, and that is what is meant by saying they have a natural movement: their natural movement is their means of getting to their proper places, of attaining their form. This is stated quite plainly by Aristotle at *De Caelo* IV. 3, 310a 34: the movement of each body to its own place is movement towards its own form, τὸ εἰς τὸν αὐτοῦ τόπον φέρεσθαι ἕκαστον τὸ εἰς τὸ αὐτοῦ εἶδός ἐστι φέρεσθαι. Such movement, such κίνησις, therefore, is exactly on a par with other κινήσεις: it is as ridiculous to ask why fire moves upwards (away from the centre of the universe) and earth moves downwards (toward the centre) as it is to ask why a thing which is curable, healable (τὸ ὑγιαστόν), when it is moved (changed) qua healable, attains health and not e.g., whiteness. And so with all other modes of κίνησις. *De Caelo* 310a 20: "The local movement of each body into its own place must be regarded as similar to what happens in connexion with the other instances of generation and change" (περὶ μὲν οὖν τοῦ φέρεσθαι εἰς τὸν αὐτοῦ τόπον ἕκαστον ὁμοίως ὑποληπτέον ὥσπερ καὶ περὶ τὰς ἄλλας γενέσεις καὶ μεταβολάς). Similarly, in the famous phrase translated by Dante, each thing becomes what it is: things γίγνεται as they do because they ἔστι what they are.

Nevertheless, the φύσις of Earth, Air, Fire, and Water is inferior to the φύσις of living creatures; and in living creatures the form, and therefore the place, and therefore the movement, of Earth, Air, Fire, and Water has to give way to higher forms and their requirements. In living creatures, these "elements" are not in their natural places. Nature, acting in a higher and more important role, makes use of them and of their characteristic properties, maybe, and to a very great extent she can bend them to her purpose, can make them subserve her τέλος; but not always, though it is surprising how wide is the field which Nature can claim for the dominion of the final cause. But not the whole; and where Nature with her final cause is defeated Necessity comes into play. "In the field of natural objects," says Aristotle (*Physics* II. 9, 200a 30–32), "Necessity is what we call matter and the κινήσεις of matter." Nature is not quickly beaten, and can often make good use of the results of Necessity, e.g., the surplus earthy matter in living organisms can be turned to good use by way of hair, teeth, and nails. But there is a residuum which cannot be controlled or put to purposive use; and if Nature sets certain movements going for her own purposes, she may find certain other movements produced which she does not need—this is simple or absolute Necessity. Similarly, we sometimes find monstrosities produced, when Nature cannot gain complete control over the material owing to its indeterminateness or its unevenness: here Necessity has won, and the form has not got embodied in the matter. The two sets of κινήσεις have contended together, and the κινήσεις of the higher form have failed to prevail.

A comparable contest (in some ways) is described by Aristotle when discussing heredity: the movements from the mother and father, or the movements from more remote ancestors, are pitted against each other. The details of this I must omit, but I should like to take up one point which is prominent in this particular discussion (*De Gen. An.* 766a 18)—what Aristotle has to say about heat, τὸ θερμόν. It is quite clear that he considers heat to be of capital importance in the formation of living things, and he can even say that it is through deficiency of heat that the material does not get brought into the form it should attain. The action of heat he describes as concoction (πέψις); and there is no doubt that here, at any rate, the action of heat is thought of as the communication or transmission of the movements proper to form. I am not sure precisely what is implied here: whether or not Aristotle is thinking again of the σύμφυτον πνεῦμα, which he sometimes describes as a special sort of θερμόν. Possibly he means a θερμόν upon which other κινήσεις have been superimposed. But there are at least two interesting passages in this connexion which are relevant to our subject. In *De Gen et Corr.* II. 2 Aristotle points out that the elements must be ποιητικά and παθητικά because in fact they act and react mutually. But it is not the quality of heavy and light which we associate with such action and reaction: it is the qualities hot and cold, moist and dry. Hot and cold are terms which imply *poietic* capability: when we say things are hot and cold we imply that they are ποιητικά, when we say they are dry and moist we imply that they are παθητικά. The two former are active principles; the two latter are passive, determinable. But this statement must not be overdone. However poietic any sort of matter may be, it is a characteristic of matter not so much to move as to be moved; to undergo, not to initiate, movement (335a, end, *De Gen et Corr.* II. 9). This is true in the arts and crafts, and in nature too, animate and inanimate. These sorts of matter are not initiators, but instruments, of movement. We must beware of speaking of them λίαν ὀργανικῶς, as though they were self-operating instruments. Fire, it is true, ποιεῖ and κινεῖ, but it does so in a manner very inferior to the artist's tools and instruments; and of course it has to be subject to the control of Form. A blowpipe is active enough, but it needs a man to hold it and control it in order to achieve a rational purpose. So Nature will use τὸ θερμόν to cause the digestion of food or the development of the embryo; but she has to supply the controlling direction of Form before the θερμόν can be a useful instrument for her purposes. Nevertheless, Nature can leave quite an amount of work to the hot and the cold: in fact, the first stage of σύνθεσις, composition, in living creatures can be dealt with by them. This stage is the formation of τὰ ὁμοιομερῆ, the "uniform parts" of the body, such as flesh, bone, hair, sinew, etc., all of which are differentiated by such qualities as hardness, softness, ability to be stretched, pulled, broken up, etc.: all of these features are derived from the hot and the cold and the commingling of their κινήσεις. Thus the movements set up by the hot and cold, as bodies are solidified by them, are sufficient to form these uniform parts. But hot and cold are not sufficient to account for the next stage of composition and development, i.e., the formation of the "non-uniform parts" (τὰ ἀνομοιομερῆ), such as head, hand, foot and so on. Similarly, he says in another field, we may admit that the hot and the cold may be reckoned to account for the formation of metals such as copper and silver, but not for the formation of a saw, or a bowl, or a box. Thus their sphere of useful operation is strictly limited, both in the natural realm and in the realm of art. It is in the first stage, the stage immediately above the four elements, that they can act without the control of a directing formal cause; beyond that they cannot. But if they can act within those limits, must they not be possessed of certain proper κινήσεις? It may be true that the dry and the moist, which are the other two ultimate constituents of the four physical elements, are just δύναμις, potentiality—παθητικά only; but hot and cold, surely, if they can do as much as they seem able to do, surely they must be characterised by κινήσεις? And may we not say that at this lowest level, the point at which form is first imposed upon matter (the hot, the cold, the moist, the dry, imposed upon prime matter), even here, that the difference between them is, as in the higher levels, a difference which is constituted by different κινήσεις? This seems probable; and if so, we should not be justified in classing Aristotle with the pre-Socratic Ionians, and their most extreme representative Anaxagoras, who made sensible characteristics in some guise or other fundamental and elementary, but we should after all have to put him a little nearer Plato's Timaeus, with his fundamental and elementary geometrical shapes and the ever-moving receptacle.

I have omitted a great deal, and I have not even attempted so far to tackle another question which I raised at the beginning, one which concerns the other end of the scale of reality, viz, the problem of the active and passive reason, though I do not think this is the only field where difficulty may arise. I will put the question in this way: can the contrast, or (better) the combination of form and matter be satisfactorily applied in cases (if any) where the matter is not physical, i.e., where it would be difficult to conceive of, or to find a place for, even the subtle κινήσεις which go on in the transparent media required for the transmission of colour, and in the mysterious though still material σύμφυτον πνεῦμα in the blood of living creatures? Or to ask the question in another way, is there a point short of the Unmoved Mover at which Form no longer needs κίνησις for its expression? Or perhaps that is putting the question too simply. Perhaps we should not say "needs κίνησις for its expression" (implying that we are concerned only with the transmission of form into new matter), but "can be independent of κίνησις, or can be dispensed from the function of transmitting its own appropriate κίνησις—or even from having one?"

It is, of course, true that the form "table" has to be apprehended by the carpenter in his ψυχή, but the κινήσεις which he sets up in his hands and tools are κινήσεις *appropriate to the form "table."* We cannot, however, say this is true in all cases; there are some in which it is not true, e.g., in the case of the Unmoved Mover causing φορά in the πρῶτον κινούμενον and of the Sun causing γένεσις and φθορά by its approach and recession, or causing spontaneous generation of animals by the heat its friction sets up, or even perhaps in the case of the human ψυχή itself causing movement, or growth, of the limbs—unless we are to think of these agents as in some way comparable with the carpenter's soul, enabling a potential matter to realize its capability. Are these agents simply the servants of some Form other than their own, and if so, what is their status with regard to it? It seems clear that in the case of the hot and the cold producing the ὁμοιομερῆ such as flesh and blood and so on, we can hardly suppose that the κινήσεις possessed by hot and cold are those proper to the Forms of flesh, bone, etc.: what controls and determines—and what supplies—the κινήσεις here? Aristotle actually says on one occasion that there are some fields (he refers to spontaneous generation) where matter can of itself supply the κινήσεις which we should normally find supplied by Form. In view of this, what are we to make of Aristotle's official contrast of Form and Matter?

It looks then as if we ought perhaps to distinguish various classes of κίνησις—not the classes we originally distinguished (as Aristotle himself does), viz, those relating respectively to γένεσις and φθορά, to ἀλλοίωσις, αὔξησις, and φορά, but using a different principle of classification, somewhat as follows:

1. κινήσεις proper to the form which is being realised, whether those κινήσεις are set up by an agent itself possessing the form concerned (as in the case of an animal generating an offspring) or by an agent not itself possessing the form but apprehending it (e.g., the carpenter). These will be κινήσεις εἰς οὐσίαν, processes leading to a complete and finished product.

2. κινήσεις which also are, but in another sense, κινήσεις εἰς οὐσίαν: the movements of the four elements to their own proper region of the universe. These κινήσεις are also closely associated with form, because it is part of the proper form of the four elements to go to certain regions of the universe; and they apparently need no agent to bring these κινήσεις about, though Aristotle seems to feel himself obliged to provide one, at least in some instances, e.g., the removal of an obstacle making the movement possible.
3. κινήσεις which also are κινήσεις εἰς οὐσίαν, set up by an agent which has no sort of connexion with the form which is being realized—e.g., hot and cold producing τὰ ὁμοιομερῆ, the Sun producing γένεσις and φθορά, the Unmoved Mover producing φορά in the πρῶτον κινούμενον, etc.
4. κινήσεις which effect not the attainment of an οὐσία but the maintenance of an οὐσία, as in the case of the fully-grown animal. These are no doubt closely related to those in class 1, the κινήσεις which produce a new individual of the same form; and according to Aristotle both are brought about by one and the same "part" of the soul, viz., the lowest and most basic part, τὸ γεννητικὸν καὶ θρεπτικόν—i.e., they are κινήσεις transmitted by the σύμφυτον πνεῦμα in the blood.

Perhaps under this same heading (4) of *maintenance* of οὐσία we ought to include the fundamental κινήσεις with which prime matter is charged, which distinguish e.g., τὸ θερμόν from τὸ ψυχρόν—for how else are we to suppose these two to be distinguished from each other? What else can be meant here, at this very first combination of form with matter, except that certain different κινήσεις subsist in the matter? Whether these κινήσεις which distinguish θερμόν and ψυχρόν are the same as those which enable θερμόν and ψυχρόν to produce τὰ ὁμοιομερῆ in a living organism may be a subject which needs investigation.

All the κινήσεις which I have mentioned so far in this reclassification are κινήσεις proper to some form, whether being realized, or already realized, in some matter; and it might therefore seem that the only way in which a form can be realized or maintained is by means of κινήσεις in matter. But then we are confronted with Forms which appear to be wholly independent of matter, and hence have no κινήσεις proper to them to set up in matter—the Unmoved Mover (and the 55 unmoved movers?), and rational soul. And this raises in a different and more acute way the question, what have the various sorts of κίνησις in common, viz, what have the various parts of *Soul* in common? We find them setting up such different sorts of κινήσεις, some of which (e.g., those set up the Unmoved

Mover) appear to have little resemblance or none to the forms which set them up.

And finally, we have to ask what is the status, from the point of view of κινήσεις, of things like tables whose manufacture has been completed, and of earth when it is at the centre—i.e., of things which have reached their οὐσία as the result of some κίνησις, and do not (as animals do) require to have their οὐσία *maintained* by some κίνησις. Is this condition of *having attained* οὐσία *as a result of* κίνησις comparable with the condition of *fully-actualized* οὐσία (such as that of the Unmoved Mover) *which is not the result of any process of* κίνησις? And does this give us any clue towards the solution of the problem of the active and passive reason?

D. A. REES
Oxford University

Aristotle's Treatment of Φαντασία

Aristotle's treatment of φαντασία, one of the most original and remarkable aspects of his psychology, is also one on which it may still be possible to say something fresh.[1] Most of this paper will be concerned with *De Anima* III, ch. 3, but other passages both in the *De Anima* and elsewhere are relevant.[2]

Fortunately we do not need to concern ourselves with the chronology of Aristotle's works, beyond noting that his treatment of φαντασία goes markedly beyond anything to be found in Plato. Nuyens, in his *L'Evolution de la Psychologie d'Aristote* (Dutch edition, 1939; French edition, 1948), distinguished a phase in which soul was thought of as a vital force functioning through the heart from a later, and final, conception of it as an εἶδος or ἐντελέχεια; he was followed, though with variations, by Lulofs in his edition of the *De Insomniis* and *De Divinatione per Somnum* (Leiden, 1947), and by Ross in his editions of the *Parva Naturalia* (1955), pp. 16 ff., and of the *De Anima* (*ed. maior*, 1961), pp. 9–12, and in his paper on "The Development of Aristotle's Thought" (*PBA*, xliii [1958]: 63—78, esp. 65—67). It is not altogether easy to extract a single view from Ross's pronouncements, but, unlike Nuyens and Lulofs, he clearly wishes to assign the whole of the *Parva Naturalia* to what he calls the biological (i.e., middle) period, and what he calls the central part of the *De Anima* to the last phase of Aristotle's work, that of his final stay in Athens.[3] More recently there has been a reaction to Ross's view, and it has been maintained that, at any rate as far as the *De Anima* and *Parva Naturalia* are concerned, no stratification of this kind is to be discerned. Block argues that the *Parva Naturalia* put forward views more mature than those of the *De Anima*.[4] Hardie's view is that Nuyens has not made out his case for distinguishing a "vital force" from an "entelechy" stage,[5] and Kahn maintains that "the *De Anima* and the *Parva Naturalia* form a continuous and progressive exposition."[6]

* Presented at the 1962 meeting of the SAGP in Baltimore, Maryland. Printed in revised form.

Plato

I have mentioned the originality of Aristotle's treatment. To appreciate this, it is necessary to contrast him with Plato—a task rendered the more difficult by the relatively more fluid character of Plato's language.[7]

Both Plato and Aristotle contrast appearance (φαινόμενα) with reality (ὄντα).[8] This distinction, however, receives a metaphysical employment in Plato but not in Aristotle. Kant, in the *Critique of Pure Reason*, undoubtedly had Plato in mind when he drew his distinction between *phenomena* and *noümena*, radically un-Platonic though the interpretation was that he gave to it in his own philosophy. The contrast does not, it would seem, occur in Plato in those terms, but there are similar expressions.[9] But the notion of φαίνεσθαι was bound to appear in a different light in Aristotle, the theory of Ideas having been abandoned, the Platonic χωρισμός denied, and substantiality (and with it the centre of intellectual interest) assigned to the physical world. The following passages in Plato, listed in (with a *caveat* about the *Timaeus*) chronological order, are relevant in one way or another:

(1) The simile of the divided line at the close of *Republic* VI, where Plato uses the imagery of shadows and reflections (τὰ ἐν τοῖς ὕδασι φαντάσματα, 510A) to clarify the ontological and epistemological distinctions he is anxious to bring out; and the further imagery of the cave and its shadows at the beginning of *Republic* VII.

(2) The metaphysical treatment of representative art in *Republic* X (to 608B). The relevant expressions are: φάντασμα 598B; εἴδωλον 598B and frequently; φαντάσματα ἀλλ' οὐκ ὄντα 599A (cf. φαινόμενα, οὐ μέντοι ὄντα γε 596E; πότερα πρὸς τὸ ὄν, ὡς ἔχει, μιμήσασθαι, ἢ πρὸς τὸ φαινόμενον, ὡς φαίνεται, φαντάσματος ἢ ἀληθείας οὖσα μίμησις; 598A–B); ὁ τοῦ εἰδώλου ποιητής, ὁ μιμητής, φαμεν, τοῦ μὲν ὄντος οὐδὲν ἐπαΐει, τοῦ δὲ φαινομένου 601B; φαίνεται 602B; εἴδωλα εἰδωλοποιοῦντα 605C. With this distinction there is significantly associated that of ἐπιστήμη from πίστις ὀρθή (δόξα ὀρθή), 601E ff. (cf. δοξάζειν and λογισμός, 602E–603A).

(3) The characterization of time at *Timaeus* 37D, where Plato says of the Divine Craftsman (δημιουργός) that he made time as a moving image of eternity (εἰκὼ . . . κινητόν τινα αἰῶνος).

(4) φάντασμα is used, as well as φαίνεσθαι, in the contrast between appearance and reality at *Parmenides* 166A–B.

(5) Plato characterizes the sophist, in the dialogue of that name, as a maker of φαντάσματα. The φανταστικὴ τέχνη, he maintains, is one of two subdivisions of the μιμητική or εἰδωλοποιϊκή, the other being the εἰκαστική (235B–D, 236B–C, 264C, 266B–D (where the term employed is

εἰδωλουργική) and 268C–D). The sophist is also called a γόης or magician (γοήτων τις, 235A), and it is noteworthy that a reference to δόξα ψευδής is introduced at 264D. Cornford[10] suggests plausibly that 234 is a reminiscence of the Allegory of the Cave in *Republic* VII, and (on p. 198) points with especial force to the way in which the language of 232 and of the passage which follows recalls the treatment of μίμησις in *Republic* X. At 264B Plato speaks of φαντασία as a σύμμειξις αἰσθήσεως καὶ δόξης.

The above passages are all metaphysical in character. But there are others of a non-metaphysical character which may be mentioned here:

(1) Speaking of dreams, Plato says at *Republic* IX. 572A–B: ἥκιστα παράνομοι τότε αἱ ὄψεις φαντάζονται τῶν ἐνυπνίων.

(2) Discussing μνήμη and ἀνάμνησις at *Philebus* 34A–B, he defines μνήμη as σωτηρία αἰσθήσεως. Neither the word φαντασία nor its cognates occur. R. G. Bury aptly quotes the parallel phrase in *Cratylus* 437B, ἡ μνήμη . . . μονή ἐστιν ἐν τῇ ψυχῇ, in an etymologizing passage.

(3) The use of φαντάζεσθαι is relevant at *Philebus* 38C–D: Τί ποτε ἄρα ἔστι τὸ παρὰ τὴν πέτραν τοῦθ' ἑστάναι φανταζόμενον ὑπό τινι δένδρῳ; ταῦτ' εἰπεῖν ἄν τις πρὸς ἑαυτὸν δοκεῖ σοι, τοιαῦτα ἄττα κατιδὼν φαντασθέντα αὐτῷ ποτε; The notion of appearing is clearly in question.

On Plato's usage as a whole, one can hardly do better than quote the words of W. H. Thompson in his article, "On the Genuineness of the *Sophist* of Plato, and on some of its Philosophical Bearings";[11] referring to *Sophist* 264B, he writes (293): "A φαντασία is . . . according to Plato a variety of δόξα." He goes on to quote Simplicius as stating that in the *Sophist* and *Philebus* φαντασία is placed by Plato ἐν μίξει δόξης τε καὶ αἰσθήσεως,[12] and refers to *Philebus* 38C. (See above on that passage and on *Sophist* 264B.)

In addition, the use of the term εἴδωλον in *Republic* X and in the *Sophist* is clearly intended to receive special point from Plato's sharply contrasting theory of εἴδη.

Aristotle's *De Memoria* looks back to *Philebus* 34A–B. Of the other passages listed above, those where the usage in no way differs from Aristotle's are clearly *Republic* IX. 572A–B and *Philebus* 38C–D, which are not metaphysical in character. But in general (not in *Philebus* 38C–D) φαντασία and allied notions seem in Plato to have a clear implication of error, not least in metaphysical contexts. The notion of φαντασία has thus (to use terminology that will be employed again below) an inherently propositional character, though resting on the experiencing of mental images.[13]

* * *

It may be useful to turn from Plato, as Aristotle's most important predecessor,[14] to glance briefly at ways in which the concept of imagination has been treated among philosophers of more recent centuries. (1) Descartes' stress on the epistemological deficiencies of *imaginatio*, and his contrast between it and clear and distinct ideas, is very much in the Platonic tradition. (2) The words of Hobbes, "Imagination therefore is nothing but decaying sense" (*Leviathan*, ch. 2)[15], are reminiscent of Aristotle, ἡ φαντασία ἐστὶν αἴσθησίς τις ἀσθενής (*Rhetoric* I. 11, 1370a 28, a passage on which Cope has a lengthy note). (3) Two aspects of Hume's theory of knowledge are relevant, his treatment of imagination as a faculty and his theory of "ideas" as products and copies of impressions, distinguishable from the latter as having less force and vivacity. This theory reminds one again of Aristotle's phrase αἴσθησίς τις ἀσθενής. The part played by imagination in Hume's theory of knowledge is a large one. (4) Kant's elaborate treatment of perceptual knowledge in the section of the *Critique of Pure Reason* entitled "The Transcendental Deduction of the Categories" sets up imagination (*Einbildungskraft*) as an essential element in its constitution. His treatment of sense-perception is in some respects far more elaborate than any to be found in Greek philosophy.[16]

But it is necessary to turn to Aristotle, and to the employment, for our interpretation of him, of an examination of the concept of imagination as we ourselves are familiar with it, so far as that may help. Ross in his *Aristotle* (pp. 142–45) first of all marks off "the passages in which Aristotle speaks of φαντασία as being at work in the presence of the sensible object" (p. 142), going on, however, to say: "But for the most part Aristotle describes imagination in a way which involves no such reversal of his doctrine of sensation; and it may be doubted whether the passages just referred to represent his deliberate view. Usually φαντασία is described as operating only after the sensible object has gone" (p. 143). He goes on to list the main functions of φαντασία as (1) the formation of after-images; (2) memory; (3) dreams; (4) imagination in relation to desire, and (5) imagination in relation to thought. This classification is useful, though we may perhaps feel reluctant to commit ourselves on the subject of what does or does not represent Aristotle's deliberate view. However, I shall attempt here a rather different approach, by way of a brief examination of uses of the English word "imagination," as that which is regularly used to translate φαντασία. The division I shall use will be, in the main, between those cases where the occurrence of a mental image is signified without any propositional implication, and those which, with or without reference to a mental image or images, are propositional in character.

Φαντασία is usually rendered in English by a word derived from the Latin "imagination," though we have also "fancy" and "fantasy," formed directly from the Greek. Coleridge, in *Biographia Literaria*, drew what he regarded as an important distinction between "imagination" and "fancy," and assigned a marked superiority to the latter in his aesthetic theory. However, it is difficult to see how the difference can be more than one of range of application, which is purely a matter of degree. In any case it belongs to the theory of artistic or poetic imagination, with which Aristotle does not concern himself when writing about φαντασία.

It may, then, prove to be of assistance to examine some uses of the English words "imagine" and "imagination," which have considerable complexity, to prepare the way for disentangling the senses which Aristotle gives to φαντασία.

(1) "Imagine" and "imagination" are sometimes used of forming or having a mental image, as when we speak of imagining a certain scene, or say (to use the Cartesian example) that a chiliagon is not something we can imagine.

(2) If, on the other hand, I ask you to imagine (or envisage) the American President's being killed in a motor crash, I am not, I think, asking you to form a mental image of a damaged automobile (though that may occur), but to make a supposition (not, be it noted, a belief as to any present or future state of affairs) and draw from it, together with the rest of your body of knowledge and beliefs about American and world politics, conclusions about what would be likely to ensue if he were so killed. This is one form of imagining such-and-such to be the case. When we express a moral criticism of some one for lack of imagination, what we are criticizing is a failure to put oneself, as we say, in the other person's shoes, a failure to form the supposition of being oneself in the other person's position and draw the correct consequences about what one would think and feel under such circumstances.

(3) To imagine is sometimes to form a tentative belief which is not indeed baseless but for which the evidence is not compelling: e.g., "I imagine that he has gone to the Post Office." "I cannot imagine that he would go without paying" clearly resembles "I cannot believe that he would go without paying." This use of the verb is particularly associated with the first person singular of the present tense; used in other persons, or in the first person of the past tense, it reports or envisages judgments by others, or by oneself in the past, of the form "I imagine . . ."

(4) To imagine is often to hold a belief which is false, and which moreover is baseless, or at any rate has little to support it. Such is the case of the man who imagines that he is Napoleon. With it may be classed those cases where the belief, though not known to be false, is, or is thought by the speaker to be, unlikely to be true; a student, for instance, who takes an unduly optimistic view of his attainments may be said to imagine that he is going to pass his examination. Naturally in these cases the use of the first person singular of the present tense is not to be found.

(5) One may wish to say that, when we see the obverse of a coin, we imagine the reverse. Here no mental image is involved. Clearly, also, to say that we imagine the existence of the reverse would be misleading, since it would suggest that the case was like those of paragraph (3) above, and not, as it is, one of firm belief; but this instance of imagining is certainly propositional.

(6) I may recount part of a narrative, whether propounded as true or fictional, and leave the rest to my hearers' imagination. Here we are dealing with conclusions about what would be likely to occur on the basis of suppositions actually or provisionally accepted.

To sum up, we need not concern ourselves with the extent to which thought involves mental imagery. Of the above uses, (1) involves mental imagery; in the others it may or may not be an accompaniment ([5] is difficult), but they are primarily propositional in character. Both aspects are found in Aristotle, and within the field of mental imagery he seems, like most people, to concentrate his attention on the visual.[17]

There are however aspects of imagination, as that term is understood in the modern world, which lie outside the scope of Aristotle's φαντασία. Ross writes as follows: "In attempting to understand Aristotle's conception of φαντασία we must not think of the scientific or the poetical imagination. He was aware of these things, but he refers to them in other terms. εὐστοχία τις ἐν ἀσκέπτῳ χρόνῳ τοῦ μέσου (*An. Post.* 89b 10) refers to the scientific imagination, and εὐφυοῦς ἡ ποιητική ἐστιν ἢ μανικοῦ (*Poet.* 1455a 32) to the poetical imagination."[18] The reminder is salutary, though the part which we today think of imagination as playing in the formation of a scientific theory, which must always be provisional and open to revision, takes us a long way from Aristotle's εὐστοχία, which is envisaged as leading to absolutely certain demonstrations (ἀποδείξεις). With the poetical imagination we may associate artistic imagination in general; nothing of this kind comes within our purview while we are examining Aristotle's treatment of φαντασία. (Contrast, however, Longinus, *De Sublimitate*, ch. 15.) If we are to speak of a religious imagination distinct from a poetical or artistic, the same will be true of it.

De Anima III. 3.

In the early part of this chapter Aristotle seems to have mental images first and foremost in his mind when he writes of φαντασία: *427b 3*. ὥσπερ ἔνιοι λέγουσι πάντα τὰ φαινόμενα εἶναι ἀληθῆ. This is clearly an allusion to I. 2, 404a 28–29, τὸ γὰρ ἀληθὲς εἶναι τὸ φαινόμενον, where Democritus is included. However, Rodier thinks Protagoras to be intended, and clearly he could be reckoned among the ἔνιοι. It is difficult to know how widely to take the term φαινόμενα here (Ross renders "everything that appears," J. A. Smith "whatever seems," Theiler "alle Erscheinungen"); Hicks translates "presentations of the senses," and in view of the context this is probably safe.

427b 14 ff. Here φαντασία clearly signifies the occurrence of a mental image. Aristotle distinguishes it both from αἴσθησις and from ὑπόληψις, in that φαντασία requires αἴσθησις, and ὑπόληψις in turn requires φαντασία. Φαντασία is a πάθος, and is contrasted with δόξα in that "true" and "false" do not, or at any rate do not necessarily, apply to it (but contrast what is said later, at 428a 1 ff., and 428a 11–12). Rodier, who criticizes Freudenthal, lays stress on ἀνάγκη, thus allowing room for the possibility that truth and falsity *may* apply to φαντασία; this is possible, but leaves Aristotle's language elliptical to the point of obscurity. Aristotle thinks that φαντασία differs from ὑπόληψις (here "belief") in being under our control, but this is clearly not always true.

There is a textual problem at 427b 16–17, where the main witnesses read ὅτι δ' οὐκ ἔστιν ἡ αὐτὴ νόησις καὶ ὑπόληψις φανερόν. Hicks retains this, and takes νόησις to include φαντασία, translating, "Clearly thinking is not the same thing as believing"; this, however, would be very awkward, in spite of 427b 27 ff. and III. 10, 433a 9–10. Hamlyn translates "That imagination is not the same kind of thinking as supposal" (similarly Theiler), which is awkward also. The recorded ms. reading which substitutes φαντασία for νόησις is clearly an attempt at a correction. Rodier, following Schneider, brackets ἡ, but the most attractive suggestion is that of Madvig, followed by Ross, that νόησις should be excised as an intrusive gloss.

427b 27 ff. Here νοεῖν is said to have two subdivisions, φαντασία and ὑπόληψις, as on Theiler's and Hamlyn's interpretation of 427b 16–17. It does not harmonize easily with εἰ δ' ἐστὶ καὶ τοῦτο (sc. τὸ νοεῖν) φαντασία τις ἢ μὴ ἄνευ φαντασίας (I. 1, 403a 8–9), and is not in accord with Aristotle's usual terminology. As Hicks observes, Aristotle's account differs in any case from that of Plato's *Sophist* (263E ff.).

428a 1 ff. Φαντασία is here the having of a φάντασμα. The cases εἴ τι κατὰ μεταφορὰν λέγομεν are contrasted; these we may take with Rodier and Hicks (following Alexander and Themistius) as involving an extension of the term to cover our mental faculties generally. But Aristotle raises the question of the ascription of truth and falsity to φαντασία—i.e., of its assimilation to judging. However, arguing that, if the terms "true" and "false" are to be applicable, it must be capable of identification with either αἴσθησις, δόξα, ἐπιστήμη or νοῦς, he proceeds to reject all these alternatives in turn.

428a 5 ff. He first distinguishes φαντασία from αἴσθησις, on the ground that in φαντασία the presence of an object is not required. Φαίνεται at 428a 7 clearly signifies the occurrence of a mental image, as is confirmed by φαίνεται καὶ μύουσιν ὁράματα at a 16 (cf. also a 10–11).

428a 11–12: εἶτα αἱ μὲν (sc. αἰσθήσεις) ἀληθεῖς αἰεί, αἱ δὲ φαντασίαι γίνονται αἱ πλείους ψευδεῖς. This is difficult. Aristotle seems to be verging on a propositional interpretation of φαντασία, or at any rate on one that includes judgment (since φαντάσματα are not being discarded). Or is it rather that mental images are thought of, in some cases as being, in others as not being, accurate copies of an original? As for the contrast with αἴσθησις, this is a considerable over-simplification of the account in II. 6, and even in the case of τὰ ἴδια Aristotle modifies his language later when he writes ἡ αἴσθησις τῶν μὲν ἰδίων ἀληθής ἐστιν ἢ ὅτι ὀλίγιστον ἔχουσα τὸ ψεῦδος (428b 18–19). It must be remembered that, though Aristotle made a serious attempt to deal with problems of perceptual error, he did not achieve a satisfactory solution. Modern treatments in terms of sense-datum and interpretation, or of sensation and perception, no doubt have difficulties, but nevertheless they have advantages over what is to be found in him. For one thing, whether a sensation or a mental image (i.e., a mental image not a sensation) is in question, the sensation or image is not in itself true or false, and must be distinguished from propositions about it or about what has given rise to it. Further, whether a mental image is an accurate copy of some percept or not, a proposition about it may be true or false. Aristotle's language at 428a 14, φαίνεται τοῦτο ἡμῖν ἄνθρωπος, clearly points to the propositional.

428a 16 ff. He contrasts φαντασία with νοῦς and ἐπιστήμη, as he has contrasted it with αἴσθησις at a 11–12 above, on the ground that these are always characterized by truth, whereas it may be false.

428a 19. On the other hand, he contrasts it with δόξα, to which he might have seemed to be assimilating it, on the ground that δόξα involves conviction (πίστις). This is difficult. He may be thinking once again of having a mental image—an interpretation supported by his attribution of φαντασία to animals (a 21, with the alternative version at a 23–24; cf. a 9–11 above). The alternative possibility would be that he is thinking of the formation of a possible belief which is suggested by the appearances but to which one does not commit oneself, as in the case of the size of the sun at 428b 2–4.

428a 24. Hicks refers to δόξη μετ' αἰσθήσεως at *Timaeus* 52A and to σύμμειξις αἰσθήσεως καὶ δόξης at *Sophist* 264B (with 264A). Aristotle is dissociating himself from these views. The text has given rise to doubts, but they do not affect the main problem of interpretation. When Aristotle objects that the formulae are inadequate, since it is necessary to add that the αἴσθησις and the δόξα must have the same object, he is not saying anything that controverts Plato's actual view (cf. *Philebus* 39B). But he alludes also to his earlier objections (διά τε ταῦτα, 428a 26–27), and then draws from the Platonic view a conclusion, τὸ οὖν φαίνεσθαί ἐστι (ἔσται —Trendelenburg) τὸ δοξάζειν ὅπερ αἰσθάνεται, μὴ κατὰ συμβεβηκός, 428b 1–2, which, he goes on to argue, is unacceptable (*Timaeus* 52A does not use the term φαντασία when speaking of the sensible world as δόξῃ μετ' αἰσθήσεως περιληπτόν, but φάντασμα occurs a little later, within the relevant context, at 52C).

428b 2 ff. (Cf. καὶ ὑγιαίνουσι δὲ καὶ εἰδόσιν ὅμως ὁ ἥλιος ποδιαῖος εἶναι δοκεῖ, *De Insomn*. 458b 28). Here, in φαίνεται μὲν ὁ ἥλιος ποδιαῖος, though sensation provides the basis, we have a propositional use of φαίνεσθαι, and "appears" (or perhaps "seems") will be the most obvious translation. It is utterly inappropriate to speak of a mental image as being a foot across, and the passage from the *De Insomniis* just quoted confirms that this is not Aristotle's meaning. It is more plausible to hold that Aristotle is contrasting a tentative judgment which the speaker feels that he might, on the evidence, be at first inclined to make, but which he rejects, and the judgment to which he commits himself on the basis of fuller consideration. Reference to the English verb "to imagine" scarcely helps, except perhaps in the form, "One would (or might) imagine that the sun was a foot across." (While we can speak of coins as looking elliptical from a certain angle, though we know they are not, it seems strange to speak of the sun as looking a foot across.)[19]

428b 10 ff. Here, in his physiological account of the nature of φαντασία, Aristotle is simply considering mental images, and visual images at that (cf. 429a 1–4: auditory images seem to be excluded.)[20]

It will be seen then that this chapter does not provide any one clear view. At times φαντασία signifies the occurrence of a mental image, at times it is propositional in character. Even when it is propositional, however, sensation provides the essential basis, and this fact gives Aristotle's treatment here such unity as it possesses. But there are passages, namely those later in Book III concerned with appetition and action, where the place of mental imagery seems to be a matter of doubt. However, we may look briefly at various passages in turn.

* * *

At I. 1, 402b 23 κατὰ τὴν φαντασίαν means "in accordance with what appears to be the case." Here no question of a mental image is involved, but the passage does not occur in any discussion of φαντασία as such. At II. 2, 413b 21–23 φαντασία is associated with ὄρεξις (cf. III. 9–11; see below). At II. 8, 420b 31–32 it signifies a mental image generally (not necessarily auditory, perhaps; but the phrase is not very clear). At III. 2, 425b 25 it signifies a mental image generally, and the words ἐν τοῖς αἰσθητηρίοις indicate that Aristotle is not confining his scope to a single sense-organ. In III. 7 there are frequent references to the part played by φαντάσματα in the operation of νόησις (cf. III. 8, 432a 12–14). The discussion of φαντασία at III. 8, 432a 10–12 is concerned with mental images likewise (cf. φαντάσματα at a 9). At III. 9, 432a 31–b 3 Aristotle says that τὸ φανταστικόν cannot be fitted into a Platonic analysis of the soul, whether a tripartition into a rational element, a spirited and an appetitive, or a bipartition into a rational element and an irrational.

III. 9–11 deals with the part played by φαντασία in the origination of movement and action (432b 15–16, 433a 9–12, a 20, a 26–29, b 11–12, b 28–29 and 434a 4–10). In one way the most interesting problems here arise out of the last of these passages, which Aristotle approaches by dividing φαντασία into that which is αἰσθητική and that which is βουλευτική or λογιστική (433b 29, 434a 5 ff.). What sort of φαντασία is that which is βουλευτική or λογιστική? Is a mental image involved? That is what seems to be envisaged in the brief and cryptic account of deliberation at 434a 7–10, which ends with the words δύναται (sc. ὁ λογισμός) ἓν ἐκ πλειόνων φαντασμάτων ποιεῖν. Deliberative imagination seems to supervene upon perceptive, and Hicks translates, "Hence we have the power of constructing a single image out of a number of images." Ross associates himself with this version ("they clearly can combine different imaginations into one"), though he adds the interpretation, "i.e., 'so that they are able to imagine a course of action which combines the advantages of two or more other courses'." Hamlyn, who translates, "Hence one has the ability to make one image out of many," comments: "The last words of this passage are obscure but involve the notion that one must be able to synthesize issues to have the idea of a single standard in terms of which the action that one is to take is assessed." Theiler ("aus mehreren Vorstellungen eine einheitliche machen") has no comment. Philoponus in his commentary (p. 592; 35–393. 2, ed. Hayduck, 1897) interprets Aristotle as meaning the unification of a plurality of mental images.

The compresence of these two aspects, that which is a matter of mental images and that which is propositional or quasi-propositional (imagining a course of action), is important and is underlined by the phrase, τὸ φαινόμενον ἀγαθόν, which occurs at 433a 28–29 and which is familiar in the *Eudemian* and *Nicomachean Ethics* and in the analysis of action in *De Motu Animalium*, ch. 6, 700b 28–29. Here the notion of φαίνεσθαι is simply that of "appearing to be the case," and the force attaching to φαντασία in the context is derivative from it. How the difference in the sense of φαντασία appeared to Aristotle—i.e., how far, if at all, he actually thought that mental imagery was essentially involved—it is difficult to be certain. The problem is not confined to him, nor to Greek; it occurs, as has been seen, in English also, and involves the term "idea" as well as "imagine." The old term "ideo-motor action," found in William James's *Principles of Psychology* (1890) and, according to him, coined by W. B. Carpenter, focusses attention on the issue.

Other works of Aristotle add further applications of his conception of φαντασία, but little that is really fresh. In the *De Memoria* he discusses the place in memory of mental imagery, to which he assigns a central importance (cf. esp. 449b 30–450a 25, 450b 11, 450b 24–451a 4, 451a 10–11, a 14–17, 453a 14–19); one may note also the term ζωγράφημά τι at 450a 29–30. Φαντάσματα in dreams are mentioned in *De Somno* 456a 24–26 and b 13–15, in *De Insomniis* 458b 22–29, 459a 6–8, a 14–22, 461a 17–19, 462a 11–19 (where the term εἴδωλα occurs three times), a 27–31, and 462b 8, and in ch. 2 of the *De Divinatione per Somnum* (463a 22, 464a 17–18 (in a discussion of Democritus), and 464b 8–14 (esp. παραπλήσια συμβαίνει τὰ φαντάσματα τοῖς ἐν τοῖς ὕδασιν εἰδώλοις.) One passage of the *De Motu Animalium* (700b 28–29) has been mentioned already. At other points too (esp. 700b 17–22) we find a difficulty in interpreting Aristotle's words, as between reference to mental imagery and to a projected course of action. The problem, in fact, runs right through: cf. ch. 6, 701a 4–6; ch. 7, 701a 29–36, b 16–19; ch. 8, 701b 33–35, 702a 17–19; ch. 11, 703b 9–11, 18–20. The problem of φαντασία in connexion with τὸ φαινόμενον ἀγαθόν arises in *Eudemian Ethics* VII (1235b 25–29 and 1236a 10); one may compare II. 1227a 18–b4. (II. 1219b 24–25 relates to dreams). The problems are similar in the *Nicomachean Ethics*, φαντασία being used in connexion with τὸ φαινόμενον ἀγαθόν at III. 1114a 31–b 3 (cf. the whole passage to 1114b 20). The other passages add little or nothing that is fresh: III. 1113a 15–b 2, VII. 1149a 32, 1150b 28, 1152b 31–33, VIII. 1155b 23–27, IX. 1166a 2–19 and X. 1176a 15–22. (VII. 1147b 5 is more strictly epistemological.)

Postscript

I have mentioned that Aristotle does not use φαντασία to denote aesthetic imagination. That application of the term seems to be much later. The writer *On the Sublime* (Pseudo-Longinus) is particularly noteworthy (ch. 3, 1 and ch. 15), using the term both in the singular and in the plural (to mean "images" or "imagery"), and connecting it with εἰδωλοποιΐα (15, 1; cf. καλεῖται μὲν γὰρ κοινῶς φαντασία πᾶν τὸ ὁπωσοῦν ἐννόημα γεννητικὸν λόγου παριστάμενον). He speaks both of ῥητορικὴ φαντασία and of ἡ παρὰ ποιηταῖς (15. 2). Somewhat later (c. A.D. 200?) is a passage in Philostratus' *Life of Apollonius of Tyana* which says μίμησις μὲν γὰρ δημιουργήσει, ὃ εἶδεν, φαντασία δὲ καὶ ὃ μὴ εἶδεν, ὑποθήσεται γὰρ αὐτὸ πρὸς τὴν ἀναφορὰν τοῦ ὄντος (VI. 19). Aristotle, on the other hand, had confined φαντασία to close dependence on that which has been perceived.

NOTES

[1] Among items in the older literature, it is still valuable to refer to the monograph of J. Freudenthal, *Ueber den Begriff des Wortes* ΦΑΝΤΑΣΙΑ *bei Aristoteles* (Göttingen, 1863), which is the fullest treatment I know. J. Frohschammer, *Ueber die Principien der aristotelischen Philosophie und die Bedeutung der Phantasie in derselben* (Munich, 1881) is less important. From among other items in the literature I shall here mention only a few. The relevant articles in Bonitz's *Index Aristotelicus* (Berlin, 1870) were not available to Freudenthal. The major editions of the *De Anima* with commentaries are those of G. Rodier (2 vols., Paris, 1900), R. D. Hicks (Cambridge, 1907), esp. pp. liii–liv and 452 ff., and Sir David Ross (Oxford, 1961), esp. pp. 38–39 and 281 ff., together with the relevant parts of his *Parva Naturalia* (1955) (pp. 32–33 and 268–69, and also those parts of the introduction generally which discuss the *De Memoria*, *De Insomniis* and *De Divinatione per Somnum*). Ross had written earlier on φαντασία in his *Aristotle* (1923; ed. 5, 1949), pp. 142–45. W. Theiler has brought out a German translation of the *De Anima* with commentary (Berlin, 1959), and most recently D. W. Hamlyn has produced an English translation of *De Anima* II and III (and parts of Book I) with a commentary (Oxford, 1968). In addition, it is still profitable

to consult what is said about φαντασία at various scattered points in E. M. Cope's edition of the *Rhetoric* (3 vols., posthumous, Cambridge, 1877; no part of the commentary composed, it would appear, later than 1869).

[2] In the *De Anima* see esp. I. 1, 403a 8–10, II. 2, 413b 22, II. 3, 414b 16. On the relation of φαντασία to νόησις see III. 7–8, esp. 431a 17, b 2–10, 432a 7–14. In III. 9–11 φαντασία is presented as involved in desire and movement. In the *Parva Naturalia* see esp. *De Memoria* 449b 30–450a 25, 450b 24–451a 17, 451b 20, 453a 14–19; *De Somno* 456a 24–26, b 13–15; *De Insomniis* 458b 22–29, 459a 6–22, 461a 17–19, 462a 11–31, b 8; *De Divinatione per Somnum* 463a 22, 464a 17–18, b 8–14. In the *De Motu Animalium* see esp. ch. 6, 700b 17–701a 6; ch. 7, 701a 29–b 19; ch. 8, 701b 33–702a 19; ch. 11, 703b 9–20. The terms τὸ φαινόμενον ἀγαθόν and φαντασία τἀγαθοῦ receive a special application in the field of ethics (*E.E.* VII. 1235b 25–29, *E.N.* III. 1113a 15–b 2, 1114a 31–b 25); one should note also *E. E.* II 1227a 18–b 4, VII. 1236a 10; *E.N.* VII. 1152b 26–33, VIII. 1155b 23–27, IX. 1166a 2–19, X. 1176a 15–22. *An. Po.* II. 19 does not mention φαντασία by name (nowhere do the *Analytics* do so), but it has relevance. There are also a few passages in the *Rhetoric* where φαντασία enters: I. 11, 1370a 27 ff., 1370b 32–1371a 24; II. 2, 1378a 30–b 10; II. 5, 1382a 21 ff., 1383a 17; II. 6, 1384a 22, with 1383b 12 ff.; and III. 1, 1404a 11.

[3] "325–4" on p. 11 of his *De Anima* must be a misprint for "335–4". Whether "the central part of the *De Anima*", *PBA*, *loc. cit.* (66), includes III. 3 is not made explicit; p. 17 of his *Parva Naturalia*, in speaking of "*De Anima* 2", would seem at first sight to exclude it, but II. may perhaps be understood as including III. 1–3.

[4] I. Block, "The Order of Aristotle's Psychological Writings," *AJP*, LXXXII (1961): 50–77, esp. 64–65 and 71.

[5] W. F. R. Hardie, "Aristotle on the Soul and the Body," *PQ*, XIV (1964): 53–72.

[6] Charles H. Kahn, "Sensation and Consciousness in Aristotle's Psychology," *AGP*, XLVIII (1966): 43–81, esp. 61–64.

[7] The word φαντασία seems not to occur in extant Greek literature earlier than the middle dialogues of Plato (plural at *Republic* II. 382E, singular at *Theaetetus* 152C).

[8] Cf. Pl. *Republic* X. 596E, and Aristotle on τὸ φαινόμενον ἀγαθόν, *E.N.* III. 1114a 32.

[9] νοεῖσθαι . . . ὁρᾶσθαι, *Republic* VI. 507B.

[10] F. M. Cornford, *Plato's Theory of Knowledge* (London, 1935), p. 195.

[11] *JPh*, VIII (1879): 290–322.

[12] Simp. on *De An.* III. 3, 428a 24; p. 211. 33–34 in Hayduck's edition (1882). See below on *De An.* III. 428a 19 ff.

[13] This is true also of *Philebus* 38C–D.

[14] A more thorough treatment would need to include the atomists.

[15] Quoted by Freudenthal (*op. cit.*, p. 24), together with other passages from Hobbes.

[16] Aesthetic imagination is handled in the *Critique of Judgment.*

[17] But see below on 420b 31–32 and 425b 25.

[18] *De Anima* (ed. maior, 1961), p. 38; cf. the similar passage on p. 32 of the introduction to his edition of the *Parva Naturalia* (1955).

[19] This passage receives an illuminating discussion in K. Lycos, "Aristotle and Plato on 'Appearing'," *Mind*, LXXIII (1964): 496–514.

[20] See Rodier on this passage.

JOHN M. RIST
University of Toronto

Notes on Aristotle *De anima* 3. 5*

Of all the Aristotelian doctrines perhaps the most difficult is that concerning the Active and Passive Intellects which we find in the short fifth chapter of the third book of the *De anima*. Interpretations of this chapter have been almost as numerous as interpreters, and it would be naive to expect at this stage to be definitive. Nevertheless it seems that progress has been delayed in many cases by a too casual approach to what Aristotle says in the chapter itself, and this at least admits of some improvement.

The chapter opens with a comparison between the Soul and the world of nature. Just as in the whole of nature, says Aristotle, there are two distinct things, matter which is potentially all things, and an efficient cause which makes all things, so distinct elements must exist ἐν τῇ ψυχῇ. Our first problem is the meaning of this phrase. Does it mean "in the case of soul" or "in each individual soul?" It is perhaps facile of Ross[1] to say that it "can hardly mean only 'in the case of the soul',"[2] even if this is in fact correct, without offering some reason for his decision. Rather he might have argued from the text of line 22. Here Aristotle speaks of the Active Intellect when it is separated (χωρισθείς). The use of the *aorist* participle (taken with the word χωριστός which, as we shall see, must have the sense of "separable" in line 17) implies a time when the Active Intellect is not separate from the Passive. There must therefore be a time when the Active and Passive Intellects are united in some way. That Theophrastus assumed the existence of such a time is shown by his remark μικτὸν γάρ πως ὁ νοῦς ἔκ τε τοῦ ποιητικοῦ καὶ τοῦ δυνάμει.[3] Now if the Active Intellect is at some time at least not separated from the Passive, it is clear that it cannot be wholly transcendent.

May we say, however, that although the Active Intellect is not entirely transcendent, it is to be regarded as a single Intellect immanent

* Presented at the 1963 meeting of the SAGP in Pittsburgh, Pennsylvania. Reprinted from *Classical Philology*, LXI (1966): 8–20, by permission of the University of Chicago Press.

in a number of human souls during their lifetime? Aristotle compares the Active Intellect to art which has an effect on matter (οἷον ἡ τέχνη πρὸς τὴν ὕλην πέπονθεν). Must we assume from this that it is Art (with a Capital *A*) which affects matter? Of course this is not the Aristotelian view. As we know from the *Metaphysics* (1071a 20–22), Man is the father of Man, but there is no such existent as Man. Rather we should say that Peleus is the father of Achilles. Similarly Art is not the efficient cause of the sculpturing of a block of marble into the form of a statue. The cause is rather the particular form of the statue in the mind of the sculptor who is the efficient cause of the product. Thus if we are to put any weight at all upon Aristotle's comparison of the Active and Passive Intellects to Art and its material, we must say that it is not Active Intellect, but a particular Active Intellect, that is, the element in the soul which "makes all things," just as it is the particular art of the particular sculptor which causes the production of the statue. Aristotle then means by his phrase ἐν τῇ ψυχῇ "inside the individual soul." Every soul therefore contains its own individual Active and Passive Intellect. The interpretations of this passage which spring from the minds of Alexander of Aphrodisias and Averroes must be rejected.[4]

Our interpretation, however, is apparently in accordance with that of Theophrastus (*ap.* Them. *in De anima* 108. 25–28 Heinze), who after wondering whether the Active Intellect is σύμφυτος or whether it has a γένεσις, decides in favor of the former alternative (ἔοικε δ' οὖν ὡς ἀγένητος). The Active Intellect is ἀγένητος and immanent (ἐνυπάρχων). We should note also the language which Theophrastus employs to describe it. It is ὁ κινῶν as well as ὁ ποιητικός; the genuinely Aristotelian nature of this terminology has been demonstrated by Barbotin.[5] The fact that the Active Intellect is a "moving" cause brings it into line with Aristotle's general theories of movement and activity, as we shall see below.

There is no need at this stage of the discussion to invoke the famous text of the *De generatione animalium* about the νοῦς θύραθεν, as so many of the commentators have done. This mistake derives from Alexander and still recurs frequently. J. A. Philip,[6] for example, writes: "The phrase ὁ θύραθεν νοῦς . . . serves us as a hint or aid to the understanding of what Aristotle meant by the νοῦς ποιητικός." Barbotin,[7] however, rightly connects Aristotle's λείπεται δὴ τὸν νοῦν μόνον θύραθεν ἐπεισιέναι with a passage of Theophrastus quoted by Simplicius. The passage runs αἱ μὲν ὀρέξεις καὶ ἐπιθυμίαι καὶ ὀργαὶ σωματικαὶ κινήσεις εἰσὶ καὶ ἀπὸ τούτου τὴν ἀρχὴν ἔχουσιν, ὅσαι δὲ κρίσεις καὶ θεωρίαι, ταύτας οὐκ ἔστιν εἰς ἕτερον ἀναγαγεῖν, ἀλλ' ἐν αὐτῇ τῇ ψυχῇ (this too seems an echo of *De anima* 3. 5) καὶ ἡ ἀρχὴ καὶ ἡ ἐνέργεια καὶ τὸ τέλος, εἴ γε δὴ καὶ ὁ νοῦς κρεῖττόν τι καὶ θειότερον, ἅτε δὴ ἔξωθεν ἐπεισιὼν καὶ παντέλειος. That this is an echo of the doctrine of the *De generatione animalium*, if not of the treatise itself, seems certain, but there is no reason to claim that it refers to the Active Intellect. Both the *De generatione animalium* and Theophrastus refer to *nous* as a whole; to both the distinction between Active and Passive Intellect is irrelevant. There will therefore be no further discussion here of the νοῦς θύραθεν.

We may say then that there are within each individual soul an Active and a Passive Intellect. The Active Intellect is the moving factor and the Passive the factor that is moved. We may perhaps compare the doctrine of the *Physics* that all souls, and indeed everything in motion, require an efficient as well as a material cause. "If then everything that is in motion must be moved by something, and that something must either be moved in its turn by something else or not, and in the latter case it is the true agent and we need go no further, but in the other case we must run it back until we do reach a primary mover not moved by something else . . . then it follows that if everything that is in motion is moved by some agent, and if the primary agent itself is in motion but is not moved by anything else, it must be moved by itself (256a 14–22)." Aristotle then of course goes on to demonstrate that the first mover is not in fact self-moved but unmoved, but this does not concern us here. We are simply concerned to recognize that the individual *nous*, not being an unmoved mover, must itself be moved in some such way by an efficient cause. Furthermore, as we know, the efficient cause is present in the *nous* itself; it is in fact the Active Intellect.

II

After determining that the Active Intellect is present in the soul, we must next consider the nature of its activity. Aristotle tells us that it functions "by making all things." We must therefore unravel the meaning of this phrase. In his book on Aristotle, Ross held that the function of the Active Intellect is to bring the Passive Intellect up from potentiality to actuality by making it actually know its objects. So far so good, but he then supposes that for this to be possible, the Active Intellect must be[8] "something in us that actually knows already, some element that is cut off from our ordinary consciousness so that we are not aware of this pre-existing knowledge." This suggestion about the pre-existing knowledge of the Active Intellect will require further investigation later. Ross, however, himself offers a different view in his recent Commentary on the *De anima*.[9] Here (p. 47) he suggests that the Active Intellect is the "faculty by which we (1) form general conceptions, (2) grasp universal truths, and (3) from two universal truths infer a third." As Philip[10] has pointed out, this view is different from any of the interpretations of the Active Intellect offered by the commentators. Furthermore, as he goes on to show, it does considerable violence to the *De anima* itself. Yet Ross himself has indicated (p. 45) that there are two suggestions in *De anima* 3. 5 itself which show how Aristotle must have understood the Active Intellect: the first is the comparison with art which "does not make its products out of nothing"; the second is that with light which raises potential colors to the status of actual colors. We know in general that Aristotle believes that nothing can be created out of nothing. We can be certain therefore that τῷ ποιεῖν πάντα cannot simply mean "by making all things." It must mean "by making things of one kind into things of another."[11] That is, the Active Intellect must work upon some "material" and must transform this "material." What is this material? We know that it is in the soul. What else, we may ask, than the Passive Intellect?

Although Ross points to the help the comparisons of the Active Intellect with art and with light can give, he is now unwilling to make use of them. With his account of the function of the Active Intellect in mind, we should not now be surprised at his denying (p. 43) that the Active Intellect acts on the Passive Intellect at all; rather, he thinks, it is concerned with the apprehension of a different class of objects. This theory is supported by a curious argument. Aristotle says, according to Ross, "not that the one Reason acts on the other, but that the one makes all things [although on Ross's interpretation it could in fact only make a limited number of "logical" or "mathematical" things] and the other becomes all things." This is certainly what Aristotle says, but the real point is that all things are "made" in the soul. All the objects of thought are "made" into characteristics of the Passive Intellect which thus "is made" or "becomes" all things. Thus when one thought gives way to the next, the Passive Intellect, now "made" of one kind of thought, is made into another. This is the only way in which it could in fact "become all things." In rejecting such an interpretation, Ross is simply despising what little help Aristotle himself gives us. He is in fact exaggerating his earlier statement[12] that "the analogy of light must not be pressed too closely." Rather it seems that neither this analogy nor the comparison with art should be used at all!

Ross's recent interpretation of the Active Intellect must therefore be denied on the grounds that it flies in the face of what little evidence we have. We must revert to something like the view that he adopted in his *Aristotle* and recognize, with the *De anima* itself, that the Active Intellect has the function of bringing potential knowledge in the Passive Intellect into actuality, just as light turns potential colors into actual colors and art transforms the block of marble into the statue. Active Intellect transforms the νοῦς παθητικός into a νοῦς νοῶν. Thus far at least the interpretation of Alexander of Aphrodisias must be pronounced correct.

The Active Intellect, we see, is an efficient cause which acts upon the Passive Intellect in the act of thinking. Since efficient causes are themselves in act, as we read in the *Metaphysics* (1049b 24) as well as in the *De anima* itself (417a 17–18), we must consider the nature of the activity of the Active Intellect. Since the Active Intellect is the efficient cause of thought, are we to suppose that as Peleus, a man in act, is the father of Achilles, so the Active Intellect, if it is to cause thought, must itself have thought?

We should realize from the start that the comparison of the Intellects with Peleus and Achilles must be misleading. Peleus is external to Achilles, but the Active Intellect and the νοῦς νοῶν are both in the soul. The efficient cause of thought in the soul is not comparable to Peleus, but to that inherited power of development handed on by Peleus to Achilles himself. After Achilles is born, his efficient cause is in himself. We may in a sense say that it is in act, since it is effective, but the immanent efficient cause in Achilles is not in actuality a man. No more need the Active Intellect be possessed of any knowledge of the external world—for if it were, it would be identical with its objects and thus also παθητικός—nor need it have any such pre-existing knowledge of which we ourselves are unaware, as Ross suggests. The efficient cause in Achilles is not a man in actuality, but a power that is capable of making Achilles, now a boy, into a man. Similarly there is no need for the Active Intellect to be possessed of actual knowledge, at any rate of the external world; rather it is the power which enables such knowledge to be abstracted by the Passive Intellect.

This rather strange nature of the Active Intellect explains very well the apparent confusion of terminology which Aristotle uses to describe it. It also explains, as we shall see, why the comparison of the Active Intellect with light is so peculiarly apt. In line 15, the Active Intellect is described as ἕξις τις, while in line 18 it is an ἐνέργεια. Commentators have found this puzzling. Hicks, after noting that in a number of passages *hexis* is practically a synonym for εἶδος, writes:[13] "That which is always actual and never potential can only be described as a ἕξις by a stretch of the term. Hence τίς." But the Active Intellect is an unusual kind of ἐνέργεια in any case. Again it seems comparable to the power to stimulate growth inherent *in* Achilles. This power might reasonably be called a kind of "positive quality" (the phrase is Hicks's) or an actuality. Peleus, of course, could only be described as an actuality, not as a kind of disposition. *Hexis* is thus also particularly appropriate to an efficient cause *in* the soul, rather than external to it. More interesting still is the fact that light itself, to which the Active Intellect is compared, is one of the activities which can at times be called a *hexis*. At *De anima* 3. 5 15 it is given as an example of a *hexis*, yet below it acts as an efficient cause and we would suppose it to be an activity. Indeed elsewhere this is almost always what it is. At *De anima* 418b 9 and 419a 11 it is an ἐνέργεια τοῦ διαφανοῦς. Yet at 418b 19 it is by implication a *hexis*. The truth of the matter is that Aristotle's terminology of "potentiality," "actuality," "disposition," is sometimes insufficently precise to achieve an exact description of the phenomena with which he is concerned.

It is well known that Alexander of Aphrodisias' attitude toward this mysterious *hexis* is very strange and cannot be acceptable as an interpretation of Aristotle. Alexander's view is that the Active Intellect is the cause of the Passive Intellect's becoming a *nous en hexei*. It has been suggested that the only reasonable explanation of this is that when he says εἶναί τινα δεῖ καὶ ποιητικὸν νοῦν, ὃς αἴτιος τῆς ἕξεως τῆς τοῦ ὑλικοῦ νοῦ γίνεται[14] he is reading a text of Aristotle different from our own, for in *De anima* 3. 5 as we have it we must certainly follow the general opinion of modern scholars that the Active Intellect is not the cause of some kind of *hexis* but that it is such a *hexis* itself. Mr. F. H. Sandbach, however, has suggested to me an explanation which accounts for the difficulty of Alexander's interpretation very well, namely that he understood ὡς ἕξις τις ⟨ᾗ⟩ in line 15. It is certain that Aristotle did not intend this sense, but had he done so I do not believe that it would have been impossible for him to omit the ᾗ. If Alexander took him this way, we can indeed accuse him of being perverse, but not of being a fool; for if such a reading of Aristotle could be understood, the Alexandrist doctrine would readily follow.

Now that we see what kind of ἕξις-ἐνέργεια the Active Intellect is, we should realize that there is no need to suppose that it has some kind of pre-existing knowledge of the external world of whose existence we are unaware. The power of growth in Achilles is not identical with Achilles the man, nor is it any kind of potentiality of Achilles the man;

rather it is the power which produces Achilles the man. We might call it ποιητικόν. Similarly light is not identical with the colors which it produces, nor is it any kind of "pre-color" in the ordinary sense of "color"; rather it is, as we shall see, the color of the transparent, which must make it different from ordinary colors. Similarly the Active Intellect does not possess ordinary knowledge (and thus is not any thought which is formally identical with the external object of thought) either in a form of which we are conscious or in any other form; rather it is the power which enables the Passive Intellect to become a νοῦς νοῶν by being made identical with the intelligible Forms of the objects of thought.

We can perhaps understand this power a little better by pushing the comparison with light (as light is understood by Aristotle) a little further. Light is not one of the colors it brings up from potentiality to actuality, but it is in a sense analogous to them. It is a color *sui generis*; τὸ φῶς οἷον χρῶμά ἐστι τοῦ διαφανοῦς (*De anima* 418b 11). Similarly perhaps the Active Intellect will not have knowledge, pre-existing or otherwise, of the same kind as that which it helps to produce in the Passive Intellect but another knowledge of a unique kind, which could therefore only be knowledge of itself, since all other knowledge could potentially be obtainable by the Passive Intellect. But we shall return to this later.

III

In line 17 Aristotle describes the Active Intellect as χωριστὸς καὶ ἀπαθὴς καὶ ἀμιγής; in line 22 he speaks of a time when it is χωρισθείς. Following Zeller, Hicks[15] remarks that "χωριστός means here not merely 'separable' but 'actually separate' i.e., 'not involved in physical life'." He thinks it is best explained by *De generatione animalium* 736b 28 where bodily activities are said to have nothing to do with the activity of *nous* (cf. *De an.* 408b 29, and 413a 4–8), and remarks that "the three predicates χωριστός, ἀπαθής, ἀμιγής were applied to νοῦς in III c. 4 before any mention had been made of the distinction between active and passive intellect." He believes that in chapter four these epithets are applied primarily to the Passive Intellect and that they must now be applied a fortiori to the Active. And, he holds, in chapter four *chōristos* means "actually separate."

Let us first look at whether we can derive much help for chapter five from chapter four. In chapter four there is no doubt that Aristotle is teaching that *nous* must be wholly free from association with the body. That is the sense he gives to *amigēs* (e.g., 429a 18, 24–25). *Chōristos* too then must, as Hicks says, mean "actually separate" at 429a 11, separate, that is, from the body-soul complex. But what relevance has this for our *chōristos* in chapter five, line seventeen? Is Aristotle there speaking of the relation of *nous* in general or even of the *Passive* Intellect to the body?

As a preliminary to the solution of this problem, we must compare χωριστός with the χωρισθείς of line 22. Most recent writers on this chapter of the *De anima* have assumed that the words χωρισθεὶς δ' ἐστι μόνον τοῦθ' ὅπερ ἐστί (ll. 22–23) refer to the Active Intellect and that it is this Intellect alone which Aristotle proclaims to be immortal. Not so Professor Mansion.[16] Criticizing Soleri, Mansion denies that Aristotle holds the Active Intellect to be divine. In fact, according to Mansion, as far as immortality is concerned "il ne s'agit plus de l'intellect agent ou actif, mais uniquement, d'après ce qu' on vient de rappeler, de la pure essence de l'intellect . . . l'intellect actif est périssable de la même façon et pour la même raison" as the passive. Mansion's notion of the "pure essence of Intellect" as something quite unconnected with the Active or Passive Intellect is a strange one which seems to derive from his pushing the idea that these two Intellects are really only aspects of the Intellect as a whole too far. Yet how can *chōristheis* not refer to the Active Intellect? Mansion's interpretation involves the supposition that *chōristheis* cannot refer to the same thing as is referred to by *chōristos* in line 17, for *chōristos* whatever it means, must refer to the Active Intellect. This is certainly a most natural interpretation of the Greek. Furthermore, Mansion's use of the phrase "pure essence of Intellect" might lead one to suppose that Aristotle refers to the idea of essence specifically. Had Aristotle wished to refer to the essence of Intellect, he had phrases for essence ready to hand which would have indicated his meaning clearly. In fact, the change from the masculine *chōristheis* to the neuter τοῦθ' ὅπερ ἐστί merely shows, as we shall see, that after death the Active Intellect no longer acts on the Passive, but just remains what it is.[17] Since therefore Aristotle does not talk about an essence of Intellect here (or anywhere else) and since what Mansion takes to refer to such an essence is more easily understood as referring to the Active Intellect after its separation from the Passive Intellect and the body at death, Mansion's suggestion must be rejected.

Now that we are assured that *chōristheis* in line 22 refers to the Active Intellect, we may revert to the exact meaning of *chōristos* in line 17. In chapter five Aristotle is in fact not only thinking of the relation of the Active Intellect to the body, but to the Passive Intellect as well. This is the clear implication of the sentence beginning ἀεὶ γὰρ τιμιώτερον.

Aristotle is reverting again to his position at the beginning of the chapter that there is an Active and a Passive element in the soul. The Active τὸ ποιοῦν is superior. Thus the words "for the active is always superior to the passive" explain the description of the Active Intellect as a χωριστός, ἀπαθής, ἀμιγής. In chapter four, as we have seen, the Intellect as a whole, including presumably the Passive Intellect, is held to be unmixed with the body and ἀπαθές (429a 15), but nevertheless the Passive Intellect, as its very name *pathētikos* shows, is receptive of the *Forms* of the objects (including the material objects) of its thought (429a 15–16). In chapter five, as we have seen, the words *chōristos* and *apathēs* are explained by a reference to the superiority of the Active Intellect to the Passive. The Passive Intellect in a sense is not *apathēs*, that is, it is *pathētikos* of the Forms abstracted in thought, while the Active is not even affected in that peculiar fashion. Since then the Passive Intellect is not in every respect *chōristos* and *apathēs* while the Active is, then Aristotle must in fact be distinguishing between them. The Active Intellect must be *chōristos* from what is not entirely *chōristos*. The Passive Intellect in fact is analogous to matter (l. 19) while the Active is an efficient cause. Efficient causes are often separate or separable from the matter on which they operate. Thus when Aristotle says that the Active Intellect is *chōristos* and *apathēs* we must conclude that these words refer not only to separation from the body, as in chapter four, but to the separation of the Active Intellect from the Passive Intellect also. The word *chōristos* then must mean here that the Active Intellect is either "separable" or "actually separate" from the Passive.

Yet in relation to the Passive Intellect it transpires that the Active Intellect cannot always be separate. If the Active Intellect were always separate, the use of the aorist participle χωρισθείς would be absurd.[18] As Ross[19] indicates, the words χωρισθεὶς . . . ὅπερ ἐστί must almost certainly mean "that after separation from the passive reason, at death, the active reason is just its true self." It is, as Hicks[20] says, now to be considered in its true self *alone*, and no longer as also acting *on* the Passive Intellect. But even if Aristotle means that *only* after separation is it its true self—which is unlikely since even when associated with the Passive Intellect it must be ἀπαθής, ἀμιγής and τῇ οὐσίᾳ ὢν ἐνέργεια—then the following argument is still valid. For Aristotle to be able to say "having been separated" implies that he supposes there is a time when the Active Intellect is not "separated." That he thinks of the separation as taking place at death is shown by the immediate raising of the question of immortality. Since then there is a time when the Active Intellect is not separated but linked in some way to the Passive, as efficient cause to matter, and since, however, separation *does* occur at death, then during a man's lifetime his Active Intellect must not be separated but separable.

IV

In his edition of the *De anima* Ross brackets out τὸ δ'αὐτό (l. 19) . . . οὐ νοεῖ (l. 22); in his German translation Theiler[21] omits τὸ δ'αὐτό . . . οὐδὲ χρόνῳ. Ross suggests that since these words (as far as *oude chronōi*) recur in chapter seven—where, as Mr. Sandbach reminded me, they are also preceded by ὕλης—and are more appropriate there, they should be excised here. He adds that they disturb the continuity of lines 17–19 with 22–25. The latter argument is subjective and could not be accepted as adequate by itself. As we shall see, the words ἀλλ'οὐχ ὁτὲ μὲν νοεῖ ὁτὲ δ'οὐ νοεῖ deleted by Ross but retained by Theiler are necessary for an understanding of the last phrase of the chapter. And even if this were not so, it would seem that Theiler is the more moderate in retaining these words which do not occur again in chapter seven, while still deleting the passage from τὸ δ'αὐτό to οὐδὲ χρόνῳ. Assuming therefore that there is no satisfactory reason for deleting as much as Ross desires, let us consider the validity of the decision to remove simply the passage that is repeated in chapter seven.

There would seem to be a clear case for deletion only if these words upset the sense of chapter five. Let us consider the idea that in the individual potential knowledge is prior to actual knowledge, though in general this is not so. How does this idea square with the following suggestion that the Active Intellect always νοεῖ? Now we know already that the Active Intellect is *in* the soul of the individual and is distinct in each individual.[22] We know too that it is in act and that it is a *hexis tis*, like light. Since this is so, the potential knowledge that is prior in the individual cannot be the knowledge of the Active Intellect. Nor, since the Active Intellect thinks (*noei*) continuously and not intermittently, can it have any potential knowledge of any kind. We must therefore assume that the words from τὸ δ'αὐτό to οὐδὲ χρόνῳ cannot refer to the Active Intellect. It seems most unlikely that Aristotle would use the word ἐπιστήμη of the Active Intellect in any case; νόησις would be more appropriate. Ross and Theiler have therefore a certain justification for excluding τὸ δ'αὐτό . . . οὐδὲ χρόνῳ from chapter five as irrelevant to the Active Intellect. Yet it will appear later that these words may serve a purpose in Aristotle's exposition—the purpose of showing what the Active Intellect is not.

V

Aristotle is quite specific that the Active Intellect alone is immortal. He then says that "we do not remember" because the Active Intellect, which is immortal, is impassive while the Passive Intellect is perishable.[23] Part of the sense of this is that because the Passive Intellect *perishes*, the power of memory must perish with it.[24] That is, he is saying that because of the perishing of the Passive Intellect, "we do not remember" *after death*. This is not quite the same position as he has adopted at 408b 28 where he says that it is because of the perishing of the body that memory ceases. But the difference between the two is not as great as Hicks[25] implies. Both share the view that the part of the complex individual man which survives death has no power of memory. Hicks mentions the further objection that οὐ μνημονεύομεν cannot mean "we do not remember after death" because "we cannot know now that we do not remember after death, but the words of the text presuppose a known fact." Yet the truth is that *ou mnēmoneuomen* is not presented as a fact but as a deduction from the facts that the Active Intellect is impassive while the Passive Intellect is perishable. We do not remember after death because "we" do not survive;[26] our Active Intellects, which do survive, are impassive and thus obviously have no memory.

It appears that the only knowledge which could conceivably be present in an Intellect devoid both of memory and of the power to abstract from sense data must be knowledge of itself, if it is continually conscious of itself and intuits itself in an eternal present without memory of the past or imagination of the future. Thus the Active Intellect which thinks continually and cannot know the external world must be thinking (if we can call it "thinking"—perhaps "being conscious" would be a better phrase) of itself. In this respect it is comparable with God who is νόησις νοήσεως in the *Metaphysics* (1074b 33).[27] Scarcely anyone nowadays is disposed to take seriously the identification of the Active Intellect with God made by Alexander of Aphrodisias, but we can at least learn to see how such an identification might have seemed plausible. We have demonstrated here certain features of the Active Intellect akin to those of God, but although to move from similarity to identity would be rash, yet at least a recognition that the highest aspect of the human mind can have no knowledge of the external world may help us to understand why the God of the *Metaphysics* a fortiori cannot have such knowledge. This God is said to be very good (1072b 30) and to think what is best (1074b 33). Clearly the best must be more akin to the Active than to the Passive Intellect of man, and clearly the thought of God must be more akin to the thought of that Active Intellect. Thus if the Active Intellect has no memory and no knowledge of the external world, we should not be surprised that Aristotle refuses to attribute such memory and knowledge to God. Perhaps we may say that Aristotle envisages both God and the Active Intellect as the power of thought understood as thought of itself.

VI

Yet in this discussion of the nature of the Active Intellect by itself is not a fundamental difficulty being neglected? We have seen already that the Active Intellect is during our lifetime "in the soul" and that it acts as a necessary efficient cause of thought. Yet since the soul is a unity and exists as a unity, how can Aristotle hold that some part of it (i.e., the Active Intellect) can exist separately after death? The human soul for Aristotle is the form of the human body; form and matter cannot exist apart except in the minds of philosophers, that is, as abstractions. If soul by itself is an abstraction, how can a mere part of that soul, the Active Intellect, be anything more than an abstraction? Yet clearly for Aristotle it is much more than an abstraction.[28] There is no easy solution to this problem. All we can do here is indicate that this difficulty about the Active Intellect is merely an extreme example of a difficulty about the Aristotelian form in general. The problem has been explained in the clearest possible terms by Gilson. Gilson[29] imagines Plato living long enough to read the first book of Aristotle's *Metaphysics* and then writing a dialogue entitled *Aristoteles* to refute the novelties of his pupil. In this supposed dialogue Socrates is made to say: "Then, my lad, I wish you could tell me how it may be that beings are, through sharing in an essence, which itself is not." The difficulty is simply that while Aristotle usually regards σύνολα (individuals) as the only realities, he also identifies *ousia* with essence in the *Metaphysics*. Essence is the cause of the existence of individuals, but essence by itself does not exist. And yet sometimes it does seem to exist apart—at least in the case of God. But not only in the case of God does this difficulty arise. We can now see that the Active Intellects, identical but distinct in individual men, exhibit the same confusion. The soul is the form of the body; the Active Intellect is in the soul during our mortal life; the form cannot exist without the matter.

If any real consistency is to be preserved for the doctrine of the *De anima*, we cannot but follow the advice of Philip,[30] who remarks: "I can see no grounds for refusing to concede that in studying and describing the human soul Aristotle recognized in it some faculty or capacity or element, not explainable as part of the body-soul complex . . ." It is certainly true that in *De anima* 3. 5 the Active Intellect does not seem to be explainable as part of such a complex; yet we must not forget that in general Aristotle holds that it is by the possession of the power of reason that man is differentiated from the animals. And he is not merely thinking of the possession of such a power, but of its use; that is, he regards νοῦς νοῶν as an essential aspect of the *form* of man.[31] We are back again to the problem of whether and in what way form in general can exist apart. The *De anima* merely exhibits in an extreme manner the difficulties in the whole Aristotelian doctrine of the reality or unreality of essence. The soul is not only a form, but as we know from 412b 10–11, an οὐσία ἡ κατὰ τὸν λόγον. τοῦτο δὲ τὸ τί ἦν εἶναι τῷ τοιῳδὶ σώματι. In view of this, it seems no easier to understand how the human mind, and *a fortiori* the Active Intellect, is not a part of the body-soul complex than it is to believe that there can be wholly immaterial substances. And yet for Aristotle there is at least one such substance.

VII

We must turn to the last phrase of the chapter, where the text reads καὶ ἄνευ τούτου οὐθὲν νοεῖ. Of this Ross wrote as follows:[32] "The last words of the chapter are capable of a variety of interpretations, viz.: (1) 'and without the passive reason the active reason knows nothing.' (2) 'and without the active reason the passive reason knows nothing.' (3) 'and without the passive reason nothing knows.' (4) 'and without the active reason nothing knows.' " Without offering any reason for his choice, Ross then approved of number (4).

It is clear that the problem in this sentence is the reference of τούτου. Considerations of grammar do not seem adequate to settle the matter one way or the other; considerations of doctrine must therefore be invoked. Now we should naturally suppose that if nothing "thinks" without the Passive Intellect, then the Active Intellect cannot think when it is separated from that Passive Intellect. And yet unless we unreasonably excise the phrase οὐχ ὅτε μὲν νοεῖ ὅτε δ'οὐ νοεῖ in line 22, we know that the Active Intellect does not merely think intermittently. Hence it would seem absurd to suppose that ἄνευ τούτου means "without the Passive Intellect." Zeller,[33] however, who is followed on this point by Rodier,[34] and whose argument in itself is accepted as reasonable by Hicks,[35] denies the contradiction. His argument is that the phrase οὐχ ὅτε μὲν νοεῖ ὅτε δ'οὐ νοεῖ does not apply to the thought of the individual, whereas it is such thought that is under discussion in ἄνευ τούτου οὐθὲν νοεῖ. Zeller's contention that the earlier passage does not deal with individuals depends on a comparison of these words with the section τὸ δ'αὐτό . . . οὐδὲ χρόνῳ immediately preceding them. Of course if this section is to be deleted (as is the view of Ross and Theiler) half our difficulties are solved, but the case for deletion is, as we have seen, insufficiently strong for us to neglect Zeller's argument. Assuming then that we accept the full text, are we to agree that Zeller's suggestion is valid? Are we to say that since in general actual *epistēmē* is prior to potential, but that this is not so in the individual, the words ἀλλ'οὐχ ὅτε . . . νοεῖ with their suggestion that the Active Intellect must qua active be in continuous thought, cannot apply to the Active Intellect in any individual soul, but must refer to the Active Intellect in general?

We are in no way bound to accept such reasoning. In the first place we must consider the Active Intellects within each individual soul. They cannot, as we have seen, be merely potential. What in that case would bring them up to actuality? Another Active Intellect? Such a regress is impossible. The Passive Intellect? That is absurd. They are in fact already τῇ οὐσίᾳ ὢν ἐνέργεια. It should thus be clear that the words τὸ δ'αὐτό . . . οὐδὲ χρόνῳ are not to be taken in the manner favored by Zeller. We cannot deduce from them that the Active Intellect in the individual has potential *epistēmē* before it has actual. Such a situation turns out to be absurd. Besides, the very use of the term *epistēmē* should indicate that the words *to d'auto* . . . *oude chronōi* do not concern the Active Intellect at all, and should not therefore be used as a guide to *all' ouch* . . . *noei*. *Epistēmē*, as we know well from the sixth book of the *Nicomachean Ethics* and elsewhere, is not the same as *nous*. The truth of the matter may be—and this is perhaps the best reason for retaining the words *to d'auto* . . . *oude chronōi*—that while in the individual potential *epistēmē* is prior in time to actual, the Active Intellect on the contrary does not experience the movement from potential to actual *noēsis* but rather is continually in act. Thus Aristotle by the whole passage *to d'auto* . . . *noei* is further emphasizing the uniqueness of the operation of the Active Intellect. This being so, Zeller's attempt to persuade us that *aneu toutou* can refer to the Passive Intellect without Aristotle's contradicting what he has just said must be accounted a failure. We are bound therefore to translate *aneu toutou* as "without the Active Intellect."

Thus of Ross's four alternatives as translations for the last phrase of *De anima* 3. 5 we can eliminate two. The words must either mean "and without the Active Intellect the Passive Intellect thinks nothing," or "and without the Active Intellect nothing thinks." It is not of great importance for our understanding of Aristotle's general doctrine to fix on one of these versions as correct, but common sense certainly points in one direction. If we ask ourselves what might for Aristotle be capable of thought of some kind, we must surely answer, "Either the Active Intellect or the Passive Intellect *and nothing else.*" If then nothing else thinks, it would be pretentious for Aristotle to write "And without the Active Intellect nothing thinks," since apart from the Passive Intellect, nothing else could be expected to think. Therefore it seems highly likely that the whole phrase means "and without the Active Intellect, the Passive Intellect thinks nothing." A second, though less likely possibility is revived by Hicks.[36] This is that νοεῖ like μνημονεύει in 408b 28, is "quasi-impersonal." This seems a less natural way of taking the Greek, but at least Hicks agrees that οὐθέν cannot be the subject of νοεῖ.

There is one final point which may be touched on briefly here, that is, the difference between sensation and thought; for my general interpretation may seem to have blurred it somewhat. If thought is analogous to sensation, says Aristotle at 429a 13–14, it must be acted upon by its object (πάσχειν ὑπὸ τοῦ νοητοῦ). We know in the case of sensation that the objects sensed are themselves the agents which stimulate the sense organ. They are themselves ποιητικά of its activity (417b 20, cf. *De sensu* 445b 7). Now there is no doubt that the Passive Intellect too needs to be brought up to activity by something that is active (cf. 417a 17–18). The question is, How far in this respect is thought analogous to sensation? There is in fact a great difference. Whereas in the case of sensation it is the objects sensed which act upon the sense organ, and thus the organ is affected by something external (417b 20), in the case of thought, that is the grasp of universals (*An. post.* 87b 37), the stimulation is provided not by the objects of thought (which are nowhere called *poiētika*) but by the Active Intellect. This is why the process of thought does not depend on the possession of "organs" (cf. 429a 26–27).

In sum then we may say that in the individual soul there is an Active and a Passive Intellect. The effect of the former is to bring the latter up from potency to act. It is itself in a rather peculiar kind of act. As for immortality, this is limited to the Active Intellect, which certainly survives, though it has no memory and no knowledge of the external world. Its strange character may perhaps best be summarized as a power to induce thought which is itself some kind of self-thinking being. If this much is clear about the nature and function of the Active Intellect, the nature and function of the Passive Intellect become easier to understand.[37]

NOTES

[1] W. D. Ross, *Aristotle*[5] (London, 1949), p. 149, n. 1.

[2] Alexander substitutes ἐπὶ τοῦ νοῦ for ἐν τῇ ψυχῇ at *De An.* 88. 17 Bruns.

[3] *Ap.* Themistium *in De an.* 108. 24–25 Heinze. For the significance of μικτόν see E. Barbotin, *La Thèorie Aristotélicienne de l'intellect d'après Thèophraste* (Louvain, 1954), pp. 163–65.

[4] Cf. G. Soleri, *L'immortalità dell'anima in Aristotele* (Turin, 1952), pp. 130–31 and the neo-Averroistic interpretation of F. Nuyens, *L'Evolution de la psychologie d'Aristote* (Louvain, 1948), pp. 299–303.

[5] E. Barbotin (see n. 3), pp. 94, 155–56.

[6] In a review of Ross's edition of the *De anima* published in *Phx*, XVI (1962): 201, n. 9.

[7] E. Barbotin (see n. 3), p. 214.

[8] W. D. Ross (see n. 1), pp. 149–50.

[9] Idem, *Aristotle: "De anima"* (Oxford, 1961), pp. 45–47.

[10] J. Philip, (see n. 6), 199.

[11] Cf. R. D. Hicks's edition of the *De anima* (Cambridge, 1907), p. 499, on a 12.

[12] W. D. Ross (see n. 1), p. 150.

[13] R. D. Hicks (see n. 11), p. 501, on a 15.

[14] *De an.* 88. 23 Bruns. Cf. *De anima Mantissa* 107. 29–30: ὁ ποιητικός, δι' ὃν ὁ ὑλικὸς ἐν ἕξει γίνεται . . . ἀνάλογον ὢν οὗτος ὁ ποιητικός, ὥς φησιν ὁ 'Αριστοτέλης, τῷ φωτί.

[15] R. D. Hicks (see n. 11), p. 502, on a 17.

[16] A. Mansion, "L'Immortalité de l'âme et de l'intellect d'après Aristote," *RPL*, LI (1953): 468.

[17] Cf. R. D. Hicks (see n. 11), p. 506, on a 22, who compares *Rep.* 611A–612A. The remark of Barbotin (see n. 3), p. 166, 2, that the Active Intellect "retrouve à la mort la simplicité de son essence" is misleading. The Active Intellect is always simple. During life however, it not only exists in itself, but also affects the Passive Intellect.

[18] If Aristotle required a word which would not naturally have a temporal sense, he could have said κεχωρισμένος (cf. 431, 18). Despite his continual translation of *chōristos* as "separate," Soleri (see n. 4), p. 132 seems to have some idea of the distinction between *chōristos* and *chōristheis* when he writes: "O si deve intendere il χωριστός in psicologia, come indipendenza di diritto e possibilità di separazione (e con separazione di fatto nell' esperienza vissuta) del nous."

[19] W. D. Ross (see n. 9), p. 48.

[20] R. D. Hicks (see n. 11), p. 506, on a 22.

[21] W. Theiler, *Aristoteles: Über die Seele* (Berlin, 1959), p. 59.

[22] For a rejection of the view that ἀλλ' οὐχ ὁτὲ . . . νοεῖ refers not to each particular Active Intellect, but to the Active Intellect in general, see below.

[23] R. D. Hicks (see n. 11), p. 508, on a 24 explains why Aristotle, who does not argue the fact here, holds that the Passive Intellect is perishable. The Passive Intellect has some potentiality (of substance) in it, and nothing

of this kind can endure (*Met.* 1050b 6–18).

[24] The punctuation with a colon after *hoti* (giving the sense "We do not in life remember that the Active Intellect is eternal") is impossible since we could not "remember" in life a fact which we never knew. The pre-existing Active Intellect, since it is impassive, obviously could not be receptive of facts.

[25] R. D. Hicks (see n. 11), p. 107, on a 23.

[26] Why does Aristotle write *mnēmoneuomen* rather than *mnēmoneuei* as in 408b 28? Because at 408b 27 ff. he has already remarked that memory is an affection of that which "holds" the mind rather than the mind itself, and therefore it is clear that at the death of the body memory ceases. At 430a 23—24, however, he has not specifically said that memory is an activity of the complex, and therefore by writing *we* do not remember, he emphasizes that when the Passive Intellect perishes (and the "we" is thus destroyed) then memory perishes with us. I am tempted to suppose that the words "We do not remember," followed by "this (the Active Intellect) is impassive" contributed to Alexander's positing a common Active Intellect for all of us.

[27] A similar comparison is made by Mansion (see note 16), p. 470, who however compares not the Active Intellect but the "pure essence of Intellect."

[28] Although in this paper we are discussing the problem of the Active Intellect only, it should be observed that *nous* as a whole is held by Aristotle in a number of passages (apart from *De an.* 3. 4 where it is *chōristos*) to be some sort of entity in its own right. It "seems" to be an *ousia* in its own right and to be imperishable at *De an.* 408b 19–20. At 413a 6–7 there are some parts of the soul which are not entelechies of the body. *Nous* comes from outside at *De gen. anim.* 736b 27 ff. and 744b 21 ff. The possibility of its survival occurs again at *Met.* 1070a 24. It goes without saying that all this is difficult to square with the perishability of the *Passive* Intellect in *De anima* 3, 5.

[29] E. Gilson, *Being and Some Philosophers* (Toronto, 1952), pp. 49–50.

[30] J. Philip (see n. 6), 201.

[31] Cf. A. Mansion (see n. 16), 466.

[32] W. D. Ross (see n. 1), p. 152.

[33] E. Zeller, *Aristotle II* (Eng. trans.; London, 1897), p. 101, n. 3.

[34] G. Rodier, *Traité de l'Ame II* (Paris, 1900), p. 467.

[35] R. D. Hicks (see n. 11), p. 509.

[36] Ibid, p. 510.

[37] I should like to thank those persons who read an earlier draft of this paper, and in particular Mr. F. H. Sandbach, without whose comments it would never have realized its present form.

RICHARD TAYLOR
University of Rochester

Aristotle's Doctrine of Future Contingencies*

ARISTOTLE believed that any statement which asserts or denies, concerning a contingent event, that it is going to occur, is neither true nor false, the world being as yet indeterminate with regard to the existence or nonexistence of such things.[1]

Few doctrines from antiquity have engendered more controversy than this one, as indicated by the rash of polemic that has broken out over it again in the last few years.[2] Medieval philosophers, following Boethius, found in it a thorny problem of reconciling liberty with divine omniscience; Lukasiewicz, more recently, revived Aristotle's arguments to provide an interpretation for his three-valued logic, while other writers still find it necessary to take account of essentially the same arguments in dealing with metaphysical problems of time. Nearly all the Scholastics discarded Aristotle's arguments as inconsistent with Christian presuppositions, while modern logicians have tended to dismiss them as paralogisms. C. A. Baylis rejected all of them, as reinterpreted by Lukasiewicz, as fallacious,[3] and W. V. Quine has disdained one of the conclusions as "Aristotle's fantasy."[4] Applying them to metaphysical puzzles, Gilbert Ryle treats such arguments as confusions of categories,[5] while Donald Williams has pronounced Aristotle's reasoning "so swaggeringly invalid that the student can hardly believe he meant it," and his conclusion "as nearly incredible as any proposition could be."[6]

The prevailing opinion, then, is and always has been, that Aristotle was muddled in these arguments and that his conclusion was false. I want to show, on the contrary, that he was exceptionally profound and that at least one important part of his doctrine is true. And if, as I believe, Aristotle was right, some far-reaching consequences follow. The conclusion yields, for instance, (1) in metaphysics, the view, much

* Presented at the 1954 meeting of the SAGP in Baltimore, Maryland. Reprinted with permission from the *Philosophical Review*, LXVI (1957): 1–28, where it appears under the title "The Problem of Future Contingencies."

fought over lately, that time has not only an intrinsic order, as does space, but also an intrinsic sense or asymmetry, as space has not; (2) in logic, an area of applicability of a three-valued system, and (3) in theology, a revision of the traditional notion of divine omniscience.

I shall proceed as follows: in the first section, to set forth Aristotle's thesis and three of the arguments for it which I regard as valid; in the second, to clarify these arguments and elicit their presuppositions; and finally, to defend Aristotle's opinion against all the important objections I know of. The reader can thus probably find in this last section his own objection, if he has one, and satisfy himself whether it has been answered.

I. ARISTOTLE'S OPINION

The thesis.—Aristotle, as I understand him, maintains that all propositions are either true or are false, with the sole exception of a limited class of propositions about the future, viz., those that assert the occurrence, or nonoccurrence, of some future contingency. Concerning these (only) he held (a) that they are, antecedently, not true and yet not false, but (b) that any disjunction of such a proposition with its denial is necessarily true.[7] And by a "future contingency" is meant any event which belongs not to the present or past, but which in the nature of things, and not merely in relation to our knowledge or ignorance of things, might or might not occur in the future.

The arguments.—There seem to be three distinct arguments for this, somewhat mixed together and admixed with other considerations. They are predicated on two assumptions, so I shall state first the assumptions and then, paraphrastically, the arguments.

The first assumption is a correspondence theory of truth, the minimum requirement of which is that in the case of any true proposition asserting some predicate of a particular individual, there is (tenselessly) a fact consisting of that individual having that predicate. This raises problems of its own, but we can ignore them. The second assumption is that there are genuine ambiguities in the future, i.e., that sometimes various mutually incompatible events are each of them future possibilities. We shall see what this means shortly.

(1) The first argument is this: Suppose all propositions, including those about future contingencies, are now either true or are false. Then if one man says today that a particular event—e.g., a sea fight—will occur tomorrow, and another denies this, what one of them says must correspond to a fact forthcoming, positive or negative, and what the

other says must fail to correspond. But in that case it must already be true that a sea fight definitely will take place, such that there is now no possibility that it might not, or else that it definitely will not take place, such that there is now no possibility that it nevertheless might. This, however, is false; for on such a view "nothing is or takes place fortuitously [ἀπὸ τύχης], either in the present or in the future, and there are no real alternatives; everything takes place of necessity and is fixed . . . for the meaning of the word 'fortuitous' in regard to present or future events is that reality is so constituted that it may issue in either of two opposite directions."[8]

Two qualifications are added to this and the following arguments. First, that it does not matter how far in advance a prediction is made: "A man may predict an event ten thousand years beforehand, and another may predict the reverse; that which was truly predicted at the moment in the past will of necessity take place in the fullness of time."[9] Second, that it is irrelevant whether such propositions about the future ever are actually stated or entertained, for "it is manifest that the circumstances are not influenced by the fact of an affirmation or denial on the part of anyone."[10]

(2) The second argument concerns propositions about past contingencies considered in relation to the time when the event in question was as yet future, and unlike the first it is stated categorically rather than disjunctively. It is this: consider an object which is now white, e.g., a table. Now on the supposition that every proposition is true, or if not true then false, it must have been true before the table became white, or even existed, that it would become white; indeed, it must have been true from all eternity. But if it was always true that it would become white, then it was never really possible that it might not, "and when a thing cannot not come to be, it is impossible that it should not come to be, and when it is impossible that it should not come to be, it must come to be." So again, "it results from this that nothing is uncertain or fortuitous,"[11] that "there are no real alternatives, but that all that is or takes place is the outcome of necessity."[12] This, however, is false, for

> in those things which are not continuously actual there is a potentiality in either direction [τὸ δυνατὸν εἶναι καὶ μή]. Such things may either be or not be; events also therefore may either take place or not take place . . . So it is therefore with all other events which possess this kind of potentiality. It is therefore plain that it is not of necessity that everything is or takes place; but in some instances there are real alternatives, in which case the affirmation is no more true and no more false than the denial.[13]

(3) The third argument is exceedingly succinct and straightforward, being but a combination of the two aforementioned assumptions and a conclusion therefrom. It is simply this: "Since propositions correspond with facts, it is evident that when in future events there is a real alternative, and a potentiality in contrary directions [τὰ ἐναντία ἐνδέχεσθαι], the corresponding affirmation and denial have the same character."[14] We could express this otherwise, but no better, by saying that if the world is such that something which has not happened nevertheless might occur or might fail to occur in the future, and if this contingency or "potentiality in contrary directions" belongs to the nature of things and is not merely relative to our knowledge or ignorance of things, then it expresses the *whole* truth about such an event to say that it might happen, or it might not.

It will be noticed that the arguments I have summarized bear only on part (a) of Aristotle's thesis, viz., that future contingency statements neither are true nor are false, and do nothing to prove part (b), viz., that any disjunction of one such proposition and its denial is nevertheless necessarily true, and it is, in fact, only the former that I shall consider. It may be that the truth of (a) would require a revision of (b), as I believe it would, but we shall have enough on our hands if we say what needs to be said concerning (a).

II. COMMENT

These arguments are valid, though terribly susceptible of misinterpretation. In this section I shall (a) formulate a more careful statement of the doctrine of real contingencies, upon which Aristotle's and my own forthcoming arguments rest, and (b) indicate the senses in which the modal terms involved should be taken.

The doctrine of real contingencies.—Most critics have tended to treat Aristotle's arguments simply as articles of logic, interpreting such key words as "necessary" as logical modalities, predicable of propositions, such that the question then becomes that of whether these arguments constitute logically valid inferences—as they plainly do not, unless further assumptions are introduced. From the mere fact that a statement is true, it hardly follows that it is logically necessary—unless one is prepared to abandon any distinction between contingent and necessary truths.[15] I should maintain, then, that Aristotle's arguments are derived from a metaphysical assumption, namely, that there are real ambiguities in nature, i.e., from a doctrine of real contingencies.

This doctrine is best understood in terms of what it *denies*, namely, universal causal determinism, which is to the effect that (as it has recently been well put) "without exception . . . the present (including the present character and behavior of human beings) is the only present that could exist, given the past that did exist, and the future will be the only future that could exist, given the particular present that now is."[16] Belief in determinism, that is, involves the belief that, for any event that ever happens, there are conditions given which nothing else could happen. And since the causal conditions of events, or the occurrences of such conditions, are themselves events, this proposition does entail that the past and present states of the world, in their totality, are compatible with only one future, that the future is unambiguous, save in reference to our powers of prediction.

The denial of this is simply that *some* events are not such as described. This view has sometimes—I think by Aristotle—been thought plausible only as applied to the choices or decisions of men. But however narrowly construed, if this view is true, then determinism, as formulated above, is absolutely false, the past and the present states of the world *are* compatible with any of several alternative futures, and "future possibilities" are real ones, not just logical or relative possibilities.

I shall give no argument for this view of real contingencies; indeed, I think it can be neither proved nor disproved, though I happen to believe it. For the purpose of the present discussion, it may be regarded as an hypothesis only, such that our problem can be formulated as the following hypothetical one: if the doctrine of real contingencies is true, was Aristotle right in believing that some propositions—viz., those asserting or denying the existence in the future of contingent things—are neither true nor false?

That Aristotle believed in real contingencies is, I think, beyond doubt, but I shall not prove it here, it being an historical question. Two articles of his philosophy do, however, deserve to be mentioned, as clarifying somewhat the doctrine in question.

The first is his rarely formulated theory of the fortuitous. According to this, as I understand it, any causally connected series of events is such that each member is caused by its predecessor, if it has a predecessor, and in this sense comes about "of necessity." The beginning of such a series, however—e.g., the ultimate cause of the choice or decision of a living being, or perhaps of a man—"no longer points to something further," and thus, Aristotle says, is "the starting-point for the fortuitous, and will have nothing else as cause of its coming to be."[17] Such a conception involves an unusual conception of causation, according to which some things—e.g., men and other active things, in the strict sense of "active"—can be "originative sources of motion," but Aristotle evidently did believe this (as I do), and whether it is unusual or not is in any case irrelevant.

The other doctrine, closely connected with the first, and alluded to in the arguments I have paraphrased, is that of rational and nonrational capacities (δυνάμεις μετὰ λόγου and δυνάμεις ἄλογοι).[18] A nonrational capacity is the disposition of something toward a unique state under given conditions—which is, of course, what philosophers normally have in mind in speaking of capacities or dispositions. Sugar placed in warm water, for instance, can only dissolve; it cannot sometimes dissolve, sometimes ignite, and sometimes do nothing. Water, heated to a certain point, can only boil, it cannot solidify; the sun can only warm us, under given conditions, not sometimes warm and sometimes chill us. Rational capacities, on the other hand, are "capacities for opposites [δυνάμεις τῶν ἐναντίων]," and characterize (together with nonrational ones) only living things, perhaps only rational beings.[19] These are dispositions to do any of two or more incompatible things under a given set of conditions, that is, dispositions that are really ambiguous. Such capacities are not utterly ambiguous—indeed, the states or acts to which a thing having such a capacity may tend, in given circumstances, may be as few as two—but the important thing is that such a disposition is not toward some unique state. Moreover, such capacities are not manifest "necessarily," i.e., from ordinary causal processes; if they were, then, being capacities for opposites, they would result in incompatible states at the same time, which is impossible. Something further is needed, then, to "decide," and this is what Aristotle calls "desire or will [ὄρεξις ἢ προαίρεσις]."[20] And this, again, is something which is not simply the actualization of another capacity, rational or nonrational, but is instead simply the act of an active being—i.e., of a being which acts and is not merely acted upon—considered as an "originative source of movement," not itself entirely determined to one thing rather than another by any fixed causal connections.

Now either of these doctrines—which really amount to much the same thing—would yield a theory of real contingencies. And both, I submit, are plausible in the light of what we take ourselves, as active beings, to be, but I shall not prove them.

Modal predicates—Nothing is so apt to mislead as Aristotle's use of such concepts as "necessary" and "possible"; so I shall now clarify these.

Given a meaning for any one of the four modal terms—"necessary," "possible," "impossible," and "contingent"—the others can forthwith be defined in terms of it. Given, for instance, a meaning for "necessary," the remaining three predicates can be explicated as follows:

x is possible $\equiv$ $\sim$ ($\sim$x is necessary)
x is impossible $\equiv$ $\sim$x is necessary
x is contingent $\equiv$ $\sim$(x is necessary). $\sim$ ($\sim$x is necessary),

substituting for "x" a statement, an event, or whatever the sense of the modal term requires, and letting "$\sim$x" designate, not simply the absence of x, but something not compossible with x, in the sense of the modality in question.

These definitions, which are of course empty until a meaning is given to the basic modal term, exhibit one important point that is easily overlooked, viz., that the possible and the contingent are *not* the same. Whatever is contingent is possible, but not vice versa; for if anything is necessary, then it is also possible, but not therefore contingent.[21]

In the light of these definitions four more or less familiar senses of necessity and hence also, derivatively, of contingency, can be distinguished in roughly the following way:

(1) *Logical necessity* is predicable of a *statement* or *proposition* and corresponds to analyticity. Thus

necessarily p $\equiv$ "p" is analytic

and a logically contingent statement is thus one which is neither analytic nor self-contradictory.[22]

(2) *Epistemic necessity* is predicable of events and states, though only in a derivative way, and corresponds to what is known to be. Thus

necessarily e $\equiv$ e is known to exist,

and an epistemically contingent event is one concerning which it is not known whether it exists (has existed, will exist) or not—one which, "for all we know," might exist, or might not. This is indeed a strange kind of contingency and is in fact no real contingency at all, being only a reflection of someone's knowledge or ignorance of things, but it is nevertheless the commonest sense of contingency embodied in ordinary speech. If, for instance, someone says before opening a drawer that it might or might not contain his necktie, he only means that he does not yet know; if someone says it might rain a week hence, he ordinarily means only that he does not know that it will not. On the other hand, one who knows, say, that Mr. Jones is in New York cannot really consider it possible that he is not.[23]

(3) *Nomical necessity*, also called "causal" and "etiological," is necessitation by causation and is predicable of an event. Thus

necessarily e $\equiv$ there is (was, will be) a cause for e, and a nomically contingent event is therefore one neither the occurrence nor nonoccurrence of which has a cause.[24] Derivatively, an event causally dependent, remotely or proximately, upon a contingent event would itself be contingent, prior to the occurrence of any member of the causal series of which it was itself a member. Of course it is customary to deny that causation does involve necessitation, and this is correct if such necessity be considered logical (and thus predicable only of statements or propositions), but on the other hand there is a fairly clear sense in which, for instance, water *cannot but* boil under certain conditions, or a man who is decapitated *must* die, and so forth, and it is simply the modality expressed by such words as "cannot but" or "must" in such uses which is here called "nomical." Also, some would deny that there *are* any contingent events, in this sense, but I have only made it an hypothesis that there are, and I am in any case not trying to prove they exist by defining them.

(4) *Temporal necessity*, which might less misleadingly be called "irrevocability" or "unalterability,"[25] applies to any event that has happened, and is thus relative to a date. Thus

necessarily e ≡ e has already occurred,

and a temporally contingent event is thus simply one which has not yet occurred, an event temporally incompatible with it having likewise not yet occurred. This is perhaps the strangest kind of contingency yet, but no questions are begged by introducing it. What this notion calls attention to is just this obvious, and in other contexts trivial, fact: that nothing that may be in the past is in any way revocable or alterable by what might happen now, whereas this is plainly not the case with such things as may be yet to come. The lapse of time by itself thus imposes a kind of necessity on things; things once capable of being otherwise, or of not existing at all, are no longer so. Until an event has happened, it is sometimes possible that it might not, but once it has happened, it is no longer possible that it did not—and this, despite the fact that it is still possible that it did not happen in any or all of the three foregoing senses of "possible." All this is surely a truism of sorts, but it does indicate an indubitable sense in which past things, but not future things, are by now "of necessity."

It must be added that none of the above distinctions purports to be an enlightening *analysis* of any modal concept. Indeed, I am sure that some senses of necessity cannot be analyzed at all without circularity; it is very doubtful, for instance, whether "cause" can be so analyzed, especially if causal statements be regarded as warranting counterfactual inferences. My only object, then, has been to distinguish these several senses sufficiently to prevent confusion in what follows.

Real and relative contingencies—To speak of an event as contingent is to say, loosely, that it might or might not happen, that its occurrence is neither necessitated nor ruled out; but this, in the light of the foregoing distinctions, can mean any of several things.

It might mean (a) that a statement asserting its occurrence is logically contingent. But this is not remotely what Aristotle was thinking. In saying that the assumption of truth for a prediction requires necessarily the occurrence of what is predicted, he emphatically does not mean that such an assumption entails that the prediction is necessary or its denial self-contradictory—it is events, not statements, which are spoken of as necessary or contingent.[26] Moreover, this interpretation would abolish any distinction between logically necessary and contingent statements, or between false and self-contradictory ones, which would be an absurdity, especially if ascribed to Aristotle.

Again, to speak of an event as contingent might mean (b) that it is uncertain, i.e., not known, whether the event has occurred, is occurring, or will occur.[27] I have called this kind of contingency "epistemic"; it can also be called "relative," being always relative to someone's knowledge of things. If, for instance, an Athenian had said in 400 B.C. that Socrates might or might not die of poisoning, he would have meant in part at least, that it was not known whether this would happen. Now being a very ordinary sense of contingency, it is exceedingly easy to force it upon Aristotle's arguments; indeed, many philosophers have insisted that this is the only kind of "contingency," other than logical, that is intelligible.[28] But it would be absurdly incorrect to so interpret Aristotle: from the mere fact that this or that person may not *know* whether something is going to happen, it hardly follows that it is neither true nor false that it *is* going to happen,[29] and Aristotle cannot be considered so dull as to have imagined that anything of this sort *does* follow.

Or again, one might mean by contingency (c) that natural causal processes are themselves ambiguous with respect to some outcome or other, that it is really undetermined by anything past or present whether an event of a given description is going to happen. This sort of contingency, which I have called "nomical," might also be called "real" contingency, being not relative to this or that man's powers of prediction but rather belonging to the very nature of things. And it is what our aforementioned Athenian could further have meant in saying that Socrates might or might not die of poisoning; that is, he might have meant, especially if he were philosophical, not only that *he* was uncertain about the outcome of things but that it was "uncertain," i.e., as yet undetermined, by nature; that the state of the world was then causally compatible with either of at least two futures, the one containing that event and the other not. And it is in *this* sense that I would understand Aristotle, since (i) I believe that some things are contingent in this sense, (ii) we have good reasons to think that Aristotle thought so too, and (iii) this interpretation is absolutely required in order that Aristotle's thesis can be rendered even plausible.

Finally, reference to an event as contingent might mean (d) that the outcome, i.e., its occurrence or nonoccurrence, has not already been decided one way or the other by the mere lapse of time—which is what I have called "temporal" contingency. One might, in short, simply be making the point that an event of a given description has not happened *yet*. Now one naturally wants to think that this is all Aristotle had in mind—else why should he have regarded contingencies as belonging to the future only, never to the past? But this, too, would be wrong. Aristotle did not hold that *all* statements having reference to the future are neither true nor false, though he can hardly have doubted that such statements do indeed have reference to things that have not happened yet.

Aristotle's doctrine should, therefore, be construed as one concerning not merely contingent events, in the sense of real or nomical contingency—as this belongs to past events no less than to future ones—and not merely events of the future, or temporally contingent things—as some of these may be already determined—but as one concerning the *combination* of these. And it is this combination of modal notions which makes his arguments so enormously liable to confusion and at the same time so profound. His claim is, therefore, that (a) if an event of a given description is really contingent in the sense given, i.e., not yet nomically determined, and (b) if the outcome of things, i.e., the occurrence or nonoccurrence of the event in question, has not already been decided merely by the lapse of time, such that it irrevocably has happened or has failed to happen—in short, if the thing in question is a future contingency—then (c) any statement asserting or denying that it will happen is not (yet) true, but also not (yet) false.

Summary.—We can now summarize the argument in this fashion. Using the general notion "incapable of being otherwise" and "necessary" interchangeably, we may say:

If the statement "*e* has happened" is *true*, given a descriptive interpretation for "*e*," then the event *e* is no longer capable of being otherwise; i.e., it is unalterable, with respect to its occurring, failing to occur, or occurring otherwise than as described, by anything that happens between the time of *e* and the present, (however nomically contingent *e* may be). Or, calling this statement "*p*,"

(1) ("*p*" is true) ⊃ (necessarily, *e*).

Note that this is *not* saying either (a) that since one proposition necessarily entails another, then it entails that that other is necessary, nor (b) that "*e* has happened" is logically necessary, nor (c) that a proposition can entail an event, nor (d) that the truth of "*p*" entails that *e* is nomically determined, nor (e) that *p* is the cause of *e*.

By identical reasoning, if the statement "*e* will happen" is *true*, given a descriptive interpretation for "*e*," then the event *e* is henceforth incapable of being otherwise; i.e., it is unalterable, with respect to its occurring, failing to occur, or occurring otherwise than as described, by anything that happens between the time of *e* and the present (however nomically contingent *e* may be). Calling this statement "*q*,"

(2) ("*q*" is true) ⊃ (necessarily, *e*).

And note here, too, that this is not to be given an interpretation similar to *any* of the five just rejected.

Now one feels no inclination to deny the consequent of (1). That is, once an event has happened, it *is* incapable of being otherwise, i.e., it is *now* impossible that it should not have happened, however nomically contingent it may have been. Hence, one feels no inclination to deny the antecedent, viz., that the statement may be true.

But we *do* deny the consequent of (2), i.e., we deny that *e* is incapable of being otherwise—for instance, that it is incapable of not occurring at all—so long as it is as yet future, *unless* something else already exists nomically sufficient for its occurrence, i.e., unless *e*, though future, is already causally necessitated by what exists already, and hence is not a real contingency. Denying the consequent (with this important qualification), then, we deny also the antecedent, viz., that the statement "*q*" is true. By similar inference, we deny also that "*q*" is false.

III: ANSWERS TO OBJECTIONS

First objection.—The truth values of propositions are no function of time. More precisely, a correspondence theory of truth, such as Aristotle assumes, does not at all require the *present* existence of facts for propositions to agree or conflict with, but only the existence of such facts at some time or other.

C. A. Baylis directed this criticism at Lukasiewicz' arguments,[30] which are essentially those of Aristotle, and Donald Williams has on the same and other grounds rejected *all* theories which deny truth about the future.[31] Baylis suggests that it is no better to argue that a proposition referring to the future cannot be true or false, on the ground that there is *not yet* any definite fact with which it can agree or conflict, than to argue that one referring to the past cannot be true or false, on the ground that there is *no longer* any fact to make it such; and both Aristotle and Lukasiewicz, like everyone else, admit that statements about the past are either true or are false. And Donald Williams, making the same point, says that "all these arguments are strangely selective . . . in making much of supposed difficulties about the future which are quietly ignored as they equally affect the past and present."[32]

Reply.—This criticism quite misses the point, for Aristotle's argument is not to the effect that because some facts do not yet exist, propositions about them are neither true nor false. It was not just their temporal distance that bothered him, but their contingency, or rather, the contingency of some of them. There is thus in Aristotle's philosophy no general denial of truth about the future. The motions of the heavenly bodies and the alterations of the seasons, for instance, are entirely "according to necessity," he thought. Hence, being uniform and determined, nothing stands in the way of there being truths about them in advance of their occurring.[33] We can thus see how little force there is in Williams' remark that "even Aristotle, when he said 'All men are mortal,' did not mean merely that all men living at the moment were mortal,"[34] or his further comment that reference to an eclipse tomorrow, rather than to a sea fight, "would not find us half so receptive of the suggestion of its unreality."[35] Neither man's mortality nor celestial motions are among those "things that can be otherwise."

Second objection.—All temporal references in statements are in principle eliminable, if replaced by explicit references to dates; that is, variations of tense, and hence explicit or implicit references to *nows* and *thens*, can be eliminated from statements altogether without changing their meanings and hence without changing their truth values. The advantage in doing so is that there is removed any temptation to think of the truth values of tensed statements as changing with the lapse of time; any proposition, when so expressed with date or time, appears as an eternal truth, if a truth at all. Instead, for instance, of saying, "Socrates was executed," and thereby having on our hands a tensed statement which it might be tempting to think could not have been true during

Socrates' lifetime, but which became true immediately thereafter, one can just say, tenselessly, "Socrates *is* executed in 399 B.C.," which amounts to the same thing. And this is fatal to Aristotle's thesis, for if the statements, e.g., "There will be a sea fight tomorrow" and "There was a sea fight yesterday," uttered on separate days with a day intervening and both referring to the same event, are equivalent to "There is a sea fight on —," the date replacing the blank, then it is obviously impossible to say that some of these are true, or are false, while one of them is neither.

St. Thomas thought that what is essentially this view holds for all propositions, necessary or contingent, known to God, since "His knowledge is measured by eternity,"[36] and logicians have tended to take the same view in order to facilitate logical analysis.[37] Bertrand Russell,[38] A. J. Ayer,[39] Nelson Goodman,[40] and J. N. Findlay[41] have all advocated the elimination of tense for certain purposes to achieve clarity and precision, the last declaring that "if we avoided the adverbs 'here' and 'there,' if we purged our language of tenses, and talked exclusively in terms of dates and tenseless participles, we should never be involved in difficulties." Indeed, it has been persuasively argued that it was only by historical accident that variations ever came to be made on verbs to indicate temporal rather than spatial direction in the first place, and that such variations can, in any case, be eliminated, just as we avoid "spatial tenses" by explicit reference, when necessary, to locations.[42] It is in terms of this view that Donald Williams is able to speak of "the totality of being, of facts, or of events as spread out eternally in the dimension of time as well as the dimensions of space"[43] and to say that "there 'exists' an eternal world total in which past and future events are as determinately located, characterized, and truly describable as are southern events and western events."[44]

Reply.—First, this argument begs the question by simply *assuming* that future contingency statements are already either true or false—precisely the thing at issue—and then offering those very statements, irrelevantly adorned with dates, as an argument.[45]

Secondly, the objection is mistaken anyway, for in fact one *cannot* convey the same information and avoid the systematic ambiguity of "now" and "then" just by substituting dates for tenses. This can be done *only* if an additional statement is supplied in order to complete the information so easily completed by the use of tense, and this additional statement must contain a temporal reference relative to *now*.[46] That is, it must be a statement to the effect that the date mentioned is earlier than, contemporaneous with, or future to *now*—precisely the thing that the use of dates was intended to avoid. Upon being told, for instance, that "Socrates is executed in 399 B.C.," I by no means get the idea that he has already *been* executed, unless I am *also* told, or happen somehow to know, that 399 B.C. is *before now*, that it is *now past*. Of course nearly everyone does know this, but only because we happen to have been taught how past and future times can be designated by numbers and what numbers designate, at various times, what is designated by "now." An ignorant man might not know this at all; but he would have to be more than ignorant to have no sense of the difference between things past and things yet to come.

Third objection.—From the truth of a statement that an event of a given description has happened, there is no temptation to infer that it *had* to happen, or that its occurrence was in any way necessitated by this posterior truth. Indeed, it might be quite *certain* that it happened, or even that it happened contingently—from which it plainly follows, not that it was not contingent after all, but that it was. But similarly, from the truth of a statement that an event of a given description *will* happen, it does not at all follow that it *must* happen, nor that its occurrence is somehow necessitated by this anterior truth, but only that it will in fact occur. Indeed, it might be quite *certain* that it will occur, or even that it will occur contingently—from which it plainly follows, not that it will not be contingent after all, but that it will. Aristotle's confusion thus results from the feeling that if it is antecedently true that an event of a certain kind will happen, then that event is by that truth *obliged* to happen and that hence there is nothing anyone can do to prevent it—whereas all that follows is that nothing will in fact be done to prevent it, that no condition nomically sufficient to prevent it will arise.[47]

More precisely, let *e* be some event, such as my coughing tomorrow, which, let us assume, is going to happen, and *f* another event, such as my taking cough medicine meanwhile, which is not going to happen but which would be such that, if it did happen, it would prevent *e*. Consider, then, these four statements:

(1) *e* will occur.

(2) If *f* were to occur, then *e* would not occur.

(3) *f* will not occur.

(4) *f* might occur.

Now it is evident (a) that the first two of these statements entail the third, and (b) all four may be true. Hence, (c) no combination of them can entail that the last is false. Therefore, the truth of (1) cannot entail that *e must* happen, or that it cannot be prevented, because (4), which we can assume is also true, entails the opposite, viz., that something might happen which would prevent it.

Reply.—This argument also begs the question, for it just *assumes* that our thesis is mistaken and conceals that assumption by applying it, not to the event *e*, to which our attention is mainly directed, but to *another* event, *f*, concerning which the very same difficulties that were initially raised concerning *e* now arise all over again.

For if, in the first place, *f* is a real and not a relative future contingency—that is, if nothing has yet occurred which is nomically sufficient either for the occurrence of *f* or for its non-occurrence—then it is not already true that it will occur, on the basis of the arguments heretofore given. By the same token, it is not yet true that it will not. Therefore, if it is assumed that statement (4) is true, and "might" is given the sense of real contingency, then it cannot be simply assumed that (3) is true also without begging the question. *If* (4) is true, then (3), according to Aristotle's and my arguments, is neither true nor false.

But if, on the other hand, *f* is not a real future contingency, then something already exists which is nomically sufficient either for its occurrence or for its nonoccurrence; i.e., either *f* or *not-f* is already nomically determined. But in that case, though (3) may indeed be true, (4) is no longer true, if "might" is given the sense of real contingency; for *f* is now by hypothesis not a contingency, whereas statement (4) asserts that it is.

So in either case, premise (b) of the argument, that all four statements may be true, must be rejected; or at any rate, it clearly cannot be used to *refute* our thesis but can be accepted only *after* our thesis has been refuted without using it.

Fourth objection.—One cannot find any general difference between past and forthcoming events, other than the difference in time, and Aristotle does not rest his thesis upon the mere futurity of future contingencies, this being something they have in common with future necessities. For when the various senses of "contingent" are examined, it is found that past and future events are contingent in the same ways and that the only difference left between them *is* a merely temporal one.

The same logical possibilities apply to both predictions and retrodictions, for instance, the only logical impossibility being, in either case, that an event of a given description both does and does not occur.[48] Again, the same epistemic possibilities apply in both cases, there being ever so many things of the past concerning which we know nothing and can only say that, for all we know, they might have existed, or might not. Indeterminacy, again, belongs to past events no less than to future ones, if it belongs to anything at all, a causally undetermined event being no less so by the mere accident of being now past. So we are left with no way of distinguishing future contingencies from past ones other than by their temporal direction from us, which is by hypothesis irrelevant.

If, accordingly, statements about future contingencies are neither true nor false, then we should accept the same conclusion as applied to past ones, or else say, as Aristotle did not, that the mere futurity of an event, unlike pastness, renders statements about it neither true nor false. Or else, conversely—and this is what most philosophers believe—if there are truths about past events, including contingent ones, there is no reason for doubting that there are truths about future ones too.[49]

Reply.—It is not the futurity of future contingencies, nor the nomical contingency of them, upon which our thesis rests, but the combination of the two. When something has *happened*, then however contingent it may have been, its occurring excludes the possibility of something incompatible with it happening at the same time, whereas in the case of some (not all) ostensibly future things, nothing has happened to exclude the possibility of something else happening then instead. In Aristotelian concepts, this is to say that when a potentiality in opposite directions has become actualized in one of these directions, there ceases to be any potentiality for the opposite, the antecedent alternative possibilities having been forever foreclosed by the one that has now become actual.[50] Nothing, however, now excludes any real contingency for the future and nothing will, *until* it is excluded by the realization of its opposite or of something nomically sufficient for the realization of its opposite; that is, until it has ceased to be a *future* contingency.

Putting this another way, we can say that there is only one possible past but many possible futures. There are, indeed, ordinary interpretations according to which this is absurd, but there is another according to which it is true. It is part of what people mean in saying, as Aristotle said, that the past cannot be "undone," no matter what indeterminism or haphazardness there may be it in.[51] The past consists of everything that has happened, and even if we should suppose that any or all of these things might easily have been otherwise, the fact that they have happened renders impossible forever after the occurrence of anything else in their place. The future, too, consists of everything that will happen; but here, nothing has happened to preclude the occurrence of *either* of two or more incompatible events. Concerning a future contingency, we can say only *if* it occurs then the occurrence of anything incompatible with it is excluded; but concerning a past contingency, we express the fact by saying *since* it occurred everything incompatible with its occurring is excluded.[52] The future *is* alterable, and not merely in the trivial sense of being alterable by our own forthcoming efforts but by the mere *lapse of time*, which itself reduces to zero what were once many alternative future possibilities.[53] One may indeed say that when tomorrow comes, we shall find its contents as fully determinate and exclusive of things incompatible with those contents as we now find the contents of yesterday, and this is true; but it only means that with the lapse of time, what were once alternative possibilities have dwindled until reduced to zero by those which have become actual.[54]

If, then, in the sense explained, there is no longer any real contingency in things past, we do not express the whole truth in any statement about the past other than by saying of an event of this or that description that it *did happen* or that it *did not*. In the case of future contingencies, however, it expresses the whole truth to say of one of them that it *might happen* or it *might not*.[55] It cannot be true now that it will, for this means more than "might," nor can it be true now that it will not, for this means more than "might not." The lapse of time, and not merely the increase of our knowledge and experience, can confute our statement that it will happen as well as our statement that it will not, whereas only the increase of knowledge, and not merely the lapse of time can confute our beliefs about things past and done.[56]

Fifth objection.—Aristotle's arguments rest on a common amphiboly, treating as equivalent certain statements which can indeed be expressed in the same way but which are really quite different in what they assert. One is

necessarily, *p* or *not-p*,

understood in the first place as meaning that the whole disjunction is necessary (which is true) but then understood to mean that one or other of the disjuncts by itself is necessary (which hardly follows). Another is

if *p*, then necessarily *p*,

understood first as meaning that the whole hypothetical statement is necessary (which is true) and then to mean that the consequent, by itself, is necessary (which is by no means the same).

Moreover, if every true proposition is in some sense necessary, then every false one must in a similar sense be impossible; indeed, Aristotle says as much: "That which is must needs be when it is, and that which is not must needs not be when it is not."[57] But if we combine these suppositions with his further claim that a proposition may be contingent, we can, by elementary rules of logical inference, get the absurd result that if a proposition is contingent, then it is false and hence impossible, but also that it is true and hence necessary. Thus, in obvious notation:

$$(1)\ p \supset Np$$
$$(2)\ \sim(Np) \supset \sim p$$
$$(3)\ Cp \supset \sim p,$$

and so on. And:

$$(4)\ \sim p \supset Ip$$
$$(5)\ \sim(Ip) \supset p$$
$$(6)\ Cp \supset p,$$

and so on. And this is absurd.

Reply.—If Aristotle had argued (1) that it is necessary that every proposition or its denial is true, and that therefore every proposition is itself necessarily true, or its denial necessarily true, or (2) that a proposition necessarily entails itself, and therefore necessarily entails that it is itself a necessary proposition, then his arguments would be as "swaggeringly invalid" as Donald Williams, who ascribes them to Aristotle, has claimed.[58] But in fact he says nothing like this. Someone might be tempted to adopt Aristotle's thesis on the basis of such amphibolies, but Aristotle did not,[59] and neither do I.

The *reductio ad absurdum* of the second part of this criticism is question begging, for it simply *assumes* that if a proposition is not true, then it is false, and if not false, then true—precisely the point at issue. Thus, the transposition of step 2 is sufficient for asserting "$\sim p$" only if this is read "*not-p*." This cannot be equated with "*p* is false" without begging the question. Again, step 5 is not even correctly symbolized; the consequent must read "$\sim(\sim p)$," meaning "it is not the case that *not-p*"—which does not mean that *p* is true. Moreover, step 3 is accomplished only by substituting "contingent" for "not necessary," and step 6 by substituting the same for "not impossible." But "contingent" means "not necessary *and* not impossible"; it does not mean "not necessary *or* not impossible." A thing which is impossible is indeed not necessary—but not therefore contingent; similarly, a thing which is necessary is indeed not impossible—but again, not therefore contingent. These distinctions are simply obliterated by this kind of criticism.

Sixth objection.—Whether or not there is any omniscient being, the conception of one involves no evident absurdity. But an omniscient being would by definition know everything, and hence everything that is going to happen, and a being less than omniscient can know something of the future. And if any man or god might know which of various alternative contingent things are going to happen, then it must already be true, though not therefore necessary, that those things will happen, and that things incompatible with them, while not impossible, will not happen.[60]

Reply.—An omniscient being would not be one who knows everything, simply, but one who knows everything that is knowable.[61] If there is anything that cannot be known—and of course there are infinitely many such things, for example, all false propositions—then even an omniscient being cannot be expected to know it. This kind of qualification was presupposed by the Scholastics when God's *omnipotence* was considered, the view of St. Thomas being, for example, that God can do only whatever is metaphysically capable of being done; if anything is inherently impossible, then it is idle to expect that God should do it.[62]

With this qualification, the question becomes whether things that are future and contingent are knowable. Now of course they are not knowable by inductive inference, but that is *not* the question. The question is whether *any* degree of prescient or sapient power would enable one to know which of several alternative contingencies will in time come about, assuming there are real contingencies.

It seems evident that it would not. For in the first place, knowledge can be only knowledge of what is true, and it has been our main point to prove that statements about future contingencies are neither true nor false. To argue, then, that such statements must be true, since they are known to God, if there is a God, is plainly circular.

Secondly, if the future is partially undetermined and in its very nature ambiguous, an omniscient being would have to comprehend it just that way. This alone would be knowledge of the future; to see it as otherwise, to comprehend it as already determinate and to judge exactly what is going to happen, is not knowledge but only the obscurity of guesswork and error.[63] Of course on this view an omniscient being would know more at one time than at another, but this need not be inconsistent with the idea of omniscience; at any time such a being would know all there is to know, and this ought surely to suffice.[64]

I think the only rejoinder that can be made to this is that, as Boethius and many others after him put it, "foreknowledge is not the cause of any necessity in things to come."[65] This point is iterated often, as if it left nothing more to be settled. Gilbert Ryle, for instance, observing that neither an "anterior truth" nor the knowledge of it could *cause* any event to happen, adds the similar point that propositions can never *entail* events but only other propositions.[66] Now all this is true, but it is irrelevant to what is here being asserted. I am not saying, nor did Aristotle, that foreknowledge would *cause* this thing or that to happen,[67] or that propositions, known or unknown, *entail* events, all of which is surely nonsense, but rather that the supposition of foreknowledge *is* inconsistent with the claim that any of several alternative futures might become real, using "might" in the sense of real and not relative contingency. For the assumption that any one of these futures, no matter which, is already known, and hence will in fact come into being, is incompatible with the theory of real contingency, viz., that some other future is no less likely to come into being than that one.

Seventh objection.—Suppose someone, "*A*," indulged in prophecy, asserting, "Henry will sneeze tomorrow," and another person, "*B*", following Aristotle's principles, replied, "No, he might, or he might not; it cannot yet be true either that he will or that he will not, this being in the realm of contingencies." Tomorrow comes, and Henry sneezes. *A*, it would seem, can now say, "I said he would sneeze, and he did, so what I said was true, while you, in denying that what I said was true, are now shown to have been wrong." This comment by *A* seems reasonable, for it certainly seems that yesterday *A* had something that *B* did not have—namely, a true opinion. Of course, *B* did not say Henry would not sneeze, but still, his opinion was not as good as *A*'s—for *A*'s opinion, we now discover, was true, while *B*'s was just noncommittal.

Reply.—The most this argument can be claimed to prove is that *either A*'s prophecy was true *or* that it *became* true, just as it became fulfilled,[68] through the lapse of time and the reduction to zero of alternative possibilities. There is nothing in it to show that it *was* antecedently true, any more than that it was antecedently fulfilled. Or to put it otherwise, all the argument shows is the trivial fact that when "tomorrow" had ceased to be tomorrow and had become today, it contained just those events which then happened; it does not show that, on the day before, it was *going* to contain those rather than alternative ones. No advantage, in the way of true opinion, can be claimed by *A* as having obtained when he first made his prediction, for all he can claim is that it was *fulfilled*—which suffices for any wagers that were made. The apparent advantage of his opinion over *B*'s is only an ex post facto sort of one—much like the advantage one might have who, by taking one path rather than another, stumbles upon a fortune. *B*, on the other hand, has had from the beginning a real advantage, for he claimed the future to be ambiguous and unsettled—as in fact it then was. His opinion, unlike *A*'s, did not have to wait to become true but was true from the start. It only *became* an inadequate opinion, but not disconfirmed, when *A*'s prediction came true, that is, when the event in question ceased to be a future contingency and to admit of any possibility of being otherwise.

It might be said that if we allow *B*'s opinion to have been true in advance, then nothing prevents *A*'s opinion from having been true as well. But this overlooks the fact that *A*'s statement concerns a future contingency, whereas there is nothing of contingency in *B*'s proposition that Henry might sneeze or he might not. We need not wait upon anything to see whether this is so.

Again, it might be said that *A*'s statement can be reformulated to say, "The belief that Henry will sneeze, while perhaps not true now, will become true" and that this assertion is about a future contingency no less than the first. But this complication introduces nothing new into the original argument; for *B* could reply that it might become true or it might not, the rest of the argument then proceeding exactly as before, only with more words.

NOTES

1 *De Int.*, ch. ix.

2 See C. A. Baylis, "Are Some Propositions neither True nor False?" *PS*, III (1936): 156–66; Donald Williams, "The Sea Fight Tomorrow," in *Structure, Method and Meaning*, eds. P. Henle, H. M. Kallen, and S. K. Langer (New York, 1951), pp.280–306; A. N. Prior, "Three-valued Logic and Future Contingents," *PQ*, III (1953): 317–26; Leonard Linsky, "Professor Donald Williams on Aristotle," *PR*, LXIII (1954): 250–52; Donald Williams, "Professor Linsky on Aristotle," ibid, 253–55; Gilbert Ryle, "It Was to Be," in *Dilemmas*, (Cambridge, 1954), pp.15–35; R. J. Butler, "Aristotle's Sea Fight and Three-valued Logic," *PR*, LXIV (1955): 264–74; G. E. M. Anscombe, "Aristotle and the Sea Battle," *Mind* n.s., LXV (1956): 1–15.

3 *Op. cit.*

4 "On a So-called Paradox," *Mind* n.s., LXII (1953): 65.

5 *Op. cit.* Cf. the introductory lecture of this collection.

6 "The Sea Fight Tomorrow," pp.284, 291.

7 Aristotle believed that "$p \vee {\sim}p$" is true for any interpretation of "*p*," including statements of future contingencies, if understood in the *sensus compositionis*. Neither "true" nor "false" can be predicated of the constituents of an interpretation of that law, however, if "p" is a statement about a future contingency. Aristotle could accordingly accept the first but not the other two of the following formulations as applying to any statements whatever, including future contingency statements: (1) "If a state-

ment is true, its denial is false, and if false, its denial is true"; (2) "Each statement is true, or, if not true, then false"; (3) "If two propositions contradict each other, one must be true."

[8] *De. Int.* 18b 5–9. All quotations are from the Oxford translation of E. M. Edghill, ed. W. D. Ross.

[9] Ibid, 18b 33–36.

[10] Ibid, 18b 36–38. Cf. Ryle, *Op. cit.*, pp.16–17.

[11] *De Int.* 18b 13–16.

[12] Ibid, 18b 30–31.

[13] Ibid, 19a 9–20.

[14] Ibid, 19a 32–35.

[15] Linsky, *op. cit.*, 252, interprets Aristotle as abolishing this distinction, comparing his philosophy to that of Leibniz in this respect. Cf. Butler, *op. cit.*, 267–68.

[16] H. Van Rensselaer Wilson, "Causal Discontinuity in Fatalism and Indeterminism," *JP*, LII (1955): 70.

[17] *Metaph.* Γ 3. Cf. *De Gen. et Corr.* II, 10, 337a 34 ff.; also, W. D. Ross, *Aristotle*, (London, 1949), p.164.

[18] Cf. *Metaph.* Θ 2, 1046a 38–1046b 25; *Phys.* 251a 28.

[19] *Metaph.* Θ. 4, 1047 1–1048a 16. Cf. also H. H. Joachim, *The Nicomachean Ethics* (Oxford, 1951), pp.108–10. This distinction is not consistently maintained, for Aristotle sometimes connects contingency with *matter* as such. Cf. also *Metaph.* Θ 8, 1050b 6–14: "Every potency is at one and the same time a potency of the opposite."

[20] *Metaph.* Θ 5, 1047b 35–1048a 11. Cf. Joachim, *op. cit.*, p.109.

[21] Cf. *De. Int.*, ch. xiii; also Yehoshua Bar-Hillel, "Mr. Weiss on the Paradox of Necessary Truth," *PSt*, VI (1955): 92–93.

[22] Cf. W. V. Quine, "Notes on Existence and Necessity," *JP*, XL (1943) 121.

[23] Cf. Nelson Goodman, "On Likeness of Meaning," in *Semantics and the Philosophy of Language*, ed. Leonard Linsky (Urbana, Ill., 1952), p.68.

[24] "Nomic necessity" has been used by R. B. Braithwaite and W. E. Johnson. "Etiological necessity" has been used by C. J. Ducasse.

[25] Cf. Butler, *op. cit.*, 269.

[26] Prior, *op. cit.*, 324, has shown that Aristotle was not thinking of logical necessity in these arguments.

[27] Cf. Anscombe, *op. cit.*, 12.

[28] Hobbes is an excellent example: "All propositions concerning future things, contingent or not contingent . . . are either necessarily true, or necessarily false; but we call them contingent because we do not yet know whether they be true or false; whereas their verity depends not upon our knowledge, but upon the foregoing of their causes" (*The Metaphysical System of Hobbes*, Open Court edition, ed, by M. W. Calkins, pp.78–79). Cf. C. J. Ducasse, "Truth, Verifiability, and Propositions about the Future," *PS*, VIII (1941): 331–33.

[29] Cf. Baylis, *op. cit.*, 163.

[30] Ibid, 162.

31 "The Sea Fight Tomorrow," pp.294 ff.

32 Ibid, pp.294–95.

33 *De Gen. et Corr.* II. 11, 337b 35; *Metaph.* Δ 5, 1015b 14; *Eth. Nic.* VI. 3, 1139b 24. Cf. Anscombe, *op. cit.*, 6–7.

34 "The Sea Fight Tomorrow," p.286.

35 Ibid, p.290.

36 *Summa Theologica*, pt. I, q.14, art.13. Donald Williams expresses the same idea ("The Sea Fight Tomorrow," p.283): "The most accidental and ephemeral proposition—that the dog's tail twitches at just such and such a moment, for example—is likewise an eternal truth, if it is true at all. It was true when the sun was formed; it will be true when the sun explodes or is extinguished."

37 Cf. W. V. Quine, *Elementary Logic* (Boston, 1941), p.6, (quoted by Williams, "The Sea Fight Tomorrow," p.286).

38 *Inquiry into Meaning and Truth* (London, 1940), p.113.

39 *Philosophical Essays* (London, 1954), p.186.

40 *The Structure of Appearance* (Cambridge, Mass., 1951), p.297.

41 "Time: A Treatment of Some Puzzles," in *Essays on Logic and Language*, ed. Antony Flew (New York, 1951), p.53.

42 Williams, "The Sea Fight Tomorrow," pp.287 ff. Cf. his "The Myth of Passage," *JP*, XLVIII (1951): 459–60.

43 "The Sea Fight Tomorrow," p.282.

44 Ibid, pp.305–06.

45 Cf. Paul Weiss, *Nature and Man* (New York, 1947), p.12.

46 Cf. Butler, *op. cit.*, 273.

47 This argument is familiar from Leibniz, who in the *Discourse on Metaphysics* (Art.13) argued that whatever is going to happen is already "assured" or "certain", but not therefore any more "necessary" than what has already happened. The same point was well made by Thomas Reid [*Essays on the Intellectual and Active Powers of Man* (1790), vol. I, Essay III, ch. ii], and more recently by Ryle, who asks, "Why does the slogan 'Whatever is, always was to be' seem to imply that nothing can be helped, where the obverse slogan 'Whatever is, will always have been' does not seem to imply this?" (*op. cit.*, p.21).

48 Cf. Baylis, *op. cit.*, 161–62.

49 Cf. Reid, *op. cit.*, vol. III, Essay IV, ch. x.

50 See G. Grote, *Aristotle* (London, 1880), pp.115–16. Cf. Paul Weiss, "The Past: Its Nature and Reality," *RM*, V (1952): 508–09.

51 *Eth. Nic.* VI. 2, 1139b: "No one deliberates about the past, but about what is future and capable of being otherwise, while what is past is not capable of not having taken place; hence Agathos is right in saying 'For this alone is lacking even to God, to make undone things that have once been done.'" Cf. St. Thomas, *S. T.* pt. I, *Q.*25, art.4, and Weiss, "The Past: Its Nature and Reality," 511.

52 Cf. Anscombe, *op. cit.*, 11.

53 Donald Williams writes that "as for the irrevocability of past time, it seems to be no more than the trivial fact that the particular events of 1902,

let us say, can not also be the events of 1952" ("The Myth of Passage," 465). But so also, the events of 2002 cannot also be the events of 1952; yet the future is alterable.

54 This point is taken from Charles Hartshorne, *Man's Vision of God* (Chicago, 1941), p.101.

55 Cf. Mary and Arthur Prior, "Erotetic Logic," *PR* LXIV (1955): 57–58.

56 Donald Williams remarks that "there is a wholly unacceptable suggestion in these passages that an event may be contingent before it happens and necessary afterward; that indeed all present and past events . . . are necessary. But in so far as he is persuaded of the truth of his first proposition, it must be by deduction from his own metaphysics of potentiality and tendency, rather than by logic or observation" ("The Sea Fight Tomorrow," pp.290–91). I think this interpretation is right but the evaluation wrong.

57 *De Int.* 19a 23–24. But notice that this is a temporal, and not an ordinary hypothetical statement.

58 "The Sea Fight Tomorrow," pp.291–92.

59 As Linsky, *op. cit.*, 251 and Butler, *op. cit.*, 267–68, have both pointed out.

60 Cf. St. Thomas, *S. T.* pt. I, *Q.*22, art.4. For a brief history of Scholastic opinion on this point, see Philotheus Boehner's edition and study of Ockham's *Tractatus de praedestinatione et de praescientia Dei et de futuris contingentibus*, Franciscan Institute Publications (St. Bonaventure, N.Y., 1945), pp.75, ff.

61 Cf. Weiss, *Nature and Man*, p.13.

62 *S.T.* pt. I, *Q*, 25, art.3.

63 Hartshorne, *op. cit.*, p.98, Cf. Boethius, *The Consolation of Philosophy* (Loeb Classical Library), p.387.

64 Hartshorne (*op. cit.*, pp.104, 139) calls this conception of omniscience "the Principle of Gersonides," after Levy ben Gerson (fourteenth century) who may have been its originator.

65 *Op. cit.*, p.385. Cf. E. Gilson, *The Philosophy of St. Thomas Aquinas* (St. Louis, 1941), p.119.

66 *Op. cit.*, pp.21–23.

67 Aristotle explicitly denied it (*De. Int.* 19b 36).

68 Essentially this point is made by Ryle, *op. cit.*, pp.19–20: "A prophecy is not fulfilled until the event forecast has happened . . . The establishment of incorrectness certainly cancels 'true' but not, as a rule, so fiercely as to incline us to say 'false.' "

69 Cr. Hartshorne, *op. cit.*, p.103.

G. VERBEKE
University of Louvain

The Aristotelian Doctrine of Qualitative Change in *Physics* VII, 3*

I

THE text that we shall try to analyze and to interpret in this exposition is of a particular philosophical interest. Aristotle wonders whether it is possible to translate into terms of qualitative change the most important activities of man, such as technical activities, care of the body, moral conduct and scientific knowledge. The question is thus one of a confrontation between the notion of qualitative change, on the one hand, and certain fundamental forms of human activity, on the other. Such a confrontation makes it possible to define even more precisely the notion of ἀλλοίωσις and to arrive at a more thorough understanding of the distinctive nature of properly human activities.

In order to answer the needs of every day life and embellishment, man makes many artificial objects, houses, beds, tapers, statues and the like. But can we say that all this results from qualitative change introduced by man into a preexisting matter? A similar question can be asked about acquired dispositions, both bodily and psychic. Can beauty and strength of body, acquired by assiduous and regular exercise, be considered as qualitative changes? Do the moral virtues introduce into human existence qualitative modifications of such kind that their acquisition or loss would constitute a change that would be situated on the level of the qualitative equipment? Finally, can the intellectual activity be considered as an ἀλλοίωσις or does it belong to another category accompanied by qualitative change? These are the principal questions Aristotle tries to answer in the text we are discussing.

Before proceeding with the analysis of the answer Aristotle offers, we have to point out that his answer has come to us in a double redaction, one considerably shorter than the other. According to Sir David Ross, the most developed version, which he calls version A, must have

* This is an extensively revised version of a paper presented at the August, 1964 meeting of the SAGP in Amherst, Massachusetts.

been written by Aristotle himself, while the other version, version B, must have been a report of the same or a comparable lecture made by a student. Indeed the general line of the exposition is the same in the two texts, but there are differences which make it difficult to admit that the two versions lead to the same exposition. The sequence of the ideas is not exactly the same in the two redactions; for instance, the example of the finishing of the house by coping and tiling is found in one text in the exposition about technical activity and in the other in the middle of the exposition about bodily dispositions. Moreover, certain other elaborations present in version A are omitted in version B. Aside from the redactional differences it should be noted that the content and the sequence of the ideas are not entirely the same in the two texts. One is tempted to conclude that this double redaction was done by Aristotle himself. On this hypothesis it is easy to understand why version A contains features absent in version B and why the sequence of ideas is not entirely the same in the two texts.

Let us look now at the context in which Aristotle's exposition about qualitative change is presented. Requisite for this purpose is an analysis of the logical structure of the arguments developed in the course of the first three chapters of book VII. The main preoccupation here is the same as in book VIII: Aristotle wants to prove the necessity of a first mover, a principle that is at the source of the cosmic movement. In other words, a first mover has to be admitted, a πρῶτον κινοῦν, since we cannot have an unlimited series of movers and movables that are subordinate to each other (μὴ βαδίζειν εἰς ἄπειρον.) This thesis is important and must be understood in the context of the Aristotelian world. Why this first mover? Experience brings us into contact with movers, which although they may be principles of movement, are not at the origin of the activity they exercise; they are able to move to the extent that they are moved by something else. Their activity exhibits dependence on another being, and as a result the movement of the mover and the moved must be simultaneous (ἀνάγκη ἅμα γίνεσθαι). The point is important in Aristotle's reasoning: if the mover is not capable of moving by itself, but only through constant dependence on something else, then it will not do anything else but communicate the movement that it receives, and the movement it imparts will be simultaneous with the one it receives. Elsewhere Aristotle admits that the movement of each of the members in the series is one numerically; this means that the movement presents itself as a finite event that is situated between two terms, the point of departure and the point of arrival; a limited time will be necessarily the result, the time that is required to travel a finite distance. Aristotle tells us that the movement happens ἔκ τινος εἴς τι. Indeed movement has been interpreted in terms of potency and act. One is in potency in relation to a determined perfection that represents act. The progress that leads from potency to the act thus constitutes a limited course in a limited time. If the point of departure is the same as well as the point of arrival, and if, moreover, the time is identical, the movement is numerically one.

If there is no first mover, the series of movers and movables is infinite. The result will be that the movement of all these movers and movables will be infinite too. But there will have to be a limited time because all these movements are simultaneous and will, consequently, end in a finite time, because the movement of each of the members of the series is limited. One ends thus in a deadlock: an infinite movement would have to be done in a finite time. Aristotle continues his argument by answering an objection: could we not escape this deadlock by admitting that each particular movement is finite, but that an infinite movement is possible in a limited time, if the number of the movers and movables is infinite? Aristotle answers that the infinite number of movers and movables constitutes a unity; all these movers and movables have to touch each other, so that they may communicate the movement to each other. It is of no importance, logically speaking, whether that unity is finite or infinite. What is important is that the movement is infinite in any case because of the infinite number of movers and movables and because such a movement cannot be done in a limited time. To the question, "Why is this movement necessarily infinite if we do not admit a first mover?" Aristotle's answer would be that the movement of an infinite is infinite. Without a first mover the series of movers and movables would be infinite and accordingly their movement would be infinite. Yet the movement of each of the members of the series is necessarily finite and occurs in a limited time; also, because the movements cause each other, they all are simultaneous and happen in a limited time. The antinomy is confirmed: an infinite movement cannot be realized in a limited time. Consequently a first mover has to be admitted as a principle of all movement. An essential point of the reasoning is without any doubt the simultaneity of the movements. If the movement of all these movers and movables is simultaneous, it necessarily is finite.

For Aristotle this simultaneity is realized not only in the case of locomotion, but also in the case of qualitative change. In this last case, mover and movable touch each other without an intermediary of any kind (οὐδέν ἐστι ἀνὰ μέσον), and because they touch each other immediately their movement is simultaneous. Each genuine alteration is produced by sensible factors that cause a determined modification by means of direct action. This is true for sensible perception (sight, hearing, smell, taste) where the extremity of the alterating principle and the beginning of the altered are together. Let us take the case of sight, since here it would seem that there is no continuity between the perceived object and the bodily organ. But such is not the case for the air is contiguous to the perceived object and the body is contiguous to the surrounding air. If a mover, itself moved, moves a movable, then they touch and in that case their movement is simultaneous. The foregoing provides the general context of Aristotle's exposition about qualitative change.

The central concern of Aristotle's exposition seems to be that of proving that in alteration the mover and the movable touch each other without intermediary and that, consequently, the movements are simultaneous. This is why he states right from the beginning of this chapter that alteration may occur in a being that is capable by nature, of being affected by a sensible cause. He wants in this way to avoid movements which, while being accompanied by qualitative changes, are not themselves qualitative changes. It is from this point of view that he wonders whether the making of a tool or the acquisition of a bodily skill, a moral or intellectual excellence can be considered an alteration. In all these cases Aristotle's answer is negative. From his point of view he wants to eliminate from his notion anything that might counteract his argument leading to proving the existence of the first mover. But at the same time he takes the opportunity to state his views on the nature of the superior activity of man, particularly with regard to the nature of knowledge. Since the discussion is on qualitative change, let us first see how quality is defined in the *Categories*.

The term "quality" is explained in different ways (chapter 7):

1. The first use of ποιότης is to indicate a habit or a disposition. According to Aristotle there is a distinction to be made between the two since a habit (ἕξις) is more lasting and permanent than a disposition (διάθεσις). The examples he gives are knowledge and virtue; they are firmly fixed in man and difficult to displace. Mere dispositions, on the other hand, like heat, cold, disease, health, and other qualities of the same kind, can be changed easily. Of course a habit is always a certain disposition, but it is not the case that every disposition is a habit.

2. The term "quality" can also mean an inborn capacity or incapacity, to be distinguished from a mere disposition. The primary examples Aristotle gives are those of the runner, the boxer and the man with good or bad health. A runner is a man who has not only a certain disposition, but also the capacity of doing something without difficulty. A man with good health is said to have the physical capacity of resisting easily all unhealthy influences.

3. The third meaning refers to the affective qualities and affections like sweetness, bitterness, sourness, heat, cold, whiteness, blackness and so on. These qualities are called "passive qualities" not because the things that possess them are affected in any way, but because each of the said qualities is able to produce an affection on the level of perception. Colours, however, are not called passive qualities in the same way as the others; they are passive because they are generated by a certain affection. There is again a distinction to be made between qualities and affections. Qualities are characteristics which last a long time, even throughout one's life. So we may say that on the level of the soul there are some firm characteristics, as irascibility or madness, which are called qualities, while the same characteristics when they are easily lost are said to be affections.

4. The fourth sort of quality is figure and the shape of a thing; also straightness and curvedness and other qualities of this type. Aristotle hesitates to state whether rarity, density, roughness, and smoothness are qualities or not. In his opinion, the term does not so much indicate in these cases a quality as a certain relative position of the parts composing a thing.

II

In *Physics* VII, 3, Aristotle does not take into consideration the second meaning of quality as stated in the *Categories*. According to Pacius the presence of a natural capacity or incapacity does not depend on alteration, but on generation (*ab ortu et generatione*). According to this interpretation, alteration would not be concerned with natural capacity or incapacity.[1] The explanation of Thomas Aquinas is quite different. He interprets Aristotle to mean that natural capacity or incapacity could only be introduced or removed by a change of nature, which is an alteration. Thomas' view is quite clear: Aristotle does not mention natural capacity or incapacity because they are evidently concerned with alteration.[2] According to Sir David Ross the fourfold division of qualities in the *Categories* is not mentioned because it had not yet been worked out.

In any case it is important to note that the correspondence between the *Categories* and the exposition of the *Physics* is not complete. The fact remains that in the latter text Aristotle does not take into account the second meaning of quality mentioned in the *Categories*, i.e., in the sense of natural capacity or incapacity. If the acquisition of a natural capacity depends on generation and consequently is not an alteration, as Pacius contends, why does not Aristotle say so? If, on the contrary, the acquisition of a natural capacity constitutes an alteration, why is this not discussed? The disagreement that we find here between the doctrine of the *Categories* and that of the *Physics* may be added to other much more important points of differences between the *Categories* and other treatises. The disagreement would strengthen the case against the authenticity of the *Categories*.

III

A. *Technical activity* (245b 9–246a 10).

First argument (245b 9–246a 4): it attempts to prove that a change in figure and shape is not an alteration. The argument can be better elucidated if we distinguish between its content and its nature.

(1) *The content*. When a certain unit of matter is moulded and given a new shape, it is not subject to alteration. Alteration is a mere change of quality; therefore the altered thing retains the same appellation as before. For instance, when water becomes warm or cold, we do not cease to call it water, for it is still called so whether warm or cold. This is not the case when a change in the external form occurs as when a ship or a bed has been made out of wood, for then the wood no longer carries the name it had before. In this case we no longer called it "wood", but "wooden bed". However, Aristotle concludes that when a certain matter is given a new shape through human activity, as in the case of the making of a bed or a ship, it is not altered.

(2) *The nature* of the argument. The argument is based entirely on predication or more generally on how we speak. Yet such a manner of reasoning occurs frequently in the writings of Aristotle. It means that he attaches great importance to common opinions and ways of speaking, especially when they are very ancient and generally accepted. Of course the very manner of speaking must be taken in account as being the expression of very ancient and universally admitted opinions. This type of argument often seems to carry great weight for Aristotle.

Second argument (246a 4–10). We have to distinguish again between the content and the nature of the argument:

(1) *The content.* Aristotle now comes to the question of generation. Can the generation of a man or a house or of whatever that can be generated be considered as a case of alteration? The answer he gives is that generation is not an alteration and things generated are not altered. Generation, however, might require a previous alteration; in other words, generation is only possible by a certain alteration of matter, for instance, condensation or rarefaction or calefaction or refrigeration. Matter must undergo previous preparation to receive a certain form. An egg has to be warmed so that the generation of a chicken may be possible. Aristotle thinks we have to distinguish between necessary conditions and generation itself.

(2) *The nature of the argument.* Aristotle clearly wants to avoid the danger of confusion between generation itself and its previous conditions. It is not because generation requires an alteration of matter in order to become possible, that generation itself is to be considered an alteration. Of course, the term "generation" is taken in a very broad sense, for it is also applied to the building of a house. Hence the term denotes more than what the realm of living beings encompasses. It also has meaning with reference to the production of artificial things. Aristotle says it would be absurd to say that a man or a house, when generated, is altered. Again the argument is based on human language; in ordinary speech, the construction of a house or the birth of a man is not called alteration, even if it is preceded by an alteration of the matter involved.

B. *Bodily habits* (246a 10-b 20).

First argument (246a 10-b 2). With regard to habits a distinction must be made between good habits, which are called virtues, and bad ones, which are called vices. According to Aristotle neither of them can be considered as an alteration. The reason is that in his opinion virtue is always a completion, a finishing or perfection. Everything is said to be perfect when it has attained its own virtue, that is, when it has realized in the highest degree what it is by nature. For instance, we have a perfect circle when we have one as good as possible. Each virtue is a kind of completion of a being according to its own nature. Every being reaches its perfection when it realizes its own nature to the utmost degree. According to Aristotle the processes of alteration and the state of perfection are not to be equated. It would be absurd to say that the coping and the tiling of a house are alterations, or to admit that a house in the process of being built is altered.

The same argument clearly applies to vices also since they are not alterations but disturbances or imperfections. The nature of the argument is clear: a habit could not be an alteration. Indeed, there are two kinds of habits, i.e., virtues and vices, and neither of them is an alteration, for virtue is a perfection, a finishing, while vice is an imperfection. The argument cannot be understood without remembering that Aristotle is talking about bodily habits, which is to say, about steady and firm qualities, according to the distinction proposed in the *Categories* between habits and dispositions. The two examples given by Aristotle, namely, a circle and a house, are taken out of the world of corporeal beings. One could object to Aristotle that he is talking again about figures and shapes, as in the first part of the chapter. Nevertheless the point of view is not the same. In our text Aristotle is not immediately concerned with the shape of a circle or a house, but with the perfection or imperfection of the two; in other words he is concerned with the virtues and vices of corporeal beings. The thesis Aristotle puts forward can be summarized as follows: the process by which the perfection or imperfection of a corporeal being is realized is not, strictly speaking, an alteration.

Second argument (246b 2-20). Here Aristotle is still talking about habits of corporeal beings. According to him all these habits exist in a certain relation. They should be thought of as a way of being in relation to something. The relation itself may be internal or external. As an example of internal relation one may cite health or well-being, which can be reduced to a balanced mixture of heat and cold; the same can be said about other virtues and vices, as, for instance, bodily beauty and strength. The relation can be external as well, viz., the relation of a corporeal being to its environment. By corporeal virtues and vices a subject is well or badly disposed towards its proper affections. By "proper affections" he means those influences that from the natural constitution of a thing tend to promote or destroy its existence.

The argument is based on the relative nature of bodily excellences and defects. Aristotle introduces a general principle: what is entirely relative cannot be subject either to alteration or to generation or to change. Bodily habits themselves could not be alterations, nor could their acquisition or loss be so regarded. However, it is quite possible for bodily habits to be generated or corrupted because of an alteration; in other words, alteration may be a necessary condition for the acquisition or loss of bodily habits. For every virtue and every vice is concerned with those things by which the subject is naturally disposed to be altered. Aristotle has in mind such things as hot and cold or wet and dry, elements through the alterations of which the health or disease of the body is produced. The virtue of a body makes its possessor to be unaffected by certain external influences or passive in a suitable way, while vice makes it affected or unaffected in the opposite way. Aristotle's argument is based on *Physics* V. 2, 225b 11. There is strictly speaking no change in a relative being, for if one of the terms is changed, there will be a change in their mutual relation, even if the other term remains what it is. Aristotle concludes that a change of a relative being is only accidental: it depends on the situation of the two terms of the relation. Taking into account that a bodily habit depends on particular relations, we may conclude that it could not be altered in itself and that the acquisition or loss of it could not be considered an alteration.[3]

C. *Habits of the Soul* (246b 20–247a 19).

First argument (246b 20–247a 2). This argument is only indicated because it has already been previously discussed. The habits of the body are a certain way of being in relation. In other words, they exist in virtue of particular relations; therefore, no alteration of them is possible. The same can be said about habits of the soul.

Second argument (247a 2). The same proof has been advanced about bodily habits: some of them, the excellences, are perfections of nature; others, the defects, departures from it. In no case can they be considered alterations, nor can the processes of losing or acquiring them be so.

Third argument (247a 3–5). This, too, is an argument previously discussed in relation to bodily habits. The virtue of the body puts its possessor in good condition to meet his proper affections, while the vice is the source of a bad condition. The same may be applied to the virtues and vices of the soul. Their acquisition or loss is not an alteration and they are not alterations themselves.

Fourth argument (247a 5–19). Virtues and vices of the soul are not alterations; nevertheless, they could not be produced in us without a previous alteration. First of all, it must be noticed that Aristotle is speaking here about moral virtues and vices. According to him they all have to do with bodily pleasure and pain, which always imply an alteration of the sense organ by sensible objects.[4] Indeed, every pleasure consists in an action, a remembrance, or a hope, which are to be traced to a certain alteration of the sense organ. This is very clear in the case of present pleasure; it is produced in us while the sense organ is moved by a pleasant object, just as pain is caused by the action of a painful object. Now it cannot be doubted that the other ways of pleasure and pain result from such present sensation; for a remembrance is no more than the memory of a past sensation, as hope is the expectation of a future one.

According to Aristotle pleasure and pain are produced by an alteration of the sensitive part of the soul, or more precisely, by the alteration of our sense organ stimulated by a sensible object Moral virtues and vices are concerned with pleasure and pain. So it is quite evident that moral virtues and vices are generated or corrupted in consequence of an alteration, i.e., the generation of moral virtues and vices is necessarily accompanied by an alteration, without being itself an alteration. Hence, the acquisition or loss of virtues and vices are not alterations, but habits, produced by the activity of man, as a result of similar actions. The core of the argument seems to be that virtue and vice, being concerned with alterations, could not themselves be alterations.

D. *Intellectual habits* (247b 1–248a 6).

First argument (247b 1–3). This is the same argument as brought forward in the discussion on the bodily habits and the habits of the soul. The intellectual habits also should be considered as a certain way of being in relation to something. Their status of being is a relative one. Although Aristotle gives only one example, namely, that of knowledge, the same can be said about other intellectual habits such as art, prudence, etc. According to the argument, a relation may be changed without any change in the subject of the relation. When I am standing at someone's right, I may come to stand at the same person's left without any movement of mine, simply because the other person has come to my right. The same occurs in the case of knowledge. It is acquired by our mind without it being changed: indeed, it is produced in us by the presence of something else, namely, by the presence of images in our imagination, the contemplation of which is knowledge. According to the *Metaphysics* (I. 1) and the *Posterior Analytics* (II. 19), an experience is formed out of many particulars whose images have been perceived by the sensitive faculty. Out of many such experiences a universal concept is generated. Such knowledge of the universal, Aristotle says, is characteristic of science and art. Therefore, the first principles are arrived at by induction and intuition. So we can say that knowledge depends on the presence of images in our imagination and on the contemplation of them by the intellectual faculty. Knowledge does not mean a change in the intellectual faculty, but a change in the imagination. So the relation of the intellectual habit is changed without any change in its subject.

Second argument (247b 3–7). This argument is based in a certain way on the similarity between intellectual activity and sense-perception. What is claimed here is that there is no generation of seeing and touching. Indeed, these powers of sense-perception depend on the presence of an object. In other words, sense-perception is not an alteration of the sense-organ. So the intellectual activity may be compared to sense-perception; there is no generation of intellectual activity. The exercise or use of knowledge is not a becoming or an alteration.

Third argument (247b 7–13). The first acquisition of knowledge is not generation. Indeed, when we are doubting and are uncertain, our mind is moving, it is searching for truth, it does not know and asks questions. But when it comes to knowing, when it reaches understanding and knowledge, it comes to rest. Knowledge means repose of mind. Aristotle says in *De interpretatione* (3, 16b 19), that verbs have a significance in themselves. The pronunciation of a verb brings the mind of the audience to rest and fixes its attention. The acquisition of knowledge is a coming to rest; that is the original meaning of the Greek verb ἐπίστασθαι. If knowledge consists in the repose of the intellectual faculty, the acquisition of knowledge would not be a generation or an alteration.

Fourth argument (247b 13–248a 6). Aristotle considers now the case of a man who, having a certain knowledge, might be prevented from using it should there be any disturbance of the imaginative faculty. Indeed, he should establish the possibility of contemplating quietly the images in the imaginative faculty. Pacius gives the example of images in water: when the water is moved, we cannot see distinctly the images reflected in it; but it is quite easy to see reflected images in calm water. So it is when our imagination is not troubled by our affections, but is kept calm and quiet by moral virtue. Aristotle offers three examples to explain his argument: drunkenness, sleep and illness. They prevent us from knowing not because they immediately influence our intellectual faculty but because they disturb the images which are contemplated by the mind. When a man awakens out of his sleep, his mind immediately comes to knowing not by a change in the mind but by a change in the imaginative faculty. In the same way when a man acquires knowledge at first; it occurs not by a change in his mind, but by a change in the imaginative faculty. Therefore children are not capable of knowing in the same way as older people, because there is much disturbance and movement in their imaginative faculty. Later on, when this trouble has been taken away by nature (becoming older) or by other factors (teaching and exercise), they also become capable of genuine knowledge. In each case knowledge is preceded by a bodily alteration without being itself an alteration. The conclusion is that alteration occurs only in sensible realities or in the sensitive faculty of the soul but not in the moral and intellectual faculties, unless accidentally insofar as the imaginative faculty has been changed.

IV

By way of conclusion it is important to analyze more profoundly some passages of our text in order to show more concretely Aristotle's conception of human activity.

1. *The nature of knowing*

Aristotle wonders whether the acquisition of intellectual knowledge may be considered a qualitative change of the knowing subject. To answer this question he is obliged to examine the nature of knowing or thinking itself. The essential problem thus is to determine whether thinking is a movement. Aristotle admits that thinking may be accompanied by an alteration. Why is it that children are less capable of knowing and judging than older persons? Because of the restlessness and multiple movements that occur in a young organism, which are only brought to peace with maturing. The exercise of thinking can thus be hindered or hampered by disturbances in the bodily organism; someone who passes from the state of sleep to the state of waking or from drunkenness to sobriety also undergoes a certain alteration. Nevertheless it remains true that thinking cannot be reduced to a case of qualitative change. Instead of being a movement, thinking (as well as moral virtue) appears to be rather a state of rest or immobility.[5] We do not pass from ignorance to knowledge as a result of a movement but by the presence of something else; namely, a sensible image, the contemplation of which constitutes a knowing. In the *De Anima* Aristotle alludes to the same doctrine; intellectual knowing looks more like a state of rest and quiet, than like a movement.[6]

In *De Interpretatione* (16b 20) we find again the same idea treated in his discussion of verbs. Aristotle says that verbs are nouns and possess a determined meaning because the person who pronounces them arrests the hearer's thinking and fixes his attention. Therefore, to know is to come to a state of completion and hence to be no longer in suspense, dissatisfied and waiting. The most fully elaborated text is found at the end of the *Posterior Analytics* (100a 6 ssq.). Aristotle treats here the different stages we must go through to reach the universal: from sense perception we develop memory, from repeated memories of the same subject comes experience, and lastly out of experience develops the stage of proper intellectual knowing, that of art and science. While art is concerned with becoming, science on the contrary looks only to being. Aristotle affirms clearly his position that the universal is entirely at rest in the soul as a unity beside the multiplicity of experiences. It resides as one and is identical in all particulars. Particular sensations serve as a point of departure in the formation of a universal. In the first degree this notion will be the notion of the species acquired from the knowledge of particular beings, because it is in the particular that we shall reach the specific nature. However, this universal notion does not signal cessation of thinking. On the contrary, it can be a new point of departure for arriving at more universal concepts, until first principles become established. Nevertheless it remains true that each universal is at rest in the soul and is the object of contemplation remaining all along identical to itself. In all these passages, knowing is represented as a rest, or at least a temporary one. Thinking is not in search of an object; it possesses the object and stops before it to contemplate it.

What is now the *origin* and the *philosphical bearing* of this doctrine? There is no doubt that the concept of knowledge as a stop and rest can be found in Plato's dialogues. In the *Cratylus* (437A) the participants in the dialogue enter a discussion of the etymology of the term ἐπιστήμη. This word seems to signify stopping (ἵστησι) the soul at things, rather than going round with them. The same etymology is proposed for the word ἱστορία. The word somehow signifies the stopping of the flow (ἵστησι τὸν ῥοῦν). The same is true for the term πιστόν, which also means a cessation of motion, a stop (ἱστάν). The word μνήμη expresses rest in the soul, and not motion (μονή in opposition to φορά). It is obvious that these etymologies have grown out of a certain conception of knowing, rather than being of themselves the origin of such a doctrine; in all the terms that have something to do with knowing a root of stability is sought.

In the *Phaedo* (96B) Socrates asks, what can be the organ of thinking in man. Is the blood the element with which we think, as Empedocles believed, or the air, as Diogenes of Apollonia thought, or the fire, as Heraclitus proposed? Another conception is put forward, probably that of Alcmaeon of Croton, according to which the organ of human thinking would be the brain. It would give birth to sensations of hearing, sight and smell, and these in their turn would produce memory and opinion, once memory and opinion have attained their fixity (τὸ ἠρεμεῖν);

real knowledge would be born through this process.[7] Plato's concern about stability is easy to understand, for any case of knowing, worthy of the name, is related to an unchanging object and since there has to be a relationship between the known object and the knowing subject, stability will be the principle of science itself.[8]

In the *Meno* (97D ff) Socrates estimates the value of true opinions as relative, because they play truant and run away from the soul. In this respect they resemble the statues of Daedalus, that have to be fixed to remain on their places. In turn, true opinions have to be linked up with a causal train of reasoning; they have the nature of knowledge only when they reach stability. Such stability can come only from the world of Ideas. It is through their connection with the world of immutable Ideas that true opinions are lifted to the level of authentic knowledge. Therefore a true opinion may not be considered as scientific knowledge, because its object is not immutable. As long as it does not transcend the changing reality of becoming, it cannot rise to the level of true knowing. Only he who grasps the Ideas is in possession of a knowledge that is above opinion. In the *Meno* Plato also speaks about a knowledge that is intermediary between opinion and knowledge; true opinion is made stable through its connection with the world of unchangeable things by means of a causal reasoning. Once connected with the immutable, true opinion becomes stable.

Plato enters upon the same problem in the *Sophist* (248E). If everything is in movement, knowing is no longer possible. Furthermore, if everything is immovable, thinking as well as life would seem to be impossible. To admit total immobilism of everything that exists is to give up all thinking. Being in its totality contains everything that is immobile and everything movable; to deny one or the other is to engage in insoluble antinomies.

Must it be admitted then that thinking is a kind of movement? Plato never says this, although he does recognize that to think is to act, and that thinking is the most intense activity that man can practise. That is why thinking is inconceivable in an entirely immobile world. Nevertheless it remains true that authentic knowing has as its object the immutable Ideas. Can the intuition of an immutable reality be a movement? What is the problem then that Plato propounds in the *Sophist*? A choice has to be made between immobilism and mobilism; neither of the two theses presented seems to be acceptable due to the nature of human thinking itself. If this nature consists of acting with the immutable as its object, why could not movement and stability be admitted at the same time? In Plato's view, thinking is not an ordinary movement, but rather an act of contemplation with the immutable forms as its object. It is at the same time an activity and a rest. Plato, like Aristotle, maintains that childhood and youth are periods that are not favorable to reflection, because the activity of the mind is hindered by the movements and disturbances of the bodily organism and by affections of all kinds. At the time of birth, when the soul is chained to a mortal body, it does not make use of its intellectual faculties (*Timaeus*, 43A–44A). This doctrine seems to be inspired by Alcmaeon of Croton. In one of the fragments attributed to him we read that man can think as long as his brain is at peace (Hippocrates, *De Morbo Sacro*, 14). According to the same author all sensations are in some way connected with the brain; when they are disturbed and in movement, the sensitive life cannot be practised normally because the channels through which sensations occur are hit and obstructed (Theophrastus, *De Sens.*, 25).

This leads us again to the other aspect of the same doctrine: if knowing is conceived as repose or rest, it might normally be hindered by disturbances of the bodily organism. If Plato and Aristotle conceive intellectual knowledge to be a kind of immobility or rest, this doctrine can be explained from three points of view: first, the etymology of the term ἐπιστήμη: secondly, the physiological conceptions of Alcmaeon of Croton; and finally the theory of Ideas. Consequently, to state that knowing is rest implies that the object of knowing must be stable and that the intuition of the knowing subject must be stable. This means particularly that knowing may not be affected by movements of the body nor by passionate elements.

2. *Psychical activity and alteration*

As Trendelenburg remarked in his commentary on *De Anima*,[9] Aristotle clings strictly to the etymological significance of the term ἀλλοίωσις. It means in fact a "becoming different," "an alteration," a "becoming other" or a "growing to otherness"; what is subject to an ἀλλοίωσις really becomes something different. "In quo premenda est graecae vocis notatio; significat enim ἀλλοίωσις quasi alienationem, ita ut res in aliam rem abeat."[10] That is the reason why alteration is a feature of the sensible world but not of the psychical activities. Aristotle views the latter as perfections. Therefore, there is in Aristotle's mind a clear distinction to be made between realizing one's own perfection, developing in the direction of one's possibilities on the one hand, and, on the other becoming different, i.e., being affected in such a way that one is transformed in one's way of being. Teleologically, each being has to realize a determined end regarding what it is in potency. To actualize this potency is not to become different, but to become more what it is: to reach the achievement of its being. In a passage of the *De Anima* (II 5, 417b 6 ssq.), Aristotle speaks of an ἐπίδοσις εἰς αὐτό (and not εἰς ἄλλο), i.e., the being in question realizes its own perfection. That is why he adds: καὶ εἰς ἐντελέχειαν. This is not so in the case of alteration. Trendelenburg translates the Greek term ἀλλοίωσις by *alienatio*. Instead of becoming entirely what it is, the being that undergoes an alteration is alienated from itself, it digresses from what it is to become different. Affected by external factors, it abandons its way of being to adopt another one. In the same context (*De Anima* II, 5, 417b 2 ssq.), Aristotle tells us that the notion of passivity is not a simple one; for one may be passive in two entirely different ways. First there is *destructive passivity* where a way of being is destroyed by means of an action of a contrary quality. In this case it is right to speak of a certain destruction (φθορά τις), for the being in question is really passive when it acquires a new quality while losing a previous one. Thus, the acquisition of a new way of being is never a pure and simple progress, but always implies a certain loss. In the case of destructive passivity we could say that a reality is destroyed by becoming different, or more precisely, that this reality suffers a destructive action produced by something else which makes it take on a new way of being.

Perfective passivity provides for the acquisition of a perfection that answers the latent potency of a given reality. In that case the being in question does not undergo the influence of an opposite quality and hence there is no destruction, but only a change from potency to act under the influence of an act. There may be external influence involved, but this influence does not work between two opposing terms, one of which prevails over the other. In the case of destructive passivity the influence originates from an opposite quality. Since such is not the case in perfective passivity, we can speak about an achievement, because the influence is exercised by a similar term that possesses *actually* the quality that the other possesses *potentially*. Aristotle applies this principle to the field of knowledge. If someone habitually possesses scientific knowledge, it is possible that at certain moments he may not use his knowledge, while at other moments he may do so. Is this an alteration? Aristotle answers negatively; it is not a question of an alteration, unless we call it another kind of alteration. In this case there is no passage to a state of privation (ἐπὶ τὰς στερητικὰς διαθέσεις), precisely because in such development nothing is destroyed. A being undergoes development in this case without a loss of any kind under the influence of an opposite quality. It might be objected that in this last case a being also becomes something different from what it was before. However, there can be no question here of "becoming different," for what causes activity is not properly the other, but the similar, and the act itself is situated in the nature of this being as potency. Therefore, the act of thinking is not an alteration, and neither is the exercise of a technical activity. For example, an architect does not undergo an alteration when he exercises his art.

In Aristotle's view movement is an activity of that which is imperfect.[11] All movement is but a progress to a terminus and takes its meaning only from the nature itself of this terminus; it is a passage going from a point of departure to a point of arrival. Aristotle's attention in his philosophical analysis of movement concentrates on the two points; the passage is not the center of his attention. He often has been criticized for this emphasis. What is true for movement in general is also applicable to alteration in particular. The issue now is whether we can say that the sensitive faculty undergoes an alteration on account of its own object. This Aristotle denies on the ground that here it is not a question of an alteration, of a true passivity, but of another kind of movement, what he calls ἁπλῶς ἐνέργεια, activity in the absolute sense. What constitutes the proper perfection of the sensitive faculty is the exercise of its activity.

The sensible object actualizes the possibilities of sensitive power. But it is not the case that this power becomes different through the exercise of perception; rather, it becomes even more what it is. Since the end of the activity is not situated outside of the exercise itself, we can say that at the same time "we are seeing and have seen, are understanding and have understood, are thinking and have thought."[12] By means of this elliptical expression Aristotle gives voice to a fundamental doctrine of his psychology; for he had wondered whether it belonged to the philosophy of nature. By stating together both the present and the perfect tenses of the verbs "to see", "to understand" and "to think," he tries to make clear that in the case of the psychical activities, the perfect (i.e., the terminus, the end) is in definite sense in the present. The exercise of the activity constitutes the end; this is not to be found outside the activity itself. In other words, the activity is not in search of a good outside itself. This is why psychical activity is not an ordinary movement, but an ἐνέργεια in the absolute sense.

Aristotle tells us that the act of seeing, as is true of all sensible knowledge, is perfect at each moment of its duration. It is not realized progressively, in terms of evolution; its proper perfection is realized entirely right from the beginning.[13] The same can be said about pleasure; it must be one of the things that are whole and complete, and hence not a movement. Pleasure is realized for shorter or longer periods. This does not mean that the proper form of pleasure would only be reached at the end of this process. At each moment of duration the essence of pleasure realizes itself fully; hence, does not become fuller during the following moments.[14]

If this is true of the sensitive activity, the same will apply to speculative thinking, for it possesses in itself its proper pleasure and is not in search of an end situated outside itself. That is why we can say that this activity is self-sufficient, enjoys a true autarchy, and can exercise itself indefinitely to the degree that man is capable of unlimited activity. Speaking about the activity of God, Aristotle tells us that the prime mover enjoys always a unique and simple pleasure, because his nature is not complex like ours. His is not only an activity of movement but also an activity of immobility (ἐνέργεια ἀκινησίας); and pleasure in this case consists more in stability than in movement. For man the same object may not always be pleasant because our nature is not simple; but there is another element in us as well, inasmuch as we are perishable beings. If the one element does something this activity is unnatural from the point of view of the other element. If man needs change, it is because he is lacking in some way. For any nature that needs change and is lacking, change is essentially imperfect.[15]

Thus, the sphere of movement, strictly speaking, is that of the material world. Man himself is subject to movement, insofar as he partakes of this world and is situated in it. But the nature of man is not simple. Even while being situated in the movement, he is able to overcome it by his physical activity. This activity may not be translated in terms of movement, for it is not something essentially imperfect which terminates in the acquisition of an end. Rather, it realizes itself fully at each moment of its exercise. It is thus an activity of immobility, so far as it is realized in purity.

Let us consider now moral action and ask whether or not it can be translated in terms of alteration. This cannot be so for the reasons already discussed. While acting morally a man does not become someone else but only fully himself; he realizes his latent possibilities. Moral good is not alien to man, nor a kind of a present or reward that is offered to him from outside himself. Moral good is situated in human nature: it is the exercise of the most perfect activity of which man is capable. To become a good man one does not have to become different because each man is above all his intellectual principle.[16]

Moreover the end of moral action is not to be found beyond this action. Aristotle repeats: the εὐπραξία is the end.[17] The moral man practises the good for itself and does not look for anything beyond this action. It is an indispensable condition of the moral action not to be subordinate to something else. He who practises the good for a reason other than the good itself situates himself outside the really moral perspective. In that respect there is a clear difference between technical activity and moral action: the former is oriented towards a distinctive product of activity (e.g., a house or a bed), while the latter finds its achievement in itself and is chosen for itself. If εὐδαιμονία or human perfection consists in the exercise of speculative thinking, that is to say, in the most noble activity of which man is capable, this activity cannot be subordinated to an ulterior finality for then it would cease being an end in itself.

Let us by way of conclusion make a brief summary of what we have said. In Aristotle's view two reasons make it impossible to translate properly human activity in terms of alteration:

(a) In exerting the activity that is proper to him, man does not become different; on the contrary, he realizes himself fully. Human activity grows from perfective passivity, through which man's possibilities are actualized.

(b) The exercise of knowing or moral activity does not have its end outside or beyond action itself. This action constitutes a whole, the essence of which is realized fully from the first instant on, precisely because the aim of action is situated in the action.

The act of seeing, conceiving, thinking, acting morally, realizes at each moment the fullness of its essence and finds its value in itself. It is along such lines that Aristotle essays to describe the world which is properly human in its own distinctive physiognomy.

NOTES

1 *Aristotelis Naturalis Auscultationis Libri VIII* (Frankfurt, 1966), p.840.

2 *In octo libros Physicorum Aristotelis*, ed. P. M. Maggiolo (Rome, 1954), VII, 5, n.914.

3 On the relative nature of bodily habits, cf. Aristotle, *Eudemus or On the Soul*, fr. 7 (Walzer); *Top.* III. 1, 116b 17; VI. 2, 139b 21; VI. 6, 145b 8; *Metaphysics* N 1, 1088a 22 ff.; also Plato, *Republic* IX, 591B; *Philebus* 26B; *Laws*, I, 631C.

[4] Cf. *Eth. Nic.* II. 3, 1104b 8–1105a 13; VII. 11, 1152b 5; X.8, 1178a 14; *Mag. Mor.* II. 7, 1204a 29; *Pol.* VIII. 5, 1340a 15.

[5] *Eth. Nic.* II. 2, 1104b 24; *Eth. Eud.* II. 4, 1222a 2.

[6] I. 3, 407a 32.

[7] Diels-Kranz, *Fragm. d. Vors.*, I, 24, A11 and A5.

[8] *Phaedo* 79D; cf. 83A. The same view is also present in the *Meno* 97D–98A, *Euthyphro* 11B–D, and also *Gorgias* 527B.

[9] (Berlin, 1877), p.299.

[10] Ibid, p.250.

[11] *De Anima* III. 7, 431 a 6.

[12] *Metaph.* Θ 6, 1048b 23 ssq.

[13] *Eth. Nic.* X. 4, 1174a 14.

[14] *Eth. Nic.* X. 4, 1174b 13.

[15] *Eth. Nic.* VII. 14, 1154b 20 ff.

[16] *Eth. Nic.* IX. 4, 1166a 17.

[17] *Eth. Nic.* VI. 2, 1139b 3; VI. 5, 1140b 6.

POST-ARISTOTELIAN PHILOSOPHY

JOHN P. ANTON
Emory University

Ancient Interpretations of Aristotle's Doctrine of *Homonyma**

I

THE main purpose of this paper is to offer an exposition and a critical examination of the ancient interpretations of Aristotle's doctrine of *homonyma*. A circumlocution of what Aristotle means by *homonyma* things is given in *Categories*, ch. 1, 1a. The ancient interpretations with which we are concerned in this paper are to be found in the extant commentaries on this treatise. Evidently, more commentaries had been written on the *Categories* than the vicissitudes of time allowed to survive, but we have only those of the following writers: Porphyrius (c. 233–303), Dexippus (fl. c. 350), Ammonius (fl. c. 485), Philoponus (c. 490–530), Olympiodorus (fl. c. 535), Simplicius (fl. c. 533), Elias (fl. c. 550). One might add here the relevant writings of John Damascene (675–749), Photius (820–91), and Michael Psellus (1018–79), which are useful paraphrases rather than full commentaries. For that reason, the interpretations they support are not discussed in this paper.

The main body of this paper is given to a discussion of the interpretations which the ancient commentators offered and to an analysis of the assumptions which underlie them. It can be stated here in anticipation of what follows that the commentators often attached to Aristotle's meaning of *homonyma* aspects that were quite foreign to his views, and that by doing so these commentators were taking extensive liberties with the text at hand. As we hope to show, the commentators brought into their discussions of this particular portion of the *Categories* issues and views that were far more relevant to their own ontologies and logical theories than to Aristotle's doctrines. In order to show how this is the

* Based on an invited paper presented at the annual meeting of the SAGP in New York City, December 27, 1965. Copyright by The Regents of the University of California. Reprinted from the *Journal of the History of Philosophy*, VII (1969): 1–18, by permission of the Regents.

case, we must first give a summary of what we believe our text permits us to say about the meaning of *homonyma*, as given in the opening chapter of the *Categories.*[1] Suffice it to add at this point that the interpretations of the doctrine of *homonyma* with which we are concerned here are only those that are discussed exclusively in the relevant commentaries on this work.

Textual tradition has preserved two versions, referred to here as V1 and V2, of Aristotle's formulation of *homonyma*. The difference between them is that while V1 preserves the key expression λόγος τῆς οὐσίας, the other, V2 omits it. V1, as established by modern textual criticism, reads as follows:

> Ὁμώνυμα λέγεται ὧν ὄνομα μόνον κοινόν, ὁ δὲ κατὰ τοὔνομα λόγος τῆς οὐσίας ἕτερος.

Not only was the inclusion of the expression *logos tēs ousias* (hereafter abbreviated as *L of O*) defended as indispensable for distinguishing Aristotle's formulation from the one propounded by Speusippus, but we also found it necessary to advance the view that Aristotle used the expression *L of O* in a definitely technical sense. We showed why the deletion of the term *ousia* would make the passage open to misinterpretation, since by omitting it one could argue that Aristotle meant to include in the class of *homonyma* such things as accidental properties and individuals with proper names. We also argued in favor of a view that delimits the meaning of *ousia* to definable substance, i.e. in the sense of secondary substance as species. Textual evidence in favor of this reading was cited from other treatises and the case was further strengthened by arguing that the meaning of the term *logos* in the sense of "definition" left no doubt that the proper application of the term could only refer to *ousia* as essence. The conclusion we drew was that the formulation of *homonyma* in V1 suited perfectly the ontological doctrine put forth in the *Categories* and also that each term occurring in the total expression was employed in a precise terminological way.

When we turn to the philosophical value of the extant commentaries on the *Categories*, three special problems deserve attention: (i) Whether each commentator shows sufficient awareness of the technical terminology in which the doctrine of *homonyma* is couched, and hence whether he phrases his interpretation of the doctrine in line with what seems to be the most acceptable reading of the text. (ii) Given the way each commentator understands what is meant by *homonyma* things, it is imperative that we identify the implications each particular formulation has for a theory of substance and definition to which the commentators subscribe. (iii) Since the miscellaneous materials which the commentators incorporate into their discussions are quite frequently alien to the issues at hand, and since their expositions cover grounds not intended by Aristotle's own theory of *homonyma*, the problem here becomes one of identifying the intellectual affiliations of the commentators and uncovering the logical and ontological views they seek to promote through Aristotle's authority.

The ancient commentators failed to appreciate the full technical import of the expression *L of O*. The reasons for this failure seem to be many. One of them is the tendency not merely to over-explicate each of the terms separately, but to do so also with the expression as a whole. When we turn to the non-Aristotelian considerations the commentators introduced in their discussion, we see that the outstanding example is that of taking *logos* to mean both *definition and description*. Now, the latter is clearly an interpolation and is found to be nowhere in the *Categories*. However, by taking such liberties with the meaning of the term *logos*, the commentators were able to change the meaning of the whole expression and to force it to appear non-technical. As a result, the denotation of the *definiendum* "*homonyma* things" became so wide as to include anything from accidental properties and first substances to highest genera, including the genera of predication. By repeatedly emphasizing this broad interpretation of *homonyma*, the commentators turned their back to the possibility that Aristotle could have intended the term in a limited sense and therefore given the expression *L of O* a technical meaning. Thus, when we leave the commentaries to return to Aristotle's own text we are hardly surprised to see that there was no plan on his part to discuss all types of *homonyma* things. Apparently Aristotle and the commentators were not doing the same thing.

II

1. *Porphyry's interpretation:* Porphyry begins his discussion by asking questions about the origin and function of *homonyma* and *synonyma*.[2] According to his theory, each thing has (a) name, (b) definition, and (c) description. Now the relations that obtain between things and their names and definitions come under four types. (i) Things may have in common both the name and the definition of what the name signifies, and when they do so these things are called *synonyma*. (ii) Things may share the name, but if they cannot claim the definition in question they are classified as *homonyma*. (iii) When two things can actually claim a

definition as common to both even if they do not have the same name they are called *polyonyma*. (iv) Things which have neither a name nor a definition in common are *heteronyma*. He also mentions a fifth type, *paronyma*, which refers to things whose names are the result of derivation; however, he considers it of little importance. Porphyry explains Aristotle's omission of (iii) and (iv) on the ground that he had no real use for either.

The next question he raises is addressed to the reason why Aristotle began the treatise with the statement on *homonyma* (61. 4 ff.). It should be noted that the explanation he gives finds no support in the *Categories* and must be regarded as Porphyry's own invention. In any event, Porphyry claims that Aristotle believed that the categories themselves, when predicated of things, are used homonymously. His explanation is prefaced with the remark that Aristotle taught that *being* (*to on*) is homonymous.[3] Hence, Porphyry argues, Aristotle should have begun with the notion of homonymy rather than *homonyma* things.[4] It is against this background that he proceeds with his support of V1 (62. 35). He takes *logos* in the sense of definition (*horistikos*), and justifies the inclusion of *L of O* by means of an argument. The term *logos*, he claims, has many meanings (definition, oral speech, reckoning, seminal reason, etc.), and if we fail to make *ousia* part of the expression, the real meaning of *logos*, i.e., in the sense of definition, becomes obscure (64. 28–65. 11). In a preceding comment on the inadmissibility of the elliptical variant *logos heteros*, vis-a-vis that of *kata tounoma logos . . . heteros*, he correctly defends the fuller version (contra Speusippus?) by pointing out that the accuracy of meaning demands it be made clear here that it is not the name which is the referent, but something else in conjunction with the name.[5] What he means is that only the fuller version expresses Aristotle's point: the denotation of a name used and the denotation of the definition of the substance named must be the same.[6]

The first sign of Porphyry's deviation from Aristotle's meaning appears with the listing of the diverse uses of *logos*. It is obvious that some of them are totally foreign to Aristotle. But the initial suspicion we form that Porphyry is about to misinterpret the text is eventually confirmed when he proceeds to give the example which illustrates his discussion of the logic of homonymy. The point is that theory and example are incompatible. The illustration he mentions is two human beings with the same name: Ajax (son of Telamon) and Ajax (son of Oileus). The definition of "man" applies to both, and though they have the same (proper) name they are not the same entities. Still, the definition of the substance underlying the name "man" is true for both Ajaxes. Next, Porphyry tells us that the only way we can logically differentiate between the two is by resorting to different descriptions. By advocating this solution, Porphyry abandons the strict approach to *homonyma* and in effect widens the term to denote also such things as the homonymous accidental properties. The terminology is shifted to accommodate a very special case: *homonymous individuals*.

If our thesis is correct, it follows that Aristotle's doctrine was not intended to cover homonymy due to proper names. If so, Porphyry is illicitly extending the initial use of the theory. The departure is so radical that it permits the term "homonyma" to refer to named species as well as individuals with proper names. Once the two views, Aristotle's and Porphyry's, are allowed to come under the formulation of *homonyma* as stated in the *Categories*, that formulation becomes at once imprecise and inconsistent; imprecise, on the ground that *L of O* is no longer a technical expression, and inconsistent because the term *logos*, in the sense of definition, is now taken to apply to both definable and non-definable things.

Porphyry's special *scholium* on *L of O* is quite revealing. He admits that in view of the many uses of *logos* the expression *tēs ousias* is needed in order to make clear that it is the defining sense of *logos* that concerns Aristotle (64. 28–65. 11). Thus, he infers, the defining *logos* (*horistikos*) which refers to the name, and *logos* which indicates substance (*ousias dēlōtikos*) are the same thing, except in the case of *homonyma* things where the definition of substance must be different in each case. Two critical reservations must be made at this point. (i) Porphyry is simply assuming that Aristotle had in mind the problem of the homonymy of the term *logos* and that *ousia* was made part of the expression primarily to avoid this particular ambiguity. Aside from the obvious anachronism about the Stoic seminal reason as one of the senses of *logos*, the list of meanings is too elementary if not irrelevant to the discussion. As a result, the explication appears contrived and the conclusions drawn far from acceptable. (ii) Though Porphyry is correct in taking *logos* to mean definition, he is far from clear as to the meaning of *pragmata*. Strict Aristotelian doctrine would demand identification of *pragmata* with definable species. However, Porphyry shows no sign of having detected here that a real ontological issue arises when the emphasis is shifted from species to individuals, an issue which touches on the very philosophical framework of syllogistic thinking. As we said in the previous section, the referents to "*homonyma*" and "*synonyma*" are substances which are both definable and predicable; they are the things which normally serve as terms in the premises of the syllogism.

Just the same, confident that he has settled the problem of the meaning of *homonyma*, he proceeds next to consider the issue of their tropes. His list of tropes (65. 12 ff.) has many merits to it, but again it turns out that it is geared to the discussion on the homonymy which is due to proper names. He lists two main tropes:[7] (a) *homonyma* by accident (*apo tychēs*), and (b) *homonyma* by intention (*apo dianoias*). The latter is further divided into four classes: from (i) similarity, (ii) analogy, (iii) unity to multiplicity, (iv) multiplicity to unity. Once again, the examples used to illustrate *homonyma* by accident leave no doubt that he was thinking of *homonyma pragmata* not in terms of Aristotelian secondary substances but in the light of the paradigmatic case of individuals with proper names.[8] What he failed to realize here is that his proposed tropes, though theoretically interesting, were explained with the aid of illustrations that could not be accommodated within the strict Aristotelian context of *L of O*, which, as Porphyry himself admits, require that *logos* be taken in the sense of definition. It is the kind of examples he offers that leads us to conclude that Porphyry did not suspect he was actually taking liberties with the text before him and that he was expressing views that violated the intent of the Aristotelian doctrine. It seems really strange that he did not observe that his and Aristotle's paradigms were at odds,[9] nor for that reason did any of the subsequent commentators. They all repeated Porphyry's error. Throughout the history of the ancient commentary practice, the source of misinterpretation remained unidentified and the error was never removed, let alone suspected.

2. *Dexippus' interpretation:*[10] He prefaces his comments on *homonyma* with a discussion on what can be legitimately considered a "category," and proposes that the following sorts of expressions be disqualified: (a) metaphors, (b) tropes, e.g., *necessity, possibility, subsistence* and (c) modifiers, e.g., *all, none, no one in particular*, etc. The criterion he employs for rejecting such expressions is that the things they stand for have no determinate nature of their own (12. 20–25).[11] Next he proceeds to show why certain principles which cannot be subsumed under any of the categories are nevertheless highly relevant to categorial theory; since they have as many uses as there are categories, such principles are cases of homonymy.[12] The third problem he considers before presenting his interpretation of *homonyma* concerns the reason why Aristotle chose to discuss *homonyma, synonyma* and *paronyma* rather than proceed directly

with the theory of categories. In giving an answer to this question he allows the discussion to sidetrack to what turns out to be an interesting bit of linguistic theory.

He remarks that things and names of things, considered as quantitative collections, are not commensurable. In some cases we have more words for the same thing, whereas in others we have more things than names available for them. Hence, in considering any given simple or non-composite word, it is necessary to determine under which of the categories it should be classified. It is on account of this peculiar relationship between words and things that, according to Dexippus, Aristotle prefaced his treatise with a brief analysis on *homonyma* and *synonyma*. Unfortunately, Dexippus does not discuss the issue in any detail. Instead, he returns to his previous point and offers the peculiar hypothesis that the real reason Aristotle opened the *Categories* with a formulation of the nature of *homonyma* is because the ten categories are themselves instances of *homonyma* (17. 25–29). His point is that each category is predicated synonymously of the species subsumed under it, and that the categories, if taken absolutely, are used homonymously. Ignoring for a moment Dexippus' numerous irrelevancies, we must pause to mention that, like Porphyry, he also gives serious attention to *homonyma* in the context of individual substances with the same proper name. This is readily seen in his paradigm of the two Ajaxes. Notwithstanding his uncritical adoption of Porphyry's interpretation, it should be noted that Dexippus was quicker in accepting the implications of that approach for the total widening of the denotation of *homonyma pragmata*. Thus, Dexippus promptly included the accidental properties. Evidently, this is in agreement with the theory that homonymy is obtainable in all the categories. However, what is not clear from his discussion is the extent to which he was aware of the liberties he was taking with the text.

Though Dexippus defends the reading *L of O*, he does not hesitate to interfere with the Aristotelian way of phrasing the nature of *homonyma*. He does so when he asks why it is that Aristotle did not say: ὁ δὲ κατὰ τοὔνομα ὅρος ὁ αὐτός. No doubt, he knows that *logos* is a wider term than *horos*. According to his explanation, Aristotle wrote *logos tēs ousias* rather than *horos tēs ousias* simply because not all things are signified through definitions: some are signified only through descriptions (20. 28–31). The explanation assumes that Aristotle was actually interested in all types of *homonyma*. Though it has an ingenious side to it, the explanation is not really original. It simply states the Porphyrian thesis in a fresh way. Since he knows that individuals are undefinable and, like

Porphyry, insists in including them in *ousia*, the only way to meet the difficulty which the term *horos* poses is by (i) saying that Aristotle never meant to use *horos*, and (ii) arguing that *logos* means both definition (*horos*) and description (*hypographē*) and that Aristotle intended *logos* in this inclusive way. What is simply amazing about all this is that the term *hypographē*, description, is to be found nowhere in the *Categories*. Just the same, he criticizes Aristotle for phrasing elliptically, i.e., not saying *hypographē tōn homonymōn*. His argument is that since Aristotle knew that *homonymy* obtains in the case of genera as well as in the other categories, he should not have said "*logos tēs ousias*".

He suggests that a good way out of this problem would be a textual reading like that of Boethus and Andronicus which omits *tēs ousias*. But he admits that this will not really do for a number of reasons, chiefly because the term *logos* is itself a homonymous expression and has different senses. It is at this point that Dexippus states his main reason for defending the acceptability of *L of O*: it is the only adequate way of showing that all things can be *homonyma*, for when we speak of *logos* we think of beings, such as substances and genera, and when we speak of *ousia* we know we can signify through this term individuals and their accidents (21. 11–29). All that can be said about the argument is that while it is a good attempt to defend V1, it fails completely as interpretation to recapture Aristotle thought.

3. *Ammonius' interpretation:* Ammonius is deeply indebted to Porphyry for his views on the subject. It is also evident that he was familiar with Dexippus' commentary. He has worked out, on his own, two formulations of *homonyma*, neither of which compares favorably to Aristotle's for brevity or precision.[13] Like his predecessors he defends the reading *L of O*, and offers extensive comments on each of these key terms. (a) He contends that Aristotle used *logos* and not *horismos* because he knew that all things cannot be defined, as for instance in the case of the highest genera (20. 15–16). Since individuals are not exempted from being *homonyma*, and are not capable of being defined, but only described, Aristotle had to use the term *logos* in order to cover all cases. The argument is a familiar one. It assumes that Aristotle intended to include in his theory homonymous individuals, and also that *logos* meant for Aristotle both definition and description. (b) In his special comment on *ousia*, he argues for its textual adoption in a way that pushes Dexippus' position a step further but in the wrong direction. First, he says, we must ask whether homonymy applies to accidental properties. Evidently, such is the case, for we do say "sharp taste" and "sharp knife." This being so

and because of the fact that accidents subsist in beings, Aristotle must have used the term *ousia* to show that he meant to cover both substances and their accidents under the denotation of *homonyma*. The surprising element in Ammonius' argument is the facility with which he abuses the meaning of *ousia* and ignores its restricted categorial sense.[14] In effect, he mistakes *ousia* for *onta*.

However, when Ammonius is not speculating or following another commentator, he shows good judgment. For instance, despite the fact that he took *logos* to mean both definition and description, in his discussion on *Categories* 1a 4, he equates it exclusively with definition. *Logos* means *horismos*. He interprets the passage correctly and suggests that *homonyma* things refers to species.

Our discussion on Ammonius could have ended on this happy note if it were not for the fact that his treatment of *homonyma* appears in two different works, his commentary on the *Categories* and in his treatise *On Porphyry's Introduction*. Our account would have been pronouncedly incomplete without at least some elementary effort to correlate what is said in these two works. The respective treatments on *homonyma* are connected by means of an extensive discussion on the relationship between definition and description. We have already seen what he said in the commentary on the *Categories*. Before turning to his analysis of Porphyry's *Isagoge*, we must point out that we are confronted here with a special difficulty since we are dealing with a commentary on another highly interpretive commentary. For this reason it is often a most cumbersome task to decide whose views it is that Ammonius is expounding. However, the fact that he is exploring the relationship between definition and description as two uses of *logos*, is sufficient to alert us that he is working with a Porphyrian issue. The key to his understanding of Aristotle's views on this matter lies in what he has to say on definition. He begins by explaining that things are signified in two ways, (i) name, (ii) definition (54. 5 ff.).[15] Discourse which is indicative of things (*logos sēmantikos*) is of two kinds: (a) with reference to what things are according to essence, and (b) with reference to accidental properties. The former gives us the definition, the latter the description. However, he argues, accidents accompany the essential nature, say, of man, even if they do not complement the essence. Next he explains what description is. It is *hypohraphē*, a sort of drawing, an imitation of likeness which succeeds in signifying something without articulating it with precision. The analogy he uses is interesting. Definition is to description what life-like painting is to drawing.

So far he has said nothing to justify the relevance of the discussion on description to Aristotle's text. What controls the analysis is Porphyry's insistence that description is part of the meaning of *logos*. One suspects here that Ammonius is accommodating Aristotle to Porphyry's theories rather than the reverse. He quotes Porphyry's dictum to the effect that "Things we cannot signify through definition we like to indicate through description" (55. 12–13). No sooner do we ask what are the things to which Porphyry's dictum refers than we discover that included in the class of such "undefinables" are, next to the accidental properties, the highest genera. Hence, Ammonius agrees with Porphyry, they are accessible only through description. But the point of real interest is that he explains the undefinability of highest genera on the familiar grounds that (a) there is no genus higher to them and (b) they are cases of *homonyma* (56. 1). The syllogism is clear: Since all *homonyma* are undefinable, and highest genera are *homonyma*, all such genera are undefinable.[16] But the significant thing here is that the undefinability of all *homonyma* was never defended by Aristotle. The only alternative is to conclude that Ammonius is expounding on Porphyry's doctrines. If his thesis claims to cover Aristotle's view on *homonyma* as well, the consequence is that it degenerates into a contradictory explanation of two incompatible theories. It is unfortunate that Ammonius neglected to state the difference between Porphyry's and Aristotle's respective approaches to *homonyma*. There are other special features in Ammonius' theory of description, but they cannot be included in this study. Had this been done we could have shown how Ammonius' neoplatonic idealism prevented him from cutting through the maze of Porphyry's philosophical assumptions to determine for himself whether Aristotle's text permitted the expansion of the meaning of *homonyma* to suit Porphyry's non-Aristotelian ontology.

4. *Philoponus' interpretation:* He opens his discussion on *homonyma* with a pious bit of theological epistemology. Had we been blessed, he remarks, with the being only naked souls have, and were free from the bondage of our bodies, we would be able to signify everything by means of concepts only. However, bodies act like clouds, cover the intelligibles and intervene with our seeing them directly. This is the reason why we need names (*In Categ.* 14. 1 ff.). Since it is not given to us to signify through concepts we enlist the help of names and definitions (*horismoi*). Next he proceeds to give a brief account of *homonyma*, *synonyma*, *polyonyma* and *heteronyma*, and states that he means by *homonyma* things which "share the name but differ according to the definition." He makes

an effort to explain why Aristotle did not refer to all four kinds of signified things. The answer he gives is that Aristotle "potentially" spoke of the other two as well, because to know a *homonymon*, for instance, is to know potentially its opposite, the *polyonymon* (14. 24 ff.). He also has an answer to the much discussed question why Aristotle decided to begin this work with a statement on *homonyma*. These things, he informs us, are actually the simplest sort, for they share one aspect only, the name; therefore, they are by nature (*physei*) prior to the *synonyma*. In fact, *being* (*to on*) is predicated of the categories homonymously, not synonymously.

Philoponus, following the example of the preceding commentators, is asking questions for which he has pat answers. The explanations he provides are at once debatable and irrelevant. Philoponus' explanation is not the only one that can be given to the last question, and more significantly, it is not basically related to the logical context of Aristotle's formulation of *homonyma*. One can not escape forming the impression that Philoponus is misled into believing that Aristotle is referring indiscriminately to all instances of *homonyma*, including "being" as a *homonymōs legomenon*. Be that as it may, Philoponus burdens his discussion with a number of trivial themes (15. 11 ff.), only to tell us what the real meaning of the opening lines is: "Let it be understood that Aristotle tells us directly in the opening statement what the purpose of the book is. He says, '*homonyma legatai* . . .' What he means by '*homonyma*' is things, and by '*legatai*,' significant sounds (*phonai*). We know things with the aid of conceptual meanings (*noēmata*)."[17] That Philoponus is straining the intent of the passage is evident from his insistence upon making the homonymy of a concept, including the concept of homonymy, a foremost and necessary part of the formulation of *homonyma pragmata*. If we keep in mind that it is this interest that dominates his itemized kind of commentary, we are in a better position to understand why he takes special pain to explicate *homonymon* as being itself a homonymous expression.[18]

More pertinent to our discussion is his comment on "legatai." His interpretation is that the subject of the verb is *pragmata*. The point is that Aristotle is actually referring to things, not concepts. Aside from the problem Philoponus has in tying this pointed explication to his previous tangential remarks on homonymy in general, he falls into the serious and repeated error of offering the Ajax paradigm (17. 26 ff.), and to make matters worse, he tries to support it through a remarkable showpiece of irrelevant erudition: a line from Plato's *Phaedrus*.[19] Since most of the comments on the itemized textual expressions are rather trivial, it is best that we give some attention to what is basic to our theme: his understanding of *pragmata*. Once again, the paradigm is individuals with the same proper name. The discussion is tied to the reasons he gives for preserving in the text the expression *kata tounoma*. The reading is justified, he thinks, because certain things which are *homonyma* with regard to one name are not so with regard to another name. Since two things may have more than one name in common, such things may turn out to be now *homonyma*, now *synonyma*. Hence, it should be plain, Philoponus argues, that Aristotle specifically meant to alert us to the need for restricting the definition called for only to that common name by virtue of which the things are *homonyma* and not any other. It would be tedious to give here the details of his analysis of the example of the two Ajaxes. What matters really is the nature of the paradigm. Aside from his questionable interpretation of the intent of the aforementioned part of the total passage, there is the further issue of the paradigm. It is here where Philoponus misunderstands the meaning of the passage. What strikes the reader is Philoponus' reluctance to as much as mention Aristotle's own examples. Instead he follows the previous commentators and supplies the illicit example of individuals with the same proper name. We have already seen what consequences follow from this sort of interpretation of *pragmata*. What we should look for next is the inconsistent view Philoponus is inadvertently forced to adopt. This matter hinges on his understanding of *logos*.

Like the other commentators, Philoponus' answer is part of his broader treatment of *L of O*. He defends the expression but interprets it as follows. Aristotle said *logos* and not *horismos* in order to cover cases of *homonyma* which are beyond proper definitions (19. 21 ff.). He repeats the familiar theory of descriptions as the only avenue to signification of *summa genera* and accidental properties. In short, *logos* means here definition and description of substance. He argues that since Aristotle used "substance" to mean something self-existent, in contrast to accidents, and also any "absolutely existing entity," the accidents are thereby part of the meaning of "*ousia*" in the passage. The surprising aspect of his discussion comes with his comment on *Cat.* 1a 4, for he gives there the impression he has forgotten what was already said about *logos*, and unaware of the inconsistency into which he is about to fall, he declares that Aristotle is asking in this passage for the definition of the species. In this respect he is doing nothing substantially different from what Ammonius did before him. What is of real interest, however, is the fact that he did not perceive the inconsistency in his interpretation, an inconsistency which would have been easier for him to detect since it did not originate with him. For all these reasons, Philoponus' commentary on the problem of *homonyma* is pronouncedly inferior to that of Ammonius.

5. *Olympiodorus' interpretation:* What he says on the subject is not radically different from any previous treatment of *homonyma*, but his commentary is interesting as a variant misinterpretation. He also defends the reading of *L of O* and comparably takes *logos* to mean both definition and description. In a general introductory comment (26. 5 ff.), he tells us that *homonyma* arise from the fact that each thing is at once one and many; as unity it has a name, as plurality it is signified through *logos*, which is of two kinds. By combining name and *logos*, we arrive at four classes of things: *homonyma*, *synonyma*, *heteronyma*, *polyonyma*. His treatment of *homonyma* presents no novel features and the illustrations are the standard ones of the two Ajaxes (27. 10–20). What is of particular interest is the facility with which he ignores his own terminology. For instance, after mentioning his example of the two Ajaxes as cases of *homonyma* he does not hesitate to use the term definition (*horismos*), despite the fact that these are individuals. He seems convinced that he is actually giving definitions when he says for instance of Ajax, son of Telamon: "from Salamis, who fought a duel with Hector and committed suicide." For his answer why Aristotle treated only *homonyma* and *synonyma* but began with the former, he borrows heavily from Philoponus (27. 25 ff.). His main points are that the categories are the most inclusive genera (*genikōtata*), that the species which come under them are all *synonyma*, and that "being" is predicated homonymously of all the categories. There are two sorts of confusion in this portion of Olympiodorus' commentary. (i) While emphasizing the synonymous character of the kinds of things subsumed under each category, he loses sight of the real differences between the sub-categorial sets. Olympiodorus the grammarian has evidently misled the ontologist. (ii) Like the others he also assumes that Aristotle's starting point and main concern of the chapter is "being" as *pollachōs legomenon*.[20]

Beginning with 31. 5, Olympiodorus offers a general treatment of the Aristotelian formulation as a whole. What he says there presents an aspect of special interest. His first question is whether the formulation contains superfluous expressions, especially in view of Aristotle's love for brevity. He draws attention to the importance of each word for the sake of clarity (*saphēneias heneka*), and also to the fact that Aristotle means to be technical: ὡς τεχνικὸς Ἀριστοτέλης τοῦτο πεποίηκεν (31. 15).

Olympiodorus' justification of his claim is not without disappointments. He says that the real reason why Aristotle did not confine his *definiens* to ὧν ὄνομα μόνον κοινόν was to prevent us from attributing to him the view that all *homonyma* are also in some sense non-*homonyma* and all *synonyma* non-*synonyma*. Consider how Plato and Alcibiades, not being *synonyma* became so when "man" is predicated of both. Again, if Aristotle had limited his formulation only to "things whose definition is different," then it would be possible to show that it permits us to say absurd things. Consider for instance, the following: since genera are predicated synonymously of subordinate species, and since we can give two distinctive accounts of the same individual, say Socrates, viz. (i) "S. animal logical and mortal," (ii) "S. bald-headed, philosopher with a protruding belly," it would turn out that by virtue of the first account Socrates and Alcibiades are synonymous, and *homonymous* by force of the second.

The intriguing thing about all this is that Olympiodorus should call Aristotle's formulation systematic and technical for reasons so foreign to Aristotle's logic and theory of definition. It did not occur to Olympiodorus that Aristotle perhaps did not mean to include as part of his denotation of *homonyma* the commentators' individuals and their accidental properties. Furthermore, it is evident that Olympiodorus did not see that it was only his loose talking about *ousia* that permitted an indiscriminate passing back and forth from *logos* as definition to *logos* as description. He is simply committing an error typical of the rest of the commentators. He is on better grounds when he argues in favor of keeping the *tēs ousias* part in the expression. Without it, he points out, Aristotle would have compromised precision and the reader would not have been able to say whether the passage is about things or words. Thus, in order to avoid any misunderstanding Aristotle distinguishes between words and their definitions on the one hand, and things signified by words and the definitions of such substantive things, on the other (32. 2 ff.). Olympiodorus' point is well taken but for one item: his implication that Aristotle is talking about all things in general; for to say so is to cancel the possibility that Aristotle's formulation has a technical side to it. But to return to Philoponus' defense of *L of O*, we must admit that it is subtle and ingenious but brings to the foreground issues which even if not irrelevant to the broader aspects of the problem, cannot be shown to have figured originally in Aristotle's discussion. Finally, it must be recognized that his comment on *Categories*, 1a 4, indicates that for once he understood correctly the intent of the formulation (37. 16–30).

Suddenly in this comment all the grammatical trivia, the preoccupation with individuals, proper names, accidental properties, theory of description and other such notions, withdraw to make room for a pointed answer to the real problem. He responds to Aristotle's own illustrations and offers appropriate essential definitions for the kinds of things that are *homonyma*. Correct though he is on this point, it cannot be said that his approach, when seen as a whole, is either unaffected by misconceptions or free from non-Aristotelian presuppositions.

6. *Simplicius' interpretation:* Simplicius opens his valuable and in many ways highly informative commentary with a remark on the importance of making appropriate distinctions that enable us to classify things signified by words under the right category. Since it is often the case that two different things may share the same signifying word, we need criteria to distinguish one from the other and to focus attention to the kinds of words that give rise to ambiguity (*In Categ*. 21. 1–10). He observes that if each thing had only one name, then it would come under only one category. But, had this been the case, there would have to be as many categories as there are things. However, we know that one and the same name is frequently used to signify a number of substantially different things. Hence the need for categorial classifications arises. He mentions as an example the name "animal" and points out how it is used to signify a man and a horse, or again, Socrates and a painting of Socrates. The manner in which Simplicius discusses the examples is quite significant. He prefers to start with homonymously predicated names rather than *homonyma pragmata*. Thus, since man and horse partake in the substance of animal, the substance is predicated synonymously and the two things are brought under the same category. But since Socrates and his portrait do not partake of the same substance, Socrates must come under the category of substance, whereas his portrait under that of quality. In order to account for such cases, Simplicius insists, Aristotle found it necessary to begin his treatise with *homonyma*.[21] Three things must be pointed out here. First, the readiness with which he substitutes his own examples of *individual* substances for Aristotle's *specific* ones. Second, his interesting speculation about *homonyma* as the key to categorial ambiguity and how this was considered by Aristotle an item of priority. Third, his diagnostic treatment of the categorial identity of the two *homonyma*, particularly his prompt classification of the portrait of Socrates under the category of quality, despite the fact that Aristotle's text does not permit such inferences. Evidently, by placing the portrait

example under quality, Simplicius gives the impression that he is presupposing that Aristotle is using (a) *homonyma* in the broadest sense, hence non-technically, and (b) *ousia* in a very loose sense to mean anything from substance to accidental properties. It is not certain whether Simplicius would have openly endorsed these implications. Regardless of what his reaction would have been, the point is that his treatment of the subject allows such inferences.

When Simplicius turns to examine "*the nature of homonyma*" (22. 14 ff.), he repeats the well known views of his predecessors how each thing can be signified through either name or *logos*, and how the latter means either definition or description. Since names in their symbolic capacity can symbolize substantially different things for which different *logoi* can be given, and since things which are essentially the same can have a variety of names, we arrive at five types of things; Aristotle, however, treated only three: *homonyma, synonyma, paronyma*. The other two, *polyonyma* and *heteronyma*, were omitted for two reasons: (i) knowledge of them is easily attained as opposites of the first two types; (ii) Aristotle actually had in mind the preparation for speechmaking (*lectika*), rather than an inventory of real things. In offering the second explanation, Simplicius admits he is following Syrianus. His endorsement of that position is intimately related to a more basic issue. He tells us that he agrees with Iamblichus who taught that Aristotle opened the *Categories* with the *homonyma*, not only because these are the simplest of expressions, but primarily because the expression "category" is homonymously predicated of the categories (23. 25–24. 5). One begins to suspect here that the neoplatonic concern for the stratification of species and genera, with the highest genera at the top, is at the back of Simplicius' explanation. What seems also to be true is his interest in pointing out that Aristotle did not assign any reality to the expression "category" or to "being." By doing so, Simplicius, like Iamblichus from whom he derives this approach, is able to contrast Aristotle's ontology from the neoplatonic theory of Being.

Faithful to the tradition he follows, Simplicius interprets *L of O* not in the strict sense of definition of *ousia*. He speculates that Aristotle purposely used the term *logos*, a broader term, to include in his formulation both the *summa genera* and the individuals. Only by means of description can we render the property of some substance (29. 16–24). We have already seen how this has become the standard treatment of *L of O*; hence it would only surprise us to read in Simplicius' account something different on the subject. But in view of his unusual erudition and familiarity with the *Categories*, we wonder why it never occurred to him to peruse the text merely for the sake of discovering the passages to which he could have appealed for his support of the interpolated meaning of *logos* as description. Nor did he realize that in order to accommodate this meaning, he was simply following the other commentators when he supplied the very examples which alone could make *logos*, in the sense of description, applicable to this non-Aristotelian situation. True, Simplicius defends the reading *L of O*, but he does so for reasons of his own. He appeals to such authorities as Porphyry, Herminus, and "the majority of scholars," but instead of arguing on his own he quotes Porphyry's full approval.[22]

Even more disappointing is the comment on an *aporia* that was raised by Nicostratus and Atticus and has to do with the claim that all *synonyma* are *homonyma*, and vice versa. Consider, for instance, the fact that there is a sense in which we can say that all *homonyma* have in common the name by virtue of which they are *homonyma*, and the definition of the homonymous name. Thus, they are *homonyma* in that sense. But in so far as they are essentially different things, they are also *synonyma*. Simplicius informs us that Porphyry resolved the difficulty by pointing out that there is nothing paradoxical about things being *synonyma* in some context and *homonyma* in another. Against this background, conspicuously unrelated to Aristotle's major theme, Simplicius proceeds to discuss Porphyry's answer by using the two Ajaxes example. Even later in the next comment, where the opportunity presents itself to focus attention on Aristotle's own examples and identify them correctly, as Ammonius and Olympiodorus at least were able to do, he forgoes it in favor of rehashing such common places of the tropes of *homonyma*. All he is able to offer there is to explain why he thinks the Aristotelian examples come under the class of "intended" *homonyma* due to similarity (31. 22–32). Simplicius is not even original when he misinterprets Aristotle. Aside from depending blindly on Porphyry and repeating characteristic neoplatonic misrepresentations of Aristotle's views he shows no signs whatever of having suspected the extent to which the doctrine of *homonyma* was strained to suit the commentator's own intellectual loyalties.

7. *Elias' interpretation:* There is hardly anything in Elias' treatment of *homonyma* that has not been said by one of the previous commentators. He shares most of their misconceptions about Aristotle and repeats the same standard errors. Like the others, he defends the reading *L of O* and assumes that *logos* means both definition and description. He begins his

commentary by saying why he thinks Aristotle was right in distinguishing between *homonyma* and *synonyma*. He argues against certain unnamed thinkers who claimed that all cases of *homonyma* are reducible to *synonyma*. He appears familiar with Simplicius' work and echoes the new emphasis this old Porphyrian problem was given by Simplicius. In fact he offers two arguments against the "reductionists," but they present little philosophical interest and have nothing to do with Aristotle's logical views. More interesting is the way in which he understands the *Categories*. He writes: "Since the main objective is to discuss the categories, and since *homonyma* is predicated of them, whereas each category is predicated synonymously of the species which come under it in the manner of the genus, . . . for these reasons Aristotle begins his treatise with the doctrine of *homonyma* and *synonyma*. If he gives priority to the former, this is because unity precedes duality" (*In Categ.* 135. 3–7). His comments abound in speculations of the sort. His is a pat explanation, typically neoplatonic and altogether unoriginal. He also ignores Aristotle's examples of *homonyma* and replaces them with the celebrated ones of the two Ajaxes. But instead of discussing any further the repetitious character of his misinterpretation, we may conclude this account with a note on Elias' original inconsistency.

Elsewhere, viz., in his *In Porphyrii Isogogen* (56. 11–14 and 4. 5–11), he explains in the familiar clichés the difference between definition and description: the former is done with reference to substance, the latter, to accidental properties and is therefore inferior to definition. His discussion of the example of the two Ajaxes as instances of homonymous substances is peculiar, to say the least. He is presumably talking about individual substances, knows that in such cases we cannot have definitions, yet uses the terms description and definition interchangeably as if there was no problem at all (138. 19–139. 6). The same careless use of terminology we find in his comment on Aristotle's examples. He has just admitted that *logos* in Aristotle's text means definition, and yet writes the following: "The real man is living substance endowed with sensation whereas the portrayed man is not substance but *symbebēkos*, not living but lifeless, not sensing but lacking in such faculty; the latter is called 'alive' in the sense of being a representation of a living and sensing substance" (139. 25–28). Why the portrait is not a substance but an accidental thing and why it is that he prefers to ignore Aristotle's text which leaves no doubt that only definitions should be given for both instances of *homonyma* mentioned, Elias' commentary offers no explanation. The inconsistency remained unnoticed.

III

When we view in retrospect the tradition of Aristotle's interpreters, starting from Elias and going back to the earlier commentators, certain major themes begin to stand out even more pronounced than when we look at these thinkers in the normal chronological order. It seems that these commentators honestly believed they were discussing and logically extending Aristotelian doctrines even after they had seriously departed from Aristotle's thoughts and had in essence abandoned some of his principal views. Whether these thinkers could have developed their philosophies without the use of the method of expounding through commentaries on major texts of the classical period is something that need not be considered here. What has been of concern was the correctness of their interpretations of an Aristotelian issue.

In general, the commentators we discussed were all Platonizing thinkers and, on the whole, well-known professors and teachers. Some of them, like Elias, taught Aristotle as a preliminary to Plato (123. 9–11).[23] Common to all the commentators on the *Categories* is the noted discrepancy between their ardent defense of the fuller version of the Aristotelian formulation of the nature of *homonyma*, one which preserves the *L of O* textual reading, and their misunderstanding of the intent of the passage. What is striking about the entire tradition that goes back to Porphyry, if not to others before him, is a common and serious effort to extend Aristotle's views and, in this particular case, to promote the belief that *logos* meant for Aristotle something more than definition. The persistent preoccupation with the meaning of *logos* in the sense of description calls for an explanation.

The new meaning the term took was appended to Aristotle's *logos* with a facility that leads one to infer that the commentators were less interested in correctness and more in using some significant text in order to bring to the foreground of their exposition certain concepts of their own. One might venture here the opinion that even more important than the extended meaning of *logos* was their eagerness to assert the view that would permit *ousia*, in the sense of individual substances, to become an object of "knowledge" even if admittedly undefinable in terms of Aristotle's logic. This view was asserted, as we saw, by means of an interpretation that rested on certain liberties the commentators took with Aristotle's text. It is difficult to know whether the commentators had actually realized the significance Aristotle had apparently attached to his way of formulating the nature of *homonyma*. The fact is that we are allowed to infer that they either ignored or suppressed the ontological and logical aspects of the doctrine and by the same token overlooked the possibility that Aristotle had conceivably stated his case through the aid of technical expressions.

It is not easy to say what it was that led the commentators to insist upon treating the two concepts, *ousia* and *logos*, in so obviously a non-Aristotelian manner. A fuller explanation of this treatment might eventually reveal that what we have here is doctrinal innovation in late Hellenistic logical theory and comparable developments in ontology. However, all we are permitted to say at this point is that no matter what new views the commentators had developed on their own it is still a fact that they failed to distinguish their own concepts from what their texts permitted.

The interpretation that takes *ousia*, as it occurs in the first chapter of the *Categories*, to mean individual substances and that such substances, if they happen to have the same proper name, are cases of *homonyma pragmata*, goes back, as far as our documents permit us to tell, to the writings of Porphyry and his pupil Iamblichus. We have no extant commentary on the *Categories* that antedates that of Porphyry. If we had the commentaries from which he was able to draw we might have been in a position to trace the origins of this misinterpretation of Aristotle's text. The way matters now stand all we can say is that the available evidence points to the fact that the misinterpretation originates with the early neoplatonists, it is transmitted through neoplatonic writers, and becomes an established approach which is shared by all the commentators whose neoplatonic affiliations cannot be doubted. Perhaps the long interpretive tradition from Porphyry to Photius and Psellus which preserved a correct textual reading only to distort its meaning and allow an error to go unnoticed for centuries, is as curious a phenomenon as is the fact that the only commentaries we have on Aristotle's *Categories* are those that were written by neoplatonists.

NOTES

1 For a full discussion of the doctrine of *homonyma* and the background against which it can be understood, see my "Aristotle's Doctrine of *Homonyma* in the *Categories* and its Platonic Antecedents," *JHP*, VI (1968): 315–26, to which the present paper is a sequel. I have tried to show in that paper how Aristotle's formulation is indebted linguistically to Plato, but was worked out not in response to Plato's usage but to his own philosophical position and as part of his logical apparatus to attack the Speusippean wing of the Academy. On the whole, the textual evidence from the Platonic writings indicates clearly that Plato had not proposed a technical use of *homonyma*. Speusippus and Aristotle, however, offered two different and

opposing technical formulations intended to fit their respective ontologies.

[2] *In Categ.*, beginning with 60. 11.

[3] Comp. Porphyry's remark in the *Isagoge* (6. 5–11): "... being is not the common genus of all things, nor, as Aristotle says, are all things of the same genus with respect to one summum genus. Still, let the first ten genera be arranged, as in the *Categories*, as ten first principles, and even if a person should call all things beings, yet he will call them, as he says, equivocally, but not synonymously, for if being were the one common genus of all things, all things would be synonymously styled beings, but the first principles being ten, the community is in name only, yet not in the definition also belonging to the name: there are then ten most generic genera." *The Organon, or Logical Treatises of Aristotle* (with Porphyry's *Introduction*), tr. O. F. Owen (London, 1883), Vol. II, pp. 615–16. Dexippus (*In Categ.* 13. 3) is in complete agreement with Porphyry. Of special interest is also the fact that Ammonius has constructed an argument of his own to support Porphyry's thesis. See Ammonii, *In Porph. Isag.* 81. 16 ff.

[4] Porphyry's explanation is interesting and deserves notice. Beginning with line 13, he proceeds to explain his views which may be summarized as follows: since there is a distinction between homonymy as a notion (*phonē*) and things (*pragmata*) which are *homonyma*, we cannot really talk about homonymy unless the claim can be made that we already know that things are ordered in a variety of ways and that all do not partake in the same definition. The cause of homonymy, then, lies in the fact that things are found to be different and that they are such that do not share the same name. Without this sort of knowledge, Porphyry remarks, we cannot conceive of homonymy.

[5] Comp. Simplicii, *In Categ.* 30. 7.

[6] Porphyry offers the following examples of the two definitions of the substance denoted by the name "man":

Df. 1: ἄνθρωπος ζῷον λογικὸν θνητόν.

Df. 2: ἄνθρωπος οὐσία ἔμψυχος αἰσθητική.

The problem now becomes one of determining whether the two definitions have the same denotation. Since Df. 2 denotes not only men but also other things such as oxen and the like, the equivalence is cancelled and one of the two definitions is declared too wide. Porphyry's rule is that a term is correctly rendered not only when properly named but also when defined in conjunction with the proper denotation of the name.

[7] The same division is adopted by Olympiodorus (*In Categ.* 34 ff.).

[8] An example of accidental *homonyma* is the case of two unrelated individuals who have been given the same proper name but without any design or planning on the part of those who gave them the name. Consider, for instance, the case of two Alexanders: Alexander, the son of Priamus, and Alexander, the son of Philippus.

[9] Porphyry's illustrations of each type within the trope of intentional *homonyma* are particularly suited to his classifications. The type of intentional trope which is of special interest to Porphyry is that from *similarity*. According to his interpretation, Aristotle's own examples mentioned in

Categories, 1a, are based on the trope from similarity (66. 22–8). *Man* and *painting of man* are *homonyma* by virtue of the fact that both are called "living," except that the painting of man is called so from similarity. This is also reflected in the language in which Porphyry couched the definitions of these *homonyma* things: (α) ἄνθρωπος, οὐσία ἔμψυχος αἰσθητική, (β) γεγραμμένον, ὁμοίωμα οὐσίας ἐμψύχου αἰσθητικῆς.

[10] Simplicius expresses serious reservations about the originality of Dexippus' commentary (*In Categ.* 2. 25–9). He remarks that the problem which Dexippus raises had been anticipated by Plotinus, and that his solutions offer nothing beyond what Porphyry and Iamblichus had already said on the subject.

[11] οὐδὲν . . . ἔχει ἀφωρισμένην ἰδίαν πραγμάτων φύσιν.

[12] He emphasizes the following principles: being (*on*), one (*hen*), plurality (*plēthos*), non-being (*mē on*), essence (*ti esti*), identity (*tauton*), otherness (*heteron*), category (*katēgoria*), property (*idiotēs*), definition (*horos*), genus (*genos*) and difference (*diaphora*) (*In Categ.* 13. 3–15. 13).

[13] Ammonius' two definitions of *homonyma* will be found in (a) *In Porph. Isag.* 6. 8 ff., and (b) *In Categ.* 17. 6–7.

[14] It is clear that Ammonius is convinced that in this context Aristotle did not mean substance in the sense in which it is contrasted to accidents (οὐ τὴν ἀντιδιαστελλομένην πρὸς τὰ συμβεβηκότα), but rather in the wider sense that would permit us to include particular existents, that is, primary *ousiai*. It follows from this, his argument goes, that Aristotle's view of *homonyma* must be understood as designed to cover the accidental properties as well. If Aristotle did not mean his theory to cover that case, he would have said φύσεως ἑκάστου καθ' ἓν ὑφέστηκεν . . . rather than *tēs ousias*. Ammonius' speculations receive no support from the text. We are dealing here with a strained interpretation but one that enables Ammonius to take *logos* to mean *hypographē*, description, and *ousia* to stand for accidental properties as well. Evidently, Elias is following almost to the letter both Porphyry and Ammonius when he states with unusual succinctness the difference between definition and description: τὸ δὲ τί ἐστιν τοῦ ὁρισμοῦ πρόσρημα ἢ ὑπογραφῆς. διαφέρει δὲ ταῦτα ἀλλήλων, ὅτι ὁ μὲν ὁρισμὸς ἐκ τῶν κατ' οὐσίαν λαμβάνεται, ἡ δὲ ὑπογραφὴ ἐκ τῶν κατὰ συμβεβηκότων. χείρων δὲ ἡ ὑπογραφὴ τοῦ ὁρισμοῦ. Eliae, *In Porph. Isag.* 56. 11–14; also *Prolegomena Philosophiae* 4. 5–32.

[15] The definition of *man*, which is the illustration he uses, is taken word for word from Porphyry as given in *In Categ.* 60. 17–18.

[16] It is reasonable to conclude that Ammonius did not see that the position which he took in his *In Porph. Isag.* contradicted what he said in the *In Categ.* In the *Isagoge* he asserted the undefinability of all *homonyma*, and this, he insisted, holds true of Aristotle's own categorial theory where it deals with *homonyma*. If so, then he should have said that *logos*, since it refers to *homonyma pragmata*, can mean only description. In other words, Ammonius commits a contradiction when on the one hand he asserts the undefinability of all *homonyma* and, on the other, that *logos* in the context of the *Categories* can mean both description and definition. He states in the

Isagoge: τῶν δὲ ὁμωνύμων οὐκ ἔστι ὅρους ἀποδοῦναι . . . ὁ δὲ ὁρισμὸς οὐσίαν σημαίνει· ὧν δὲ οἱ ὁρισμοὶ οἱ αὐτοί, τούτων καὶ τὰ πράγματα τὰ αὐτά· οὐκ ἄρα ἐνδέχεται τῶν ὁμωνύμων ἕνα κοινὸν ὁρισμὸν ἀποδοῦναι (56. 2–6).

[17] Philoponi, *In Categ.* 16. 15–8.

[18] The point is that Philoponus purports to alert his reader to the fact that the term "*homonymon*" has many senses. He adopts Porphyry's two main tropes of *homonyma* and introduces certain minor changes in the types of intentional *homonyma.* Actually, all he does is to replace Porphyry's class of *homonyma* from similarity with two sub-classes, each related to a different underlying motive: (i) intention to commemorate, viz., a father who names his son after himself, and (ii) intention to indicate expectation, viz., a man who names his son after Plato (*In Categ.* 16. 20–17. 25).

[19] At 206A: ἴσον θυμὸν ἔχοντες ὁμώνυμοι.

[20] The reason, he says, Aristotle begins with the *homonyma* is because they are the simplest things, meaning that they have only one thing in common, unlike the *synonyma* which have two. This, he argues, is as it should be, for the simple must always precede the complex. Furthermore, it just so happens that the most general thing is itself a *homonymon:* "I speak here of *to on* . . . [hence] the theory of *homonyma* must have priority" (*In Categ.* 28. 8 ff.). Olympiodorus abounds in such irrelevancies and speculations. For his comment on the phrase "*homonyma legatai,*" he borrows heavily, according to his own admission, from Iamblichus' lost commentary. More often than not, Olympiodorus fails to keep his discussion within the boundaries of basic issues. His irrelevancies run the gamut from a Homeric verse to Attic syntax.

[21] Simplicius never doubts the usefulness of the discussion on *homonyma.* He quotes from Iamblichus and Plato's *Euthydemus* to show the seriousness of the subject (22. 1–9). Plato, according to Simplicius, had to deal with ambiguity which is due to the lack of proper distinctions in the use of names (22. 9–13). The important thing is that Simplicius depends rather heavily on Iamblichus' lost commentary (*In Categ.* Proemium, 2. 10 f.), and also refers to Porphyry's work which had already exerted considerable influence on Iamblichus. Simplicius credits Iamblichus for being the first to observe that *to katēgorein* is homonymously predicated of the ten categories and that they have the name "category" in common only as a homonymously predicated name. Iamblichus is further reported to have taught that it was only proper for Aristotle to open the *Categories* with a brief discussion on the nature of *homonyma.* Simplicius is also eager to inform us that there were certain commentators, like Nicostratus and his followers, who had expressed serious reservations about the relevance of the first chapter of the *Categories* to the main doctrine presented in this treatise. Since we have no reason to doubt the historical accuracy of this information it is reasonable to say that we can speak with certainty about the existence of two schools opposing each other on the issue of the relevance of the doctrine of *homonyma* to the rest of Aristotle's categorial theory: the school of Nicostratus on the negative side and the neoplatonists Porphyry and Iamblichus defending the other.

[22] *In Categ.* 30. 5–15. The quotation is most likely from Porphyry's

lost work "*Tois pros Gedaleion.*" Porphyry argues that Aristotle added *tēs ousias* in order to leave no doubt about the exact meaning of *logos*, i.e., definition and description. Without *ousia*, *logos* might have also been taken to mean such things as eduction, syllogism, an affirmation, or a denial.

[23] Elias states that it is necessary for the exegete of Aristotle to πάντα εἰδέναι τὰ Πλάτωνος, ἵνα σύμφωνον ἑαυτῷ τὸν Πλάτωνα ἀποδείξῃ τὰ 'Αριστοτέλους τῶν Πλάτωνος εἰσαγωγὴν ποιούμενος (cf. 110. 28–30). See L. G. Westerink, *Anonymous Prolegomena to Platonic Philosophy* (Amsterdam, 1962), p. xx.

PHILLIP DeLACY
University of Pennsylvania

Οὐ μᾶλλον and the Antecedents of Ancient Scepticism*

IN the post-Aristotelian period of ancient philosophy οὐ μᾶλλον or οὐδὲν μᾶλλον, expressing the relation, "no more this than that," appears as a philosophical term in the Pyrrhonists, Plutarch, and the Aristotelian commentators. It is found also in Aristotle's criticisms of certain presocratic philosophers and in Plato's analysis of Heraclitus. Even earlier, Democritus employed it on more than one occasion; and it may be assigned with some plausibility to Gorgias and Nausiphanes. The meaning of οὐ μᾶλλον underwent a number of changes during this long period. Yet its more prominent uses were not unrelated, for it came to be associated with certain persistent problems in Greek thought, the history of which its use in some measure reflects.

For Democritus οὐ μᾶλλον carries no suggestion of scepticism. There is, of course, an element of paradox in his statement that being is no more real than not-being,[1] but the paradox is only apparent, as Democritus means to say that atoms are no more real than void. Also Democritean is the statement, "nothing is any more of one kind than of another"; and as this is used, according to Simplicius, as an argument for the infinite variety of atoms, it probably means that there is no limit to the differences among things.[2] Still a third use of the formula, assigned by Theophrastus (*De Sens.* 69) to Democritus, by Sextus Empiricus (*P. H.* 1. 213) to Democritus and his followers, has to do with the relativity of sense-perception; and Plutarch (*Col.* 1109 ab) implies that the Epicurean Colotes concurred in this interpretation. Moreover, Nausiphanes, who was considered a Democritean,[3] is said to have held that "ex his quae videntur esse nihil magis esse quam non esse."[4] But Plutarch (*Col.* 1109a) emphatically denied that Democritus used οὐ μᾶλλον of sense-perception, and it is possible that he misinterpreted Colotes, who may

* An earlier version of this paper was presented in December, 1956 before the SAGP. The author has profited greatly from the many helpful comments made at that meeting. From *Phronesis*, III (1958): 59–71. Reprinted by permission of Royal Van Gorcum Ltd.

well have been criticising the Democritean view that things are infinitely various.[5] Nausiphanes, who came under Pyrrho's influence (D. L. IX. 69), may have got the phrase from that source, and Theophrastus could have been alluding to a passage in Aristotle's *Metaphysics* which might be taken to refer ahead to Democritus, though it must also refer back to Protagoras: "the one set is no more true than the other, but both are alike."[6] One must conclude, therefore, that while Democritus gave some currency to the phrase he may not have associated it with the problem of knowledge.

Whether Protagoras used οὐ μᾶλλον to express the relativity of sense-perception must remain in doubt. Plutarch (*Col.* 1109a) is alone in assigning it to him, though Aristotle also used it (in the passage just cited) to describe the Protagorean view. It is possible that Plutarch had in mind either the Aristotelian passage or Plato's *Theaetetus* 182E, where the phrase, though used of Heraclitus, might easily be taken to refer also to Protagoras.[7] Presumably if Protagoras had used the formula it would have been as a double affirmation: the statement that honey is no more sweet than bitter means that honey is both sweet and bitter; while for Democritus it would have been a double negation: honey is neither sweet nor bitter.[8] In either case it would be intended as a statement about the nature of things.

But it was soon recognized that the relativity of sense-perception, when expressed in propositional form, raises certain difficulties; for if an object appears to be no more of one description than the opposite, one can hardly be said to have knowledge of it. It is just such "unsound" perceptions, according to Plato (*Republic* 523BC), that give rise to thought; for sense-perception reports the same thing as hard and soft, or heavy and light, or one and many, "so that a thing appears no more one than also its opposite" (524E).

Another statement of the relativity of sense-perception brings out the contradiction even more clearly: honey no more *is* than *is not* sweet. This formulation apparently lies behind the paradox attributed to Gorgias in *MXG* 979a 26–27: "For that which is not is *not*, and that which is, is, so that things will no more be than not be."[9] There is some question, however, whether Gorgias actually used the phrase, as it does not appear in Sextus' version of the Gorgian argument (*A.M.* VII. 65 ff.).

In *Theaetetus* 182E Plato uses οὐ μᾶλλον of a relation between contradictories. Socrates argues that on a Heraclitean view seeing "has no right to be called seeing, any more than not-seeing, nor is any other perception entitled to be called perception rather than not-perception, if everything is changing in every kind of way"; and as Socrates and Theaetetus had said that perception is knowledge, "in that case, our answer to the question, what knowledge is, did not mean knowledge any more than not-knowledge" (Cornford's translation). Here, as in the presumed Gorgian usage, οὐ μᾶλλον has become a formula of refutation, as a view which has been shown to be self-contradictory has been discredited.[10]

But Plato's concern here is perhaps less with a violation of the law of contradiction than with the loss of identity that follows on the admission of contrary or contradictory predicates: "nothing is one thing just by itself, nor can you rightly call it by some definite name, nor even say it is of any definite sort."[11] Things without a determinate character cannot be known (*Cratylus* 439D–440A), and οὐ μᾶλλον easily conveys the sense of indeterminateness. This may be seen again in *Timaeus* 49B: "It is hard to say, with respect to any one of these, which we ought to call really water rather than fire, or indeed which we should call by any given name rather than by all the names together or by each severally, so as to use language in a sound and trustworthy way" (Cornford's translation).

In *Met.* Γ and K οὐ μᾶλλον is once more a formula of refutation, now associated quite explicitly with the charge that certain systems are self-contradictory, that they make knowledge impossible by destroying the differences among things, and, in consequence, that they remove the grounds of action and moral choice. *Met.* Γ. 5 1009b 10–11 has already been cited, and Alexander's commentary on *Met.* Γ interprets several other passages from this book in terms of οὐ μᾶλλον.[12] A more generalized statement appears in K. 5 1062a 23–30: "Further, if the affirmation is no more true than the negation, he who says 'man' will be no more right than he who says 'not-man.' It would seem also that in saying the man is not a horse one would be either more or not less right than in saying he is not a man, so that one will also be right in saying that the same person *is* a horse; for it was assumed to be possible to make opposite statements equally truly. It follows then that the same person is a man and a horse, or any other animal."

In his refutation of Heraclitus, Aristotle speaks as if this philosopher admitted contradictory predicates not only in statements about the properties of objects but in any statements whatever. This means that he would have to admit the truth of statements contradicting his own doctrine. If an affirmation is no more true than its negation, then the affirmation that 'an affirmation is no more true than its negation' is itself no more true than its negation.[13] It follows that οὐ μᾶλλον as a universal principle is self-contradictory and hence untenable. In the refutation of Anaxagoras, Aristotle makes a similar transition from statements about objects to statements generally, and so concludes that Anaxagoras makes all predication impossible.[14] This universalization of οὐ μᾶλλον to apply even to statements about statements (and so to itself) is a prominent feature of its post-Aristotelian use.

In *Met.* K Aristotle touches on the implications of οὐ μᾶλλον for action (K. 6 1063a 28–35): "Further, when the doctor orders people to take some particular food, why do they take it? In what respect is 'this is bread' truer [μᾶλλον] than 'this is not bread'? And so it would make no difference whether one ate or not. But as a matter of fact they take the food which is ordered, assuming that they know the truth about it and that it is bread. Yet they should not, if there were no fixed constant nature in sensible things, but all natures moved and flowed for ever." And in Γ. 4 1008b 14–20 Aristotle asks, "For why does a man walk to Megara and not stay at home, when he thinks he ought to be walking there? Why does he not walk early some morning into a well or over a precipice, if one happens to be in his way? Why do we observe him guarding against this, evidently because he does not think that falling in is alike good and not good? Evidently, then, he judges one thing to be better and another worse. And if this is so, he must also judge one thing to be a man and another to be not-a-man, one thing to be sweet and another to be not-sweet." We hardly need Alexander to tell us (p. 299. 13–15 Hayduck) that the supposition that not falling in is good, and falling in is bad, and that the two are not alike but one is better and the other worse, is incompatible with the position that the thing is "no more this way than not this way" (οὐδὲν μᾶλλον οὕτως ἢ οὐχ οὕτως). A few lines later, commenting on Aristotle's statement that "all men make unqualified judgements, if not about all things, still about what is better and worse" (1008b 26–27), Alexander again uses the formula: "He says that all who say of everything, οὐδὲν μᾶλλον, and who assert that both of two contradictories are true, nevertheless make unqualified judgements in their suppositions, if not about all things, at least about the better and worse, expedient and inexpedient, and in general, matters that have to do with action" (p. 299. 30–33 Hayduck). Theophrastus' refutation of the Democritean οὐ μᾶλλον (*De Sens.* 69–70) also rests in part on an appeal to ethical judgements.

Finally, in Aristotle's words, "There is a more and a less in the nature of things" (*Met.* Γ. 4 1008b 32–33); this means, according to

Alexander (p. 301. 9–10 Hayduck), that we cannot say of all things indiscriminately, "no more this than that."

Thus for Aristotle and his school οὐ μᾶλλον was linked with the untenable position that two contradictory or otherwise incompatible propositions may both be true, that there is no essential nature in things, that good and bad, better and worse, have no basis in nature—a position to which presocratics and sophists, whether intentionally or not, came dangerously close to committing themselves. Of course, as a common Greek phrase, οὐ μᾶλλον is not limited to these contexts; one fairly frequent philosophical usage is simply to indicate that a philosopher has failed to make his case, as opposed to some alternative view.[15] Perhaps Aristotle did not yet think of οὐ μᾶλλον as a technical term; that Alexander did so is evident from his use of it with the article, τὸ οὐδὲν μᾶλλον (e.g., p. 285. 3 Hayduck).

The philosophical issues associated with οὐ μᾶλλον continued to be of central importance in the post-Aristotelian period, and the several Hellenistic schools may in large part be differentiated in terms of their method of handling the οὐ μᾶλλον predicament. They appear to have owed much to Aristotle's formulation.

In early Pyrrhonism οὐ μᾶλλον had a prominent place. Pyrrho gave it a universal application, with complete suspension of judgement (ἐποχή) as its consequence. It is said that he lacked even a basis for action and, like Aristotle's adversary, was in danger of falling over precipices.[16] Timon, his successor, explained οὐδὲν μᾶλλον as "to determine nothing, but to withhold assent" (D. L. IX. 76); and it is possible that the phrase "to determine nothing" echoes the indeterminate (ἀόριστον) which Aristotle associated with those who fail to choose between opposites and so have no principle of individuation (*Met.* Γ. 4. 1007b 26–29). Timon was also said to have maintained the doctrine of ἀφασία, the avoidance of assertion;[17] compare Aristotle's "for he says nothing" of the person who admits contradictories to be true.[18] Other aspects of Pyrrhonism may best be discussed in connection with the later Pyrrhonism of Aenesidemus and Sextus Empiricus, but first it is necessary to trace our problem through the other Hellenistic schools.

The avoidance of precipices (cf. Lucr. IV. 509) is a basic consideration in Epicureanism. If precipices are to be avoided, that is, if life is to be lived at all, there must be distinctions among things, and these distinctions must be knowable. But the things with which action deals are particulars, and these are known by sense-perception; hence the Epicurean insistence that sense-perception is accurate and reliable. And if things are to have distinct natures, their qualitative differences must rest on some firm foundation. Although not properties of individual atoms, such qualities as sweet and bitter are properties of combinations of atoms—here the Epicureans depart from Democritus—and thus provide an objective ground for practical judgements. Qualities cannot be ultimate, because they are unstable and tend to change into one another. Nor would the atoms produce an orderly universe if their possible combinations were infinitely various. The Epicurean limitation both of the kinds of atoms and of their possible combinations appears therefore as a deliberate attempt to escape the οὐ μᾶλλον predicament.

The phrase itself occurs infrequently in Epicurean texts, and only in the refutation of rival philosophers, for example in Lucretius' rejection of the four qualitative elements on the ground that in a continual process of qualitative change it is impossible to say what is the element of what: "how can they be called the first-beginnings of things any more than things the first-beginnings of them?" (I. 765–66, Bailey's translation). Colotes, one of Epicurus' early followers, charged that Democritus "confounded life" by saying that "each thing is no more of one kind than of another" (Plut. *Col.* 1108f); and indeed the whole of Colotes' attack on the philosophers is centered on the demands of everyday life. Parmenides destroyed the real differences among things; Empedocles ruled out generation; Socrates and the sceptics, by calling into question the validity of sense-perception, were left with no means of distinguishing food from fodder, or the wall from the door. Colotes' argument is thus an extravagant elaboration of certain aspects of the Aristotelian οὐ μᾶλλον and testifies to the Epicureans' desire to avoid its pitfalls.

But the Epicureans found themselves vulnerable to charges of οὐ μᾶλλον from other quarters. Stoic logicians attacked Epicurean inference from similar to similar by asking why inference holds between some sets of similars more than others (Philod. *Sign.*, col. V. 8–36); Epictetus (*Diss.* II. 20. 26) charged that the Epicurean neglect of moral principles makes slavery no more shameful than honorable, and freedom no more honorable than shameful; and Plutarch pointed out that the Epicurean insistence on the accuracy of sense-perception involves them in the old Protagorean predicament (*Col.* 1109a–1110e; cf. *Mor.* 651f–653b and Sextus, *A.M.* VII. 369) and reduces all things to ἀφασία (*Col.* 1123c). That the Epicureans were not unaware of the difficulties of their position is seen in Lucretius' remarkable statement (IV. 500–06) that it is better to give faulty explanations of optical illusions than to shake the foundation on which life and safety rest.

The Stoics, like the Epicureans, escaped some of the difficulties of οὐ μᾶλλον, only to fall into others. In the Stoic universe *being* (ὄν) is equated with body (σῶμα), which is characterized by power to act or be acted upon. The specific character of individual bodies is determined largely or perhaps entirely by their relation to other bodies, and all parts of the universe are related to each other and to the whole. Knowledge is secured through a special kind of appearance, the φαντασία καταληπτική, which is itself relational; it could not appear as it does if its object were not such as the appearance shows it to be.

Stoicism thus escaped a Protagorean relativity without recourse to a Platonic dualism; it provides a principle of individuation and the discernment of differences that practical judgements require.[19] Its weakness lies in the uniqueness that is required if every knowable object is to present to us its own identifiable appearance. How is it possible, the Academic Sceptics asked, to perceive the differences between eggs, for example, or between identical twins, and how can we be sure that there is not for every true appearance a false appearance indistinguishable from it.[20] Nor is there any subjective test by which true appearances may be distinguished from false; those that are true receive no more credence than those that are only thought to be true (Cic. *Luc.* 90). The Academics may also have asked how the Stoics could maintain the individual identity of things in the face of their doctrine of mixture (κρᾶσις).[21]

In self-defense the Stoics appealed to the practical situation. The New Academy "throws everything into confusion" (Plut. *Mor.* 1077c) by questioning the power to differentiate; and however difficult it may be to explain perception, there can be no doubt, says Epictetus (*Diss* I. 27. 17–19), "that you and I are not the same person." "Never, when I wish to eat something, do I carry the morsel of food there, but here; never, when I want bread, do I take chaff, but I always go to the bread like an arrow to its mark. And you who deny perception, do you do otherwise? Who of you goes to the mill-house, meaning to go to the bath?"[22] Scepticism, in short, is a Medusa that turns men to stone.[23]

If it was difficult for the Epicureans and Stoics to explain how they detected the μᾶλλον in things, it was in a way more difficult to hold that this μᾶλλον does not exist or cannot be known; for, as Aristotle had shown, οὐ μᾶλλον, when raised to the status of a universal principle, sooner or later removes itself along with everything else and so becomes untenable.

Arcesilaus, the first of the Academic Sceptics, apparently paid little attention to this problem. His aim was to find for every argument an opposing argument of equal weight, and such positive views as are assigned to him may all be explained as developed merely to counter Stoicism. The "dogma" ascribed to the Academy by Antiochus (Cic. *Luc.* 29), A. Gellius (XI. 5. 8) and Sextus Empiricus (*P.H.* I. 226), that "nothing is comprehensible," is no more than the contradictory to the Stoic view that some things are comprehensible. The analysis of action preserved by Plutarch in the reply to Colotes (1122b–d), that appearances give rise to impulses and impulses to action, is a demonstration that the Stoic psychology makes possible action without assent. Suspense of judgement is itself defended as a consequence of the Stoic view that the wise man will not have opinions (Cic. *Luc.* 77); and perhaps the appeal to the εὔλογον as a guide in practical matters is intended to show that it is possible to act in accordance with reason without commitment.[24]

Carneades, like Arcesilaus, did not regard scepticism as a position, as he insisted that even the statement "nothing can be comprehended" cannot be comprehended (Cic. *Luc.* 28), and he continued the device of constructing for every argument an opposing argument of equal weight. Against Stoicism he held that there is no appearance which might not be false (*Luc.* 27), and presumably he is to be counted among those who "cry out that those things [which they themselves defend] are no more true than false" (*Luc.* 43). There was a dispute among Carneades' followers whether or not he held that the wise man would have opinions. Cicero, I think rightly, agrees with Clitomachus that Carneades must have maintained this for the sake of argument (*Luc.* 78, cf. 59), doubtless against the Stoic view that the wise man never errs.

Apart from *Luc.* 43 Cicero's accounts of Academic Scepticism attest the use of οὐ μᾶλλον only in restricted contexts;[25] two other passages, however, assign it specifically to the Academy. One is from Numenius' account of Carneades (Euseb. *Praep. Ev.* XIV. 8. 7): "Having taken on one side something false but like the truth, and on the other a like thing apprehended by the φαντασία καταληπτική, and having balanced them against each other, he granted neither the true nor the false, or no more the one than the other—or rather, that which rested on the probable."[26] The second is a much emended passage from Hippolytus, *Haer.* I. 23. 3: "Some followers of the Academy say that one should make no assertion at all about things, but only construct arguments about them, then let them be. Others added οὐ μᾶλλον, saying that fire is no more fire than something else. Indeed they did not assert of anything *what it is* but that it is *of such a sort*."[27] If, as seems possible, this latter passage ultimately derives in part from *Timaeus* 49B–E, it may reflect some authentic Academic tradition.

In the ethical sphere Carneades avoided the overthrow of life (*vitae eversio*, *Luc*. 99) by his doctrine of the πιθανόν, which Cicero translated *probabile* or *veri simile* (*Luc*. 32, with Reid's note). It does not carry with it the assent to the truth of anything, as the "probable" may be, and often is, false; it means merely that under the proper circumstances certain appearances receive our approval and provide a basis for action (*Luc*. 104). Nevertheless, this doctrine in a sense reintroduces a μᾶλλον into things (one thing is more persuasive than its opposite) and is unacceptable to Sextus (*P.H*. I. 226), to whom even a statement of preference is a departure from scepticism (*P.H*. I. 223). So Aristotle (*Met*. Γ. 4 1008b 31–1009a 5) had said that even a "more true", that is, the recognition that one proposition is closer to the truth than another, eliminates οὐ μᾶλλον.

The later Pyrrhonists accepted οὐ μᾶλλον as one of their characteristic formulas (*P.H*. I. 187; Photius, *Bibl*. 169b 29–30). It appears in two of the ten tropes (D.L. IX. 81–82; cf. *A.M*. VIII. 54), but even more prominently in the juxtaposition of conflicting dogmas, for example (*A.M*. IX. 50): "some say that there is a god, some that there is not, some [i.e., the Pyrrhonists, cf. 59] that there no more is than is not"; or again (*A.M*. X. 45), "some say that motion exists, some that it does not, some [i.e., the Pyrrhonists, cf. 49] that it no more exists than not." Other examples include the indicative sign (*A.M*. VIII, 201), proof (*A.M*. VIII. 328), cause and effect (*A.M*. IX. 228–29), wealth as a good (*A.M*. XI. 147), and the choice among authorities in philosophy (*A.M*. VII. 328).[28]

As the Pyrrhonists thought of their scepticism as a *position*, it was necessary for them to find an answer to the logical difficulties inherent in οὐ μᾶλλον. For one thing, the statement that one of two contradictories is no more true than the other may be taken either affirmatively (both are true) or negatively (both are false); but neither alternative is tenable, as Aristotle had pointed out that of any two contradictories one must be true and the other false (*Met*. Γ. 8 1012b 10–13). Moreover, either alternative would commit the sceptic to the truth or falsity of something. Diogenes Laertius (IX. 75) says that the Pyrrhonists, recognizing that οὐ μᾶλλον could be taken in either an affirmative or a negative sense, chose to use it negatively; perhaps the formulation preserved by Eusebius (*Praep. Ev*. XIV. 18. 3) is more accurate: "saying of each thing that it no more *is* than *is not*, or *both is and is not*, or *neither is nor is not*." Here I take the concluding compounds to be parallel to *is not*, giving the formulations, "each thing no more *is* than *both is and is not*," and "each thing no more *is* than *neither is nor is not*." Compare the truncated formula in A. Gellius (xi. 5. 4): "this is no more this way than that way or neither way."

A second logical difficulty had been pointed out by Aristotle: if an affirmation is no more true than its negation, then the affirmation, "an affirmation is no more true than its negation," is itself no more true than its negation. Hence οὐ μᾶλλον destroys its own validity.[29] Carneades, similarly, had held that the statement, "nothing can be comprehended," cannot be comprehended; and of course the opponents of scepticism had seized on the point:

> Denique nil sciri siquis putat, id quoque nescit
> an sciri possit, quoniam nil scire fatetur.[30]

Compare also Photius, *Bibl.* 170a 11–12: "Universally the Pyrrhonist determines nothing, not even the very fact that he determines nothing";[31] and the paradox in Euseb. *Praep. Ev.* XIV. 18. 7: "Furthermore, if all things are indifferent and one should therefore hold no opinions, these things too are indifferent—I mean, being indifferent or not, and holding opinions or not. For why are they any more of this kind than not? Or, as Timon says, why "yes," and why "no," and why the very question, "why?"?[32]

That οὐδὲν μᾶλλον "includes itself" is recognized by Sextus (*P.H.* I. 14); it thus eliminates itself and does not constitute a tenable position.[33] And yet (Photius, *Bibl.* 169b 36–170a 38) the Pyrrhonists claim to avoid the self-contradiction into which the Academic Sceptics fall when they hold that nothing is comprehensible. They can make good this claim only by giving to οὐ μᾶλλον and the other formulas of scepticism some special status differentiating them from the dogmas they attack. Having accepted the Aristotelian formulation, they were not able to do this simply by stating that οὐ μᾶλλον is not a member of the class of propositions to which it refers. Such a solution (for the statement, "nothing can be comprehended") had apparently been suggested by the Stoic Antipater (Cic. *Luc.* 28), but had been rejected by the Academic Sceptics as impairing the universality of their scepticism. Instead, the Pyrrhonists give a special meaning to οὐ μᾶλλον, or even transform it into another kind of sentence. It is not assertive. It makes neither an affirmation nor a denial, but merely reports the speaker's failure to assent to one alternative rather than the other. As Timon had said, it means "to determine nothing, but to withhold assent" (D.L. IX. 76). Elsewhere Diogenes

Laertius describes it as a "confession" (ἐξομολόγησις, IX. 104) and Sextus terms it "interrogative."[34] Again, one may say that οὐ μᾶλλον and the other formulas give information about the sceptic; they report a πάθος (*P.H.* I. 190), revealing the way in which things appear to the sceptic at the time he utters them (*P.H.* I. 191–93, 197). Hence they may be called narrative or descriptive (cf. *P.H.* I. 15, 197, 200). Thus understood, οὐ μᾶλλον and the other formulas are no longer self-contradictory.

Having thus disposed of the logical difficulties of οὐ μᾶλλον, the Pyrrhonist can now accept a Protagorean relativism without falling into the Protagorean contradictions. He can agree with Aristotle in rejecting the view that all appearances are false or that all are true (*A.M.* VIII. 55) yet agree with Protagoras that all is relative[35] and can appropriate as "tropes" the considerations that were presumed to have led Protagoras and Democritus to their mistaken views. He can further agree with Aristotle that this relativism destroys individuation, proof, and meaningful assertion. "No form, no words, no object of taste, smell, or touch, no other object of perception has any distinctive character";[36] and terms used by the dogmatists, such as "proof" (*A.M.* VIII. 327), "definition" (*P.H.* II. 212), and "genus" (*P.H.* II. 219–27), have no precise meaning.

Appearance, not reality, is for the Pyrrhonist the proper locus of human thought and action. With the Academic Sceptics (Cic. *Luc.* 103; Plut. *Col.* 1118ab) he protests that he does not deny to appearances their apparent qualities (*P.H.* I. 19–20, 22; D.L. IX. 103–06), and he maintains that observation and memory give to these appearances a kind of order. It is as if he accepted the lower regions of Plato's cave as the true picture of human life and decided to make the most of it. Necessary relations between things, as expressed by indicative signs, give way to observed and remembered relations, or admonitive signs (*P.H.* II. 100, 102; *A.M.* VIII. 152, 156–58), and proofs give way to reminders (ὑπόμνησις is used as a substitute for ἀπόδειξις in *A.M.* VIII. 444; X. 15, 85; *P.H.* II. 130, 206; III. 20). Words regain their meanings as signifying those appearances with which we agree to associate them (*A.M.* VIII. 202, 289), and even arts and sciences become possible (cf. *A.M.* I. 49; V. 2). So life is not overthrown (*A.M.* VIII. 157).

The problem of action thus finds its solution on the phenomenal level. Some of our activities come to us naturally, as the satisfaction of hunger or the act of perceiving. Others are in pursuance of empirical arts and sciences. In the strictly ethical sphere nothing is by nature more to be desired than to be avoided (*A.M.* XI. 118; cf. D.L. IX. 101); we therefore follow human laws and customs without commitment, that we may not be inactive.[37]

Whatever one may think of the adequacy of the Pyrrhonic analysis, it seems safe to conclude that the terms of the problem which they were attempting to solve were in large part dictated by Aristotle and his predecessors.

NOTES

[1] Aristot. *Metaph.* A. 4 985b 8: οὐδὲν μᾶλλον τὸ ὂν τοῦ μὴ ὄντος εἶναί φασιν. Cf. Plut. *Col.* 1109a: μὴ μᾶλλον τὸ δὲν ἢ τὸ μηδὲν εἶναι.

[2] Frags. 67A 8, 68 A 38 Diels-Kranz; cf. Zeller, I. 2^6, pp. 1063 f.

[3] Frags, 75 A 1, 4, 5 Diels-Kranz.

[4] Sen. *Epist. Mor.* 88.43; 75 B 4 Diels-Kranz.

[5] Cf. *AJP*, 77 (1956): 434.

[6] *Met.* Γ. 5 1009b 10–11: οὐδὲν γὰρ μᾶλλον τάδε ἢ τάδε ἀληθῆ, ἀλλ' ὁμοίως. Cf. Theophr. *De Sens* 69: μηδὲν μᾶλλον ἕτερον ἑτέρου τυγχάνειν τῆς ἀληθείας. The Oxford translation of the *Metaphysics* has been used throughout.

[7] At 166C Plato puts the phrase in the mouth of Protagoras, but not as indicative of the relativity of sense-perception.

[8] Cf. E. Pappenheim, *Die Tropen der griechischen Skeptiker* (Berlin, 1885), p. 8 n. 1; Sextus, *P.H.* I. 213; II. 63.

[9] Kerferd's translation, *Ph*, I (1955): 10; see also V. Di Benedetto, "Il περὶ τοῦ μὴ ὄντος di Gorgia e la polemica con Protagora", *RML*, Ser VIII, vol. X (1955): 287–307.

[10] οὐδὲν μᾶλλον is used of a rejected view also in *Theaetetus* 181E and *Republic* 340B.

[11] *Theaetetus* 152D Cornford's translation; cf. 156E–157A and *Republic* 523C.

[12] At 1007a 20 he says that Aristotle is here giving further proofs that it is not possible to say universally that each thing no more is than is not (p. 285. 3–4 Hayduck; cf. 285. 21–25). At 1008a 2 he formulates the position that Aristotle is refuting as "no more man than not-man" (p. 293. 1–2), and again at 1008a 7 he characterizes Aristotle's opponents as wanting to say of all things no more the affirmation than the negation (p. 294. 1–2). On 1010b 19 (p. 315. 14–18) he points out that if everything can be said to be no more one thing than its opposite, there is no οὐσία of anything. For other instances see 305. 30, 312. 18, 319. 36–37, 320. 23; I have not attempted to compile an exhaustive list.

[13] *Met.* K. 5, 1062b 2–7: καθάπερ γὰρ καὶ διῃρημένων αὐτῶν οὐδὲν μᾶλλον ἡ κατάφασις ἢ ἡ ἀπόφασις ἀληθεύεται, τὸν αὐτὸν τρόπον καὶ τοῦ συναμφοτέρου καὶ τοῦ συμπεπλεγμένου καθάπερ μιᾶς τινος καταφάσεως οὔσης οὐδὲν μᾶλλον ⟨ἢ⟩ ἡ ἀπόφασις [ἢ] τὸ ὅλον ὡς ἐν καταφάσει τιθέμενον ἀληθεύσεται.

[14] *Met.* K. 6 1063b 26–35: ὅταν γὰρ ἐν παντὶ φῇ παντὸς εἶναι μοῖραν, οὐδὲν μᾶλλον εἶναί φησι γλυκὺ ἢ πικρὸν ἢ τῶν λοιπῶν ὁποιανοῦν ἐναντιώσεων, εἴπερ ἐν ἅπαντι πᾶν ὑπάρχει μὴ δυνάμει μόνον ἀλλ' ἐνεργείᾳ καὶ ἀποκεκριμένον. ὁμοίως δὲ οὐδὲ

πάσας ψευδεῖς οὐδ' ἀληθεῖς τὰς φάσεις δυνατὸν εἶναι, δι' ἄλλα τε πολλὰ τῶν συναχθέντων ἂν δυσχερῶν διὰ ταύτην τὴν θέσιν, καὶ διότι ψευδῶν μὲν οὐσῶν πασῶν οὐδ' αὐτὸ τοῦτό τις φάσκων ἀληθεύσει, ἀληθῶν δὲ ψευδεῖς εἶναι πάσας λέγων οὐ ψεύσεται. Cf. *Met* A. 8 989b 6–12; Γ. 4 1007b 25–26; Γ. 7 1012a 24–28.

[15] Cf. *Met.* A. 8 990a 15; A. 9 991a 3; B. 2 996b 33; Theophr. *De Sens.* 13, 33.

[16] D.L. IX. 61–62. It is chronologically possible that Pyrrho, as a younger contemporary, influenced Aristotle's use of the phrase.

[17] Euseb. *Praep. Ev.* XIV. 18.4.

[18] *Met.* Γ. 4 1008a 31; cf. K. 6 1063b 10–11.

[19] Cf. Sextus, *A.M.* VII. 252. There is, to be sure, an area of "indifferents" in ethics, where presumably discrimination is not required, e.g. in selecting one of two identical coins. Our inclination is to select one, but is "no more toward this than toward that." Cf. Sextus, *P.H.* III. 177; Plut. *Mor.* 1045 ef.

[20] Cic. *Luc.* 56–58; Sextus, *A.M.* VII. 409–410.

[21] Plut. *Mor.* 1077e–1078e. Compare Aristotle's criticism of Anaxagoras. The Stoic category of "relative disposition" (πρός τί πως ἔχον) also results in οὐ μᾶλλον: *A.M.* XI. 118.

[22] Cf. II. 20 28–31, where the τί μᾶλλον formula occurs.

[23] Plut. *Mor.* 1122a; Epict. *Diss.* I.5.2.

[24] Sextus, *A.M.* VII. 158. Cf. Epictetus' description of ethical situations as hypotheses which in themselves we do not admit to be either good or bad, but the consequences of which we work out, as of mathematical problems, and act accordingly: *Diss.* I. 25. 7–13.

[25] E.g. *Luc.* 96, 128; *Nat. Deor.* III. 36; *Div.* II. 9, 37, 62, 65, 67, 106, 126.

[26] παραλαβὼν γὰρ ἀληθεῖ μὲν ὅμοιον ψεῦδος, καταληπτικῇ δὲ φαντασίᾳ καταληπτὸν ὅμοιον καὶ ἀγαγὼν εἰς τὰς ἴσας, οὐκ εἴασεν οὔτε τὸ ἀληθὲς εἶναι οὔτε τὸ ψεῦδος, ἢ οὐ μᾶλλον τὸ ἕτερον τοῦ ἑτέρου ἢ μᾶλλον ἀπὸ τοῦ πιθανοῦ. The concluding clause indicates that Numenius found the Carneadean theory of probability inconsistent with the principle of οὐ μᾶλλον.

[27] I follow Wendland's text: οἱ μὲν οὖν τῶν 'Ακαδημαϊκῶν λέγουσιν μὴ δεῖν τὴν ἀρχὴν περὶ μηδενὸς ἀποφαίνεσθαι, ἀλλ' ἁπλῶς ἐπιχειρήσαντας ἐᾶν. οἱ δὲ τὸ ⟨οὐ⟩ μᾶλλον προσέθεσαν, λέγοντες οὐ μᾶλλον τὸ πῦρ ⟨πῦρ⟩ εἶναι ἢ ἄλλο τι. οὐ μέντοι ἀπεφήναντο αὐτὸ ⟨τὸ⟩ τί ἐστιν, ἀλλὰ τὸ τοιόνδε. It is true that Hippolytus draws no distinction between Academic and Pyrrhonic scepticism.

[28] This last is used against the Pyrrhonists in Euseb. *Praep. Ev.* XIV. 18. 14, 17.

[29] Cf. *Met.* Γ.8 1012b 14f.: αὐτοὺς ἑαυτοὺς ἀναιρεῖν. The idea is doubtless older than Aristotle; cf. Sen. *Epist. Mor.* 88. 43: Protagoras ait de omni re in utramque partem disputari posse ex aequo et de hac ipsa, an omnis res in utramque partem disputabilis sit.

[30] Lucr. IV. 469–70; cf. D.L. IX. 102. The idea was earlier expressed by Metrodorus of Chios, frags. 70A 25, B1 Diels-Kranz.

[31] καθόλου γὰρ οὐδὲν ὁ Πυρρώνιος ὁρίζει, ἀλλ' οὐδὲ αὐτὸ τοῦτο, ὅτι οὐδὲν διορίζεται. Cf. D.L. IX. 104; Gellius XI. 5. 8.

32 ἔτι γε μὴν εἰ ἐπ' ἴσης ἐστὶν ἀδιάφορα πάντα καὶ διὰ τοῦτο χρὴ μηδὲν δοξάζειν, οὐκ ἂν οὐδὲ ταῦτα διαφέροι· λέγω δὲ τὸ διαφέρειν ἢ μὴ διαφέρειν, καὶ τὸ δοξάζειν ἢ μὴ δοξάζειν. τί γὰρ μᾶλλον τοιαῦτα ἔστιν ἢ οὐκ ἔστιν; ἤ, ὥς φησι Τίμων, διὰ τί ναὶ καὶ διὰ τί οὒ καὶ αὐτὸ τὸ διὰ τί διὰ τί;

33 D.L. IX. 76: ἀναιροῦσι δ' οἱ σκεπτικοὶ καὶ αὐτὴν τὴν οὐδὲν μᾶλλον φωνήν· ὡς γὰρ οὐ μᾶλλόν ἐστι πρόνοια ἢ οὐκ ἔστιν, οὕτω καὶ τὸ οὐδὲν μᾶλλον οὐ μᾶλλόν ἐστιν ἢ οὐκ ἔστι. Cf. *P.H.* I. 206; Euseb. *Praep. Ev.* XIV. 18. 21.

34 *A.M.* I. 315 (πυσματική). Cf. the alternate formula, τί μᾶλλον (*P.H.* I. 189).

35 Cf. Aristot. *Met.* Γ. 6 1011a 17; Sextus, *P.H.* I. 216; Gellius XI. 5. 7; and the anonymous commentary on the *Theatetus*, col. 63. 1–4.

36 Comm. on *Theaet.*, col. 63. 6–11; cf. the Pyrrhonic ἀφασία: *P.H.* I. 192–93.

37 *P.H.* I. 23–24, 231, 237–38; D.L. IX. 61. See also the reply to this position in Euseb. *Praep. Ev.* XIV. 18. 20.

DAVID J. FURLEY
Princeton University

Knowledge of Atoms and Void in Epicureanism*

THERE is an obvious paradox in the theories of the Atomists. They held that nothing exists but atoms and void, and that the atoms are imperceptibly small, and invariant in quality. The thinking part of a man is composed of these materials and no others; his thinking can only be a function of the motions of invariant atoms. Knowledge of the external world must be some kind of reaction between the atoms of the external world and the atoms of the thinking man; and the only reaction in the atomist's theory is simply collision. That is to say, the connexion between the thinking subject and the external world is nothing but touch: "tactus enim, tactus, pro divum numina sancta" as Lucretius strenuously insists (2. 434). The Atomists are then ready to show how all our senses are really varieties of the sense of touch; each faculty of sense is stimulated by actual contact with suitable formations of atoms proceeding from the external world.

It is a picture which has a certain plausibility as a theory of sensation. And the atomists liked to say that sensation is indeed the basis for all our contact with the external world. The paradox of course is this: if knowledge comes to us by means of sensation, how are we to explain the atomist's knowledge of the basic propositions of his special theory: that the world consists of void, which is called "the intangible," and atoms, which are said to be imperceptibly small? It is a question which arises with regard to the earlier Atomists and the post-Aristotelians; but this paper deals only with the latter.

One answer to the question has acquired authority during the last few decades of classical scholarship, and I want first to examine it. Its best known statement is in the work on Epicurus by Cyril Bailey. According to Bailey, the Epicureans believed in a form of direct knowledge

* A revised version of a paper entitled "Problems in the Epistemology of the Greek Atomists," presented at the 1967 meeting of the SAGP in Boston, Massachusetts.

of the external world which by-passed sense perception. It was a sort of focussing of the mind analogous to focussing the eyes, straining the ears, dilating the nostrils (and presumably doing whatever one does do to the tongue and the skin for the other two senses).

Bailey correctly drew attention[2] to a striking difference in what Epicurus said about the two classes of subjects which he grouped together under the heading *adela* (non-evident). Meteorology and the stars were one such class; Epicurus asserted that since we cannot get the close view and since many explanations of the same phenomenon are often equally in conformity with our observations, the philosopher must hold all these explanations to be equally true. To prefer one to the others, he said, would be to plunge into mythology.[3] And everybody knows that the Epicureans exhibited something like relish in offering multiple explanations for these things.[4]

However, the fundamental principles of the atomic theory, such as the statement that there exist atoms, that there is void, that there is no third sort of being, and so on—these are also *adela*, in that they are not accessible to direct sense-perception. But in this case, the Epicureans accepted no multiple explanations: just one theory was right, and one could accept it confidently.

What was the Epicureans' justification for this certainty? Bailey thought he had found the answer in the expression used by Epicurus with some frequency but without definition: "*epibolē tēs dianoias.*" I quote from Bailey:[5] "Thought—or reasoning—about the ultimate realities of the world is conducted by the comparison and combination of 'clear' concepts, each stage in the process being a new concept recognized as self-evident. These concepts are grasped by 'an act of apprehension on the part of the mind' (*epibole tes dianoias*) exactly similar to that by which the senses apprehend the 'clear vision' of the near object, or the mind the subtle images which penetrate to it."

This assertion was defended in a long appendix on *epibole tes dianoias* which Bailey put at the end of both of his books on Epicurus.

Striking use of Bailey's explanation was made by Cornford, in the second chapter of his *Principium Sapientiae*, where he attacks the verdict of some writers that Epicureanism was one of the most "scientific" of ancient philosophical systems. Cornford says:[6]

> A system which professes to rest on the testimony of the infallible senses might be expected to put forward only a tentative hypothesis about the wholly imperceptible, and to recommend suspension of

> judgment . . . But Epicurus' attitude is exactly the reverse of this sceptical caution: he is more dogmatic in this field than in either of the other two . . . "Atomism is not one among several possible theories of the universe, nor with regard to any of its details is there a hint that any other view than that expounded by Epicurus himself could be true," (Bailey *GAE* 265). Epicurus is content to assert roundly that his atomism is the only theory consistent with phenomena.

A curious feature of this appreciation of Epicurus is the way in which it ignores some of the evidence, and distorts the rest. "How did Epicurus suppose we come by our knowledge of atoms and the void?" Bailey asks. But he does not look for the answer in the obvious place: namely, in the text in which Epicurus defends his basic propositions. Instead he seizes upon the obscure phrase *epibole tes dianoias* and manipulates the contexts[7] in which it appears until they seem to justify his theory of direct mental apprehension.

It must be conceded first that the notion of direct mental apprehension *does* play a part in Epicureanism. What I want to deny is only that it plays the supremely important part in the foundations of the atomic theory that Bailey has given to it.

There is enough textual evidence in Epicurus himself and Lucretius to show that the Epicureans held that certain *eidola*, of the same kind as the *eidola* which cause sense-perception, do not stimulate the senses, because they are too fine (*leptos*), but rather penetrate directly to the soul-atoms of the mind.[8] There they may produce a phantasia or image, which is similar to the images produced by sensation. The experiences which the Epicureans hoped to explain by this thesis were dream-visions, certain types of imagination (in the modern sense), and especially ideas about the gods.

The texts which serve as our evidence for *this* theory do not speak of the fundamental propositions about atoms and the void. It is my belief that this theory was strictly limited to the explanation of those experiences with which it is associated in the surviving texts.

The inflation of *epibole tes dianoias* into a kind of intuitive knowledge which includes knowledge of the fundamental propositions of atomism can be punctured by the study of one text in particular. This text is in the right place: that is, it is no obiter dictum, but centrally placed in the *Letter to Herodotus*, §50–51, in the passage that deals with our knowledge of the external world. To my mind all the editors misunderstand it.[9]

A

καὶ ἣν ἂν λάβωμεν φαντασίαν ἐπιβλητικῶς τῇ διανοίᾳ ἢ τοῖς αἰσθητηρίοις εἴτε μορφῆς εἴτε συμβεβηκότων, μορφή ἐστιν αὕτη τοῦ στερεμνίου, γινομένη κατὰ τὸ ἑξῆς πύκνωμα ἢ ἐγκατάλειμμα τοῦ εἰδώλου.

Whatever image, of shape or of properties, we get by apprehension of the mind or the senses, this is the shape of the solid object, when it comes about because of the successive repetition of the *eidolon*, or because of the remaining effect of the *eidolon*.[10]

B

τὸ δὲ ψεῦδος καὶ τὸ διημαρτημένον ἐν τῷ προσδοξαζομένῳ ἀεί ἐστιν . . . .

But falsehood and error always lie in the addition made by *doxa* . . . .[11]

C

ἥ τε γὰρ ὁμοιότης τῶν φαντασμῶν οἱονεὶ ἐν εἰκόνι λαμβανομένων ἢ καθ' ὕπνους γινομένων ἢ κατ' ἄλλας τινὰς ἐπιβολὰς τῆς διανοίας ἢ τῶν λοιπῶν κριτηρίων οὐκ ἄν ποτε ὑπῆρχε τοῖς οὖσί τε καὶ ἀληθέσι προσαγορευομένοις, εἰ μὴ ἦν τινα καὶ ταῦτα πρὸς ἃ ἐπιβάλλομεν.

For there would have been no similarity between the appearances seen as if in a picture or occurring in dreams or in any of the other apprehensions (*epibolai*) of the mind or of the other criteria, and things which really exist and are called true, unless these things that we apprehend really existed.[12]

D

τὸ δὲ διημαρτημένον οὐκ ἂν ὑπῆρχεν, εἰ μὴ ἐλαμβάνομεν καὶ ἄλλην τινὰ κίνησιν ἐν ἡμῖν αὐτοῖς συνημμένην μὲν τῇ φανταστικῇ ἐπιβολῇ, διάληψιν δὲ ἔχουσαν· κατὰ δὲ ταύτην, ἐὰν μὲν μὴ ἐπιμαρτυρηθῇ ἢ ἀντιμαρτυρηθῇ, τὸ ψεῦδος γίνεται· ἐὰν δὲ ἐπιμαρτυρηθῇ ἢ μὴ ἀντιμαρτυρηθῇ, τὸ ἀληθές.

But the error would not have happened if we did not have a second motion, in ourselves, connected with the apprehension of the image, but different from it; in this motion, if there is no confirmation, or refutation, error arises, and if there is confirmation or no refutation, truth.[13]

Sentence A of this text is about reliable perception and mental apprehension. It might perhaps be thought that the word *epibletikos* mentions the necessary and sufficient condition for reliable perception; but this need not be so. The conditions for reliable perception are mentioned in the clause beginning *ginomene*. Mental images (*phantasiai*) are reliable when they are produced by the successive repetition of the *eidolon* (that is, when a constant stream of *eidola* comes from the external object to the perceiver, as when one is directly looking at the object), or when they come about through what is left behind by the *eidolon* (that is, the pattern left behind as a memory by previous sense-experience).[14] The word *epibletikos* means no more than "by the apprehensive process," the process by which the mind or the senses "get hold of" something. This is confirmed by a fragment of the lost work of Epicurus *On Nature*, where the *epibletikos tropos* is contrasted with "proceeding from oneself alone" (29.15.8).

Sentences B, C, and D are *all* about illusion. This is the point missed by the editors, who believe that C is about reliable perception. The passage as a whole is telling us something essentially simple, and it runs like this:

Sentence A (following a description of the *eidola* and their reception by the perceiver): the image that results from the apprehension of *eidola*, when it comes from a succession of *eidola*, not just a random one, or when it corresponds to a memory image, reproduces the shape of the external object which produced the *eidola*.

Sentence B. Error is not in the act of apprehension, but in a subsequent movement of the soul, called *doxa*.

Sentence C. The misleading resemblance between dream-images and other illusory appearances[15] on the one hand and what is true and real on the other—the resemblance which leads into the error of supposing that the illusion is the truth—exists because illusory images, as well as reliable images, are produced by the apprehension of real *eidola* (real *eidola*, we have to understand, but not in a steady succession).[16]

Sentence D. Error occurs when such an image is wrongly assessed by *doxa*—the "second motion" (*sc.* of soul atoms) "in ourselves": it is treated as a clear image, resulting from a steady stream of *eidola*, when it is not.

Here, then, *epibole tes dianoias* occurs in the explanation of illusions of many kinds. This surely should have been enough to give Bailey pause. What kind of a concept is it that is *both* the explanation of illusory dreams and visions, *and* the guarantee of scientific truth? If this phrase is to mean "an act of deliberate attention" is it not disconcerting to find it in an account of dreams?

At this point we can turn to the other approach to Epicurus' idea of his knowledge of the atomic theory: that is, the method of argument used to defend it. First, it may be worth saying that Bailey and Cornford were probably distracted from this approach by the notion, which seems to me mistaken, that we must look for the distinguishing characteristics of an empirical theory in the manner in which the theory is first reached, rather than the manner in which it is defended. As against this, I agree with Popper, who wrote at the beginning of his *Logic of Scientific Discovery*, "The question of how a new idea occurs to a man . . . may be of great interest to empirical psychology; but it is irrelevant to the logical analysis of scientific knowledge."[17]

The relevant section of the *Letter to Herodotus* is preceded by a methodological note: "We must control all our investigation by the sensations and by the immediate apprehensions (*epibolai*) either of the mind or the various other criteria, likewise by the immediate feelings, so that we can make inferences about that which is in suspense and about things which are unclear."[18]

He continues at once: "About things that are unclear, we must get the following points made and keep them in mind. First, that nothing comes to be out of that which does not exist; for everything would in that case be coming into being with no need of seeds."

Notice the very simple method: he asserts his thesis, then makes its contradictory the protasis of a conditional statement, of which the apodosis is a proposition falsified by sense-perception. "P. For, if not-P, then Q, which is observed to be false."

We have very nearly the same pattern repeated frequently, and especially in the argument for the existence of void, which became famous and much talked about in antiquity—indeed it was famous before Epicurus used it at all, for it was used in the reverse direction by the Eleatics,[19] and was almost certainly borrowed from them by Leucippus and Democritus.[20]

First Epicurus notes that the existence of *somata* is confirmed by the direct evidence of the senses, "which we must use for making inferences about what is unclear by reasoning (*logismos*)." He goes on, "If there did not exist that which we call void and space and untouchable nature, bodies would have nowhere to be or to move, as they are observed to move."

The schema is this: "Void exists: for if void did not exist, there would be no motion, which we observe to be false."

A century or more after Epicurus, when *Stoic* logic was developed into a systematic study, this pattern of inference was formalized and grouped with other similar patterns. It is in fact the second of the undemonstrated arguments collected by Benson Mates (*Stoic Logic*, p. 71): "If the first, then the second. Not the second; therefore not the first," with negative propositions substituted for the propositional variables.

The Stoics, with their new interest in logic and epistemology, attacked the Epicureans. Although the Epicureans were probably never much interested in logic as such, they evidently felt impelled to offer some sort of reply to Stoic criticism. We have evidence of their replies in the Epicurean work by Philodemus, called *On Signs*, which partly survives in the form of badly mutilated papyrus fragments. It was published by Gomperz in the 1860s, and there was a further study of it by Philippson in 1909 and 1910, so there was no excuse for Bailey's total neglect of it in his books on Epicureanism; though of course he did not have the advantage of Professor DeLacy's edition of it. This book should at least be scrutinised for any evidence it may provide on the way the Epicureans thought about the epistemological basis of their theory. Like all the Herculaneum papyri which contain Epicurean material (at least, those so far unrolled and read), Philodemus' *On Signs* has very limited value. What it does show is that a debate went on about the validity of inductive inference. The Stoics, it appears, wanted a logic of science based on the model of Aristotelian *apodeixis*, in which only necessary truths would be admitted. Hence they claimed that the implication, "If there is motion, then there is void," was valid only if it was contradictory to deny the second and assert the first; i.e., only if void were somehow involved in the definition of motion. The Epicureans replied with an insistence that the inference is empirical, not analytic. "We study all the things that move in our experience and we reckon up the accompanying conditions, without which we see nothing move; and we claim that everything that moves, moves like these things, and so infer that there cannot be motion without void."[21]

Now, these Epicurean arguments are no doubt naive and lacking in scientific precision. But they do not, so far as I can see, suggest that knowledge of the proposition, "there is void," and of the other basic proposition of the atomic theory, was thought to depend upon some kind of direct mental perception called *epibole tes dianoias*. Of course, the Stoics had a point when they said that the arguments which moved from instances in our experience to instances outside our experience depend on the assumption that there are uniformities in nature. But this is clearly only a weakness if you demand analytic truth in the realm of empirical knowledge.

However let us look at some Epicurean arguments of a different type, where the appeal to sense-perception is less obvious.

One example is the argument with which Epicurus supports his theory of τὸ ἐν τῇ ἀτόμῳ ἐλάχιστον, or *minimae partes*, as Lucretius calls them.[22] There are other ways of reading this argument, but if I am right about it, it includes the following: Suppose that an atom contains infinitely numerous parts, each of them having size: *it is impossible*, in that case, *to see* how it can still be finite in size, since the parts must all be of some size, and if they are infinitely numerous, the total must be infinitely large. Hence we must not suppose that the atom is infinitely divisible.

This argument contains the expression *ouk esti noesai*, "it cannot be thought," "it is impossible to see." Does this indicate some appeal to a kind of direct intuition? Are we perhaps supposed to make use of the *epibole tes dianoias*, and rely on its negative report: "It is not possible to see how a finite body can have infinitely numerous parts"?

No. Epicurus continues at once with an appeal to sense-perception. There is a minimum visible quantity: one cannot—experience shows that one cannot—divide a *visible* area into infinitely numerous parts. We must believe that the sub-visible area, which is accessible only to the theorising mind, follows the same pattern as the visible one.

It is interesting that there are two analogies in this argument, one of which is supposed to hold while the other is not. Epicurus uses the analogy between the visible and the intelligible: he regards this as valid. But we might suppose that there is likewise an analogy between the minimum and multiples of the minimum in the visible field, and conclude that because we can distinguish parts of something that is larger than the minimum we must be able to distinguish parts of the minimum itself, since it is the same kind of stuff. This analogy obviously has to be rejected. Epicurus goes on at once to reject another one: if we say the atom has parts, we might be tempted to think that it could be resolved into its parts like compound bodies in the sensible range: but this again is obviously false. The reason why the analogy can be seen to be invalid on both these cases is just that the conclusion yielded by the analogy has already been falsified by another argument. We know already that there is a minimum visible quantity, and that atoms are indissoluble.

This passage may perhaps throw some light on another part of the *Letter to Herodotus*: an obscure remark which Bailey used as the main prop to support his argument about *epibole tes dianoias*.[23]

The subject is this. Epicurus has just asserted that atoms moving in the void all move at the same speed, in whatever direction they are moving. Compound bodies, however, are seen to move at different speeds. How can this be? The answer is that though the compound appears to move all in a solid mass, it is in reality composed of atoms and void, and within its surfaces its component atoms *are* moving to and fro in all directions all at constant speed. The speed of motion of a compound body depends on the overall direction taken by its component atoms during a stretch of time. Now, suppose we have a compound moving from A to B, a distance of one metre, in 100 seconds. Then all its component atoms have moved one metre in that direction in 100 seconds. It is natural to suppose that each atom therefore moves one centimeter in that direction in one second, one millimeter in one tenth of a second, and so on. But this would be false. If we take the smallest time-intervals, each atom may be moving in any direction whatever.

This is how Epicurus concludes the paragraph:

τὸ γὰρ προσδοξαζόμενον περὶ τοῦ ἀοράτου, ὡς ἄρα καὶ οἱ διὰ λόγου θεωρητοὶ χρόνοι τὸ συνεχὲς τῆς φορᾶς ἕξουσιν, οὐκ ἀληθές ἐστιν ἐπὶ τῶν τοιούτων· ἐπεὶ τό γε θεωρούμενον πᾶν ἢ κατ' ἐπιβολὴν λαμβανόμενον τῇ διανοίᾳ ἀληθές ἐστι.

"The inference of *doxa* about the invisible, namely that the time intervals that can be examined (only) by means of theoretical reasoning will also retain that continuity of motion (sc. which is observed during perceptible time intervals), is false in such cases as these; for everything that is studied or grasped by apprehension is true."[24a]

Bailey seizes upon this statement because it appears to say that *epibole tes dianoias* is infallible. He makes the statement into an entirely general one by taking *theoroumenon* to mean "that which is grasped by the senses when 'looking' at the close view"; thus he makes it a general statement of the two sources of knowledge according to his view of Epicureanism: the close view, and the direct mental apprehension. But in fact *theoroumenon* must mean studied: the same root has occurred 16 words before, precisely to distinguish what is studied theoretically from what is observed by the senses. Whatever this concluding sentence says, it is all about thought. However, it still appears to say that the processes of thought are infallible. The contribution of *doxa* is false, since what is grasped by thought is true. "Why is *doxa* liable to produce false results, while the other (*epibole*) can only give us what is true?" Bailey asks;[24] and he answers, "with some hesitation," that it is because the mind moves by one *epibole* after another, from one clear and distinct concept to another, each of these concepts being clear in the same technical sense as that in which the unimpeded view of a near object is clear.

I think the clue to understanding this cryptic sentence of Epicurus lies in the passage quoted above.[25] What we have in both passages is a contrast between the operation of *doxa*, and the *epibole* of the senses or the mind. The important thing is to realize the exact nature of the contrast. Bailey takes it to mean that *doxa* goes wrong, whereas *epibole* is always right. But we have seen in the earlier passage that *epibole* is responsible for dreams and illusions, as well as for truth-telling apprehensions. The point of the contrast is that when we experience a mental image, it always pictures accurately the *eidolon* or set of *eidola* which cause it. Error never arises because of a lack of correspondence between the mental picture and the atomic configuration which caused it. The possibility of error (and of being right, too, we ought to add) arises only at the second stage, when *doxa*, a second movement of the mind, distinct from the *epibole*, pronounces upon the relation between the mental picture and the external world.

Epicurus should not use the word *alethes* of the primary impressions of the senses or the mind. It would be better to say they are neither true nor false. But it is quite clear that he does use *alethes* in this sense, since he is quoted as saying that "the illusions (*phantasmata*) of madmen and dream-visions are true." The explanation is added: "they are true because they move (the sufferer), and what does not exist does not cause movement."[26]

So I suggest that Epicurus is not saying, as Bailey thought, that *doxa's* inference from the seen to the unseen in this case is wrong, whereas the inference of *epibole* to the unseen is always right: he is saying that it must be *doxa's* inference to the unseen that is wrong in these cases, because the error never lies in the mental picture itself. He is not saying that direct mental apprehension infallibly tells the truth about the external world, but only that our mental images are not the level at which mistakes occur.

So, what are we left with?

An examination of all the evidence, of which the greater part has been discussed here, offers no ground for accepting Bailey's view of Epicurus.[27] Epicurus did not claim to have some kind of direct insight which led to clear and distinct ideas about the structure of the world. He tried to present arguments for his basic propositions, based on the evidence of sense-perception. Admittedly, his arguments were extremely simple minded, for the most part. But I do not see any fundamental inconsistency in his position. In particular, he is not liable to the charge laid against him by Cornford, that he dogmatically ruled out multiple explanations in his atomic theory, while accepting them in his meteorology. His method was to set up a pair of contradictories—either there is void or there is not, either matter is infinitely divisible or it is not—and then to present an argument for rejecting one of them.

NOTES

References are given as follows:

Epicurus *Letter to Herodotus* (*Her.*), *Letter to Pythocles* (*Pyth*), *Kyriai Doxai* (*KD*), *On Nature* (*Nat.*), in the edition of G. Arrighetti, *Epicuro* (Turin, 1960).

Philodemus *On Signs* in the edition by P. and E. A. De Lacy, *Philodemus: On Methods of Inference* (American Philological Association, 1941).

C. Bailey, *Epicurus* (Oxford, 1926)—*Ep.*

C. Bailey, *The Greek Atomists and Epicurus* (Oxford, 1928; N.Y., Russell and Russell, 1964)—*GAE.*

---

1 *GAE* 265, 559–76.

2 *GAE* 264–65.

3 *Pyth.* 87.

4 Many examples in *Pyth.* and Lucretius 6.

5 *GAE* 265.

6 *Principium Sapientiae* (Cambridge, 1952) p. 26.

7 E.g. the quotation at the top of *GAE* 565, which is not "extracted" but rewritten: note the substitution of τὰς for ἄλλας τινάς.

8 *Her.* 49, 8 εἰς τὴν ὄψιν ἢ τὴν διάνοιαν. *Her.* 51, 2 καθ' ὕπνους γινομένων (on which see below). Lucretius 4, 722–822.

9 Bailey (*GAE* 563) treats sentence A as an instance of ἐπιβολὴ τῶν αἰσθητηρίων, ignoring διάνοια for the moment. "This is exactly," he says, "the idea of ἐπιμαρτύρησις which Epicurus has just been expounding in the preceding context." We get first a mere passive sensation, but it is not until we have *looked* closely that we can be sure the image is clear; "ἐπιβολή is required for the confirmation (or non-confirmation) of the δόξα founded on the original passive perception."

It is not true, however, that Epicurus has been expounding the idea of ἐπιμαρτύρησις. He has been *using* the criterion of ἀντιμαρτύρησις in sections 48–49; but that is a very different thing. He has been saying that there is nothing in our sense experience to contradict his statements about the εἴδωλα that they are incomparably fine textured, move as swiftly as thought, and so on. But there is *nothing* in the preceding context that warrants a distinction between the first passive sensation and the subsequent act of looking.

Bailey then argues (*GAE* 564–65) that sentence C is about normal, reliable sense perception. His method is to remain silent about the previous sentence, which is concerned with error, and to substitute a row of dots for ἢ καθ' ὕπνους γινομένων.

Arrighetti puts sentence B in square brackets. But this seems to be only because he has accepted the wrong interpretation of C.

[10] For the meaning of ἐγκατάλειμμα, see n. 14.

[11] The words which follow these in the text are disputed. They fill out the meaning of "the addition made by *doxa*" by referring to the concepts of confirmation and non-confirmation. None of the likely readings would alter the logic of the passage as a whole; the important point is that sentence A is about reliable sense perception, sentence B is about error, and sentences C and D explain B.

[12] The MSS have πρὸς ἃ (or ὃ) βάλλομεν. Bailey reads τοιαῦτα προσβαλλόμενα with Usener. I have adopted the emendation of Schneider followed also by Arrighetti.

[13] The words τῇ φανταστικῇ ἐπιβολῇ are supplied here by all recent editors from 50, 11–12, where they are probably misplaced.

[14] "The remaining effect" (ἐγκατάλειμμα) is mysterious. There is no doubt that in Epicurean theory the *eidola* leave some mark on the soul atoms—presumably some more or less durable pattern of motion. This is probably what ἐγκατάλειμμα refers to (although there have been other interpretations of it). It would take too much space to examine the possibilities fully. I believe Epicurus is thinking of the role of πρόληψις in his theory of knowledge. See further Bailey *GAE* 245–47; K. Kleve, *Gnosis Theon* (Oslo; Symbolae Osloenses Fasc. Supplet. XIX, 1963): 23–29; D. J. Furley, *Two Studies in the Greek Atomists* (Princeton University Press, 1967) pp. 202–08.

[15] There is much obscurity in "the appearances seen as if in a picture (ἐν εἰκόνι)." Centaurs, Scyllas, Cerberuses, as in Lucretius 4, 732–33?

[16] Note the similar argument in Lucretius 4, 750–51: "quatenus hoc simile est illi, quod mente videmus/ atque oculis, simili fieri ratione necessest." And 757–59 "nec ratione alia, cum somnus membra profudit,/ mens animi vigilat, nisi quod simulacra lacessunt/ haec eadem nostros animos quae cum vigilamus." The occurrence of this in Lucretius is a strong confirmation that we are now interpreting C correctly.

[17] Karl R. Popper, *The Logic of Scientific Discovery* (London, Hutchinson, 1959) p. 31.

[18] *Her.* 38, 3–7. The text is disputed, but none of the variations proposed would affect the present discussion.

[19] Melissus B 7.7.

[20] Leucippus A 7 (Aristotle *GC* 325 a 4).

[21] VIII 32 – IX 3 (p. 42). Lucretius' way of handling this argument is interesting. In 1, 370–97, he gives reasons for rejecting the proposition that there *can* be motion without void. The second seems the better argument: if two flat bodies are in contact, surface to surface, and are then separated suddenly, then if a void space is impossible the air must fill the newly created gap instantaneously.

[22] *Her.* 56–59. Lucretius 1, 599–634. See my *Two Studies in the Greek Atomists*, pp. 7–43 for a defence of the explanation given here.

[23] *Her.* 62.

[24] *GAE* 569–70.

[24a] I am grateful to Father T. J. Tracy, S. J., for some helpful comments on this passage.

[25] *Her.* 50–51.

[26] Diogenes Laertius 10, 32. Rather than chiding Epicurus for misusing *alethes*, I ought rather to say that the Greek word itself is not strictly equivalent to the English word "true." See the article by E. Heitsch, "Die nicht-philosophische ἀλήθεια" *Hermes* 90 (1962): 24–33, and the bibliography cited there. There have been some interesting studies of Plato's use of ἀληθής—H. D. Rankin, "'Α-λήθεια in Plato," *Glotta* 41 (1963): 51–54; S. Bernardete, "The Right, the True and the Beautiful," *Glotta* 41 (1963): 54–62; G. Vlastos, "Degrees of Reality in Plato" in *New Essays on Plato and Aristotle* (London: Routledge, 1965), pp. 1–19.

[27] Other relevant passages are *Her.* 35 and 38, *KD XXIV*, *Nat.* 29, 14–15.

A. N. M. RICH
University of Bristol

Body and Soul in the Philosophy of Plotinus*

BEFORE the time of Aristotle, there had been no serious philosophical enquiry into the relation existing between the body and the soul. Admittedly, in those Dialogues of Plato in which the problem of Motion begins to assume importance, something approaching a scientific interest in the question starts to emerge. In the *Phaedrus*, for instance, the soul is considered as the source of all bodily movement and change,[1] and in the *Timaeus*, the interaction of body and soul is given some attention and a special bodily organ allotted to each phase of the tripartite soul (69C–71A). But it is fair to say that on the whole, Plato does not give the impression of being vitally concerned about the soul-body relation. In fact, in the *Phaedo*, he makes it abundantly clear that he views such an association as morally regrettable rather than scientifically interesting; at this stage of his thought, he prefers, like Socrates, to ignore such questions as those discussed by Empedocles and Alcmaeon, namely, "whether we think with the blood, or whether it is the brain that is the seat of sensation" (96B). Thus, to some extent Plato merits the censure of Aristotle who, in the *De Anima* (I: 1, 407b 15–18), ranks him among those who "associate the soul with and place it in the body without specifying why this is so and how the body is conditioned." In Aristotle's opinion, examination of the soul-body connection is essential: "for it is by this association that the one acts and the other is acted upon, that the one moves and the other is moved; and no such mutual relation is found in haphazard combinations" (407b 18–21).

Now there is a strong likelihood that Aristotle's criticism of Plato on this point may have led Plotinus to take up the problem to some extent neglected by his master. He must have known the *De Anima*, probably through the commentaries of Alexander of Aphrodisias which, we know,

* Presented at the 1961 meeting of the SAGP in Atlantic City, New Jersey.

were read in his school along with the writings of other Peripatetics like Aspasius and Adrastus[2]; and although he did not himself envisage the soul-body relation in Aristotelian terms, neverthelsss his whole enquiry into the subject is deeply colored by the language and influence of the *De Anima*. Of course, Plotinus is much too loyal a Platonist to remain untouched by the dualism of the *Phaedo*, and the undertone of suspicion and hostility toward the body which is lacking in the *De Anima* but present in much of Plato, runs right through the *Enneads* of Plotinus. In fact, almost the last words of his final treatise on psychology reveal that this uneasy attitude persists to the end: "Life in the body," he says, "is in itself evil."[3] Strictly speaking, however, the extreme dualism of a Dialogue like the *Phaedo* has no real place in Plotinus' system. In his view, both body and soul are alike descended from the primal Absolute or One; each represents a different stage in the evolution of plurality from unity: soul is an earlier stage, body, a later; and though soul does not require body in order to exist, nevertheless, without body, it could never come forth from the intelligible realm to display its powers in the visible universe (IV: 3. 9). Thus, because body is, in a sense, necessary to soul, because, figuratively speaking, it is the only "place" appropriate for the soul's occupation (IV: 3. 9), it is impossible to view the relation between body and soul as one of unmitigated hostility. For to some extent, body and soul imply each other. On the cosmic level indeed, they never exist apart. For though we may speak of the "ensoulment" (ἐμψύχωσις) of the cosmos, because the cosmos is, in fact, eternal and uncreated, there never was a time when its soul and its body were dissociated (IV: 3. 9). In the case of the human soul and body, however, matters are rather different, since it is evident that the two were separate before birth and will be parted again by death. The union between human souls and bodies is therefore only temporary. When the soul "descends" into the lower world, it finds a body already awaiting its occupation, a "residence" prepared for it by the World Soul (IV: 36). But it does not enter in its totality into its prearranged dwelling, for souls, according to Plotinus, are "amphibious" (ἀμφίβιοι; IV: 8. 4). In their lower phase only are they in contact with the body; in their higher aspect, they live a purely intellectual life divorced from the body altogether. In fact, what "descends" to the body is only a phantom (εἴδωλον) of the higher soul, comparable, in mythical language, to the Shade of the hero Heracles which lingers in the Underworld while the real Heracles enjoys the company of the gods in Heaven.[4]

Though Plotinus talks in terms of a higher and a lower soul, he believes, in fact, that the soul has three main phases, the purely intellectual, which is concerned only with the divine and the suprasensible, the discursive aspect, characteristic of the rational human being, and the irrational phase, corresponding to the "mortal" soul of Plato's Timaeus and to the ἄλογος ψυχή of Aristotle. This third division, which is the one with which we are chiefly concerned in this discussion, includes the faculties of growth, nutrition and sensation, and it is this that unites with the body to form what Plotinus calls the ζῷον or συναμφότερον, that complex of body and soul which, if we add to it the faculty of discursive thought, is conventionally regarded as "the man himself."[5] Plotinus' intense interest in the συναμφότερον and the relation of its two components is revealed by the incident described in Porphyry's *Life*. Plotinus, we are told (c. 13), once spent three days discussing with Porphyry the question: πῶς ἡ ψυχὴ σύνεστι τῷ σώματι. In the course of the discussion, a certain Thaumasius appeared, who, after listening to the conversation, remarked that he would much prefer to hear a general exposition of Plotinus' views rather than a series of questions and answers. To this Plotinus replied that without questions there would be no objections to resolve and therefore no material for an exposition of the type required. From what Plotinus eventually wrote on this topic, we can judge fairly accurately the tenor of the arguments put forward on this occasion and the kind of solutions offered to Porphyry's questions. But before we can even begin to consider in detail how Plotinus finally envisaged the κοινωνία of soul and body, we ought first to reflect briefly upon the causes originally responsible, in his view, for the initial embodiment of the soul.

It is misleading, Plotinus insists, to talk of the soul "descending" into the body. For descent implies a downward movement in space, which the soul never actually experiences (VI: 4. 16). This must be looked upon simply as a manner of speaking; the entry of the soul into the body cannot legitimately be described in spatial terms at all. However, in the spirit of Platonic myth, Plotinus continues to employ the metaphor of descent in his efforts to account for the departure of the soul from its original disembodied state. It is guilty, he suggests, of some error (ἁμαρτία) which consists in a desire to be independent of the Universal Soul (IV: 8. 4), a voluntary inclination (IV: 8. 5) toward the material world which results in its "fall" and the loss of its wings. Or to use a different metaphor, the soul beholds its own image in the mirror of matter, becomes enamored of it and plunges downward.[6] But though this entry into the material world can be regarded as voluntary in so far as it is the soul's own act, and "sinful" in so far as it involves separation from the perfection of the Whole, nevertheless, on a higher level, it is seen to be determined. For it is a universal law in the Plotinian system that the higher must give itself to the lower, and that soul must impart itself to body in order to realize its own implicit powers and to contribute to the perfection of the Cosmos. This means that the "sin" of the soul in entering the body proves to be, as it were, the "felix culpa" that is necessary to the divine economy. The incarnation of the soul is therefore no more the result of genuine sin than is the casting of a shadow.[7]

When we say that the soul "enters" the body, we imply that it is the soul that takes the initiative. It would be more accurate, however, Plotinus points out, to say that body approaches soul, as long as we do not take this to suggest any local movement (VI: 4. 16). Indeed, body has what Plotinus calls an "aptitude" (ἐπιτηδειότης; VI: 4. 15) for soul. This differs with different types of body; some are more suitable recipients than others; but that which is not capable of receiving soul in its entirety, shares in it as far as it can (VI: 4. 15). But in what sense can any organism, vegetable, animal or human be said to "possess" or "participate in" soul? How are soul and body connected? This is difficult to discover. For though body and soul are both ultimately derived from the same source, they are nevertheless completely different in character. Body is composite and therefore liable to dissolution; soul is the animating force that holds the bodily constituents together. Any theory that makes the soul itself corporeal ignores this distinction; and Plotinus takes great pains in this connection to refute the Stoic view that the soul is a special kind of body, the πνεῦμα in a particular state, (πως ἔχον) and the Epicurean theory that the soul is the product of a concourse of lifeless atoms (IV: 7. 18). To counter these materialistic doctrines he draws on various stock arguments which can be traced back, in many cases, to chapters II and V, Book I, *De Anima* of Aristotle. We need not linger over these although they are relevant to the problem in hand, but will give some detailed attention to the objections brought by Plotinus against two other theories; firstly, the view set forth in the *Phaedo* (85E ff.) that the soul is an "attunement" (ἁρμονία) of bodily elements; and secondly, the Aristotelian definition[8] of the soul as the ἐντελέχεια or "fulfilment" of the body. Both of these theories attempt some sort of explanation of the body-soul connection.

The attunement theory, which Plotinus attributes to the Pythagoreans (IV: 7. 8[4]), makes the soul analogous to the ἁρμονία produced upon the strings of the lyre, the πάθημα that supervenes when the instrument is duly tuned. Plotinus points out, with an obvious allusion to the

Phaedo, that this theory has already been proved untenable. But his own objections, curiously enough, are not based upon this dialogue, but, as Jaeger has shown,[9] upon the *Eudemus* of Aristotle. Certain arguments deriving from the *De Anima* of Aristotle are also, apparently, utilized for purposes of refutation.[10] The first point that Plotinus makes is that soul is prior to body, whereas the attunement theory presupposes the prior existence of the lyre. Second, the soul rules, guides, and often resists the body; this a mere attunement could not do, since it depends entirely upon the bodily constitution. In the third place, the soul is a substance in its own right, whereas an attunement is merely an accidental πάθημα. Fourth, a due blending of bodily elements would produce not soul but health. Fifth, there would have to be a plurality of souls in each individual, on the theory of an attunement, since each part of the body, being blended in different proportions, would require a distinct soul. Sixth, prior to the soul that supervenes upon the body after the manner of an attunement, there would have to be another soul to produce this condition, just as, in the case of a musical instrument, a musician is required to tune the strings: neither musical instruments nor human bodies are capable of putting themselves in tune. Finally, those who hold the attunement theory derive life and arrangement (τάξις) from what is lifeless and disordered; but this is manifestly impossible. For all these reasons, therefore, the soul cannot be related to the body as an attunement to its instrument.

The Aristotelian definition of the soul as the ἐντελέχεια of the body can be just as effectively disposed of. In the first place, Plotinus says (IV: 7. 8[5]), if the soul is related to the body as the shape (μορφή) of a statue is related to its matter, the bronze, it follows that when the body is divided, the soul, its "form" will be divided with it; so that if any fragment of the body is severed from the whole, a portion of the soul will be severed too. In the next place, it is imperative that an ἐντελέχεια should be inseparable from that of which it is the fulfillment or realization; but if it is inseparable, the result will be that the soul will be incapable of withdrawing from the body in sleep, and this will make sleep an impossibility. Again, if the soul is an ἐντελέχεια, conflict between reason and bodily desire is ruled out completely, since the whole organism must have one uniform experience and there can be no discord between the body and the soul that informs it. Furthermore, on the ἐντελέχεια definition, there can be no pure thought, since thought is an activity that does not involve the body in any way. (And it is precisely for this reason, Plotinus notes, that the Peripatetics have to postulate another soul over and above the ἐντελέχεια to account for the purely intellectual functions of the soul.) There are further objections in similar vein. The final conclusion reached by Plotinus is that the soul does not depend for its existence upon serving as the "form" or realization of something else; it is an essence quite separate from any particular entity and it exists as soul pure and simple before it becomes the soul of such-and-such an individual.

Much of what Plotinus has to say about the body-soul problem seems purely negative. In what is perhaps his most important discussion of the topic, (IV: 3. 20) his main concern is to emphasize that however body and soul are related, they are not to be thought of as spatially connected. Soul is not in a body as in a space, for the definition of space is that which contains body, and soul, not being corporeal, cannot be contained. The body is not, in any sense, the "vessel" (ἀγγεῖον) of the soul. For if it were, and if the relation were a spatial one, the body itself would still remain devoid of soul, since container and contained are two entirely separate things. Of course, one might assume that soul could transmit something of itself to its container, but this would mean that the body's gain would be the soul's loss. In any case, space, being the container of body, is not itself corporeal. Thus body which is corporeal, could scarcely be the τόπος or "space" in which the soul is contained. Besides, if the soul were "in" the body in a spatial sense, the body would be in contact with the soul only at its surface and not throughout its entire mass; while yet another consequence of assuming a spatial connection would be that the soul *qua* contained by the body, would be carrying its own space about with it, which would be not only absurd, but actually impossible, according to the Peripatetic description of space as ἀκίνητος. And even if we adopted the Stoic definition of space as the "interval" separating physical objects (διάστημα), a spatial relation between body and soul would still be impossible. For such an interval, Plotinus points out, would have to be a void. Body, however, is not a void; rather, it is itself in a void. So that even on Stoic premises, body cannot contain soul in a spatial sense.

Having established this point, Plotinus now tries to explain the presence of the soul in the body in non-spatial terms. He first considers the possibility of an analogy between the soul "in" the body and a color or shape in a substrate. But this suggestion is at once rejected on the grounds that color and shape are mere accidents of that which exhibits them, whereas the soul is not an accident of anything but an independent substance. Nor will Plotinus admit the possibility that the soul may be in the body as a part is "in" the whole; for the soul, he says, is not a part of the body. It would be equally absurd to say that it is in the body as a whole is "in" its parts. Nor can the soul be related to the body as immanent form to matter, for such a form is inseparable from matter and logically posterior to it. Besides, the soul is not itself a form but that which produces form; and even if we fall back upon the suggestion that it is analogous to a transcendent Platonic form and not an Aristotelian εἶδος ἐν ὕλῃ, we are still no nearer solving the problem of how this "form" is present to the body.

In spite of the many logical objections that should deter us from talking about the body-soul relation in spatial terms, we still persist in saying that the soul is "in" the body or that the body "has" a soul. The reason, Plotinus concludes, is that while the body is visible, the soul is invisible. Only from the behavior of the body can we observe the presence of the soul. But if we could see the soul, we would perceive that it is not merely coextensive with the body but "extends" far beyond the body. So that to be accurate, we ought to say not that soul is in body but that body is in soul. Would it be a satisfactory solution of the problem to say that soul is related to body as the pilot to his ship? But this, Plotinus objects, would not really explain the mode of the soul's presence in the body (IV: 3. 21). All it would indicate is that the soul and the body are potentially separable from one another, as is the case with the pilot and his vessel. In any case, the analogy is inadequate because the pilot is not omnipresent in the ship, whereas the soul penetrates to every point in the body. This difficulty might be avoided by comparing the soul not to the pilot himself but to his τέχνη which operates through the helm, and so, in a sense, extends its power throughout the entire ship. But the pilot's τέχνη Plotinus points out, is in actual fact, external to the instrument it employs, whereas, if we are to apply this analogy to the soul, we shall have to regard it as immanent in the helm; and even if, accordingly, we think of the soul as immanent in the body, its instrument, the actual mode of its presence is still left unexplained.

Finally, after all his efforts, Plotinus is forced back upon a spatial metaphor to explain how soul is present to body. Their true relation is analogous, he says (IV: 3. 22), to that between light and air. Light is both present and not present to air (παρὸν οὐ πάρεστι), for though it completely penetrates the air, it is not blended with it at any point. While the air flows past, it remains immobile; and when the air passes beyond the region of illumination, it takes no light away with it. Therefore, just as the air is in the light and not vice-versa, the body is in the soul and not the soul in the body. But there is no objection to saying that the soul is "present to" the body, as long as we do not imply that any mixture has taken place between them. The soul is no more mixed with the body than light with air. Nor is it divided by contact with the body any more than light is divided by association with air. Of course, Plotinus is prepared to admit that the soul can be described as divisible in body in so far as it is present in every separate part of the body; but because it is present also at every point in its totality, it can also quite legitimately be designated indivisible (IV: 2. 1). The powers of the soul are various and different powers are associated with different organs, but every soul is present entire at every point. For if it were not omnipresent, it would not be a unity. If, like the body, it could be divided into distinct parts, each part would be cut off from the experiences of its fellows; thus the organism would never be affected as a whole by anything occurring in one particular part, and the body would be under the control, not of a single soul, but of a plurality of souls (IV: 2. 2). However, Plotinus adds, if the soul were completely indivisible, nothing would ever be ensoulled. Only when body approaches soul, can it participate in life; and such contact inevitably brings with it an element of apparent multiplicity. But this division, this μερισμός, Plotinus reminds us, is not really an affection of the soul itself but a πάθημα of bodies (IV: 2. 2).

By comparing the soul to light and the body to air, Plotinus makes clear both that the soul is indivisible and omnipresent in the body and that it is not confined within bodily limits. He is well aware, however, that he has still not found a satisfactory scientific explanation of the soul-body connection, and for this reason we find him still wrestling with this problem in the last of his psychological writings, *Ennead* I: 1. The specific question which he is discussing in the relevant part of this treatise is to what extent body and soul share in the experiences of sensation, desire, emotion and thought. We are reminded at once of Aristotle's query in *De Anima* I: 1 (403a 3–5) as to whether all the attributes of the soul are common to the living body, or if some are peculiar to the soul. It was a question that had also been discussed by Plutarch, who had concluded that in the case of the desires and emotions it was to the compound organism, to soul combined with body, that such experiences should be assigned.[11] This is precisely the position assumed by Plotinus. He insists, of course, that the higher soul which stands aloof from the body, remains quite unaffected by the experiences of the body-soul complex. But he believes that between the lower soul and the body which together make up the ζῷον or συναμφότερον, a genuine community of experience exists. The standard academic definition of Man as a "soul using a body"[12] will not, however, allow for a sympathy between body and soul within the living organism. For it implies that body and soul are two quite unrelated things, the one corresponding to the workman's tool, the other to the workman himself. On this analogy, the soul will certainly have no share in the experiences of the body, for the workman does not actually feel the παθήματα of his tool. And if this objection is countered by the argument that the soul will at least be aware of what is happening in the body, just as the workman knows how his tool is being affected, it is still impossible to see how the body could transmit its experiences to be shared by the soul. However, some sort of sympathy between the two might be established if one regarded them as mixed together. But the objection here is that as a result of any such mixture, the original characters of the two components would be modified; soul would become something less than soul and body something more than body; and, of the two, it would be body rather than soul, that would gain in power by assuming the faculty of sensation and the experiences that result from it. In any case, as Plotinus proceeds to point out, the metaphor of mixture is probably absurd, since soul and body may be, in fact, absolutely incongruous, so that to regard them as mixed together is as nonsensical as to say that a line can be mixed with whiteness (I: 1. 4). Perhaps then as an alternative to the notion of a blend of soul and body, we might adopt the suggestion of Plato that the soul is interwoven (διαπλακεῖσα) with the body. But this will not help either, if we wish to explain how soul and body can share common experiences. For the soul might penetrate right through the body and yet not share its states, in just the way that light can penetrate air and yet remain unaffected by it (I: 1. 4).

So far Plotinus has drawn a blank in his attempt to find some relation that will allow for sympathy between body and soul. But his next suggestion looks more promising. We may perhaps think of the soul, he says, as analogous to an immanent form inseparable from its matter, as for instance, the axe-shape in the axe. Now of course, it is not the axe-shape that performs the task of the axe and experiences the act of cutting, but the iron, the matter of the axe, on which the form has been imposed. So that on this analogy, it will be the body, not the soul, that is the subject of actions and states. But we should note that in the case of the axe, the effectiveness of the iron depends upon the fact that it has been modified by the axe-shape. So that if we apply this reasoning to the body-soul relation, we may conclude that it is not the body in isolation that is affected by desire, sensation and feeling, but rather, the living body, body modified, as it were, by soul. It is in fact, the ζῷον or συναμφότερον that is the subject of these experiences. Body by itself is inert and soul by itself impassible (III: 6). But when body and soul combine to produce some distinct entity which is neither the one nor the other, then we can quite legitimately say that body and soul are in sympathy and are sharing common experiences and affections.

Particular attention is given by Plotinus to the various ways in which soul and body co-operate and interact within the living organism. He lays special emphasis upon the mechanism of sense-perception which he regards as the connecting link between the body and the discursive reason. The power of sensation has been given to the soul, he says, in virtue of its association (κοινωνία, IV: 4. 24) with the body. It is the κοινὸν ἔργον (IV: 3. 26) of body and soul. That phase of the soul which transcends the body is quite incapable of perceiving anything in the sense world by direct means, because it lacks the necessary bodily organs of sight or hearing (IV: 3. 19; 23; V: 1. 10). However, it is made aware of events in the physical world through association with the sensitive faculty which transmits data to it (I: 19). In the *Timaeus*, Plato had actually assigned this discursive phase of the soul a definite physical location within the head. But Plotinus parts company with Plato here, since he does not regard the reasoning faculty as actually resident in the body. However, he continues to attach particular importance to the head since he believes that the brain is the central organ of certain psychic functions with which the discursive soul is intimately connected. It is from the brain, in his view (IV: 3. 23), that the nerves take their origin, and it is to the brain that the nerve-endings which occur all over the surface of the body, transmit what we should call tactual sensations and motor impulses. The more specialized sensations like sight or hearing, are not specifically associated by Plotinus with the brain and he seems to think of eyes and ears as independent organs of perception. But this does not mean that there is no co-ordination of the different types of sensation. Plotinus never tires of insisting upon the omnipresence of the soul in the body and its essential unity. Though different powers operate at different points, the soul, though apparently dispersed, is one. Thus all its functions must be inseparably connected, whatever their instruments may be and wherever situated (IV: 9. 3). The various sense organs cannot all admit the same impressions, but all perceptions terminate in one center where the data provided are sifted by the discursive reason (IV: 3. 3).

As for the desires experienced by the body-soul compound, these, according to Plotinus, should be connected with the very lowest phase of the irrational soul, the vegetative element or φυτικόν (IV: 4. 20). This is present in all living things from plants to human beings, is responsible for their growth, nutrition and propagation, and is a reflection in the individual organism of the cosmic φύσις, the lower aspect of the World Soul. Now though the term φυτικόν is borrowed from Aristotle, it is from Plato that Plotinus has taken the idea that the desires belong to this particular faculty. In the *Timaeus* (77A, B), when discussing vegetable life, Plato assigns to plants the third form of soul which has to do with sensation, pleasant or painful, and the appetites. Plotinus is ready to accept this connection between the vegetative soul and the desires because he believes that the principle which causes birth and nourishment and growth must also desire these things. He agrees with Plato too in making the liver the special organ of desire, since it is in the liver that the veins and the blood that are the vehicles of the φυτικόν have their point of origin (IV: 3. 23). Plotinus' account of the way in which desires are experienced is somewhat complicated (IV: 4. 20). Neither body alone nor soul alone can be the subject of desire, he insists, for body by itself cannot give rise to appetite, and soul in isolation from body has no interest in what is desirable or the reverse. Desire for such objects must clearly belong to something that is bodily but chooses to be more than mere body, that is, to a living organism, a body animated by a soul. Now is it this living body that initiates the desire? And is the desire transmitted thence to the desiring faculty of the soul? Or does the desiring faculty itself take the lead? Plotinus' reply is that it is hard to see how anyone could experience desire except through prior activity in the faculty of desire, but on the other hand, the desiring faculty cannot take the initiative unless the body is first in the appropriate condition (I: 1. 5). In fact, Plotinus distinguishes three stages in the operation of desire within the body-soul complex. First there is a vague and unconscious προθυμία felt by the body. This is transferred to the φυτικόν where it becomes a fully conscious ἐπιθυμία; and finally, an image of this is conveyed by means of sensation, to the reasoning phase of the soul which alone has power to satisfy or to resist the desire (IV: 4. 20). That desires originate in this way, within the living body, is proved, Plotinus argues (IV: 4. 21), by the fact that they differ according to the condition of the body in respect of age or health. Furthermore, there are some desires that never get beyond the stage of unconscious προθυμίαι of the body, simply because the φυτικόν refuses to admit them. But when the needs of the body are conformable to this principle, like a human mother, it tries to satisfy the needs of the organism and to relieve its pain by identifying itself as far as possible with the sufferings of its offspring (IV: 4. 20).

Closely bound up with the desires are pleasure and pain, also affections of the συναμφότερον. Body by itself could experience neither, since by itself it is devoid of life (IV: 4. 18); and soul in isolation is ἀπαθής. Pleasure and pain are the direct result of their union. Because the two members of the compound are different in character, there is a constant tension as the organism is drawn in two opposite directions at once. When it is drawn toward the body it suffers pain; when directed toward the soul, it feels pleasure. Pain is thus defined as our perception of the body deprived of the soul's image, pleasure as the realization that this image is restored (IV: 4. 19), in other words, that body and soul are again in harmonious relation to one another. When pain occurs, the πάθος is felt directly by the body and perceived by sensation which then makes it known to the central sense on which all perceptions converge. It is of course, the living body that actually feels the pain. The soul, though aware of it, does not experience it directly. And this, Plotinus says, is proved by the fact that if the soul actually suffered the pain, being omnipresent in the body, it would not be able to localize the affection in one particular area, but would feel it at every point all over the body. A distinction must be made, in fact, between the actual pain and the perception of that pain, which is what the soul experiences. This perception of pain is a kind of knowledge (γνῶσις) and the phase of soul that acquires this awareness, if it is to report its findings correctly, must be ἀπαθής. A messenger who is himself overwhelmed by emotion either fails to communicate his news at all or else transmits it inaccurately.

Finally we should consider the emotions experienced by the συναμφότερον. Only anger receives any detailed treatment in the *Enneads*, and this, following Plato, Plotinus connects with the passionate element of the soul, the θυμοειδές (IV: 4. 28). Like the desiring faculty, the θυμοειδές is also closely connected with the φυτικόν, the principle of physiological life. But since anger also implies some subject capable of sensation and judgment, this association might not at first sight seem obvious or appropriate. The Stoics who say that anger arises from the judgment that some injury has been incurred, might well be correct in assigning to it a purely mental origin. However, Plotinus argues, anger usually has a physical rather than a mental source, since a predisposition to anger is a consequence of the organization of the body. People in whom the blood and the bile are particularly active are especially prone to anger, while those who are not of a bilious temperament (ἄχολοι) are less irascible. Animals get angry, not because they judge that they are victims of injury, but simply because of their bodily κρᾶσις; sick people are more prone to anger than those in full bodily health; the hungry are more irritable than the well-fed. All this goes to suggest (against the Stoic view) that the starting point of anger is not a mental perception, but rather a predisposition of the body. Anger actually arises, Plotinus says, in the blood around the heart which, being swift and subtle, is a suitable vehicle for passion. The blood and bile becoming active, impel the body to go through the motions of anger; sensation then follows; an impression (φαντασία) is submitted to the reasoning faculty, and the source of the suffering is then attacked. Thus a mere disturbance in the body is transformed through the agency of the soul into an impulse (ὁρμή) to action. That anger, like desire, is connected primarily with the vegetative phase of the soul and is of like nature, (ὁμοούσιον) is indicated by the fact that people who are less inclined to bodily pleasures are also less irascible. The ἀπάθεια which they display is not due to the exercise of reason, but is simply a matter of physical temperament. It might be argued of course, that anger cannot be associated with the φυτικόν because plants, in which only this phase of soul is present, are not subject to anger. But this objection does not deter Plotinus. Plants do not feel anger, he explains, simple because there is no blood or bile in their constitution. They therefore lack the essential preconditions, the vehicles through which the θυμοειδές operates. Of course, Plotinus does not deny that there can be cases where anger arises as the result of a mental judgment alone, and where a physical reaction follows and does not precede. But the vital point is that a feeling of anger can never be confined to the soul by itself. The body is always involved at some stage and its κρᾶσις will invariably determine the intensity of the emotion in each individual case.

Plotinus' interest in the συναμφότερον as the meeting point of soul and body was undoubtedly inspired by the psychological studies of Aristotle. But it is likely too that it was also to some extent dictated by an interest in medical science. We know from Porphyry[13] that Plotinus numbered several ἰατρικοί among his close associates, Paulinus of Scythopolis, Zethos, an Arab, and Eustochius of Alexandria, who attended Plotinus during his last years and became an ardent disciple. Perhaps it was through such professional medical practitioners as these that Plotinus became familiar with the psychological theories of the great physician Galen, whose influence can be detected at several points in his examination of the soul-body problem, particularly in his discussion of the nerves and the brain,[14] and in his emphasis on the importance of bodily "temperament." Plotinus' strange theory of the πνεῦμα "around the soul" may also have come from some medical source. According to Inge,[15] Plotinus envisaged this πνεῦμα as the connecting link between body and soul. Let us consider what evidence there is to support this view. In Ennead II 2. 2, Plotinus introduces the πνεῦμα in a discussion of the circular motion of the Cosmos. Why, he asks, since the Cosmic Soul revolves around God, do not human souls and bodies also revolve? The reason given is that while bodies are characterized by movement in a straight line, the human soul is hampered in its circling motion by the earth that clogs it. But perhaps, Plotinus adds, the πνεῦμα around the soul revolves. In IV: 4. 26, there is a clue as to what Plotinus means by this πνεῦμα. Here he describes it as διαφανὲς καὶ ἐλλαμπόμενον παρὰ τοῦ κύκλου, and represents it as the container of the vegetative principle. Now presumably this πνεῦμα can be equated with the celestial body which, in IV: 3. 15, souls are said to assume when they first emerge from the intelligible world, and by means of which they proceed into "more earthy bodies." Already in the same treatise (c. 9), Plotinus has described the soul as born into an earthy body ἐκ σώματος ἀερίνου ἢ πυρίνου. Perhaps we have in these texts a clue to the origin of Porphyry's[16] theory of a celestial πνεῦμα which the soul retains even after death. In the same way we can probably trace to another Plotinian passage (III: 6. 5) the definition of the πνεῦμα put forward by Proclus.[17] He calls it the ὄχημα or "vehicle" of the soul. This could be a direct interpretation of Plotinus' remark that the soul can only be separated from the body when that which contains it (τὸ ἐν ᾧ) is tenuous (ἰσχνόν) and not swollen from gluttony or excess, so that the soul can ride peacefully upon it (ὡς ἐπ' αὐτοῦ ὀχεῖσθαι ἡσυχῇ; III: 6. 5). As Inge observes, this πνεῦμα probably has little philosophical importance in Plotinus' system, but at least it seems to be an attempt to bridge the gap between body and soul. We realize of course, that the notion of a kinship between the human soul and the celestial regions goes back to Plato's *Timaeus* where the Demiurge is represented as "sowing" each soul into a star at its first birth (41E). But it also seems possible that the notion of a celestial πνεῦμα in Plotinus may owe something to Aristotle too. In his *De Generatione Animalium*, we remember, Aristotle establishes an analogy between the vital heat or σύμφυτον πνεῦμα in animals and the ether, "the elements of the stars" (II: 3, 737al). Now one of the main functions of this σύμφυτον πνεῦμα is to explain locomotion and sensation in animals. Could this be the role Plotinus intends for his πνεῦμα in the *Enneads* and has the

Aristotelian connection of the πνεῦμα with the ether, which is characterised by circular motion, suggested to him an equation of the πνεῦμα "round the soul" with the star-bodies of the *Timaeus*? Further research into this question might lead to interesting results.

The final theme of this discussion concerns the fate of the irrational aspects of the soul after the body-soul association has been terminated by death. Does the irrational soul perish with the body? Plotinus answers this question in the negative. When the body is discarded, he says, "all powers merge into one soul" (IV: 9. 3). Thus, desire, feeling and the power of sensation lose their specific character when their raison d'être has gone, and like the discursive faculty, become absorbed into the higher phase of the soul that has always held itself aloof from the body. Even the φυτικόν, the source of physical life, survives bodily death. For a brief time it may actually linger within the body after death has occurred; this is evident from the fact that hair and nails may continue to grow upon a corpse (IV: 4. 29). But eventually, it abandons all connection with that particular organism and returns to its source in the World Soul, only to re-emerge as the animating force in some other individual. In this way life can arise again even in the carcass of a dead animal. The soul that originally inhabited the beast's body is, of course, no longer present, since that particular body has long since ceased to be receptive of the life force. But the decayed matter in time becomes suitable material for some other form of life, and is thus, once more, ensoulled, because, as Plotinus says, "Soul is nowhere lacking, though a suitable recipient may be" (IV: 3. 8). Although Plotinus does not use the term in this context, we might almost be justified in talking of the reincarnation of the φυτικόν. But such a rebirth would, of course, have to be distinguished from the μετενσωμάτωσις that is the fate of individual souls who have failed during life in their moral duty of purifying themselves from the body. In the case of such souls, irrational elements are not laid aside even after death. If they have succeeded during life in preserving their specifically human character, they are born again into human bodies. But those who have lived on the level of sensation alone take animal forms, while those who have lived stupid and unreflective lives are reincarnated as plants (III: 4. 2). In each case, the faculty most fully developed during one life will determine the type of body that the soul will assume in the next. However, the final goal for which the soul must strive, is to be free of the body altogether; the true awakening of the soul is not with the body but from the body (III: 6. 6). The soul that finally achieves emancipation is compared by Plotinus to an actor who, while others continue to make their exits and entrances, takes his last bow from the stage, never to reappear (III: 2. 15).

Plotinus' remarks on the theme of reincarnation show up the more "Platonic" strain in his approach to the body-soul problem. He tends, in this context, to stress the ill effects the body can have on the soul, and elsewhere, in language reminiscent of the *Phaedo*, he complains of the way in which the body impedes thought and fills the soul with its follies. His attitude to the body is not, however, consistently hostile. Admittedly the story told by his pupil Porphyry[18] that he refused to sit for his portrait because "he seemed ashamed of being in the body" reveals Plotinus in an ultra-Platonic mood. But one wonders if this was the actual reason for the refusal or simply the ascetic pupil's interpretation of it. The excuse Plotinus actually made was that he did not want to transmit "an image of an image" to posterity. He might conceivably have meant this humorously. At any rate, an attitude of hostility to the body is quite out of keeping with the general tone of Plotinus' treatise *Against the Gnostics* (II: 9). Here he vindicates the entire visible Cosmos as an expression of the powers of Soul, and roundly castigates the Gnostic dualism which would condemn the bodily and the material, and which declares the world to be the creation of an evil Demiurge. In fact as we noted at the beginning of this discussion, a dualistic view of the body is incompatible with Plotinus' philosophy as a whole. Body, no less than soul, is, in his view, a necessary consequence of that "procession" whereby the powers of the Absolute Unity are made manifest. If body is less perfect than soul or mind, this is simply because it is further removed from its source than they, not because it is inherently evil. The primary source of evil is explicitly stated to be not body, but matter (I: 8. 8); and though, admittedly, the soul which defers to its bodily temperament becomes corrupted,[19] nevertheless, even when in the body, it is possible to avoid evil. Embodiment in itself is not a degradation, and the man who is truly wise will treat the body as the musician treats his instrument, with respect:

> he will care for and bear with it as long as possible, just as the musician cares for his lyre as long as he can use it. When this is not possible, he will change the lyre or will give up the use of the lyre and will refrain from playing it, since he has a different task to perform without the lyre; so he will let it rest at his side while he sings on without instruments. Yet it was not in vain that the instrument was originally bestowed upon him; for he has made use of it many a time in the past.[20]

NOTES

[1] 245C-E; cp. *Laws* X: 898C 5.

[2] Porphyry, *Life of Plotinus*, c. 13.

[3] I:7.3. But note that in I:8.4, body is described as a δεύτερον κακόν, matter being the primary evil.

[4] I:1.12, cp. IV:3.27.

[5] Though strictly speaking, this title should be reserved for the higher soul, the Ideal Man, which exists in the intelligible realm and is never associated with the body in any way. See A. H. Armstrong, "Man's Higher Self in Plotinus," *DR*, 206 (1948).

[6] IV:3.12. cp. III:9.3.

[7] IV:8.5; I:1.12. For an excellent discussion of Neoplatonic views on the Fall of the Soul, see A. J. Festugière, *La Révélation d'Hermès Trismegiste*, Vol. III, (Paris, 1953), pp. 65–95.

[8] *De Anima* II:1. 413a 2.

[9] *Aristoteles* (Berlin, 1923), p. 43.

[10] Notably the fourth and fifth arguments which are based on *De Anima* I:4.3 and I:4.5.

[11] In chapters IV and V of his discussion *Whether Desire and Pain belong to the Soul or the Body*, Plutarch gives evidence of a controversy on this topic between those who supported Strato's view that these states were the province of the soul alone, and those (perhaps Platonists) who attributed them to the body. See Bréhier's edition of Plotinus, Vol. IV, p. 39.

[12] Plato, *Alcibiades* I: 129C; *Phaedrus*, 246B; *Phaedo*, 79C; *Timaeus*, 30B.

[13] *Life of Plotinus*, c.7.

[14] See Bréhier's edition, Vol. IV, (Paris, 1928), 90, n.l, and F. Solmsen, "Greek Philosophy and the Discovery of the Nerves," *MH*, 18, fasc. 4 (1961): 169–97.

[15] Dean W. R. Inge, *The Philosophy of Plotinus*, Vol. I, (London, 1918), p. 219.

[16] *Sententiae*, 32.

[17] *Institutio Theologiae*, 207. cp. Macrobius, *Comm. in Somnium Scipionis*, I:11.

[18] *Life of Plotinus*, c.1.

[19] III:1.8. cp. I:2.3.

[20] I:4.16, cp. II:9.18.

Subject Index

Name Index